A FIELD GUIDE TO
WARBLERS
OF NORTH AMERICA

THE PETERSON FIELD GUIDE SERIES®

A FIELD GUIDE TO

WARBLERS

OF NORTH AMERICA

JON L. DUNN

and

KIMBALL L. GARRETT

Illustrated by
THOMAS R. SCHULTZ
and CINDY HOUSE

Maps by
SUE A. TACKETT and LARRY O. ROSCHE

SPONSORED BY THE NATIONAL AUDUBON SOCIETY,
THE NATIONAL WILDLIFE FEDERATION, AND
THE ROGER TORY PETERSON INSTITUTE

HOUGHTON MIFFLIN COMPANY
BOSTON   NEW YORK

PETERSON FIELD GUIDES and PETERSON FIELD GUIDE SERIES
are registered trademarks of Houghton Mifflin Company.

For information about this and other Houghton Mifflin trade and reference
books and multimedia products, visit The Bookstore at Houghton Mifflin
on the World Wide Web at http://www.hmco.com/trade/.

LIBRARY OF CONGRESS CATALOGING-IN-PUBLICATION DATA

Dunn, Jon, 1954–
A field guide to warblers of North America / Jon Dunn and
Kimball Garrett: illustrated by Tom Schultz and Cindy House.
p. cm. — (The Peterson field guide series ; 49)
"Sponsored by the National Audubon Society, the National
Wildlife Federation, and the Roger Tory Peterson Institute."
Includes bibliographical references (p.   ) and index.
ISBN 0-395-38971-2 (cloth).   ISBN 0-395-78321-6 (pbk.)
1. Wood warblers — North America — Identification.   I. Garrett, Kimball.
II. National Audubon Society.   III. National Wildlife Federation.
IV. Roger Tory Peterson Institute.   V. Title.   VI. Series.
QL696.P2438D85   1997
598.8'72'097 — dc21   97-12213

Book design and icons by Anne Chalmers
Typeface: Linotype-Hell Fairfield; Futura Condensed (Adobe)

PRINTED IN THE UNITED STATES OF AMERICA

RMT 10 9 8 7 6 5

The authors dedicate this book to Ralph Hoffman,

whose excellent early guides, particularly

Birds of the Pacific States, were

influential and inspirational.

The artists dedicate their work in this book to their families,

without whose support and patience this book

would not have been possible.

The legacy of America's great naturalist, Roger Tory Peterson, is preserved through the programs and work of the Roger Tory Peterson Institute of Natural History. The RTPI mission is to create passion for and knowledge of the natural world in the hearts and minds of children by inspiring and guiding the study of nature in our schools and communities. You can become a part of this worthy effort by joining RTPI. Just call RTPI's membership department at 1-800-758-6841, fax 716-665-3794, or e-mail (webmaster@rtpi.org) for a free one-year membership with the purchase of this Field Guide.

Contents

LIST OF PLATES   x

Introduction   1
The Natural History of Warblers   5
How to Identify Warblers   31
How to Use This Book   34

PLATES   43

SPECIES ACCOUNTS
FAMILY PEUCEDRAMIDAE
    Genus *Peucedramus*
        Olive Warbler   109
FAMILY PARULIDAE
    Genus *Vermivora*
        Bachman's Warbler   117
        Blue-winged Warbler   125
        Golden-winged Warbler   133
        Tennessee Warbler   145
        Orange-crowned Warbler   154
        Nashville Warbler   166
        Virginia's Warbler   174
        Colima Warbler   180
        Lucy's Warbler   185
    Genus *Parula*
        Crescent-chested Warbler   190

Northern Parula 195
Tropical Parula 204
Genus *Dendroica*
Yellow Warbler 210
Chestnut-sided Warbler 232
Magnolia Warbler 240
Cape May Warbler 248
Black-throated Blue Warbler 257
Yellow-rumped Warbler 267
Black-throated Gray Warbler 282
Golden-cheeked Warbler 291
Black-throated Green Warbler 298
Townsend's Warbler 307
Hermit Warbler 316
Yellow-throated Warbler 325
Grace's Warbler 334
Pine Warbler 340
Kirtland's Warbler 349
Prairie Warbler 356
Palm Warbler 366
Bay-breasted Warbler 375
Blackpoll Warbler 383
Blackburnian Warbler 392
Cerulean Warbler 401
Genus *Mniotilta*
Black-and-white Warbler 411
Genus *Setophaga*
American Redstart 418
Genus *Protonotaria*
Prothonotary Warbler 427
Genus *Helmitheros*
Worm-eating Warbler 435
Genus *Limnothlypis*
Swainson's Warbler 442
Genus *Seiurus*
Ovenbird 448
Northern Waterthrush 457
Louisiana Waterthrush 468

Genus *Oporornis*
    Kentucky Warbler   475
    Connecticut Warbler   484
    Mourning Warbler   493
    MacGillivray's Warbler   502
Genus *Geothlypis*
    Common Yellowthroat   512
    Belding's Yellowthroat   525
    Bahama Yellowthroat   529
    Gray-crowned Yellowthroat   535
Genus *Wilsonia*
    Hooded Warbler   541
    Wilson's Warbler   549
    Canada Warbler   560
Genus *Cardellina*
    Red-faced Warbler   568
Genus *Myioborus*
    Painted Redstart   573
    Slate-throated Redstart   579
Genus *Euthlypis*
    Fan-tailed Warbler   584
Genus *Basileuterus*
    Golden-crowned Warbler   589
    Rufous-capped Warbler   593
Genus *Icteria*
    Yellow-breasted Chat   598

Acknowledgments   611
Glossary   618
Bibliography   623
References   626
Index   654

List of Plates

1. Bachman's and Prothonotary warblers
2. Blue-winged and Golden-winged warblers
3. Blue-winged × Golden-winged hybrids
4. Tennessee and Orange-crowned warblers
5. Nashville and Virginia's warblers
6. Colima and Lucy's warblers
7. Northern and Tropical parulas
8. Migratory Northern Yellow Warbler
9. "Golden" and "Mangrove" Yellow warblers
10. Chestnut-sided and Black-throated Blue warblers
11. Magnolia and Cape May warblers
12. Yellow-rumped Warbler
13. Black-throated Green and Golden-cheeked warblers
14. Townsend's and Hermit warblers and their hybrids
15. Black-and-white and Black-throated Gray warblers
16. Blackburnian and Cerulean warblers
17. Yellow-throated and Grace's warblers
18. Bay-breasted and Blackpoll warblers
19. Pine and Prairie warblers
20. Kirtland's and Palm warblers
21. Worm-eating and Swainson's warblers,
    Ovenbird, Waterthrushes,
22. Connecticut and Kentucky warblers
23. Mourning and MacGillivray's warblers
24. Common Yellowthroat
25. Bahama, Belding's, Gray-crowned yellowthroats
26. Wilson's and Hooded warblers
27. Canada Warbler and American Redstart
28. Painted and Slate-throated redstarts, Red-faced Warbler
29. Mexican vagrants
30. Olive Warbler and Yellow-breasted Chat
31. Undertail patterns, I
32. Undertail patterns, II

A FIELD GUIDE TO
WARBLERS
OF NORTH AMERICA

INTRODUCTION

North American warblers, or wood-warblers, have long captivated birders with their diversity, bright plumages, sprightly behavior, and spectacular migrations. They have also been the subject of considerable scientific investigation, including pioneering studies of migration strategies, behavior, population and community ecology, niche separation, habitat associations, and human-induced population declines. At the same time, these warblers have presented a challenge for field identification for several reasons. First, some plumages of related species are very similar, particularly of females and immature birds. Second, warblers are small and very active, often foraging at high levels and in dense foliage, where subtle markings are hard to discern. Third, general field guides have simply pointed out the confusing nature of many warbler plumages, especially in fall, without attempting to thoroughly treat identifying characters. In this volume we bring together considerably more information on plumages, vocalizations, behavior, habitats, and distribution of warblers than can be accommodated in a standard field guide to birds. It is our conviction that details of distribution, migration patterns, and habitats, along with discussions of appearance, voice, and behavior, will provide the reader with a better framework for working through difficult identifications and understanding the significance of particular sightings.

The fascinating warblers have been treated by several excellent and indispensable previous works. Only one has had field identification primarily emphasized—Curson, Quinn, and Beadle's *Warblers of the Americas, an Identification Guide* (1994); this excellent guide describes and illustrates all of the wood-warblers, including those of Central and South America. Among the important general references on North American warblers are Frank Chapman's *The Warblers of North America* (1907), A. C. Bent's

Life Histories of North American Wood Warblers (1953, reprinted 1963), Ludlow Griscom and Alexander Sprunt's *The Warblers of America* (1957, revised 1979), and Hal Harrison's *The Wood Warbler's World* (1984). Especially recommended is Douglass Morse's *The American Warblers* (1989), a current and comprehensive review of the behavior and ecology of wood-warblers. Several monographs and review papers have treated aspects of wood-warbler biology in detail. Particularly important are those by Spector (1992) on vocalizations, Morse (1985) on habitat selection, Ficken and Ficken (1962) on behavior, and Burtt (1986) on the adaptive aspects of warbler colors and patterns. Vocalizations are described and presented in spectrographic and recorded form in Borror and Gunn's indispensable *Songs of Warblers* (1985). Behavior and songs of eastern North American wood-warbler species are presented in the video *Watching Warblers* (Male and Fieth, 1996). The Birds of North America series, jointly published by the Academy of Natural Sciences, Philadelphia, and the American Ornithologists' Union, has produced several thorough and up-to-date species accounts of wood-warblers; as of February 1997, accounts for 22 warbler species have been published.

WHAT IS A WARBLER?

The warblers treated in this guide, correctly called wood-warblers, are small, primarily insectivorous songbirds, which recently have usually been treated as a subfamily, Parulinae, of the vast family of nine-primaried songbirds, Emberizidae. Scientists had long classified wood-warblers in their own family, the Parulidae, and very recently the American Ornithologists' Union has reverted to family-level treatment for the wood-warblers. The one exception is the Olive Warbler, *Peucedramus taeniatus,* an evolutionary outlier that is best placed in its own family, the Peucedramidae. The family Parulidae has been considered closely related to the tanagers (Thraupidae) as well as the honeycreepers (Coerebidae). However, these three groups merge morphologically in almost imperceptible ways. The honeycreeper family, in fact, appears to be a rather artificial amalgam of superficially similar tanager-like birds specialized for nectar feeding.

The family Emberizidae has also been considered to include not only the wood-warblers but the tanagers and everything formerly subsumed under the Coerebidae, as well as the New World buntings, cardinals, grosbeaks, the New World blackbirds and orioles, the emberizine sparrows (including the Old World buntings), and other groups. In their 1992 book *Distribution and Taxonomy of the Birds of the World,* Charles Sibley and Burt Monroe included all of the emberizid complex within the family Fringillidae, reducing the wood-warblers to the rank of a tribe (Parulini) within the fringillid subfamily Emberizinae. Anthony Bledsoe's study of nuclear DNA suggests that the wood-warblers may be closest to the blackbirds and orioles within the emberizid complex.

Ornithologists are now almost universally agreed that the Olive Warbler (*Peucedramus taeniatus*) is well removed from the other wood-warblers. Some remove it completely from the nine-primaried songbird complex and ally it tentatively with the Old World warblers (itself a complex and almost certainly unnatural grouping). Sibley and Monroe were not able to resolve the position of the Olive Warbler within the fringillid complex and tentatively consider it the "sister group" of all other fringillids. Thus the Olive Warbler has now been given family rank of its own.

The status of the Yellow-breasted Chat as a wood-warbler has at times been questioned, with some suggesting a relationship with the mockingbirds and thrashers; but recent work confirms the position of the chat within the wood-warblers. Among several enigmatic Neotropical nine-primaried songbirds, the Wrenthrush (*Zeledonia*) is almost certainly allied with the wood-warblers. Others, including the Bananaquit (*Coereba flaveola*) and the Pardusco (*Nephelornis oneillei*) appear to be allied with the tanagers. Finally, the endemic West Indian genera *Microligea* and *Xenoligea*, traditionally considered wood-warblers, may in fact be tanagers.

Defining the American warblers is also confusing nomenclaturally. The term *warbler* is applied to many unrelated groups of small insectivorous songbirds. Australian "warblers" are in fact part of a great radiation of crowlike birds in that long-isolated part of the world. "Old World warblers" are relatives of the thrushes, comprising the leaf warblers, reed warblers, and other warblers that have radiated throughout Eurasia and into the Afrotropical, Indomalayan, and Australo-Papuan regions. Dominant genera of Old World warblers include *Phylloscopus, Acrocephalus, Locustella, Sylvia, Cisticola, Cettia, Hippolais*, and *Bradypterus*; one species, the Arctic Warbler (*Phylloscopus borealis*), breeds marginally within North America, and four other species have been recorded as vagrants to Alaska and the West Coast. None of the above groups of "warblers" are closely related to the warblers that are the subject of this book. Note that American warblers of the family Parulidae are often called wood-warblers to distinguish them from the other warblers of the world.

To confound the nomenclatural issue, there are wood-warblers covered in this book that are not called "warblers." Some are called "chats" (unrelated to various thrushlike Old World birds called chats), "redstarts" (unrelated to the Old World thrushes called redstarts), "waterthrushes" (not true thrushes!), "parulas" (which is Latin for warbler, or, more literally, the diminutive form of Parus, or titmouse), "yellowthroats," and "Ovenbird" (unrelated to the Neotropical "ovenbird" family, Furnariidae).

GEOGRAPHICAL SCOPE

We limit the scope of this guide primarily to warblers that have been recorded in North America north of the United States/Mexico border, exclusive of the West Indies; additionally we include the Baja California peninsula, biogeographically related to "Alta" California (warbler ranges in Baja California are not mapped, however). We also include the endemic yellowthroat (*Geothlypis rostrata*) of the Bahamas because of its geographical proximity to our area and the existence of possible sight records in Florida; we also include distinctive subspecies of the Yellow-throated Warbler from the Bahamas. The species accounts discuss the distribution, habitats, and geographical variation in North American warblers outside of our area of coverage.

THE NATURAL HISTORY
OF WARBLERS

There are some 115 species of New World warblers, of which slightly more than half occur in North America north of Mexico. The greatest diversity of breeding wood-warbler species occurs in eastern North America and in montane regions of Central America and northern South America. Maps of gradients in species richness in North American warblers in both *The Summer Atlas of North American Birds* by Jeff and Amy Price and Sam Droege and an article by R. Cook in *Systematic Zoology* show that the highest species numbers are found in the Appalachian, Canadian maritime, and northern Great Lakes regions. Most warbler species breeding north of Mexico are moderately to highly migratory and occur in the nonbreeding season in Mexico, Central America, or the West Indies, and in many cases south to northern South America as well (exceptionally as far south as Brazil and northern Chile).

WARBLER GENERA

The following 18 genera of warblers occur in the area covered in this guide.

Peucedramus: A taxonomic outlier to the other species covered in this guide. One medium-small, pine-dwelling species of northern Central America and Mexico, ranging north into the southwestern United States. Sexually dimorphic, with males not attaining full adult plumage until over one year old. Unique voice, tongue musculature, kingletlike wing-flicking and other characteristics suggest a relationship to the Old World warblers, but biochemical evidence appears to confirm a relationship, albeit a distant one, to the New World nine-primaried songbirds, including the wood-warblers. It is best assigned family rank of its own (Peucedramidae).

Vermivora: Very small to medium-small warblers with sharply pointed bills; plumage without strongly contrasting pattern in most species. Sexual dimorphism minor in most species. Several species specialize on nectar in nonbreeding season; some species routinely forage at dead leaf clusters. Songs usually simple trills or buzzes, more complex in some species. Most nest on or near the ground, with the exception of the cavity-nesting Lucy's Warbler. This genus may not be a natural grouping: the Bachman's, Blue-winged, and Golden-winged warblers are quite distinct from the others.

Parula: Very small to small warblers with green or black patches on the back, pale mandibles; sexual dimorphism strongest in northernmost species. Songs buzzy. Two Central American species (one of which, Crescent-chested Warbler, occurs casually in our area) are sometimes placed in *Vermivora;* these two genera are very closely related and merged by some authors. Four species, three in our area (but only one, the Northern Parula, is widespread in North America).

Dendroica: The most diverse warbler genus, with nearly all species showing contrasting plumage marks such as wing bars, tail spots, flank streaks, and patterning around the eyes. Sexual dimorphism varies from slight (e.g., Yellow-throated Warbler) to extreme (Black-throated Blue Warbler). Medium-small to medium-large. Nests are placed from near the ground to high in trees. Songs range from buzzy or wheezy to clear and rather musical; some are extremely high in pitch. Twenty-seven moderately to highly migratory species, all occurring in our area except six species endemic to the West Indies.

Mniotilta: One medium-sized, contrastingly marked black and white species uniquely specialized for creeping along trunks and branches. Closely related to *Dendroica,* and perhaps best merged into that genus.

Setophaga: One medium-sized "redstart" that is another close offshoot of *Dendroica.* Strong sexual dimorphism; males do not reach adult plumage until over one year old. Wing and tail fanning and flycatching behavior convergent with members of the diverse Neotropical warbler genus *Myioborus,* but the two genera are not closely related within the wood-warblers.

Protonotaria: One medium-large species noteworthy for its bright golden color, large bill, short tail, and cavity-nesting habit within swampy woodlands. Song of clear, sweet notes.

Helmitheros: One medium-sized species with a spikelike bill and relatively short tail; sex and age classes have similar olive and buff plumage with bold head stripes. Most commonly forages by probing into clusters of dead leaves; hops on ground. Song a simple trill. Many characters suggest *Vermivora,* and this species may in fact be closely related to that genus.

Limnothlypis: One large, brownish, terrestrial species with an exceptionally long and heavy bill. Shuffling gait on ground; typically feeds on the ground, often by flipping over dead leaves. Sex and age classes similar. Song loud and ringing. Although some experts merge this genus into *Helmitheros,* the marked differences in locomotion, behavior, vocalizations, structure, nest site, and nest structure suggest to us that the two are probably not closely related.

Seiurus: Three large, walking, terrestrial species with brown or olive upperparts and streaked or spotted underparts. Strong supercilium and tail-bobbing behavior shown by the two species of waterthrushes; a bold eye-ring and tail-cocking behavior typify the Ovenbird. All post-juvenal plumages similar. Song loud and ringing, with clear slurred notes (waterthrushes) or chanting rhythm (Ovenbird). The waterthrushes differ in many respects from the Ovenbird (locomotion, juvenal plumage, songs, etc.) and may in fact be only distantly related; they almost certainly deserve separate generic rank.

Oporornis: Medium-large warblers that feed on or near ground (the most divergent species, the Connecticut Warbler, walks on the ground, whereas the others hop); olive above and yellow below, often with an eye-ring and other facial markings. Moderate sex and age differences in plumage. Chanting songs. Four species, all found in our area. *Oporornis* is sometimes merged into the following genus; in many respects Mourning and MacGillivray's warblers do suggest *Geothlypis,* but Kentucky (though superficially yellowthroat-like) and Connecticut do not.

Geothlypis: Nine medium to medium-large species of "yellowthroats," one of which is widespread in North America; one endemic species each from Baja California and the Bahamas, are also treated in this guide, along with the Gray-crowned Yellowthroat, a vagrant to southern Texas. Skulking, wrenlike birds of marshy, weedy, or dense understory habitats. Generally olive above and yellow below, with males showing a black mask. Rhythmic, chanting songs. We follow AOU 1983 in including the Gray-crowned Yellowthroat here, but it is probably best placed in its own genus, *Chamaethlypis.* It is similar to *Geothlypis* yellowthroats in plumage but has a thick bill with a distinctly curved culmen. Males lack a black mask but have black lores. Its vocalizations (especially call notes), postures, and habitat (grassy areas, meadows) are quite distinct from *Geothlypis.*

Wilsonia: Small to medium-sized warblers, green or gray above and bright yellow below, with black markings on the head or chest most prominent in males. Active, flycatching warblers with well-developed rictal bristles. The long tail is expressively flipped or flicked. Three species, all found in our area; the Hooded Warbler does not appear to be especially closely related to the other two species.

Cardellina: One medium-sized species, gray and white on the body with unique red and black face pattern; bill stout, chickadee-like. Sexes generally similar. Found in mountains of Mexico to southwestern United States. Long expressive tail like *Wilsonia,* and thought by some to be closely related to that genus as well as to the Neotropical genus *Ergaticus.*

Myioborus: Twelve medium-sized flycatching "redstarts," of which two occur (one casually) in our area. Our species are distinctly marked with red on the lower breast and bold white flashes in the tail; sexes are generally similar. Both of our species are very active, often fanning the tail. The English name "whitestart" is sometimes used for the members of this genus. The name "redstart" is an Old German language reference to a red tail, not present in any member of this genus; it was originally applied to Palearctic chats of the genus *Phoenicurus,* not to our wood-warbler "redstarts." We strongly concur, however, with Robert Ridgely and Guy Tudor, who wrote in *The Birds of South America,* that it is undesirable to replace a long-accepted group name with a contrived one with little immediate descriptive value (who, after all, commonly associates "start" with the tail?).

Euthlypis: One large Central American species, occurring as a casual vagrant along our southwestern border. A ground-dwelling species that flicks and fans its white-tipped tail. This genus is closely related to, and perhaps best merged with, the genus *Basileuterus,* but shares some features with *Myioborus* as well.

Basileuterus: The second largest warbler genus, with some 24 Neotropical species, two of which occur as vagrants along the southern border of our area. Most species are olive to gray above, yellow to whitish below, with some patterning on the crown or face. Usually found near the ground in brushy habitats or forest understory; most diverse in northern South America. As Ridgely and Tudor write, the limits of this genus are somewhat controversial; two streamside species are now usually placed in their own genus, *Phaeothlypis.*

Icteria: One unique, very large species with an exceptionally thick bill, long tail and unwarbler-like loud, rich, and often harsh voice. Olive above, bright yellow on the breast, with black (or slaty) and white markings about the eyes. Although some workers have postulated relationships with the mockingbirds and thrashers, biochemical evidence shows this chat to be an aberrant wood-warbler.

The remaining wood-warbler genera are restricted to the Neotropics. Five genera (*Catharopeza, Microligia, Teretistris, Leu-*

copeza, and *Xenoligia*) are endemic to the Greater and Lesser Antilles. The red warblers of the genus *Ergaticus,* probably allied with *Cardellina* and perhaps also *Wilsonia,* occur from northern Mexico to Guatemala. The three *Granatellus* chats occur in tropical lowlands from coastal Mexico to Belize and in Amazonian South America. The Wrenthrush (*Zeledonia*), perhaps an offshoot of *Basileuterus,* is endemic to the mountains of Costa Rica and western Panama.

The generic limits of wood-warblers, as suggested above, are not always well defined or understood. Most of the northern genera (and certainly at least *Vermivora* through *Setophaga* in the sequence followed in this book) appear to be especially closely related to one another. Divergent morphological trends may be noted within a single genus. For example, in the large genus *Dendroica,* the thin, somewhat decurved bill of the Cape May Warbler appears to be an adaptation to the species' nectar-feeding habits in the nonbreeding season; other *Dendroica* show long, probing bills or relatively wide "flycatching" bills. Morphological variation in structures related to foraging can be especially "plastic" evolutionarily (for example, the bills in *Dendroica*), so closely related species can be rather different in these structures. Analyses of the relationships among wood-warblers should concentrate upon more conservative characters that do not change so readily. Call notes, mitochondrial DNA, and juvenal plumage may be examples of such characters. Thorough phylogenetic studies to trace the evolutionary relationships of the wood-warblers are sorely needed.

SPECIES LIMITS

With a few exceptions, there is little controversy about the species limits of North American warblers, even though the scientific definition of a species itself remains somewhat controversial. Unresolved questions about wood-warbler species limits fall into two main categories. First are the cases of populations that are distinct in appearance (and often behavior and vocalizations) but have been demonstrated to interbreed to some degree where their ranges overlap. In some cases, where there is free interbreeding in zones of contact, these forms have been lumped into a single species, as in the "Myrtle," "Audubon's," and "Goldman's" warblers (collectively known as the Yellow-rumped Warbler); in others, where mating is most often only with conspecifics, they have been maintained as separate species (e.g., Blue-winged and Golden-winged warblers, or Townsend's and Hermit warblers). To some extent, hybridization in these groups may have been accelerated by human-caused habitat changes. Taxonomic decisions at the species level depend on the nature of the interbreeding data available, as well as on subjective assessments that depend on one's concept of a species.

A second group of species-limit problems concerns geographically isolated ("allopatric") forms that share most morphological and behavioral characteristics but differ in some; here the test of interbreeding is not applicable. One example is the Nashville Warbler, in which the geographically separated eastern *ruficapilla* and western *ridgwayi* subspecies differ slightly in plumage, behavior, and vocalizations as well as genetically. There has not yet been a serious suggestion by recent ornithologists that eastern and western Nashville Warblers represent different species, but they clearly represent distinguishable separate evolutionary lineages and would perhaps qualify as "phylogenetic species." Under the phylogenetic species concept, such separate evolutionary lineages, when distinguishable from one another, are afforded species status. With the more traditional biological species concept (in which reproductive isolation is the main criterion for species status), such "phylogenetic species" are usually equivalent to subspecies status within a species. The Yellow Warbler has three groups of subspecies (Northern, "Golden," and "Mangrove" groups) which may involve numerous "phylogenetic species," but perhaps includes two or three "good" biological species as well (and have sometimes been so treated in the past).

HYBRIDIZATION

Closely related species with a recent common evolutionary ancestor are often termed "superspecies," a concept useful for identifying close relatives within a genus. We refer, for example, to the *Dendroica virens* superspecies (the Black-throated Green Warbler and its close allies) and the *Vermivora ruficapilla* superspecies (Nashville and Virginia's warblers; some workers would include the Colima Warbler in this superspecies as well). The two waterthrushes, two parulas, and Blue-winged and Golden-winged warblers also form superspecies or "species pairs." Hybridization is frequent within the last pair, but unknown (or at least exceedingly rare) in the first two.

Hybridization poses clear field identification problems, and these are treated in the text. Hybridization may occur within species pairs, as noted above. However, hybrid pairings often involve more distantly related warbler species and even members of different genera. Such intergeneric hybrids include Blue-winged × Kentucky warbler, Nashville Warbler × American Redstart, and Northern Parula × Yellow-throated Warbler ("Sutton's Warbler"). These combinations point to the close evolutionary relatedness of most North American warbler genera.

Many warbler species show variation in morphological and behavioral characters through their range. Of the 60 species treated in this guide, about half have subspecies, or geographical "races"; such species are termed polytypic, in contrast with monotypic species with no recognized subspecies. Subspecies are given trinomials, or three-parted scientific names; the third part of the name, following the genus and the specific epithet, is the name of the subspecies. Two of our warblers, the Yellow Warbler and the Common Yellowthroat, show exceedingly complex geographical variation, with 43 and 13 currently recognized named subspecies respectively (and many more yellowthroat races, according to the views of some workers). Taxonomists often disagree on the validity of particular subspecies, and some have even questioned the utility of naming subspecies altogether. The geographic variation shown by many of our warblers is minor, gradual ("clinal"), or without clear pattern over the species' geographical range; in such species (e.g., American Redstart, Northern Waterthrush, and Black-throated Gray Warbler) the validity of named subspecies might rightly be questioned. Even if the naming of subspecies has been carried to extremes by some workers, we still find subspecies a useful tool for describing geographical variation.

North American wood-warblers show several patterns of geographical variation. In two species, Nashville Warbler and Yellow-breasted Chat, there are eastern and western subspecies (although some workers recognize additional subspecies of the chat). Within eastern North America, two species (Pine and Prairie warblers) show minor differentiation in peninsular Florida. Also within the East, a few species show interior vs. coastal plain variation (Yellow-throated, Black-throated Green). The Palm Warbler is strongly differentiated into a subspecies breeding over much of boreal Canada (and adjacent portions of some Great Lakes states) and another in easternmost Canada and adjacent New England.

Two species, the Orange-crowned and Wilson's warblers, show parallel patterns of differentiation into boreal, interior West, and Pacific coastal forms (with the Pacific Coast races being brightest). Other variation within the topographically diverse West is shown by the MacGillivray's Warbler and Common and Belding's yellowthroats. The highly variable Yellow Warbler shows east-west variation across the boreal regions, variation within the West, and considerable variation within tropical and subtropical regions. Most of the species that are widespread in the Neotropics show geographical variation south of our area, e.g., the Tropical Parula, *Myioborus* redstarts, Grace's Warbler, Gray-crowned Yellowthroat, and the *Basileuterus* warblers. Finally, some subspecies represent divergence resulting from isolation on islands, as in the Orange-crowned Warbler of the California Channel Islands and the Bahama subspecies of Yellow-throated Warbler.

PLUMAGES AND MOLTS

The plumage sequences of most North American warblers are generally similar, but important variations do occur. An excellent summary of molts and plumage sequences is given in the book *Identification Guide to North American Passerines* by Peter Pyle, Steve Howell, Robert Yunick, and David DeSante. The first plumage developed by the nearly naked hatchlings is the juvenal plumage. This is usually the dullest plumage shown by a species, with dull olive, brown, buff, and gray colors often predominating. Juveniles (birds wearing juvenal plumage) often show more streaking, mottling, or spotting in the plumage than older birds, and many show buff or light brown wing bars, even in species that lack wing bars in subsequent plumages. Juvenal plumage is also more lax in texture, and wears more rapidly than post-juvenal feathering.

The juvenal body plumage is usually only worn for a brief period. In some species, such as American Redstart, juvenal plumage may begin to be replaced even before the young bird leaves the nest. In almost all of our species, juvenal plumage is seen only on the breeding grounds, usually only for a couple of weeks after fledging. Specimens of warblers in full juvenal plumage are rare in collections. For this reason, we do not illustrate this plumage for most species. A few species, such as the Orange-crowned Warbler and Yellow-rumped Warbler, may disperse well away from the natal territory while still in juvenal plumage; in the Painted Redstart, juvenal plumage persists for weeks after fledging. Juvenal plumage is less persistent in the Ovenbird, but it differs substantially from that of the waterthrushes, with which the Ovenbird is traditionally considered congeneric. We illustrate juvenal plumage for these four species. Juvenal plumages of most species are illustrated in *Warblers of the Americas* by Jon Curson, David Quinn, and David Beadle.

Juvenal plumage is partially replaced by a first prebasic molt which almost always occurs on the breeding grounds. The first prebasic molt results in the acquisition of first basic ("first fall") plumage. In nearly all of our species, the first prebasic molt involves the contour feathers covering the body, along with most of the wing coverts. The tail feathers (rectrices) and the primaries, secondaries, and tertials (collectively, the remiges) of juvenal plumage are usually retained until the following year's

JUVENAL	ADULT
Tend to be more tapered and more pointed at the tip. Entire feather may average slightly narrower than on adults of the same species.	Often more truncate, less pointed. The feathers may be slightly broader, on average, than on first-year birds of the same species.

Figure 1. Aging Warblers by Rectrix Shape

prebasic molt. The juvenal primary coverts are usually retained also. Juvenal rectrices are usually more pointed or tapered (less rounded) than the corresponding feathers of older birds (see Figure 1); this difference is important for aging birds in the hand and may be striking in some species (but subtle in most and useless for aging in many); in many *Vermivora*, the juvenal primaries are also more pointed than those of older birds. In a few species, the first prebasic molt involves some or all of the rectrices.

The prebasic molt of birds one year old or older is complete, with all feathers replaced over a several-week period, again almost always after nesting but while still on the breeding grounds. In a few species, such as the Tennessee Warbler, the prebasic molt of flight feathers is largely completed on the breeding grounds but may be suspended during migration and completed on the wintering grounds. The prebasic molt of warblers older than their first year results in the definitive basic ("fall adult") plumage.

Most warblers show a partial prealternate molt into an alternate ("breeding" or "spring") plumage. This molt does not involve flight feathers (except the tertials in some species), but rather affects only contour feathers and often wing coverts as well. The prealternate molt may be extensive in many species of *Dendroica*, such as Yellow-rumped, Magnolia, Blackpoll, and Bay-breasted Warblers; these are the warblers that show strikingly different spring and fall plumages. In most warblers the prealternate molt is less extensive, resulting in only minor changes in appearance; in some species, such as the Yellow-breasted Chat and Prothonotary, Worm-eating, and Hooded warblers, as well as most Neotropical species, there is no significant prealternate molt. The prealternate molt is begun on the wintering grounds, as early as late December or January in many species (e.g., Tennessee Warbler); it is often completed by the onset of spring migration and nearly always completed by the time of arrival on the breeding grounds.

For simplicity, the text accounts and plate legends use a more accessible plumage terminology: spring adult (the definitive alternate plumage in those species with a prealternate molt; worn definitive basic plumage in the others); first spring (first alternate plumage in those species with prealternate molt, worn first basic plumage in the others); fall adult (fresh definitive basic plumage); and first fall (fresh first basic plumage).

It is important to bear in mind that seasonal changes in appearance may be the result of feather wear, rather than the replacement of feathers. For example, the black color of the throats, heads, and back streaks of many *Dendroica* warblers is veiled by thin pale tips (olive, yellow, gray, buff, or whitish) in fresh plumage after the prebasic molt, but wear through the course of the winter results in clean black coloration before the start of the breeding season. Even over the course of a season there can be significant change in appearance with plumage wear and bleaching; "fresh" basic plumaged individuals in early fall may be noticeably brighter than in midwinter. Change in appearance can also result from soiling of plumage with nectar, pitch, pollen, or soot; this is often seen on the faces of warblers that probe for nectar in the winter and can be extensive on species feeding at eucalyptus

Plumage wear through winter and early spring is especially evident on wings (including wing bars) and tail of Dendroica *warblers. (Photo: Brian E. Small)*

flowers (as in coastal California). Change in appearance can also result from loss of feathers.

Bill colors often change seasonally and with age. In many warblers the bill is darker during the breeding season than in fall and winter; a striking example is the Prothonotary Warbler, in which spring males have black bills but fall males have pale pinkish brown bills (see Plate 1); a similar seasonal difference is also found in Blue-winged and Golden-winged warblers. In many *Dendroica*, Prothonotary Warbler, Yellow-breasted Chat, and some other species, the bill of the male averages darker than that of females of like age.

HABITATS

Wood-warblers are generally birds of woodlands, forests, or dense brush, but habitat preferences vary widely among species, as well as geographically and seasonally within a species. Many species breed in coniferous forests; several species, for example, may inhabit the same spruce forests in New England or eastern Canada (where pioneering studies by Robert MacArthur, Douglass Morse, and others have demonstrated how warbler species coexist by utilizing these forests in measurably different ways). Other species are typical of deciduous woodlands, or of mixed conifer-hardwood associations. Whereas some species (such as Blackburnian, Cerulean, or Hermit warblers) require mature forests in the breeding season, others (for example, Blue-winged, Golden-winged, Chestnut-sided, and Kirtland's warblers) reach peak abundances in early successional woodland habitats. A few western species breed in relatively arid, brushy habitats, though within western North America, riparian (streamside) woodlands and montane forests harbor the greatest densities of breeding warblers.

Wood-warbler species vary in their degree of habitat specialization. The Kirtland's Warbler has narrow requirements — successional jack pine woodlands only 5 to 15 years old. Conversely, American Redstarts nest in a wide range of woodlands with some hardwood component, and Common Yellowthroats thrive in dense vegetation in a variety of moist areas, whether brushy forest edges or monotonous cattail marshes. In some species, very specific components of the habitat are critical for survival and reproductive success (for example, the Golden-cheeked Warbler of central Texas requires the presence of Ashe juniper for nest material).

Winter habitat requirements, in general, are more poorly known for our wood-warblers than are breeding habitats. The literature suggests that most of our warblers winter in a variety of second growth, woodland edge, and mature forest habitats, but the requirements of individual species are undoubtedly more specific than this. Extensive rain forests are generally not important winter habitats for our wood-warblers; on the other hand, foothill and montane forests from Mexico south through northernmost South America host a great diversity of North American warblers in winter. The hardiest warblers (for example, Yellow-rumped, Palm, and Orange-crowned) winter commonly within the United States and can indeed be quite broad in their habitat tolerances.

Most warblers will use a variety of habitats in spring and fall migration; many take advantage of rich food sources at flowering or budding trees and shrubs in spring; fall migrant warblers abound in rank annual vegetation as well as in high mountain meadows (which may be inhospitable in spring). The energetic stresses of migration amplify the importance of stopover habitats (such as in coastal woodlands and cheniers along the Gulf Coast, bayberry thickets on the Atlantic Coast, and desert oases in the West).

Habitats are an important part of the puzzle of warbler identification, but we caution observers that even breeding warblers may occur in atypical habitats. Also, habitats often blend and interdigitate in complex ways that may not be evident to the human observer. Often, the way a warbler uses its habitat is the better clue to identification.

FORAGING AND FOOD

Warblers employ a variety of techniques to obtain their food, and their diets are surprisingly complex. Arthropod prey, especially

· *Figure 2. Grace's Warbler*

THE NATURAL HISTORY OF WARBLERS

Figure 3. Black-and-white Warbler

insect larvae, are overwhelmingly important in the diets of all warblers, but fruit and nectar are seasonally important in the diets of many species. Not only do the methods of obtaining prey differ somewhat among species, but foraging sites may differ as well. James V. Remsen Jr. and Scott Robinson developed a useful terminology for describing foraging maneuvers by terrestrial birds; wood-warblers primarily employ the following techniques: gleaning, reaching, hanging, probing, gaping, sallying, flutter-

Figure 4. Swainson's Warbler

chasing, and flutter-pursuing. Although we generally use more familiar and accessible terms, such as "flycatching," we urge warbler observers to apply the more rigorous terminology as well.

As the food searching and attack techniques of wood-warblers vary, so, too, do the substrates from which food is obtained. Some warblers may glean leaves or twigs while others probe needles (for example, Grace's Warbler, Figure 2), bark or crevices; bark gleaning is carried to the extreme by the Black-and-white Warbler (Figure 3), which creeps in nuthatch fashion along branches. Among the leaf gleaners, some (e.g., Worm-eating, see photo below) virtually specialize, at least seasonally, on clusters of dead leaves suspended above the ground. Ground-foraging warblers concentrate especially on the leaf litter, and some species such as Swainson's Warbler (Figure 4), Ovenbird, and the waterthrushes often flip over dead leaves for prey. Sallying into the air ("flycatching") is part of the foraging repertoire of many warblers; many warblers also sally-strike and sally-stall, gleaning prey from a surface, such as the bottom of a leaf, while hovering in the air. Observers will readily note that some warblers (e.g., Blackpoll and Bay-breasted warblers, Ovenbird) appear relatively lethargic or deliberate while foraging, whereas others are intensely active (e.g., redstarts, Wilson's Warbler).

Animal food other than arthropods (insects, spiders, and related groups) is rare in warbler diets, but mollusks (small snails, slugs) and worms are sometimes an important food source. Vertebrate prey is exceptional, although waterthrushes often take small fish from shallow water. Palm, Yellow-rumped, and "Mangrove" Yellow warblers, at least, have been noted foraging in intertidal habitats along ocean shores.

Worm-eating Warbler
(Photo: Giff Beaton)

Figure 5. Cape May Warbler

Fruit and nectar can be critically important food for many wood-warblers in the fall and winter months. Many *Vermivora* warblers, as well as the Cape May Warbler (Figure 5), are regular nectar-feeders for much of the year. Small fruits sustain many warblers during fall migration and the winter months; bayberry and poison ivy thickets often teem with berry-eating Yellow-rumped Warblers in fall. Lingering warblers wintering well north of their normal range often visit suet feeders and other feeding stations.

Vocalizations

Vocalizations of wood-warblers mainly fit into two categories. Songs are generally more complex vocalizations, given almost exclusively by males, which serve such functions as mate attraction and territory advertisement. Call notes, in contrast, are relatively simple vocalizations, often single syllables, which serve a variety of functions but primarily signify the location and temperament of the calling bird.

Wood-warbler songs vary from series of thin, high-pitched notes, through lower-pitched trills or buzzes, to complex whistled or chanting crescendos. Male warblers sing almost incessantly early in the breeding season, and often in spring migration as well (especially as the breeding grounds are approached); many species begin singing before departing the wintering grounds. There is often a resurgence in song after the young have fledged in midsummer. Female song is documented for only a few North American wood-warbler species. Especially within *Dendroica* and related genera, male warblers have several song types which usually fall into the major categories of "accented ending" and "unaccented ending" (terms that hint at the main structural differences between the two types of song). These song types are given under different circumstances, and one type may predominate during certain times of day or certain phases of the breeding season. To generalize a complex situation: accented-ending songs appear to function mainly in pair formation and are given most often during pair bonding; unaccented-ending songs function in territorial advertisement and are often most frequent at dawn and dusk. There may be a great deal of individual variation in the structure of songs, but a given individual tends to sing a predictable repertoire. Geographical variation in songs has been reported for many wood-warbler species, and isolation on islands may have profound effects on the song repertoire.

Special song types include various muted songs and "subsongs," and also "flight songs," which are given routinely by several wood-warblers, most notably Yellow-breasted Chat, Common Yellowthroat, waterthrushes, and Ovenbird. Some species occasionally give rather faithful renditions of the songs of other warbler species; the function of such mimicry, if any, is unknown.

The posture and location of a singing warbler is often quite unlike the species' normal behavior: the singer may select a high, open perch (even if it is normally a skulker) and adopt a rather vertical posture with the tail down (see Figure 6 of Common Yellowthroat). Species that routinely bob their tails or have other distinctive body, wing, or tail movements generally abandon such behaviors while singing.

Call notes of wood-warblers are often referred to as "chip"

Figure 6. Common Yellowthroat

notes, since the commonly given notes that announce location are variations on that syllable. The "chip" calls of different warblers vary in loudness, quality (e.g., "sweet," "metallic," or "hard"), and "shape" (e.g., flat vs. down-slurred). Few birders would agree on the adjectives that best describe a given warbler's "chip"; for this reason we often compare the "chip" call to those of other species. Call notes show little variation within populations and can be excellent clues to species identification. However, the quality and repetition rate of calls can vary with the state of agitation of the calling individuals. Some call notes which the observer would do well to learn as standards include the sweet slurred *tsip* of the American Redstart, the huskier slurred *tchip* of the Yellow or Chestnut-sided warbler, the hard *stik* of the Orange-crowned Warbler, the loud *chink* of the Northern Waterthrush, the soft *tip* of the Black-throated Green Warblers and its close relatives, and the mellow *chup* of the Kentucky Warbler. Call notes of some species, including the Yellow-breasted Chat, Painted Redstart, Wilson's Warbler, and Magnolia Warbler are so distinctive as to be termed unique, though often hard to describe.

Flight notes are simple, high-pitched calls given during short flights and also long (usually nocturnal) migration flights. Rarely are flight notes species-specific, but a few differences in quality will enable the observer to narrow down the identity of the calling bird. Some species, such as Yellow, Blackpoll, and Connecticut warblers give a buzzy *zzeet* call in flight. Others, including all species in the Black-throated Green Warbler complex, give a high, sweet *see*. Notes resembling flight notes are sometimes given by perched birds; conversely, "chip" notes are frequently given in flight, especially upon takeoff.

The repertoire of simple calls given by warblers goes well beyond the common "chip" and flight notes, but most of the other calls are tied to specific situations (e.g., alarm, begging, stress) and are not discussed in the species accounts.

Behavior

Beyond the obvious foraging behavior (discussed above), birders are most likely to be struck by species differences in locomotive behavior and body movements among our warblers. Body, wing, and tail movements are often quite distinctive. For example, Palm, Kirtland's, and Prairie warblers bob their tails in a rapid up-and-down movement (this is often referred to as "tail wagging," which misleadingly connotes a side-to-side movement). Many other wood-warblers (e.g., Yellow, Virginia's, western Nashville) routinely bob the tails, but to a lesser degree. Rufous-capped Warblers carry the tail cocked upward (often nearly vertically),

Hooded Warbler. Tail flashing, exposing the mostly white outer rectrices, is a characteristic behavior of this species. (Photo: Brian E. Small)

and Chestnut-sideds carry the tail at about a 30° angle, well above the slightly drooped wingtips.

Tail fanning and wing spreading is characteristic of our two *Myioborus* redstarts as well as the American Redstart. The Hooded Warbler has the distinctive behavior of flashing open and shut its outer tail feathers, displaying the large white patches on these feathers (see photo above).

Ground locomotion in wood-warblers usually involves hopping, but a few species walk: the waterthrushes, Ovenbird, and Connecticut Warbler (the latter two with distinctive, high-stepping gaits). The Swainson's Warbler employs a peculiar shuffle, seemingly between a walk and a hop. The largely terrestrial waterthrushes exaggeratedly bob the tail and rear quarters in an up-and-down or nearly circular motion.

Most warblers raise their crown feathers when disturbed or excited; around the nest many give exaggerated distraction displays, drooping or spreading the wings and tail and calling excitedly.

BREEDING BIOLOGY

The body of literature on the social and reproductive behavior of wood-warblers is vast and fascinating, from territorial establishment and maintenance through courtship and mating systems to post-fledging behavior of the young. The traditional notion that warblers establish monogamous pair bonds for the breeding season has been challenged by recent research on populations of marked individuals. Polygyny (in which a male mates with more than one female during a breeding season), while not the norm, is certainly not rare. Males of migratory wood-warblers typically arrive on the breeding grounds about a week before the females, claiming and maintaining a territory through singing and hostile interactions with rival males. Pair bonds may form quickly after the arrival of females, and (at least in the northernmost breeders) the whole breeding cycle occurs in only about a three-month period.

Nest-building is performed by the female. Nearly all warblers construct their nests of plant downs, fibers, strips of bark, grasses, spider webs, and other rather fine materials. Many add dried leaves to the outside of the nest, which is an open (or sometimes domed) cup. A few species select highly specialized nest materials; parulas, for example, use Spanish moss, *Usnea* lichens, and similar materials for nest construction. Nest placement varies greatly among our wood-warblers. Many species place the nest on the ground, even some species (e.g., Black-and-white Warbler) whose foraging sites are usually high in the trees; ground nests are usually hidden well within grass tussocks, clumps of dead leaves, or under exposed roots. Only two of our warblers, Lucy's and Prothonotary, habitually nest in cavities.

Warbler eggs are pale (usually whitish) with variable spotting; in a few species, eggs are unmarked or nearly so. Clutch sizes range from two eggs to as many as eight, with clutch size generally decreasing with decreasing latitude. Incubation is performed almost exclusively by the female; the incubating female is sometimes fed by the male. Most of our warblers normally lay only one clutch of eggs per breeding season, but in a few species, especially those of more southerly distribution, there may be a second clutch after the first brood is successfully fledged. Incubation generally takes 11 to 13 days.

Nestlings grow rapidly, and they may fledge as early as the ninth day, before they are capable of sustained flight. Fledglings are often easily located by their incessant thin begging calls; typically the fledged young will split up, with one or more cared for by each adult.

The breeding biology of many North American wood-warblers is well studied; detailed studies of the Prairie Warbler by Val Nolan make that species perhaps the best known. In contrast, little is known of the breeding biology of our species whose primary breeding range is in the Neotropics, south of the United States.

In the nonbreeding season, wood-warblers vary greatly in their social behavior. Some, like the Yellow-rumped Warbler, may gather in large single-species flocks, and many other warblers join mixed-species foraging flocks (whose members include warblers and nonwarblers alike). Other species, such as the Hooded Warbler, are solitary and defend winter territories.

Among the most memorable birding events in North America are the spring and fall migrations of warblers along our coasts and Great Lakes shores, along mountain ridges, through midwestern valleys, and at western desert oases. With few exceptions, the wood-warblers treated in this guide are migratory, and most are highly so. Their movements are massive, routes complex, and timing predictable. The scatter is great as well, with species occurring well out of range on a regular basis, and exceptionally far out of range on occasion. Only some of our southernmost populations are sedentary (some populations of Pine Warbler and Common Yellowthroat, for example), and even the Neotropical species that are largely resident show some degree of annual movement.

Warblers migrate primarily at night, "refueling" during the day, although there can be significant migratory movement through the daylight hours as well. Those taking overwater routes (as over the Gulf of Mexico) must keep flying until a shore is reached; when encountering headwinds, migrants flying across the Gulf of Mexico often become exhausted, and many perish in the ocean (some may land on ships and oil-drilling platforms). Those reaching the coastline (with the greatest concentrations reaching the upper coast of Texas and the coast of southwestern Louisiana) concentrate in the first patches of shrubs and live oaks they encounter (hence, migration "fallouts" at well-known localities such as High Island, Texas). Similar concentrations of warblers at the beginning or completion of overwater crossings are noted around the Great Lakes and elsewhere. Weather conditions profoundly affect the magnitude of migratory movements of warblers, with birds often awaiting favorable conditions before attempting a particular leg of the journey. Conditions promoting massive "fallouts" may occur when large numbers of birds depart for a night's journey but encounter headwinds and overcast conditions during the night. Many other birds die at communications towers, tall buildings, and lighthouses during migration, particularly on overcast nights.

Spring migration routes in eastern North America fall into some generalizable patterns (see map at right). Species that winter primarily in the West Indies and/or Amazonian South America (e.g., Blackpoll, Connecticut warblers) take a spring route through Florida, or from the Bahamas to the southern Atlantic coastal states. Most species whose winter ranges are mainly in Central America and adjacent northern South America are trans-Gulf migrants, crossing from the Yucatán peninsula region of Mexico to the Gulf Coast from the upper Texas coast east to the western Florida panhandle; examples include Blue-winged, Gold-

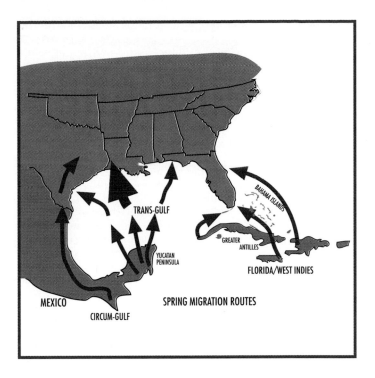

TRANS-GULF

BAHAMA ISLANDS

YUCATAN
PENINSULA

GREATER
ANTILLES

FLORIDA/WEST INDIES

MEXICO

CIRCUM-GULF

SPRING MIGRATION ROUTES

en-winged, Blackburnian, and Bay-breasted warblers. Other species, whose winter ranges are mainly in Mexico and northernmost Central America, tend to be circum-Gulf migrants, skirting the Gulf of Mexico by moving northward through southern and east-central Texas; Nashville Warbler is a classic circum-Gulf spring migrant. There are many exceptions to these generalizations (for example, the Mourning Warbler, which winters in Central America and northern South America, is a circum-Gulf spring migrant). Many species with large wintering ranges (Northern Parula, Black-and-white Warbler, Northern Waterthrush, and Common Yellowthroat, for example) migrate in spring on a broad front, although particular populations of those species undoubtedly use narrower routes than those of the species as a whole.

Spring arrival dates at a given locality are predictable, and of course are generally later at higher latitudes. During strong southerly winds and warm fronts, one often finds early arrivals at the latitude of the Great Lakes shortly after the first birds arrive on the Gulf Coast. Spring overshoots of southerly-breeding warblers north of their normal breeding range often coincide with strong southerly storms as well.

Most warblers breeding in western North America south of the boreal regions winter in Mexico and northern Central America. Their spring migration routes through the West vary, with species whose breeding ranges are mainly in the Pacific Coast states (e.g., Townsend's and Hermit warblers) generally moving northward through southern California and southern Arizona (from the San Pedro River Valley west), while those with more extensive breeding ranges (e.g., MacGillivray's Warbler) move north on a broader front.

Fall migration routes also vary among species. Through eastern North America, fall migration routes are usually more easterly than in spring. Many circum-Gulf spring migrants, for example, are not uncommon in fall along the Gulf Coast of Louisiana. Trans-Gulf spring migrants that are rare at that season in Florida and along the eastern Gulf Coast may be numerous in those same areas in fall; many, like the Cerulean Warbler, are casual in fall along the upper Texas coast where they are numerous in spring. Some species (Blackpoll and Connecticut warblers, for example) have a strong eastward component to their fall migration, east to New England and the Mid-Atlantic Coast; one view is that these species then launch on an overwater route to the West Indies and northern South America. A few species, notably Palm and Black-throated Blue warblers, are actually more numerous in fall along the Texas coast than in spring.

In the West, many warblers move southward along north–south-trending mountain ranges in fall. Many species have an easterly shift in their fall migration routes; for example, Hermit Warblers are numerous in fall in the mountains of extreme southeastern Arizona and southwestern New Mexico, where they are very rare in spring.

Individual warblers commonly linger in the northern states and provinces into the late fall. In Newfoundland, for example, individuals of at least 20 species have lingered as late as December (in some cases January or even through the winter) around St. Johns. It goes without saying that overwinter survival at these latitudes is low, and individuals that do survive often rely on feeding stations. The migrations of some species, notably the Yellow-rumped Warbler, may vary with existing conditions, with the timing and magnitude of movements being governed by weather and food availability.

Vagrancy, the occurrence of individuals well outside of the "normal" range, is a hallmark of wood-warblers and a corollary of their large-scale annual migrations. Indeed, at least 21 species have been recorded in Britain and Europe, where none normally occurs. As the states and provinces of North America receive more and more thorough coverage, warbler lists invariably climb. Centrally located Texas has recorded 53 of the 60 species treated in this guide. Lists of 46 warbler species in California and 43 in Massachusetts attest to the phenomena of western, northward, and eastward vagrancy. Certain factors appear to promote the occurrence and the discovery of out-of-range vagrants; these include isolation of habitat (e.g., a desert oasis, small offshore island, or even a park within an extensive urban region), thoroughness of observer coverage (the extreme being intensive netting and trapping operations in an isolated and extremely limited habitat, such as at Southeast Farallon Island, California), and geographical position (e.g., on a coastline or peninsula). In the species accounts, California (totals complete through 1995) is often used as indication of vagrancy patterns to the west because of the extensive data base amassed there over the years.

CONSERVATION

Several lines of evidence suggest that many Neotropical land bird migrants, including wood-warblers, have experienced significant population declines over the past 30 years or so. Such evidence comes from long-term monitoring of breeding bird populations, especially from the United States Fish and Wildlife Service's Breeding Bird Surveys, and of migrants. Although there are clearly multiple causes of these declines, the primary factor is the loss, fragmentation, and decline in quality of breeding habitat. In addition to the direct decrease of populations with the loss of breeding habitat, there are insidious indirect effects of the reduction and fragmentation of forests and woodlands. The increasing ratio of edge to interior as forest patches diminish in size accelerates rates of nest predation by adaptable native predators as well as feral cats and dogs and brood parasitism by cowbirds. Even seemingly intact nesting habitats may suffer from more subtle loss of quality due to exotic plants, exotic or feral predators, and pesticides and other environmental toxins.

Wood-warblers that require old-growth forests as breeding habitat have been severely affected by loss of these forests; these include the Cerulean Warbler of old river valley forests in the Mississippi and Ohio valleys and Allegheny region, and perhaps the Townsend's Warbler of coniferous forests of the Pacific states. Other warblers with narrow habitat specializations have suffered as well, with the ultimate victim being the almost certainly extinct Bachman's Warbler, which bred only in southern bottomland forests (and may have been largely limited to cane brakes there). The deforestation of much of the hardwood forests of eastern North America in the 1700s and 1800s undoubtedly led to the range fragmentation and population declines of many wood-warbler species, although forest preservation and regeneration in the present century has largely reversed this trend. Some species (e.g., Chestnut-sided and Blue-winged warblers) that favor successional forest stages and forest edges have greatly benefited from human-caused habitat changes over the past century.

Many view cowbird parasitism (see photo below) as perhaps the major factor in wood-warbler declines in North America. Brown-headed Cowbirds (locally also Bronzed Cowbirds, and potentially Shiny Cowbirds) lay their eggs in the nests of host species (often warblers), and the young cowbirds are raised by the "foster parents" to the detriment of the host species' own young. Few warbler young are successfully fledged from nests containing cowbird chicks. Cowbirds can thus severely reduce reproductive success in warblers and other small, open-cup nesting birds. The disastrous effects of increasing cowbird populations (and increasing cowbird access to warbler nests due to habitat fragmentation) are undeniable. Intensive cowbird control programs have led to vastly increased reproductive success of Kirtland's Warblers in Michigan. It is important to realize, however, that cowbird effects are a symptom of more general losses of habitat size and quality.

The loss and fragmentation of wintering habitat has also been implicated in the population declines of our wood-warblers. Winter habitat loss would be expected to affect mainly those species with narrow requirements, especially those requiring mature forests. Fortunately, most (but by no means all) of our North American wood-warblers winter in a range of habitats that includes disturbed and second-growth woodlands.

Migrating warblers face a host of human-induced problems,

Blue-winged Warbler feeding cowbird fledgling (Photo: Steven and Dave Maslowski)

from loss of critical stopover resting and foraging habitats to massive mortalities from structures such as skyscrapers, glass-fronted buildings and walkways, television and radio towers, and lighthouses. The numbers of birds killed by collisions with human-built structures is staggering, but the importance of such kills relative to habitat-related problems is uncertain.

Several wood-warblers have officially been designated as endangered by the United States Fish and Wildlife Service; these are Golden-cheeked Warbler, Kirtland's Warbler, and Bachman's Warbler (already probably extinct). Several additional species, subspecies, or populations are on the special concern, management concern, rare, or endangered listings of individual states.

A NOTE ON RESEARCH METHODS

We relied heavily on the examination of museum specimens of warblers during the development of the plates and species accounts in this book. We conducted most of this work on specimens at the National Museum of Natural History in Washington, D.C. This work was supplemented by examination of warbler specimens at the Natural History Museum of Los Angeles County and the Moore Laboratory of Zoology (Occidental College) in Los Angeles. Additional specimens were examined at or borrowed from the Carnegie Museum of Natural History, Pittsburgh; Museum of Vertebrate Zoology, Berkeley; San Diego Natural History Museum; Field Museum of Natural History, Chicago; Burke Memorial Museum at the University of Washington, Seattle; the Cincinnati Museum of Natural History; the University of Wisconsin at Madison; and the Royal Ontario Museum in Toronto.

In order to work out plumage criteria and select representative specimens for the plates, we (including the two artists, who were in many ways coauthors on this project) sorted series of specimens by age and sex. Label data rarely provided information sufficient to determine age or sex (gonad description or measurement, skull ossification); many prolific collectors from the late 1800s and early 1900s, in fact, appear to have determined the sex of their specimens by plumage rather than by gonadal data, resulting in a high rate of "mis-sexing" (see Ken Parkes's article "Sex ratios based on museum collections—a caution" and D. Scott Wood's article "Color and size variation in eastern White-breasted Nuthatches").

Despite having examined over 10,000 warbler specimens during our research, we were struck by the inadequacy of specimen collections and the need for additional sampling with careful recording of such features as degree of skull pneumatization, size and condition of gonads, and colors of bare parts. Fading, sooting, and discoloration were frequent problems in older specimens; the brilliant orange coloration of spring male Blackburnian Warblers, for example, appears to be ephemeral in specimens. We salute those institutions such as the Museum of Natural Science at Louisiana State University, Baton Rouge, which have amassed extensive collections of modern specimens with exhaustive label data and careful gonadal sexing. We point out that these "modern" collections can be developed in large measure through salvage programs at sites of recurring tower or building kills in migration, rather than solely through active collecting.

We attempted to examine all important literature on North American warblers. Douglass Morse's *American Warblers* was an especially valuable entry point to the extensive literature on warblers. We did not, however, make an exhaustive search of local and regional journals.

How to Identify Warblers

Despite the fearsome concept of "confusing fall warblers," the identification of North American warblers is generally straightforward given adequate views. Furthermore, most species are quite vocal and usually have species-specific songs and call notes. Problems in warbler identification arise most often under two circumstances. First, a very few species pairs truly are very close in appearance, at least in nonbreeding and, especially, immature plumages. Perhaps the most difficult pair is Mourning and MacGillivray's warblers, but others include Bay-breasted and Blackpoll warblers (except in alternate plumage), Northern and Tropical parulas, and the Northern and Louisiana waterthrushes. A second group of identification problems involves less closely related species that share many characters in the less distinctive (usually immature) plumages; examples include dull Yellow Warblers vs. Orange-crowned Warblers, immature female Cerulean vs. immature Blackburnian, and Wilson's vs. immature female Hooded.

An observer will soon learn several natural groups within the wood-warblers. Waterthrushes, for example, are easily told from all other warblers, even if distinguishing the two species is often difficult. Most *Vermivora* are distinctive, with their sharply pointed bills, acrobatic foraging, and lack of obvious streaking in the plumage. Two major and useful groupings of wood-warblers are those species (usually arboreal) with bold wing bars and tail spots and those less patterned species, which often are more in undergrowth, or on ground; bear in mind, however, the many exceptions to this dichotomy.

When viewing a warbler (itself often a difficult thing!), the observer should consider the following characters:

- Are there contrasting wing bars and tail spots? (Most *Den-*

droica and some members of other genera show these markings prominently.)

- What head pattern is present? (Look for lateral crown stripes, supercilium, a dark line through the eye, an eye-ring, a contrastingly dark cheek patch.)
- Is the back plain or striped/spotted?
- Is there a contrasting pale patch on the rump?
- Are there stripes or spots on the sides and flanks? Across the breast?
- What is the shape and relative size of the bill?
- How long is the tail, and how far does it extend past the undertail coverts? (compare Blackpoll and Pine warblers in Figure 7).
- How far do the wingtips (primary tips) extend beyond the tertials and secondaries? (See Figure 10 on page 41.)
- What is the overall size of the bird?
- Vocalizations (What is the quality of the "chip" note? of the song?).
- How does the bird behave? (Are there distinctive postures, tail movements, or foraging techniques? Does it walk or hop?)

A knowledge of distribution, migration timing, and habitat requirements will enhance one's ability to identify warblers, but keep in mind that warblers do occur out of range, in seemingly inappropriate habitats, and outside of their normal seasons.

Once a warbler is identified to species, it is often possible to determine its sex and age class (first year or adult). The sexes are often distinguishable, at least as adults, by plumage (as well as by behavior—bear in mind that normally only males of most wood-

Figure 7. Tail Projection Past Undertail Coverts

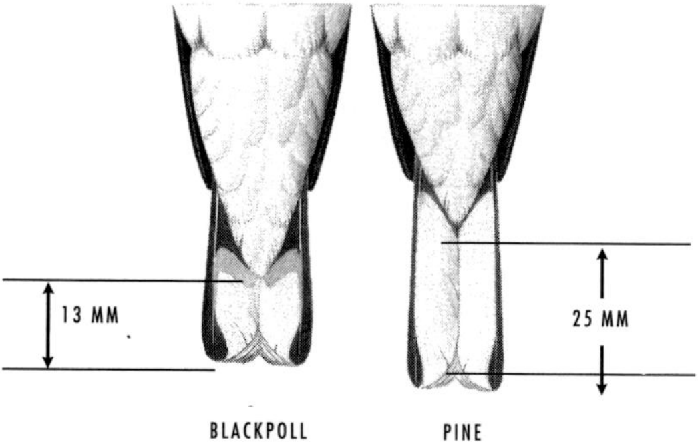

13 MM   25 MM

BLACKPOLL   PINE

warbler species sing). In many species there are three easily distinguished sex and age categories: adult males, immature males and adult females, and immature females. Refer to the species accounts and plates for the aging criteria for warblers, including overall color pattern, rectrix shape and degree of wear, primary shape, flight feather and wing covert color and wear. Many of these criteria are difficult if not impossible to apply under field observation conditions, so one should not attempt to designate the age and sex of a great many individuals encountered. Likewise, some well-marked subspecies of wood-warblers are often identifiable in the field, given adequate studies; "Myrtle" and "Audubon's" warblers, for example, can readily be distinguished by plumage and by call notes (although the issue is confounded by the occurrence of intergrades). Many of the subspecies treated in this guide are based on minor geographical variation in size or plumage, and we do not recommend attempting to name them in the field.

4

How to Use This Book

The 60 species accounts follow the sequence adopted by the American Ornithologists' Union in the sixth edition of their *Check-list of North American Birds* (1983), with the exception of our placement of Olive Warbler in its own family before the "typical" wood-warblers and of Blackburnian Warbler near the end of *Dendroica* next to Cerulean Warbler. Each account is formatted as outlined below.

The Species Accounts

ENGLISH AND SCIENTIFIC NAMES: Nomenclature follows the AOU *Check-List of North American Birds,* sixth edition, and published supplements through 1995; we follow the treatment of the AOU (in press) of placing the Olive Warbler in its own family. Although we adhere to AOU taxonomy, we do suggest alternate treatments, such as the placement of the Gray-crowned Yellowthroat (or "Ground-Chat") in its own genus, *Chamaethlypis.* Alternate English names, where well entrenched, are given in the introductory statement, and alternate taxonomic and nomenclatural treatments are discussed in the Taxonomic Relationships section. Spanish names can be found in Escalante et al. (1996), and French names in the Commission Internationale des Noms Français des Oiseaux (1993).

INTRODUCTORY STATEMENT: Each species account begins with a capsule statement summarizing the species' most important characteristics, including appearance, behavior, distribution, relationships to other species, ecology, and outstanding identifying features. Additional information on conservation status, etymology, etc. is sometimes presented here. Length—from bill tip to tail tip, in inches and centimeters—is given here, but should be used only for a sense of relative size; posture, shape, and proportion are among the many factors that affect apparent size.

DESCRIPTION: This section is a summary of features shared by all post-juvenal individuals of the species, including color, pattern, markings, shape, and structure. Seasonal, sexual, geographical, and age variations in plumage are noted here.

SIMILAR SPECIES: This important section, to be used in conjunction with the color plates, explains the characters that best distinguish the species from similar "confusion" species; such characters may include plumage color and patterns, shape and structure, vocalizations, and behavior, along with additional clues from habitat, range, and season. We usually begin with the most similar species. Note that in a few cases the confusion species are not even warblers.

VOICE: The song is described first, beginning with more typical songs followed by a discussion of song variations. Simpler call notes (or "chip" notes) are described next, followed by a mention of the flight note. Warbler vocal repertoires are considerably more complex than this simple scheme suggests, but our emphasis is on vocalizations that are commonly heard and aid in identification. We acknowledge the inherent difficulties of describing warbler vocalizations, either through description or rendition. An invaluable resource is Borror and Gunn's recording *Songs of Warblers*. Other references include Morse (1989), Getty (1993), and Spector (1992).

BEHAVIOR: The emphasis here is on habits useful to field identification, such as locomotive behavior (walking vs. hopping on ground, creeping along limbs, etc.), and wing, tail, and body movements (tail flicking, bobbing, flashing, or cocking; tail and wing spreading, etc.). Foraging behavior and typical foraging heights are described. For reproductive biology, we describe general nesting behavior and nest placement and structure but do not include descriptions of eggs (which show little variation among wood-warblers anyway) or nestlings; readers are referred to Hal Harrison's excellent *Field Guide to Birds' Nests* for egg descriptions. We certainly do not attempt to catalog the species' entire behavioral repertoire. General references used for this section include Harrison (nests), Bent (1953), Morse (1989), and Ficken and Ficken (1962).

HABITAT: This section details breeding habitat first, then describes habitats used in winter and migration. Some warbler species are likely to be found only in very specific habitats, whereas others may occur in a wide variety of habitats. Habitat preferences may vary somewhat throughout a species' range. We strive to describe the common characteristics of a species' habitat requirements as well as geographical differences. There is more published information about breeding habitat requirements than winter and migration requirements for most species. Important references include the various state and regional works and breeding bird atlases, as well as Morse (1985).

DISTRIBUTION: The breeding range is described first; the range map should always be consulted in conjunction with the text. The text description of breeding range amplifies rather than repeats the information presented in the map, including discussions of breeding range borders, rare or irregular breeding sites, etc. Next, the full winter range is described. For those species wintering in Central and South America, the winter ranges south of the United States and Mexico are not mapped; West Indian winter ranges are also not mapped. There follows a discussion of spring and fall migration, including a summary of migration routes, timing of migration, and abundance. Vagrant records are summarized at the end of the distribution section; we generally refrain from giving numbers of vagrant records by state or region except when such records are extremely unusual or numbers are illustrative of interesting patterns (in well-worked California, for example, we usually give totals, following Roberson's 1980 *Rare Birds of the West Coast* for records through 1979, and *American Birds/National Audubon Society Field Notes* reports from 1980 through 1995). We recognize that numbers we do provide will quickly become out of date. The following terms are frequently used in the discussion of vagrancy: *rare* (occurs annually, but in very small numbers); *very rare* (one or two individuals occur most years); *casual* (very few records, but these records reflect a regional pattern of vagrancy); and *exceptional* (for those records that do not conform to presently understood patterns of vagrancy for that species; this is analogous to the term *accidental* used in many works). References for the distribution section include relevant state and regional distributional works and breeding bird atlases, AOU (1957 and 1983), Howell and Webb (1995), and DeSante and Pyle (1987). We note that the criteria for acceptance of sight records varies somewhat among the states and provinces.

STATUS AND CONSERVATION: Significant population trends within the range of the species are discussed here, along with a brief discussion of factors influencing population declines (including susceptibility to cowbird parasitism), population increases, and range adjustments. Federal threatened or endangered status is noted here. Important references include various regional and state works and breeding bird atlases, and data from the Breeding Bird Surveys supplied by the United States Fish and Wildlife Service. Cowbird parasitism data come primarily from Friedmann and Kiff (1985) and references therein.

SUBSPECIES: Any known geographical variation within the species is described here, whether or not it involves named subspecies. Subspecies are briefly diagnosed and their distribution is summarized. For two species with well-marked subspecies, the Yellow and Yellow-rumped warblers, some of the other text sections above are divided to treat each major subspecies group. Important references include AOU (1957), Behle (1985), Lowery and Monroe (1968), Mengel (1965), Oberholser (1974), Phillips et al. (1964), Rea (1983), Sutton (1967), and Unitt (1984). Geographical variation outside of our North American area of coverage is noted only briefly.

TAXONOMIC RELATIONSHIPS: Knowledge of the species' evolutionary relationships to other species in the genus, or to other warbler genera, is briefly summarized here; in the absence of any thorough study of warbler phylogeny, however, much of the discussion of interspecific relationships remains conjectural. An important reference is Mayr and Short (1970). Instances of hybridization are noted here. In the few cases where hybridization is regular or frequent (e.g., Golden-winged × Blue-winged or Townsend's × Hermit), descriptions of the most commonly encountered hybrid phenotypes are provided.

PLUMAGES AND MOLTS: The plumages are treated individually here: spring males, spring females, fall males, fall females, and juveniles. In cases where first spring or first fall birds are distinguishable from their older counterparts, such plumages are also described; such age differences are apparent in most warbler species, although distinctions are often slight and may only be detectable in the hand. For geographically variable species, this section describes one indicated key subspecies (usually, but not always, the nominate subspecies); distinctions of other subspecies are noted in the Subspecies section. Major references for the Plumages section (in addition to those cited in individual species accounts) are Pyle et al. (1987), Oberholser (1974), and the museum collections cited in the Acknowledgments. Also given are bare part colors—those of the eyes, bill, legs, and feet—including age, sex, and seasonal variation.

The timing and extent of prebasic and prealternate molts are briefly discussed in this section, based on Pyle et al. (1987, and draft of revised edition kindly provided by the author) and other works as cited.

REFERENCES: Selected references that treat aspects of the identification and biology of the species are listed here by author and year of publication; they are grouped by general subject matter. Full literature citations are given in the References section on page 626.

RANGE MAPS: The last 15 years have seen the publication of many state, provincial, and even county breeding bird atlases. This abundance of distributional information enabled our map researcher, Sue A. Tackett, to render precise breeding range maps. All pertinent published state, provincial, and regional literature, including breeding bird atlases, were consulted in our research for the maps and the distribution and habitat accounts. Initial maps were county by county, state by state, and province by province. In a number of cases we received access to unpublished material from atlas works in progress, some of which have now been published. This detailed information allowed a more detailed mapping of occupied areas and range gaps alike (previous works have generally shaded in vast areas on range maps, not taking into account distributional complexity on a smaller scale). For some regions, no atlases or detailed distributional works exist, and more precise mapping was not possible. The maps were greatly improved by a team of state, provincial, and regional reviewers (see Acknowledgments), particularly in those regions

LEGEND

■ Regular Breeding
■ Permanent Resident
■ Regular Wintering
■ Rare Wintering
⌒ Limit of Rare Wintering
? Breeding status uncertain or (in subspecies maps) breeding subspecies uncertain

Some maps have tints of magenta or purple to indicate subspecies differences. This is a generic map.

where atlas information did not exist. The detailed drafts were digitized into final maps by Larry O. Rosche.

Areas of sporadic breeding or wintering are generally not mapped; the Distribution section should be consulted for each species. We show winter ranges north of the Mexico border for those species that occur regularly; winter ranges outside of the United States and Canada are not mapped, but a full description is provided in the text. We have not mapped migration ranges and routes; the text gives detailed accounts of migration routes and timing and should always be consulted.

COLOR PHOTOGRAPHS: Photos were chosen to show selected plumages in an attempt to encompass the brightest (usually adult male) and dullest (e.g., first fall female) plumages shown by a species; in some cases we provide photographs of more than one subspecies. We have refrained from providing definitive age and sex information on many of the photos, acknowledging the difficulty of analyzing a single photograph for definitive aging and sexing characters.

THE PLATES

The plates were researched using the extensive specimen collections of the National Museum of Natural History at the Smithsonian Institution, Washington, D.C., with supplemental research at other museum collections. Nearly all figures were painted from a particular specimen or a combination of two specimens. (The list of specimens used is not included here but is available from Houghton Mifflin, Guidebooks, 222 Berkeley Street, Boston, MA 02116.) We have tried to encompass all significant variation found within North American populations of each species, and to group similar species together whenever possible.

In general we depict spring adults on the upper left (males above females), and fall birds on the right (adults usually above immatures). Where geographic variation is depicted, we often show age and sex variation only within a "key" subspecies. All figures on a plate are depicted at the same scale (except as noted for the Townsend's × Hermit warbler hybrids on Plate 14 and the Bahama subspecies of Yellow-throated Warbler on Plate 17). We include two plates of undertail covert patterns (from below).

We employ the "Peterson System" of arrows pointing to important field marks, including field characters that help identify the species and those that suggest the bird's sex, age, seasonal plumage, or subspecies. Accurate species identification (and particularly subspecies identification, aging and sexing) often requires a more holistic approach than the mere recognition of key field marks, so we urge readers to consult the species accounts for further detail.

Cindy House painted plates 1–7, 21, and 24–30. Thomas Schultz did plates 8–20, 22, 23, 31, 32, and the black and white illustrations.

PLATE LEGENDS

The legends opposite each plate give basic identification criteria for each species (often including brief notes regarding distribution and habitat) and then list the figures shown for each species (with brief notes on aging and sexing criteria, subspecific characters, and seasonal plumage differences). In all cases the reader is urged to consult the more detailed treatments in the species accounts. Especially important field marks are given in italics.

Terms used in this guide for the parts of a warbler are illustrated in the diagrams on pages 41–42. Note that the "wing bars" shown by many warblers are usually the tips of the median and greater secondary coverts, which we simplify to the terms *median coverts* and *greater coverts*. The relative state of wear of the primary coverts, secondaries, and primaries may be important characters for determining a warbler's age.

Wood-warblers have six pairs of tail feathers (rectrices). In the text we frequently refer to different pairs of rectrices using the numbering system in Figure 9 (the central rectrices being r1 and the outer rectrices being r6). Note (Figure 8) how on the folded tail viewed from below one usually only sees the outermost rectrices.

See the Bibliography on page 623 for books referred to in this Introduction.

Figure 8. Tail Underside

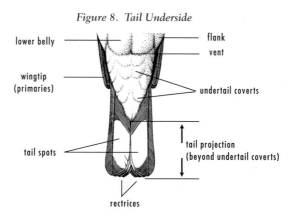

lower belly — flank — vent

wingtip (primaries)

undertail coverts

tail spots

tail projection (beyond undertail coverts)

rectrices

Figure 9. Numbering of Rectrices

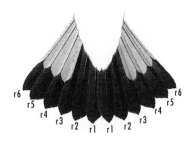

r6 r5 r4 r3 r2 r1 r1 r2 r3 r4 r5 r6

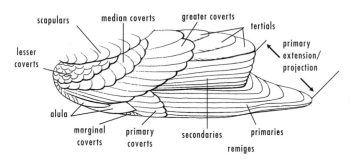

scapulars
median coverts
greater coverts
tertials
lesser coverts
primary extension/projection
alula
marginal coverts
primary coverts
secondaries
primaries
remiges

Figure 10. Wing

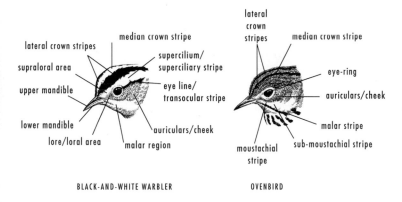

lateral crown stripes
median crown stripe
supraloral area
supercilium/superciliary stripe
upper mandible
eye line/transocular stripe
lower mandible
auriculars/cheek
lore/loral area
malar region

lateral crown stripes
median crown stripe
eye-ring
auriculars/cheek
malar stripe
moustachial stripe
sub-moustachial stripe

BLACK-AND-WHITE WARBLER

OVENBIRD

Figure 11. Head

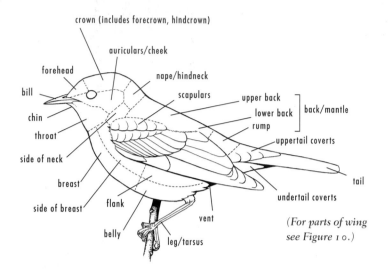

crown (includes forecrown, hindcrown)

auriculars/cheek

forehead

nape/hindneck

bill

scapulars

upper back

chin

lower back

back/mantle

throat

rump

side of neck

uppertail coverts

breast

tail

side of breast

flank

undertail coverts

belly

vent

leg/tarsus

(For parts of wing see Figure 10.)

Figure 12. *Parts of a Warbler*

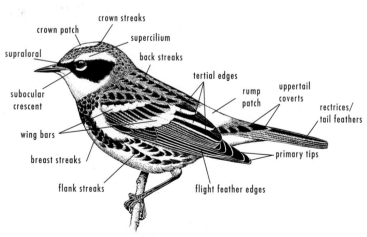

crown streaks

crown patch

supercilium

supraloral

back streaks

tertial edges

rump patch

uppertail coverts

subocular crescent

rectrices/ tail feathers

wing bars

breast streaks

primary tips

flank streaks

flight feather edges

Spring Male Yellow-rumped ("Myrtle") Warbler

PLATES

PLATE 1

BACHMAN'S WARBLER   *Vermivora bachmani*   p. 117

4.25" (11 cm). Almost certainly *extinct*; bred in swampy se. lowlands. *Bill thin, slightly decurved.* Yellow forehead contrasts with black or gray cap in all but immature females. Males show at least hint of *black breast patch*. All show small yellow or whitish mark at the edge of the forewing.

SPRING ADULT MALE. Black forecrown patch contrasts with yellow forehead; hindcrown gray. Extensive solid black chest patch. All males show yellowish eye-rings.

FIRST SPRING MALE. Black on crown and chest variably reduced (a, b). Black on crown may be nearly absent (b), but forehead still contrasting yellow. Yellow of underparts duller, more reduced than in spring adult male. White tail spots, shown in (b), present in all plumages except immature females.

SPRING ADULT FEMALE. Black chest patch absent, replaced by gray wash on chest. Some yellow on forehead contrasting with crown. Adult females show slightly yellowish eye-rings.

FIRST FALL MALE. No black on forecrown; forehead washed olive.

FIRST FALL FEMALE. Drab; no yellow on forehead; eye-ring whitish; tail spots lacking. Brighter (a) and duller (b) examples shown. Compare with immature female *celata* Orange- crowned Warbler (Pl. 4) and immature female *gundlachi* Yellow Warbler (Pl. 9).

PROTHONOTARY WARBLER   *Protonotaria citrea*   p. 427

5.25" (13.3 cm). Bright golden warbler of southern lowland swamps. *Long, heavy bill*; eye stands out prominently on blank face. *Blue-gray wings contrast with green back. White undertail coverts, large white spots in short tail.*

SPRING ADULT MALE. Typical bird (a) has rich golden head and underparts; sharp contrast between yellow hindneck and greenish back. Bill black in spring males. Variant (b) shows deeper orangish head and breast (females may also show orange).

FIRST SPRING MALE. Resembles spring adult male, but olive tips to crown feathers (which are usually lacking in adults).

SPRING ADULT FEMALE. Crown, nape stongly washed green. Some brown at base of mandible. Yellow of underparts less intense than in males.

FALL ADULT MALE. All fall birds show pale bills. Some olive tips to hindcrown feathers, but otherwise like spring adult male. First fall males similar.

FIRST FALL FEMALE. Dullest plumage. Forehead, crown, neck, and face washed olive. Yellow underparts paler than other plumages.

BACHMAN'S WARBLER

first spring ♂
a

b
first spring ♂

first
fall
♂

spring adult ♂

first fall ♀
a

first fall ♀
b

spring adult ♀

PROTHONOTARY WARBLER

b
spring adult ♂

first spring ♂

a

spring adult ♀

fall adult ♂

first fall ♀

PLATE 2

BLUE-WINGED WARBLER   *Vermivora pinus*   p. 125

4.75" (12 cm). All show *black or blackish line through eye,* yellow underparts contrasting with *white undertail coverts,* large *white spots in tail,* white or pale yellow *wing bars.* Hybridizes with Golden-winged Warbler (see hybrids, Pl. 3).

SPRING ADULT MALE. Broad white wing bars. Extensive bright *yellow crown* sharply contrasting with nape. Black eye line. Brightest yellow underparts of all plumages.

SPRING ADULT FEMALE. Eye line less black than in spring adult male, wing bars thinner, crown less extensively yellow (may be nearly all green in some first spring females).

FIRST FALL MALE. Some blending of green into yellow crown. All fall birds show some pale on mandible. Wing bars of all plumages may be tinged yellowish, and all show extensive white in tail.

FIRST FALL FEMALE. Crown extensively washed with green; yellow remaining on head appears as supercilium, joining across forehead. Dullest yellow underparts of any plumage.

GOLDEN-WINGED WARBLER   *Vermivora chrysoptera*   p. 133

4.75" (12 cm). Chickadee-like; unique head pattern shows *black or gray throat* and *auricular patches, yellow on crown. Yellow wing patch* or wing bars. Grayish upperparts and wash on sides and flanks. Large *white spots in tail.*

SPRING ADULT MALE. Crown extensively bright yellow; facial patches black. Large yellow wing patch in all males. Back clear gray.

SPRING ADULT FEMALE. Crown less yellow than male; back with slight greenish wash. Auriculars and throat patch gray but distinct. Yellow wing bars (not solid patch).

FIRST FALL MALE. Crown with some dull olive tipping. Trace of green wash on back. All fall and winter birds show much pale on bill. Many Golden-wingeds show a hint of yellow below throat patch; this is not necessarily a sign of hybridization with Blue-winged. Extensive white in tail in all plumages.

FIRST FALL FEMALE. Crown dull greenish yellow; back washed with green.

BLUE-WINGED WARBLER

spring adult ♂

first fall ♂

first fall ♀

spring adult ♀

GOLDEN-WINGED WARBLER

spring adult ♂

first fall ♂

first fall ♀

spring adult ♀

PLATE 3

BLUE-WINGED/GOLDEN-WINGED WARBLER HYBRIDS
Vermivora pinus × *V. chrysoptera*

4.75" (12 cm). These two species hybridize extensively. Refer to text (p. 140) for a fuller account of hybridization.

"BREWSTER'S WARBLER" *"Vermivora leucobronchialis"*

Includes Blue-winged × Golden-winged hybrids (F1 generation) and backcrosses of these F1 to either Blue-winged or Golden-winged phenotype (F2 generation). Resembles Golden-winged but shows head pattern of Blue-winged, including *black eye line. Double yellow wing bars.*

SPRING ADULT MALE, F1. Yellow wash on white underparts; black eye line. Gray back washed with yellow. Crown yellow.

SPRING ADULT MALE, F2, BACKCROSS. Lacks yellow wash on back and underparts; heavy black eye line and double wing bar.

FIRST FALL MALE, F1 Greenish crown, gray back tinged greenish; gray eye line. Pale yellow wing bars. Yellow wash on underparts, grayish flanks.

FIRST FALL FEMALE, F2, BACKCROSS. Crown and back tinged greenish. Whitish underparts tinged buff; flanks gray-brown.

VARIANTS

Many birds (a, b) do not match "Brewster's" or "Lawrence's" phenotypes but still combine characters of parental species.

"LAWRENCE'S WARBLER" *"Vermivora lawrencii"*

Shows recessive features. Much less common than "Brewster's." Most show *yellowish underparts* of Blue-winged but *face pattern of Golden-winged.*

SPRING ADULT MALE. Like Blue-winged but with black face pattern of Golden-winged. Double white wing bar.

SPRING ADULT FEMALE. Gray face pattern. Back, crown tinged green; underparts whitish tinged yellow. Wing bars whitish, washed with yellow.

FIRST FALL FEMALE. Like spring adult female but flanks buffier, washed yellow; undertail coverts slightly buffy.

BREWSTER'S WARBLER

spring adult ♂
first generation

first fall ♂
first generation

spring adult ♂
second generation
(backcross)

first fall ♀
second generation

VARIANTS

spring adult ♂

a

spring adult ♂

b

LAWRENCE'S WARBLER

spring adult ♂

first fall ♀

spring adult ♀

PLATE 4

TENNESSEE WARBLER   *Vermivora peregrina*   p. 145
4.75" (12 cm). Small, short tailed. *Bright green back, white un-dertail coverts, strong eye line and supercilium* in all plumages.
SPRING ADULT MALE. *Blue-gray crown*; green back. Underparts whitish.
SPRING ADULT FEMALE. Back duller than spring adult male; crown washed with olive. Tinge of pale yellow on breast.
FALL ADULT MALE. Like spring adult male but crown duller, some pale yellow on breast. Short, thin wing bar. *White spots in tail* (smaller in females). Primaries with distinct pale tips in all fall plumages.
FIRST FALL. Yellowish underparts; greener on crown than fall adults. Variation in extent of yellow shown by (a) and (b). Contrasting undertail coverts are white (a) or whitish washed with yellow (b). Thin yellowish wing bars.

ORANGE-CROWNED WARBLER   *Vermivora celata*   p. 154
4.75" (13 cm). Widespread, with four distinct subspecies. Compared with Tennessee, Orange-crowned has longer tail, shorter primary tip extension. All Orange-crowneds show a *split eye-ring, yellow undertail coverts,* and some *blurry breast streaking.* Orange crown patch concealed or absent. Adults similar year-round.
SPRING ADULT MALE *celata.* Northern and eastern subspecies. Generally dull grayish olive above, yellowish below. Split eye-ring yellowish.
SPRING ADULT FEMALE *celata.* Duller, grayer than male; eye-ring paler.
FIRST FALL FEMALE *celata.* Dullest, grayest plumage. Trace of *pale yellow* on breast, *undertail coverts.* Whitish split eye-ring.
JUVENILE *celata.* Buffy wing bars; juvenile *orestera* similar.
SPRING ADULT MALE *orestera.* Breeds in Rocky Mtns., Great Basin. Intermediate between duller *celata* and brighter *lutescens.*
FIRST FALL FEMALE *orestera.* Gray-headed; compare with MacGillivray's Warbler (Pl. 23). Like *celata,* but yellow on sides/breast slightly brighter, may extend to lower throat. Whitish split eye-ring.
FIRST FALL MALE *orestera.* Gray-headed, yellow extends to chin. Compare with Nashville (Pl. 5).
SPRING ADULT MALE *lutescens.* Pacific coastal slope. Brightest subspecies; underparts yellow with indistinct olive streaking. Yellow split eye-ring in all plumages. Adult female very similar.
FIRST FALL MALE *lutescens.* Similar to adults; no gray-headed effect (compared to two subspecies above). Eye-ring yellowish.
JUVENILE *lutescens.* Buffy wing bars. Yellower than *celata* or *orestera.*
HEAD OF ADULT MALE *lutescens.* Extensive orange crown patch in adult males of all subspecies is rarely visible. Adult females and immature males show less orange, immature females none.
SPRING ADULT MALE *sordida.* Southern California islands, adjacent coast. Similar to *lutescens* but darker overall, more *extensive* streaking on underparts (including undertail coverts). Longest bill.

TENNESSEE WARBLER

spring adult ♂

fall adult
♂

spring adult ♀

first fall
a

first fall
b

ORANGE-CROWNED WARBLER

spring adult ♀
celata

first fall ♀
celata

spring adult ♂
celata

juvenile
celata

first fall ♀
orestera

spring adult ♂
orestera

first fall ♂
orestera

spring adult ♂
lutescens

first fall ♂
lutescens

spring adult ♂
sordida

juvenile
lutescens

adult ♂
lutescens

PLATE 5

NASHVILLE WARBLER   *Vermivora ruficapilla*   p. 166
4.5" (11.5 cm). *Conspicuous white or whitish eye-ring. Gray head contrasts with yellow throat.* Greenish upperparts, wing coverts, and flight feathers. Mostly yellow underparts. *Undertail coverts bright yellow.* Two subspecies; eastern *ruficapilla* shown except as noted.

SPRING ADULT MALE. Clear blue-gray head, bold white eye-ring. Deep chestnut cap, often difficult to see.

SPRING ADULT MALE *ridgwayi.* Pacific states. Differs from *ruficapilla* in clearer, *brighter yellow-green rump and uppertail coverts* contrasting more with back, which is slightly washed grayish. Slightly clearer yellow on underparts, often showing slightly more white in the vent area. Pumps tail, unlike eastern birds.

SPRING ADULT FEMALE. Head dull gray; underparts duller than adult male. Chestnut on crown much reduced.

FALL ADULT MALE. Head slightly washed olive-brown; chestnut cap largely obscured by feather tips.

FIRST FALL FEMALE. Head strongly washed olive. Eye-ring tinged buffy. Underparts variable; yellow may be extensive (a) or more restricted (b). Dullest plumage (b) best told from Virginia's by *greenish wing coverts and edges to flight feathers.*

VIRGINIA'S WARBLER   *Vermivora virginiae*   p. 174
4.5" (11.5 cm). Southern Rocky Mtns. and Great Basin relative of Nashville; also shows bold white eye-ring and *yellow undertail coverts. Gray above,* with contrasting yellow-green rump, uppertail coverts. *Yellow of underparts usually restricted to breast, undertail coverts. Flight feathers and wing coverts gray,* never greenish. *Tail relatively long,* frequently pumped. Compare with Colima and Lucy's (Pl. 6).

SPRING ADULT MALE. Chestnut cap, often obscured. Typical bird (a) shows large yellow breast patch. Yellow may be restricted to center of breast (b); in some birds (c), yellow extends onto the chin and back to flanks. Yellow extreme always distinguished from Nashville by gray flight feathers and wing coverts, longer tail.

SPRING ADULT FEMALE. Yellow of breast pale and restricted; crown patch paler and less extensive than in adult males.

FALL ADULT MALE. Some veiling of yellow breast patch, and slight brownish wash on upperparts. Chestnut of cap mostly obscured by gray feather tips.

FIRST FALL MALE. Like fall adult male, but slightly browner above. Chestnut of cap much reduced, generally not visible in field.

FALL FEMALE. Yellow on breast very restricted, tinged buff (or completely absent). Rufous on crown limited and hidden in fall adult female, absent in first fall female.

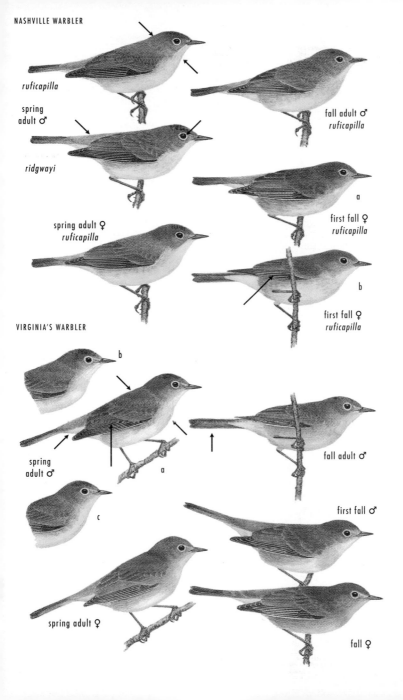

NASHVILLE WARBLER

ruficapilla

spring
adult ♂

ridgwayi

spring adult ♀
ruficapilla

fall adult ♂
ruficapilla

a

first fall ♀
ruficapilla

b

first fall ♀
ruficapilla

VIRGINIA'S WARBLER

b

spring
adult ♂

a

c

fall adult ♂

first fall ♂

spring adult ♀

fall ♀

PLATE 6

COLIMA WARBLER *Vermivora crissalis* p. 180
5.25" (13.3 cm). Local breeder in lush montane woodland of Chisos Mtns., Texas, and adjacent Mexico. Like *large,* long-tailed Virginia's (Pl. 5) but moderately to strongly *washed with brown on the back, sides, and flanks.* Lacks yellow on breast. *Undertail coverts deep orange-yellow.* Seldom pumps tail. Rufous crown patch often hidden. Cannot be reliably aged or sexed. Typical breeding bird (a) and a browner bird from wintering grounds (b) shown.

LUCY'S WARBLER *Vermivora luciae* p. 185
4.25" (11 cm). Very *small* warbler of southwestern desert riparian habitats, especially mesquite. Mainly *gray above and creamy white below. Chestnut or tawny rump patch.* Indistinct face pattern, with eye standing out prominently. *Lacks yellow on undertail coverts,* which always separates it from Virginia's (Pl. 5). The rather short tail is pumped frequently.
SPRING ADULT MALE. *Deep chestnut crown patch and rump.*
SPRING ADULT FEMALE. Chestnut on crown reduced, largely hidden; rump patch rufous (not deep chestnut).
FALL ADULT MALE. Underparts strongly washed buffy, especially on breast, flanks. Crown patch somewhat obscured by gray feather tips.
JUVENILE. Buffy wing bars; tawny rump patch. Buff wash on underparts. No rufous in crown. First fall birds (after July–August) resemble fall adults.
JUVENILE Verdin (*Auriparus flaviceps,* Family Remizidae).
Broadly co-occurs with Lucy's Warbler, and juveniles (summer months) may be mistaken for them. Note *deep-based, sharp bill* with obvious *pinkish yellow base to mandible.* Acrobatic, often clings to twigs chickadee-fashion.

COLIMA WARBLER

a

b

LUCY'S WARBLER

spring adult ♂

fall adult ♂

spring adult ♀

juvenile

VERDIN

juvenile

PLATE 7

NORTHERN PARULA *Parula americana* p. 195
4.25" (11 cm). Small and *short tailed,* with *bold white wing bars,* white tail spots, and a *split white eye-ring.* Generally *bluish above,* yellow on breast (variably marked with *chestnut and black in males). Bronze-green patch on back. Yellowish mandible* in all plumages.

SPRING ADULT MALE. Blue upperparts with distinct green back patch. Black lores. Breast markings variable. Some show much chestnut across chest and sides (a). Typically the upper chest has a black-ish band, bordered below by broader chestnut band (b). Some show a broader black chest band (c).

SPRING ADULT FEMALE. Less blue (more gray) above than spring males, with only a trace of chestnut across the chest. Crown tinged green; lores gray.

FALL ADULT MALE. Green wash through blue crown and neck. No black in lores. Chest bands somewhat veiled with yellow.

FIRST FALL MALE. More extensively washed with green above than fall adult male; secondaries edged greenish.

FIRST FALL FEMALE. Crown, neck and uppertail coverts strongly washed green. No hint of chestnut or black across breast; yellow of throat is constricted by gray. Wing bars tinged greenish; secondaries edged green.

TROPICAL PARULA *Parula pitiayumi* p. 204
4.25" (11 cm). Widespread in Neotropics, but restricted in our area mainly to southern Texas (*nigrilora,* illustrated below, except as noted); the one record for Arizona likely pertains to the sub-species *pulchra.* Similar to Northern Parula in bluish upperparts, green back patch, yellow throat and breast, bold white wing bars and tail spots . Typically *lacks white* around eye. More yellow at sides of throat than in Northern; yellow also extends farther down through underparts. Variable tawny wash across breast, but no dark chest bands.

ADULT MALE. Strong tawny wash on breast, blended into yellow throat. Black lores extending in narrow band across forehead and down along sides of upper throat. Similar throughout year.

ADULT FEMALE. Black in face replaced by gray; only slight suffusion of tawny on breast.

FIRST FALL FEMALE. Crown, neck, rump washed greenish. No tawny wash on breast. Secondaries edged greenish in all first-year birds.

ADULT MALE *pulchra.* Similar to *nigrilora* but *wing bars broader, particularly on greater coverts.*

NORTHERN PARULA

maximum chestnut

spring adult ♂

a

b

fall adult ♂

maximum black

c

first fall ♂

spring adult ♀

first fall ♀

TROPICAL PARULA

adult ♂ *nigrilora*

adult ♀ *nigrilora*

first fall ♀ *nigrilora*

adult ♂ *pulchra*

PLATE 8

YELLOW WARBLER: MIGRATORY NORTHERN
SUBSPECIES   *Dendroica petechia (aestiva* group)   p.210

4.75" (12 cm). Yellow Warbler is a widespread and variable species with three distinct subspecies groups. Highly migratory *aestiva* group breeds over much of mainland North America south to central Mexico. The "Golden" *(petechia)* and "Mangrove" *(erithachorides)* groups, resident on subtropical and tropical coasts, are shown on Pl. 9. Males are olive to yellowish green above and yellow below, with variable *red streaking on underparts.* Females generally duller, with red streaks reduced or lacking. All show *yellow edges to flight feathers, tertials, and wing coverts,* and *yellow tail spots; tail is relatively short.* Dark eye stands out on blank face. The top six figures show variation in East; bottom six show various western subspecies.

SPRING ADULT MALE *aestiva.* Cen. and e. United States. Bright yellow-green upperparts, brilliant yellow underparts with red streaks. Broad yellow edges to wing coverts, tertials. Birds from western part of subspecies' range in Great Plains (a) are brightest; northeastern birds (b) slightly duller. Fall and winter adult males similar.

SPRING ADULT FEMALE *aestiva.* Red streaks below greatly reduced. Fall and winter adult females similar.

FIRST FALL MALE *aestiva.* Much like adult female. A few short red streaks below.

FIRST FALL FEMALE *aestiva.* Red streaks lacking; yellow of underparts paler than in other plumages.

FIRST FALL FEMALE *amnicola.* Darker subspecies breeding across much of boreal Canada. Quite dull and olive.

SPRING ADULT MALE *rubiginosa.* Highly migratory, far northwestern breeders that show longer primary extension past tertials. Very green above, up to the forehead.

FIRST FALL FEMALE *rubiginosa.* Dull, brownish plumage; tertial edges pale buffy, not yellow.

SPRING ADULT MALE *morcomi.* Great Basin and Rocky Mtns. areas (*brewsteri* of Pacific Coast very similar). Much like eastern *aestiva* adult male, but red streaks paler.

FIRST FALL FEMALE *morcomi/brewsteri.* Usually paler and duller than young female *aestiva.* Paler than far northern birds.

SPRING ADULT MALE *sonorana.* Southwest. Palest subspecies in our area. Back pale and yellowish, typically with some thin chestnut streaks. Red streaking below pale, thin, almost absent on some spring males.

FIRST FALL FEMALE *sonorana.* Very pale above, whitish below. Spring females similar.

spring adult ♂
aestiva

first fall ♂
aestiva

a

b

first fall ♀
aestiva

spring adult ♀
aestiva

first fall ♀
amnicola

spring adult ♂
rubiginosa

first fall ♀
rubiginosa

spring adult ♂
morcomi

first fall ♀
morcomi/brewsteri

spring adult ♂
sonorana

first fall ♀
sonorana

PLATE 9

"GOLDEN" YELLOW WARBLER   p. 210
Dendroica petechia (*petechia* group)

5″ (12.7 cm). Resident in mangroves of tropical Caribbean coasts and islands. In our area subspecies *gundlachi* (shown here) is resident on Florida Keys and extreme south Florida mainland. Note *rounded wings with short primary extension*. Males show *broad red streaking below* and may show some pale chestnut in cap (also present in variants in *aestiva* group). First fall birds can be quite gray.

SPRING ADULT MALE. Red streaking on underparts broader than in *aestiva* group. Some show pale chestnut on crown. *Upperparts olive green through forehead.*

ADULT FEMALE. Uniformly dark olive above; little or no red streaking below. Fall bird shown; spring adult female similar, but bill darker.

FIRST SPRING FEMALE. Some green on back and yellow on underparts appears by late winter or early spring. Suggests Tennessee (Pl. 4).

FIRST FALL MALE. Variable. May show much gray on head and upperparts (a), or be more generally green and yellow (b). Ventral streaking usually evident. First spring males resemble (b).

FIRST FALL FEMALE. Gray above and whitish below. Even in dullest plumage note pale edges to wing coverts, tertials, and flight feathers. Distinct pale eye-ring.

"MANGROVE" YELLOW WARBLER   p. 210
Dendroica petechia (*erithachorides* group)

5″ (12.7 cm). Resident in mangroves from the coasts of n. Mexico south to w. South America. Subspecies *castaneiceps* of Baja California shown here. Records for coast of Texas likely pertain to similar *oraria*. Similar in structure to "Golden" group.

ADULT MALE. *Entire head chestnut.* Fine *reddish streaks on underparts* (*oraria* with very slightly heavier streaks). Many show fine chestnut streaking on back.

ADULT FEMALE. Much like adult female Golden. A few *chestnut spots on face* (a), or even chestnut patch on crown (b).

FIRST SPRING MALE. Patchy chestnut on head; fine chestnut streaking below.

FIRST SPRING FEMALE. Generally dull and pale, but always shows pale tertial edges. First fall females (not shown) grayer, much like first fall female Golden.

"GOLDEN" YELLOW WARBLER

spring adult ♂

first fall ♂

b

adult ♀

a

first spring ♀

first fall ♀

"MANGROVE" YELLOW WARBLER

adult ♂

first spring ♂

a

adult ♀

b

first spring ♀

PLATE 10

CHESTNUT-SIDED WARBLER   *Dendroica pensylvanica* p. 232
5" (12.7 cm). *Chestnut on sides and flanks* of most plumages. *Yellow-tinged wing bars. Tail often held slightly cocked upward.*

SPRING ADULT MALE. All have *yellow crown.* White cheek partly framed by black. *Deep chestnut extending from upper sides to flanks.* Back streaked yellow and black.

FIRST SPRING MALE. Chestnut less extensive, not extending to flanks. Black of face less solid.

SPRING ADULT FEMALE. All have greenish crowns. Chestnut on sides less solid than spring males. Back streaked olive and black.

FIRST SPRING FEMALE. Dark areas on face not as black as on spring adult female. Chestnut of sides more reduced and broken; a few show no chestnut at all.

FALL ADULT MALE. All fall birds show a *white eye-ring on a gray face, distinct yellow-green crown.* Yellow-green upperparts with heavy black spotting. Extensive rich chestnut on sides and flanks.

FIRST FALL MALE. Chestnut variable, always more reduced than in fall adult male. Back spotting narrower. Fall adult females similar.

FIRST FALL FEMALE. Sides, flanks grayish; chestnut absent. Back appears unstreaked.

BLACK-THROATED BLUE WARBLER   p. 257
Dendroica caerulescens
5" (12.7 cm). Center of breeding abundance is in Appalachian Mtns. *Striking sexual dimorphism. Blue, black, and white pattern* of males distinctive. *Females drab;* most show at least a small *white patch at base of primaries* (well developed in all males). Males show distinct white tail spots, females little or none.

SPRING ADULT MALE. *Deep blue upperparts.* Black face, throat, sides, flanks. *Large white wing patch.* Fall adult male similar.

SPRING ADULT MALE *cairnsi.* Mainly s. Appalachians. Variable black mottling on back, black streaking in crown.

SPRING ADULT FEMALE. No black or deep blue present in any females. *Distinct whitish supercilium* and arc under eye. *Small white patch at base of primaries.* Slight bluish tinge to crown.

FIRST FALL MALE. Resembles adult male, but primary coverts and flight feathers browner (less black); tertials edged greenish rather than blue-gray. White patch on wing averages smaller. Some (a) are much like adult male except for duller, browner wings. Most (b) show some white tips to black feathers, whitish in uppermost chin, slight greenish wash on back, and yellowish tint on belly sides. First spring males look like (a).

FIRST FALL FEMALE. Olive above, buffy or whitish below. Little or no white at base of primaries. No hint of blue in plumage. First spring female similar, but may show some bluish in crown.

CHESTNUT-SIDED
WARBLER

spring adult ♂

first spring ♂

spring adult ♀

first spring ♀

fall adult ♂

first fall ♂

first fall ♀

BLACK-THROATED BLUE WARBLER

spring adult ♂

spring adult ♂
cairnsi

spring adult ♀

first fall ♂

a

b

first fall ♀

PLATE 11

MAGNOLIA WARBLER   *Dendroica magnolia*   p. 240
4.75" (12 cm). All show *yellow rump patch*. Underparts mostly yellow, breast usually streaked; white undertail coverts. *Distinctive tail pattern: basal half of tail appears white from below.* Most spring birds show *distinct white supercilium, white wing patch.* Fall birds have white eye-ring and wing bars, gray chest band.

SPRING ADULT MALE. Extensively black back, auriculars, forehead. Blue-gray crown. *Bold black streaking on bright yellow underparts.*

FIRST SPRING MALE. Similar to adult male, but black on back reduced.

SPRING ADULT FEMALE. Crown, forehead dull gray. Auriculars not solidly black. Black on back can approach that of first spring male, but more green usually shows.

FIRST SPRING FEMALE. *White eye-ring* on often plain gray face; compare to Kirtland's (Pl. 20).

FALL ADULT MALE. Heavy black side and flank streaking. Well-developed (but veiled) black spots on back.

FIRST FALL MALE. Black flank streaking evident, but thinner, less extensive than fall adult male. Fall adult female very similar.

FIRST FALL FEMALE. Plain greenish back. Ventral streaking indistinct, mostly limited to flanks.

CAPE MAY WARBLER   *Dendroica tigrina*   p. 248
4.75" (12 cm). Small and short-tailed, with *fine, slightly decurved bill. Yellow to greenish rump.* Extensive *ventral streaking* in all plumages (indistinct in first fall females). *Greenish edges to flight feathers;* white tail spots. Even dullest immatures usually show trace of pale *yellow on the sides of the neck* and on the breast. All show narrow eye line.

SPRING ADULT MALE. Bold head pattern includes *bright chestnut cheeks* and *yellow patch on sides of neck; black streaks through bright yellow underparts.* Clear yellow rump patch. White wing patch.

FIRST SPRING MALE. Similar to spring adult male but yellow areas paler, yellow on sides of neck slightly obscured.

SPRING ADULT FEMALE. Lacks chestnut in cheek; thin whitish wing bars.

FIRST SPRING FEMALE. Can be very drab, much like first fall females.

FALL ADULT MALE. Chestnut in face present (a), or sometimes absent (b).

FIRST FALL MALE. Crown and back spots average finer than in fall adult male (back spotting largely veiled in all fall males). Cheeks lack chestnut. Yellow of underparts paler than in fall adult male.

FALL ADULT FEMALE. Like first fall male, but back lacks spotting, yellow of underparts less extensive, and median coverts less solidly white.

FIRST FALL FEMALE. Drabbest plumage. Largely gray above, obscure grayish streaking below. Greenish yellow rump. *Greenish edges to remiges.* Most (a) show traces of pale yellow on breast, sides of neck; yellow lacking in some (b).

MAGNOLIA WARBLER

spring adult ♂

fall adult ♂

first spring ♂

first fall ♂

spring adult ♀

first spring ♀

first fall ♀

CAPE MAY WARBLER

spring adult ♂

fall adult ♂

a

b

first spring ♂

first fall ♂

fall adult ♀

spring adult ♀

a

first fall ♀

first spring ♀

b

PLATE 12

YELLOW-RUMPED WARBLER   *Dendroica coronata*   p. 267
5.25" (13.3 cm). Large, hardy, abundant. All show *bright yellow rump*, white tail spots. "Myrtle" Warbler breeds in boreal regions and is widespread in winter. "Audubon's" breeds, winters in West.

"MYRTLE WARBLER"   *Dendroica coronata* (*coronata* group)
Dark auricular region, bordered above by *pale supercilium* and below and behind by extension of the white or creamy throat.

SPRING ADULT MALE. Auriculars black, bordered above by white broken supercilium, below by white throat. Black may form patch on chest, sides (a), or be broken into streaks (b). First spring males similar.

SPRING ADULT FEMALE. Auriculars brownish (a) to slaty (b). Back washed with brown. Black of underparts appears as long rows of spots.

FALL ADULT MALE. Upperparts with gray tint and broad black streaks, veiled with brown. Distinct brown auricular (with limited black in some). Uppertail coverts blue-gray with large black centers.

FIRST FALL MALE. Told from fall adult male by finer back, breast, and flank spotting, and lack of any gray tones on upperparts (except gray-fringed uppertail coverts). Fall adult females similar.

FIRST FALL FEMALE. Dullest plumage, rich brown above, buffy below. Streaking above and below duller. Told from dull Audubon's by *hint of supercilium, pale throat patch curving up behind auricular.*

JUVENILE. Heavily streaked above and below; no yellow on rump.

"AUDUBON'S WARBLER"   *Dendroica coronata* (*auduboni* group)
Yellow throat in males and most females. Told from Myrtle by plainer face, lack of supercilium, differently shaped throat patch.

SPRING ADULT MALE. *Bright yellow throat. Chest, sides black.* In spring (a), black partly veiled by whitish feather tips. By late spring/summer (b), more solid black below and on back. Birds near Mexican border (c) may show more extensive black. *Greater coverts extensively white,* often forming nearly solid patch.

SPRING ADULT FEMALE. Upperparts with brownish cast; underparts streaked with black. Throat usually yellow. Yellow patch on sides paler, smaller than in spring male.

FIRST SPRING FEMALE. Like spring adult female, but back browner. Many spring females show mostly whitish throat.

FALL ADULT MALE. Upperparts washed brown, but some gray present. Large black back spots partly veiled with brown. Black spots on breast and sides partly veiled with white. Large black centers on blue-gray uppertail coverts.

FIRST FALL MALE. Back and underpart streaking finer and more veiled than in fall adult males. Fall adult females similar.

FIRST FALL FEMALE. Variably brown above. Back and breast streaking fine, indistinct. Throat pale yellow (a) or creamy (b).

"MYRTLE" WARBLER

a
spring adult ♂

b

fall adult ♂

first fall ♂

a
spring adult ♀

b

first fall ♀

juvenile

"AUDUBON'S" WARBLER

a
spring adult ♂

b

c

fall adult ♂

first fall ♂

spring adult ♀

first fall ♀

a

first spring ♀

b

PLATE 13

BLACK-THROATED GREEN WARBLER   p. 298
Dendroica virens

4.75" (12 cm). Mainly in East. *Bright green back* with little or no streaking. *Face largely yellow,* framing a suffused *greenish auricular outline. Yellow wash on vent* in all plumages.

SPRING ADULT MALE. *Solid black chin, throat, and upper breast.* Bold black streaks on sides, flanks. Indistinct back spotting. May show pale yellow wash on lower breast.

SPRING ADULT FEMALE. Similar to spring male, but black of throat veiled by whitish feather tips, flank streaking less bold. Typically (a) chin and upper throat pale yellow. Many with more black (b); first spring male similar to (b). No females show black spotting on back.

FIRST SPRING FEMALE. Black often limited to small area on lower sides of throat, but in some birds approaches pattern of spring adult female (a) above. Side and flank streaks thin.

FALL ADULT MALE. Like spring adult male, but throat and upper breast with pale feather tips.

FIRST FALL MALE. Throat and chest mostly black, veiled with whitish. Fall adult female (not shown) similar.

FIRST FALL FEMALE. No black on throat or breast. Thin dusky streaks on sides, flanks. Even this dullest plumage shows *yellow wash in vent area.*

GOLDEN-CHEEKED WARBLER *Dendroica chrysoparia*   p. 291

4.75" (12 cm). Hill country of central Texas. Like Black-throated Green, but all show clear yellow cheeks with *distinct eye line* that angles up posteriorly, joining dark nape; no dark lower border of cheeks. Back of males black, or olive with heavy black streaking; females have dull olive backs. *Lacks yellow in vent area.*

SPRING ADULT MALE. *Crown and back usually solid black;* heavy black streaking on sides and flanks.

FIRST SPRING MALE. Some olive on back, but otherwise resembles spring adult male. Thin yellow streak on forehead is found in all plumages.

SPRING ADULT FEMALE. Back and crown olive, streaked with black. Some pale on chin.

FIRST SPRING FEMALE. Like spring adult female but usually less black on throat; streaking on upperparts finer, less conspicuous.

FIRST FALL FEMALE. Like first fall female Black-throated Green but *cheeks clearer yellow,* unbordered below; more distinct eye line connects with nape. Back slightly duller olive. Black limited to smudge on lower sides of throat.

FIRST FALL MALE. Like adult female; larger black spots on back.

BLACK-THROATED GREEN WARBLER

spring adult ♂

fall adult ♂

a
spring adult ♀

first fall ♂

b

first
spring ♀

first fall ♀

GOLDEN-CHEEKED WARBLER

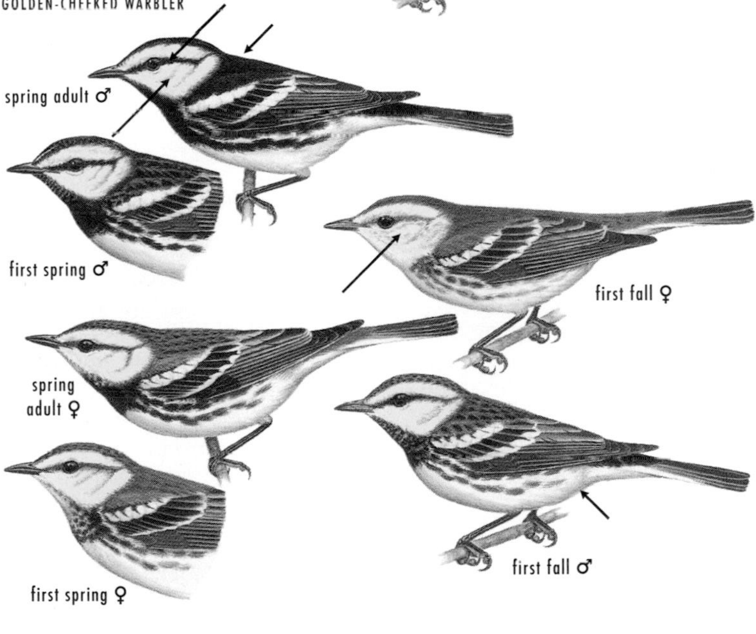

spring adult ♂

first spring ♂

first fall ♀

spring
adult ♀

first spring ♀

first fall ♂

PLATE 14

TOWNSEND'S WARBLER   *Dendroica townsendi*   p. 307
4.75" (12 cm). Western. All show *dark cheek outlined by yellow,* streaked sides/flanks, *yellow breast,* greenish back. All species on Pls. 13, 14 show *extensive white in the rectrices.*

SPRING ADULT MALE. Crown, cheek, and throat black. Bold black streaking on sides, flanks. Distinct black spotting on back.

SPRING ADULT FEMALE. Cheeks and crown mottled with olive. Reduced black on throat and reduced back spotting. Thin black streaks on sides, flanks. First spring female (not shown; see photo p. 14) largely lacks black on throat, is paler yellow below.

FALL ADULT MALE. Like spring male but black areas on head with slight olive tips, back spotting somewhat obscured.

FIRST FALL MALE. Chin yellow; variable black on lower throat. Black spotting on back mostly veiled with green. Fall adult female similar.

FIRST FALL FEMALE. No black spots on back or black on sides of throat. Dark streaking on sides and flanks dull and somewhat veiled with yellow. Yellow of underparts paler than in other plumages.

TOWNSEND'S × HERMIT WARBLER HYBRIDS
NOTE: Hybrids shown approximately ⅘ size of other figures.
Some adult males resemble Townsend's but lack yellow below throat (a). More frequently they combine Hermit head pattern with yellow breast and greenish back of Townsend's (b). Spring adult females (c) and some fall immatures (d) resemble Black-throated Green (Pl. 13); note lack of yellow in vent area. Some immature males (e) are more extensively yellow below but lack distinct cheek patch of Townsend's.

HERMIT WARBLER   *Dendroica occidentalis*   p. 316
4.75" (12 cm). Mainly Pacific Coast states. *Head mostly yellow;* no other yellow in plumage. Most show some *black on throat, grayish upperparts.* Streaking on underparts absent; *breast whitish.*

SPRING ADULT MALE. Clear yellow head, black throat. Variable blackish on nape. Bold black spotting on gray (or slightly olive-tinged) back.

FIRST SPRING MALE. Like spring adult male, but usually some white on chin; spotting on yellow crown may be extensive. Gray of upperparts washed with olive-brown. Back spotting may be extensive.

SPRING ADULT FEMALE. Black of throat limited (virtually absent in some first spring females, or more extensive but not including chin). Plain gray upperparts. Slight dark tinge to cheeks.

FIRST FALL MALE. Back with olive cast. Black on throat largely veiled with white. Fall adult female similar (see text).

FALL ADULT MALE. Black throat slightly veiled with whitish tips.

FIRST FALL FEMALE. Unstreaked brownish olive back. No black on throat. Dark shadow on auriculars. See Olive Warbler (Pl. 30).

TOWNSEND'S WARBLER

spring adult ♂

fall adult ♂

spring adult ♀

first fall ♂

first fall ♀

TOWNSEND'S × HERMIT HYBRIDS

a

b

c

d

e

HERMIT WARBLER

spring adult ♂

first fall ♂

first spring ♂

fall adult ♂

spring adult ♀

first fall ♀

PLATE 15

BLACK-AND-WHITE WARBLER   *Mniotilta varia*   p. 411

5" (12.7 cm). Distinctive *nuthatchlike creeping behavior. Heavily streaked black and white.* All show bold white wing bars, *white tertial edges,* dark spots on undertail coverts, and distinctive head pattern of *white median crown stripe* and supercilium, and black lateral crown stripes. Males (except in first fall) show black cheeks; all females show pale auriculars and a black eye line.

SPRING ADULT MALE. *Black cheeks and throat* (some can show white on chin).

FIRST SPRING MALE. Similar to above, but black on chin and throat reduced or absent in many birds.

FALL ADULT MALE. Like spring males, but chin typically whitish (a). Pattern variable; some birds have black throat with white veiling (b) or fully white throats (c). Variable black on auriculars separates adult males from other fall plumages.

SPRING ADULT FEMALE. *Cheeks pale; distinct black eye line.* Underpart streaks less distinct than in males. Slight buff wash on flanks. Fall adult female similar.

FIRST FALL MALE. Face pattern like adult female, but flanks white, with broader, blacker streaking.

FIRST FALL FEMALE. Like adult female, but averages buffier on flank and vent area.

BLACK-THROATED GRAY WARBLER   p. 282
Dendroica nigrescens

4.75" (12 cm). Gray western member of the *virens* complex (Pls. 13, 14). Resembles Townsend's, but greens and yellows replaced by gray and white. Dark auricular connects with gray hindneck. All show *distinct yellow supraloral spot.*

SPRING ADULT MALE. Solid black crown, auriculars, chin, and throat. First spring male similar, but black on crown usually less extensive.

FALL ADULT MALE. Like spring adult male, but back spotting more veiled, throat feathers tipped white. Black of crown slightly veiled with gray.

FIRST FALL MALE. Variable. Black on throat less solid than in adult male. Cheek varies from blackish to slaty brown. Black of crown mostly restricted to sides, center of crown gray. Slight brownish wash on upperparts.

SPRING ADULT FEMALE. Typically (a) with black area on sides of lower throat, forming a band across the lower throat. Some (b) show more extensive black on throat; these resemble males, but auriculars grayish, not solid black.

FIRST FALL FEMALE. Completely white throat. Gray-brown upperparts, auriculars, and crown. Flanks with fine streaks, slight buff wash.

BLACK-AND-WHITE WARBLER

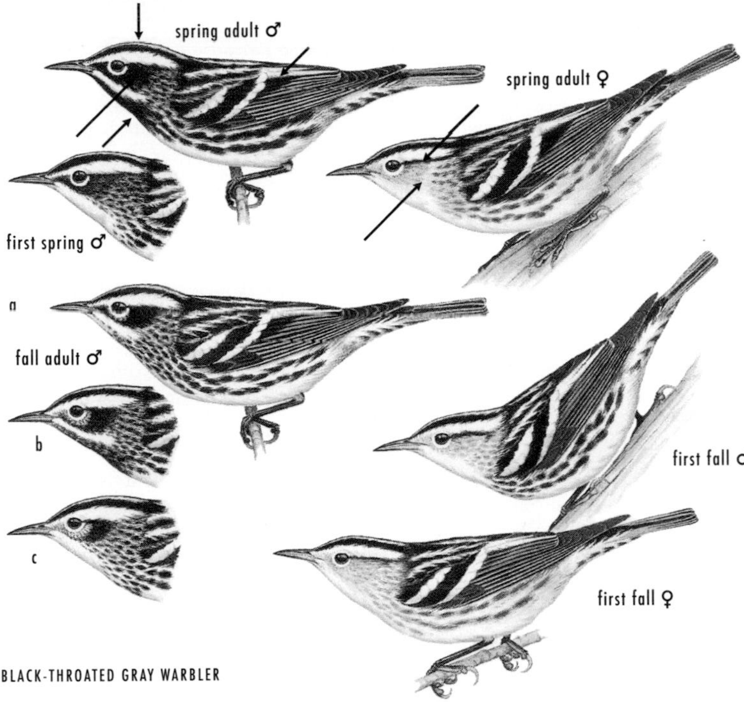

spring adult ♂

spring adult ♀

first spring ♂

a
fall adult ♂

b

c

first fall ♂

first fall ♀

BLACK-THROATED GRAY WARBLER

spring adult ♂

b
spring adult ♀

fall adult ♂

a

first fall ♂

first fall ♀

PLATE 16

BLACKBURNIAN WARBLER   *Dendroica fusca*   p. 392
4.75" (12 cm). *Throat* varies from *brilliant orange* to pale buffy yellow; all show *angular cheek patch, broad supercilium* which connects to the pale sides of the neck, and *pale stripes on the back.*

SPRING ADULT MALE. *Throat fiery orange.* Back black with yellowish braces. Prominent white patch on wing. Auriculars and flank streaks black.

SPRING ADULT FEMALE. Orange areas paler, duller than in male. Auriculars and flank streaks grayish.

FALL ADULT FEMALE. Similar to spring female; upperparts washed with olive.

FALL ADULT MALE. Orange areas paler, more yellow than spring male. Black areas variably veiled with olive. Inner greater coverts usually with less white, yielding two wing bars rather than a solid white wing patch.

FIRST FALL MALE. Resembles fall adult female, but eye line blacker, back and ventral streaking stronger. Throat and supercilium more yellow, less orange. See Townsend's (Pl. 14) and Yellow-throated (Pl. 17).

FIRST FALL FEMALE. Throat and supercilium more buffy, less yellow (a) than in first fall male. By late September or October some are paler, nearly whitish (b). Compare with first fall female Cerulean and with Bay-breasted and Blackpoll (Pl. 18).

CERULEAN WARBLER   *Dendroica cerulea*   p. 401
4.5" (11.5 cm). Small and *short-tailed.* Distinctive *blue or blue-green upperparts* in most plumages. *Bold white wing bars,* white tail spots. Dark eye line and *prominent supercilium* in all female and first fall plumages.

SPRING ADULT MALE. Upperparts cerulean blue, brightest on crown. *Narrow chest band* varies from blue-gray to black, often veiled with white. Short black stripe on side of crown.

FIRST SPRING MALE. Many show slight whitish supercilium behind eye. Blue upperparts duller than in spring adult male.

SPRING FEMALE. All females have unstreaked backs. Streaking on sides and flanks diffuse. Underparts variably washed with pale yellow. Upperparts vary from pale bluish (a) to greenish (b). First spring females resemble adults.

FIRST FALL FEMALE. No blue in plumage; upperparts plain greenish. Underparts clear pale yellow. Compare with Blackburnian. Note supercilium, not joined to pale areas on sides of neck.

FIRST FALL MALE. Resembles first fall female but with variable bluish tint to crown and upperparts, streaks on sides of crown and upperparts, and stronger streaking on sides and flanks.

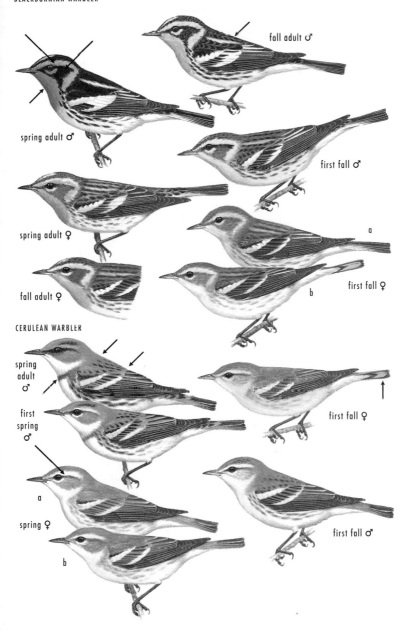

BLACKBURNIAN WARBLER

fall adult ♂

spring adult ♂

first fall ♂

spring adult ♀

a

fall adult ♀

b

first fall ♀

CERULEAN WARBLER

spring adult ♂

first spring ♂

first fall ♀

a

spring ♀

b

first fall ♂

PLATE 17

YELLOW-THROATED WARBLER   *Dendroica dominica*   p.325
5" (12.7 cm). Pine and sycamore woodlands, mainly in the Southeast. *Bright yellow throat.* Distinctive face pattern with *white patch behind black auriculars,* bold white supercilium (yellow supraloral in some populations). Geographical variation in bill length and supraloral color. More easterly subspecies *dominica* shown except as noted.

SPRING ADULT MALE. Yellow supraloral portion of white supercilium. Strong black streaks on sides, flanks. In *dominica,* bill length moderate in South (a) to *very long* on Delmarva peninsula (b). Subspecies *stoddardi* of Florida panhandle similar to (b), bill more slender.

SPRING ADULT FEMALE. Like male but with less black on forehead, flank streaks duller.

FIRST FALL MALE. Resembles adult male, but underparts washed slightly buff, back and tertials browner. Fall adult female similar.

FIRST FALL FEMALE. Upperparts browner than other plumages; stronger buff wash on flanks. Least amount of black on forehead. Cheek patch less distinct than other plumages.

SPRING ADULT MALE *albilora.* Western part of range. Bill length as in shorter-billed *dominica* (upper left). Supercilium usually white (a). Some show limited pale yellow in supraloral area (b). In *albilora,* many spring males have extensive black on forecrown (b).

FIRST FALL MALE *flavescens.* (Shown ⅘ size of other figures.) Resident in n. Bahamas. *Very long bill, extensive yellow on underparts; reduced white* in supercilium and *on sides of neck.*

GRACE'S WARBLER   *Dendroica graciae*   p.334
4.75" (12 cm). Sw. mountain pines. Suggests small, short-billed version of Yellow-throated, but *short yellow supercilium is whitish at rear; yellow arc under eye. Lacks strong face pattern* of Yellow-throated.

SPRING ADULT MALE. Breast, arc below eye, and broad supercilium bright yellow (white at rear). Lores and moustachial area blackish. Clear gray upperparts with black spotting on back and crown. Early spring birds (a) still have some gray veiling to back and crown. By June (b), wear reveals more black on back, forecrown.

SPRING ADULT FEMALE. Upperparts duller gray than spring male; black streaks on crown, back and flanks finer. Lores and moustachial area gray. First spring male resembles spring adult female.

FALL ADULT MALE. Black streaks on back and crown mostly veiled by gray.

FIRST FALL MALE. Gray of upperparts tinged brownish; buff wash on flanks. Some black spotting on sides of crown.

FIRST FALL FEMALE. Upperparts strongly washed brown; back unstreaked. Flanks strongly washed buffy; flank streaks fine. Some buff tint through belly. Grayer overall in late fall, early winter.

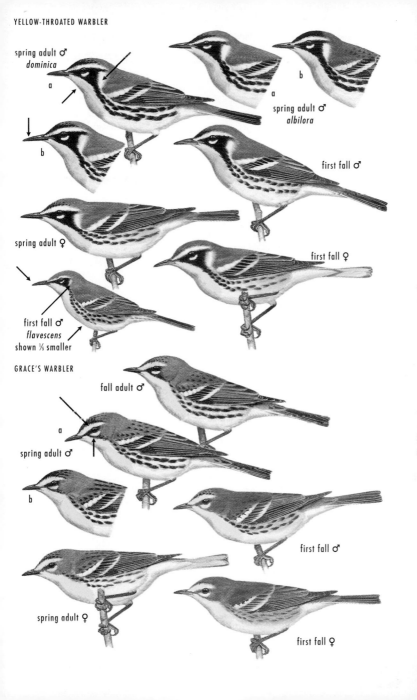

YELLOW-THROATED WARBLER

spring adult ♂
dominica

a

b

b

spring adult ♂
albilora

a

first fall ♂

spring adult ♀

first fall ♀

first fall ♂
flavescens
shown ⅓ smaller

GRACE'S WARBLER

fall adult ♂

a

spring adult ♂

b

first fall ♂

spring adult ♀

first fall ♀

PLATE 18

BAY-BREASTED WARBLER   *Dendroica castanea*   p. 375

5.25" (13.3 cm). Large, heavy, with conspicuous wing bars. Short tail and long primary extension. Spring birds show *buffy patch on sides of neck* and *bay or buff color on sides.* On fall birds, upperparts are bright yellow-green; some bay or buff on the rear flanks. Fall birds show whitish primary tips. *Legs and feet usually dark.*

SPRING ADULT MALE. *Deep bay on crown, throat, sides, and flanks.* Black forehead and face.

FIRST SPRING MALE. Duller than spring adult male; bay of underparts paler, face less solidly black (many are blacker cheeked than shown).

SPRING ADULT FEMALE. Told from males by *split buffy eye-ring* and *mottled blackish cheeks.* Chestnut crown patch. Bay color below washed out.

FIRST SPRING FEMALE. Duller than spring adult female, with more blended pattern. Chestnut crown limited (a) or absent (b). Dullest birds (b) show only slight buff on breast.

FALL ADULT MALE. Conspicuous patch of bay on flanks; some show limited bay in crown also. Gray rump. Breast clear buff. Indistinct, blended face pattern in all fall birds.

FIRST FALL MALE. Back streaks fainter; bay of sides reduced.

FIRST FALL FEMALE. Streaking above obscure. Generally lacks chestnut on flanks. Compare to first fall Blackpoll and also Pine (Pl. 19). Note indistinct face pattern, *brighter green upperparts, clear breast,* and *buff wash on flanks and vent.*

BLACKPOLL WARBLER   *Dendroica striata*   p. 383

5.25" (13.3 cm). Built like Bay-breasted. *Legs yellowish* in spring birds, *darker in fall birds but still yellow posteriorly and on soles of feet.* Fall birds olive green above, variably yellow-olive below with white edges to tertials, white primary tips and undertail coverts.

SPRING ADULT MALE. *White cheek bordered by black cap and black malar stripe* (compare with Black-and-white and Black-throated Gray, Pl. 15). First spring male similar.

SPRING ADULT FEMALE. Variable; all appear streaked with bold white wing bars. Streaking light in first spring birds and many adults (a, c), heavy in other adults (b). Some strongly washed with yellow-olive (c) and resemble fall birds, with more streaking and yellowish legs.

FALL ADULT MALE. Some show strong streaking.

FIRST FALL. Typical plumage of both sexes shown by (a). Compare closely with Bay-breasted and with Pine (Pl. 19). Told from Bay-breasted by duller olive upperparts, slightly stronger eye line, more yellowish breast with *diffuse olive streaking on sides.* No buff or bay tones on flanks. Usually with *pure white undertail coverts.* Told from Pine by lack of distinct cheek patch, white primary tips and tertial edges, and shorter tail. Fall birds, especially first fall females, rarely show fine dark stippling across the breast (b).

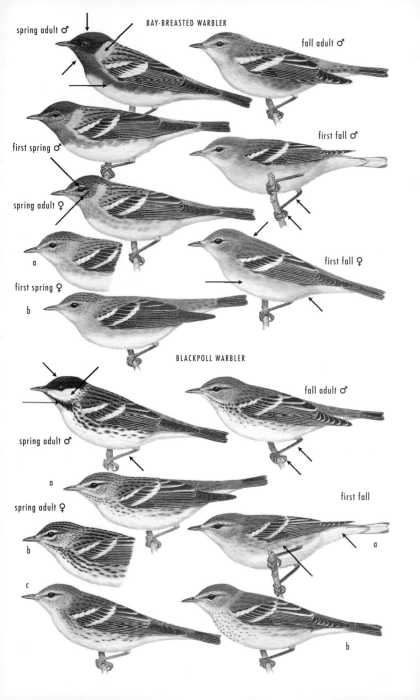

BAY-BREASTED WARBLER

spring adult ♂

fall adult ♂

first spring ♂

first fall ♂

spring adult ♀

a

first spring ♀

b

first fall ♀

BLACKPOLL WARBLER

spring adult ♂

fall adult ♂

a

spring adult ♀

first fall

b

a

c

b

PLATE 19

PINE WARBLER   *Dendroica pinus*   p. 340
5.25" (13.3 cm). Strong preference for pines. Large and heavy-billed, with *long tail extension* past undertail coverts. Upperparts olive to brownish, unstreaked. *Cheeks sharply set off from throat* and bordered behind by *pale upward extension from rear of throat.* Elongated white tail spots. Brighter birds superficially resemble Yellow-throated Vireos and are frequently mistaken for them.

SPRING ADULT MALE. Upperparts bright olive green. Underparts extensively bright yellow; lower belly, undertail coverts white. Variable streaking on sides of breast, from olive (a) to blackish (b).

SPRING ADULT FEMALE. Similar to adult male but yellow is paler and less extensive; eye-arcs whitish; streaks on sides of breast less evident.

FIRST FALL MALE. All fall males browner above than spring males (brown stronger above and on flanks in first fall males). Compare to Bay-breasted and Blackpoll (Pl. 18). Note *dull brownish edges to tertials,* dull wing bars, and lack of white tips to primaries.

FIRST FALL FEMALE. Drab. Yellow on chest limited and pale. Upperparts brownish. Note contrasting cheek area and distinctive structural features. First spring females are similarly dull.

JUVENILE. Smoky brown with pale wing bars.

PRAIRIE WARBLER   *Dendroica discolor*   p. 356
4.5" (11.5 cm). Small, fine-billed; habitually *pumps tail. Distinct pale crescent under eye,* with dark moustachial crescent below. Streaks on sides, flanks. Yellow on underparts including *pale yellow undertail coverts.* Most show some reddish spotting on back.

SPRING ADULT MALE. Black eye line, yellow crescent under eye, and black moustachial crescent. Bold black streaks on sides, flanks. Distinct red spots on back. Yellowish wing bars.

SPRING ADULT FEMALE. Similar to spring male but black areas of face replaced by olive (may show some black feathers in moustachial crescent); red spots on back reduced. Flank streaks narrower, more diffuse. First spring females similar, can be paler on throat; in some, grayish feathers on nape contrast with green crown.

FALL ADULT MALE. Like spring male, but red back spotting veiled with green.

FIRST FALL MALE. Narrow, split *whitish eye-ring* separates all fall immatures from adults. Typically (a) there is some gray in auriculars; supercilium and crescent under eye pale yellow. Very little black in moustachial crescent. Some (b) are brighter yellow and closely resemble fall adult males. Fall adult females similar but have face pattern like spring adult females; note split yellow eye-ring.

FIRST FALL FEMALE. Chin and undertail coverts very pale yellow; supercilium and crescent under eye pale gray. Moustachial crescent grayish. Wing bars dull. Side and flank streaking obscure. Compare with first fall Magnolia (Pl. 11).

PINE WARBLER

spring adult ♂

a

b

first fall ♂

spring adult ♀

first fall ♀

juvenile

PRAIRIE WARBLER

fall adult ♂

spring adult ♂

first fall ♂

a

b

spring adult ♀

first fall ♀

PLATE 20

KIRTLAND'S WARBLER *Dendroica kirtlandii* p. 349

5.5" (14 cm). *Endangered.* Breeds locally in Michigan; winters in Bahamas, seldom seen in migration. Largest *Dendroica; frequently pumps long tail. Split whitish eye-ring.* Grayish or graybrown above, streaked with black. Yellow below with white undertail coverts; sides and flanks spotted. Indistinct wing bars.

SPRING ADULT MALE. Head and back with bluish cast. Underparts mostly yellow; strong black streaks on sides, flanks. *Black in lores and anterior cheeks.*

FIRST SPRING MALE. Black in face reduced, mainly confined to lores. Yellow underparts paler; streaking on sides, flanks averages thinner. Slight brown tint to back, nape, wings. Fine black stippling across chest found in many spring males (adults and immatures).

SPRING ADULT FEMALE. All females lack black in face. Yellow underparts paler than in males. Slight brown wash on back. Stippling on breast variable; spring females of all ages can have clear breasts.

FIRST SPRING FEMALE. Back, nape, crown browner than spring adult female. Back streaking less black; underparts buffier.

FIRST FALL FEMALE. Strongly washed with brown above, stippled with dark on throat and breast. Wing bars buffy brown.

PALM WARBLER *Dendroica palmarum* p. 366

5" (12.7 cm). *Vigorously pumps tail.* Usually on or near ground. All show bright *yellow undertail coverts, strong eye line, and distinct supercilium.* Difficult to age and sex in the field. Two distinct subspecies, "Western" Palm Warbler (*D. p. palmarum*) and "Yellow" Palm Warbler (*D. p. hypochrysea*).

SPRING ADULT *palmarum.* Sexes similar. *Supercilium and throat yellow; crown chestnut.* Lower breast and belly only faintly tinged yellow. Thin chestnut streaks on sides of breast. Spring immatures may be duller, resembling fall and winter birds.

FALL/WINTER *palmarum.* Supercilium and throat dull whitish. Age and sex classes similar. Chestnut in crown lacking or reduced to a few spots, mostly on feather bases. Only bright yellow in plumage is on undertail coverts. Typical birds (a) show little or no yellow on the belly. Some (b) have a pale yellow suffusion on underparts; compare to fall and winter *hypochrysea.* By midwinter (c), some red appears in cap.

SPRING *hypochrysea. Underparts entirely yellow,* with broad, bold *chestnut streaks down sides and flanks.* Back tinged with warm brown.

FALL/WINTER *hypochrysea.* Duller than spring birds; chestnut in crown reduced or lacking. *Supercilium yellowish.* Underparts duller but still yellowish throughout, with little contrast with undertail coverts. Wing bars, tertial edges richer, more reddish brown than in fall/winter *palmarum.*

KIRTLAND'S WARBLER

spring adult ♂

first spring ♂

spring adult ♀

first spring ♀

first fall ♀

PALM WARBLER

spring adult
palmarum

spring
hypochrysea

c

fall/winter
palmarum

fall/winter
hypochrysea

a

b

PLATE 21

WORM-EATING WARBLER   *Helmitheros vermivorus*   p. 435
5.25" (13.3 cm). Olive above, buffy below with *bold blackish head stripes* (eye line and lateral crown stripes). *Heavy, sharp bill* and rather short tail. Forages at dead leaf clusters.

Many (a) are rather bright olive above and *rich orange-buff on breast*. Others (b) are grayer above and paler buff below.

SWAINSON'S WARBLER   *Limnothlypis swainsonii*   p. 442
5.25" (13.3 cm). Southeastern; breeds in lowland swamps and locally in montane rhododendron thickets. *Long spikelike bill* with slight upturn to mandible; flat forehead. *Warm brown crown*, slightly duller upperparts. *Pale supercilium and dark eye line.*

Many show yellowish tint to underparts, more extensive wash of gray-olive on chest and flanks (a); others (b) are slightly grayer.

OVENBIRD   *Seiurus aurocapillus*   p. 448
5.75" (14.6 cm). *Walks; tail often cocked.* Shows peaked crown when agitated. Large eye with *bold white eye-ring. Olive upperparts.* Thrushlike *black spotting on white underparts. Orange crown patch* (often difficult to see) bordered by black stripes.

Typical fresh birds (fall to early spring) *olive green above* (a). Western *cinereus* grayer (b), as are worn summer birds elsewhere. Juvenile (c) streaked above and below; not to scale.

NORTHERN WATERTHRUSH   *Seiurus noveboracensis*   p. 457
5.75" (14.6 cm). Waterthrushes are usually found near streams and pools; distinctive *tail-bobbing behavior* and walking gait. Little age or seasonal variation in plumage.

Northern shows *supercilium of even width throughout,* usually pale yellowish. Dense *blackish brown spots on underparts aligned to form streaks. Throat usually spotted.* Most are washed slightly (a) to strongly (b) with yellowish on supercilium and underparts. Some (c) are whiter below with whitish supercilium. Immature *Seiurus* show inconspicuous cinnamon tips to tertials (a).

LOUISIANA WATERTHRUSH   *Seiurus motacilla*   p. 468
6" (15.2 cm). More partial to running streams than Northern. Plumages parallel Northern; slightly larger overall with *longer bill.* Tail bobbing slower, with more side-to-side motion. *Supercilium tinted buff anteriorly and long, broad, and pure white behind eye;* flanks, vent, and undertail coverts washed warm apricot-buff in most birds; *legs brighter pink;* spotting below sparser, slightly paler, and less neatly arranged into rows; *throat usually unspotted.*

Flank color varies from bright (a) to whitish (b). Some individuals (b) are more sparsely spotted below.

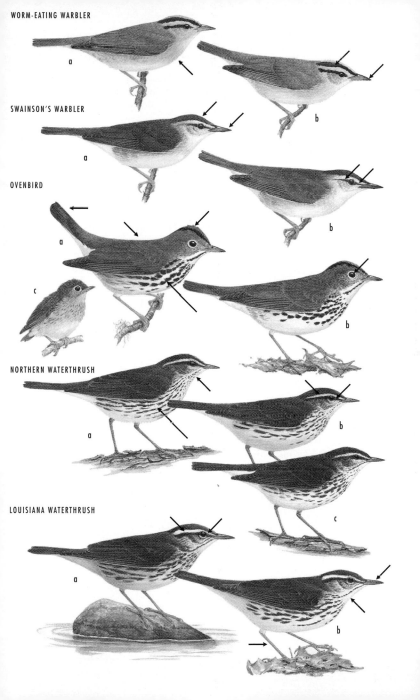

WORM-EATING WARBLER

SWAINSON'S WARBLER

OVENBIRD

NORTHERN WATERTHRUSH

LOUISIANA WATERTHRUSH

PLATE 22

CONNECTICUT WARBLER   *Oporornis agilis*   p. 484
5.5" (14 cm). Robust and short-tailed; long undertail coverts and primary extension. Retiring habits. *Walks* on ground, limbs. Plumage shows *hooded appearance* and distinctive *complete eye-ring* (slightly broken at rear in some birds). Compare with Mourning Warbler (Pl. 23); Connecticut shows *paler yellow underparts* in all plumages.

SPRING ADULT MALE. Distinct gray hood; olive nape. First spring males are slightly duller on hood with more olive in crown.

SPRING FEMALE. Hood less distinct, strongly washed olive. Throat buffy; lower hood forms grayish band across chest.

FALL ADULT MALE. Resembles spring adult male but crown and forehead strongly washed olive.

FIRST FALL. Eye-ring tinged buffy. Many (a), especially males, are nearly identical to adult females. Others (b), especially females, have *brownish hood* with buff throat that may have slight yellow tinge.

KENTUCKY WARBLER   *Oporornis formosus*   p. 475
5.25" (13.3 cm). Distinctive face pattern with *yellow supercilium curling behind and under eye. Black on sides of face* in most plumages. Olive green upperparts and bright yellow underparts. Chunky and short-tailed. Legs pale pink. Hops when on ground. Compare with immature male Common Yellowthroat (Pl. 24).

SPRING ADULT MALE. Crown black, with gray feather tips toward rear. Large black patch on face.

SPRING ADULT FEMALE. Black on crown, sides of face reduced; olive tips to crown feathers. Some individuals of both sexes show some orange tint to yellow of underparts, as shown here.

FALL ADULT MALE. Much like spring adult male but more extensive gray tips to black crown feathers.

FIRST FALL MALE. Much like females; black crown feathers variably veiled with slate gray and olive-brown tips. Black in face somewhat reduced compared to fall adult male.

FALL FEMALE. Most fall females cannot be aged in the field. Black of crown feathers variably veiled with olive or olive-brown rather than slate gray.

FIRST FALL FEMALE. Many first fall females show mainly olive forecrown; dark face patch reduced, heavily veiled.

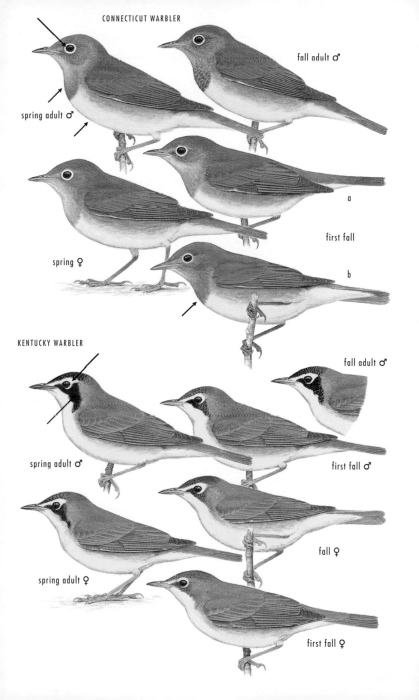

CONNECTICUT WARBLER

spring adult ♂

fall adult ♂

spring ♀

first fall

a

b

KENTUCKY WARBLER

spring adult ♂

fall adult ♂

first fall ♂

spring adult ♀

fall ♀

first fall ♀

PLATE 23

MOURNING WARBLER   *Oporornis philadelphia*   p. 493
5.25" (13.3 cm). Easily confused with closely related Mac-Gillivray's. Both are similar in structure, though Mourning has shorter tail, which extends less past undertail coverts. Immature and some adult female Mournings show whitish eye-arcs which are thinner and more complete than the blunt arcs shown by all MacGillivray's. Mourning and MacGillivray's also told by species-specific call notes. Compare also with Connecticut (Pl. 22), which has paler yellow underparts and walks rather than hops.

SPRING ADULT MALE. Blue-gray hood, typically (a) with *black most visible on lower portion of hood* (but gray-veiled black area extends onto throat) and gray lores. Some (b) show more black on chin, throat, lores. *Most lack eye-ring.* First spring males average duller.

SPRING ADULT FEMALE. Upper part of hood gray, often with a slight olive tint; slight buff wash on throat, chest. No black feathering any-where. May show thin whitish eye-rings.

FIRST SPRING FEMALE. Many females show *thin and nearly complete white eye-rings*. First spring females more extensively washed olive on nape and crown.

FIRST FALL MALE. First fall Mournings usually show *yellowish extending through breast onto throat*. Some first fall males show veiled black marks on lower throat.

FIRST FALL. Typical fall immature (a) lacks black markings and shows *yellow throat* washing through breast to yellow underparts. All show short tail extension beyond undertail coverts. A few (b) show only a slight hint of yellow on throat and closely resemble first fall MacGillivray's; best told by eye-ring shape, chest pattern, calls.

MACGILLIVRAY'S WARBLER   *Oporornis tolmiei*   p. 502
5.25" (13 cm). Western counterpart of Mourning. *Prominent white or whitish eye-arcs.* Longer tail and greater tail extension past undertail coverts compared with Mourning. Slight geograph-ical variation (not shown), mainly in tail length.

SPRING ADULT MALE. Blue-gray hood and *black lores*. Variable dark slate mottling on lower throat.

SPRING ADULT FEMALE. Gray hood, paler on chin and throat.

FIRST FALL MALE. Many show a *gray chest*, unlike any first fall Mourning. Crown strongly washed olive-brown.

FIRST FALL. From Mourning, typical birds (a) told by *breast band separat-ing yellow underparts from pale gray-buff throat*. A few birds (b) show some dirty yellow on throat and closely resemble first fall Mournings.

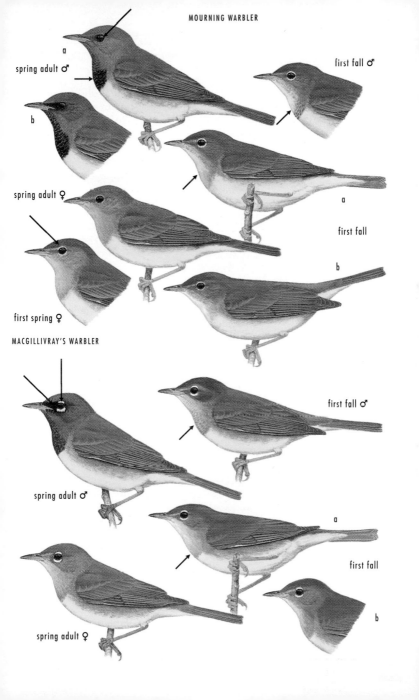

MOURNING WARBLER

a

spring adult ♂

b

first fall ♂

spring adult ♀

first fall

a

first fall

b

first spring ♀

MACGILLIVRAY'S WARBLER

first fall ♂

spring adult ♂

a

first fall

spring adult ♀

b

PLATE 24

COMMON YELLOWTHROAT   *Geothlypis trichas*   p. 512

5" (12.7 cm). Widespread in marshy and weedy areas; geographically variable. *Wrenlike; tail often cocked. Black mask* in adult males, trace of mask in first fall/winter males; males show *bright yellow throat.* Females nondescript but usually yellow or buffy on throat and breast. Compare with related *Oporornis* (Pls. 22, 23). Shown here are various plumages of an eastern subspecies, *trichas,* and selected subspecies from western North America.

SPRING ADULT MALE *trichas.* Eastern subspecies show *pale gray frontal band* above *black mask.* Yellow of throat moderate in extent.

SPRING FEMALE *trichas.* Yellow of throat duller than males. Suggestion of dark mask (a) in many birds, especially spring adult females. Most (b) lack darker cheeks, but all show sharp contrast between lower border of auriculars and yellow throat.

FALL ADULT MALE *trichas.* All fall birds have flanks strongly washed with brown and upperparts with brownish tinge. Some pale tips to black forehead feathers in fresh fall males.

FIRST FALL MALE *trichas.* Forehead, crown olive-brown. Black mottling on cheeks, with suggestion of a pale rear border.

FALL ADULT FEMALE *trichas.* Like spring female but upperparts and flanks strongly washed brownish.

FIRST FALL FEMALE *trichas.* Like fall adult female but underparts strongly washed buffy; cheek area less distinctly set off from pale throat.

SPRING MALE *campicola.* Typical of many western interior populations. *Frontal band whitish.* Upperparts paler than in *trichas.* Yellow breast does not extend as far toward belly as in other subspecies.

SPRING FEMALE *campicola.* Paler and grayer than female *trichas.* Yellow of throat pale and often quite limited.

SPRING FEMALE *occidentalis.* Some spring females of interior West (*occidentalis, campicola, yukonicola*) can lack yellow on throat and breast; yellow is restricted to undertail coverts. Sides of breast, flanks dull brownish.

SPRING MALE *scirpicola.* Typical of West Coast birds in having extensive yellow on lower breast, upper belly, and upper flanks. Frontal band whitish as in other western subspecies.

SPRING MALE *chryseola.* S. Arizona to sw. Texas. Extensively yellow underparts. Frontal band tinged pale yellow. Largest subspecies in our area.

COMMON YELLOWTHROAT

spring adult ♂
trichas

a

spring ♀
trichas

b

spring ♀
trichas

fall adult ♂
trichas

first fall ♂
trichas

fall adult ♀
trichas

first fall ♀
trichas

spring ♂
campicola

spring ♀
campicola

spring ♂
scirpicola

spring ♂
chryseola

spring ♀
occidentalis

PLATE 25

BAHAMA YELLOWTHROAT   *Geothlypis rostrata*   p. 529
5.5" (14 cm). Endemic resident on Bahamas; unconfirmed reports for
s. Florida. *Large* yellowthroat with *long, heavy bill*. Differs from
Common in vocalizations, behavior, and habitat. Geographical
variation primarily in crown and upperpart color.

SPRING MALE *tanneri*. Grand Bahama and Abaco. Limited gray on crown;
distinctly yellow frontal band does not extend across forecrown.

ADULT FEMALE *tanneri*. Extensively yellow below; many show hint of pale
border to rear of auricular.

SPRING MALE *rostrata*. New Providence. Pale gray tinge to crown; frontal
band meets across forehead; yellower on back and flank. Andros
Is. *exigua* (not shown) similar, but darker gray on crown, less yellow above, frontal band does not extend across forecrown.

SPRING MALE *coryi*. Eleuthera and Cat Island. Brightest race; yellow
green crown and yellow frontal band.

COMMON YELLOWTHROAT   p. 512
Spring adult male of subspecies *trichas* for comparison; see Pl. 24.

BELDING'S YELLOWTHROAT   *Geothlypis beldingi*   p. 525
5.5" (14 cm). Resident on s. half of Baja California peninsula. *Large,*
with longer bill than Common Yellowthroat. Compare especially
with sw. *chryseola* Common Yellowthroat (Pl. 24). Extensively yellow below. Males show *yellow in frontal band*. Two subspecies:
goldmani of s.-cen. peninsula and *beldingi* of Cape district.

FALL ADULT MALE *goldmani*. Frontal band tinged yellow.

FALL ADULT FEMALE *goldmani*. Yellow supercilium; lacks black mask.

ADULT MALE *beldingi*. Frontal band entirely bright yellow.

GRAY-CROWNED YELLOWTHROAT   p. 535
Geothlypis poliocephala
5.5" (13.3 cm). Neotropical species; grayest, northeastern subspecies
ralphi formerly resident in grassy and shrubby habitats near
Brownsville, Texas; recent records from there, perhaps involving
only one bird. *Heavy bill with curved culmen;* pale mandible.
Black or dark gray lores. Fresh fall birds browner. High slurred
call and buntinglike song very different from Common Yellowthroat's.

SPRING MALE. Black lores

ADULT FEMALE. Grayish lores.

FALL MALE. Extensive olive-brown wash on crown; lores variably black to
slaty.

BAHAMA YELLOWTHROAT

spring ♂
tanneri

spring ♂
coryi

spring ♀
tanneri

spring ♂
rostrata

COMMON YELLOWTHROAT

spring adult ♂
trichas

BELDING'S YELLOWTHROAT

fall adult
♂ *beldingi*

fall adult ♂
goldmani

adult ♀

GRAY-CROWNED YELLOWTHROAT

fall ♂

spring ♂

adult ♀

PLATE 26

WILSON'S WARBLER *Wilsonia pusilla* p. 549
4.75" (12 cm). Small, active. Green above, yellow below with *complete or partial black cap* in most plumages.

SPRING MALE *pusilla*. Boreal; only subspecies expected in East. Underparts, forehead, and short, broad supercilium yellow. *Auriculars and upperparts olive green. Complete shiny black cap.*

SPRING MALE *pileolata*. Alaska through montane West. Similar to *pusilla*, but slightly brighter, above and below.

SPRING MALE *chryseola*. Pacific Coast region. More golden than *pileolata*. Auriculars and upperparts brighter and yellower.

SPRING ADULT FEMALE *pileolata*. Cap smaller, less shiny than male. Black limited mainly to front of crown (a) or nearly as extensive as in male (b) but blended with olive at rear. A few lack black entirely.

FIRST SPRING FEMALE *pileolata*. Variable; many lack black in crown.

FALL ADULT MALE *pileolata*. Olive tips to feathers at rear of cap.

FIRST FALL MALE *pileolata*. Like fall adult male, but olive tips more extensive, usually found throughout black cap.

FALL ADULT FEMALE *pileolata*. Head tinged olive, little contrast with cap. Black cap absent or limited to front of crown.

FIRST FALL FEMALE *pileolata*. Black usually absent in crown. Forehead yellow-olive, not contrasting sharply with crown.

FIRST FALL FEMALE *pusilla*. Yellow of underparts dull, washed with olive. *Forehead olive, not contrasting with crown.* Auriculars with much dull olive, setting off yellow eye-ring.

FIRST FALL FEMALE *chryseola*. Relatively bright above and below; forehead yellow, contrasting with cap. Many show some black at front of cap. Cheeks washed yellowish.

HOODED WARBLER *Wilsonia citrina* p. 541
5.25" (13.3 cm). *Unique hood frames yellow face* in males and adult females. *Extensive white in tail* revealed by repeated rapid spreading and closing of tail feathers. All show olive upperparts, bright yellow underparts, and black or olive in lores. *Bill and eye large.* Usually remains within understory.

SPRING MALE. *Solid black crown and throat,* connected along sides of neck and framing yellow face and forehead.

ADULT FEMALE. Typically (a) throat is extensively yellow, bordered below with black; some (b) show extensive blackish nearly to bill and closely resemble males. Some (c) show little black and resemble first fall female. *Rear crown mostly olive* rather than black adult males.

FIRST FALL MALE. First fall males average more pale fringing and may show yellow under the bill.

FIRST FALL/FIRST SPRING FEMALE. No black on crown. Face extensively yellow, bordered with olive; prominent black eye. Dark in lores.

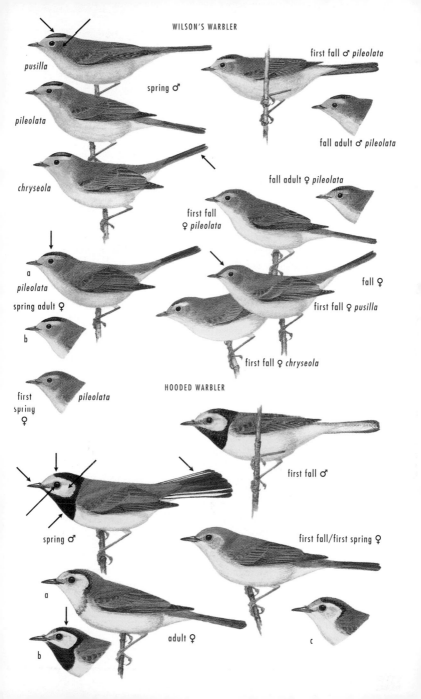

WILSON'S WARBLER

pusilla

spring ♂

pileolata

chryseola

a
pileolata

spring adult ♀

b

first
spring
♀ *pileolata*

first fall ♂ *pileolata*

fall adult ♂ *pileolata*

fall adult ♀ *pileolata*

first fall
♀ *pileolata*

fall ♀

first fall ♀ *pusilla*

first fall ♀ *chryseola*

HOODED WARBLER

first fall ♂

spring ♂

a

b

adult ♀

first fall/first spring ♀

c

PLATE 27

CANADA WARBLER   *Wilsonia canadensis*   p. 560
5.25" (13.3 cm). Size, shape, and actions suggest Wilson's (Pl. 26); also flips long tail. Gray upperparts, yellow underparts with *white undertail coverts. Necklace of streaks across breast* varies from black to inconspicuous olive-gray. *Distinct whitish eye-ring.* Necklace width and darkness, face pattern may vary within age and sex classes.

SPRING ADULT MALE. Extensive black in crown and face. *Bold black necklace.* Upperparts pure gray.

FIRST SPRING MALE. Black in crown, face, and necklace reduced.

SPRING ADULT FEMALE. Black absent in face and crown; necklace streaks dusky. First spring birds show brownish tinge to wings.

FALL ADULT MALE. Like spring adult male, but black of face and crown veiled gray; necklace with some yellow veiling.

FIRST FALL MALE. Crown and face suffused with olive. Black of necklace dull and reduced. Wings tinged brownish.

FIRST FALL FEMALE. Resembles first fall male but necklace streaks indistinct (nearly absent in some birds).

AMERICAN REDSTART   *Setophaga ruticilla*   p. 418
5" (12.7 cm). Active, flashy warbler with *orange* (adult male) *or yellowish patches in wings and tail* especially visible during characteristic wing-drooping and tail-spreading behavior.

ADULT MALE. Typical birds (a) are black with *orange patches on sides of breast,* bases of primaries and secondaries, and basal ⅓ of outer several pairs of rectrices. Orange may extend to wash through lower breast and upper belly on some birds (b). Extent of black on lower breast and belly also varies, with (a) more typical. Some adult males (c) show variable warm brown tips to back feathers and grayish tips to black areas on head and underparts. These tips are more evident in fresh fall plumage.

SPRING FEMALE. No black in plumage; head gray, upperparts tinged olive. Patches on sides of breast, wings, and tail yellow. White eye-ring and lores.

FIRST SPRING MALE. *Blackish always present in lores* (a). Some show variable black spotting on head and breast (b). Most show orange tint to patch on sides of breast (a); others (b) have patches very similar to female's. Uppertail coverts blackish.

FIRST FALL MALE. Much like female, lacking black in lores. Patch on sides of breast often orangish, as shown, but many have yellow patches on sides of breast and cannot be told from females. Extent of yellow at base of remiges averages greater in immature males than in immature females.

CANADA WARBLER

first spring ♂

spring adult ♂

spring adult ♀

fall adult ♂

first fall ♂

first fall ♀

AMERICAN REDSTART

adult ♂

c

b

a

first spring ♂

a

b

spring ♀

first fall ♂

PLATE 28

PAINTED REDSTART *Myioborus pictus* p. 573
5.25" (13.3 cm). Pine-oak canyons of sw. mountains. *Flashy white patches in wings and tail;* wings slightly spread and *tail often held fanned* when foraging (see plate). *Bright red lower breast patch.* White lower eye-arc.

MALE. All post-juvenile birds resemble figure shown; females, on average, show slightly paler red breast patch.

JUVENILE. This plumage held longer than in most warblers; seen June–August on breeding grounds. Lacks red; lower underparts sooty. Conspicuous white patch in wings and white outer tail feathers. Later juveniles show patches of red molting on lower breast.

SLATE-THROATED REDSTART *Myioborus miniatus* p. 579
5.25" (13.3 cm). Widespread Neotropical montane species; a few records for sw. border region. Like Painted Redstart, tail often held fanned. More graduated tail shows less white. *Upperparts slaty,* not black. *No white wing patch or arc under eye. Red of underparts paler.* Chestnut patch on crown.

MALE. Forehead and throat black, contrasting with slaty upperparts. Well-defined *deep chestnut patch on crown.*

FEMALE. Underparts slightly duller than male's. Throat and forehead slaty like upperparts. Chestnut crown patch paler, more poorly defined.

RED-FACED WARBLER *Cardellina rubrifrons* p. 568
5" (12.7 cm). Sw. montane species with *unique red and black face pattern. White patches on rump and nape.* No white in tail; white wing bar on median coverts only. Bill short; tail long, often flipped. Head appears peaked.

FALL MALE. *Brilliant red on forehead, eye-ring, throat, and sides of neck. Black from crown through sides of face.* Clear gray back. Fresh fall birds may show pink wash on underparts and on white nape patch.

SPRING MALE. Like fall male, but lacks pink wash.

SPRING FEMALE. Red of face averages slightly paler than that of male.

FIRST FALL FEMALE. Red of face even duller, more orangish; slight brown cast to upperparts, sides of breast. First fall males brighter, closely resembling adult males.

PAINTED REDSTART

juvenile

♂

SLATE-THROATED REDSTART

♂

♀

RED-FACED WARBLER

fall ♂

spring ♀

spring ♂

first fall ♀

PLATE 29

CRESCENT-CHESTED WARBLER   *Parula superciliosa*   p. 190
4.25" (11 cm). Neotropical montane species; three confirmed records for se. Arizona presumably representing palest subspecies *sodalis. Prominent white supercilium.* Parula-like patch of green on back; *lacks wing bars. Bright yellow throat and breast;* variable *chestnut band on chest.*

ADULT MALE. Chestnut chest band broadest.

ADULT FEMALE. Chestnut band thinner.

FIRST FALL FEMALE. Chestnut band absent or present only as a faint wash; this plumage held through first spring.

RUFOUS-CAPPED WARBLER   *Basileuterus rufifrons*   p. 593
5" (12.7 cm). Males, females similar. Northern member of diverse Neotropical genus, found in brushy montane habitats. Recorded in se. Arizona (one attempted nesting) and w. and cen. Texas. Striking head pattern with *rufous on crown and auriculars, white supercilium.* Gray-olive upperparts, *yellow throat and breast,* and white belly. *Long, thin tail is cocked in wrenlike fashion.*

Subspecies *jouyi* of ne. Mexico has more extensive rufous cap, approaching (a). Northwestern *caudatus* (b) has paler and more restricted rufous.

GOLDEN-CROWNED WARBLER   p. 589
Basileuterus culicivorus
5" (12.7 cm). Widespread neotropical species; northernmost, grayest race *brasherii* recorded several times in southernmost Texas. Skulking habits; superficially suggests Orange-crowned Warbler. *Yellow* (a) *to orangish* (b) *crown bordered by black lateral crown stripes.* Partial yellow eye-ring. Yellow underparts brightest on breast.

FAN-TAILED WARBLER   *Euthlypis lachrymosa*   p. 584
5.75" (14.6 cm). Another Mexican species recorded casually in se. Arizona and once in n. Baja California. *Large; flicks white-tipped tail open and shut.* Usually found on or near ground. Tawny orange breast and yellow underparts. *Yellow crown patch, white markings around eye.* Loud, high call note.

Some (a) are slightly paler and grayer on the upperparts. Others (b) are darker above; birds in fresh plumage may show dark feather tips on crown. Birds as dark as (b) are more typical of more southerly populations.

CRESCENT-CHESTED WARBLER

adult ♂

first fall ♀

adult ♀

RUFOUS-CAPPED WARBLER

a

b

GOLDEN-CROWNED WARBLER

a

b

FAN-TAILED WARBLER

♀

a

♂

b

PLATE 30

OLIVE WARBLER   *Peucedramus taeniatus*   p. 109

5" (12.7 cm). Mainly resident in pine-fir forests of sw. mountains. *Masked appearance;* mask more solid in males. Kingletlike wing pattern with rather distinct wing bars, *yellow-green edges to secondaries,* and *pale patch at base of primaries. Bill long and thin.* Distinctive vocalizations. Distantly related to other warblers.

ADULT MALE. *Unique, bright, tawny orange head* and breast, with *blackish mask.* Grayish upperparts.

ADULT FEMALE. Dark outline of mask. Head and breast buffy yellow. Compare with female Hermit Warbler (Pl. 14); note stronger mask and different wing pattern of Olive.

FIRST SPRING MALE. Head and breast yellow, with variable traces of tawny orange feathering. Solid dark gray mask.

FIRST FALL FEMALE. Resembles adult female, but buffy yellow of head and breast paler; back more brownish.

YELLOW-BREASTED CHAT *Icteria virens*   p. 598

7" (17.8 cm). Unique, *very large* warbler with *heavy bill* and long tail. All show bright yellow throat and breast contrasting with white belly and undertail coverts, *white spectacles.* Upperparts uniform olive. Secretive, though singing males may be conspicuous. Unique, loud, varied song. Minor geographical variation. Birds shown are eastern *virens,* except upper figure of western *auricollis.*

SPRING MALE *auricollis.* Western birds are *longer tailed* and have olive upperparts grayer, less green, more white on sides of throat.

SPRING MALE. All spring males show black bills and black lores. A few may show black in auriculars and crown also. Typical birds resemble (a), but some birds of both sexes can show patchy orange on breast (b).

SPRING FEMALE. Lores slaty, not black. Yellow breast paler than in adult male. Bill shows some pale on mandible.

FALL ADULT MALE. Similar to spring male, but slight olive tipping on yellow underparts. Bill shows some pale. First fall males similar, but olive tipping more extensive, lores less black, and flanks more strongly washed brownish.

FIRST FALL FEMALE. Yellow of underparts extensively tipped olive; flanks of all first fall birds washed brown.

OLIVE WARBLER

adult ♂

first spring ♂

adult ♀

first fall ♀

YELLOW-BREASTED CHAT

spring ♂
auricollis

spring ♂

a

b

fall adult ♂

spring ♀

first fall ♀

UNDERTAIL PATTERNS

In many cases, various features presented by the underside of a warbler's tail may be helpful or diagnostic for species identification.
Included for these purposes of comparison are the undertail
coverts, which often add important clues as well. These illustrations depict primarily *adult males in breeding plumage,* with exceptions noted. Females and immatures of each species often exhibit similar characteristics to the males, but see the individual
text accounts for additional detail.

• **TAIL SPOTS:** These pale portions of otherwise dark rectrices (tail feathers) are not present in all species, so their presence or absence
may be significant in ruling out other warblers. Their *size, shape,*
and sometimes *color* are factors to note. Typically, in the field,
one can observe the tail spot patterns of only the two outer feathers, since the tail is usually folded and viewed from below.

• **UNDERTAIL COVERTS:** The *color* and the *length* of the undertail coverts can
vary considerably from species to species, so their appearance
can often be very useful to note. They are generally white or yellow, often contrasting with the color of the rectrices, and the
presence or absence of dark spots or other markings may be significant. The *length* of the undertail coverts should be noted in
relation to the total length of the tail, for the relative proportions
of these may be distinctive.

• **TAIL PROJECTION** (beyond undertail coverts): As noted above, the length
of the tail and of the undertail coverts often vary significantly
from species to species, resulting in varied *tail projections.* These
are defined as the distance the rectrices (tail feathers) extend beyond the undertail coverts. Some species may have long tails with
short undertail coverts (e.g., Pine Warbler), producing a *long* tail
projection. Other species (e.g., Blackpoll Warbler) have relatively
shorter tails with longer undertail coverts, resulting in a *short* tail
projection. With experience, these relative lengths can be judged
in the field, providing clues that help one with identification.

• **VARIATION:** Although the illustrated undertail patterns may be "typical"
for each species, individual variation does exist and may result in
differing appearances — especially in the size and intensity of
markings on the undertail coverts. For example, many
Townsend's Warblers have bold, black, triangular streaks here,
but some individuals have only faint shaft streaks, and many others are intermediate. In Hermit Warbler, most individuals lack
markings on the undertail coverts, but some may show streaks
here.

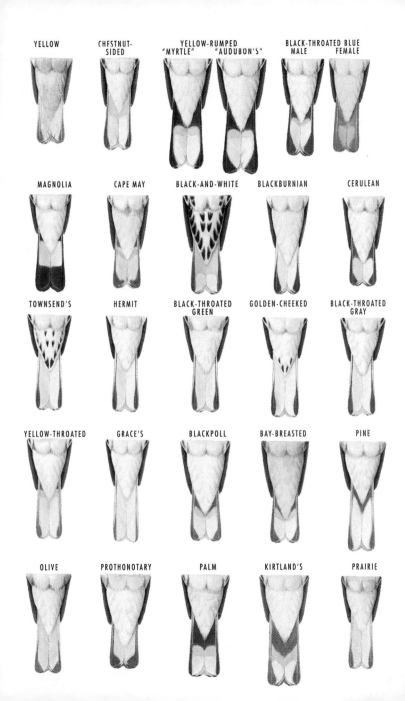

YELLOW

CHESTNUT-SIDED

YELLOW-RUMPED
"MYRTLE" "AUDUBON'S"

BLACK-THROATED BLUE
MALE FEMALE

MAGNOLIA

CAPE MAY

BLACK-AND-WHITE

BLACKBURNIAN

CERULEAN

TOWNSEND'S

HERMIT

BLACK-THROATED
GREEN

GOLDEN-CHEEKED

BLACK-THROATED
GRAY

YELLOW-THROATED

GRACE'S

BLACKPOLL

BAY-BREASTED

PINE

OLIVE

PROTHONOTARY

PALM

KIRTLAND'S

PRAIRIE

BLUE-WINGED GOLDEN-WINGED ORANGE-CROWNED TENNESSEE
FEMALE MALE

NASHVILLE VIRGINIA'S COLIMA LUCY'S NORTHERN PARULA

KENTUCKY CONNECTICUT MOURNING MACGILLIVRAY'S TROPICAL PARULA

COMMON YELLOWTHROAT HOODED WILSON'S CANADA RED-FACED

WORM-EATING SWAINSON'S AMERICAN REDSTART
AD. MALE FEMALE/IMM. MALE PAINTED REDSTART SLATE-THROATED REDSTART

SPECIES
ACCOUNTS

Peucedramus taeniatus

5 in. (12.7 cm) The Olive Warbler is a pine-loving species of montane forests from Arizona and New Mexico south to Nicaragua. It possesses many traits unusual among our warblers, and anatomical and biochemical studies suggest that it is only distantly related to the wood-warblers. The combination of a whistled call, titmouselike song, kingletlike wing-flicking, and strongly notched tail also set it apart from our other warblers. In U.S. populations, males do not attain definitive plumage until after one year of age. At least some (perhaps most) of the U.S. population appears to withdraw south into Mexico for the winter, but at least a few birds remain. The species is essentially unknown in the U.S. away from its limited breeding habitat. The rather inappropriate name "Olive Warbler" derives from the scientific name originally applied to the species, *Sylvia olivacea*, a name subsequently found to have been already in use.

 DESCRIPTION

Sexually dimorphic, with first spring males (at least in northernmost subspecies) more similar to females than to adult males. No seasonal changes in appearance apart from the effects of plumage wear. Adult males have a tawny head and black mask; the head of females and immature males is yellowish but retains a suggestion of the mask at the rear of the auriculars. The upperparts are grayish (tinged olive in some portions of the range, brownish in fresh immatures), and the underparts are unmarked grayish white.

There are two white wing bars and a variable patch of white at the base of the primaries. The primaries, secondaries, and rectrices are edged with yellowish olive. There is extensive white in the outer two pairs of rectrices.

Structure is distinctive. The bill is long and thin but not especially sharp; the culmen is slightly decurved. The tail shows a decided notch (about 5–6 mm difference between tips of central and outer rectrices, more than any other wood-warbler). The wing is relatively long compared to the tail, and the wingtips are long and pointed (possibly related to foraging behavior, since the species is largely sedentary).

 ## SIMILAR SPECIES

Adult males with bright tawny heads and black masks are unique among our warblers. Note superficial resemblance to some immature male **BULLOCK'S ORIOLES** *(Icterus bullocki)*, which are much larger, with conical bills and very different voice and behavior. Female and immature Olive Warblers are more obscure. Important identifying characters include the slight masked effect (especially behind the eye), whitish patch at the base of the primaries (which can be obscured by primary coverts), light yellow-green edges to the secondaries, strongly notched tail with extensive white in the outer rectrices, and long and slender bill. Most likely to be confused with **HERMIT WARBLER**, particularly immature female Hermits, which lack dark on throat. Hermit Warblers may be numerous as migrants in the southwestern montane breeding habitat of Olive in late July through September. Note the essentially all-yellow face of Hermit, with much yellow enclosed within the indistinct dusky auricular patch. The primaries and secondaries of Hermit are essentially plain, lacking the whitish base to the primaries and yellow-green edges to the secondaries that are evident in Olive. The tail of Hermit is only shallowly notched, and the bill is shorter and somewhat thicker. The "tip" call of Hermit differs from the rich whistled note of Olive. Because Olive Warbler is essentially unknown in the U.S. away from its limited breeding range, any extralimital claim must be carefully separated from the much more likely Hermit. Confusion with other warblers is unlikely, but see immature female **PINE** (larger, with heavy bill, dull streaks on sides of breast). Immature female **TOWNSEND'S** and **BLACK-THROATED GREEN WARBLERS** have green upperparts.

General plumage of females and immatures can suggest **KINGLETS** *(Regulus)*, but note different head patterns and kinglets' smaller size and different calls.

♪ VOICE

All vocalizations differ strongly from those of other warblers. The **SONG** is variable in pattern but distinctive in quality, being a series of rich, titmouselike notes of 2–3 syllables: *peeta peeta peeta pee-ta.* Variants include *pit-cheer pit-cheer pit-cheer* or *whit-er'-a whit-er'-a whit-er'-a.* Occasional renditions are buzzier, but still of rich quality. Song is not likely to be confused with that of any other warbler; titmice with similar songs that share range (Plain, *Parus inornatus,* and in ne. Mexico, Black-crested, *P. [bicolor] atricristatus* occur at lower elevations, mainly in oaks, not pines. Female song in Olive Warbler has been reported, but most or all reports may pertain to first-year males in femalelike plumage. Males are known to sing through the winter as well as in the breeding season.

CALL NOTE is a short, rich, downslurred whistle, *kew* or *phew;* it suggests call of Western Bluebird (*Sialia mexicana*). A hard *pit* note is also given. **FLIGHT NOTE** unknown.

⚥ BEHAVIOR

Typically forages by gleaning for insects high in conifers, often well into the interior of the branchwork but frequently at terminal needle clusters as well. It is a slow and deliberate feeder, often creeping methodically along the branches. The long, slender bill may aid in the probing of crevices and needle clusters; such ability may facilitate overwintering in montane forests within the U.S. In the nonbreeding season, foraging tends to expand into non-conifer understory trees and shrubs and occasionally even to the ground. Flight between foraging trees is swift and erratic, and large distances may be covered. Often found in pairs and, in late summer, family groups. Gregarious outside of the breeding season, forming small flocks of up to 15 or more birds and readily joining mixed-species flocks.

The **NEST** is located high in a conifer, usually at least 30 ft. up; it is placed near the tip of a branch and often concealed in mistletoe clumps. The nest is a soft, compact, deep cup of fine materials, often incorporating the silvery fibers of the undersides of the silverleaf oak. The eggs are heavily smudged with dark, unlike the paler and more finely marked eggs of typical wood-warblers. The occupied nest becomes heavily soiled by droppings; such soiling is reminiscent of many cardueline finches but is unknown among paruline warblers.

BREEDS (and primarily resident) in rather open coniferous forest of high elevations (usually above 7,000 ft.). Found primarily in pines (especially ponderosa) and white fir, often along ridges. In Mexico, range may occur in rather arid, high-elevation pine and fir forests and is not especially tied to the vicinity of water anywhere in its range. Only rarely descends (mainly in **WINTER**) to the lower altitudinal limit of pines.

 DISTRIBUTION

Mainly **RESIDENT** from cen. Ariz. and sw. N.M. south through Mexico to n.-cen. Nicaragua, although northernmost populations are partially migratory. In Ariz., **BREEDS** north locally to the Mogollon Rim, the Sierra Prieta just west of Prescott, and in the mountains west and south of Flagstaff; also breeds in the Pinal Mtns. (Gila Co.), Mazatzal Mtns. (Maricopa Co.), and in all of the higher

OLIVE WARBLER
Peucedramus taeniatus

ranges of the Southeast. Breeds in w. N.M. north to the Mogollon Mtns., San Francisco Mtns. and Black Range, and Pinos Altos Mtns., and south to the Animas Mtns. in the extreme Southwest. South of the U.S. it breeds through the high mountains of n. Mexico (n. Sonora, n. Chihuahua, n. Coahuila, and sw. Tamaulipas) south to the Isthmus of Tehuantepec, and also in the mountains of Chiapas, Guatemala, Honduras, and n.-cen. Nicaragua.

WINTERS throughout breeding range, but some (or perhaps most) birds withdraw from northernmost breeding range (Ariz., N.M., Sonora, Chihuahua, n. Coahuila) for the winter.

There are few records of **MIGRANTS**, and it only rarely descends to middle elevations (5,000–6,000 ft.) in the ranges where it nests, or to adjacent ranges lacking breeding habitat (as in the Dragoon and Patagonia mtns. in Ariz.). There is a well-documented record for the Davis Mtns., Texas: a singing immature male on Mt. Livermore on 19 May 1992. Other accepted Texas records are from Presidio Co. on 7 September 1994, and an adult male in Briscoe Co. in the Panhandle on 30 April 1995. There are two winter records along the Rio Grande in s. N.M., and one from early May in s. Luna Co., N.M.

▟ STATUS AND CONSERVATION

No information on population trends; most breeding habitat within the U.S. is on at least nominally protected public land. Unknown as a cowbird host.

▜ SUBSPECIES

Up to seven subspecies have been recognized, with a confusing history of racial taxonomy in this species. The rather subtle geographical variation involves dorsal color (plain gray to darker blackish gray, variably tinged olive), ventral color (whitish to grayish), richness of the tawny head in males, and size. U.S. birds belong to the northernmost, palest subspecies, *arizonae*, which ranges south in Mexico to Sonora and cen. Chihuahua, and n. Coahuila. Plumages of *arizonae* are described below. In this subspecies, first spring males have a femalelike plumage, whereas many or most males of remaining subspecies attain an adult male plumage with the first prebasic molt. From n.-cen. Mexico south to Guatemala occur several similar forms: *jaliscensis* (s. Chihuahua, cen. Coahuila, and s. Nuevo Leon south to sw. Jalisco, Colima, and Zacatecas); *giraudi* (cen. Mexico); and nominate *taeniatus* (considered to include "*aurantiacius*," and usually also "*georgei*"; cen. Guerrero east to w. Guatemala). These subspecies are very similar to one another, differing slightly in size (*taeniatus* is smallest) and the amount of olive tones to the upperparts. They are darker gray above than *arizonae*, often tinged more strongly with olive, especially on the rump and uppertail coverts. The head and throat of males are a brighter tawny orange color, and there is a partial yellow-olive collar behind the tawny hindneck. The primaries and secondaries are more boldly edged with yellow-olive, and the underparts are grayer, less white, with deeper olive-gray flanks. Overall size is similar to or slightly smaller than *arizonae*. The neck and throat of adult females is a deeper yellow. The smallest and brightest subspecies is *micrus*, found in El Salvador, Honduras, and Nicaragua; this race is bright tawny orange on the face and throat, slightly paler golden-tawny on the crown and nape, with a yellow collar behind the nape; it is relatively pure white below and blackish gray above, and there is slightly more white in the primaries and tail than in other races.

TAXONOMIC RELATIONSHIPS

The relationships of the Olive Warbler have long been controversial. The genus *Peucedramus* was long considered a member of the Parulidae, with suggested affinities with *Dendroica*. Some authors even suggested merging *Peucedramus* into *Dendroica*. One detailed study enumerated important distinctions in the anatomy of *Peucedramus*, especially bone and muscle characters relating to the tongue; these, along with some behavioral traits, suggested that the Olive Warbler was not a wood-warbler but might better be placed in the Muscicapidae, a large assemblage including thrushes and Old World warblers. Evidence based on DNA-DNA hybridization raises questions regarding the relationship with the Muscicapidae (along with the composition of the Muscicapidae itself) and tentatively indicates that the Olive Warbler is a "sister group" to a branch containing all of the nine-primaried songbirds. It is best, perhaps, to give the Olive Warbler family rank of its own (Peucedramidae).

PLUMAGES AND MOLTS

SPRING ADULT MALE: Entire head pale tawny orange except for a mask of dull black extending from the loral region back through the auriculars. Chin paler tawny buff. The tawny orange color of the head is slightly tinged with olive-yellow at the rear, which gives an indistinct collared effect. Remaining upperparts medium gray, tinged slightly with olive on the rump. Upper breast tawny orange like the head; lower breast, belly, and undertail coverts dull whitish. Sides tinged with gray; flanks and vent

Olive Warbler. Adult male in Arizona in June. (Photo: John Hoffman/Frank S. Balthis)

area tinged with gray-buff. Wing coverts blackish, with very broad white tips to the median coverts and bold (but somewhat less broad) white tips to the greater coverts; the effect is of two bold wing bars, the anterior one broader; plumage wear through spring and early summer reduces the boldness of the wing bars. Remiges blackish, with olive-yellow edges evident on the secondaries; edges of primaries paler, more whitish. A white patch at the base of the middle primaries is visible behind the blackish primary coverts. The tail is mostly blackish slate. The outer rectrices are white on the basal half of the outer web and all but the tip of the inner web; there is nearly as much white on r5, but white on r4, if present, is limited to a small patch on the inner web. **FIRST SPRING MALE:** Forehead and crown yellow, variably obscured with gray feather tips, especially on the center and rear of the crown. Nape grayish, with an indistinct collar of olive-yellow across the uppermost back. Lores and auricular area slaty gray, with some pale buff or whitish mottling in the center of the auriculars, contrasting with the slaty rear auricular. Chin whitish. Supercilium, sides of neck, throat, and breast rather rich tawny yellow; a few flecks of tawny orange may be present on sides of throat, sides of neck. Remainder of plumage as in adult male, although white patch in primaries and white in outer two pairs of rectrices may average slightly more restricted. **SPRING ADULT FEMALE:** Forehead, crown, and hindneck yellow-olive with a variable wash of gray, especially toward hindneck. Lores gray, auriculars mottled gray and buffy white; rear of auriculars dark gray, standing out on the face as a patch. Supercilium and sides of neck, behind auricular, buffy yellow. Chin buffy white. Throat pale yellow, blending into gray-buff lower breast, sides, and flanks. Belly dull grayish white; undertail coverts whitish. Back medium gray, slightly paler and more olive on the rump. Tips to median coverts narrower than in adult male, so the two wing bars are of roughly equal width. Olive-yellow edges to the flight feathers, somewhat paler on the primaries. White patch at the base of the primaries small and mostly or completely hidden by the blackish primary coverts. White on r5 much more restricted than in adult male, occasionally lacking; white lacking on r4. **FIRST SPRING FEMALE:** Similar to spring adult female, but yellow of head, throat, and breast averages even paler and duller. White primary patch not visible beyond greater coverts; usually no white in r5. **FALL ADULT MALE:** Nearly identical to spring adult male but plumage fresher; upperparts may show slightly more olive in this fresh plumage. Tawny orange of rear crown and nape is somewhat obscured by gray feather tips. Gray wash on sides and gray-buff of flanks and vent stronger in fresh fall plumage. Olive-yellow edges to secondaries and whitish edges to primaries more conspicuous. **FIRST FALL MALE:** Resembles first spring male, but plumage fresher, with a noticeable tinge of olive-brown on the upperparts. Generally lacks any flecks of tawny orange color (these presumably gained in limited prealternate molt in late winter or early spring). **FALL ADULT FEMALE:** Similar to spring adult female, but plumage fresher; upperparts tinged somewhat more brownish olive, and sides, flanks, and vent with a deeper wash of gray-buff. Edges to flight feathers more conspicuous. **FIRST FALL FEMALE:** Very similar to first spring female, but yellow of throat, breast, and sides of head paler and duller; crown and forehead more strongly washed with olive-brown; upperparts more brownish olive. Probably not safely distinguishable from first fall male, but yellow averages paler and buffier, white primary patch completely obscured, and white lacking in r5. **JUVENILE:** Crown and upperparts dull brownish olive. Face pattern indistinct, with brownish auricular and dull buff supercilium. Throat and breast dull pale yellowish, obscurely mottled with gray. **BARE PARTS:** Bill of adults blackish, with some pinkish brown at the base of the lower mandible; bill of first fall birds duller slaty brown, with more extensive pale on the lower mandible. Eyes brown. Legs and feet slaty gray; soles of toes yellowish.

The prebasic molt takes place from July to August; it is complete in adults and partial in hatching-year birds (not involving flight feathers). There is a limited prealternate molt (February to April), at least in birds in their first winter and spring. Definitive adult plumage is not attained in male northern birds of the race *arizonae* until the second prebasic molt, at 1 ¼ years of age. Many or most males of the remaining subspecies attain definitive plumage at the first prebasic molt.

 # REFERENCES

ECOLOGY, BEHAVIOR, VOCALIZATIONS, AND CONSERVATION: Webster 1962.
SYSTEMATICS: George 1962, Harshman 1994, Miller and Griscom 1925, Phillips 1966, Sibley and Ahlquist 1990, Webster 1958 and 1962, Zimmer 1948.

Vermivora bachmanii

4.25 in. (11 cm). This enigmatic warbler of bottomland forests of the southeastern U.S. is probably extinct; the last certain sightings (of a single bird) were in the Charleston, South Carolina, region in 1962. The Bachman's (pronounced "BACKman's") Warbler was a habitat specialist, breeding in shrubby edges and canebrakes within bottomland forests; it wintered almost exclusively in Cuba. Habitat degradation on its breeding grounds and perhaps also on its wintering grounds was certainly the main factor in the species' decline. Hamel's works summarize what little is known of the biology and decline of this species. This small *Vermivora* shows a uniquely thin and decurved bill; males combine a black bib with a yellow chin and yellow or olive-yellow forehead.

DESCRIPTION

A small, rather short-tailed warbler showing fairly strong sexual dimorphism, moderate age variation, and minor seasonal variation. The bill is distinctly shaped, thin and slightly decurved. The upperparts are olive to olive gray. The underparts are extensively yellow in males and adult females, but generally grayish in the dullest immature females; the undertail coverts are whitish in all plumages. A black bib is characteristic of males and present to a limited extent in adult females; all plumages show gray on the nape. The rectrices of males and adult females show at least some white.

SIMILAR SPECIES

Black-bibbed males bear a superficial resemblance to male (and some adult female) **HOODED WARBLERS**. The Hooded is a larger warbler that flashes conspicuous white patches in the outer tail feathers. The cheeks of Hooded are bright yellow, as are the underparts all the way through the undertail coverts (Bachman's have whitish undertail coverts). Compare also with male **"LAWRENCE'S WARBLER"** (Golden-winged × Blue-winged warbler hybrid), which shows white or yellowish wing bars and dark cheek patch.

Females, particularly immatures, are much less distinctly marked and might be confused with several other warbler species. The combination of a fine, slightly decurved bill and a yellowish forehead contrasting with the gray crown and nape should identify adult females, but drab immature females require careful scrutiny. These drabbest birds are mostly grayish, with a wash of olive above (especially on the rump) and just a hint of yellow in the face; note again the distinctive bill shape. An immature female Bachman's suggests ORANGE-CROWNED WARBLER but has a complete whitish eye-ring on a rather blank face (Orange-crowned shows a split eye-ring and at least a hint of a dark transocular line) and whitish undertail coverts; even the dullest Orange-crowned shows a yellow wash through the undertail coverts. Orange-crowneds also show diffuse streaking on the sides of the breast, lacking in all plumages of Bachman's. NASHVILLE WARBLERS show distinctly yellow undertail coverts in all plumages and have a straighter culmen. Compare also with immature female YELLOW WARBLERS, particularly *gundlachi* (resident in Bachman's wintering grounds), which can be quite grayish. Yellow Warblers are larger than Bachman's, and all show distinctive pale edges to the greater coverts and tertials, yellow tail spots, and heavier bills. Female COMMON YELLOWTHROATS are considerably longer tailed than Bachman's and (except when worn) more brownish in plumage, especially on the flanks. Because this species is probably extinct (and quite possibly has been for several decades), any future claims would require extensive photographic documentation and confirmation.

 ## VOICE

The SONG is a rapid series of buzzy notes, sometimes ending with a sharp slurred note, *bzz-bzz-bzz-bzz-bzz-bzz-bzz-zip*. Songs contain 6–25 *bzz* notes, delivered at a rate of 5–10 per second. The quality of the buzzy notes is suggestive of type B songs of Blue-winged and Golden-winged warblers. The rapid delivery and monotone pitch of the song suggests Worm-eating Warbler but is far buzzier than the Worm-eating's simple trill. The rapid buzzy series given by the Northern Parula has a distinctive rise in pitch toward the end and usually ends with more pronounced slurs. Beware, however, variation in the song of Northern Parula, a species that can be abundant in the former haunts of the Bachman's Warbler.

Information on CALL NOTES is scant and confusing. Notes attributed to this species include a low, hissing *zee-e-eep*, a soft *tsip*, a *twee* or *chee* note, and a *zeep* (given singly or in series). Some of these may refer to FLIGHT CALLS.

There is little first-hand information on the behavior of this species. Most foraging took place at rather low heights (especially 3–10 ft.), although spring migrants have been noted foraging high in the canopy in Florida. Foraging techniques included gleaning and probing into leaf clusters. Its penchant for probing into leaf clusters has led to speculation that it might have specialized on foraging among dead leaves within canebrakes and other bottomland associations. Like many *Vermivora* it has been noted foraging in acrobatic, chickadee-like fashion, hanging upside down and probing the undersides of leaves. Food consisted almost entirely of caterpillars, spiders, and other small arthropods; the extent to which it might have fed on nectar on the wintering grounds, if at all, has not been determined.

Although not habitual tail-waggers, Bachman's were noted to jerk the tail when alarmed; they frequently raised their crown feathers slightly to give the head a fluffed appearance.

Males would sing vigorously upon arrival on the breeding grounds, but singing during spring migration was evidently rare. Preferred song perches were often fairly high in the trees. Information on nesting and breeding biology comes primarily from South Carolina and Missouri.

NESTS were usually placed from 1 to 4 ft. off the ground in the dense understory of bottomland forests, among stalks of cane, blackberry brambles, palmettos, etc.; they were often placed over or near pools of water. The nest was rather deep and bulky, with dead leaves, grasses, moss, and weed stalks on the outside; the neat inside cup was lined with fine fibers from *Ramalina* lichen and Spanish moss (*Tillandsia*). The pure white eggs, sometimes finely marked at the large end, were unusual among wood-warblers.

 HABITAT

BREEDING habitat consisted of timbered bottomland swamps with pools of still water; dominant trees were deciduous and included cypress, black gum, sweet gum, tupelo, hickory, dogwood, and red oak. It is uncertain exactly what specialized habitats within these swamps were important to Bachman's Warblers, but it appears that they favored small openings and edges with a dense understory of cane or "bamboo" (*Arundinaria gigantea*), palmettos, and brambles of blackberries and other thorny vines. It is possible that this species was a specialist on cane, a strategy found in many insectivorous passerines within Neotropical forests (see Remsen's

1986 paper). The clearings that appeared to be so important to these warblers might have been created by storms, fires, or insect damage and were probably somewhat ephemeral in nature. Small- scale, selective logging of southern forests late in the 1800s might actually have increased Bachman's Warbler habitat for a short period. Whatever the particulars of its habitat, it is clear that habitat modification contributed to a steep decline shortly after the turn of the century. See Status and Conservation for more details.

WINTER habitat on Cuba apparently consisted of a range of forest associations, but little information is available. Recorded habitats varied from dry, semideciduous forest to wooded swamps and even forests within urban regions. Majagulales (forests of *Hibiscus*) were sometimes important.

In **MIGRATION**, bottomland forests were apparently favored, but migrants also occurred in relatively low, scrubby habitats in regions such as the Florida Keys.

 DISTRIBUTION

Known **BREEDING** localities are few and were located mainly in two regions: the southern Atlantic coastal plain (at least in S.C. in the vicinity of Charleston, but perhaps originally north to Va. and south to Ga.), and from the Gulf states (cen. Ala., but with breeding season records from s. Ala., n. Miss., and La.) north in the southern Mississippi R. drainage (primarily in the "sunken lands" along the St. Francis R. of ne. Ark. and se. Mo.) and Ky. (north of Russellville in Logan Co.). This species' dramatic decline occurred before many portions of the se. U.S. received thorough ornithological coverage; its apparent abundance at some known sites suggests that it may have bred more widely than the relatively few areas cited above, although many early authors commented on this species' colonial nature. There were a few breeding season records for La., n. Miss., s. Ala., N.C. (two specimens from Raleigh), and Va. (four records) but no proven breeding in those regions. There are no reports for Tenn., and the few e. Texas and Okla. reports are not fully acceptable.

WINTERED for certain only in Cuba, and probably also on the nearby Isle of Pines (one specimen, which was subsequently lost). There is a 27 January 1898 specimen from Melbourne, Fla., suggesting that this species may have occasionally wintered on the Fla. peninsula. Winter reports (including a specimen) cited by Bent in the Okefenokee Swamp, se. Ga., cannot be confirmed.

MIGRATION data were limited, with the only records of migrants occurring in significant numbers from Fla. (mainly the west coast and Keys) and se. La. (mainly on the n. shore of Lake Ponchartrain). Both spring and fall migration were quite early.

SPRING MIGRATION was primarily through the Fla. peninsula, but apparently with some movement across the eastern Gulf of Mexico as well. Migration began as early as late February, and numbers of migrants were noted in s. Fla. and se. La. by the first week of March. Peak spring movement was during the first three weeks of March in s. Fla. and se. La., and in the third to fourth weeks of March farther north on the west coast of Fla. The latest spring migrant recorded in Fla. was 9 April. Birds arrived on the S.C. breeding grounds by mid-March (and even as early as the end of February). Arrivals at the northern end of the breeding range in sc. Mo. were probably in mid to late April. There is one record for Cay Sal Bank, Bahamas (13 March 1901), which is on a direct line between Cuba and s. Fla.

FALL MIGRATION was again poorly documented, with the greatest numbers of migrants recorded at Key West, Fla. The earliest fall migrants were recorded on 4 July in s. Miss. and 17 July at Key West, and peak fall movement was likely from the end of July to about 25 August. The latest date from the S.C. breeding grounds was 19 July, and the latest known migrants were 18 September in Key West and 24 September in coastal Ga.

Possibly **VAGRANT** north of known breeding range; records for Va., N.C., and nw. Ark. might apply to spring overshoots or small breeding populations. There are old reports from Ill. and Ind. (the latter involves a specimen of unknown whereabouts). There are a few erroneous or undocumented reports for e. Texas and a dubious report from 1960 in Okla.

⠿ STATUS AND CONSERVATION

The Bachman's Warbler is probably extinct, although several unconfirmed sightings from the southeastern U.S. and Cuba since about 1970 perhaps offer a slim hope that the species might still survive. The first specimens were obtained by Bachman in 1832, and the species was formally described by Audubon in 1833. It remained virtually unknown until the mid-1880s, after which it was encountered in fair numbers at the breeding localities noted above (and, as migrants, in s. Florida) until about 1910. As noted under Habitat, it is possible that selective logging of bottomland forests late in the 19th century briefly benefited this species by creating small openings where cane and other dense growth could flourish; this was followed, however, by wholesale clear-cutting of these forests. By 1920, Bachman's had become scarce over most of its range, and only a handful of breeding birds or migrants were encountered after 1930. The last certain records from the winter grounds were in 1938 and 1940, although unconfirmed reports persisted into the 1980s; a published report of a female in Cuba in 1980 appears to pertain to a Common Yellowthroat. The last specimens taken were a male, 21 March 1941 at Deer Island, Mississippi (specimen at the University of Michigan Museum of Zoology), and a female at Ship Island, Mississippi, on 28 February 1949. Breeding populations may have persisted in the "sunken lands" of se. Missouri and ne. Arkansas into the 1940s; the last Missouri record was in 1948. The last certain Florida record was of a male in Calhoun Co. on 30 March 1951. A few birds persisted at I'On Swamp near Charleston, South Carolina, until 1953. The only well-documented records after that were of individual singing males in Fairfax Co., Virginia, in 1954 and 1958, and a few sightings near Charleston in the 1950s. The last undisputed sighting was of a singing male seen by a number of observers at Moore's Landing, near I'On Swamp, in April 1962. An immature female photographed 30 March 1977 in Brevard Co., Florida, a region of the state where the species was rarely recorded even in its "heyday," appears to us more likely a ("Golden"?) Yellow Warbler. The true time table of this species' demise is unclear.

The decline and probable extinction of the Bachman's Warbler was due largely to the destruction of the bottomland deciduous woods on the breeding grounds, superimposed on the warbler's specialized habitat requirements. Habitat destruction came about through large-scale clearing of forests (and replacement with agriculture), and the channelization of watercourses and resulting draining of swamps. It is uncertain to what extent habitat alteration on the wintering grounds was also a factor. Always localized in its breeding distribution, this species apparently could not withstand the extensive loss of appropriate habitat. Hamel speculates that a series of destructive fall hurricanes crossing over Cuba in the early 1930s might have dealt the species its final blow; populations may have subsequently been so much reduced that breeding birds simply could no longer find each other.

 ## SUBSPECIES

No subspecies recognized; no geographical variation described.

 ## TAXONOMIC RELATIONSHIPS

No close relatives within *Vermivora* have been identified, but its relationships appear to lie with the Blue-winged/Golden-winged warbler complex.

SPRING ADULT MALE: Forehead, supraloral area, short supercilium, and arc under the eye yellow; lores and postocular line dusky olive. Forecrown black, center of crown black with gray fringes. Rear crown and nape olive-gray; auriculars washed with olive-gray. Remaining upperparts olive green, brightest on the rump. Chin, uppermost throat, and malar area yellow. Center of throat and bib across upper breast black, sharply demarcated from the yellow lower breast and belly. The black of the bib and forecrown is variable in extent. Some males may not acquire the full extent of black until two years of age. The black may still show grayish or olive veiling in early spring. Undertail coverts whitish, lightly washed with pale yellow on the sides of the vent. Median and greater secondary coverts and primary coverts olive green; lesser coverts yellow (often hidden); bend of wing yellow. Flight feathers dusky, narrowly edged with olive. Rectrices grayish olive with extensive white patches on the inner webs of the outer pair of rectrices and successively smaller white patches on r5 to r2; the central rectrices lack white. **FIRST SPRING MALE:** Similar to spring adult male, but with black areas on the crown and bib less extensive. The lesser wing coverts show less yellow. In the hand, the rectrices and outer primaries are more tapered than in adults. **SPRING ADULT FEMALE:** Forehead and supraloral area light yellow, blending into a grayish crown and nape. The remaining upperparts are olive green, brightest on the rump. Lores and auriculars grayish olive; complete whitish eye-ring. Chin and throat light yellow. The sides of the neck are grayish, and this color extends down somewhat onto the sides of the upper breast. There is a variable grayish olive wash across the center of the lower throat and chest, and some (older?) females show a few black feathers in this region. The lower breast and belly are pale yellow, paling to whitish on the lower belly and

Bachman's Warbler. Adult male at St. Andrews Parish, Charleston County, South Carolina (1958, probably May). (Photo: J. H. Dick/VIREO)

undertail coverts. The flanks are washed with grayish. Wing coverts olive, brighter yellowish olive on the lesser coverts and the bend of the wing. Flight feathers dusky with narrow olive edges. Rectrices grayish olive; most birds show indistinct whitish patches on the inner webs of the outer two or more pairs. **FIRST SPRING FEMALE:** Resembles first fall females, but plumage more worn, often appearing grayer and duller. The extent of any prealternate molt in females is unknown. Some brighter birds may resemble spring adult females but never show black feathers on lower throat and chest. In the hand, the rectrices and outer primaries are more tapered than in adults; inner webs of rectrices usually lack any white. **FALL ADULT MALE:** Similar to spring adult male, but black feathers of forecrown extensively veiled with grayish, and those of the bib edged with yellowish olive. **FIRST FALL MALE:** Resembles fall adult male, but yellow of the underparts is paler and duller, and the black of the breast is more heavily veiled with olive. The forehead is strongly washed with olive, not contrasting strongly with the crown. The forecrown is olive, nearly or completely lacking the black feather centers visible in fall adult males. White in the tail is limited to a small diffuse spot on the edge of the inner webs of the outer rectrices. **FALL ADULT FEMALE:** Similar to spring adult female, but plumage fresher. Any black mottling on the bib is nearly obscured by grayish olive feather tips; the yellow of the forehead is heavily tinged with olive. **FIRST FALL FEMALE:** Variable; the dullest plumage and the one most likely to be confused with other species. Forehead dull olive-yellow, not forming a contrast with the grayish olive crown and nape. Remaining upperparts olive green, duller than in adult. Dull whitish eye-ring, contrasting with olive-gray lores and auriculars. Throat and breast variably marked with yellow. In the dullest birds, yellow is nearly lacking, with underparts dull grayish white, washed with grayish olive on the breast and flanks; brighter birds show a pale yellow wash on the throat and breast. White on inner webs of rectrices usually lacking; when present, white is diffuse and limited to inner edge of the outermost rectrices. **JUVENILE:** Dusky brown on head and upperparts; pale brownish buff below, paling to dull whitish on the lower belly and undertail coverts. Wings dusky with pale brown wing bars. Some whitish on the outermost rectrices, at least in males. **BARE PARTS:** Bill blackish brown in adults, browner in young birds, especially at the base of the lower mandible. Legs grayish brown to dark brown. Eyes dark brown.

The prebasic molt occurs on the breeding grounds and is exceptionally early. Hatching-year birds acquire their first basic plumage as early as May; juvenal flight feathers are retained. Adults begin their complete prebasic molt as early as the beginning of June; this molt is usually completed by August, but a few September specimens from the winter grounds show traces of molt. A prealternate molt appears to be absent in adults; the more solid black bib and forecrown of spring males is the result of wear of the pale feather tips of fresh basic plumage. The plumage of first spring birds suggests that there is a limited prealternate molt in birds that age.

 REFERENCES

GENERAL: Hamel 1995, Shuler 1977c, Stevenson 1978 and 1982.
DISTRIBUTION: Barber 1985, Burleigh 1944a, Brewster 1891, Chamberlain 1958, Hamel and Hooper 1979, Ripley and Moreno 1980, Sciple 1950, Scott 1888, Shuler 1977a, Shuler et al. 1978, Stevenson 1938 and 1972.
ECOLOGY, BEHAVIOR, VOCALIZATIONS, AND CONSERVATION: Brewster 1891, Embody 1907, Hamel 1986, Hamel and Hooper 1979, Hooper and Hamel 1977, Remsen 1986, Shuler 1977b, Stevenson 1938 and 1972, Wayne 1907, Widmann 1897.
IDENTIFICATION: Hamel and Gauthreaux 1982.

BLUE-WINGED WARBLER   PL. 2

Vermivora pinus

4.75 in. (12 cm). This inhabitant of successional habitats in eastern North America has dramatically expanded its range to the north and northeast in the 1900s. Although the Blue-winged is very different in plumage pattern from the more northerly-breeding Golden-winged Warbler, these two species are closely related and frequently hybridize in the shifting zone where their ranges come into contact. Hybrids are discussed under Golden-winged Warbler (p. 133). The Blue-winged Warbler has a long, sharp bill and a bold, dark line through the eye in all plumages, along with white undertail coverts that contrast with the yellow underparts. The blue-gray wings with whitish wing bars and mostly extensive white in the outer three pairs of tail feathers are distinctive among warblers with plain olive upperparts and unmarked yellow underparts.

 DESCRIPTION

Generally green above and yellow on the crown and underparts, becoming white on the undertail coverts; all plumages show a dark line through the eye and pale (usually whitish) wing bars. Age and sex differences are slight; there is little seasonal change in plumage.

The Blue-winged is a medium-sized warbler with a moderately long tail and a rather long and sharply pointed bill; there is a strong seasonal change in bill color.

Distinctive, with its combination of unmarked yellow underparts, white undertail coverts, conspicuous dark eye line, pale wing bars, and large white tail spots. Other warblers that are mostly yellow below, such as YELLOW WARBLER and PROTHONOTARY WARBLER, lack the dark eye line and broad whitish wing bars. Bright ORANGE-CROWNED WARBLERS (subspecies *lutescens*), which show a hint of a dark eye line, are easily told by the lack of white in the wings, tail, and undertail coverts.

The main identification cautions concern hybrids and intergrades with GOLDEN-WINGED WARBLER. These might be mistaken for "pure" Blue-winged, and some individuals vaguely resemble other warbler species. Identification problems posed by hybrids are covered under Golden-winged Warbler.

 VOICE

The typical SONG is a distinctive and easily learned *beeee, bzzzz,* a dry buzz followed by a longer, sizzling buzz on a slightly higher (or sometimes lower) pitch. Only the song of the Golden-winged Warbler is similar, but the Golden-winged song contains two or more short notes following the introductory buzz. The alternate (or "type B") song is more complex than the typical song, with a variable number of short, somewhat musical notes given rapidly after the buzzy notes; these songs are sometimes given in flight, especially early in the morning. Alternate songs may closely resemble those of the Golden-winged Warbler. Songs of Blue-winged × Golden-winged hybrids may resemble those of either parental species; see Golden-winged Warbler account for a discussion of songs of hybrids.

CALL NOTE is a sharp *tsik* or *swik*, indistinguishable from the call note of Golden-winged. The FLIGHT NOTE is a high, somewhat buzzy *zweet* or *tzzii,* often doubled.

 BEHAVIOR

Feeds rather deliberately, often hanging upside-down to glean leaf and twig surfaces. It uses its spikelike bill to open curled leaves within dead leaf clusters and to open new leaf buds; often probes along climbing vines. Occasionally hover-gleans to pick insects from leaf surfaces. Most feeding is at low to moderate heights within the vegetation; ground feeding is rare. Blue-wingeds seem to feed, on average, at lower heights than Golden-wingeds, but the foraging behavior of the two species is quite similar. In migration and winter this species joins mixed flocks of warblers and other insectivorous birds. Although some have suggested that Blue-winged Warblers dominate Golden-wingeds during hostile encounters between the two species (which might help explain the expansion of the former species at the expense of the latter), several studies have found this not to be the case. Males often sing from high, exposed perches at the edge of a field.

The **NEST** is a deep, bulky cup placed among forbs or grasses on or (usually) just above the ground. It is constructed of leaves and bark shreds, supported by a foundation of dried leaves, and lined with fine bark shreds, grass stems, and hair.

HABITAT

BREEDS in a wide variety of successional habitats such as old pastures, woodland clearings and slashings, power line right-of-ways, and woodland edges. The Blue-winged is more generalized in its habitat requirements than is the Golden-winged, tolerating later stages of succession. The common element of the breeding habitat is an abundant undergrowth of shrubs, herbs, and weeds. In much of the southern part of the breeding range it occupies relatively dry, brushy hillside habitats with emergent growth including red oak, locust, walnut, and elm. In parts of the southern Midwest it occupied, at least formerly, rich bottomland woods with an abundant undergrowth of cane. Other important associations include clearings within oak-hickory, oak-pine, and even pure pine forests. In the northern part of the range breeding habitats are relatively moist, including streamside thickets, aspen and pin cherry woodlands, mature lowland deciduous forest, old apple orchards, and old weedy/brushy pastures; a thick understory (such as catbrier, *Smilax*) and a ground layer of forbs and sedges is typical. Breeding habitats are mostly below 1,000 ft. in Pennsylvania, up to 1,500 ft. in New York, and up to 2,000 ft. in w. North Carolina.

WINTERS in woodland clearings, brushy woodland borders, and fields overgrown with weeds and shrubs; perhaps somewhat more partial to second-growth and open habitats in winter than the Golden-winged. **MIGRANTS** are encountered in woodlands and woodland edges and openings.

DISTRIBUTION

BREEDS presently from se. Minn., cen. Wisc., cen. Mich., s. Ont., sw. Que. (not confirmed), cen. N.Y., cen. Vt., and s. N.H. (annually also in extreme s. Me. in recent years) south to n. Ark., Tenn.,

n. Ala., n. Ga., and w. N.C. Also breeds south on the Atlantic coastal plain to s. N.J., n. Del., and probably se Md. There are a few summer records for the Piedmont and mountains of S.C., but no documented breeding yet. Has nested in e. Okla. and probably formerly nested in e. Kans.; breeding not proven for Neb. There has been considerable change in the breeding range during the present century; this is detailed under Status and Conservation below.

WINTERS primarily in Mexico and n. Central America, occurring from se. San Luis Potosi (rarely s. Tamaulipas) south through the Atlantic slope of Mexico to Costa Rica (uncommon) and cen. Panama (rare). Farther south there is a single record for e. Panama and a 21 March specimen for the Santa Marta Mtns. in n. Colombia. Very rare in winter in the West Indies, where recorded in the n. Bahamas, the Greater Antilles, and the larger Virgin Is. Casual in winter (also spring, fall) on Bermuda. This species is surprisingly rare in the U.S. in winter, given how far north it winters in Middle America. There are some 20 winter sightings for Fla., but the species occurs only exceptionally anywhere else in the U.S.: 29 December 1972 in Brazos Co., Texas; 9–10 January 1973 in Medina Co., Texas; 20 December 1980 in Frankfort, Ky.; 10 December 1899 to 6 January 1900 near New York City; 2 January to 7 March 1993 in Humboldt Co., nw. Calif.; 25 February 1995, Winston Co., Miss.; and different birds were banded and photographed in Oriental, N.C. 30 January through February 1994 and on 5 March 1995. There are numerous records of fall birds lingering into November in eastern North America.

This is a classic trans-Gulf **MIGRANT** in spring, common at migrant traps on the upper Texas coast and La. but rare in Fla. There is a slight easterly shift in the fall migration route, when the species is more numerous in regions such as Fla. and the coastal Carolinas.

SPRING MIGRATION is early, with the earliest birds appearing along the Gulf Coast by the last week of March, and small numbers occurring (in Texas and La.) by the first week of April. More exceptional early records extend back nearly to mid-March (a 3 March record for Fla. might represent a locally wintering bird). Late March sightings extend as far north as n.-cen. Texas, Tenn., and Ky., and there are 1 April records for Ark. and s. Mo. From Ark. east to Tenn. and the n. portions of the Gulf states, spring arrivals are during the second week of April. From cen. Ill. east to s. Ohio, first arrivals are usually during the third week of April, and in the Mid-Atlantic region during the last week of April. At the northern end of the breeding range, spring arrivals are during the first half of May. There are scattered earlier records at northern latitudes (e.g., 19 April in Mich., 15 April in N.Y., and 21 April in Mass.); exceptional was a 7 April record for w. N.Y. and one on 14 April on Sable Is., N.S. Spring movements on the Gulf Coast peak during the second and third weeks of April, and during the first third of May over a broad front from Mo. to Md. Small numbers may linger on the Gulf Coast through the first week of May, and a few migrants are found in late May farther north.

FALL MIGRATION is poorly defined but is generally early. There are scattered records of fall migrants through the latter half of July over much of the East. Fall movement through the Mid-Atlantic region is heavier and more prolonged than that through the Midwest; peak movements in these regions are in mid- to late August, with a few still passing through in early September. Peak movements in the Gulf states are during the middle third of September. This species is generally absent from the northern states and Midwest after mid-September, and from the Mid-Atlantic coast after the end of September; even on the Gulf Coast it is rare after September. Late dates extend well into October over much of the

BLUE-WINGED WARBLER
Vermivora pinus

East (and into November along the Gulf Coast). Exceptionally late were birds in the New York City region on 29 November, Mass. on 6–27 November, Ont. on 27 November and 1–2 December, and w. N.Y. on 30 November.

VAGRANT or very rare migrant on the e. Great Plains (casual in the Dakotas), mainly in spring. Casual north of the breeding range, e.g., Man. in late fall, n. Ont. (May and October, exceptionally north to James Bay), and Nfld. (now nearly annual). Casual in spring in the Canadian Maritime Provinces, but probably regular there in fall (and on islands off Me.). Casual in w. North America, mainly in May and September. In Colo. there are some 30 spring and 10 fall records, plus a record of a summering pair. Recorded in Alta. (fall), Sask. (four records), Wyo. (June), Nev. (twice, May), Wash. (September), Ore. (twice, May), N.M. (about 12 records), and Ariz. (five September and early October records, four May and June records). Of the 20 Calif. records, half are for spring (mainly late May) and the remainder are fall (mostly during the latter half of September) except the winter record noted above.

ⅢⅢ STATUS AND CONSERVATION

This species has accomplished a tremendous northward and northeastward range expansion. Historically this species was restricted to west of the Appalachians and did not occur much north of the Ohio River Valley. Expansion into the Delaware and lower Hudson river valleys took place by the late 1800s, and much of s. New England was colonized during the first part of the 20th century. Breeding was first established in Vermont in 1976 and in Maine in 1980. Farther west, Blue-wingeds spread rapidly up the Ohio River Valley during the early 1900s, reaching n. Ohio and the Niagara frontier region of w. New York by the 1930s. In Michigan, populations were established in the southwest in the 1940s, and this species was widespread over s. Michigan by the 1950s. Breeding was established in Minnesota and Ontario in the 1950s. Occupation of cen. Pennsylvania in the 1970s connected the expanded populations in New England and the northern Midwest. Much of the expansion of this species occurred in areas occupied earlier by expanding Golden-winged Warbler populations, with a general replacement of the latter by Blue-wingeds. The expansion at the northern edge of the range continues today. Increases of this species are reflected in the pattern of vagrancy to w. North America; all but two of the accepted records for California are after 1982.

Local decreases have been noted in regions of intensive agriculture in the Midwest, e.g., in w. Missouri.

SUBSPECIES

None described.

 TAXONOMIC RELATIONSHIPS

Genetically very similar to the Golden-winged; the two compose a superspecies; the closest recent relative of this superspecies may be the Bachman's Warbler. A full discussion of the Blue-winged × Golden-winged hybrid complex is given under the latter species account. Blue-winged Warblers have hybridized with Kentucky Warbler, a combination (represented by two specimens) that apparently explains the enigmatic "Cincinnati Warbler"; one of these hybrids was originally considered to be a Blue-winged × Mourning. A probable pairing between a Blue-winged and a Nashville Warbler in Walworth Co., Wisconsin, in 1899 (clutch of six eggs and both adults collected) has been recorded.

 PLUMAGES AND MOLTS

SPRING ADULT MALE: Forehead to midcrown bright yellow, contrasting fairly sharply with the yellow-olive hindcrown and nape. Remaining upperparts yellow-olive, slightly brighter on rump and darker and duller on uppertail coverts. Lores black, extending through the eye as a short postocular streak, pointed at the rear. This black line through the eye is about the same width as the eye. Sides of the neck and rear portion of the auricular yellow-olive. Chin, throat, breast, and belly bright yellow, tinged slightly olive on the sides and flanks. Undertail coverts white. Wing coverts gray, with median and greater coverts broadly tipped with white; these white wing bars may be slightly tinged with yellow. Flight feathers slaty, edged

Blue-winged Warbler. Male in Florida in May. (Photo: Herbert Clarke)

Blue-winged Warbler. Female in Texas in May. (Photo: Brian E. Small)

with pale blue-gray. The inner greater coverts and tertials may show a thin edging of yellow-olive. Rectrices dark gray; white spots on inner webs of outer three rectrices, extending to tip of r4 and r5, but not of outer rectrices; r3 may show a small white spot. **FIRST SPRING MALE:** Nearly identical to spring adult male. In the hand, the outer primaries and rectrices are more tapered and the primary coverts appear more worn. Many first spring males have the olive of the hindcrown blending into the yellow forecrown, thus showing less contrast than in spring adult males. Some show duller (slate black) lores than adult males. On average there is less white in the rectrices. **SPRING ADULT FEMALE:** Very similar to spring males, differing as follows: Yellow of forecrown duller, blending into the olive of the hind crown. Lores and eye line slaty gray rather than black. Underparts average slightly duller yellow. Wing bars average thinner, and white in the tail averages slightly more limited than in spring adult male. **FIRST SPRING FEMALE:** Resembles spring adult female, but averaging duller (many birds closely resembling first fall female). Aged in the hand by primary, rectrix, and primary covert criteria given above under First Spring Male. White in rectrices relatively diffuse and limited. **FALL ADULT MALE:** Plumage essentially identical to spring adult male, but the midcrown may show slight olive feather tips. Note differences in bill color (below). **FIRST FALL MALE:** Like first spring male, but many show a more slaty (less jet black) eye line, suggesting that there must be some prealternate molt in this region); olive on crown slightly more extensive and blended with the yellow forecrown. Generally brighter than first fall female, with more yellow on the forecrown and darker eye line. Outer primaries and rectrices tapered. **FALL ADULT FEMALE:** Very similar to spring adult female, but crown slightly more extensively blended with olive. **FIRST FALL FEMALE:** Yellow forehead and crown extensively blended with olive, with little contrast between the forecrown and the hindcrown. There is a slight effect of a yellow supercilium between the extensively olive crown and the eye line, which is dusky or gray in this plumage. The rear of the auriculars and sides of the neck are strongly tinged with olive. Yellow of the underparts relatively dull; undertail coverts washed with light yellowish. Wing bars thin and often tinged dull yellow. Outer primaries and rectrices tapered. White in rectrices relatively diffuse and limited. **JUVENILE:** Head, throat, and upperparts dull olive, tinged yellow; lores dusky. Remaining underparts dull buffy yellow. Wings and tail as in first fall birds; thin pale yellowish wing bars. **BARE PARTS:** Bill black in spring and summer males, changing to dull pinkish brown with a dusky black culmen in fall and winter. Spring and summer females have blackish bills showing some brown on the sides; in fall and winter their bills resemble those of fall/winter males. First fall and winter birds have dull pinkish brown bills, darker on the culmen. Legs and feet slaty black, dull yellowish on the soles. Eyes blackish brown.

The prebasic molt takes place on the breeding grounds from June to August; it is complete in adults, partial in hatching-year birds (not involving remiges, or rectrices). The prealternate molt (January to April) is probably limited to the feathers of the head.

 REFERENCES

See also those listed for Golden-winged Warbler (p. 145).
DISTRIBUTION: Gochfeld 1974.
ECOLOGY, BEHAVIOR, VOCALIZATIONS, AND CONSERVATION: Ficken and Ficken 1968e, Robbins 1991 (Blue-winged × Nashville pairing).
SYSTEMATICS: Graves 1988, Short 1963.

GOLDEN-WINGED WARBLER PL. 2

Vermivora chrysoptera

4.75 in. (12 cm). Primarily an inhabitant of early successional habitats. In recent decades, the Golden-winged Warbler has been declining in the southern portion of its breeding range, where the closely related Blue-winged Warbler is largely replacing it. The current stronghold of the Golden-wing is at higher elevations in the Appalachians and in the states and provinces along the eastern U.S./Canada border. Hybridization with the Blue-winged Warbler has been intensively studied for decades; the two species are similar in behavior and vocalizations. Hybrids are discussed at the end of this account. Golden-winged Warblers are slightly later spring and fall migrants than Blue-wingeds, and their winter range is somewhat farther south. The yellow crown and wing patch, combined with the chickadee-like head pattern, make the identification of males simple; females also show enough of this pattern to be readily identified in the field.

Description

Generally grayish above and whitish below, with yellow to yellow-olive forecrown and forehead and a distinctive facial pattern of dark auriculars and throat (black in males, gray to dark slaty in females); all plumages show a yellow patch on the wing coverts that may appear as two broad yellow wing bars in many females. Age differences are slight, and there is little seasonal change in plumage.

Shape and size similar to those of Blue-winged Warbler, with moderately long and sharply pointed bill; there is strong seasonal change in bill color.

Similar Species

The distinctly patterned males are unmistakable, and confusion with other warblers (apart from BLUE-WINGED × GOLDEN-WINGED HYBRIDS) is unlikely. The active and acrobatic foraging behavior combined with the black throat patch might suggest a CHICKADEE (*Parus*) if views are poor, but the yellow forehead and wing patch, dark cheeks, white in the tail, and sharply pointed bill easily distinguish this species from any chickadee. Male BLACK-THROATED GRAY WARBLERS are similar if viewed from below, but show strong black streaking on the sides and flanks. Although more subtly patterned, females are still distinctive with their yellow wing patches, yellow-olive to olive forecrown, and hint of dark cheeks and throat.

Voice

SONGS are of two main types. The typical "type A" song consists of a high buzzy note followed by one to four (usually three) buzzes slightly lower in pitch: *bzee-bzz-bzz-bzz*; the introductory buzz is often but not always longer in duration than the subsequent notes. The quality of the notes is similar to that of the Blue-winged Warbler song, but the pattern differs. This type of song is heard mainly from spring migrants and unmated males on the breeding grounds, but also from paired males accompanying females and during mild territorial conflicts. An alternate ("type B") song is given on the breeding grounds by unmated males in bouts around sunrise and during high-intensity territorial encounters; it is also the predominant song late in the nesting season. This song may have three or more syllable types, often starting with a high stuttering series and ending with a low buzz. Type B songs of Golden-winged and Blue-winged warblers are probably indistinguishable. A modified version of the type B song may be given as a flight song. Songs of hybrids may match those of either parental species, rather than combining elements of the two. Rarely, phenotypically "pure" Golden-wingeds may sing a song typical of Blue-winged. **CALL NOTE** is indistinguishable from that of Blue-winged, a sharp *chip* or *tsik* suggestive of a Chipping Sparrow. The **FLIGHT NOTE** is a high, slightly buzzy *tzii*, often doubled (and indistinguishable from Blue-winged's flight note).

BEHAVIOR

This species mirrors the Blue-winged Warbler in its behaviors. It gleans leaves and twigs, often concentrating its foraging at dead leaf clusters. Foraging is acrobatic, and birds often hang upside-down in the manner of a chickadee. At least in migration, foraging may average slightly higher than that of Blue-winged, with considerable overlap. Migrants and wintering birds join mixed species flocks.

Territorial males often sing from a fixed, conspicuous perch high on a bare branch or treetop.

The **NEST** is often placed on the ground (unlike most Blue-wingeds) or attached to plant stems a few inches (up to 1 ft.) above the ground. The nest cup is shallower than that of Blue-winged, and the outside of the nest is less neatly woven.

HABITAT

BREEDING habitat broadly overlaps that of the Blue-winged Warbler, though the Golden-winged generally prefers an earlier stage of successional growth, and the range of habitats it occupies is somewhat narrower. Habitats include abandoned pastures, shrubby stream borders, openings in woodlands, power line right-of-ways, wet fields with clumps of shrubs, swamp edges, and young stands of oak-hickory. In West Virginia (and undoubtedly elsewhere), Golden-wings formerly bred in brushy cut-over chestnut sprouts with scattered old dead chestnuts for song perches (such habitats are now largely gone). In the northernmost portions of the breeding range, habitats include alder bogs (with taller trees such as black ash, spruce, and tamarack present), and young willow-aspen-tamarack associations adjacent to spruce-tamarack bogs; open stands of jack pine and poplar are used in se. Manitoba, and young conifer plantations are sometimes occupied in Michigan. A common characteristic of breeding habitat is the presence of patches of dense herbaceous growth (without woody plant cover) along with extensive patches of dense shrubs. Locally, as in s. Michigan, the planting of exotic autumn-olive for game has caused the disappearance of Golden-wingeds from formerly suitable shrub habitats.

In **WINTER**, Golden-wingeds are found in evergreen woodlands and woodland edges from sea level to over 7,000 ft. (2,300 m) in Middle America, but generally occur above 1,500 ft. (500 m) in n. South America. Habitats include rain forest, cloud forest, and high-elevation dwarf woodlands. In general the Golden-winged is more tied to woodland habitats in winter than the more generalized Blue-winged Warbler. **MIGRANTS** are usually noted in woodlands and are often encountered feeding high in mature associations.

DISTRIBUTION

BREEDS from sw. (Riding Mt.) and se. Man. (and probably adjacent e. Sask., Duck Mountain Provincial Park), n. Wisc., n. Mich., s. Ont., sw. Que., and s. N.H. south to ne. N.D. (once, 1981), cen. Minn., s. Wisc., n. Ill. (very local), s. Mich. (local), extreme n. Ind. (rare), n. N.J., and nw. Conn. Also breeds south through the higher portions of the Appalachian Mtns. to n. Ga. (approaches the Ala. state line in nw. Ga., but no Ala. nesting records). Formerly nested farther south, at least to cen. Ill., nw. and ne. Ohio, and s. Conn. There are 19th-century breeding records for Mo., se. Iowa, and w. S.C. There are two probable breeding records for Me. in the early 1900s, and this species nested rarely in R.I. until the 1950s. The breeding range has been expanding north but at the same time withdrawing from the south; this northward shift has been occurring for decades.

WINTERS from s. Mexico (Chiapas) south through Central America (primarily on the Caribbean slope and in the mountains) to Panama, and in n. South America in w. Colombia (not recorded in the lowlands east of the Andes), n. and w. Venezuela, and nw. Ecuador (once, Pichincha). There are a very few winter reports from the Greater Antilles (Cuba, Jamaica, Hispaniola); apparently a rare but regular winter visitor to Puerto Rico, with an additional winter record for St. John. Not recorded in winter in the Lesser Antilles or islands of the western Caribbean; there are winter sight records for Trinidad.

CASUAL within the U.S. in midwinter, with records for s. La. (5 January 1971), the lower Rio Grande Valley of Texas (24 January 1979), s. Ariz. (twice), and Calif. (two mid-December records, plus late winter records almost certainly pertaining to wintering birds in Los Angeles and in Orange Co.).

This is a classic trans-Gulf **MIGRANT**, with an easterly shift in the migration route in fall. It is a rare migrant on the s. Great Plains, with most records for spring. **SPRING MIGRATION** arrivals on the Gulf Coast are typically in early April, especially during the second week of April. Exceptionally early are records for 31 March in Fla. and 29 March in Ala. In the northern portions of the Gulf states and across the southern Midwest, arrivals are usually in late April, with scattered records to mid-April. First arrivals over the northern portion of the breeding range are mainly during the first third of May, but as late as mid-May at the northernmost sites (e.g., Man.). There are a few exceptional April records for the north, e.g., a singing bird in cen. Sask. on 17 April 1981. Peak spring numbers on the Gulf Coast occur about 15–25 April; over much of the Midwest, peak numbers are about 5–15 May. This species is never very numerous east of the Appalachians, particularly in spring. Even over the Midwest, peak counts seldom exceed a

GOLDEN-WINGED WARBLER
Vermivora chrysoptera

dozen birds per day. A few birds can still be seen on the Gulf Coast during the first week of May, and casually to mid-May. Across the Midwest, few Golden-wingeds are seen after the third week of May, but exceptional records extend into early June. Overall, the spring migration is decidedly later than that of Blue-winged Warbler.

FALL MIGRATION is also later than that of Blue-winged. Exceptionally early migrants have been recorded on 23 July in La., 28 July on the Miss. coast, 30 July in Mo., and 3 August at Cape May, N.J. Fall arrivals south of the breeding range are more typically during mid-August, with peak counts occurring at the end of August and beginning of September over the southern Midwest and Mid-Atlantic region. Numbers diminish rapidly after mid-September in most of e. North America except on the Gulf Coast, where peak fall counts are from mid- to late September. Small numbers of migrants are noted in the Gulf states through the first third of October. Casual in October in the north, with exceptional records to 10 October in Man. and 27 October in Ont. There are a few November records north of the Gulf Coast and Fla., e.g., 13 November in Mass. and 21 November in Ohio.

VAGRANT west and north of the normal range. Recorded rarely but annually (mainly in fall) in the Canadian Maritime Provinces (but unrecorded on Prince Edward Is.); casual in Nfld., with two of the five records there from spring (late May). A rare but regular vagrant to Bermuda, recorded mainly in fall from 30 August to 28 October (with a peak of six in a day in late September); also a very scarce transient in the Bahamas. Casual (mainly in spring) in Sask.; there are two summer/fall sight records for Alta. Unrecorded in B.C., Yukon, Northwest Territories, or Alaska. There are records for all western states except Wash. and Ut. Most of the 70+ Colo., records are for spring (May), and there are at least six late May records for Wyo. One confirmed nesting near Denver, Colo. in 1993. The single records for Nev. and Idaho are for late spring, as are the two Ore. records. Most of the 10+ N.M. records are for May; about half of the 20+ Ariz. records are for fall, but there are also several spring and summer records including four birds, possibly a family group, seen near Prescott in late August and early September 1992, and the two winter records noted above. Of some 52 Calif. records, 21 are for spring (20 May to 5 June, plus 5 and 15 July) and 27 are for fall (16 August to 30 November, with a third of these after mid-October); several winter records are noted above.

Recorded exceptionally in w. Greenland (fall 1966) and in the United Kingdom, a wintering bird seen by thousands of observers in Kent from 24 January to 10 April 1989.

Population expansions and declines and range shifts of this species have been studied thoroughly; trends in this species are closely linked with those of the Blue-winged Warbler. Because the Golden-winged Warbler is a specialist in early successional habitats, its range is expected to be dynamic. Little is known of the distribution of this species before the large-scale clearing of forests for agriculture in late 1700s and 1800s. A northward expansion of Golden-wingeds into much of New England is documented for the late 1800s and early 1900s, probably in response to farmland abandonment; the species has decreased in New England since then. Golden-wingeds have shown a gradual northward shift in their range during the 1900s, expanding through much of s. Ontario (first Ontario breeding documented in 1912), n. Minnesota, n. Wisconsin, n. Michigan, and sw. Quebec by the 1970s; at the same time the species has decreased in or disappeared from much of its range in the southern parts of Minnesota, Wisconsin, and Michigan, as well as n. Indiana. The major factor in the decline of Golden-wingeds from the southern and New England portions of the breeding range is the reduction of early successional second-growth habitats; competition with the Blue-winged Warbler is often cited as another important factor, since Blue-wingeds, which are more generalized in their habitat requirements, usually replace Golden-wingeds after a few decades of coexistence. Blue-wingeds are still absent as breeders from the higher Appalachian Mtns. and from the northern part of the Golden-winged's range (on or near the Canadian Shield).

Breeding Bird Survey data show a continuing decline of Golden-winged Warblers over most of the species' range, and the species is considered one of management concern by the U.S. Fish and Wildlife Service. Proposed management strategies include regular burning cycles and cowbird control.

Subspecies

None described.

Taxonomic Relationships

Closely related to the Blue-winged Warbler, with which it frequently hybridizes (see below); this species pair, in turn, may be most closely related to the Bachman's Warbler.

BLUE-WINGED × GOLDEN-WINGED HYBRIDS

Frequent hybridization between these two species in a shifting zone of overlap has resulted in two basic hybrid phenotypes: the more commonly seen hybrid with white underparts and a thin black eye line, called "Brewster's Warbler" (*"V. leucobronchialis"*), and the less common "Lawrence's Warbler" (*"V. lawrencii"*), which shows yellow underparts and a dark throat and auricular patch. Brewster's Warbler is the result of a hybrid pairing between a "pure" Golden-winged Warbler and a "pure" Blue-winged Warbler; the Brewster's phenotype can also result from a second-generation hybrid pairing between a Golden-winged and a Brewster's. The "Lawrence's Warbler" phenotype usually results from second-generation backcrosses; see below.

Since the initial discovery of these forms (subsequently proven to be hybrid offspring) in 1870, there has been a great deal of study of the underlying genetics and of the dynamics of the hybrid zone.

Habitat modifications, including those caused directly or indirectly by humans, have led to a gradual northward shift in the ranges of Blue-winged and Golden-winged warblers. As Blue-wingeds (the more southerly of the two) expand north into the range of Golden-wingeds, the initial result is a population of mostly Golden-wingeds, with a few Blue-wingeds and a very few "Brewster's" hybrids. Soon Blue-wingeds balance Golden-wingeds in numbers, and the number of hybrids (mostly "Brewster's") increases. Eventually the population consists mainly of Blue-wingeds, with a few pure Golden-wingeds and a broad range of intermediates, including some "Lawrence's Warblers." Golden-wingeds later disappear altogether, with only a few hybrids pres-

"Brewster's Warbler." Male F1 in Ontario in May. (Photo: Arthur Morris/Birds as Art)

"Brewster's Warbler." Male F₂ backcross in Texas in May. (Photo: B. Schorre/VIREO)

ent. Finally, the population consists wholly of Blue-wingeds, with an occasional "Lawrence's" present. The entire process takes about 50 years or less.

To understand the genetics underlying the "Brewster's" and "Lawrence's" hybrids, it is necessary to establish the dominance of the genetic traits. The white underparts of Golden-winged is a dominant trait, as is the reduced head pattern (eye line only) of Blue-winged. Conversely, the yellow color of the Blue-winged's underparts is recessive, as is the bold head pattern (throat and auricular patch) of Golden-winged. The pattern shown by "Brewster's Warbler" exhibits the dominant traits, and that by "Lawrence's" the recessive traits. A hybrid pairing between a Blue-winged and a Golden-winged yields offspring that show the dominant traits, i.e., the "Brewster's" phenotype. Subsequent pairings between a "Brewster's" and a Golden-winged that carries the recessive gene for underpart color can produce the "Lawrence's" phenotype, as can a pairing between a "Brewster's" and a Blue-winged carrying the recessive gene for head pattern. "Lawrence's" can also arise from a pairing between two Golden-wingeds carrying recessive genes for underpart color, or (a 1 in 16 chance) from the rare mating of two "Brewster's Warblers."

Hybrid offspring only rarely mate with other hybrids; there are only about four known pairings between "Brewster's Warblers," and none between "Lawrence's." Although there is considerable variation in the phenotypes of hybrid offspring, we do not see a general averaging of characters in the zone of overlap.

Hybrid phenotypes are noted on the breeding grounds, particularly where the two species overlap, but also within the normal migration range of the two parental species. There are records of

"Brewster's Warblers" west to the Dakotas, Colorado, w. Texas (Big Bend National Park), New Mexico, and California (three records). A "Lawrence's Warbler" was banded in Albuquerque, N.M., on 15 May 1996.

PLUMAGES OF HYBRIDS: "Brewster's Warbler." Adult male has a yellow forehead and forecrown, gray nape and upperparts (variably tinged with olive-yellow), and a black line through the lores and eye, extending back along the top of the auriculars. The chin and throat are white, and the remaining underparts may be pure white (tinged gray along the sides and flanks) but are usually washed with yellow, often strongly so on the breast. Birds with some yellow on the underparts are in the majority; those with pure white underparts are probably backcrosses between "Brewster's" and Golden-winged. "Brewster's" usually show double wing bars that vary from off-white to rather strongly yellow. Females are similar to males in pattern, but the forehead and crown are yellow-olive, the upperparts are more strongly washed with olive, the eye line is dark gray or slaty (instead of black), and the underparts are more extensively washed with yellow or creamy yellow. Age and seasonal variation of hybrids is subtle, and parallels that described for the parental species.

"Lawrence's Warbler." Adult male has black lores and auriculars and a black throat patch. The forehead and forecrown are bright yellow, and the nape and remaining upperparts are olive green. The malar region, breast, and belly are bright yellow, becoming white on the undertail coverts. The grayish wings (tinged olive-yellow on the tertials and secondaries) have two bold white wing bars that are tinged yellow in many birds. Females show the same basic pattern as males, but the black facial pattern is replaced by dark gray, and the forehead and forecrown are tinged with olive (strongly so in first-year females).

Other variants occur, including individuals that closely resemble Blue-winged Warblers but show some black on the throat, and birds that look like Golden-wingeds but have whitish throats and some white mixed into the black of the auriculars.

PLUMAGES AND MOLTS

SPRING ADULT MALE: Forehead and forecrown bright yellow, bordered sharply at the rear by the gray hindcrown and nape; the rear portion of the yellow is slightly tinged olive. Entire upperparts gray, with a slight tint of olive in the center of the back and nape in some individuals. Supercilium white. Lores and auricular patch black, bordered below by a white malar stripe that broadens on the side of the face. Chin and throat black, forming a sharp lower border contrasting with the whitish breast. Remaining underparts white, washed with clear gray on the sides of the breast, sides, and flanks. Upper breast and sides of the vent slightly tinged with pale yellow in some individuals. Wings gray, tinged with yellow-olive on the outer webs of the tertials and secondaries. Median and greater coverts broadly edged and tipped with bright yellow, forming a large yellow wing patch. Tail gray; the outer three pairs of rectrices are extensively white. **FIRST SPRING MALE:** Closely resembles spring adult male; many birds show more restricted black on the throat, with some white mixed in on the chin. Some have the auriculars more slaty, less black, than adults. In the hand the rectrices and outer primaries are more tapered and appear more worn. The amount of white in the rectrices is not useful for aging males. The extent of yellow-olive on the outer webs of the tertials and secondaries and on the center of the back does not appear to be clearly related to age,

Golden-winged Warbler. Male in Texas in May. (Photo: B. Schorre/VIREO)

Golden-winged Warbler. Female in Ontario in May. (Photo: Jim Flynn)

although some sources suggest that first-year birds average more olive, less gray. **SPRING ADULT FEMALE:** Auriculars and lores dark gray, with a whitish supercilium and malar stripe. Throat medium gray, not contrasting strongly with the underparts; chin often lighter gray or whitish. Forehead and forecrown yellow tinged with olive, washing into the gray upperparts, which are variably tinged with olive. Sides of breast and flanks grayish; center of breast, belly, and undertail coverts dull whitish. Median and great coverts yellow, forming two broad wing bars, but rarely appearing as a solid patch of yellow. Tertials and secondaries washed with yellow-olive on the outer webs. Rectrices gray with white spots on the inner webs of the outermost three pairs; the amount of white in the rectrices averages less than that of males. **FIRST SPRING FEMALE:** Very similar to spring adult female; rectrices and outer primaries more tapered and worn. **FALL ADULT MALE:** Nearly identical to spring adult male, but may average more strongly washed with olive on the back and on the tips of the yellow crown feathers. **FIRST FALL MALE:** Similar to fall adult male and much like first spring male, but plumage fresher than in latter and slightly more washed with olive on the upperparts; the chin is usually whitish. Lower breast may be slightly washed with pale yellow. **FALL ADULT FEMALE:** Similar to spring adult female, but often more strongly washed with olive on the upperparts, and with more olive mixed into the yellow forehead and forecrown. **FIRST FALL FEMALE:** Duller than fall adult female and first spring female. No sharp contrast between the dull gray throat and dull grayish white breast. The chin, malar stripe, and underparts are faintly washed with yellowish cream. Crown yellow-olive, showing little contrast with the olive-washed upperparts. White in the tail is limited to the inner webs of the outermost three rectrices and is limited and obscure in the outermost rectrix. **JUVENILE:** Upperparts olive; head, throat, and breast grayish olive, becoming paler gray on the remaining underparts. There is a hint of a dark auricular and lores, bordered by a paler supercilium and malar stripe.

Wings grayish with two dull wing bars. **BARE PARTS:** Bill color varies seasonally. In spring, both sexes have black bills; all fall and winter birds have dusky flesh bills, darkest along the culmen. Eyes dark brown. Legs and feet dark brown.

The prebasic molt occurs on the breeding grounds; it is complete in adults and partial in hatching-year birds (not involving the tertials, remiges, or rectrices). There is apparently no prealternate molt.

 REFERENCES

GENERAL: Confer 1992.
DISTRIBUTION: Doherty 1992, Gochfeld 1974.
ECOLOGY, BEHAVIOR, VOCALIZATIONS, AND CONSERVATION: Confer and Knapp 1979 and 1981, Crook 1984, Ficken and Ficken 1968a, b, d, Gill and Murray 1972b, Highsmith 1989, Murray and Gill 1976, Russell 1976.
SYSTEMATICS: Ficken and Ficken 1968c, Gill 1980 and 1987, Gill and Murray 1972a, Parkes 1951 and 1991, Short 1963.

TENNESSEE WARBLER

Vermivora peregrina

4.75 in. (12 cm). This small, indistinctly marked warbler has a fine, sharp bill and a short tail. It breeds in boreal forest, where it is a spruce budworm specialist; overall it is abundant, although numbers vary from year to year, particularly in the Northeast. In spring it can be heard singing vigorously from shade trees throughout the Midwest. In all plumages it is rather bright green above, with a dark eye line and pale supercilium. The underparts vary from whitish to clear yellow or olive-yellow on the throat and breast; the undertail coverts are always whitish, occasionally with a pale yellowish tinge. This is one of our warblers that favors nectar and fruit in the winter season. This species winters mainly in Central America and northern South America; the spring migration of the Tennessee Warbler is largely across the Gulf of Mexico; the fall passage averages more easterly. It is one of the most frequent "eastern" warblers to occur in the West.

 DESCRIPTION

In all plumages the upperparts are bright olive green, brightest on the lower back and rump. The crown and hindneck vary from gray, contrasting sharply with the back, to bright olive like the back. A pale (whitish to yellowish) supercilium and indistinct grayish eye line are present in all plumages. Breast color varies from dull whitish to clear yellow-olive, depending on season, sex, and age; there is also a great deal of individual variation within sex and age classes. In all plumages the lower belly and undertail coverts are either pure white or whitish tinged slightly with pale yellow. The olive wings show one or two very thin and indistinct pale yellow wing bars; the primaries of fresh fall birds are narrowly tipped with whitish. Variable small whitish spots are present on or near the tips of the inner webs of the outer one or two pairs of rectrices; these are inconspicuous or absent in many birds, including some males and most females.

Structurally, the Tennessee Warbler appears rather short-tailed, with a noticeably shorter tail extension beyond the undertail coverts than is found in other *Vermivora*. The bill is sharply pointed, with a straight culmen. The primary extension is slightly longer than in other *Vermivora*. As in most warblers, males average slightly larger than females in most measurements, especially wing and tail length.

 ## SIMILAR SPECIES

Confusion is most likely with ORANGE-CROWNED WARBLER. Orange-crowned is always told by yellow or greenish yellow (often contrastingly so) undertail coverts; this region is whitish or only faintly washed with yellow in Tennessee. Orange-crowned is longer-tailed, with noticeably longer tail extension past the undertail coverts; the wingtips of Orange-crowned are more rounded and lack the prominent pale primary tips of fresh plumaged Tennessees. Orange-crowneds show a pale patch at the bend of the wing, an excellent distinction from Tennessee when visible. Face pattern of Orange-crowned is more subdued, with less distinct eye line and supercilium; Orange-crowned does have stronger split eye-ring. Tennessee averages much brighter green on the upperparts, and fall birds are clearer yellow on the breast, without the subdued streaking on the sides of the breast visible in most Orange-crowneds. The sharp *tik* call note of Orange-crowned is very different from the soft *tsit* and sweet *chip* notes of Tennessee. Beware especially juvenile Orange-crowneds, which show faint pale wing bars (resembling thin pale wing bar on greater coverts of Tennessee) and may approach Tennessee in underpart color. Compare with female CERULEAN (which shows bold wing bars); adult female and immature male PINE (much larger and longer-tailed, with stronger wing bars, blurred streaks on sides of breast, different face pattern); and duller YELLOW (plain face pattern, yellow spots in tail, and yellow to whitish edges of wing coverts and flight feathers).

Confusion has occurred with PHILADELPHIA and WARBLING VIREOS (*Vireo philadelphicus* and *V. gilvus*); note heavier, hooked bills, stouter legs, larger overall size, and more sluggish behavior of vireos. Spring female Tennessees with a yellow wash across the breast are superficially similar to Philadelphia Vireo; note shape and behavior characters above plus yellowish undertail coverts of vireo. Warbling Vireo, especially smaller Pacific Coast birds, may suggest Tennessee but are much duller and paler on the upperparts. Both vireos show an indistinct pale arc under the eye, absent in Tennessee Warbler.

Confusion also possible with some Old World warblers, especially ARCTIC WARBLER (*Phylloscopus borealis*) which nests in cen. and w. Alaska. Note different bill shape (not as fine and sharp as Tennessee), yellowish pink (rather than pale gray) base to mandible. Arctic call is a sharp, buzzy *tchick* or *tziet*. In hand, all Old World warblers show a tenth primary.

Compare winter birds and migrants in tropics with *Hylophilus* greenlets, especially LESSER GREENLET (*H. decurtatus*), which shows a thicker, paler bill and duller green upperparts.

 ## Voice

A very vocal species. SONG is a loud, persistent and staccato three-part (sometimes two- or four-part) series, often given only partially several times until the singer gears up to deliver the full song. The third part of typical three-part song is much faster than the introductory parts. Typical descriptions include *ticka ticka ticka ticka, swit swit, sit-sit-sit-sit-sit-sit* or *sidit-sidit-sidit sidit swit-swit-sit-sit-sit-sit-sit-sit*. The song is most likely to be confused with that of Nashville, especially eastern nominate birds. Nashville's song is less staccato, usually only two-parted, and ends in a softer trill.

Several CALL NOTES are frequently given. These include a sharp *tsip, tsit,* or *tit* which may be given while perched or in flight, and a high, sweet, slurred *chip* reminiscent of Cerulean Warbler, American Redstart, or some notes of Yellow Warbler. Typical FLIGHT NOTE a thin, clear *see*. May be extremely vocal with *tsit* and *see* notes around flowering trees on the winter grounds and in migration.

Behavior

A quick, nervous, and active species (unlike vireos, some of which are superficially similar in plumage). Unlike some other *Vermivora* (e.g., Virginia's, some Nashvilles), it does not habitually bob its tail. Gleans for insects at all foliage heights, but typically forages well up in trees in spring migration and in lower growth in fall migration. Spring birds frequently probe into new, furled leaves, flowers, and catkins. The sharp bill is well adapted for piercing grapes, berries, and other fruits, and on the winter grounds the species frequents nectar-rich flowers; some seeds may also be taken. The vine *Combretum fructicosum* is especially favored in winter, and these warblers are important pollinators of that plant; *Inga, Erythrina,* and *Eucalyptus* blossoms are also probed. May be quite gregarious in winter and migration, but can be aggressive and territorial in winter around nectar sources. Has been observed probing flowers with small sticks, presumably for insects. Birds that spend much time foraging at flowers on the winter grounds often become stained by red pollen on the head; some of this staining may persist during the northward migration in spring.

The **NEST** is placed on or near the ground, often in sphagnum moss or hummocks in bogs but sometimes on drier hillsides; the nest is usually concealed from above. It is woven from grasses and fine stems.

⛰ HABITAT

BREEDS in a variety of boreal woodlands, coniferous, mixed, or deciduous, as long as there is a brushy and mossy understory. Over much of the breeding range, bogs of black spruce, tamarack, or balsam fir are preferred, although there is usually deciduous growth mixed in or nearby. Preferred forests are usually open or regenerating. More westerly populations, such as those in Alberta and British Columbia may be in primarily deciduous associations of aspen, willow, alder, or poplar, usually along streams. In the northern Rocky Mountains, spruce forests are occupied. The key to breeding habitat throughout the range is a well-developed mossy or herbaceous ground layer along with some brushy under-story.

In **WINTER**, found in a variety of woodlands and forest edges where flowering trees are abundant; also coffee plantations, gardens, and secondary scrub. Most numerous at middle elevations, but extends from lowlands to high mountains (in some areas, there is upslope movement late in winter to take advantage of flowering and budding of oaks). Important flowering trees include native *Inga* and *Erythrina* and introduced *Eucalyptus*; flowering *Combretum* shrubs and vines can be a very important habitat component.

In **SPRING MIGRATION**, they feed high in deciduous trees and are often abundant in towns and residential areas. **FALL MIGRANTS** use a variety of habitats, including low brushy and herbaceous growth.

BREEDS across most of Canada, from n. and cen. B.C. (has bred in se. Alaska), s. Yukon and w. and s. Dist. of Mack. east across n. and cen. Alta., n. Sask., Man. (except sw.), Ont. (except s.), cen. and s. Que., and the Maritime Provinces (including Lab. and Nfld.). The breeding range extends south very locally in nw. Mont. (rare, irregular), n. Minn., northernmost Wisc. (Apostle Is.), n. Mich. (upper peninsula; scarce), ne. N.Y. (Adirondacks), ne. Vt., n. N.H., and cen. Me. Generally rare to uncommon in the southern part of the breeding range, including the northern U.S. (except Me., where they are more numerous). Singing birds are often noted south of the mapped breeding range. Population size on breeding grounds may vary from year to year in response to spruce budworm fluctuations.

WINTERS mainly from s. Mexico (Oaxaca and Veracruz) south through Central America into n. South America (Colombia, n. Venezuela, a few to n. Ecuador). The center of winter abundance is in Costa Rica, w. Panama, and the mountains of nw. Colombia.

TENNESSEE WARBLER
Vermivora peregrina

A few winter in Bermuda, and the species is rare but regular in winter in coastal Calif. (north to Eureka), especially around flowering eucalyptus trees; one remained in coastal Wash. until early January. Casual in early winter in s. and coastal Texas and Fla.; there are a few December records from the interior Southwest. Very few winter records elsewhere in the East, but there are mid- to late winter records for Tenn., Ga., Ill., and the New York City area. One bird remained at a N.S. feeder to 2 December.

SPRING MIGRATION is mainly trans-Gulf, with the bulk of the passage moving from the Gulf Coast up through the Miss. and Ohio river valleys; spring migrants are uncommon east of the Appalachians. A few may arrive on the Gulf Coast and s. Fla. in late March (exceptionally to the second week of March), but more typically arrival is in early April, with peak spring passage along the Gulf in mid- and especially late April. Numbers fall off after early May, with a few birds passing through in mid-May and stragglers occurring to late May and early June. For much of the southern Midwest, spring arrival is at the end of April, exceptionally in early April in Tenn.; peak spring movement at the latitude of Kans., Mo., and Ky. is around 10 May. In the northern Midwest and Great Lakes region, spring arrival is typically during the first week of May (less commonly in late April), with peak passage during the third week of May. Arrival on the breeding grounds is from mid-May to late May, perhaps even early June at northernmost sites, such as Churchill and the Mackenzie River Valley. Large numbers of migrants are still passing through the Midwest to about 20–25 May, with a few birds into early June (casually to late June).

FALL MIGRATION averages more easterly than spring migration; it can begin quite early, as many adults migrate south before completing the prebasic molt. This species is frequently recorded in July south of the breeding range, even to late June and early July on the lower peninsula of Mich. and Lake Erie shore; these undoubtedly pertain to migrating adults and should not be considered "summer" records. The earliest Gulf Coast record is 2 August (Ala.). Fall migration does not normally pick up just south of the breeding range until mid-August, and arrivals over the rest of the East are typically in late August and early September. Most birds have left the far north by early September. The peak fall movement is prolonged, from late August to mid-September in the northern U.S. and from about 20 September to early October along the Atlantic Coast and southern Midwest. The peak on the Gulf Coast is even later (the first half of October), and significant movements have been recorded in early November (for instance, 150 in coastal Miss. on 2 November after a hurricane). Lingering migrants routinely occur through the end of October and into mid-November; these late fall migrants are more frequent than in most other warbler species that winter in the Neotropics. Very late stragglers occur even into late December in Fla., but these birds do not overwinter.

VAGRANT throughout the western states, Baja Calif., and Sonora; also recorded on Clipperton Is. off sw. Mexico. Averages nearly 100 birds per year (over 2,300 in all) in Calif., about three-fourths in fall. Spring peak in Calif. is late May/early June, while fall peak is mid-September to early October. Some occur in Calif. by late August, and they are routinely found to mid-November, with some remaining to winter along the coast; the Farallon Is. show an interesting second peak of fall vagrants in late November and early December. Casual in cen. Alaska, mainly in summer. In West Indies, mainly a scarce fall transient, wintering in small numbers in the western Caribbean. Strictly accidental on the Lesser Antilles. Recorded in Greenland (three records), Iceland, and the Faeroe Is.; four fall records for Britain.

STATUS AND CONSERVATION

Often extremely abundant, both in migration and on the breeding grounds; abundant enough on breeding grounds to appear highly concentrated in good habitat. Populations on breeding grounds fluctuate from year to year in response to fluctuations of spruce budworms, as in several "spruce-woods warblers" (including Cape May and Bay-breasted warblers). Overall numbers have probably increased since the 1800s, but spraying for spruce budworms has probably caused some local declines.

Tennessee Warbler. Male in Florida in April. (Photo: Kevin T. Karlson)

No subspecies described, but some slight geographic variation in bill and tarsus length in samples found dead beneath towers has been noted.

 Taxonomic Relationships

Although close in appearance to the Orange-crowned Warbler, its relationships within *Vermivora* are unclear. Has been considered a distant relative to a complex including the Orange-crowned Warbler and the Nashville Warbler superspecies. One hybrid with Nashville Warbler is known from Westmoreland Co., Pennsylvania, 26 August 1979.

 Plumages and Molts

SPRING ADULT MALE: Forehead, crown, and hindneck clear medium gray, contrasting with remaining upperparts. A few rufous feathers, not visible in the field, are rarely present in the crown of adult males. Supercilium, including supraloral area, whitish, contrasting with dark gray to blackish eye line. Auriculars mottled grayish and white. Remaining upperparts olive green, brightest on the lower back, rump, and uppertail coverts. Underparts dull whitish or grayish white, variably tinged with gray on the sides of the breast and sometimes very slightly tinged yellowish across the breast and on the flanks. Primaries and rectrices are grayish and relatively fresh. **FIRST SPRING MALE:** Not always distinguishable from spring adult male, although the primaries and rectrices average browner and more worn than in adult. **SPRING ADULT FEMALE:** Forehead, crown, and hindneck

Tennessee Warbler. Female in Texas in May. (Photo: Brian E. Small)

Tennessee Warbler. First fall in Ohio in October. (Photo: Steve and Dave Maslowski)

olive-gray, contrasting only slightly with olive upperparts. Supercilium and auricular area tinged light yellow. Throat, breast, sides, and flanks variably washed with light yellow. This yellow may be limited to a band across the breast or may be much more extensive through the underparts (with only the belly and undertail coverts white). Primaries and rectrices as in spring adult male. **FIRST SPRING FEMALE:** Not always distinguishable from spring adult female, although the primaries and rectrices average browner and more worn than in adult. **FALL ADULT MALE:** Very similar to spring adult male, but the gray feathers of the crown, hindneck, and sides of neck are extensively tipped with olive, and there is a variable pale yellowish wash across the breast and throat. The flanks of fall adult males are grayish or pale olive; the flanks of most fall immatures and fall adult females are extensively washed with yellow-olive. The primaries and rectrices are gray with greenish edging. Variability in fall (some males appearing nearly as bright as spring males) may be accounted for in part by birds moving south before the prebasic molt of body plumage is completed. **FIRST FALL MALE:** Entire upperparts, from forehead to uppertail coverts, olive green, brightest on lower back, rump, and upper tail coverts. Supercilium yellowish; auriculars washed with olive-yellow. Chin, throat, breast, sides, and flanks lightly to strongly washed with light yellow or yellow-olive. Center of belly and undertail coverts white; in rare individuals, undertail coverts and center of belly may be very lightly washed with yellow, but these are still whiter than the remaining underparts. On average, first fall birds are yellower than fall adult females, with slightly more distinct thin yellowish wing bars. However, these age and sex classes are not safely distinguished in the field. The primaries and rectrices of first fall birds are browner than in fall adults, with less greenish edging. **FALL ADULT FEMALE:** Not safely distinguishable from first fall male in the field, but many may be told in the hand by broader, blunter shape of primaries and rectrices. **FIRST FALL**

FEMALE: Not safely distinguishable from first fall male or fall adult female in the field. **JUVENILE:** Dull olive above, dull yellowish buff below. Thin yellowish buff wing bars. **BARE PARTS:** Bill slaty along culmen, pale gray on cutting edge and base of mandible. Eyes dark brown. Legs and feet dark gray, soles of feet tinged yellowish.

The prebasic molt is partial in hatching-year birds, complete in adults. This molt occurs mainly on the breeding grounds (July, August), but adults may suspend the molt (especially flight feathers) before fall migration, completing it on the winter grounds. The limited prealternate molt may begin in midwinter (exceptionally as early as December) and is usually completed sometime between February and April.

 REFERENCES

DISTRIBUTION: Gochfeld 1974.
ECOLOGY, BEHAVIOR, VOCALIZATIONS, AND CONSERVATION: Bohlen 1989 (Tennessee Warbler tool use), MacArthur 1958, Morton 1980, Tramer and Kemp 1980.
IDENTIFICATION: Bradshaw 1992.
PLUMAGES, MOLTS, AND MORPHOLOGY: Baird 1967, Dick and James 1996.
SYSTEMATICS: Raveling 1965, Raveling and Warner 1965, Sealy 1985.

ORANGE-CROWNED WARBLER PL. 4

Vermivora celata

4.75 in. (13 cm). This widespread and geographically variable species is far more abundant in the West than in the East. It is a rather obscurely marked warbler, varying from drab olive-gray to olive-yellow and usually showing some indistinct streaking on the underparts; the orange crown that gives the species its name is nearly always obscured by olive feather tips but may be visible on bathing or scolding birds. Its spring migration is quite early, especially in West Coast subspecies *lutescens;* fall migration of boreal nominate birds is very late for a warbler. These are relatively hardy warblers that winter farther north than most of our species. Orange-crowneds are easily confused with a number of indistinctly marked warbler species and with a few nonwarblers.

 DESCRIPTION

No strong patterning in the plumage. Generally olive green on the head and upperparts, with an indistinct dark eye line, a weakly developed pale yellowish supercilium, and a narrow, split, yellowish or dull whitish eye-ring. Upperpart color is brightest in Pacific Coast *lutescens* and dullest in nominate *celata;* the head and upperparts may be tinged grayish in fall birds, especially immatures. The rump and uppertail coverts are a brighter yellow-olive than the remainder of the upperparts. The underparts vary from pale olive with a hint of yellow to rather bright yellow (brightest in Pacific Coast birds); if the yellow of the underparts is limited, it is brightest on the undertail coverts. Variable dull olive or grayish streaking is present at least on the sides of the breast and sometimes more extensively across the underparts. The wing coverts are olive and the flight feathers dusky; a small whitish or pale yellow mark, often conspicuous in the field, is found at the bend of the wing on the marginal wing coverts. The rectrices are dusky, edged with olive. There are no wing bars or tail spots (except in juveniles, which show thin wing bars).

There is little seasonal change in plumage, apart from a slight veiling of the head and upperparts with grayish or olive in fresh fall and early winter plumage; the primaries have thin whitish tips in fresh fall plumage. Males are slightly brighter than females and have a larger patch of orange (usually concealed) on the crown. First fall birds average somewhat duller than adults, and in the races *celata* and *orestera* appear somewhat gray-headed. Worn adults in summer often show the orange crown patch more conspicuously.

Structurally, the Orange-crowned shows a typical sharp-pointed *Vermivora* bill, although the culmen is very slightly decurved, giving the bill a less spiky shape than in Tennessee Warbler. The bill of *sordida* is somewhat longer than bills of other races. The tail is moderately long, with considerable extension beyond the undertail coverts. There is moderate primary projection beyond the tertials, shorter in Pacific Coast birds than in boreal *celata,* with *orestera* intermediate.

 ## SIMILAR SPECIES

The most similar species is the **TENNESSEE WARBLER**; it is likely that most if not all of the early fall (August, early September) reports of Orange-crowneds from the eastern U.S. and se. Canada actually pertain to Tennessees. Tennessee always shows a much brighter green back than eastern (*celata*) Orange-crowneds, and lacks the split eye-ring of Orange-crowned. Even Tennessees that are extensively yellowish below show contrastingly white or whitish undertail coverts; in dull eastern Orange-crowneds the undertail coverts are always yellow, contrasting with the duller remaining underparts. Gray-headed individuals of Orange-crowned in fall are easily told from immature Tennessees, which have bright green crowns. Structurally, Tennessee differs from all Orange-crowneds in its shorter tail, more pointed wingtips, and spikier bill.

Brighter Orange-crowneds, particularly West Coast *lutescens*, may be mistaken for some of our unmarked yellow warblers such as YELLOW, WILSON'S, and MACGILLIVRAY'S WARBLERS. Wilson's and Yellow both show plainer face patterns with the dark eye standing out prominently on the face. The unmarked underparts of Wilson's Warbler are brighter than those of even the brightest Orange-crowned; Wilson's has a distinctively long tail, which is frequently flipped about. Yellow Warbler, particularly the dull olive and gray immature *amnicola,* is told by pale edges to wing coverts, tertials, and flight feathers, and yellow tail spots.

Gray-headed individuals of the nominate race and *orestera* are often mistaken for MacGillivray's or MOURNING WARBLERS; these two *Oporornis* are brighter yellow through the underparts, have pale mandible and legs, are larger and proportionally larger-headed, and are skulking species often found on the ground. These gray-headed immature birds, particularly those of the Rocky Mountain race *orestera,* in which underparts may be quite yellow, are often mistaken for NASHVILLE WARBLER. Nashville always shows a complete eye-ring and a shorter tail, which is frequently wagged in *ridgwayi..*

Compare also with female BLACK-THROATED BLUE WARBLER, which shows a dark cheek patch and has a small whitish patch at base of primaries (not to be confused with the pale mark at the bend of the wing in Orange-crowned). Nonwarblers that might be confused with Orange-crowned include BELL'S and PHILADELPHIA VIREOS (which are plumper and thicker-billed).

♪ Voice

SONG is a rapid, colorless trill that seems to lose energy toward the end, usually dropping in pitch and volume. Many songs rise in pitch in the middle. Some song variations do not drop at the end, but there is almost always some variation in pitch through the song. There is some geographical variation in song quality, with boreal *celata* giving a slightly thinner and slower trill than at least West Coast *lutescens.* The song of *sordida* of the California Channel Islands is consistently slower and lower pitched than those of *lutescens.*

CALL is a hard *stick* or *tik,* unlike that of any other North American warbler and quite distinctive once learned. Slight variations among the subspecies. FLIGHT NOTE is a high, thin *seet* or *seep.*

A rather deliberate warbler that forages mostly from understory growth and weedy ground cover up to the middle story of trees and shrubs. They often probe into dead leaf clusters, catkins, and flower heads. The wrenlike probing behavior along branches and trunks may be one factor allowing the species to winter successfully farther north than most of our warblers. Most of their food is invertebrate material, but they will sometimes take fruit, especially in winter. Late fall and winter birds may visit feeding stations, and in some areas this species readily visits hummingbird feeders. Winter birds may show strong territoriality and are only rarely encountered in pure flocks with conspecifics (unlike the related Tennessee Warbler, which routinely forms flocks). Migrants and wintering birds are often encountered with sparrows along brushy field edges. Orange-crowneds are very vocal warblers and are inquisitive birds, quite responsive to pishing. They do not show any strong tail-wagging or bobbing behavior.

The **NEST** is a cup of grasses, fibers, and down usually placed on the ground under a bush and well hidden by ground cover. Nests may sometimes be placed low in a shrub or tree; this is typically the case for the race *sordida* on the California Channel Islands.

 HABITAT

BREEDING habitat varies somewhat with subspecies; habitat throughout the range characteristically includes brushy areas, especially deciduous thickets. Nominate *celata,* breeding in boreal regions, occupies dense deciduous brush and thickets, second growth in cleared woodlands, shrubby growth following burns, and a variety of other low shrubby habitats. Rocky Mountain region *orestera*, breeds in streamside thickets in canyon bottoms (such as willows and chokecherries), and in aspen groves at higher elevations; they may range up to about 9,000 ft. elevation. Pacific Coast *lutescens* breeds in dense mature chaparral on canyon slopes, especially around live oaks; it also breeds in foothill, canyon, and coastal riparian thickets, often with oaks or conifers intermixed; *lutescens* breeds mainly below 5,000 ft. The race *sordida* breeds widely in brushy and wooded habitats on the California Channel Islands and locally in brushy thickets along the adjacent mainland coast.

WINTERS in a variety of brushy habitats, in open woodlands with a brushy understory, and in parks and gardens. On the Gulf Coast and southern Atlantic Coast, *celata* winters mainly in thickets of oaks but also in magnolias, red cedars, wax myrtle, and the brushy understory of swampy woods; many winter in gardens, hedges, and other landscaping. Western wintering birds are found widely in brushy lowland habitats, from riparian thickets, chaparral, and oak woodland understory to desert scrub such as saltbush, mesquites, and exotic salt cedars; they are often seen around exotic flowering shrubs in parks and gardens.

Widespread in **MIGRATION** in a variety of open woodlands and brushy habitats. Spring birds often feed high in budding trees at woodland edges in the East and in live oaks and budding mesquites in the West; fall birds mostly shun woodlands and prefer weedy fields and brushy areas.

 DISTRIBUTION

BREEDS across the boreal regions of Alaska and Canada and south through the Rocky Mountains, Great Basin region, and Pacific Coast states to the Mexican border region. The boreal race *celata* breeds from cen. and w. Alaska (west to 166° latitude on the Seward Peninsula; south to the Alaska Peninsula and Kodiak), n.-cen. and se. Yukon, w. and s.-cen. Dist. of Mack., and n. and cen. Alta. east through n. and cen. Sask., n.-cen. and ne. N.D., Man., n. and cen. Ont. (mainly north of 50° N), cen. Que., and s. Lab. In the interior West, the race *orestera* breeds from sw. Yukon, interior B.C., sw. Alta., and the Cypress Hills (Alta. and Sask.) southeast of the coastal mountain ranges but mainly west of the Continental Divide to e.-cen. Calif., cen. Nev., se. Ariz. (Santa Catalina and Graham mtns.), and w. Texas (Guadalupe Mtns., recently also in Davis Mtns.); it is rather local and uncommon through most of its breeding range. In the Pacific Coast region the race *lutescens* breeds commonly from s. coastal Alaska (Cook Inlet area, but not Kodiak Is.) and se. Alaska south through the coastal areas and islands of B.C., w. Wash., w. Ore. (locally east of Cascade crest), westernmost Nev. (Lake Tahoe area), and Calif. (south on coast to Los Angeles area and in mountains to n. Baja Calif., where breeding not documented). The subspecies *sordida* nests on the Channel Is. off s. Calif. and on the Coronados Is. and Todos Santos Is. off nw. Baja Calif.; *sordida* also nests locally on immediate coast of s. Calif. from Los Angeles to San Diego.

As a whole, the species **WINTERS** mainly from the southern U.S. south through Mexico to Guatemala; this is a hardy species, however, and a few regularly winter north on the Atlantic Coast to New England, in the southern Midwest states, and north on the Pacific Coast to B.C. Casual in winter in south coastal Alaska. Nominate *celata* winters primarily from the Gulf Coast and Fla. south in Mexico to Veracruz and more sparingly to Belize and

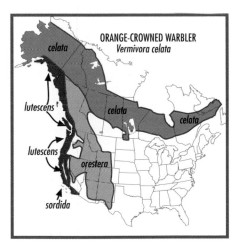

Guatemala. Also winters regularly in small numbers north to ne. Texas, Okla., s. Ark., the northern portions of the Gulf states, and along the Atlantic Coast north to se. Va. (and very sparingly north to Mass.). There are a number of winter records north to Neb., Ill., Ind., Ohio, and s. Ontario, but very few of these birds successfully overwinter. Has been recorded in early winter north to Wisc. and N.S. Nominate birds also winter sparingly west to cen. and s. Calif., s. Nev., and cen. Ariz. They winter very sparingly on Bermuda and in the Bahamas. The subspecies *orestera* winters from s. Calif., s. Nev., cen. Ariz., and s. Texas south through Baja Calif. and west Mexico to Oaxaca. The subspecies *lutescens* winters from cen. Calif. and sw. Ariz. south through Baja Calif. to sw. Mexico; very small numbers winter along the Pacific Coast north to n. Calif. and Ore., and there are winter records north to B.C. A few winter east to s.-cen. Ariz., and this subspecies has been recorded as far south as Guatemala. The subspecies *sordida* disperses through the coastal lowlands of s. Calif. in winter, and has been recorded from nw. Calif. south to n.-cen. Baja Calif.

MIGRATION of this species is complicated by striking differences in timing between subspecies. West Coast *lutescens* is a relatively early migrant in spring and fall, with *orestera* being somewhat later. Nominate *celata* is noteworthy for being a very late fall migrant, with migration through the e. North America peaking from late September to late October. The main movements of nominate *celata* are through the e. Great Plains and western portions of the Midwest; it is quite scarce in spring east of the Appalachians, but more numerous in fall (where usually recorded on the immediate coast or offshore islands). Small numbers of *celata* occur in the West in late fall. In the West, migrant *lutescens* move northward from sw. Ariz. and s. Calif. up through the Pacific states; fall movements of *lutescens* spread somewhat farther east. The race *orestera* moves primarily through the western interior in spring, but is regular in fall along the Pacific Coast.

SPRING MIGRATION of nominate *celata* in e. North America begins with the departure of wintering birds from the Gulf Coast and s.-cen. Texas beginning in mid- to late March, with most being gone from these areas by the end of April. Over much of the Midwest spring arrivals are from mid-April to the third week of April; the few birds that are found in the Northeast in spring are usually recorded in very late April and May. Birds arrive on the breeding grounds from mid-May to the first of June. The spring peak of migration throughout the Midwest is in very late April or early May (slightly later in the northernmost areas). Migrant *orestera* through the interior West are first noted in early April, and birds of this subspecies arrive on the breeding grounds at the end of

April (and probably in May at high elevations and in the northern part of the breeding range). Pacific Coast *lutescens* is an early spring migrant, with the first birds appearing away from wintering areas in very early March or even late February on the deserts and late February on the coast. Arrivals in w. Ore. and Wash. are during the latter half of March, and birds begin to arrive at the north end of the subspecies' breeding range in south coastal Alaska in early May. The peak movement of *lutescens* in s. Calif. is in late March and early April, and a few still pass through into early May.

FALL MIGRATION of Orange-crowneds in the East is strikingly late, with the earliest fall arrival at Pt. Pelee, Ont., being 17 September, and in. s. Nfld. on 23 September; typical arrivals over much of the East are in late September. A very few of the numerous reports in early September and late August may be correct, but the vast majority likely pertain to misidentified Tennessee Warblers. Fall migration peaks are from late September (e.g., Wisc.) through the first half of October, with numbers still passing through the s. Midwest and New England in late October. Strictly casual north of the wintering range after early November. Fall movements in the West are far earlier than in the East. Migration of *orestera* in the West begin as early as August, but timing for this subspecies is poorly known. Western *lutescens* begin to depart breeding areas by early June (often moving upslope), and are recorded well away from the breeding areas by late July (with a few back to early June); fall migration is protracted, continuing well into October (with a peak in late August and September).

VAGRANT to the western tip of the Alaska Peninsula, the Pribilofs, and the north slope of Alaska, in far northern Canada, and in Greenland; all of these probably pertain to *celata*. A bird found dead in Costa Rica on 26 October 1974 had been banded in N.Y. on 13 September 1972, but the identification of this bird cannot be confirmed; the very early date of banding in N.Y. suggests that it may have been a Tennessee Warbler.

STATUS AND CONSERVATION

Quite abundant along the Pacific Coast, but generally uncommon in the boreal and eastern portions of its range. Populations appear to be stable, except for the decline of the insular subspecies *sordida* on some islands off the coast of Baja California and, conversely, expansion of the limited mainland breeding range of *sordida* during this century.

This is one of our more geographically variable North American warblers, with four rather well-marked subspecies.

V. c. celata breeds in boreal regions and is the only subspecies normally occurring in eastern North America. It is the palest and grayest subspecies, with dullest immatures appearing mainly gray with only a hint of olive above and yellow in the undertail coverts. The plumages of *celata* are described below.

Orestera of the Rocky Mountain and Great Basin region is marginally the largest race. Adults are intermediate in plumage between *celata* and *lutescens*, being more yellowish olive above and yellower below than the former but duller than the latter. First fall *orestera* have grayish heads like *celata*, but the head usually shows more contrast with the olive back than in *celata*. First fall *orestera* average brighter, clearer yellow below than *celata*, with more yellow in or near the throat region, often showing a noticeable contrast with the gray sides of the head. The dullest fall immature *orestera* are not separable in the field from *celata*.

Lutescens, breeding along the Pacific Coast, is marginally the smallest subspecies; adults are considerably brighter than *celata* and somewhat brighter than *orestera*; the upperparts are rather bright olive-yellow, and the underparts are relatively bright yellow, with limited dull olive streaking. Winter adults show a slight gray cast to the upperparts. Dull immature *lutescens* show much less gray on the sides of the head than *celata* and *orestera* and are more extensively yellow on the underparts, though the yellow can be rather dull and pale. The supercilium, split eye-ring, and mark at the bend of the wing are yellowish even in the dullest immature

Orange-crowned Warbler. Subspecies celata *in Texas in February. (Photo: Kevin T. Karlson)*

lutescens. Juvenile *lutescens* are considerably yellower below than juvenile *celata* and *orestera* but also show rather distinct buffy wing bars.

Sordida of the California Channel Islands is darker and duller than *lutescens*, with broader and more extensive dusky olive streaking on the throat, breast, sides, and flanks, and dusky olive centers to the undertail coverts. The sides of the head are dull olive, and this color extends well down through the malar region and constricts the pale yellow of the throat. Winter adults show a grayish cast to the upperparts, and first fall birds have paler and less extensive yellow on the underparts. *Sordida* is somewhat longer billed than the other subspecies.

TAXONOMIC RELATIONSHIPS

Relationships within *Vermivora* not well understood, but perhaps most closely allied with the *ruficapilla* complex (Nashville/Virginia's/Colima).

PLUMAGES AND MOLTS

The following descriptions apply to the nominate *celata*. **SPRING ADULT MALE:** Crown and upperparts olive, slightly brighter yellow-olive on the rump and uppertail coverts. Feathers of the center of the crown extensively orange at the base, but this color is nearly always hidden by olive feather tips. Indistinct supercilium pale yellow; split eye-ring whitish. Sides of neck and auriculars dull olive. Underparts dull and rather pale yellow, indistinctly streaked and washed with grayish olive on the throat, breast, and sides. Yellow of the underparts usually clearest on the belly and

Orange-crowned Warbler. Subspecies celata *in New York in October. (Photo: Arthur Morris/Birds as Art)*

brightest on the undertail coverts. Wing coverts dusky, edged with olive. Feathers at the bend of the wing pale yellow. Remiges dusky, edged with olive on the secondaries and inner primaries and with pale gray on the outer primaries. Rectrices dusky with olive edges. **FIRST SPRING MALE:** Indistinguishable from spring adult male in the field; in the hand, usually distinguishable by browner, more worn and tapered rectrices and by browner and more tapered outer primaries. **SPRING ADULT FEMALE:** Very similar to spring adult male, but average duller and grayer on the upperparts and duller and less yellow on the underparts; background color of chin and throat, supercilium, and split eye-ring often whitish or very pale yellow. The orange crown patch is much reduced, a character that can be useful for sexing adult birds in the hand. **FIRST SPRING FEMALE:** Indistinguishable from spring adult female in the field; in-hand distinctions from adult female as for first spring male. **ALL ADULT MALE:** Much like spring adult male, but crown, auriculars, nape, back, and sides washed with gray. Primaries with thin grayish white tips. **FIRST FALL MALE:** Like fall adult male, but duller and more extensively gray-brown on the upperparts and duller, less yellow on the underparts; yellow below usually very inconspicuous except on undertail coverts. Supercilium and split eye-ring whitish. Tawny orange crown patch very small or occasionally absent. Many first fall males are indistinguishable from first fall females (below). **FALL ADULT FEMALE:** Much like spring adult female but somewhat duller and more gray-brown on upperparts and flanks; primaries with thin grayish white tips. **FIRST FALL FEMALE:** Duller than fall adult female. Upperparts completely dull olive-gray, indistinct supercilium and split eye-ring whitish. Face and sides of neck grayish. Underparts pale grayish with dull olive-gray streaking on the throat and breast. A faint yellow wash on the breast, sides, and belly; undertail coverts pale yellow. The dullest, grayest birds show only a slight hint of pale yellow on the chest and undertail coverts.

Orange-crowned Warbler. Subspecies lutescens *in California in September.* (*Photo: Jon L. Dunn*)

Orange-crowned Warbler. Subspecies orestera *first fall female in California in October. (Photo: Larry Sansone)*

Small mark at bend of wing whitish. No tawny orange present at bases of crown feathers. **JUVENILE:** Dull olive-brown above, paler and yellower on the rump. Dull gray-buff on the underparts, with a slight wash of pale yellow on the breast, sides, and undertail coverts. Pale grayish white supercilium and split eye-ring. Dull olive wings show two thin but fairly conspicuous buffy wing bars formed by the tips to the median and greater coverts. **BARE PARTS:** Bill dusky black on maxilla and tip of mandible, duller brown to grayish at base of mandible and along cutting edge; bill generally somewhat darker in spring birds. Eyes dark brown. Legs and feet slaty brown, grayish, or pale brown, palest on soles of feet and toe pads.

The prebasic molt is complete in adults; it does not usually include flight feathers or greater primary coverts in first-year birds, though some juvenal rectrices and remiges may be replaced in occasional individuals. Prebasic molt takes place mainly on the summering grounds, although birds retaining much juvenal plumage have often dispersed well away from breeding habitats (and completion of most of the prebasic molt on the wintering grounds may be the rule for *sordida*). The prealternate molt is very limited, usually only involving the chin and head; it takes place from February to May.

 REFERENCES

GENERAL: Sogge et al. 1994.
DISTRIBUTION: Bradley 1980 (song of *sordida* Orange-crowned), Stiles and Smith 1980.
ECOLOGY, BEHAVIOR, VOCALIZATIONS, AND CONSERVATION: Remsen et al. 1989.
PLUMAGES, MOLTS, AND MORPHOLOGY: Foster 1967a, b.

Vermivora ruficapilla

4.5 in. (11.5 cm). A widespread *Vermivora* with a grayish head, conspicuous complete white or whitish eye-ring, and a partly concealed chestnut crown patch; closely related to the Virginia's Warbler. The tail is rather short and, at least in western populations, is frequently bobbed. This warbler is always greenish on the upperparts, wing coverts, and edges of the flight feathers, and shows much yellow below. There are two rather distinct subspecies, one in the midwestern and eastern parts of North America and the other mainly in the Pacific Coast states; the eastern race is one of the few warblers that is a circum-Gulf migrant. Overall, a rather early spring migrant.

 ## DESCRIPTION

Head gray, contrasting with olive upperparts and yellow throat and underparts. Deep chestnut patch on crown in males, smaller or absent in females, is largely concealed. Conspicuous white or whitish eye-ring in all plumages; some whitish in loral region, but this does not form a conspicuous line connecting with the eye-ring as sometimes portrayed in guides. Throat, breast, and undertail coverts always bright yellow, variably paling to whitish in the belly and vent region. Wing coverts and flight feathers edged yellow-olive in all fresh plumages. Sexes are generally similar, with females slightly duller; little seasonal variation in plumage, although fall birds are slightly duller and show thin whitish tips to the remiges.

Structurally a small, rather short-tailed warbler with typical sharply pointed *Vermivora* bill.

 ## SIMILAR SPECIES

The small size, gray head (varying from blue-gray to dull gray-brown) with a complete white eye-ring, and extensive yellow on the underparts are conspicuous in all plumages. Always told from the related **VIRGINIA'S WARBLER** of the Southwest by more extensive yellow on the underparts, by the greenish tint to the back, wing coverts, and flight feathers, and by the shorter tail.

CONNECTICUT WARBLER shares gray head (adult males) and conspicuous white eye-ring, greenish upperparts, and yellowish underparts, but is very different in shape and behavior. Connecticut is a large, heavy thrushlike warbler that walks on ground or tree limbs. Most fall Connecticuts encountered have brownish heads;

all have duller, paler yellow underparts than Nashvilles and lack strong yellow on the throat and white on the belly. Immatures of eastern *(celata)* and some western *(orestera)* **ORANGE-CROWNED WARBLERS** have grayish heads and can be confused with Nashvilles. All Orange-crowneds show a split eye-ring and dark line through the eye; *celata* immatures are much duller on underparts than any Nashville, but *orestera* can show underparts approaching the color of Nashville. Orange-crowneds do not bob their tails as western Nashvilles often do. Female **COMMON YELLOWTHROATS** can show an indistinct whitish eye-ring but differ in their much longer tail, thicker and blunter bill, and wrenlike actions (skulking, tail cocking).

VOICE

SONG varies between eastern nominate birds and western *ridgwayi*, but always starts with a series of two-syllable notes. In eastern birds, beginning series is usually followed by a rapid, short trill, usually slightly lower in pitch, e.g., *see-pit see-pit see-pit see-pit titititi*. Some songs, including occasional flight songs, are slightly longer and more elaborate. Western *ridgwayi* song also starts out with a series of double notes, but overall quality is richer, with less of a tendency to have a distinct trill at the end in most songs: *see-pit see-pit see-pit sweet-sweet-sweet tyu*.

CALL is a distinctive sharp *plink* or *pink;* calls of western birds are very similar to the calls of Virginia's and Lucy's but average slightly clearer, less scratchy. Calls of eastern nominate birds are softer, less metallic. **FLIGHT NOTE** is a high, thin *tsip* or *seet* without any buzzy tones.

BEHAVIOR

A rather active warbler, often feeding at tips of twigs or weed stalks. Western birds *(ridgwayi)* frequently bob their tails in a down-up motion with a slight lateral component so that the tail bob describes a deep arc; this tail-bobbing behavior is much less frequent in eastern nominate birds. Spring migrants often feed high up in budding trees, but fall birds are often lower, frequently even feeding on low weed stems. Singing perches on the breeding grounds are high and often exposed. A flight song is sometimes given, with slow, fluttering wingbeats. Feeds primarily on insects but will take berries and nectar in nonbreeding season. Winter birds often occur in small flocks and will also join mixed-species flocks. The **NEST** is located among dense cover on the ground, usually well hidden within a hummock or under a bush or clump of ferns, grasses, or mosses.

Eastern *ruficapilla* **BREEDS** in a variety of wet or dry open wood-lands with brushy understories. Wet habitats, where the species reaches highest densities, include the edges of swamps or bogs of tamarack, cedar, or spruce. Dry habitats are often successional, following burns or deforestation. Dominant trees may be birches, alders, or aspens; also breeds in pine barrens, including jack pines. In some areas, breeds in early successional stages of beech-hemlock-maple forests. Undergrowth in dry habitats may include sphagnum, grasses, sedges, and Labrador-tea. Western *ridgwayi* primarily montane, breeding in brushy understory of open conif-erous forest or along shrubby riparian zones adjacent to conifers; often in successional habitats following burns or logging. Domi-nant trees within breeding habitat may include ponderosa pines, white firs, and oaks, particularly black oaks; important understory shrubs include manzanita and *Ceanothus*.

In **WINTER**, widespread in humid forests, shrubby areas, forest edges, coffee plantations, parks, and gardens. Winter birds north of Mexico have mostly been found in exotic flowering plantings, coastal woodlands.

SPRING MIGRANTS partial to budding and flowering trees; western *ridgwayi* especially partial to flowering mesquites and palo-verdes in deserts and live oaks in foothill and coastal regions. For *ridg-wayi* there is some upslope post-breeding movement into high montane meadows and willow thickets.

 # DISTRIBUTION

V. r. ruficapilla: **BREEDS** from cen. Sask., cen. and s. Man., cen. Ont., s. Que., and the Canadian Maritimes south to ne. N.D., n.-cen. Minn., s. Wisc., e. Mich., Pa. (sparse), Mass., nw. Conn., R.I., and N.Y. (mainly highlands); also south locally in Appalachians to w. Md., W. Va., and rarely w. Va. Formerly bred farther south, to southernmost Wisc., Ill., Ohio (one recent record), s. Conn. Has recently bred in sw. Nfld.

WINTERS mainly from ne. Mexico south to Belize, Guatemala, and cen. Honduras. Sight records farther south (two from Costa Rica, one from Panama) cannot be assigned to subspecies. Win-ters occasionally in the Bahamas. Small numbers winter in s. Texas (rarely north to Houston); casual along the Gulf Coast from La. to s. Fla. Also casual in winter north to the Midwest (Kans., Ill., Ohio, s. Ont.), and along the Atlantic Coast north to Mass. and N.S. Most of these northern winter records are for December (especially early December), with very few birds having successfully remained through the winter.

SPRING MIGRATION is circum-Gulf and quite early. Rare in the southeastern states at all seasons, but especially in spring. Most spring movement is north through the Miss. and Ohio valleys, west to the e. Great Plains and east to the Appalachian Mtns. Quite scarce on the Atlantic Coast south of N.Y. in spring. Migration begins in s. Texas in late March (a few in mid-March), continuing through late April and early May. Most arrive at the latitude of Ark. and Okla. in April, peaking in late April and early May. Through most of the Midwest, arrives in late April or very early May, peaking in mid-May; numbers drop off rapidly after about 20 May, with a few records into early June. Arrives on northernmost breeding grounds (N.S., Man.) during the second week of May, earlier than most sympatric warblers.

FALL MIGRATION may begin as early as mid-July just south of the breeding grounds, but typical fall arrivals are from mid- to late August. Peak movements over most areas are rather drawn out,

NASHVILLE WARBLER
Vermivora ruficapilla

usually from early September to early October; small numbers occur into late October, and stragglers are regularly noted into November and casually into early winter. Arrives in Texas and the southern states usually in early September. Quite rare in fall in the Southeast, but more regular along the southern Atlantic Coast in fall than in spring. Rare but regular fall migrant in Bermuda (occasionally winters; also recorded there in spring) and in Bahamas.

VAGRANT to West Coast (specimen from Los Coronados Is., Baja Calif.), Lab., Greenland (two records), Jamaica, Cuba, Mona Is. (off Puerto Rico).

V. r. ridgwayi: BREEDS from s. B.C., Idaho, extreme w. Mont. (quite local), and the mountains of e. Wash. and ne. Ore., south through the Cascade Mtns. of Wash. and Ore. (especially on eastern slopes) and through the mountains of nw. Calif. and through the Sierra Nevada. Small numbers breed in the mountains of cen. and s. Calif. (San Benito Mtn., Mt. Pinos, San Gabriel Mtns., San Bernardino Mtns.). Most breed from 3,000–5,500 ft. in the north, but s. Calif. birds have been at 5,500–7,000 ft.

WINTERS from w. Mexico south to Guatemala. Very small numbers winter along the coast of Calif., with winter records north on the coast to Wash. and Vancouver Is. There are interior winter records from se. Calif. and s. Ariz., and exceptionally to sw. Idaho.

SPRING MIGRATION is noted mainly in s. Ariz. and s. Calif., with a few seen east to s. N.M. and w. Texas. Arrives by late March or early April, with peak movements in mid- to late April. There is a rapid drop in numbers of migrants after early May; casual by mid-May in coastal areas and late May in the northern deserts of s. Calif. Arrives in nesting areas of Sierra Nevada and nw. Calif. as early as mid-April, and on the northernmost breeding grounds in very late April or early May.

In FALL there is some upslope movement into high mountain meadows by mid-July; fall migrants may be noted away from breeding mountain ranges by late July. Migrants are widely noted by mid-August. Uncommon fall migrant through the Great Basin. Decidedly scarcer along the coast in fall than in spring, except on northern coast (Vancouver Is. to Wash.), where rare at all seasons but recorded most often in fall. Migration continues in small numbers through September and into October; mostly gone from northern parts of range by the first of October. Frequent late stragglers along coast into early winter.

VAGRANT to cen. and s. Texas. Birds of unknown subspecies are rare migrants along the w. Great Plains and Rocky Mtn. states; also recorded in Alaska (sight records from Middleton Is., September 1981).

STATUS AND CONSERVATION

Populations appear to be stable, and overall numbers have probably increased in many areas where vegetation succession has followed deforestation. Some contraction of the breeding range has
been noted in the southern parts of breeding range in the east.
Significant year-to-year population fluctuations have been noted
in portions of the range (for example, Wisconsin). Because this
species winters commonly in modified habitats such as gardens
and coffee plantations, it has probably not suffered significant
declines from the loss of wintering habitat.

SUBSPECIES

The ranges of the two subspecies are outlined above; note the differences in vocalizations and tail-bobbing behavior indicated
above. Plumages of nominate *ruficapilla* are described below.
Western *ridgwayi* (sometimes called "Calaveras Warbler," and
referred to as *V.r. guttaralis* in older literature) differs in the following respects: the back (especially upper back) is slightly grayer, less green, and the rump is a brighter yellow-green. In the field
this gives the effect of reduced head and back contrast but
stronger back and rump contrast compared to nominate birds.
The yellow of the underparts is slightly clearer and brighter, less
washed with greenish. On average there is more white in the vent
area and belly of *ridgwayi*, but this character appears to be quite
variable. Finally, *ridgwayi* averages slightly longer-tailed than *ruficapilla*; the tail is frequently bobbed (rarely if ever bobbed in
nominate *ruficapilla*). Intergradation between the two forms is

Nashville Warbler.
Subspecies ruficapilla
in Texas in May.
(Photo: B.
Schorre/VIREO)

not known; the small numbers summering in s. Alberta (one proven nesting) likely pertain to *ridgwayi*, but *ruficapilla* could occur.

Taxonomic Relationships

Closely related to the Virginia's Warbler, and has been considered conspecific with it by some authors; no known areas of sympatry reported, although limited sympatry is now known from s. California mountains. Some have lumped Colima Warbler with the Nashville/Virginia's "species," a decision that ignores Colima's strikingly different morphology, songs, and behavior. Nashville has hybridized with Tennessee Warbler; additionally a female hybrid with Black-throated Blue Warbler was collected in Kalamazoo Co., Michigan, in September 1984.

Plumages and Molts

The following descriptions apply to the nominate subspecies from eastern North America. **SPRING ADULT MALE:** Forehead, crown, hindneck, sides of neck, and auricular region clear gray, contrasting noticeably with greenish back and yellow throat. Deep chestnut crown patch, largely veiled by gray feather tips. Complete and conspicuous white eye-ring; inconspicuous whitish supraloral streak. Back olive green with a slight yellowish wash; rump and uppertail coverts brighter yellow-olive. Chin, throat, breast, and undertail coverts bright yellow with a very slight greenish tint; paler yellow through belly and flanks. Some whitish in extreme lower belly and vent area. Wing coverts, primaries, and secondaries dusky, strongly edged with olive. Rectrices dusky olive with brighter yellow-olive edges. **FIRST SPRING**

Nashville Warbler. Male ridgwayi *in California in April. (Photo: Larry Sansone)*

Nashville Warbler. First fall female ridgwayi *in California in September. (Photo: Herbert Clarke)*

MALE: Not safely distinguishable from spring adult males, although averaging duller. Primaries and rectrices average browner and more worn than in adult. **SPRING ADULT FEMALE:** Gray of head duller than in spring males, washed slightly with brown; hindneck shows little contrast with back. Chestnut in crown greatly reduced and paler, more rufous; usually limited to just a few feathers and not visible in the field. Conspicuous eye-ring, slightly tinged buffy. Yellow of underparts paler than in spring males; a few spring females are whitish on the chin. More extensively whitish around the lower belly, vent, and flanks. **FIRST SPRING FEMALE:** Similar to spring adult females but averaging slightly duller. Primaries and rectrices average browner and more worn than in adult. **FALL ADULT MALE:** Like spring adult male, but chestnut crown patch is further obscured by gray feather tips, back lightly washed with gray, somewhat obscuring contrast between nape and back. Underparts more strongly tinged with olive. Thin whitish tips to remiges on all fall birds. **FIRST FALL MALE:** Resembles fall adult male, but crown, cheeks, and hindneck are slightly duller, contrasting little with back; chestnut crown patch less extensive. Yellow of underparts slightly paler, often very pale on chin and throat. Primaries and rectrices browner and more tapered than in adult. **FALL ADULT FEMALE:** Like spring adult female but slightly washed with pale gray on back and more strongly washed with olive-brown on crown and hindneck. Yellow of underparts slightly tinged olive. **FIRST FALL FEMALE:** Dullest plumage, showing little contrast between hindneck and back. Generally resembles first fall male, but averaging even duller, with chestnut absent in crown. Eye-ring buffy. Yellow of underparts pale, and often shows an orange-buff cast on the breast; many birds are whitish on the chin and throat and have extensive white in the lower belly, vent, and flanks. Primaries and rectrices browner and more tapered than in adult. **JUVENILE:** Upperparts brownish olive, underparts buffy yellow, chin whitish; fairly distinct pale buff wing bars. **BARE PARTS:**

Bill dark gray or blackish on maxilla, paler (dull yellow pinkish to whitish) along cutting edge and at base of mandible. Eyes dark brown. Legs and feet dark gray-brown to dull blackish; soles of feet dull yellow.

Prebasic molt takes place on the breeding grounds; complete in adults, partial in hatching-year birds. The limited prealternate molt (February to April) mostly occurs in the head region and does not result in a significant change in appearance.

 REFERENCES

GENERAL: Brush et al. 1976, Williams 1996.
DISTRIBUTION: Gochfeld 1974, Grinnell 1914, Johnson 1976.
ECOLOGY, BEHAVIOR, VOCALIZATIONS, AND CONSERVATION: Lawrence 1948, Robbins et al. 1996 (Blue-winged × Nashville pairing).
SYSTEMATICS: Johnson 1976.

VIRGINIA'S WARBLER   PL. 5

Vermivora virginiae
4.5 in. (11.5 cm). This close relative of the Nashville Warbler breeds on brushy mountain slopes within or adjacent to arid coniferous forests in the Great Basin mountain ranges and Rocky Mountains. It is like a grayer version of the Nashville, lacking that species' green wash on the wing coverts and flight feathers. The yellow on the underparts, when present, is much less extensive than in Nashville, but the undertail coverts are always contrastingly bright yellow. The complete white eye-ring is distinctive in all plumages. The relatively long tail is habitually bobbed.

 DESCRIPTION

Generally gray above with a bold white eye-ring, rufous crown patch (may be obscured) and a yellow-green rump. The underparts are pale grayish or gray-buff, with a variable yellow patch on the breast and bright lemon yellow undertail coverts. The sexes are generally similar, but males average more yellow on the breast and more rufous in the crown. In first fall birds, the upperparts are washed with brown, the rufous cap is greatly reduced or lacking, and the yellow on the breast may be lacking. Structurally much like the related Nashville Warbler, but noticeably longer tailed (tail averages 3 mm longer than *ridgwayi* Nashville).

SIMILAR SPECIES

Very similar to **NASHVILLE WARBLER** but considerably grayer overall. Some immature Nashvilles, especially the western subspecies *ridgwayi*, can be quite dull and pale-throated, resembling brighter Virginia's; the amount of yellow on the breast of Virginia's is variable and can approach that of Nashville in extent. Even the dullest Nashvilles are always distinguished by traces of olive green on wing coverts, back, and the edges of the flight feathers. Virginia's are longer tailed than Nashville. Particularly in late summer and early fall, Virginia's Warblers outside areas of regular occurrence should be identified with extreme caution.

COLIMA is superficially similar but is considerably larger and strongly washed with brown on the upperparts and flanks; the undertail coverts of Colima are tinged tawny orange, not clear yellow. Colimas rarely wag their tails. Within the U.S. Colima is restricted to the Chisos Mountains of w. Texas, where Virginia's is an uncommon migrant usually found in more arid habitats. **LUCY'S** is also similar but lacks bright yellow undertail coverts and has a tawny or chestnut rump (not greenish yellow) and shorter tail. Compare also with palest female **COMMON YELLOWTHROATS** of western interior subspecies.

VOICE

SONG usually consists of two series of 3–6 slurred notes, with the first series usually more strongly disyllabic: *s-weet, s-weet, s-weet, s-weet, s-weet, sweet-sweet-sweet,* or *seedle seedle seedle sweet-sweet.* Some songs have only a single series of notes, while others may have three series. Song closely resembles some songs from western (*ridgwayi*) Nashville Warblers, but slightly lower in pitch and not as distinctly structured. Song can also suggest Yellow Warbler. **CALL** is a sharp *plink* or *chink,* very much like western Nashville call but slightly huskier and louder; quite similar to call of Lucy's. Calls very frequently. **FLIGHT NOTE** is a very high, clear *seet.*

BEHAVIOR

A rather shy warbler, at least on breeding grounds; singing birds can be hard to track down. Quite active, and almost constantly bobs its tail in a down-up movement. Although males may sing from high in pine or other trees, most foraging is rather low. Migrants habitually forage in low brushy or weedy habitats. The **NEST** is placed on the ground on a steep slope, well concealed in a hollow or under a clump of vegetation.

HABITAT

BREEDS in dense brush of mountain slopes where there is adjacent or intermixed taller growth such as pinyon pines, yellow pines, Douglas-fir, Gambel oaks, or aspen. Dominant shrubs may include mountain-mahogany, serviceberry, manzanita, currant, snowberry, chokecherry, and scrub oak. Most breeding localities are from 4,000 to 9,000 ft. Breeding habitats are, on average, much more arid than those of Nashville Warbler. **WINTER** birds occur in mesquite thickets, second growth, and other arid sub-tropical scrub. **SPRING MIGRANTS** may use brushy habitats such as scrub oak and mesquite below breeding elevations. **FALL MIGRANTS** tend to occur in brushy or weedy habitats; vagrants on the coast are often in patches of fennel (*Foeniculum*) or tree tobacco (*Nicotiana*).

DISTRIBUTION

BREEDS from extreme s. Idaho, cen. and sw. and cen. Wyo. south through appropriate montane habitat in e. and s. Nev., Ut., Colo., Ariz., and N.M.; the southernmost nesting localities are in the border ranges of se. Ariz. and in the Guadalupe and Davis mtns. of w. Texas. Small populations also breed west to e.-cen. and s. Calif. (White Mtns., se. slopes of Sierra Nevada in Mono and Inyo cos., N.Y., Clark, San Bernardino and San Gabriel mtns., occasionally other ranges). Arrival on breeding grounds is mostly from early April to early May (but note late concentrations of migrants below).

WINTERS mainly in w. Mexico from Jalisco and Guanajuato south to the interior of Oaxaca. There are sight records for Belize and n. Guatemala. Winters casually in coastal s. and cen. Calif.

Uncommon in **SPRING MIGRATION** away from breeding grounds. The first migrants usually noted in s. Ariz. in late March, with passage continuing through mid-May; peak passage in Colo. somewhat later, with some migrants noted to the first of June. Large concentrations of migrants have been reported in Ariz. in early May and Colo. in mid-May.

Most **FALL MIGRATION** is through mountains, with relatively few birds seen in lowlands of Southwest. Some altitudinal movement may occur in late July, but main southward migration begins in August and probably peaks from late August to mid-September; there is some movement to early October.

Regular fall **VAGRANT** to coastal southern Calif., mainly in late August and September; much scarcer inland in Calif. and on the n. and cen. Calif. coast. Casual spring vagrant in s. Calif. (and on

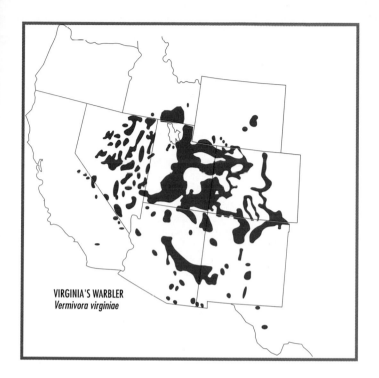

VIRGINIA'S WARBLER
Vermivora virginiae

Farallon Is.). Recorded casually in Ore. and on the Great Plains (e. Colo., Okla., Kans., n. Texas). Casual on the Texas coast in migration; one winter record for the lower Rio Grande Valley. Farther east, there are three May records for s. Ont., a spring record for Mich., a mid-December record for La., two fall records for N.J., fall records for N.B. and N.S., and exceptional records for Goose Bay, Lab. (21–22 September 1994) and the Bahamas (8 March 1993, Grand Bahama Is.).

STATUS AND CONSERVATION

Populations appear stable; some range expansion noted into California since the 1960s. Known cowbird host, but parasitism does not appear to have significantly affected populations.

SUBSPECIES

No subspecies; no geographical variation described.

Closely related to Nashville Warbler; the two have even been considered conspecific by some authors. And one author even included the Colima Warbler in this expanded species, confusingly suggesting the species names "Gray-headed" or "Rufous-capped" warbler (both in use for other, Neotropical warblers). Although vocalizations are similar between Virginia's and Nashville, they differ significantly in habitat, behavior, and shape (Virginia's is longer tailed), and there is no strong evidence to support lumping the two. No interbreeding between Nashville and Virginia's is known, although the species marginally overlap in the Transverse ranges and s. Sierra Nevada in California. Curiously, one author actually removed Virginia's Warbler from *Helminthophila* (*Helminthophila* = *Vermivora*) to the genus *Oreothlypis* based on subtle differences in primary shape, a placement not followed by other authors.

Plumages and Molts

SPRING ADULT MALE: Head clear gray with bold white eye-ring and pale gray supraloral area. Extensive chestnut cap only slightly obscured by gray feather tips. Hindneck and back gray, very slightly tinged brown. Rump and uppertail coverts yellow-green. Chin pale grayish, tinged pale yellow in some birds. Lower throat and center of breast extensively bright lemon yellow, this color extending variably into the upper throat and down to the upper sides. Lower breast and belly dull whitish, very faintly tinged pale yellow-buff. Sides and flanks gray. Undertail coverts bright yellow. Wing coverts gray; flight feathers dark gray, edged with pale gray. **FIRST SPRING**

Virginia's Warbler. Male in Arizona in May. (Photo: Anthony Mercieca/Root Resources)

Virginia's Warbler. In California in October. (Photo: Mike Danzenbaker)

MALE: Probably indistinguishable from spring adult male but averages slightly duller, with slightly less extensive yellow on breast. Some spring males, presumably first year, have yellow barely visible on breast. The primaries and rectrices are browner and more worn than in adult. **SPRING ADULT FEMALE:** Much like spring males, but crown patch paler rufous and less extensive; yellow on breast less extensive, usually confined to center of breast. **FIRST SPRING FEMALE:** Indistinguishable from spring adult female, but averages slightly duller with even less yellow on breast. The crown patch may be absent in some birds. The primaries and rectrices are browner and more worn than in adult. **FALL ADULT MALE:** Like spring adult male, but chestnut of crown mostly obscured by gray feather tips, upperparts washed with mouse brown, some gray-buff tips to yellow of breast, and a slightly stronger wash of buff on the lower breast, belly, and sides. **FIRST FALL MALE:** Upperparts mouse brown. A few chestnut feathers in crown, but these largely obscured. Yellow of center of breast varies from nearly absent to fairly extensive, but slightly obscured by gray-buff feather tips. Sides and flanks strongly washed with buff. Eye-ring slightly tinged buff. **FALL ADULT FEMALE:** Like spring adult female, but back washed with mouse brown, yellow of breast partly obscured by gray-buff feather tips. **FIRST FALL FEMALE:** Much like first fall male, but yellow nearly or completely absent on breast (breast washed buffy); rufous usually completely lacking in cap. **JUVENILE:** Gray-brown above with dull yellow on rump and uppertail coverts; light gray-brown below, dull whitish on belly and undertail coverts. Pale buffy wing bars. **BARE PARTS:** Bill dull gray-black, paler on cutting edge and mandible. Eyes dark brown. Legs and feet dull gray-brown; soles of toes yellowish.

Prebasic molt occurs on breeding grounds; complete in adults, partial in hatching-year birds. A limited prealternate molt takes place February–May.

 **REFERENCES**

DISTRIBUTION: Johnson 1976, Smith et al. 1994.
PLUMAGES, MOLTS, AND MORPHOLOGY: Brush and Johnson 1976.
SYSTEMATICS: Brush and Johnson. 1976.

COLIMA WARBLER

Vermivora crissalis

5.25 in. (13.3 cm). This is a large, long-tailed *Vermivora* with a very limited breeding range in lush montane woodlands of the highlands of northeastern Mexico, barely reaching into our area in the Chisos Mountains of Big Bend National Park, Texas. It is unrecorded in our area away from its limited breeding grounds. Colima suggests a large Virginia's Warbler but has browner tones to the plumage, lacks clear yellow on the breast, and does not habitually wag its tail. The English name derives from the locality of the type specimen, a winter bird collected in Colima, Mexico.

 ## DESCRIPTION

All plumages quite similar; head grayish with a rufous crown patch and whitish eye-ring; upperparts brownish to gray-brown, becoming bright yellow-olive on the rump and uppertail coverts; throat gray, with underparts becoming more brownish on the breast and flanks. Lower belly dull whitish. Undertail coverts deep tawny yellow with a slight orangish tint. Wing coverts gray-brown; remiges and rectrices dusky. No white markings in wings or tail. Plumage criteria for aging and sexing uncertain because of scarcity of specimens.

Structurally, the largest *Vermivora*, with longest bill and tail (tail even longer than Virginia's); overall shape more like an Orange-crowned Warbler than like Nashville or Virginia's.

 ## SIMILAR SPECIES

Most similar to the **VIRGINIA'S WARBLER**, a scarce migrant through the Chisos Mountain region, below the habitat of Colima. Colima is substantially larger, with a longer bill. It is much browner overall, particularly on the back and along the sides and flanks. It shows less contrast between the face and throat than Virginia's. The undertail coverts are more tawny orange, less clear yellow. The crown patch tends to be more extensive and paler (more rufous, less deep chestnut) in Colima. First fall Virginia's, which have a brownish cast to the upperparts and lack yellow on the breast, are most similar to Colima but can always be told by the characters above. Additionally, Colima does not normally bob its tail (Virginia's is a vigorous tail-bobber).

 ## VOICE

SONG is a somewhat musical trill very similar to that of an Orange-crowned Warbler, with slight changes in pitch through the course of the song. It is quite different from the slower and more varied series given by Virginia's and Nashville warblers. Sometimes the trill two-parted, with notes at the end given on a lower pitch. The trill lasts about 1.5 seconds and consists of about 12–24 notes. The **CALL NOTE** is a loud, sharp *plink* or *plisk,* similar to the calls of Virginia's, Nashville *(ridgwayi),* and Lucy's, but perhaps somewhat scratchier.

 ## BEHAVIOR

A rather confiding bird that responds well to pishing. Feeds rather sluggishly, often fairly high in oaks. Primarily feeds by gleaning insects from leaves, buds, twigs, and flowers; only occasionally makes aerial sallies. Has been known to take nectar from agaves. As noted above, Colima does not normally wag or bob its tail, unlike the Virginia's and Nashville warblers. Winter birds in Mexico tend to be solitary, apparently maintaining winter territories.

The **NEST** is built on the ground, well concealed by grasses, undergrowth, or root systems; it is constructed of grasses, rootlets, and mosses and may be partly domed-over by dead leaves.

 ## HABITAT

In the Chisos Mountains. **BREEDS** from about 6,000–7,700 ft., usually in humid canyons with an overstory of oaks, maples, pinyon pines, madrone, junipers, or Arizona cypress; occurs mainly on north-facing slopes. Some inhabit more open slopes and ridges of scrub oak and pinyon-juniper. Preferred habitat usually has extensive bunch grass and leaf litter at the ground level. **WINTERS** in habitat similar to breeding habitat and in other lush montane oak-conifer associations, usually keeping to the understory.

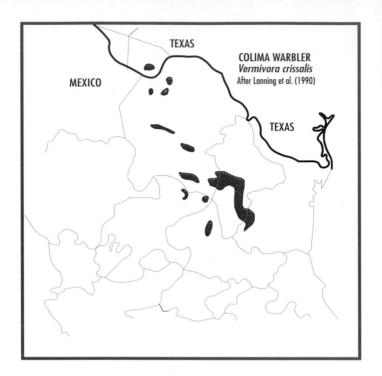

COLIMA WARBLER
Vermivora crissalis
After Lanning et al. (1990)

TEXAS

MEXICO

TEXAS

 DISTRIBUTION

BREEDS from the Chisos Mtns., Big Bend National Park, Texas, south in appropriate montane habitat through the Sierra Madre Oriental of e. Mexico from Coahuila, Nuevo Leon, and sw. Tamaulipas to n. San Luis Potosi and ne. Zacatecas. Within Chisos Mtns., most occur in Boot Canyon drainage, but breeds more widely following plentiful late-winter precipitation (in Laguna Meadows area, numbers fluctuate from year to year).

WINTERS in lush montane woodland in central and sw. Mexico, primarily from se. Sinaloa south through Jalisco, Colima, Michoacan, and Guerrero; also recorded in states of Morelos, Mexico, and the Distrito Federal; recently photographed in cen. Oaxaca (see photo p. 184). In general, winters in higher and more humid habitats than the Virginia's Warbler. Winter populations quite sparse, with only 4 birds per week encountered during one intensive study.

MIGRATION routes and timing uncertain. Has been recorded in the Chisos Mtns. as early as 15 March, but generally does not arrive until the first 10 days of April. Spring arrivals probably prolonged, with peak numbers not reached until early May; has been recorded in May on the wintering grounds. Birds begin leaving the breeding grounds in mid-July; the latest record for the Chisos Mtns. is 19 September.

STATUS AND CONSERVATION

Generally quite numerous within its limited breeding range; population estimates for the Chisos Mtns. range from about 100 to 150 birds. U.S. breeding range is fully protected, and northern part of Mexican range is thinly occupied by people. Fire is a potential threat throughout the species' range; overgrazing and deforestation are significant threats in the southern part of the breeding range and on the wintering grounds. No documented cowbird parasitism on this species. Because of its rather limited range, this species should be closely monitored.

SUBSPECIES

No geographic variation described; no subspecies recognized.

TAXONOMIC RELATIONSHIPS

Published works indicate that the Colima Warbler belongs to the *ruficapilla* complex (along with the Nashville and Virginia's Warblers); some authors have suggested that Colima, Virginia's and Nashville are conspecific, an assertion dismissed by subsequent workers. More recently, some experts feel that Colima may be closely related to the Orange-crowned Warbler, based on characters of size, shape, songs, and habitat; call notes of the two species differ, however.

PLUMAGES AND MOLTS

SPRING MALE: As described in Description; head grayish with an extensive rufous crown patch (partly veiled with gray). Hindneck and upperparts mouse brown except for yellow-olive rump and uppertail coverts. Breast washed slightly with brown (a few show a very slight wash of yellow-olive on the breast, but never clear yellow); stronger brown wash on flanks than on breast. First spring males presumably similar to adult. **SPRING FEMALE:** Not safely distinguished from spring males; may average less rufous in crown and slightly browner below. First spring females presumably similar

Colima Warbler. In Oaxaca, Mexico, in December. (Photo: R. K. Bowers/VIREO)

to adult; primaries and rectrices likely browner and more worn in first-year birds than adults, as in other *Vermivora*. **FALL MALE:** Like spring males, but breast, flanks, crown, hindneck, and back more strongly washed with brown. Rufous crown patch more strongly veiled with gray. First fall birds similar to adult but probably with more restricted rufous in crown. **FALL FEMALE:** Like spring females but browner above and below. First fall females presumably represent the brownest plumage, with rufous in crown most restricted and veiled. **JUVENILE:** Resembles adults but with buffy wing bars and paler, more yellowish undertail coverts. Rufous of crown said to be absent in juveniles but can rarely be evident by mid-July in birds still showing juvenal wing bars. **BARE PARTS:** Bill dark gray, paler and browner along the cutting edge and base of the mandible. Eyes dark brown. Legs and feet grayish.

The prebasic molt occurs on the breeding grounds from June to August; it is complete in adults but probably does not involve flight feathers in hatching-year birds. There is a limited prealternate molt from February to April, but most change in appearance between fall and spring seems due to plumage wear.

REFERENCES

GENERAL: Bangs 1925, Wauer 1985.
DISTRIBUTION: Lanning et al. 1990.
ECOLOGY, BEHAVIOR, VOCALIZATIONS, AND CONSERVATION: Blake 1949, Lanning et al. 1990.
SYSTEMATICS: Phillips et al. 1964.

Vermivora luciae

4.25 in. (11 cm). This smallest of the wood-warblers is a pale gray bird of the southwestern deserts, very much tied to the presence of mesquite *(Prosopis)* over much of its breeding range. It builds its nest primarily in crevices and cavities, a trait shared only with Prothonotary among our warblers. Lucy's appears to be closely related to the Nashville/Virginia's complex, sharing the chestnut crown patch and tail-bobbing behavior, and having similar vocalizations. In all plumages, the dark eye stands out prominently on the plain face and the uppertail coverts are chestnut or tawny.

 ## DESCRIPTION

Plumage generally gray above and white to creamy white below, with a variable chestnut crown patch and chestnut or tawny uppertail coverts. The face pattern is very plain, with only a diffuse creamy white eye-ring contrasting slightly with the gray (or gray and chestnut) crown. Face patterns do vary somewhat among individuals, however, although this variation does not appear to be linked to age, sex, or season. The smallest warbler, kinglet-sized, lightly built and very short-tailed.

 ## SIMILAR SPECIES

The overall pale silvery gray coloration above and more whitish underparts, with the dark eye standing out boldly on the plain face, give this species a distinctive appearance, even when the diagnostic chestnut or tawny rump is not seen. VIRGINIA'S WARBLER, superficially similar, always shows yellow undertail coverts and a greenish yellow rump and has yellow on the breast in most plumages; the eye-ring of Virginia's is thin and well-defined, whereas Lucy's shows a broader, less contrasting pale eye-ring. Lucy's is distinctly shorter-tailed than Virginia's.

Beware superficial similarity of very pale female YELLOW WARBLERS of the race *sonorana* which share some of Lucy's southwestern range. These warblers are larger, even shorter-tailed, and always show some pale yellow edging to the wing coverts and flight feathers and pale yellow spots in the tail.

Lucy's is perhaps most likely to be confused with certain non-warblers. Western races of BELL'S VIREO *(Vireo bellii)*, especially *pusilla* of California and Baja California, are quite gray; beware also pale WARBLING VIREOS. These vireos have stronger head patterns and heavier, hooked bills; they lack any chestnut or tawny patches above. Juvenile **VERDIN** *(Auriparus flaviceps)* (Plate 6), completely gray in plumage, is often mistaken for Lucy's Warblers and is usually common in the same habitats. Note the much sharper, deeper based bill of the Verdin, with pale yellowish pink at the base of the mandible. The Verdin is also longer tailed.

 VOICE

SONG is loud, sweet, and vigorous, usually consisting of two or three fairly rapid series on slightly different pitches: *tee-tee-tee-tee-tee-sweet-sweet-sweet* or *swee-swee-swee-swee tee-tee-tee-sweet-sweet.* Simpler and more rapid songs may suggest Orange-crowned or Colima; many songs suggest Virginia's but usually without distinctly two-parted syllables. Most complex songs recall Yellow Warbler but are less emphatic. **CALL NOTE** is a sharp *plink* or *chink,* much like note of Virginia's. **FLIGHT CALL** a weak *tsit.*

 BEHAVIOR

An active warbler, moving rapidly and bobbing its tail in a down-up motion. Gleans insects from foliage and twigs; often seen probing into blossoms of saguaro cactus and ocotillo. Can be rather shy and hard to approach in its thorn-scrub habitat, but family groups in late spring or early summer can be quite conspicuous.

Its **HOLE-NESTING** habit is quite different from related species; it is the only warbler besides Prothonotary to nest regularly in tree cavities. The nest may be in a natural crevice, under loose bark, or in a woodpecker cavity. Occasionally Lucy's Warblers will use old Verdin nests. Rarely, nests may be in holes in stream banks or in matted clumps of dead leaves.

 HABITAT

BREEDS mainly in thickets of mesquite, mainly velvet (honey) mesquite but also screwbean mesquite, frequently along water-courses or near ponds where there are also low willows and cottonwoods; they shun mature cottonwood-willow riparian associations. They range into sparser thorn-scrub of palo verde, ironwood, and catclaw acacia where such habitat borders stands of mesquite. Locally, as in the mountains of se. Arizona, they range up canyons to 4,500 ft. or more, using mixed woodland of walnut, sycamore, ash, and live oak (in these areas they may marginally overlap with Virginia's Warblers). In the lower Colorado River Valley, Lucy's will frequently use and sometimes even nest in exotic salt cedar (*Tamarix*). **WINTERS** mainly in second growth and thorn-scrub habitats, up to about 5,500 ft. **MIGRANTS** are infrequently noted but are usually in low scrub, thorn-scrub, tamarisks, or riparian vegetation.

 ## DISTRIBUTION

BREEDS from s. Ut., s. Nev., and se. Calif. (mainly lower Colorado River, but locally north to Death Valley National Monument and west to Morongo Valley, Borrego Valley) south through Ariz., cen. and sw. N.M., to n. Sonora and extreme ne. Baja Calif. Also nests along the Rio Grande from Big Bend National Park to e. Hudspeth Co., Texas. An old nesting record for extreme sw. Colo., where now strictly accidental.

LUCY'S WARBLER
Vermivora luciae

WINTERS mainly in w. Mexico, from Nayarit (and less commonly farther north) south to Guerrero. Very rare north to the mesquite groves along the Rio Grande in the Big Bend region in Texas, and there are December records for s. Ariz. There are over a dozen winter records for coastal Calif., north to Sonoma Co. Recorded once in winter in Lane Co., Ore.

SPRING MIGRATION is little understood, as the species is rarely encountered in spring away from breeding and wintering grounds. Arrival on the breeding grounds is early, from about 10 March on the lower Colorado River to about 20–25 March in the northern breeding localities. *En masse* arrival of birds in March coincides with the leafing out of the mesquites.

FALL MIGRATION is also poorly understood. Birds begin dispersing away from breeding localities by late July or early August, with most birds gone by early September; a few have been noted as late as early October. A few linger in riparian nonbreeding areas in se. Ariz. through September. It is an annual fall vagrant to coastal Calif., especially from Santa Barbara Co. south; most records are from late August to early November; casual in fall on the northern Calif. coast.

CASUAL along Pacific Coast as noted above; there is a May report from Idaho, two early winter (December) records for La., and an *exceptional* early December record for Mass.

STATUS AND CONSERVATION

Lucy's Warblers have declined over much of their range (especially in s. Arizona and along the lower Colorado River) with the felling of mesquite woodland and other riparian associations. Overgrazing has caused the spread of mesquite scrub into grassland habitats, but the extent to which Lucy's use such scrub is uncertain. Much of its current New Mexico range, however, has only been occupied since the 1920s. Even though it is a cavity nester, it is occasionally parasitized by cowbirds.

SUBSPECIES

No geographic variation described within the rather limited range; no subspecies recognized.

TAXONOMIC RELATIONSHIPS

A close relative of the Nashville/Virginia's species complex, though differing in several important respects, including its cavity-nesting habits.

SPRING ADULT MALE: Upperparts entirely silvery gray except for a deep chestnut crown patch, partially obscured by gray feather tips, and chestnut uppertail coverts. The rump is slightly paler gray than the back. Loral region and broad indistinct eye-ring creamy white; auriculars washed with pale gray. Entire underparts creamy white, shaded slightly with gray on the sides of the breast and the flanks. Wing coverts and remiges gray-brown, edged pale gray. Rectrices gray-brown, with an indistinct white spot on the distal third of the inner web of the outer pair of rectrices. **FIRST SPRING MALE:** Generally not distinguishable from spring adult male, but in the hand the primaries and rectrices appear browner and more worn. **SPRING ADULT FEMALE:** Very similar to spring adult male, but chestnut crown patch paler and less extensive, often almost completely obscured by gray feather tips; chestnut of uppertail coverts paler, more orangish. White spots in outer rectrices average less extensive. **FIRST SPRING FEMALE:** Essentially indistinguishable from spring adult female, but perhaps averages even less chestnut on crown. In the hand, the primaries and rectrices appear browner and more worn. **FALL ADULT MALE:** Much like spring males, but in this fresher plumage there is a stronger buffy wash to the underparts, and the chestnut uppertail coverts are slightly veiled by pale buff feather tips; the upperparts are slightly tinged brownish. **FIRST FALL MALE:** Like fall adult male, but uppertail coverts pale tawny rufous, chestnut in crown less extensive. Averages even browner above and buffier below. **FALL ADULT FEMALE:** Like spring adult female but more strongly washed with buff below; uppertail coverts slightly veiled with pale buff feather tips. The upperparts are slightly tinged brownish. **FIRST FALL FEMALE:** Probably indistinguishable from first fall males, but the very limited pale chestnut in the crown is more or less completely obscured, and the uppertail coverts are

Lucy's Warbler. Male in Arizona in March. (Photo: Jim Flynn)

even paler tawny rufous. **JUVENILE:** Resembles first fall birds but chestnut in crown lacking, uppertail coverts tawny, and with indistinct buffy wing bars. **BARE PARTS:** Bill dusky black, paler and grayer on the mandible; eyes dark brown; legs blackish.

The prebasic molt occurs in July (or even late June) and August; it is complete in adults and partial in hatching-year birds. The prealternate molt is absent or extremely limited.

 ## REFERENCES

IDENTIFICATION: Kaufman 1990b.

CRESCENT-CHESTED WARBLER PL. 29

Parula superciliosa

4.25 in. (11 cm). This Neotropical montane species occurs primarily from northern Mexico to northern Nicaragua but has strayed at least three times into southeastern Arizona; there are additional unconfirmed sight records for the lower Rio Grande Valley in Texas. The bright coloration includes a bright yellow throat and breast with a variable crescent of chestnut on the lower throat, a yellow-green patch on otherwise blue-gray upperparts, and a bold and broad white supercilium. Some authorities place this species in the genus *Vermivora*; other English names sometimes used include "Spot-breasted Warbler" and "Hartlaub's Warbler."

 ## DESCRIPTION

Head and upperparts mostly gray to blue-gray, with an extensive patch of yellow-green on the back and a conspicuous white supercilium. This supercilium broadens behind the eye. There is a small white crescent under the eye. The throat and breast are bright yellow, marked with chestnut in the center of the chest in the shape of a wide spot or short crescent (and absent or reduced to an inconspicuous blur in some individuals). The remaining underparts are white, washed with dusky on the flanks. The wings and tail are unmarked gray.

The sexes are similar, although females average slightly paler and show a reduced crescent on the chest. First-year birds have the reddish chest crescent reduced (males, some females) or absent (many females). Seasonal variation is slight.

SIMILAR SPECIES

The broad and pure white supercilium should prevent confusion with most other yellow-breasted warblers. In combination with the blue-gray head and yellow-green back patch, this supercilium is diagnostic. The reddish or chestnut mark on the chest is also diagnostic but may be difficult to see and is absent in some immature birds. Compare with **NORTHERN** and **TROPICAL PARULAS**, both of which lack the bold white supercilium and show strong white wing bars. The **RUFOUS-CAPPED WARBLER**, another straggler along the Mexican border, shares the white supercilium and yellow breast, but has a rufous cap, lacks the chestnut chest mark, and is a skulking bird with a long, thin tail that is cocked in wrenlike fashion.

 VOICE

SONG is an unassuming, quick dry buzz, *tz-z-z-z-z-z* or *zzzzirrrrrrr*, insectlike in quality and delivered with the tail vibrating exaggeratedly. The song completely lacks the rising, crescendo effect of the songs of our other *Parula*, suggesting instead the buzzy songs of certain *Vermivora*. The **CALL NOTE** suggests the *tik* note of an Orange-crowned Warbler, but is somewhat softer, indicated as *ship* or *sik*. **FLIGHT NOTE** is a high, thin *sip*.

 BEHAVIOR

Forages by gleaning at medium heights in trees and shrubs, with actions rather deliberate for a warbler. Often hangs acrobatically to examine the undersides of leaves, and frequently forages in clusters of dead leaves. In fall and winter up to several dozen individuals may join loose flocks of insectivorous passerines, including other warblers, titmice, gnatcatchers, and vireos. Occasionally will flick wings and tail when excited. The **NEST** (unknown in our region) is placed on or near the ground along banks and ravines (in contrast to other arboreal-nesting *Parula*, but like most *Vermivora*); it is an unroofed cup of grasses, mosses, and pine needles. The eggs are usually pure white, unusual among wood-warblers.

 HABITAT

Primarily **RESIDENT** in montane pine-oak woodlands and in cloud forests of firs, pines, and cypresses. The spring and fall records for Arizona are from pine-oak woodlands in mountain canyons. There is at least a limited downslope movement into foothill and

lowland riparian habitats in the nonbreeding season. The **WINTER-**
ING bird in Arizona occupied a willow-dominated woodland, and
the one lowland record for Sonora was in willow-cottonwood
riparian forest.

 ## DISTRIBUTION

Mainly **RESIDENT** in the mountains from n. Nuevo Leon, Tamaulipas, Chihuahua, and se. Sonora (possibly farther north, but certainly within about 200 miles of the Ariz. border) south through
the montane regions of Mexico to Honduras and n.-cen.
Nicaragua. In at least the northern populations, there is some
downslope movement to the base of the mountains in fall and
winter, although the species is very rare in the lowlands.

In our area, recorded three times in southeastern Ariz.: 3–15
September 1983 in Garden Canyon, Huachuca Mtns.; two birds,
apparently a mated pair, 28 April to 17 May 1984 in Ramsey
Canyon, Huachuca Mtns.; and one wintering along Sonoita
Creek in Patagonia, 11 September 1992 to 28 March 1993, and
returning 13 November 1993 to 17 January 1994. There are two
additional unverified sight records for Texas: one at Falcon Dam
in the lower Rio Grande Valley on 10 May 1970 and one in Boot
Canyon in the Chisos Mtns. on 2 June 1993; the latter record has
been provisionally accepted by the Texas Bird Records Committee. This species is a fairly common resident in the Sierra Picachos near Cerralvo in n. Nuevo Leon, Mexico, within sight of Falcon Dam.

 ## STATUS AND CONSERVATION

Generally uncommon within its range. Little information on population trends, although populations in Mexico appear to be relatively stable.

 ## SUBSPECIES

Geographic variation in this species is rather slight, involving
slight size variation and a general progression from paler northern
forms to darker, more deeply blue-gray southern forms. The
records for Arizona and the Big Bend, Texas, sight record (if correct) undoubtedly pertain to the palest, northwesternmost subspecies *sodalis*. The sight record for Falcon Dam, Texas, may pertain to the race *mexicana* of the Sierra Madre Oriental region. *P.
s. sodalis* ranges from Sonora and s. Chihuahua south through the
mountains of w. Mexico to at least Nayarit. The race *mexicana*
breeds from Nuevo Leon and w. Tamaulipas south through the

Sierra Madre Oriental to the isthmus region of Mexico. It is slightly larger and darker than *sodalis,* with the blue-gray of the upperparts a bit deeper; the green of the back is deeper, less yellowish; these differences are minor, and the validity of *sodalis* has been questioned. Another pale subspecies, *palliata,* is resident in sw. Mexico. Nominate *superciliosa* is resident south of the Isthmus of Tehuantepec from Chiapas and Guatemala to El Salvador, and the similar race *parvus* is described from Honduras and Nicaragua at the southern limit of the species' range; both of these subspecies are darker blue-gray on the head and upperparts than *mexicana* and even deeper green on the back.

TAXONOMIC RELATIONSHIPS

This species was formerly placed in the genus *Vermivora* and perhaps belongs there, as suggested by the sharply pointed bill, which is not strongly bicolored, and by its ground-nesting habits. Its green back patch and buzzy song suggest *Parula,* but the song even more closely resembles the songs of certain *Vermivora*; call notes also resemble those of certain *Vermivora.* Any generic realignment would have to take into account the Flame-throated Warbler *(Parula gutturalis)* of Central America, which may also be a *Vermivora.* These two genera are clearly closely related.

PLUMAGES AND MOLTS

SPRING ADULT MALE: Forehead, crown, lores, auriculars, sides of neck, and nape deep gray with a slight bluish tint. Back and rump yellow-green. Uppertail coverts gray. A bold white supercilium extends from the supraloral region back beyond the auriculars, widest and boldest behind the eye. There is a small white crescent under the eye. The chin, throat, and breast are bright yellow. At the lower border of the throat is a thick crescent-shaped patch of deep chestnut that is usually isolated in the yellow from the gray sides of the throat. The belly, sides, and flanks are dull whitish, with a slight gray-buff cast on the flanks. The wing coverts are unmarked gray, and the flight feathers are dusky gray with pale gray edges. The gray tail has an inconspicuous white edge to the inner webs of the outer two pairs of rectrices. **FIRST SPRING MALE:** Probably not distinguishable from spring adult male, but chestnut patch on chest may average smaller. **SPRING ADULT FEMALE:** Similar to spring adult male, but the chestnut crescent on the chest is somewhat thinner and paler, and may be very inconspicuous on some birds. The gray of the head and the yellow of the throat and breast average very slightly paler. **FIRST SPRING FEMALE:** Very similar to spring adult female, but chestnut on chest averages even less extensive and may be reduced to just a slight dull orange wash; presumably

Crescent-chested Warbler. Subspecies supercilosa *in Chiapas, Mexico, in February. (Photo: E. F. Knights/VIREO)*

most spring birds showing very faint or no chestnut on the chest are first-spring females. **FALL ADULT MALE:** Very similar to spring adult male, but plumage fresher, chestnut of chest slightly veiled with yellow feather-tips, the sides of the breast tinged with olive, and the flanks more strongly washed with brown. **FIRST FALL MALE:** Resembles fall adult male, but gray of upperparts slightly duller, green of back somewhat more blended with the gray of the hindneck, and chestnut patch on chest averaging slightly smaller and thinner. **FALL ADULT FEMALE:** Very similar to spring adult female, but plumage fresher, with any chestnut present on the chest partly veiled with yellow feather tips, yellow of the sides of the breast tinged olive, and the flanks more strongly washed with brown. **FIRST FALL FEMALE:** Resembles fall adult female but gray of the upperparts very slightly tinged with brown, uppertail coverts tipped with olive, green back more blended with the gray of the nape, and chestnut on the chest absent or present as an indistinct pale orange wash. **JUVENILE:** Whitish supercilium evident, but upperparts gray-green, underparts dull grayish buff; buffy wing bars. Yellow appears on throat and breast soon after fledging. **BARE PARTS:** Bill blackish with extensive fleshy yellow at the base of the lower mandible. Eyes dark brown. Legs and feet gray to gray-brown; soles of feet pale yellow.

Presumed to be similar to other *Parula/Vermivora*, with a complete prebasic molt (adults) or incomplete prebasic molt (hatching-year birds) occurring after breeding and a partial prealternate molt occurring in late winter.

 # REFERENCES

DISTRIBUTION: Heathcote and Kaufman 1985, Terrill 1985.
IDENTIFICATION: Heathcote and Kaufman 1985.
SYSTEMATICS: Hardy and Webber 1975 (suggests *Parula superciliosa sodalis* and *P.s. mexicana* are inseparable), Moore 1941.

Parula americana

4.25 in. (11 cm). Also known as the Parula Warbler or Northern Parula Warbler, this species is among the smallest American warblers; it is compact in shape and noticeably short-tailed. All individuals show bold wing bars, a bright yellow breast, and a distinct blue or blue-gray color on the head and portions of the upperparts; there is a yellow-green patch on the back. Males give their distinctive rising buzzy song with great frequency during the breeding season. Northern Parulas breed primarily in two situations—woods in the Deep South that are laden with Spanish moss, and northern boreal woodlands with extensive *Usnea* lichen. The Spanish moss and lichen are important in nest construction and placement.

 ## DESCRIPTION

Blue to blue-gray on the head and upperparts except for a triangular yellow-green patch in the center of the back. White arcs above and below the eye form a split eye-ring. Chin, throat, and breast bright yellow, variably marked in males with a band of chestnut and often a band of slate gray or blackish across the uppermost chest. Remaining underparts whitish. Wings blue-gray with two bold, broad white wing bars. Tail blue-gray with white spots on the inner webs of the outer two or three pairs of rectrices. Males are brighter than females and show chest bands (indistinct in immature males). Plumage shows little seasonal change, but fresh fall and winter adult males are tinged greenish on the head and rump and have the chest bands somewhat veiled with yellow.

This is a very small warbler with a short tail and a rather sharply pointed bill reminiscent of a *Vermivora* but slightly decurved on the culmen. Specimens of leucistic birds exist.

 ## SIMILAR SPECIES

The closely related **TROPICAL PARULA** is found in small numbers in south coastal Texas and casually elsewhere along the Mexican border; it is similar in plumage and vocalizations; distinctions are discussed under that species.

The very small size, short tail, bluish tone to the upperparts, broad, conspicuous wing bars, and bicolored bill (blackish above, fleshy yellow below) should make identification of parulas from other warblers straightforward. Possible confusion species include **NASHVILLE WARBLER**, which is also small and short-tailed and shows a combined grayish head and yellow throat. Nashville lacks white in the wings and tail, has yellow undertail coverts, and has a complete (not split) eye-ring. Confusion could also occur with immature female **MAGNOLIA WARBLERS**, which may have very indistinct flank streaking; note the complete eye-ring and more extensively yellow underparts of Magnolia, as well as its completely different tail pattern.

Other warblers showing bluish color on the upperparts (**CERULEAN** and **BLACK-THROATED BLUE**) differ in face pattern and underpart coloration and are not likely to be confused with parulas.

♪ VOICE

The most frequent **SONG** type is a rapid buzzy trill that climbs the scale then drops suddenly with an explosive ending note. This type of song may have several shorter introductory notes, which are usually also buzzy. Renditions of songs include *zzzzzzzzzzzz-zip* and *zh-zh-zh-zheeeeeeeeeee-up*. A second, less frequent song type consists of a rising series of separate buzzy notes and a sharp, slurred ending. This song is quite suggestive of the Cerulean Warbler's song but ends in a sharp note rather than a long buzz.

Western populations of Northern Parula, corresponding to the subspecies *ludoviciana* discussed in Subspecies, differ from eastern populations in having a buzzier, less emphatic, and slightly upslurred terminal note to the song.

The **CALL NOTE** is a rather sharp *tsip*. The **FLIGHT NOTE** is a high, weak, descending *tsif*, sometimes frequently repeated.

BEHAVIOR

In general, the Northern Parula feeds at moderate to high levels in the foliage, but particularly in fall it may descend to feed in weed patches and scrubby thickets; there is a slight tendency for males to forage higher than females. This species' small size may facilitate foraging at the tips of twigs and sprays of foliage, where it gleans methodically and often hangs in chickadee or kinglet fashion. Hover-gleaning and flycatching is sometimes performed. The tail may be held slightly cocked. Behavioral subordinance to other warblers and even kinglets may explain a tendency to forage at forest edge rather than forest interior. Their probing of flowering catkins in spring is reminiscent of many *Vermivora*. Foraging behavior has been shown to be more generalized on offshore islands that lack competing warblers and kinglets, as well as in the southern part of the range, where breeding *Vermivora* are absent. On the wintering grounds it usually occurs singly but may mix with other species.

The distinctive **NEST** is placed within and is constructed of *Usnea* lichen in the northern part of the breeding range and Spanish moss (a bromeliad in the genus *Tillandsia*) in the South. The few nests found in California have been constructed of the lichen *Ramalina reticulata*. The nest is a basketlike cup with an opening near the top, recalling the nest construction of a Baltimore Oriole (*Icterus galbula.*) Nest height is variable, from 6–60+ ft., and the nest is usually placed well out from the trunk. Where preferred nest materials are absent, a variety of materials including dead leaves, shreds of bark, down, grasses, and pine needles are used in nest construction.

 HABITAT

BREEDING habitat varies considerably through the species' range, but it nearly always includes trees laden with the lichens or Spanish moss noted above. In the northern portion of the breeding range it is generally associated with rather moist boreal forests including spruce, hemlock, balsam fir, white cedar, tamarack, and various hardwoods; *Usnea* lichen abounds in these habitats. Often associated in the north with streams or slow-moving rivers, or coastal fog belts. Appalachian populations favor wet ravines dominated by hemlocks; in the upper Ohio River Valley, they may occur locally in sycamore and oak woodlands along streams. Southern populations favor cypress swamps but also occupy pine-oak woodlands, hardwood forests, and other wet woodland types with abundant Spanish moss. At least in the northern part of the range, Northern Parulas occur more frequently near woodland edges than in deep forest interior. **WINTER** habitat includes a variety of semi-arid and tropical evergreen woodlands, plantations, mangroves, and gardens. **MIGRANTS** occur widely but show a preference for deciduous woods; they are occasionally even found in overgrown fields and hedgerows.

 DISTRIBUTION

BREEDS in the boreal region from se. Man. and n. Minn. east through cen. Ont. and s. Que. to the Canadian Maritime Provinces (and possibly sw. Nfld.), Me., most of Vt. and N.H., and the Adirondack Mtns. of N.Y. Breeds uncommonly and locally south through the Midwest (west to se. Iowa, e. Kans., e. Okla., very locally in extreme e. Neb.) and along the Atlantic Coast from s. New England to Md., and south through the length of the

Appalachian Mtns. Absent as a breeder over portions of the Midwest (see map). A common breeder over the Deep South, south to cen. (locally s.) Fla. and west to s.-cen. Texas. Has occasionally bred well outside of its normal range, as in the Rio Grande Valley of Texas, cen. New Mexico, n. Sonora, and coastal Calif. (several breeding records for the central coast from Marin Co. to Santa Barbara Co., but also once in the San Bernardino Mtns. of s. Calif.).

WINTERS primarily in the West Indies, where common in the Bahamas, Greater Antilles, and n. Lesser Antilles, but only in small numbers in the s. Lesser Antilles (casually south to Tobago and to Los Roques Is. off Venezuala); also winters uncommonly on Bermuda. On the mainland it winters uncommonly to fairly commonly in e. and s. Mexico (mainly from Veracruz south), south to Guatemala and Belize, and in small numbers to Nicaragua and Costa Rica. Casual in winter in Panama; unrecorded from the mainland of South America. North of Mexico, the Northern Parula is regular only in s. Fla., where uncommon. It is rare to casual farther north in Fla. and along the Gulf Coast to the lower Rio Grande Valley; very rare but nearly annual, in winter in Ariz. and s. Calif. North of the border region and Gulf Coast there are a few records of lingering birds in December from Virginia north to N.S., Ont., and Nfld., a January record from Arkansas, and a bird surviving to early February at a feeder in Illinois.

SPRING MIGRATION begins quite early and is prolonged; it occurs on a broad front along the Gulf of Mexico and through Fla. In general this species is much more numerous in spring along the Atlantic Coast than farther west; it is an uncommon migrant through much of the Midwest. Occasional small waves of spring arrivals have been noted as early as mid-February, but typical arrivals are at the end of February and in early March. Typically arrives in late March from most of the Carolinas west through Ark., and in early April in Mo., and arrivals in Okla., s. Mo., Tenn., s. Ky., and coastal Va. Arrivals in the Great Lakes region are usually in late April or early May, but very early spring "overshoots" have been noted (18 March in Wisc.). Birds arrive on the northwesternmost breeding grounds around mid-May. On the northern Atlantic Coast, arrivals are from late April to early May; peak migration movements in the Cape May area are during the first half of May. Late spring migrants are noted through late May over much of the East and into early June in the Great Lakes region.

FALL MIGRATION is similarly prolonged and is strongly biased toward the Atlantic Coast. The earliest birds may be noted away

NORTHERN PARULA
Parula americana

from breeding areas in the South in late June or early July. Fall migrants are found away from breeding areas in the Midwest during the latter half of August; migrants are found uncommonly there through the end of September and occasionally into October. The peak movement on the Atlantic Coast, where the species is common, is from mid-September to early October. Fall migrants pass through Fla. in numbers through mid-October, with a few to the end of the month and even into early November. Straggling migrants are noted north of regular wintering localities well into November, and occasionally later (as noted under Winter above).

Frequent **VAGRANT** to western North America, with a majority of records for spring. Regular on the Great Plains, in the Southwest, and especially in California (855 records; about two-thirds in spring, peaking in late May). Casual in Alta. and B.C., Great Basin and in the northwestern states; (unrecorded in Idaho). One mid-June record for Churchill, Man. One late-September sight record for Middleton Is., Alaska. Casual in Greenland, Iceland, United Kingdom (about 15 records, making it the third most numerous American warbler there), and France; all of these records are for September through November.

STATUS AND CONSERVATION

Populations overall appear to have been fairly stable, and some increases have been reported in the boreal and northeastern portions of the range. Local declines or extirpations in the southern Great Lakes states and Atlantic Coast (s. New England south to New Jersey) in the early 1900s may be attributable to loss of required *Usnea* lichen because of air pollution; acid precipitation may pose a more current threat to this habitat component. Cowbird parasitism is relatively infrequent in this warbler.

SUBSPECIES

No subspecies are recognized by the American Ornithologists' Union. However, subspecies delineated by some authors reflect slight variation found among the western, northeastern, and southeastern parts of the species' range. In this scheme, nominate *americana* occupies the wet wooded habitats of the southeastern states, west to the Alabama-Mississippi border and north to Virginia and Maryland. It is said to be intermediate in size and shows relatively poorly developed chestnut and black breastbands. The race *pusilla*, weakly differentiated from *americana*, occupies the northeastern portions of the range, from the upper Ohio River Valley, Appalachians (from e. Tennessee), and coastal New Jersey north to the northern limits of the species' eastern range. It is marginally the longest-winged subspecies, and has better developed breast-bands than *americana*. The western part of the species' range, from the northwestern Great Lakes region south to s.-cen. Texas and sw. Alabama, is occupied by the subspecies *ludoviciana* (given the name *ramalinae* in older literature); it is said to average slightly smaller than the other subspecies but is intermediate in breast-band characters. None of these described differences are noticeable in the field, and there is considerable variation even within populations in the strength of the black and chestnut breast-bands of male Northern Parulas. No genetic differences have been detected between eastern and western populations.

Songs of birds from the described range of *ludoviciana* are clearly distinguishable from those of eastern *pusilla/americana* (see under Voice). Recent authors recommend recognition of *ludoviciana*, but merge *pusilla* into the nominate subspecies. *P. a. ludoviciana* may winter primarily in Mexico and Central America, with *americana/pusilla* wintering in the West Indies, but winter ranges of the forms are not well understood.

TAXONOMIC RELATIONSHIPS

This species is closely related to a complex of tropical populations, collectively called the Tropical Parula, which includes several island-endemic forms. Some workers have suggested that Northern and Tropical parulas are conspecific; a combined species has been known as the Parula Warbler. Relationships of the genus *Parula* lie with *Dendroica* and *Vermivora*, but the exact phylogenetic relationships of these genera, and even their validity, are uncertain. *Parula* was formerly known as *Compsothlypis*. The Northern Parula has hybridized with the Yellow-throated Warbler (with hybrids known as "Sutton's Warbler"; see under Yellow-throated), American Redstart, and Yellow-rumped Warbler.

PLUMAGES AND MOLTS

SPRING ADULT MALE: Head, hindneck, uppermost back, rump, and uppertail coverts deep blue-gray. Triangular patch in the center of the back yellow-green, tinged slightly reddish in some individuals. Lores slaty black; small but conspicuous white arc under the eye, with a slightly smaller arc above the eye. Chin and upper throat bright yellow; this region is somewhat constricted by the blue-gray of the sides of the head, which extends down through the malar region. Chest pattern quite variable. A variable band of slaty blackish extends across the lower throat, this color merging into the blue-gray of the sides of the lower throat; this blackish band may be nearly absent, or consist of a few scattered feathers, or be complete and of variable width. Below and often mixed with the blackish band is a band of chestnut, which is similarly variable in extent. It is wider than the blackish band in most individuals, and at least a trace is present in all individuals. A few chestnut feather tips are often found on the yellow throat as well. The remainder of the breast is bright yellow, with some yellow often mixed with the chestnut chest band. There is a trace of pale chestnut on the sides of the lower breast in many individuals. The remainder of the underparts is whitish, with a gray wash on the flanks. The median and greater wing coverts are broadly tipped with white, forming two thick and conspicuous wing bars. Otherwise the wing coverts and flight feathers are slaty, edged with light blue. The rectrices are slaty, edged blue, with white spots on the inner webs of usually the outer three pairs. **FIRST SPRING MALE:**

Similar to spring adult male, but flight feathers slightly duller; edges to flight feathers, especially the tertials and secondaries, duller and more greenish. Rectrices slightly more tapered and worn. On average, first spring males may show less extensive bands of blackish and chestnut on the chest, but this feature is quite variable. The blue-gray of the upperparts averages slightly duller, sometimes tinged slightly greenish. **SPRING ADULT FEMALE:** Head and upperparts blue-gray, but duller than in spring males and slightly tinged with greenish. Triangular green patch on back, as in males, but somewhat less defined. Lores grayish, with a hint of a pale supraloral streak. Chin, throat, and breast yellow, lacking the distinct blackish and chestnut chest bands of males (but usually washed with tawny across the center of the chest, and sometimes with an indistinct chestnut band). As in males, the yellow of the lower throat is constricted by encroaching gray from the sides of the neck. Yellow of the breast merges into the dull whitish remaining underparts; sides and flanks washed with gray-buff. Wings and tail as in spring adult male, but edgings slightly duller and white spots in tail average less extensive. **FIRST SPRING FEMALE:** Very similar to spring adult female, but averages slightly duller and more extensively washed greenish above. Flight feathers and rectrices duller and more worn. **FALL ADULT MALE:** Similar to spring adult male, but blue-gray of crown, hindneck, rump, and uppertail coverts with light green feather tips, and chest bands somewhat veiled with yellow feather tips. White eye-arcs more extensive, lores paler. **FIRST FALL MALE:** Resembles fall adult male, but more extensive green veiling to the blue-gray coloration above and with chest bands even less evident. Whitish or pale yellowish supraloral streak. Secondaries are edged greenish (bluish in adult male). **FALL ADULT FEMALE:** Not safely distinguishable in the field from duller first fall males, although upperparts generally more extensively washed

Northern Parula.
Male in Florida in
May. (Photo: Herbert
Clarke)

Northern Parula. First fall in New York in October. (Photo: Arthur Morris/Birds as Art)

with greenish, and edges of tertials and secondaries not quite as greenish (more gray-green). In the hand, the rectrices are less pointed than in first fall birds. **FIRST FALL FEMALE:** Resembles fall adult female, but upperparts even more strongly tinged greenish, with the green back patch the least sharply defined of any plumage. Throat and breast yellow, completely lacking dark chest bands. **JUVENILE:** Upperparts grayish, with a wash of olive green on the back. Thin grayish white supercilium and dark gray eye line. Underparts lack yellow, being grayish on the breast and whitish on the belly. Remiges and rectrices show blue-green edging; there are two thin but conspicuous white wing bars. Most young birds out of the nest show at least some yellow of first-basic plumage coming in on the chin and throat. **BARE PARTS:** Bill is blackish on the upper mandible and bright fleshy yellow or yellow on the cutting edge and the lower mandible, imparting a distinctive bicolored appearance. Eyes are dark brown. Legs and feet are brown, paler and yellower on the toes.

Adults undergo a complete prebasic molt on the breeding grounds in July and August; this molt is partial in hatching-year birds, not involving the flight feathers. A limited prealternate molt occurs from February to April.

 REFERENCES

GENERAL: Moldenhauer 1992.
ECOLOGY, BEHAVIOR, VOCALIZATIONS, AND CONSERVATION: Moldenhauer 1992, Morse 1967a, 1968, 1971, 1977, Regelski and Moldenhauer 1996.
SYSTEMATICS: Burleigh 1944b (American Redstart × Northern Parula), Chapman 1925, Graves 1993, Parkes 1951, Paynter 1957 (considers Northern and Tropical parulas conspecific).

Parula pitiayumi

4.25 in. (11 cm). This very close relative of the Northern Parula is also known as the Olive-backed Warbler, and the northeastern-most subspecies that occurs in Texas is sometimes called the "Sennett's Warbler." This is one of the most widespread Neotropical warblers; its breeding range extends from the U.S.-Mexico border region farther south into South America than that of any other warbler. It is scarce and local in our area, although it was more numerous in the early 1900s. Here it is limited mainly to bromeliad-draped live oak woodlands in southernmost Texas. In all plumages it is very similar to the Northern Parula, best distinguished by the lack of a split eye-ring and the more extensive yellow on the underparts, particularly on the sides of the throat. Like the Northern Parula, it is tiny and short-tailed, shows a green patch on the back, and has a bill that is blackish above and yellowish below.

 DESCRIPTION

Generally deep blue-gray to gray above, with a triangular yellow-green patch on the back. Underparts mostly bright yellow, with a variable tawny orange wash on the lower throat, breast, and flanks; lower belly and undertail coverts whitish. Two wide white wing bars on blue-gray wings; tail with white spots on inner webs of outer 2–3 pairs of rectrices. Normally there are no white markings around the eye in any plumage. Moderate sexual dimorphism; males are a deeper, bluer color above, show a black mask, and have a wash of tawny orange on the breast; little seasonal change in appearance. Structurally a small, fairly short-tailed warbler with a sharp beak. Some subspecies, especially certain island subspecies outside of our region, are somewhat larger and have relatively longer tails.

 SIMILAR SPECIES

Very similar to the **NORTHERN PARULA**, but nearly all our birds (of the northernmost subspecies *nigrilora* and *pulchra*) are readily told by the lack of prominent white markings around the eye (Northern Parulas show an obvious split white eye-ring in all plumages). Some have limited arcs of white above and below the eye; these should be told from Northerns by the remaining characters. The yellow of the underparts is more extensive, including the lower breast, uppermost belly, and a wash on the flanks. Most importantly, a rather straight border divides the yellow of the throat from the gray or deep blue-gray of the sides of the face; this gray does not extend downward to constrict the yellow of the lower throat. The lower throat and breast may be strongly washed with tawny orange, but Tropicals always lack the well-defined dark chest bands of male Northerns. In males, the black of the face extends into the auricular region, giving a masked effect.

The subspecies *graysoni* of Socorro Is., off w. Mexico, has been reported from the Cape region of Baja California, where the Northern Parula is a potential vagrant. It resembles a dull female Northern and has the yellow of the throat somewhat constricted by gray, but it is larger and longer tailed, has more extensive yellow on the underparts and thinner and duller wing bars, and lacks white around the eye.

CRESCENT-CHESTED WARBLER is easily told by strong white supercilium and lack of wing bars.

♪ VOICE

The songs and calls of Texas birds (*nigrilora*) closely resemble those of the Northern Parula. Songs vary through the species' range. The typical **SONG** is a buzzy trill that winds upward in pitch and ends with a separate, abrupt, buzzy note. The ending note is buzzier than that of eastern Northern Parula songs, but only slightly different from that of the western (*ludoviciana*) song type of Northern. Alternate song types begin with two or three separate short buzzes, then a quicker rising buzzy trill, and a final buzzy note. Songs vary through the species' range. Western Mexican birds (*pulchra*) sing a somewhat more varied, higher and thinner song that may end with an upslurred note. South American races have many nonbuzzy songs. **CALL NOTE** is a thin slurred chip very similar to that of the Northern Parula.

🦅 BEHAVIOR

Habits generally resemble those of the Northern Parula. Wings often slightly drooped, with tail angled slightly upward. An active and restless warbler, often gleaning insects from the tips of twigs and branches; hover-gleans insects from the undersides of leaves. During the winter in south Texas often associates with small flocks of passerines, including other warblers, Blue-gray Gnatcatcher (*Polioptila caerulea*), and Black-crested Titmouse (*Parus bicolor* complex). Feeds mainly on insects, but with more vegetable matter recorded in the diets of some of the more southerly subspecies.

The **NEST** is built into a clump of *Tillandsia* bromeliads (mainly

T. baileyi in live oaks of coastal plain and Spanish moss, *T. usneoides* along the Rio Grande floodplain); the inconspicuous opening to the ball-shaped nest is on the side. Nests are placed at heights of about 10–40 ft.

HABITAT

BREEDS in our area mostly in lush live oak woodlands interspersed with open grassland; the presence of *Tillandsia* bromeliads for nest construction and placement is an important habitat component. Breeding birds in the lower Rio Grande Valley, where now largely extirpated, occurred in wooded resacas, river bottom thickets, and mesquites where Spanish moss or other bromeliads were available. Through most of its Neotropical range it occurs in upper tropical and subtropical habitats in foothills and lower montane areas.

WINTER habitats are slightly more variable; at present most birds in resaca and river bottom habitats in the lower Rio Grande Valley are found in winter; at this season they are often found in residential areas where large native trees survive development.

DISTRIBUTION

RESIDENT widely through the Neotropics from Tamaulipas and s. Sonora south through the lowlands and foothills of Mexico (but not the Yucatán peninsula), and locally through Central America to Panama. Also breeds in South America south to Peru, Bolivia, and n. Argentina.

BREEDS in our area in southernmost Texas, primarily in live oak thickets on the King Ranch (north to Kingsville) and very rarely in woodlands of the lower Rio Grande Valley. Formerly much more numerous in the Rio Grande Valley, with the major declines occurring shortly after 1950. Primarily resident, but there is some dispersal in **WINTER,** at which season it is somewhat more widespread. There is perhaps limited withdrawal toward the south at this season from King Ranch oak thickets. Very rare or casual in fall and winter north to Corpus Christi (once in early summer at Aransas), Freeport, the vicinity of Houston, and s. La. (five records). Casual in spring in the s.-cen. Texas hill country.

VAGRANT (30 April to 1 May 1994, and 26–27 April 1996) to Rio Grande Village, Big Bend National Park, Texas. One exceptional photographic record of a male (and, briefly, a female) in Madera Canyon, se. Ariz., 14 July to 13 September 1984; this record probably pertains to *pulchra*.

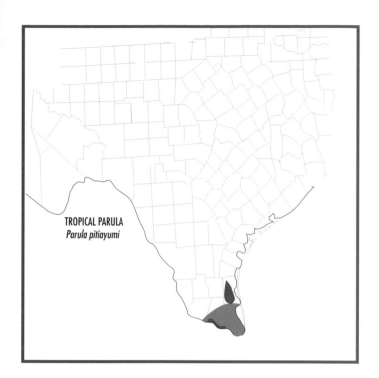

TROPICAL PARULA
Parula pitiayumi

 ## Status and Conservation

Populations in south Texas declined precipitously after a major freeze in the early 1950s and resultant changes in agricultural practices later that decade; before this time it was considered fairly common. Population levels remain low and continue to be threatened by pesticides, destruction of woodlands of *Tillandsia*-laden trees, and perhaps the increasing population of Bronzed Cowbirds. U.S. populations of *nigrilora* are candidates for federal threatened or endangered species listing. This species is still widespread and common in most of its Neotropical range.

Subspecies

There is pronounced geographical variation through the extensive range of this species, with some 14 subspecies described. It is likely that two subspecies occur in our area. The breeding race in south Texas is *nigrilora*; the one documented record for s. Arizona probably pertains to the subspecies *pulchra*. The plumage descriptions below pertain to *nigrilora*, which breeds south through eastern Mexico to n. Oaxaca.

P. p. pulchra differs from *nigrilora* in being slightly larger and longer tailed and showing more white on the greater wing coverts, with only a narrow dark region between the white tips to the median and greater coverts; males have a more extensive cinnamon or tawny wash on the flanks. This subspecies breeds from e.-cen. Sonora south through western Mexico to sw. Oaxaca; it is almost certainly the race that has occurred in s. Arizona.

The subspecies *graysoni* of Socorro Is., off w. Mexico, is the dullest and palest form, being grayish above and pale yellow below, fading to whitish on the lower belly. It lacks black on the face, lacks tawny across the breast and flanks, and has greatly reduced white in the tail. The white wing bars are thin and poorly defined. The gray of the sides of the neck is more extensive in *graysoni* than in other races of Tropical Parula, somewhat constricting the yellow of the lower throat in a Northern Parula-like pattern. Specimens of *graysoni* (not located by us) have reportedly been taken in the Cape region of the Baja California peninsula, about 300 miles north of Socorro. Another slightly brighter island subspecies, *insularis,* is resident on the Tres Marias Is. off Nayarit, Mexico. Unlike *graysoni*, male *insularis* show black in the lores and some tawny orange on the breast and flanks; there is no constriction of the yellow of the lower throat by gray. Both of these island subspecies are longer-tailed than the mainland forms. Both *insularis* and *graysoni* may well prove specifically distinct from Tropical Parula.

The six South American subspecies, including nominate *pitiayumi,* are characterized by their brilliant deep blue upperparts, extensive bright yellow underparts through the belly, and a strong wash of tawny orange across the throat and breast. Nominate *pitiayumi* nests as far south as n. Argentina. Central American subspecies (such as *speciosa*) resemble South American birds but virtually lack white wing bars. *P. p. inornata* of Chiapas and Guatemala resembles *nigrilora* but is paler and has the white of the wing coverts lacking or virtually lacking.

TAXONOMIC RELATIONSHIPS

The Tropical Parula is closely related to the Northern Parula, and is considered conspecific by some authors. The near sympatry of these species in southern Texas and the occasional summering and nesting of the Northern Parula southwest of its normal range suggest the possibility of occasional hybridization. At least one specimen (ANSP 41694) shows some intermediate characteristics, but may be an exceptionally dull Tropical Parula. The Mexican subspecies *insularis* of the Tres Marias Is. and *graysoni* of Socorro Is. might both be best considered distinct species; the relationships of *graysoni* may, in fact, prove to lie most closely with the Northern Parula. See also comments under Northern Parula on relationships of the genus *Parula*.

PLUMAGES AND MOLTS

SPRING ADULT MALE: Crown, hindneck, uppermost back, rump, and uppertail coverts are deep blue-gray. Sharply defined triangular patch in the center of the back is bright yellow-green. Lores, anterior portion of the auricular region, and a narrow strip across the forehead are black; remainder of auriculars dark slaty. Chin and throat bright, deep yellow. Breast and sides yellow, strongly washed with tawny orange; some clear yellow extends below this tawny orange wash to the center of the belly. Flanks tinged with tawny; lower belly and undertail coverts white. Flight feathers slaty, strongly edged with blue-gray. Outer median and greater wing coverts broadly edged with white, forming two thick but short white wing bars. Rectrices dark gray, with the outer webs edged with blue-gray; large subterminal white spot on the inner web of the outer rectrix, and progressively smaller white spots on the next two pairs of rectrices. **FIRST SPRING MALE:** Very similar to spring adult male, but slightly less blue above and with slightly duller and more worn flight feathers and rectrices. **SPRING ADULT FEMALE:** Resembles spring adult male, but upperparts are grayer, less blue, and may be very slightly washed with green. The lores are dull slaty gray, and the anterior auricular area is blue-gray rather than black. The

Tropical Parula.
Adult male nigrilora
in Texas in April.
(Photo: Brian E.
Small)

breast is yellow with only a slight hint of a tawny wash. **FIRST SPRING FEMALE:** Very similar to spring adult female but averaging slightly duller. Flight feathers and rectrices slightly duller and more worn. **FALL ADULT MALE:** Closely resembles spring adult male, but fresher plumage shows a very slight wash of olive green on the head and rump; tawny orange of the breast slightly veiled with yellow feather tips. **FIRST FALL MALE:** Resembles fall adult male, but slightly duller and more washed with green on the upperparts. Not readily distinguished from fall females, but grays of the upperparts average slightly bluer, and the lores and region under the eye are often darker slaty black. Flight feathers are duller and browner than in adult. **FALL ADULT FEMALE:** Closely resembles spring adult female, but upperparts more strongly tinged with olive green. **FIRST FALL FEMALE:** Probably not distinguishable from duller first fall males and duller fall adult females. Gray of upperparts strongly washed with green, especially on the crown and rump. Lores slaty, but auricular region dull grayish. Underparts yellow without any trace of tawny on the breast or flanks. Flight feathers duller and browner than in adults, edged dull gray-green. **JUVENILE:** Grayish olive above; dull whitish below with some dull olive-yellow on the chin and throat. Light brownish wing bars. **BARE PARTS:** Bill blackish or dark brown on the upper mandible, yellow or yellow-pink on the cutting edge and lower mandible. Eyes dark brown. Legs and feet brownish.

The northerly subspecies undergo a prebasic molt on the breeding grounds in July and August (complete in adults, but not involving the flight feathers in hatching-year birds). A partial prealternate molt occurs between February and April. Molt schedules undoubtedly differ in equatorial forms outside of our area.

 REFERENCES

GENERAL: Oberholser 1974.
DISTRIBUTION: Lamb 1925.
SYSTEMATICS: Brewster 1889, Chapman 1925, Phillips 1962.

YELLOW WARBLER PLS. 8, 9

Dendroica petechia

4.75 in. (12 cm). This familiar and abundant bird of broadleaf woodlands and thickets has the most widespread breeding range of any of the wood-warblers, and it shows the strongest geographical variation. The 43 subspecies fit into three main groups: the highly migratory "Northern Yellow Warbler" (*aestiva*) group of continental North America, the "Golden Warbler" (*petechia*) group of the Caribbean (including extreme s. Florida), and the

"Mangrove Warbler" (*erithachorides*) group along the coasts of Mexico, Middle America, n. South America, Cocos Is., and the Galápagos Is. The three groups were formerly treated as separate species, and there is still debate over whether one, two, or three species are involved. The yellow coloration is distinctive in all individuals of the widespread subspecies of eastern North America; adult males of all subspecies show distinct but variable chestnut ventral streaking. Immatures of the western and northern continental subspecies and of the Golden and Mangrove groups are usually much less yellow and thus more difficult to recognize, but on all individuals note the "blank" face on which the dark eye stands out prominently, the yellow or yellowish white edges to the wing feathers, and the long undertail coverts that nearly reach the tip of the short tail. This is our only *Dendroica* with yellow tail spots. Yellow Warblers habitually bob their tails and are usually quite vocal. These warblers have been the subject of numerous studies relating to ecology, behavior, vocalizations, and cowbird parasitism. Strong declines have been noted in the southwestern U.S. where the species is limited to narrow riparian corridors.

DESCRIPTION

Generally green to yellow-green above and yellow below, with males showing variable chestnut on the underparts (as streaks) and on the crown (Golden group) or entire head (Mangrove group). All sex and age classes show yellow spots on the inner webs of the rectrices (though these are nearly whitish in worn females of some subspecies), and pale edges to the wing coverts and flight feathers. The face has little pattern, showing only an indistinct pale eye-ring. There is only minor seasonal variation in plumage. Most adults are easily sexed, especially when comparing birds of known subspecies. Age variation can be substantial, with immature females of some populations being rather yellow and others being dull olive-brown to grayish above and buffy yellow to whitish below.

This is a fairly large and rather compact warbler, with a moderately short tail and long undertail coverts. Primary extension is longer in the Northern group than in the Golden and Mangrove groups, and generally increases with higher latitude within the Northern group.

In the descriptions below the Northern group is represented by the widespread eastern North American subspecies *aestiva*, the Golden group by the subspecies *gundlachi* of Cuba and s. Florida, and the Mangrove group by the subspecies *castaneiceps* of s. Baja California. Additional variation is discussed under Subspecies below.

Distinctive with its compact shape, rather short tail with long undertail coverts, yellow tail spots, and yellow or pale yellowish white edges and tips to the wing coverts and flight feathers. Males are easily told by the chestnut streaking on the breast, although the extent of this streaking varies geographically. Only female and immature male **AMERICAN REDSTARTS** share the yellow spots in the rectrices; in redstarts the yellow forms patches at the base of the rectrices, whereas in "Yellow Warbler" the yellow forms long spots on the inner webs of the outer five rectrices. The lack of any facial markings other than a complete but indistinct yellow eye-ring imparts a "beady-eyed" look that eliminates most other extensively yellow warblers. **ORANGE-CROWNED WARBLER** (especially brightest *lutescens*) might be mistaken for Yellow, but on Orange-crowned, note stronger face pattern formed by dark eye line, pale eye-arcs, and hint of pale supercilium, the uniformly olive wings, and the olive-gray underside of tail that extends well beyond the undertail coverts. **HOODED** and **WILSON'S WARBLERS** are longer tailed, lack the pale edges to the wing coverts and remiges, and lack yellow in the tail (Hooded has white tail spots); Wilson's appears dark-capped, and the yellow face of Hooded contrasts with the olive rear crown and nape. Some females of the southwestern subspecies *sonorana* are very pale, and largely whitish below; immature **LUCY'S WARBLERS** may be superficially similar but are much smaller and have a buffy or rufous rump patch and a fine, sharp-pointed bill.

Male "Mangrove" Warblers are highly distinctive with their mostly or entirely chestnut heads. Female "Mangrove Warblers" and, particularly, "Golden Warblers" may be extensively gray on the upperparts (especially the head and hindneck) and whitish on the underparts; compare these to immature female **CHESTNUT-SIDED WARBLERS** (which differ in having strong wing bars, much white in the tail, and much greener upperparts) and to spring **TENNESSEE WARBLERS** (which are smaller, show a strong eye line and supercilium, and lack yellow in the tail). Distinctions between the Mangrove, Golden, and Northern groups of Yellow Warblers are discussed under Subspecies.

BEHAVIOR

Yellow Warblers frequently pump their tails in an up-and-down motion, although the motion is not as exaggerated as in Prairie and Palm warblers. They are often tame and confiding, even on the breeding grounds. They respond vigorously and vocally to pishing. Most foraging is by gleaning, though they sometimes engage in bouts of sallying and hover-gleaning. They often forage low (e.g., within willow clumps), but also range high into cotton-woods, alders, and other tall trees; much of their foraging is concentrated on open, outer portions of the foliage. Food consists almost entirely of insects (particularly larvae) and spiders. Singing birds may perch high in tall deciduous trees. Mangrove and Golden warblers forage along mangrove stems, often just above the water's surface; sometimes they forage on the mud at the base of the mangroves and even in intertidal zones of nearby shores. Foraging usually involves deliberate gleaning movements; sallying and hovering is less frequent than in Northern birds. Males sing from the tops of mangroves.

These warblers are not especially gregarious, particularly in winter when individuals maintain foraging territories; loose concentrations may be noted in migration. Resident Mangrove Warblers defend territories from each other, but not from migrants of the Northern *aestiva* group.

The **NEST** is a deep cup placed on an upright fork in a small deciduous tree or shrub, usually from 3 ft. to 5 or 6 ft. off the ground, but rarely as high as 50 ft. The nest is neat and compact, built of grasses, plant fibers, plant down, and strips of bark. The outside is covered with plant down and fine fibers, giving most nests a pale, cottonlike appearance. The inside of the nest cup is also lined with fine fibers, down, and feathers. Nests of far northern populations are larger and better insulated than those farther south. Mangrove and Golden warblers build within the foliage of mangroves, placing the cup nest in a fork about 2 to 12 ft. off the water. Clutch size varies geographically, being lowest in tropical Mangrove and Golden populations and largest in the northernmost populations of the *aestiva* group. North American populations regularly raise two broods.

Northern Yellow Warblers are frequent and well-studied Brown-headed Cowbird hosts. Unlike most other wood-warblers, Yellow Warblers have had a long association with Brown-headed Cowbirds because of the warbler's wide breeding range across the Great Plains. Many Yellow Warblers recognize cowbird eggs and either abandon the nest or "bury" the eggs (often along with one or more warbler eggs) with another nest layer; nests with up to six tiers have been recorded. Cowbird parasitism rates of 30–40 percent have been recorded in some regions, and locally they may range much higher. One study showed that cowbird parasitism rates are quite low when Yellow Warblers nest in swamps that host nesting colonies of Red-winged Blackbirds (*Agelaius phoeniceus*). "Golden" Warblers are heavily parasitized by Shiny Cowbirds (*Molothrus bonairensis*) in the West Indies, but cowbird parasitism is not recorded for the s. Florida populations. No cowbird parasitism of Mangrove Warblers has been recorded.

SONG is bright and emphatic, beginning with 2–5 clear *sweet* notes followed by two or more quick notes and, usually, a strongly upslurred or downslurred ending note. There are numerous variations of the song which fall mainly into "accented" and "unaccented" categories, although intermediate song types occur. Typical renditions of accented-ending songs include *sweet sweet sweet, I am so sweet, sweet sweet sweet see-see whew!,* and *tseet tseet tseet sitta-sitta-see.* The accented end of the song may slur up or down, though songs of eastern birds usually are in the former category. Unaccented-ending songs can vary greatly even in an individual's repertoire; these songs are longer and more complex than accented-ending songs and lack the emphatic slurred ending. Unaccented-ending songs may be quite similar to analogous songs of Chestnut-sided and Magnolia warblers and American Redstarts. There is a great deal of literature concerning the song types of this species and the circumstances under which the various songs are used. Female song was documented in one dense population in Manitoba.

The songs of the Mangrove and Golden groups resemble those of the Northern migratory birds, particularly the "unaccented" songs (i.e., they usually lack the emphatic endings of the "accented" songs of Northern birds). Resident "Golden Warblers" in s. Florida may begin singing as early as late January.

CALL NOTE is a downslurred *tchip* which is variable in quality. This chip note is usually rather husky and emphatic, closely resembling the chip of the Chestnut-sided Warbler. Often, however, it is thinner, approaching the soft *tsip* of an American Redstart. This is an extremely vocal warbler; call notes are often delivered rapidly (as in response to pishing). The calls of the Golden and Mangrove groups are similar, but a bit huskier. **FLIGHT NOTE** is a buzzy *zeet,* similar to the flight notes of many eastern North American warblers, but differing from all common species in the West.

 Habitat

Birds of the Northern (*aestiva*) group **BREED** in a great variety of habitats, the common denominator being wet deciduous thickets, especially of willows. Across much of the Midwest and the Northeast they breed in abandoned fields, overgrown pastures, reclaimed strip mines, and reservoir margins that have grown up to young willows and other deciduous trees. In the northern part of the breeding range in eastern North America, they occur in old orchards and disturbed areas within boreal forests (such as regenerating clear-cuts). Both Yellow Warblers and Chestnut-sided Warblers are birds of disturbed and successional habitats in these regions, with the Yellow generally occurring in earlier succession-al stages and in lowlands, and Chestnut-sideds preferring upland habitats. Farther south in the East, breeding habitats are usually near shrub-dominated wetlands such as willow-lined creeks. Across the Great Plains they mostly occupy watercourses lined with willows and cottonwoods, but also occur in towns with tall trees and shrubbery, as well as in shelterbelts. In the Rocky Mountains and Great Basin region, favored habitats are willow-lined streams and other brushy riparian associations; densities are greatest along ungrazed watercourses. They breed in shrublands to over 10,000 ft., including willow thickets, young aspens, wet shrubby meadows, and regenerating burns and avalanche slopes. Along the Pacific Coast they occupy riparian woodlands dominat-ed by willows, which may also include cottonwoods, maples, syca-mores, and alders; also, groves of aspens and alders at higher ele-vations. Locally in the Sierra Nevada of California they breed in montane chaparral and young monocultures of reseeding pines. In the desert Southwest, they breed locally in riparian groves of willows and cottonwoods. In the far northern part of the breeding range, Yellow Warblers occupy dense willow or willow-alder thick-ets.

Northern Yellow Warblers WINTER in a great variety of wooded and scrubby habitats, including gardens, town plazas, second growth, brushy pastures, forest edge, streamside woodlands, and other semi-open habitats. They commonly winter alongside and within mangrove associations, thus widely overlapping birds of the Golden and Mangrove groups in winter. The Yellow Warbler is probably less tied to pristine forest than any other migratory wood-warbler wintering widely in the Neotropics. In *migration*, Northern Yellow Warblers use a great variety of habitats, though they shun the deep interior of woodland. They are more apt to use weedy fields and marshes in fall migration than in spring.

Within the U.S., the Golden (*petechia*) group — represented by the subspecies *gundlachi* — is RESIDENT in black and red mangroves along the shores of small islands, canals, and tidal streams. They are more apt to be found in small to medium-sized mangroves or at the edges of mature stands than in the interior of extensive stands of tall trees. Through the rest of its range, the Golden group is found in coastal mangroves, but also extends into dry scrub, freshwater swamps, riparian scrub, and even humid forest on many islands of the Caribbean.

Birds of the Mangrove (*erithachorides*) group are restricted to coastal mangroves throughout their range, except on the Galápagos and Cocos islands, where the subspecies *aureola* occurs more widely through scrub habitats. One of the two U.S. records is for coastal black mangroves, but the other record is from a patch of scrubby live oaks (also coastal).

 DISTRIBUTION

NORTHERN YELLOW GROUP
BREEDS across North America from Alaska (west to Alaska Peninsula and Unimak Is. and north to the northern limits of shrubby habitats) across Canada (south of the tundra regions) to Nfld. and s. Lab. The breeding range extends south to nw. and ne. (formerly) Baja Calif., the central plateau of Mexico (south to Guanajuato, cen. Michoacan, Mexico, Distrito Federal, n. Guerrero, and Puebla), w., cen. and ne. Texas (formerly), cen. Okla., cen. Ark., n. Ala., n. Ga., extreme nw. S.C., cen. N.C., and Va. It has been extirpated as a breeder from much of its range in the Southwest; there have also been declines and northward range contractions in the Southeast.

WINTERS primarily from s. Baja Calif., coastal w. Mexico (Sinaloa), coastal e. Mexico (Veracruz), and the interior of Mexico (south of the Isthmus) south through Middle America to n. South America (e. and w. bases of the Andes in Colombia, south to cen. Peru; n. Brazil; and the Guianas; recorded in Bolivia and at Manaus, Brazil). At the southern end of its winter range it is common along the northern fringe of the Amazonian forest but rare farther south in Amazonia. A common winter visitor on Trinidad and Tobago but scarce in winter through most of the West Indies; the status of the northern forms in this region is complicated by the presence of resident "Golden Warblers." Birds wintering in the southern Lesser Antilles may actually arrive from the south, in view of the scarcity of Northern birds through the remainder of the West Indies in migration.

North of Mexico, Yellow Warblers are rare but regular in winter in se. Calif. (Salton Sea and lower Colorado R.) and coastal s. Calif. Elsewhere in the West the species is extremely rare in s. Ariz. (away from the lower Colorado R.) and coastal cen. Calif. and casual in nw. Calif. and coastal Ore. There is a single record of an overwintering bird in sw. Utah, and a mid-December record for w. Wash. Northern Yellow Warblers are casual in winter along the Gulf Coast (perhaps regular in coastal and s. Texas) and Fla. Elsewhere in the East, there are scattered winter records north to Ill., Ind., Mich., s. Ont., and W. Va., and along the Atlantic Coast north to Del., s. N.J. (Cape May region, two December records), Mass. (one early December record), N.S., and Nfld. Most of these records are for December, with only the records for Ont. and W. Va. extending later (to January and February, respectively). Also casual in winter on Bermuda.

MIGRATIONS of the "Northern Yellow Warblers" are complex because of the species' extensive breeding range. We discuss migration in eastern and western North America separately. Yellow Warblers may migrate during the daytime to a greater extent than most other warblers, so nocturnal tower kills are not always a good index of the magnitude of migration.

Eastern migrants are mainly *D. p. aestiva*, with *D. p. amnicola* apparently an uncommon migrant in the East (this based on rather meager specimen evidence). Eastern Yellow Warblers are rather early spring migrants and one of the earliest of all species in fall. This timetable applies to *aestiva*; migrations of *amnicola* are considerably later in both spring and fall. The major spring movements of Yellow Warblers in the East are circum-Gulf or across the western Gulf. The southbound movement in fall is on a much broader front. The species is much less common in spring than fall in coastal La., and in peninsular Fla. it is rare to very uncommon in spring but can be abundant in fall.

SPRING MIGRANTS *in the East* arrive in the Deep South and Gulf Coast as early as the last few days of March, but not consistently noted until mid-April. There are some exceptionally early records far to the north, such as a 28 March record and two mid-April records for N.S. Northern Yellow Warblers are casual anywhere in eastern North America before late March; some early to mid-March records for Texas and Fla. could pertain to overwintering birds. Over much of the Midwest and Mid-Atlantic region, spring arrivals are in mid-April; arrivals around the Great Lakes, Niagara region, and New York City region are from late April to early May. In southern Canada and northern New England, typical arrivals are in mid-May. Arrivals of *amnicola* in Nfld. and Lab. are usually in late May, and that subspecies doesn't reach Churchill in n. Man. until early June. Peak movements through the Gulf states are in late April, with an exceptional early concentration of 65 in coastal Ala. on 7 April. In the Midwest and Mid-Atlantic region peak movements are during the first three weeks of May (100 at Cape May, N.J., on 26 April was an unusually early high count). Large movements occur through the northern Midwest and New England into late May. Late spring migrants occur through late May and early June nearly throughout eastern North America. Small concentrations of migrants (likely *amnicola*) have been noted as late as the second week of June on Sable Is., N.S.

FALL MIGRATION *in the East* begins extremely early, with migrants recorded in the Great Lakes region as early as 19 June. Fall arrivals are more typically in the first or (especially) second weeks of July throughout the East, even as far south as Fla. Migrants are numerous by the end of July, and the fall movement peaks in early August in most regions; fall peaks along the Gulf Coast and in Fla. peak from mid-August to early September. Only small numbers continue to pass through in the Midwest, Northeast, and Mid-Atlantic region by the end of August; migrants are rare in most areas away from the Deep South after the first week of September, but a few persist through the month; small numbers are noted along the Gulf Coast into the second week of October. Northerly-breeding *amnicola* departs the breeding grounds late, with small numbers lingering through September and occasionally into early October. It is likely that many or most of the Yellow Warblers passing through eastern North America in September and early October are *amnicola*. Yellow Warblers are casual anywhere in eastern North America (away from the Gulf Coast and Fla.) after mid-October. There are scattered November records over much of the East (records for December or later are noted under Winter).

SPRING MIGRATION *in the West* varies with subspecies. Breeding populations of *sonorana* in the Southwest arrive as early as the second week of March in se. Ariz. and early April in cen. Ariz. *D. p. brewsteri* arrives in coastal southern Calif. by the last few days of March or very early April. Farther north, *brewsteri* arrives on the breeding grounds in mid- to late April (nw. Calif.) or late April (w. Ore. and w. Wash.). Breeding ground arrivals over much of the interior West (mainly *morcomi*) are in early May (Colo., Wyo., Idaho, s.-cen. B.C.) to mid-May (Mont., Alta.). The first arrivals over much of Alaska (mainly *rubiginosa, banksi*) are during the latter half of May. True migrants are rarely noted away from breeding areas in the Southwest before late April. Spring migration peaks in s. Calif. in the first half of May, and around 20 May in coastal n. Calif. and the northern deserts of Calif. Peak migration through the Okanagan Valley of interior s. B.C. is during the third week of May. A few late migrants are regularly noted at migrant traps in the West during the first few days of June, and casually into the second week of June.

FALL MIGRATION *in the West* is later and more extended than that of the East, not normally being evident until the last third of July; migrants are widespread by early August. Fall peaks over much of the West are in late August and early September, but somewhat later (through the month of September) along the Calif. coast. Moderate numbers remain in Calif. into early October, with a few through mid-October. Scarce over most of the interior West after early September. As in the East, the later September and October

YELLOW WARBLER
Dendroica petechia

YELLOW WARBLER
Dendroica petechia

banksi

parkesi

rubiginosa

amnicola

amnicola

brewsteri

aestiva

sonorana

gundlachi

*Subspecies boundaries
based on Browning
(1994).*

migrants probably represent the more northerly subspecies. Recorded in se. Alaska as late as 31 October and 12 November; recorded into November in N.M. and December in interior Ore.

There are numerous November and early December records for coastal Calif., with some birds remaining through the winter (see Distribution).

VAGRANT in fall north to St. Lawrence Is. (Bering Sea), Southampton Is. (Northwest Territories) and Baffin Is. There are two records (summer and fall) for w. Greenland, one fall record for Iceland, and at least three fall records for the United Kingdom.

GOLDEN (*petechia*) GROUP

RESIDENT in southernmost Fla. and through most of the islands of the Caribbean from the Bahamas south through the Greater and Lesser Antilles and along the northern coast of Venezuela and its offshore islands. They are absent from some of the West Indies (Saba, St. Vincent, Grenada, Swan Is., and most of the Grenadines) and from Trinidad and Tobago. Populations also occur in the w. Caribbean on Is. Providencia, Is. Andres, and Cozumel Is. In the U.S., birds of this group are limited to mangroves of extreme s. Fla., throughout the Florida Keys (but not the Dry Tortugas), and the Florida Bay islands north to se. Collier Co. and ne. to Virginia Key. They are more numerous on the small islets of Florida Bay than on the Florida Keys. Most of the locations where they currently occur are accessible only by boat. There are no records of vagrancy within the U.S.

MANGROVE (*erithachorides*) GROUP

RESIDENT from cen. Baja Calif. (San Ignacio and Pond lagoons on the Pacific Coast, about 27° N on the Gulf of California coast), Sonora (Tepopa Bay, north of Kino Bay) south along the Pacific Coast of Mexico and Central America to w. Colombia and nw. Peru (to near Lima); also on the Galápagos Is. and Cocos Is. "Mangrove Warblers" are resident on the Gulf Coast of Mexico from s. Tamaulipas southward (except Cozumel Is., where resident birds belong to the Golden group), and along the entire Caribbean coast of Central America and the northern coast of Colombia (east to the Paraguana Peninsula in nw. Venezuela).

There are two well-documented records of "Mangrove Warblers" in the U.S., both from south coastal Texas. One was in scrubby live oaks north of Rockport on 26 May 1978, and the other was photographed in black mangroves at the mouth of the Rio Grande at Boca Chica, 20 March to 6 April 1990. Possibly correct is a sight record of two birds at Port Isabel, Texas, on 13 July 1992. Texas birds undoubtedly represent the subspecies *oraria* of ne. Mexico. There are two sight records of "Mangrove Warblers" from Isla Socorro in the Revillagigedo chain off western Mexico.

 ## STATUS AND CONSERVATION

Conservation status varies greatly through the species' range. In ideal habitat, populations can be very dense, with up to 60 pairs in a 25-acre (10 hectare) area. Within the Northern group, populations appear to be stable in eastern North America, although there has been some decline in the Southeast and the southern Great Plains; it has been extirpated as a breeder in Texas. In some regions (e.g., Michigan, Pennsylvania, and the Canadian Maritime Provinces) there have been substantial increases. In the West, there have been some declines in the northern Rocky Mountain region and significant and steady declines in the Pacific states. Particularly decimated has been the subspecies *sonorana*, which formerly bred from se. California to w. Texas. This subspecies was common along the Rio Grande in the Big Bend region of Texas as well as along the lower Colorado River, but has been extirpated from these areas since the 1960s (a few possible breeders have appeared along the lower Colorado River in recent years); it has also disappeared from most of its former range in s. New Mexico and is much more localized than formerly in s. Arizona. Declines of populations in n. Mexico seem likely as well. Declines in the West are largely attributable to the loss or modification of lowland riparian habitats through river channelization, overgrazing, and replacement of native riparian growth by salt cedar. Brown-headed Cowbirds have also been implicated in declines of Yellow Warblers in the West, and cowbird control has resulted in local warbler increases (e.g., Kern River, California). Destruction of mangrove habitats has undoubtedly caused some declines in the Golden and Mangrove groups. Concern has been expressed about the vulnerability of the small s. Florida population of "Golden Warblers" (subspecies *gundlachi*) with the recent arrival of breeding Brown-headed and Shiny cowbirds in that region; a recent study, however, found no evidence of brood parasitism of "Golden Warblers."

SUBSPECIES

The Yellow Warbler shows a great deal of geographical variation, with more named subspecies than any other wood-warbler. A recent review recognizes 43 subspecies, 9 in the Northern (*aestiva*) group, 18 in the Golden (*petechia*) group, and 16 in the Mangrove (*erithachorides*) group; many of the subspecies within the latter two groups are island endemics.

Within the northern *aestiva* (or "Yellow Warbler") group, there is variation in the extent of yellow on the crown (males), the darkness of the green in the dorsal plumage, the intensity of the yellow underparts, the extent of the red ventral streaking, overall size, and wing length (including primary projection). The general color trend is toward darker birds in the north and paler birds in the south. Geographical variation in female and, particularly, immature plumages has been largely unstudied but seems to be at least as pronounced as that of adult males. In particular, even the dullest immature females encountered over much of eastern North America (subspecies *aestiva*) are strongly washed with yellow below and on the face and eye-ring; immature females of the boreal and far northwestern subspecies tend to be dark and dull, whereas those from the Southwest are quite pale and dull.

Intergradation is often extensive at the boundaries of subspecies distributions, which are roughly outlined below. All of the subspecies in this group are migratory, and all but the southernmost subspecies, *sonorana* and *dugesi,* are characterized by a relatively long, pointed wingtip (with the ninth primary distinctly longer than the sixth; this is most pronounced in the far northern subspecies). Northern Yellow Warblers are somewhat smaller than the "Golden" and, especially, "Mangrove" warblers; within the Northern group the smallest birds breed in subarctic Alaska and northwest Canada, and the largest are in the Southwest.

The most widespread subspecies in eastern North America is *aestiva*. Even within *aestiva* there are clinal trends in coloration. For example, there is a trend toward darker green upperparts in birds in the northern part of the subspecies' range, versus brighter upperparts in the Southeast (e.g., Georgia) and the southern Great Plains. Adult male *aestiva* show bolder and more extensive red streaking on the underparts than any of the western subspecies; some adult males show an orangish wash to the yellow crown. Female *aestiva* (even immatures) are brighter yellow than females of other subspecies. D. p. *aestiva* breeds north through the Great Lakes region, the southern Canadian Prairie Provinces, New England and s. Nova Scotia; it breeds west to s. Alberta.

To the north of *aestiva*, the similar but darker *amnicola* breeds from most of Quebec, Newfoundland, and s. Labrador west through n. Ontario, cen. Manitoba, cen. and n. Saskatchewan, southernmost District of Mackenzie, n. Alberta, and ne. British Columbia. Male *amnicola* are darker and greener on the upperparts than *aestiva,* and more washed with green on the crown and forehead. To the north of *amnicola*, in n. Manitoba and cen. and w. District of Mackenzie (and north to the northern limit of the species' Canadian range), is the subspecies *parkesi*, which is even darker and greener above, duller yellow below, and has darker chestnut streaks on the underparts; *parkesi* shows the darkest green upperparts of all Northern Yellow Warblers. The subspecies *banksi*, breeding from cen. and w. Yukon west through much of interior and western Alaska (north and west to the limits of the species' range), is paler and more yellowish above than *parkesi* and *amnicola*. All three of these northern subspecies migrate later in spring and fall through eastern North America than does *aestiva*. Details of their wintering range are not known.

From the Alaska Peninsula south and east through coastal Alaska and British Columbia is the subspecies *rubiginosa*, characterized by a dorsal color intermediate between *banksi* and *parkesi*, a crown and forehead the same greenish color as the upperparts, and a slightly longer bill than adjacent subspecies to the northeast. On average, the reddish ventral streaking of *rubiginosa* is narrower than that of *banksi, parkesi, amnicola,* and *aestiva*. North-coastal *rubiginosa* is a later spring and fall migrant through western North America than *brewsteri* and the widespread *morcomi*. Many of the purported specimens of *rubiginosa* from eastern North America probably pertain to far northern *parkesi* instead, although specimens showing the characters of *rubiginosa* exist from Louisiana, Pennsylvania, and elsewhere.

The most widespread western subspecies is *morcomi*, breeding from the Rocky Mountain region west through the Great Basin to eastern California, north through much of interior British Columbia to s. Yukon and south to the Texas Panhandle, n. New Mexico, ne. Arizona, and e.-cen. California. Compared to eastern *aestiva*, adult male *morcomi* are greener above and paler yellow below, with the chestnut streaks on the underparts narrower and more blended than in all the eastern and far northern subspecies. Females are paler above and below than *aestiva*. This subspecies intergrades with *rubiginosa* in sw. British Columbia, and extensively with *sonorana* in s. Utah, n. Arizona, New Mexico, and w. Colorado.

The breeding subspecies of the western portions of the Pacific Coast states from nw. Washington south to nw. Baja California is *brewsteri*; this race is often included with *morcomi* and closely resembles some populations of that subspecies; however, males differ from those of the geographically nearest populations of *morcomi* on the eastern slopes of the Cascade and Sierra Nevada ranges in being more yellow (less green) on the back, brighter yellow on the forehead, rump, and tertial edges, and in having narrower and sparser chestnut streaks below.

Perhaps the most distinctive subspecies in our region is southwestern *sonorana*, breeding from s. Arizona and sw. New Mexico south to n.-cen. Mexico (interior Nayarit, Zacatecas). This subspecies formerly bred west to se. California, north to extreme s.

Nevada, and east to w. Texas. It intergrades extensively with *morcomi*. Males are yellower (less green) on the upperparts and paler yellow on the underparts than any other race in the Northern group. The chestnut streaking below is quite narrow, pale, and sparse (often nearly lacking); the upperparts may be marked with thin dark chestnut shaft streaks. Females are distinctively pale, and immature females (even through their first spring and summer) are grayish above and gray-buff below, with only faint traces of yellow in the plumage.

Outside of our area, the southernmost subspecies of the Northern group is *dugesi*, breeding on the central plateau of Mexico from s. San Luis Potosi and Guanajuato south to Michoacan, Guerrero, and Puebla and wintering in the southern part of that range. It resembles *sonorana* but is slightly longer winged; males are somewhat greener above, with reduced dorsal streaking, and females are paler and grayer above than *sonorana*.

Much remains to be learned of the winter ranges and migration routes and timing of the nine subspecies of "Northern Yellow Warblers." In general the boreal and eastern subspecies winter from e. Mexico south to n. South America; Pacific Coast subspecies winter mainly from w. and s. Mexico south to nw. South America.

The *petechia* ("Golden Warbler") group is primarily Caribbean. Only the Cuban subspecies, *gundlachi*, occurs in our area. All birds of the Golden group are distinguished from Northern (*aestiva*) birds by their larger overall size and shorter primary projection (more rounded wing), with the outermost primary generally shorter than the sixth primary. Males of most subspecies have a well-defined orange to dark chestnut crown, but this is restricted or absent in many individuals of the northernmost subspecies *gundlachi* (described under Plumages) and *flaviceps*. Note that some adult males of the Northern group, particularly D. p. *aestiva*, show a suffusion of orange on the crown; they are best told from "Golden Warblers" by their slightly smaller size and longer primary projection. The range of *gundlachi* in s. Florida is outlined under Distribution; this subspecies is also resident in Cuba and the Isle of Pines. The subspecies *flaviceps*, resident on the Bahama Islands, is closely similar to *gundlachi*, differing in being slightly more yellow (less green) above and below and in having a slightly longer tarsus. Sixteen other subspecies occur through the West Indies, along the n. Venezuela coast, and on islands in the western Caribbean. General trends in these regions include: (1) the chestnut crown becomes darker and greater in extent to the south, with birds of the Greater Antilles (including our *gundlachi*) having the palest crowns; (2) chestnut ventral

Yellow Warbler, Male aestiva *in Ohio in June. (Photo: Ron Austing)*

streaking is more prominent in western Caribbean populations than in the remainder of the range; (3) the upperparts are duller and greener in the northernmost populations; and (4) measurements vary, with more southerly populations being relatively small and long-tailed. Most distinctive is the subspecies *ruficapilla* from Martinique in the Lesser Antilles; males have entirely chestnut hoods (and therefore resemble birds of the Mangrove group), though they are similar to other "Golden Warblers" of the Lesser Antilles in measurements.

In the *erithachorides* ("Mangrove Warbler") group of the Neotropical coasts, the northernmost forms are *castaneiceps* of the southern half of Baja California, *rhizophorae* of the northwestern Mexico mainland coast, and *oraria* of the Gulf Coast of Mexico (the last is presumably the subspecies that has wandered to Texas). All "Mangrove Warblers" are distinguished from Northern (*aestiva*) types by their larger overall size and shorter primary projection (more rounded wings), but the Mangrove and Golden groups are similar to one another in this regard. Except for the subspecies *aureola*, male "Mangrove Warblers" are distinguished from all "Golden Warblers" (except those on Martinique in the Lesser Antilles) by their entirely chestnut heads. "Mangrove Warblers" along the Pacific Coast of Mexico and South America are distinctly smaller billed than any "Golden Warblers." The three northernmost subspecies of "Mangrove Warbler" are quite similar to one another, with males having complete, dark chestnut hoods and narrow chestnut streaking below. The subspecies *oraria* is resident along the coasts of s. Tamaulipas south through Veracruz to Tabasco at the foot of the Yucatán peninsula. In western Mexico, *rhizophorae* is resident from coastal cen. Sonora south to the

Yellow Warbler. Male of one of the north-western subspecies in California in May. (Photo: Larry Sansone)

vicinity of Mazatlan, Sinaloa, where it intergrades with the similar *phillipsi,* which is resident s. to Honduras. On the Baja California peninsula is the subspecies *castaneiceps,* males of which are slightly greener (less yellow) above than *rhizophorae* or *oraria* and show even narrower and sparser chestnut streaking below. South through Central and w. South America, "Mangrove Warblers" show wider chestnut streaking below, and the chestnut hood is paler and less well-defined. In the subspecies *aureola* of Cocos Is. and the Galápagos Is., the chestnut on the head is limited to the crown; these birds superficially resemble birds of the Golden group.

TAXONOMIC RELATIONSHIPS

The relationships of the three subspecies groups of Yellow Warblers continue to be studied; these groups were frequently treated as separate species in the earlier literature. The Golden and Mangrove groups were once considered conspecific, but the Northern birds were treated as a separate species; all of the forms were lumped into a single species in 1942 and have been so treated since. As noted above, patterns of geographic variation are complex, and some characters, such as the amount of chestnut on the head in Neotropical forms, do not vary in a simple geographical pattern. Within *Dendroica,* the Yellow Warbler is perhaps most closely allied to Chestnut-sided Warbler (vocalizations, in particular, are similar in these two species). A possible hybrid between a bird of the Northern *aestiva* group and Black-throated Blue Warbler has been described.

Aestiva Group ("Northern Yellow Warbler")

SPRING ADULT MALE: Forehead and forecrown yellow to yellow-orange, sometimes slightly streaked with chestnut. Rear crown and nape yellow-green. Back yellow-olive, often with thin chestnut shaft streaks; rump and uppertail coverts yellow, tinged with olive. (Boreal and far northwestern subspecies darker green on the upperparts; see Subspecies.) Face and throat unpatterned bright yellow, or slightly tinged with olive on the auriculars; diffuse pure yellow eye-ring setting off the dark eye. Remaining underparts bright yellow, strongly and broadly streaked with chestnut across the breast and on the sides and flanks; undertail coverts pure yellow. (In western subspecies, chestnut streaking of underparts is thinner and sparser; see Subspecies.) Median and greater coverts dusky, broadly edged with yellow, forming two diffuse wing bars. Tertials broadly edged with yellow; secondaries and primaries more narrowly edged with yellow on the outer webs. Rectrices dusky olive on the outer webs (and on the entire central pair); r2 to r6 extensively pale yellow on the inner webs, forming large yellow tail spots. **FIRST SPRING MALE:** Similar to adult male; yellow tail spots slightly less extensive than in adult male. Crown averages a little greener than adult male, and chestnut streaking below may be slightly reduced (but always broader and more distinct than in spring females). First spring birds of both sexes may be reliably aged by retention of worn juvenal outer greater secondary coverts and outer greater primary coverts; their rectrices are also more tapered and worn than those of spring adults, with more limited yellow in the outer rectrix than in adults. **SPRING ADULT FEMALE:** Forehead and forecrown greenish yellow, contrasting slightly or not at all with greenish nape and remaining upperparts. Face,

Yellow Warbler. Male sonorana in Arizona in May. (Photo: Rick and Nora Bowers)

Yellow Warbler. First fall female of one of the western races (probably Northwestern) in California in October. (Photo: Herbert Clarke)

throat, and entire underparts yellow, but duller and more greenish than in spring males; thin, inconspicuous reddish streaks on the sides of the breast (variable; often nearly lacking and always less broad and conspicuous than in spring males). Yellow edgings of wing coverts and flight feathers duller and more greenish than in spring males. Yellow tail spots similar to those of adult males. (Females of boreal subspecies duller and darker; those of western and especially southwestern subspecies paler; see Subspecies.) **FIRST SPRING FEMALE:** Resembles spring adult female, but reddish streaks below are essentially lacking; the crown is even more greenish, not contrasting with the back. May be aged by same criteria as first spring male. **FALL ADULT MALE:** Very similar to spring adult male, but chestnut streaks of underparts somewhat veiled by yellow, so less evident than in spring birds; crown and auriculars slightly washed with green, accentuating the yellow eye-ring. **FIRST FALL MALE:** Crown heavily washed with greenish, only slightly yellower than the remaining upperparts; much less yellow on crown than fall adult male. The yellow of the underparts is paler and greener than in adult males. Some have rather extensive red streaking below, but most have limited and indistinct red streaking, and many lack streaking altogether. Yellow less extensive on the inner web of the outer rectrix than in adult males (tail pattern may overlap with first-year females). **FALL ADULT FEMALE:** Essentially identical to spring adult female but a little duller, more washed with green; the thin reddish streaking of the underparts is largely veiled with yellow. Yellow tail spots extensive, as in adult males. **FIRST FALL FEMALE:** Forehead, crown, and entire upperparts dull, pale olive-yellow, slightly brighter olive-yellow on the rump and uppertail coverts. Face shows an indistinct whitish eye-ring. Underparts rather pale greenish yellow, with no trace of chestnut streaking. Edges of wing coverts and tertials dull, pale yellowish to buffy white. Tail as in first fall male but averaging even less yellow in the outermost rectrix. (This plumage is extremely variable geographically. First fall females of eastern *aestiva* are rather yellow below and greenish above, but upperparts of far northern birds are darker and duller, and those of southwestern birds are grayer and paler; the color of the underparts in these subspecies can vary from pale olive to pale buffy yellow or nearly whitish.) **JUVENILE:** Brownish overall, obscurely streaked with dusky on the back and rump. Underparts light grayish olive to buffy white; two buffy yellow wing bars. Flight feathers as in first fall birds. **BARE PARTS:** Bill of spring adult males black, tinged grayish on the cutting edge and lower mandible; spring females and fall adults have a duller bill with some yellowish on the mandible, and the bills of immatures are more extensively pale. Eyes very dark brown, appearing beady on the "blank" face. Legs and feet pinkish yellow to light olive-brown; soles of feet yellow.

Petechia Group ("Golden Warbler")

ADULT MALE: Forehead and crown olive-yellow, with the crown variably washed with orange in many individuals. (All adult males of more southerly subspecies of "Golden Warblers" show distinct orange or chestnut patches on the crown.) Auriculars and sides of the neck yellowish with a slight olive wash, showing some contrast with the darker crown and the diffuse yellow eye-ring. Remaining upperparts olive-yellow, not contrasting with the crown. Underparts entirely bright yellow, strongly streaked with chestnut on the lower throat, breast, and sides. Wings dusky; wing coverts and tertials broadly edged with yellowish; edges of primaries and secondaries dull yellowish olive. Extensive pale yellow on the inner webs of the outer three pairs of rectrices. No significant seasonal change in appearance, although chestnut breast streaking may be slightly veiled with yellow in fresh basic plumage. **FIRST YEAR MALE:** Variable. Younger birds have an olive-gray forehead and crown and grayish auricu-

"Golden" Yellow Warbler. Immature male flaviceps *on Grand Turk, Bahamas, in June. (Photo: Bruce Hallett)*

lars and nape, with the remaining upperparts olive (blending to olive-yellow on the rump). The throat and inconspicuous eye-ring are whitish and the remaining underparts are pale yellow, with inconspicuous thin reddish streaks on the breast and sides. In many birds, especially later in winter and spring, the head is more strongly washed with yellowish olive, the eye-ring and throat are pale yellowish; these birds resemble adult females but show more extensive and distinct thin reddish streaking below. In the hand, they may be told from adult females by the more tapered and (by spring) more worn rectrices. **ADULT FEMALE:** Forehead, crown, and upperparts uniformly olive. Face olive-yellow, with an inconspicuous yellow eye-ring. Underparts yellow, slightly tinged greenish; some birds show a slight hint of pale reddish streaking on the breast. Wings dusky; coverts and flight feathers with less conspicuous yellowish edges than adult male. Yellow in rectrices more limited than in adult male. **FIRST YEAR FEMALE:** Younger birds in summer and fall are generally gray above, with a variable olive cast to the lower back and rump (and upper back of some birds). Thin whitish eye-ring on a "blank" grayish face. Underparts dull whitish, grayer on the sides and flanks. Wing coverts and tertials edged with dull whitish; primaries and secondaries narrowly edged with olive. Rectrices show limited pale yellowish white on the inner webs of the outer two pairs. Through the winter and early spring, young females acquire some olive on the back and patches of pale yellow on the underparts. **JUVENILE:** Probably similar to juveniles of Mangrove group, below. **BARE PARTS:** Resemble those of Mangrove group, below.

Erithachorides GROUP ("MANGROVE WARBLER")

ADULT MALE: Entire head deep chestnut (slightly paler on throat), contrasting sharply with the green upper back and yellow breast. Upperparts deep yellow-green, with inconspicuous chestnut shaft streaks on the back. Entire underparts bright yellow, very finely streaked with chestnut on the breast and sides. The yellow of the sides of the breast extends up the sides of the neck, forming a partial yellow collar. Wing coverts and flight feathers broadly edged with yellowish olive. Tail dark dusky-olive; extensive yellow spots on the inner webs of the outer four pairs of rectrices do not reach the tip of the tail. There is no significant seasonal change in plumage, apart from the slight veiling of the chestnut ventral streaks by yellow and of the thin dorsal streaks by yellow-olive. **FIRST YEAR MALE:** Adultlike plumage is gradually acquired through the first year. Younger birds resemble adult females but by winter (or earlier?) show solid patches of chestnut on the sides of the face and crown, and may show some inconspicuous thin reddish streaking on the breast. Many immature males may not be safely distinguishable from adult females with maximum chestnut except in the hand by the more tapered rectrices. Some immature males are extensively gray on the nape and upper back and whitish on the breast and may resemble many immature females until

"Mangrove" Yellow Warbler. Adult male oraria on 6 April 1990 at mouth of Rio Grande at Boca Chica, Cameron County, Texas. (Photo: Edward Greaves)

they begin to molt in considerable chestnut on the head. **ADULT FEMALE:** Forehead and crown olive; many individuals show some chestnut feathering on the crown. Remaining upperparts generally olive to olive-yellow, brightest on the rump and uppertail coverts; many birds are strongly washed with gray above, especially on the nape and upper back. Face unmarked olive-yellow, with an indistinct yellowish eye-ring. Face contrasts with the darker olive crown and contrasts slightly with the yellow throat; many birds show a hint of diffuse chestnut streaking on the throat and some dull chestnut in the moustachial region. Remaining underparts yellow with an olive wash on the sides and flanks; some birds are paler and grayer on the breast. Wing coverts and primaries edged with yellowish olive; tertials and primary tips edged whitish. Tail dusky olive with some pale yellow on the inner webs of the outer three pairs of rectrices. **FIRST YEAR FEMALE:** Variable. The brightest birds approach adult females in plumage but lack any hint of chestnut in the crown and throat, are paler yellow below, and are washed with grayish above. Duller birds are sooty grayish on the upperparts, tinged slightly with olive on the back and rump, and grayish white on the underparts, with a hint of pale buffy yellow on the throat and undertail coverts; such birds have dull whitish eye-rings, grayish olive edges to the wing coverts, and grayish white edges to the flight feathers. The tail is grayish olive, with limited yellow-white on the inner edge of the inner webs of the outer two pairs of rectrices. Plumage differences among immature females may be due in part to variation in fledging dates over the presumably prolonged breeding season, with adultlike plumage being attained slowly over the first several months after fledging. However, some authors refer to distinct yellowish and gray color morphs of immature females in some northern races of "Mangrove Warblers." **JUVENILE:** Upperparts dull grayish olive, underparts dull grayish white; wing coverts and flight feathers edged with pale grayish olive. **BARE**

PARTS: Bill of adult male black, tinged grayish on the cutting edge. Bill becomes dusky gray in nonbreeding males. Bills of females and immatures dusky, tinged yellowish on the lower mandible. Eyes dark brown. Legs and feet brownish, tinged yellow on the soles of the feet.

The prebasic molt of Northern birds occurs primarily on the breeding grounds, beginning as early as June; this molt is complete in adults and partial in hatching-year birds. Some individuals may complete flight feather molt on the wintering grounds. A partial prealternate molt of body plumage, sometimes also involving the tertials and greater coverts, takes place from February to April. There is little information on the molt schedules of the Golden and Mangrove groups; the first prebasic molt in at least some populations of "Mangrove Warbler" may begin as early as April or May, probably reflecting an early breeding season.

 REFERENCES

DISTRIBUTION: Duncan and Weber 1985, Parkes 1968.
ECOLOGY, BEHAVIOR, VOCALIZATIONS, AND CONSERVATION: Bankwitz and Thompson 1979, Briskie 1995, Busby and Sealy 1979, Clark and Robertson 1981, DellaSala 1986, Ficken and Ficken 1965 and 1966, Hobson and Sealy 1972, Morse 1966, Spector 1991, Spector et al. 1989, Wiedenfeld 1992.
IDENTIFICATION: Kaufman 1991, Prather and Cruz 1995.
PLUMAGES, MOLTS, AND MORPHOLOGY: Rimmer 1988.
SYSTEMATICS: Aldrich 1942, Browning 1994, Ducharme and Lamontagne 1992, Hellmayr 1935, Klein and Brown 1994, Olson 1980, Parkes 1968, Parkes and Dickerman 1967, Raveling and Warner 1978, Van Rossem 1935, Wiedenfeld 1991.

CHESTNUT-SIDED WARBLER   PL. 10

Dendroica pensylvanica

5 in. (12.7 cm). The distinctively plumaged Chestnut-sided Warbler is somewhat reminiscent of the Yellow Warbler in shape and vocalizations, but it habitually holds its somewhat longer tail partly cocked and wings slightly drooped. Because it is a bird of second growth, scrub, and disturbed woods, it underwent a spectacular increase in range and abundance with the clearing of eastern hardwood forests in the 1800s. The yellowish crown and chestnut markings on the sides and flanks are distinctive in spring adult plumages; the combination of bright lime green upperparts, whitish underparts, and yellowish wing bars are diagnostic for other plumages.

Description

In all plumages the underparts are mostly whitish or very pale gray, with some deep chestnut on the sides and flanks in spring birds, winter adults, and most first-winter males. The wing bars are yellow or tinged yellow in all birds. There is a strong seasonal plumage change, with spring birds showing a yellow or yellow-green crown, a black-and-yellow-streaked back, and some black on the face and fall birds being more uniformly yellow-green or lime green above, with a distinct green cap sharply set off from the face and a clean white eye-ring. A heavy-looking warbler, with a moderately long tail and fairly heavy bill. Aging and sexing not always clear-cut; in fall birds note the extent (or absence) of chestnut on the sides and the back and uppertail covert spotting.

 ## Similar Species

All plumages are quite distinctive and are not likely to be confused with other species. Spring birds, with their yellow crowns and mostly white underparts, might briefly be confused with GOLD-EN-WINGED WARBLERS if not seen well. Fall females could be mistaken for BAY-BREASTED and BLACKPOLL WARBLERS, which are shorter tailed and have duller upperparts and white wing bars, and lack the contrast between the cap and the underparts. Beware of some female YEL-LOW WARBLERS with essentially white or pale gray underparts; Yellows lack clear wing bars and show yellow tail spots and a shorter tail (often wagged, but not held cocked). Posture, eye-ring, and white underparts might recall BLUE-GRAY GNATCATCHER (*Polioptila caerulea*), a species quickly ruled out by its gray upperparts.

 ## Voice

SONG is a series of rich whistled notes, usually with a distinctive drop at the end, a feature that distinguishes it from similar songs of the Yellow Warbler. Several one- or two-syllable notes precede the upslurred notes and final downslurred note of the ending. Songs may be rendered *Very very very pleased-to-meet-you*, or *zee zee zee zee meet-meet-ya*. Alternative song lacks the sharp slur at the end and is more variable in phrasing; some may be indistinguishable from unaccented Yellow Warbler songs. Chestnut-sideds have been known to countersing with nearby territorial Yellow Warblers. Subdued songs are occasionally heard in fall migration. CALL NOTE is a husky slurred *chip*, very similar to some of the lower-pitched chips given by Yellow Warblers. FLIGHT NOTE is a distinctive, very burry, slightly musical *breeet*.

Behavior

The distinctive habit of holding the tail partly cocked, often with wings slightly drooped, is characteristic for this species and is reminiscent of a gnatcatcher; it does not normally bob or wag its tail. Often quite tame, allowing close human approach when feeding and around nest. Most foraging is at mid-levels under the canopy or in undergrowth. Much food obtained by probing or hover-gleaning on undersides of leaves. Winter birds generally solitary, quite territorial.

The **NEST** is usually located a few feet off the ground in a deciduous shrub or small tree, a tangle or berry briar. The nest is rather loosely constructed and relatively easy to locate.

Habitat

For **BREEDING**, occupies second growth over much of its range, most typically deciduous brush and young growth in abandoned farms, orchards, and pasturelands, cut-over forests, roadsides, and clearings; also in streamside thickets and, at higher elevations, mountain laurel thickets. In portions of Appalachian region, found in thickets of young chestnuts (which die before reaching maturity). Generally avoids conifer-dominated habitats and mature deciduous forests, although westernmost populations from Manitoba west to Alberta occur in mature deciduous woodland with an understory of dogwoods and cranberries. Avoids towns and areas of intensive agriculture, and has decreased where such development has replaced or fragmented brushy habitats. Before extensive felling of deciduous forests in the 1800s, this species was probably quite uncommon and local.

WINTER habitat includes disturbed areas within tropical forests, forest borders, second growth, and shaded gardens. **MIGRANTS** are found in a variety of brushy habitats and open woodlands.

Distribution

BREEDS in ne. B.C., e.-cen. Alta., cen. Sask., and s. Man. (except southwest corner) east to cen. Ont., s. Que., and the Canadian Maritimes, and south to se. Sask., n. N.D., the Great Lakes region, N.J. and n. Del., and in the Appalachians to n. Ga. Rather scarce and local along the southern edge of the breeding range, in Iowa, n. Ill., n. Ind., and nw. Ohio. May breed sporadically south to Mo., Ark., and n. Ala. Breeds mainly at 2,500–3,000 ft. in ne. Tenn., se. Ky., w. N.C., w. S.C., and n. Ga. Considerable range adjustments during the 1900s have included the species' near disappearance in some regions (e.g., s. Wis., s. Minn., St. Louis area) and expansion into others (including Long Island). Summers very rarely along the east slope of the Rocky Mtns. in n.-cen. Colo. (two nestings). There are scattered summer occurrences to the south and west of the regular breeding range, or below normal breeding elevations in the Appalachian states.

WINTERS from s. Mexico and Guatemala south through Central America to e. Panama, with the great majority of birds from the Caribbean slope of Honduras and Costa Rica to the Panama Canal Zone area. Casual in winter south to Colombia, Venezuela, and Trinidad. Generally absent from West Indies in winter, but has wintered in Puerto Rico. North of the regular winter range it has been recorded about 10 times in winter in Fla. and once each in coastal Miss., La., and s. Texas. It is casual (almost regular) in winter in s. Calif. and s. Ariz.; one winter record for cen. Calif. There are many additional late fall and early winter records for the southern U.S. that do not pertain to overwintering birds.

CHESTNUT-SIDED WARBLER
Dendroica pensylvanica

SPRING MIGRATION is primarily trans-Gulf, with arrivals on the Gulf Coast in mid-April (a few by early April) and a peak there from late April through the first few days of May; lingering migrants on the Gulf Coast occur as late as mid-May. Arrives in the southern interior states (Ark., Mo., Tenn.) around 20 April, peaking there in the second week of May. Reaches the Great Lakes region and southern New England around the first of May (with exceptional records to mid-April), with peak occurrence about 10–20 May. Generally arrives on northernmost breeding ground by the third week of May. Late migrants away from breeding areas may be seen as late as the first of June.

FALL MIGRATION is somewhat more easterly; much more numerous along s. Atlantic Coast in fall than in spring, and correspondingly scarcer on w. Gulf Coast. The first movement away from breeding areas is usually noted by mid-August, and the species becomes fairly widespread and numerous by late August. A prolonged fall passage lasts through the first three weeks of September, with most birds gone from the northern states and Canada by the end of September or beginning of October (stragglers recorded as late as mid-November in these areas). In the southern states the peak fall passage is in late September and early October; an exceptional tower kill of 115 birds occurred in Tenn. in mid-October.

CASUAL in the western states and B.C. in spring and fall, but regular in Calif., where there are 972 records, about 80 percent from fall (mainly coastal, September and October) and 150 records from spring (mainly in the interior and Farallon Is., from late May to early June). Uncommon in fall and casual in spring in Bermuda, with one winter record there; in Lesser Antilles, recorded on Antigua and Barbados. Recorded in Alaska (sight record from Middleton Is., September), Greenland (three records), and United Kingdom (Shetland, September; Devon, October).

⦚ STATUS AND CONSERVATION

This species clearly underwent a great increase in both range and abundance in the 1800s, following the felling of vast acreages of mature deciduous forest. Local increases also occurred with forest loss from chestnut blight and where open farmland and pastures have regrown to scrub and second growth. Because of its preference for brushy, second-growth, or disturbed habitats, it has declined with regeneration of mature forests in some regions. It does not adapt well to urbanization or habitat fragmentation and has experienced local declines in portions of its range in recent decades. Still a rather common bird over much of its range. A rather frequent cowbird host.

None described.

TAXONOMIC RELATIONSHIPS

No clear close relationships within *Dendroica* but may perhaps be closest to Yellow Warbler, with which it shares close similarities in vocalizations.

PLUMAGES AND MOLTS

SPRING ADULT MALE: Forehead and crown bright yellow, becoming whitish in supraloral area. Lores and malar region black, with black eye line extending around to nape and hindneck, which are black streaked with white. Auriculars and adjacent lower rear orbital ring white. Upper back streaked, with black feather centers and grayish white fringes; center of back and rump yellow-green with black streaks and yellow-green fringes. Uppertail coverts mostly black with clear gray fringes. Upper sides (continuous with black malar region in many birds), lower sides, and flanks deep chestnut (extending back to or just beyond the legs). Underparts otherwise white, unstreaked. Lesser wing coverts black centered with gray fringes; median and greater coverts broadly tipped with pale yellow, forming distinct wing bars. Remiges dull blackish, secondaries and tertials edged yellow-green. Rectrices dull blackish, with extensive white spots on inner webs of outer three pairs. **FIRST SPRING MALE:** Closely resembles spring adult male, but averaging slightly duller, with flight feathers brownish black and more worn. Chestnut on sides averages slightly less exten-

Chestnut-sided Warbler. Adult male in Texas in May. (Photo: Brian E. Small)

sive, usually not extending onto flanks. At anterior end, chestnut usually not connected with black malar area. Yellow of crown slightly duller. **SPRING ADULT FEMALE:** Resembles spring males, but generally duller and with less chestnut on the sides. Forehead and crown greenish yellow, not sharply contrasting with nape and hindneck (which are tinged greenish and streaked with slaty). Malar and loral region and ocular stripe dull black or slaty, with dark areas less well defined and less extensive than in spring males. Auricular region dull whitish. Upperparts much more strongly green than spring males, with moderate black streaking. Chestnut of sides less extensive than in adult male; chestnut often somewhat broken, not extending posteriorly beyond lower wing bar and not extending forward to slaty malar stripe. Black centers of uppertail coverts average smaller than in males. White spots in rectrices average slightly less extensive than in males. **FIRST SPRING FEMALE:** Closely resembles spring adult female, but many individuals considerably plainer, with chestnut on sides very limited or even absent. Slate or dull black of face more restricted, sometimes nearly absent. The primaries and rectrices are browner and more worn than in adult. **FALL ADULT MALE:** Forehead and crown bright yellow-green to lime green, contrasting rather sharply with plain gray face and auriculars. Bold, complete white eye-ring. Upperparts bright lime green, spotted or streaked with black (upperpart streaking averages bolder than other fall age and sex classes). Uppertail coverts with broad black centers, gray fringes. Underparts white with extensive rich chestnut on the sides and flanks; anteriorly the chestnut continues nearly to the malar region. Wing bars tinged pale yellow. **FIRST FALL MALE:** Closely resembles fall adult male, but streaking on upperparts averages finer and less extensive, and chestnut of sides less extensive anteriorly, usually not extending forward of the wing bars; chestnut often so restricted as to be difficult to

Chestnut-sided Warbler. Adult female in Texas in May. (Photo: Brian E. Small)

Chestnut-sided Warbler. First fall (probably male) in California in October. (Photo: Brian E. Small)

discern in the field, and may occasionally be absent. **FALL ADULT FEMALE:** Probably indistinguishable in the field from first fall males, but back more extensively green, with only fine dusky streaks. Chestnut on sides variable in extent: absent in a very few birds, a thin streak on the flank in others, and nearly as extensive as in fall adult male on some birds (but chestnut paler, more broken, less extensive anteriorly). In hand, told from first fall male by blunter rectrix tips. **FIRST FALL FEMALE:** Forehead, crown, and entire upperparts yellow-green to lime green, with faint dusky streaks on back barely evident. Dusky centers on uppertail coverts mostly obscured by green and gray fringes. Underparts silky white, grayer on face and sides. Chestnut absent, but many birds show a yellowish suffusion on the rear flanks and vent. **JUVENILE:** Dull olive-brown above; buffy on chin and throat, otherwise whitish below; buffy wing bars; no distinctive markings. **BARE PARTS:** Bill of spring birds black; may be slightly duller in females. In fall and winter, maxilla dusky blackish, mandible dull brown, paler at base. Eyes dark brown. Legs and feet dull blackish to slaty brown; soles of feet dull yellowish.

Prebasic molt occurs on the breeding grounds; complete in adults, but not involving flight feathers, rectrices in first-year birds. Anomalous individuals of this and some other *Dendroica* species show a bright basic plumage that nearly matches alternate plumage. A partial prealternate molt from February to April includes most of the body feathers.

REFERENCES

GENERAL: Richardson and Brauning 1995.
ECOLOGY, BEHAVIOR, VOCALIZATIONS, AND CONSERVATION: Ficken and Ficken 1965, Greenberg 1984, Kroodsma et al. 1989, Lein 1978, Morse 1966.

Dendroica magnolia

4.75 in. (12 cm). Striking black, yellow, and white spring Magnolia Warblers and the more subdued fall adults and immatures share the unique tail pattern, which in the field gives the impression of a white tail base. All plumages show white markings around the eye and a yellow rump patch. This common breeding species in boreal and Appalachian coniferous and mixed evergreen forests is numerous in migration through the East. Alexander Wilson secured the first specimen from a magnolia tree, hence the rather inappropriate scientific and English names (although Wilson did recommend the more descriptive English name "Black-and-Yellow Warbler.") Another suggested name, "Spruce Warbler" indicates one of the species' preferred breeding habitats.

DESCRIPTION

Like several other *Dendroica* warblers, the Magnolia shows strikingly different basic and alternate plumages. Color pattern ranges from strikingly black, white, and yellow in spring males to more subdued gray, olive, white, and yellow in fall birds. Generally gray above with a black saddle across the back (adult males), black spotting on the back, or plain, yellow-olive back in dullest plumages. Lores and cheek patch black in spring adults; olive-gray to sooty in other plumages. Underparts yellow on the breast and upper belly, with a necklace of streaks across the breast in spring. Wing coverts with white tips or a solid white patch. Distinctive tail pattern in all plumages: a broad white band across the central third of the rectrices, so that tail appears to have a white band at the base from below in the field.

Aging and sexing of some plumage classes can be difficult.

SIMILAR SPECIES

Immature **PRAIRIE WARBLERS** are the main source of confusion, resembling the dullest fall Magnolias. All Magnolias in fall show complete white eye-rings, very different from the yellowish to whitish superciliary and under-eye arc of Prairie. The tail patterns differ, the white central band being diagnostic for Magnolia (as noted above, this is only evident when the tail is viewed from below). Prairies lack the diffuse grayish white band across the upper chest shown by dull Magnolias; the yellow on the underparts is more extensive in Prairie. Prairie lacks the yellowish rump patch of Magnolia. Prairies frequently wag or bob their tails;

Magnolias do not, but may occasionally spread the tail. Magnolias do not give *chip* note of Prairie.

In spring, first alternate female Magnolias have been mistaken for KIRTLAND'S WARBLERS. In these birds the supercilium may be reduced or absent, leaving only an eye-ring similar to that of Kirtland's. Kirtland's is always told from Magnolia by its vigorous tail-bobbing behavior, larger size, and different tail pattern.

Otherwise the Magnolia is quite distinct from other warblers; beware the superficial similarity to other "eye-ringed" species, such as NASHVILLE WARBLER (which always lacks wing bars and white in tail). The eye-ring and breast streaking may also recall CANADA WARBLER (which also lacks white in wings, tail).

 ## VOICE

SONG is short and rather musical, usually consisting of two or three slurred phrases followed by a more emphatic note that is higher in pitch but usually downslurred, such as *wee-o, wee-o, wee-chee* or *weeta weeta wit-chew.* There is a great deal of variation in the songs of this species; males give the "accented-ending" songs described above and a simpler "unaccented-ending" song. Spring migrants may give many variations of these songs. Songs may recall those of Chestnut-sided (but are shorter, with a less emphatic ending) or Hooded (but less rich and emphatic).

The CALL NOTE is unique among our warblers, being a rather nasal, dry chip represented variously as *nieff, schlepp, tlep,* or *tzek.* This call note is frequently heard in fall migration, but less often in spring and on the breeding grounds; it is frequently given on the wintering grounds. Additional calls given at least on the breeding ground include a high, soft *chip* and a high *tit.* FLIGHT NOTE is a high, buzzy *zee.*

 ## BEHAVIOR

Usually feeds at low or medium levels within undergrowth, thickets, and young trees, but often found in treetops as well. Foraging is primarily by gleaning of leaves, with some hover-gleaning and sallying. It is moderately active, often with fidgety movements; occasionally spreads open its white-banded tail, redstart fashion; on the breeding grounds wing and tail spreading is given during courtship and (by males) in territorial encounters. Songs may be given from a high, exposed perch, but more often from within the foliage while foraging. In winter, solitary and territorial, but individuals do join mixed foraging flocks of other species.

NESTS are mostly placed in a conifer (or sometimes deciduous tree) with dense foliage, varying in height from less than 1 ft. to 35 ft. (but usually less than 10 ft.). The nest is well concealed and cradled by small branches, usually close to the trunk. It is a relatively flimsy structure, nearly always lined with fine black rootlets; the male may sometimes participate in nest construction.

HABITAT

BREEDS mainly in moist coniferous forests of spruces (the species has sometimes been nicknamed "Spruce Warbler"), firs, hemlocks, or pines, especially in young trees, second growth, forest edges, openings, and ravines. Maximum densities occur in dense second-growth stands of spruce and other conifers, but this species tolerates a wide range of disturbance (from young regenerating clear-cuts to edges and openings in older undisturbed forests). Generally avoids deep, mature forests, but will occupy such habitats if there is sufficient dense undergrowth. Specifically favored in the North are associations of balsam-fir and spruce, whereas south in the Appalachians eastern hemlock is characteristic dominant tree species. The conifers which form the key component of the breeding habitat are often intermixed with maples, alders, birches, beeches, willows, and other hardwoods. Locally they may occupy steep wooded ravines, tamarack swamps, and even pure hardwood associations. Breeding habitats range down to sea level in Maine and eastern Canada, and to over 4,500 ft. in the Appalachians.

In **MIGRATION**, the Magnolia Warbler is quite generalized in habitat, from conifer and hardwood forests to scrubby habitats and (particularly in fall) even weedy fields.

WINTERS in lowland and foothill second growth, forest borders, woodland clearings, and gardens; also in evergreen forests, tropical deciduous woods, and peripherally in arid tropical scrub.

DISTRIBUTION

BREEDS from Yukon, ne. and cen. (very locally also w.-cen.) B.C., and w.-cen. Dist. of Mack. east through the boreal forests of Canada to s. Lab. (Goose Bay and vicinity), Nfld., and N.S. Breeds south to n.-cen. Minn., n. Wisc. (and in the Baraboo Hills of s. Wisc.), w.-cen. Ind. (very local), n., cen. and sw. Mich., e. Ohio (very local), n. N.J., s. N.Y., and nw. Conn., and south in the Appalachian Mtns. to W. Va., and locally in high mountains of ne. Tenn. and w. N.C. It is especially common in the northeastern part of its range. Possibly breeds in extreme se. Alaska (singing males noted annually in recent years around Hyder).

WINTERS mainly from e. and s. Mexico (including the Yucatán peninsula) and in small numbers in w. Mexico (Nayarit south), south to Honduras, Costa Rica (uncommon), and w. Panama (rare to uncommon). Within this range, most common in s. Mexico, Belize, Guatemala, and Honduras. Casual to e. Panama and n. Colombia, with single sight records for n. Venezuela, Trinidad, and Tobago. Also winters uncommonly in Bermuda (where a rare but regular fall migrant), the Bahamas, and the Greater Antilles; rare in winter in the Virgin Is., and casual in the Lesser Antilles.

Given the relatively northerly winter range, the Magnolia Warbler is surprisingly rare in the U.S. in winter. It is regular only in s. Fla., where rare. It is very rare through December in s. coastal Texas and the lower Rio Grande Valley, but there are few records here of overwintering birds. December records are scattered over much of e. North America (as far north as Mich., Ont., N.Y., and N.S.). There are four winter records for Calif. (including some overwintering) and a single winter record for w. Ariz.

This is a trans-Gulf migrant, with an easterly shift in the fall migration route at which season it is more numerous along the

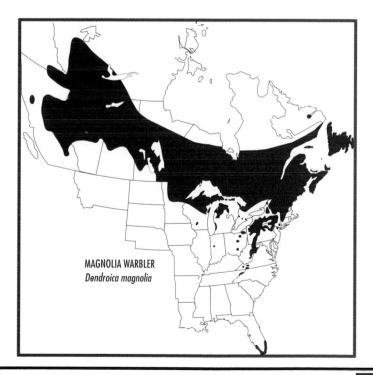

MAGNOLIA WARBLER
Dendroica magnolia

mid- and s. Atlantic coast and in Fla. than in spring but, conversely, scarcer in Texas and the s. Great Plains.

SPRING MIGRATION is late, with the species being casual before mid-April on the Gulf Coast and in Fla. The earliest arrivals on the Gulf Coast are normally around 20–25 April, but there are scattered records for the third week of April as far north as the Great Lakes and New England. Arrivals across most of the South and s. Midwest are in the last few days of April and the first week of May; birds arrive in the Great Lakes region in the second week of May and at the northern end of the breeding range after mid-May. Peak movements on the Gulf Coast are around 5 May, with large numbers recorded through mid-May. Peaks over much of the Midwest and east to s. N.Y. are in the third week of May, with good numbers to 25 May. Peaks in the n. Great Lakes region and much of New England are around 20 May. Spring movements diminish sharply after late May on the Gulf Coast, with a few recorded through early June. Small numbers move through the remainder of e. North America through the end of May and early June and casually to the third week of June.

FALL MIGRATION begins around the middle of August, with exceptional early records in the Great Lakes region as early as late July. The earliest fall records for the Deep South are at the very end of August (with birds arriving more typically around 5–10 September. Through much of the n. U.S. and s. Canada there is a protracted fall migration peak from late August through the first three weeks of September, with small numbers continuing through the first week of October. Peak movements in the Deep South are about 5–15 October, with smaller numbers through the end of the month. Recorded rarely but regularly over the Midwest and Northeast until mid-October, with many records into November (and casually later; see above). There are numerous December records for the Gulf states.

Rare migrant on the w. Great Plains; there are summer records in the Colo. Rockies. Recorded as a **VAGRANT** in all western states, even in Idaho (two records) and Ut. (five records) where coverage is relatively poor; also recorded in Baja Calif., and on Clipperton Is. (off sw. Mexico). There are 985 records for Calif. through 1995, with three-fourths being in fall and one-fourth in spring (see also under Winter above). The fall peak in Calif. is in late September and early October, and the spring peak is at the very end of May and beginning of June; there are four summer records, but no indication of nesting. Vagrant well north of the breeding range in n. Man. (rare at Churchill in late spring and summer) and in Alaska (twice at Middleton Is., once in n. Alaska, and three times in the Bering Sea, all in fall). Recorded in the

Davis Strait and three times in Greenland (including a spring record, 20 May 1880). The only record for the Palearctic is for one in late September on the Isles of Scilly, United Kingdom.

 ## STATUS AND CONSERVATION

Numbers have increased in some regions (such as New England) with the regrowth of coniferous woodlands following the abandonment of pastures and with forestry practices in which short logging cycles promote a dense growth of young trees. Some local declines (especially in the Appalachians) could potentially result from the continued spread of introduced insects that threaten eastern hemlock forests. Although Magnolia Warblers do exploit outbreaks of spruce budworms, their populations are not as strongly cyclic as those of other "spruce-woods" warblers.

This species is a relatively infrequent cowbird host, although parasitism rates may be increasing.

 ## SUBSPECIES

No subspecies recognized; no geographic variation described.

TAXONOMIC RELATIONSHIPS

Perhaps close to the Yellow-rumped Warbler complex, but the limited molecular data do not confirm this; there is no strong evidence establishing relationships within *Dendroica*.

Magnolia Warbler. First spring male in Texas in May. (Photo: Brian E. Small)

SPRING ADULT MALE: Crown clear gray. Lores, auricular patch, and narrow strip across forehead black. Supercilium (beginning above eye) and narrow arc under eye white. Solid black patch across the back, continuous on neck with black auricular patch; lowermost back olive with black feather centers. Rump clear yellow; uppertail coverts solid black. Underparts bright yellow, becoming white on the lower belly and undertail coverts. A series of thick black streaks across the chest often merge to form a black patch sharply set off from the yellow throat. Bold black streaks down the sides and flanks. Median and greater secondary coverts broadly tipped with white, forming a nearly solid white wing patch. Flight feathers blackish, edged clear gray. Central rectrices black; remaining rectrices black with a broad patch of white on the middle third of the inner web. **FIRST SPRING MALE:** Very similar to spring adult male, but black on back less extensive, not reaching uppermost back and not joining black of auriculars. Black streaking on underparts averages less bold, less often forming solid area on uppermost chest. Edges of secondaries more olive, less gray. Rectrices and primaries browner and more worn than in adult. **SPRING ADULT FEMALE:** Crown and hindneck gray, tinged with olive. Auriculars and lores dull black, not extending across forehead; white arc under eye and posterior supercilium as in male. Back mostly yellow-olive with heavy black spotting, but not extensively solid black. Yellow rump patch less extensive than in male. Uppertail coverts tipped with grayish. Yellow of underparts slightly paler than in adult male; black ventral streaking averages less bold, and less solid on the uppermost chest. White in wing coverts less extensive than in adult male, usually forming two broad wing bars. White in rectrices slightly less extensive than in adult male. **FIRST SPRING FEMALE:** Very similar to spring adult female but slightly duller. Lores

Magnolia Warbler. First spring female in Texas in May. (Photo: Brian E. Small)

Magnolia Warbler. First fall females in Newfoundland in August. (Photo: Shawneen E. Finnegan)

and auriculars dark gray; there is a white eye-ring, but the white supercilium behind the eye is reduced or absent. Black back spotting and ventral streaking even more limited. Rectrices and primaries browner and more worn than in adult. **FALL ADULT MALE:** Black much reduced from spring plumage. Back feathers black with broad yellow-olive feather tips giving a black-spotted appearance; if present, gray fringes on the black upper tail coverts are very narrow. Black on head absent; crown and face gray with thin white eye-ring, sometimes a hint of white supercilium behind eye. Yellow of underparts slightly paler than on spring birds, often with a suffusion of grayish white across the upper chest. Black streaking below is greatly reduced, being heaviest on the flanks, and is partly veiled with yellowish. White on median and greater secondary coverts reduced to form two wing bars instead of a more solid patch. **FIRST FALL MALE:** Crown and hindneck gray, slightly tinged olive. Back olive-yellow with sparse, inconspicuous black chevrons or spots. Uppertail coverts broadly tipped with yellowish olive and gray. Sides of face grayish olive with thin white eye-ring. Throat, breast, and belly yellow, paler than in fall adult male; pale grayish white band across upper chest. Underparts with partly veiled black streaking, mainly confined to the flanks. Two thin white wing bars. **FALL ADULT FEMALE:** Resembles fall adult male but crown slightly washed with olive; black very much reduced, ventral markings reduced to a few fine streaks on flanks; much less black on uppertail coverts. **FIRST FALL FEMALE:** Essentially indistinguishable from first fall male, though back spotting is usually completely absent, and streaking on underparts is very fine and limited to the flanks. Black of uppertail coverts very broadly tipped with gray or olive. White in rectrices least extensive of any age or sex class, but these differences not likely to be ascertained in the field. **JUVENILE:** Upperparts strongly washed brownish; wing bars buffy. Underparts dull yellowish buff, washed with grayish brown on the breast. Tail still shows diagnostic pattern for species. **BARE PARTS:** Bill mostly black in spring adults, or with limited brown at the base of the mandible. Bill more extensively pale on the mandible in fall adults. Fall immatures with brown maxilla, fleshy mandible. Iris dark brown. Legs dusky blackish, soles of feet yellowish orange.

A complete prebasic molt occurs in adults on the breeding grounds; hatching-year birds undergo a partial prebasic molt that does not involve the flight feathers. The prealternate molt (February to April) is extensive, involving some body and head feathers, wing coverts, and sometimes tertials and greater coverts.

 ## REFERENCES

GENERAL: Hall 1994.
DISTRIBUTION: Enright 1995.
ECOLOGY, BEHAVIOR, VOCALIZATIONS, AND CONSERVATION: Morse 1976, Nice 1926.

CAPE MAY WARBLER

Dendroica tigrina

4.75 in. (12 cm). The Cape May Warbler is an arboreal species that is closely associated with spruces in the breeding season; its populations fluctuate with cycles of abundance of a moth larva called the spruce budworm (*Choristoneura fumiferana*). This is a pugnacious warbler, often vigorously defending food sources, which in migration and winter may include fruit and nectar. In all plumages it is notable for the extensively streaked underparts. Nearly all show at least a hint of a pale yellowish patch behind the auriculars; the rump is contrastingly yellow to yellowish green in all plumages, and all show at least a hint of greenish edges to the flight feathers. The bill is fine and slightly decurved for a *Dendroica*.

 ## DESCRIPTION

Cape May Warblers are distinctly streaked on the underparts in all plumages, with the ground color of the breast varying from bright yellow to dull grayish white. Males are streaked with blackish on the crown and back; this streaking is indistinct or absent on the upperparts of females. The ground color of the upperparts varies from rather bright olive green to dull olive-gray, with the rump contrastingly brighter (bright yellow to olive-yellow). Adult males have a bold face pattern with chestnut auriculars, a black eye line, a yellow and chestnut supercilium, and a large yellow patch on the side of the neck behind the auricular. This face pattern is progressively duller in fall adult males, immature males, adult females, and immature females, and some young females in fall can completely lack yellow. Aberrant plumages (one bird with extensive yellow patches on the head, back, and rump, and with excessive white in the wing; and another leucistic bird) have been reported.

Structurally, Cape May Warblers are rather short-tailed, and the bill is slender, sharp-pointed, and slightly decurved. They are small but rather chunky in overall shape.

 ## SIMILAR SPECIES

In most plumages quite distinctive, but confusion of first fall females with first fall females of other *Dendroica* possible, particularly with dull Yellow-rumped, Pine, and Palm warblers.

Very dull YELLOW-RUMPED WARBLER told by distinct, bright yellow rump patch, browner (less green) upperparts (at least in Myrtle subspecies), more distinct face and throat pattern, larger size, longer tail, and heavier bill; *chip* calls of Yellow-rumped different from any Cape May calls. Immature female PINE WARBLER is much larger and longer tailed, browner (less gray) above, has broader, more distinct wing bars, and lacks the contrasting greenish rump and flight feather edgings. Dull PALM WARBLERS are easily told by their tail-pumping behavior, yellow undertail coverts, and more distinct transocular line and supercilium. Confusion also possible with first fall female CERULEAN and BLACKBURNIAN (both have striking supercilia, bolder wing bars), YELLOW (grayest immatures from far northwest and "Golden" and "Mangrove" groups may suggest Cape May but show yellow tail spots and a bold dark eye on a pale face), BAY-BREASTED and BLACKPOLL (greener above, with bold white wing bars), and TENNESSEE (which lacks streaking on underparts and has brighter green back).

 ## VOICE

The weak SONG most commonly a series of 3–12 (usually 5–6) very high-pitched, sibilant, upslurred notes of even cadence (3–4 per second) and volume. These songs suggest those of Golden-crowned Kinglet *(Regulus satrapa),* but do not speed up and lack the kinglet's jumbled ending. Alternate songs may consist of slightly lower and more slurred notes, given at a rate of 6–8 per second; these are most likely to be confused with that of Bay-breasted, but notes in song of latter are more distinctly two-parted. A given bird may sing both song types.

CALL NOTE a distinctive high, thin, sharp *seet* or *tsip.* **FLIGHT NOTE** a soft buzzy *zeet,* slightly softer than similar flight notes of Yellow, Blackpoll, Bay-breasted.

Behavior

On the breeding grounds, Cape Mays are largely treetop warblers, feeding high in the outer branches of conifers; their foraging mostly involves gleaning of needles at the tips of branches, but they do occasionally pursue insects in the air. They consume a variety of insects, particularly spruce budworms. Singing birds choose high, exposed perches, often singing from the top of a spruce spire for extended periods. This is an aggressive, pugnacious species, often chasing other birds away from favored feeding areas at all times of the year.

During migration and in winter, they feed to a larger extent on nectar and fruits than most other warblers. Migrants and winter birds habitually defend local food sources, spending considerable time defending nectar sources. The thin, sharp, slightly decurved bill is related to the species' habit of feeding on nectar and puncturing small fruits, as is the relatively tubular and brushy-tipped tongue. Late fall and early winter stragglers in far north may use suet feeders, hummingbird feeders, and sap wells drilled by sapsuckers (*Sphyrapicus*).

The **NEST** is placed high (30 to 60 ft., occasionally lower) in a conifer such as a spruce or fir, often near the trunk within a few feet of the treetop. The nest is built of grasses, small twigs, and sphagnum moss, and is lined with fine grass, hair, and feathers. This species lays large clutches, often six or seven eggs, though clutch size may be smaller in years of food scarcity.

Habitat

BREEDING birds occupy mature or medium-age coniferous forests or bogs dominated by spruces, especially black spruce. Other important conifers include balsam fir, northern white cedar, and white spruce. Throughout their breeding range they are locally irregular in numbers; large concentrations are found where spruce budworm outbreaks occur. Within these forests Cape Mays usually occupy openings or edges.

In **MIGRATION**, conifers (especially spruces) are preferred, but will utilize a variety of trees and shrubs. In spring, Cape May Warblers commonly frequent exotic flowering trees such as silk-oaks and bottlebrush, and also flowers and catkins of hardwoods such as oaks, hickories, and honey locusts. Fall migrants often occupy berry-producing shrubs and small vineyards within woodlands.

In **WINTER**, occupies open woodlands and exotic shade trees (for example, palms, eucalyptus, casuarinas) over a wide elevational range; such habitats include towns, ornamental gardens, montane forest, mangroves—wherever flowering trees are numerous.

 DISTRIBUTION

BREEDS across the boreal forests from se. Yukon, ne. B.C. (scarce), sw. Dist. of Mack., and n. Alta. east to cen. Que. and sw. Nfld.; breeds south to n. Minn., n. Wisc., n. Mich., s. Ont. (rarely to Bruce Peninsula), n. N.Y., n. Vt., n. N.H., cen. Me., and the Maritime Provinces. Abundance varies within breeding range; it is generally more common in eastern portions of the range. Casual in summer south of breeding range.

WINTERS primarily in the Bahamas and (especially) Greater Antilles, with small numbers in Bermuda, the Lesser Antilles, and islands in the w. and s. Caribbean (regular on Cozumel). Uncommon in winter from Veracruz (rarely n. to San Luis Potosi) and the Yucatán peninsula, Mexico, south along the Caribbean coast (and especially offshore islands) to Honduras; a few also winter in along the Pacific slope from Oaxaca to El Salvador; recorded casually from Sonora to Jalisco. Rare in winter in Costa Rica (from both coasts to over 4,000 ft.) and in Panama (east to Canal Zone). Casual on Tobago and Trinidad, the Netherlands Antilles, and the islands off Colombia and Venezuela.

In the U.S. winters in very small numbers in s. Fla., with a few records in n. Fla. There are numerous early winter records of Cape Mays in eastern North America, and in fact it is the most likely warbler (after Yellow-rumped) at that season in some northern regions; there are multiple early winter records for most states in the East, and for N.S. and Nfld. This species' propensity for occurring well north of the normal winter range is underscored by several remarkable early winter records from Alta. (with one remaining into February). Few of these birds in the far north survive after December. Has wintered casually in Calif., s. Ariz., and the Gulf states.

MIGRATION is through Fla. and the West Indies; in spring it moves up both sides of Fla. (and regularly west on the Gulf Coast to Ala.) and northward mainly through and west of the Appalachian Mtns., through the Ohio and upper Mississippi river valleys and the Great Lakes region. Smaller numbers move through New England and N.Y., but it is uncommon to rare on the Atlantic Coast from the Mid-Atlantic states south through the Carolinas. Rare in spring on the western Gulf Coast (usually after east winds), the lower Mississippi River Valley and the s. Great Plains. The fall migration route is much more easterly; the species is much more numerous along the Atlantic Coast in fall than in spring, but rare through the interior Southeast and very rare on the Gulf Coast.

SPRING MIGRATION begins with a few birds in late March (very rarely mid-March) in Fla.; more typically birds arrive in Fla. in the second week of April. There are March records for the Gulf Coast and S.C., but more normal arrivals there are 10–20 April. Arrivals across the s. Midwest are at the beginning of May, and around 5–10 May in the Great Lakes states. For the northern Great Lakes and New England the earliest arrivals are in mid-May. Peak spring movements in Fla. are during the last third of April, with some movement through the first week of May. Peaks over most of the Midwest and Northeast are during the middle two weeks of May (the latter half of May in the n. Great Lakes region). Spring stragglers occur through the end of May and into June.

In **FALL MIGRATION** occasionally noted south of breeding grounds

CAPE MAY WARBLER
Dendroica tigrina

by the last third of July, but normal movement does not begin until the latter part of August. This species builds to a peak rapidly over much of the Great Lakes region and New England by the end of August and early September, with peak numbers continuing through much of September. In the Appalachians and Mid-Atlantic region the fall peak is in the latter half of September (with much movement continuing through early October); in Fla. the peak is from late September through the first half of October. Most of the few fall records for coastal La. are around 10–25 October. Small numbers move through much of the Midwest through the first week of October, and along the East Coast to the end of the month. Scattered records exist for much of e. North America well into November and even later (see Winter).

Rare migrant on the e. Great Plains; there are numerous records (mostly for spring) on the w. Great Plains and Rocky Mountain region. Farther west, recorded in all states, with most records for fall. There are some 209 records for Calif., with over two-thirds for fall (mainly late September and early October) and 11 for winter; the remainder are in spring (mostly very late May and early June). The numbers of vagrants in Calif. appear to cycle with overall population cycles in relation to spruce budworms; yearly averages from 1974 to 1977 (coinciding with a spruce budworm epidemic in the heart of the breeding range) were nearly three times the averages since 1979.

Casual in s. and s.-cen. Alaska, and recorded in fall on Socorro Is. off w. Mexico. Recorded exceptionally in Barrow, Alaska (6 June 1976), and in Great Britain (a singing male in Strathclyde, Scotland, on 17 June 1977).

STATUS AND CONSERVATION

Populations of Cape May Warblers fluctuate more than populations of most warblers, with highest breeding densities reached during outbreaks of spruce budworms. These fluctuations are often apparent in migration as well. Breeding Bird Survey population trends show increases in the 1970s and declines thereafter, but these might reflect population cycling rather than long-term population trends. Some local increases over historical numbers have been noted, as in n. Michigan. This species has sometimes been considered a pest in vineyards in portions of its migration range, but no direct control measures have been taken. Intensive spraying programs to control spruce budworms could have a negative impact on this and other warblers that specialize on this food source.

None described; no geographical variation reported.

 TAXONOMIC RELATIONSHIPS

Clearly a *Dendroica*, but specializations for nectar feeding (especially thin, slightly decurved bill) set it slightly apart structurally from others in the genus and suggest some *Vermivora*. Certain plumage characters suggest Magnolia, or perhaps Yellow-rumped, may be most closely related species. A purported hybrid Blackpoll Warbler × Northern Waterthrush might perhaps instead pertain to a Cape May Warbler × Northern Waterthrush. A hybrid with Yellow-rumped ("Myrtle") Warbler was taken in Florida. Audubon's "Carbonated Warbler" is suspected to be based on a first spring male Cape May, a hybrid between Blackpoll Warbler and Cape May Warbler, or an aberrant Blackpoll Warbler.

 PLUMAGES AND MOLTS

SPRING ADULT MALE: Forehead and crown blackish (the former tinged chestnut on a minority of individuals), becoming olive on the hindneck. Supercilium bright yellow in front of the eye, yellow (tinged chestnut) behind the eye. Black lores and eye line. Auricular patch bright chestnut, contrasting with the bright yellow throat, sides of neck, and patch behind the auricular region. Uppermost throat tinged chestnut in some individuals. Breast and upper belly bright yellow, with a variable suffusion of yellow on the flanks and vent area. Bold black streaks across the entire breast and sides, extending well down the flanks. Some short black streaks extend to

Cape May Warbler. Adult male in Florida in April. (Photo: Brian E. Small)

*Cape May Warbler.
First fall female in
New York in October.
(Photo: Arthur Mor-
ris/Birds as Art)*

the center of the throat on most individuals. Upperparts olive green with
black feather centers on the back; rump bright yellow but not in a well-
defined patch, grading to yellow-olive on the black-centered uppertail
coverts. Median and greater secondary coverts broadly edged and tipped
with white, usually forming a single large patch rather than two distinct
wing bars. Primaries and secondaries blackish, edged with greenish. Tail
blackish, with thin greenish edges to the outer webs; white patches on the
inner webs of the outer four pairs of rectrices. **FIRST SPRING MALE:** Resembles spring adult male, but crown more extensively olive, with black spotting; chestnut patch of auriculars smaller and slightly paler, often suffused with yellow; rear portion of supercilium often has yellow present,
with reduced chestnut. Lores and eye line dark gray rather than black. Yellow patch on sides of neck suffused with olive, showing less contrast with
crown and hindneck. Whitish edges and tips to greater coverts less extensive, so wing patch appears smaller and more broken. Slightly more greenish tinge to yellow rump. White in rectrices slightly less extensive, with
only a small white spot on r4. Rectrices and primaries browner and more
worn than in adult. **SPRING ADULT FEMALE:** Crown and upperparts dull olive
green, with fine black spotting on the crown. The back shows only blurry,
inconspicuous streaks; rump fairly bright yellowish olive. Face pattern
much duller than that of males, with yellow supercilium, thin gray
transocular line, gray wash on auriculars (with a hint of chestnut in rare
individuals), and pale yellow suffusion on the sides of the neck behind the
auricular area. Throat and breast washed with moderately bright yellow,
continuous with yellow neck sides; extent and brightness of yellow variable, but less extensive than in males. Thin blackish streaks across the
breast and sides, becoming blurred on the flanks. Lower belly and undertail coverts dull whitish. Wing bars thin and not especially conspicuous.
White in rectrices more limited than in adult males, with very little white

Cape May Warbler. First fall female in Maine in August. (Photo: Shawneen E. Finnegan)

on fourth rectrix. Thin greenish edges to flight feathers. **FIRST SPRING FEMALE:** Duller than spring adult female, with yellow of chin, throat, and breast largely replaced by whitish, with a wash of pale yellow on the supercilium and below and behind the grayish auricular area. Upperparts and flight feather edges grayer, less green, than those of adult. Rump more olive, less pure yellow. Rectrices and primaries browner and more worn than in adult. **FALL ADULT MALE:** Generally resembles spring adult male but with the following differences: crown less solidly black, with much olive feather tipping; chestnut of auriculars and rear portion of supercilium paler and more limited, sometimes lacking altogether; gray feather tips on hindneck. The yellow of the sides of the neck behind the auricular patch still forms a bold patch, only slightly veiled with gray feather tips. Back with large black spots, often veiled with olive tips. The yellow in the underparts of all fall males is brighter and more extensive than that of fall females. **FIRST FALL MALE:** Somewhat duller than fall adult male but generally brighter than brightest fall adult females. Told from fall adult male by thinner black streaking on underparts and paler yellow of underparts and face; they usually lack chestnut (but note some fall adult males can lack chestnut as well); there is a more extensive grayish tint to crown and hindneck, and the inner greater primary coverts are less pure white (washed olive-gray). Told from bright fall females by short black streaks on back (often heavily veiled), and yellower underparts with blacker and more extensive streaking. **FALL ADULT FEMALE:** Resembles spring adult female, but upperparts more strongly suffused with gray and lacking any hint of streaking on the back; yellow on sides of neck duller, streaking of underparts less distinct. Very similar to first fall male, but yellow of underparts more restricted to the breast, with only a pale wash of yellow onto the belly; wing patches less conspicuous. **FIRST FALL FEMALE:** The dullest, grayest plumage, with just a hint of pale yellow across the chest and below and behind the gray auricular area. Blurry gray streaks across the breast. Extremely dull first fall females can completely lack yellow in this plumage, except for a yellow-olive wash on the rump. They show some greenish edgings to the flight feathers. Wing bars are thin and tinged with gray. White in tail more limited than in adults or young males, with white usually absent from fourth rectrix. **JUVENILE:** Dull olive-brown above, dull brownish gray below, with a tinge of buff on breast and sides and pale buffy yellow on the belly. Two buff wing bars. **BARE PARTS:** Bill of breeding male black with some pale at base of lower mandible; winter male and adult female more extensively brown on lower mandible; first fall birds slaty on upper mandible, pale brown on lower mandible. Eyes dark brown. Legs and feet blackish, toes brown, soles yellowish.

A complete prebasic molt occurs in adults on the breeding grounds; the prebasic molt of hatching-year birds does not involve the flight feathers. The partial prealternate molt is generally completed on the wintering grounds.

 REFERENCES

DISTRIBUTION: Byers and Galbraith 1980, Mason 1976.
ECOLOGY, BEHAVIOR, VOCALIZATIONS, AND CONSERVATION: Bohlen and Oehmke 1993, Emlen 1973, Kale 1967, Kendeigh 1947, MacArthur 1958, Morse 1978, Schnell and Caldwell 1966, Sealy 1988.
PLUMAGES, MOLTS, AND MORPHOLOGY: Schnell and Caldwell 1966.
SYSTEMATICS: Lucas 1894, Parkes 1978 and 1985 ("Carbonated Warbler" may be first spring male Cape May), Short and Robbins 1967.

BLACK-THROATED BLUE WARBLER   PL. 10

Dendroica caerulescens

5 in. (12.7 cm). Male Black-throated Blue Warblers are strikingly marked in deep blue, black, and white, but this species is the most highly sexually dimorphic of all wood-warblers, and females are quite drab. Nearly all plumages exhibit a unique white flash at the base of the primaries. This species nests primarily in fairly mature deciduous or mixed woods, usually in uplands, and winters mainly in the Bahamas and Greater Antilles. Away from the eastern Great Lakes, Appalachians, and Atlantic Coast, it is generally scarce both as a breeder and a migrant. Despite its easterly distribution, the Black-throated Blue Warbler is surprisingly regular as a vagrant to western North America in fall.

Description

Highly sexually dimorphic. The striking male is unique: deep bluish on the upperparts (with geographical variation in the extent of black markings on the back) and with an extensive black area on the underparts from the auriculars, chin, and throat back along the entire sides. A conspicuous patch of white is located at the base of the primaries; wing bars are completely lacking. There is a flash of white in the corners of the tail. The female is quite different, plain olive-brown above and buffy below, with a thin, pale superciliary line and (usually) a suggestion of the white flash at the base of the primaries. There is only minor age variation, with immatures generally resembling adults of their respective sex. Seasonal differences are slight. One bird, resembling a male on its left side but showing predominately femalelike plumage on its right side, was observed in California in 1987.

Similar Species

All males are unmistakable, with the distinctive combination of deep bluish upperparts, a black throat and sides, and a large flash of white at the base of the primaries which is conspicuous in flight. The drably colored females could possibly be mistaken for plain warblers of the genus *Vermivora,* such as the ORANGE-CROWNED and TENNESSEE WARBLERS. Female Black-throated Blues always told from Orange-crowned and Tennessee warblers by the contrast between the dark auriculars and the pale throat and by the brownish tones to the plumage. The white flash at base of primaries, when present, is diagnostic for Black-throated Blue. Orange-crowned has a less conspicuous supercilium than Black-throated Blue, always lacks white in the rectrices, and has the pale color of the wing limited to the edge of the bend of the wing. Tennessee is told by its bright green back, trace of wing bar on the greater coverts, short-tailed look, and contrasting white in the undertail coverts.

The dullest immature female PINE WARBLERS, which show brownish plumage tones, always have evident pale wing bars and more extensive white in the tail.

Immature female CERULEAN WARBLERS show strong wing bars, lack brown tones to the plumage, and show a strong superciliary that widens toward the rear.

Throughout the wintering grounds there is the possibility of confusion of females with drabber immature (particularly juvenal) plumages of BANANAQUIT (*Coereba flaveola,* a warblerlike tropical species); similarities include the olive upperparts, pale supercilium, and small whitish patch at base of primaries. The Bananaquit is shorter tailed and has a distinctly decurved bill. Female STRIPE-HEADED TANAGERS (*Spindalis zena*) in portions of their range (Bahamas, Cuba) suggest female Black-throated Blue Warbler in plumage, but are easily distinguished by their thicker bill, whitish edges to flight feathers, and larger overall size.

♪ VOICE

SONG is a lazy series of 3–5 buzzy *zwee* notes, even in pitch or slightly descending but concluding with a strong, ascending buzz: *zwee zwee zwee zweeee?* or *zur zurr zreee*. Some notes are occasionally clearer, less buzzy. It is a distinctive and easily learned song, but perhaps could be confused with song of Cerulean (which usually has several short notes in the terminal ascending part of the song) or Black-throated Green (which is higher, with shorter and more rapidly delivered notes, and lacks the prolonged upslurred terminal note).

Common **CALL NOTE** is a soft *tik, thik,* or *dit,* strikingly similar to the call note of Dark-eyed Junco (*Junco hyemalis*); this note is often given in a rapid series (when alarmed?). **FLIGHT NOTE** is a distinctive, prolonged *tseet*.

🦅 BEHAVIOR

Often tame and confiding, spending much time foraging low in brush and foliage. Males forage higher than females on average; they spend much time in the subcanopy at 15–45 ft. while females usually forage below 15 ft. There is some habitat segregation by the sexes on the wintering grounds, with males more partial to primary forest and canopy feeding and females occupying younger, lower growth. Foraging involves gleaning of leaves and short sallies for flying insects; often quite deliberate in its movements, but sometimes more active. Frequently holds its wings partly spread, suggestive of an American Redstart. In addition to insects, the diet includes fruits (particularly in fall and winter) and occasionally seeds. In fall, often seen feeding at sapsucker (*Sphyrapicus*) drillings. Late fall and winter birds in the East often feed on suet and peanut butter at feeding stations. Males on the breeding grounds often sing from a low, inconspicuous perch, but will ascend in response to song playback.

The **NEST** is placed low (usually below 3 ft., but rarely to 20 ft.) in a dense bush or sapling deep in the forest interior. The bulky nest often has wood and bark woven into the outer structure and is bound with spider webs. The nest cup is deep and lined with fine grasses, leaves, and rootlets. Frequently double-brooded. Polygyny is rare, but was recorded regularly at a New Hampshire study site.

Habitat

BREEDS in upland deciduous or mixed deciduous-coniferous forests with a dense understory, most characteristically on mountain slopes and ridges. Important trees include maple, beech, birch, oaks, spruce, and hemlock. Undergrowth often consists of thickets of rhododendron (especially in the Appalachians), mountain laurel, hobblebush, yew, and various saplings. In most areas, pure coniferous forest is shunned, but in West Virginia and elsewhere it may occupy forests dominated by spruces, either in dense young stands or in mature stands where edges or clearings permit a dense understory to grow; oak-pine woodlands and hemlock-dominated ravines are inhabited in some parts of the Appalachians. Deciduous woods of birch, beech, and especially maple are important in the northwestern part of the breeding range. Breeding elevations are generally above about 2,100 ft. (usually above 2,400 ft.) in the southern Appalachians, but down to about 600 ft. (usually 1,200 ft.) in Pennsylvania and even lower in New England. Summering males found below optimal elevations and in more fragmented forests are usually second-year birds and probably only rarely find mates.

WINTER birds inhabit wet and dry forests, forest edges and undergrowth, shaded gardens, and mangroves; wintering elevations range from sea level to the highest portions of the Greater Antilles, but on most islands this species is more numerous at higher elevations.

MIGRANTS are most often found in woodland or woodland edge habitats, but are often in scrubby deciduous growth. They are frequently seen in the company of Canada Warblers.

Distribution

BREEDS from ne. Minn. (scarce), n. Wisc., n. Mich. (mainly upper peninsula), s.-cen. Ont. (west along the n. shore of Lake Superior), east through s. Que. to the Canadian Maritimes. Breeds south in New England to Conn., and southward through the Appalachian Mtns. and adjacent highlands from N.Y. to northernmost Ga., including highland areas of n. N.J. In the Great Lakes region it formerly bred south to s. Mich. and ne. Ohio. There are records of summering birds west to Sask. (nesting proven) and

Man. There are also summer records for Anticosti Is. and the Madeleine Is. in the Gulf of St. Lawrence. The greatest breeding densities are found in the cen. Appalachians from N.Y. to w. N.C.

WINTERS mainly in the Bahamas and the Greater Antilles, including the Cayman Islands. It is less numerous on the Virgin Islands and islands of the western Caribbean, but still regular. Winters casually on Bermuda and in the Lesser Antilles (recorded St. Martin, Antigua, Guadeloupe, and Dominica). Small numbers winter (regularly?) along the Caribbean coast from s. Veracruz and e. Yucatán peninsula south to Honduras, Costa Rica, Panama, and northernmost South America (Colombia and Venezuela); there is a 29 December 1971 specimen from Nuevo Léon in n. Mexico. Arrives on the wintering grounds mainly in late September and early October.

Within the U.S. a very few winter annually in s. Fla., and it is casual elsewhere in the southern states. Most birds recorded in early winter do not remain (or survive) through the entire winter, but birds have remained to at least midwinter as far north as Minn., Ind., Ont., the New York City region, and Del. In the West, there are over a dozen winter records for Calif., three for Ore., two for w. Wash., one for B.C., four for Ariz., and a January specimen from Idaho.

MIGRATION routes in spring and fall lie primarily from the Appalachian Mtns. east, through Fla. and the West Indies. The spring and fall passages follow similar routes, with perhaps a slightly more easterly component in spring. This species is always a scarce migrant in the Great Plains states and south to Texas and La., but is far more frequent in those regions in fall than in spring.

SPRING MIGRATION through Fla. occurs mainly from the Keys up the East Coast. This species is increasingly rare along the Gulf Coast from the Fla. panhandle west. The earliest migrants have been noted in s. Fla. in mid-March, but most arrivals are during the first half of April. The first arrivals in the Mid-Atlantic states and s. Appalachians (Tenn.) are around 25 April, but there are a scattering of early to mid-April records from these regions. In the upper Midwest, s. Ont., and s. New England, the earliest arrivals are usually during the first few days of May, rarely to late April; again, earlier overshoots have been noted in mid-April in these regions. In n. New England and the Canadian Maritime Provinces, the earliest birds are usually noted in the second week of May. Peak movements in Fla. are during the last week of April and first week of May, with peaks occurring the first two weeks of May in the Mid-Atlantic region, and mid-May in the upper Midwest and s. New England (with high counts sometimes found in the last week of May). Migration has largely ceased in the Southeast by mid-May, but stragglers have even been found in early June in s. Fla. and elsewhere in the East. There is one late June record for Churchill, Man., well north of the normal range.

FALL MIGRATION is rather late, with peak movements from mid-September to mid-October. The earliest fall transients are noted in mid-August (rarely earlier) in the Great Lakes, New England, and Mid-Atlantic states, with numbers building in late August and early September. Even in Fla., records extend to the first half of August. Peak fall movements in much of e. North America are from mid-September to the second week of October. Peak movements are somewhat later in Fla.; the high count for Fla. (700) was recorded on 17–18 October 1887 at Sombrero Key. Only a few stragglers occur over much of the East after the second week of October (late October in the Deep South). There are numerous November records throughout the East, and some individuals may even remain into mid-December (see Winter above). Much

RACIAL BOUNDARY

caerulescens

cairnsi

BLACK-THROATED BLUE WARBLER
Dendroica caerulescens

more regular in fall than in spring in the Great Plains and Gulf Coast, but still scarce. An uncommon fall transient on Bermuda.

VAGRANT in fall north to the Belcher Is., Northwest Territories. Also rare to casual in w. North America, with the great majority of records from fall. Records for most western states are in double figures. Regular in Calif., with 634 records. Most Calif. records are in October and early November (with a few as early as mid-September), and only about 5 percent of the records are for spring or winter. There are a few summer records for the West (e.g., Colo., Ariz., Ore.); a 12 August record in Kern Co., Calif., might have pertained to a locally summering bird. There are three fall records for Greenland, and a male was off s. Iceland, 14–19 September 1988. There are no records for Great Britain or Europe.

📊 STATUS AND CONSERVATION

There has undoubtedly been considerable reduction in range and numbers with the extensive cutting and fragmentation of eastern deciduous forests. Some recovery has occurred, particularly in New England, with the regrowth of forests. Breeding Bird Survey data show no strong population trends since 1966.

A relatively infrequent cowbird host, at least in relatively unfragmented forest. Nest failure rates from predators such as squirrels and jays are higher in fragmented forests than in more pristine forests.

🦋 SUBSPECIES

The nominate subspecies occupies the species' breeding range except for the Appalachian Mtns. from sw. Pennsylvania south, where the subspecies *cairnsi* occurs. Some male *cairnsi* are distinctive in having slightly darker blue upperparts which are heavily scalloped or blotched with black in the center of the back, along with fine black streaking on the crown. Female *cairnsi* may average slightly darker and duller above, with darker olive color on the flanks, than nominate females. Individual male nominate birds from throughout the range can show black markings on the back, sometimes nearly as extensively as "typical" *cairnsi*; furthermore, some individuals well within the breeding range of *cairnsi* lack black on the back. *D. c. cairnsi* is thus weakly differentiated, and many authors suggest that this species may best be considered monotypic. Field identification to subspecies is not advised.

TAXONOMIC RELATIONSHIPS

No close relatives within the genus have been shown; a relationship with Cerulean Warbler has been postulated. A possible hybrid with Yellow Warbler was described from Quebec.

PLUMAGES AND MOLTS

These descriptions are of nominate *caerulescens*. **SPRING ADULT MALE:** Deep blue to blue-gray on the entire upperparts, from the forehead to the uppertail coverts. The back is unmarked or very lightly marked with black scalloping; black is present in the form of heavy scalloping or even a solid patch in Appalachian populations (see under Subspecies) and occasionally elsewhere. Chin, throat, auricular region, sides, and flanks black. Remainder of underparts pure white, forming an irregular border with the black of the sides. Remiges blackish, edge bluish; tertials black on the inner web, deep bluish on the outer web. Wing coverts black, broadly edged bluish; primary coverts jet black with narrow deep blue margins. Bold white patch on wing, formed by the bases of the primary feathers, usually 9–14 mm long but rarely as short as 7 mm. Tail blackish with large white spots on the inner webs of the outer three rectrices. **FIRST SPRING MALE:** Similar to spring adult male, but differences are observable in the hand, and usually in the field. Alula and primary coverts brown, edged greenish. Remiges and rectrices duller than in adult, with edging more greenish, less blue; tertials dusky, tinged with greenish on the outer web. White at the base of the primaries averages slightly less extensive, usually 5–10 mm. Upperparts with dull brownish or olive tinge to the blue. Slight grayish tipping to the black feathers of the chin and throat. White of underparts not as pure as in adult male, often with a tinge of buffy or even pale yellow in the vent area. **SPRING ADULT FEMALE:** Olive to brownish olive

Black-throated Blue Warbler. Adult male caerulescens *in Florida in April. (Photo: Kevin T. Karlson)*

Black-throated Blue Warbler. Female caerulescens *in Texas in April. (Photo: Brian E. Small)*

on the entire upperparts, with the forehead being more bluish or bluish green. Uppertail coverts usually have a bluish tint. Thin but distinct whitish supercilium, tinged yellowish; small whitish arc below the eye. Auricular patch brownish olive, slightly darker than upperparts, and contrasting with throat, supercilium, and paler bluish forehead. Underparts pale lemon yellowish, with olive wash on the sides of the breast. Dusky wings show olive edges to the remiges; the primary coverts are blackish brown with narrow olive edges. Dull white patch at the base of the primaries usually 2–7 mm. Dusky gray rectrices have narrow bluish edges; only faint grayish spots in the tail. **FIRST SPRING FEMALE:** Very similar to spring adult female, but remiges more brownish, and primary coverts brownish with virtually no olive edging. Wing patch averages even smaller, usually 1–4 mm, and is occasionally absent. Tail spots often lacking entirely; when present rather dull and poorly defined. **FALL ADULT MALE:** Resembles spring adult male but occasionally shows slight olive veiling of the blue of the back and rump. **FIRST FALL MALE:** As in first spring male but more extensively washed with olive above. Black of chin, throat, malar region, and sides a bit duller, nearly always with whitish tips to feathers; chin sometimes completely white. Readily told from fall adult male in the field by the presence of an olive wash on the upperparts (sometimes hard to see), whitish tips on the black of the chin and throat, brown tinge to the primary coverts and inner web of the tertials, olive (rather than blue) edges to the remiges, and duller white of the underparts. Rectrices more tapered than in adults. **FALL ADULT FEMALE:** As spring adult female, but appearing slightly richer yellow-buff on underparts, with sides and flanks more strongly tinged olive. **FIRST FALL FEMALE:** Olive green to olive-brown on upperparts, averaging slightly more brownish than in fall adult female; forehead and upperparts completely lack any bluish tones. Dull yellowish buff below, sometimes paling to dull whitish on center of abdomen, and rarely with richer buff undertail coverts. Supercilium dull yellowish to yel-

Black-throated Blue Warbler. First fall female in New Jersey in September. (Photo: Brian E. Small)

lowish white; on exceptional birds supercilium may be nearly lacking. Face and auriculars more olive green, closely matching color of crown. Pale patch at base of primaries very small (less than 5 mm) or completely absent (in about 10 percent of birds). Primary coverts paler brown than in adult females, with virtually no olive edges evident. Lesser upperwing coverts olive, lacking any bluish tint. Rectrices edged with olive (bluish in adult females) and are relatively tapered. Tail spots dull grayish white and indistinct if present at all. **JUVENILE:** Brownish above, dull whitish buff below with brownish olive mottling on the breast; suggestion of buff supercilium and dark cheek patch. **BARE PARTS:** Bill blackish in spring birds, but with some brown on the base of the lower mandible in the non-breeding season; immature males show a tinge of brown on the bill, and immature females have extensively brownish bills. Eyes blackish brown. Legs and feet vary from dark brownish to paler olive-brown.

The prebasic molt occurs on the breeding grounds, from July to September; it is complete in adults, involving all feathers except remiges and rectrices in juveniles. A very limited prealternate molt takes place from February to April.

 REFERENCES

GENERAL: Holmes 1994.
DISTRIBUTION: Contreras-Balderas et al. 1995, Monroe 1968.
ECOLOGY, BEHAVIOR, VOCALIZATIONS, AND CONSERVATION: Black 1975, Holmes 1986, Holmes et al. 1989 and 1992, Hubbard 1965, Lack 1976, Petit et al. 1988, Sherry and Holmes 1985, Wunderle 1992.
PLUMAGES, MOLTS, AND MORPHOLOGY: Graves et al. 1996, Parkes 1979, Patten 1993.
SYSTEMATICS: Ducharme and Lamontagne 1992.

Dendroica coronata

5.25 in. (13.3 cm). Perhaps our most abundant and widespread warbler, the Yellow-rumped Warbler is especially evident in late fall, winter, and early spring, when its hardiness and adaptable feeding behavior (from ground foraging and berry eating to tree-top flycatching) make it the dominant warbler over much of the continent. Yellow-rumps winter in large numbers farther north than any other warbler; in the colder seasons at northern lati-tudes they are often the only warbler present. The species com-prises two distinct groups, which were formerly recognized as full species and perhaps still deserve that rank. The "Myrtle Warbler" (*D. [coronata] coronata*), is widespread across boreal regions, being an abundant migrant and winter visitor in the East and uncommon to locally common in winter in the West; the "Audubon's Warbler" (*D. [coronata] auduboni*) of western and Mexican coniferous forests is abundant in the West in winter and migration, and a rare vagrant in the East. The relatively large size, bright yellow rump patch, and white tail corners are obvious in all plumages, but the species' geographic variability and striking sea-sonal plumage change produce a confusing variety of plumages.

 DESCRIPTION

A large warbler of average proportions, characterized in all post-juvenal plumages by a distinct bright yellow rump patch. A small yellow crown patch is mostly concealed and often lacking in duller plumages, as is a patch of yellow on the sides. The throat is white to buffy in Myrtle, usually yellow in Audubon's. An auricu-lar patch, eye line, and supercilium are evident in most Myrtles, but the face is plainer in Audubon's. The breast has a variable amount of black in spring males, being most extensive in Audubon's, especially in the southern portion of the range. The upperparts and breast of spring males appear blacker with wear. All plumages show white or whitish eye-arcs. The amount of white in the tail varies with age, sex, and race. Myrtles have the white tail spots usually limited to the outer three rectrices, but the white is more extensive on the outer rectrix than in Audubon's; Audubon's shows white in the outer four or five rec-trix pairs. Spring birds are fairly easily sexed (males with gray backs and much black on breasts, females with brownish backs and streaked breasts), but fall birds generally fall into three less easily distinguished classes: adult males, immature females, and all others. A pure white bird (with yellow spots) was photographed in Connecticut.

"Myrtle" and "Audubon's" warblers are distinguishable in the field by vocal and plumage characters, though a small minority of individuals, some of them probably intergrades, are not identifiable. Spring adult male Myrtle and Audubon's are easily told by several characters: throat color (white in Myrtle, yellow in Audubon's); face pattern (white supraloral spot present in Myrtle, absent in Audubon's; black auricular patch in Myrtle, contrasting with thin white postocular stripe and whitish upward extension at the rear of the throat; gray to black in Audubon's but not contrasting because of lack of supercilium and throat patch extension); wing coverts (more extensively white in Audubon's); and underparts (more extensively black in Audubon's, especially in southwestern breeders). Face pattern is the best mark for distinguishing Myrtle from Audubon's in other plumages. Even the dullest Myrtles show a suggestion of a dark auricular patch outlined by a weak, pale supercilium above and a pale extension of the whitish throat patch extending behind the auricular. Myrtles show a white or dull creamy white throat in all plumages, whereas immatures and basic adult females of the Audubon group can show pale yellow, buffy, or even white throats. Myrtles, especially eastern nominate birds, average considerably richer brown on the upperparts in immature plumages than corresponding plumages of Audubon's; they also appear more streaked on the underparts. Within a given age or sex group, Myrtle shows white in fewer rectrices than Audubon's, with white limited to r4–6 (Audubon's almost always show at least some white on r3, and many on r2 as well); on the folded tail from below, Myrtle shows more extensive white than Audubon's. Birds of the two groups are consistently separable by call notes (see below), but beware of variation within groups and possibility of intergrades with intermediate calls. Also, intergrades may give call notes typical of one group or the other.

Note on intergrades: Intergrades between Myrtle and Audubon's groups may show intermediate or mosaic characters of the parental forms, particularly in face pattern and the amount of white in the tail (by age and sex class). Individuals showing plumage characters of one group but giving call notes of the other may also be intergrades.

Drab immatures in fall and winter may be mistaken for immature Pine and Cape May warblers, and perhaps for Palm Warblers. The dull *chup* call note of Myrtle differs from that of all of these species. Dull Myrtle Warblers, in particular, may suggest dull brownish immature female **PINE WARBLERS** because of the contrast between the auriculars and the pale extension of the throat behind the auriculars. The rump of Pine Warbler is the same color as the back, lacking the bold yellow patch of all Yellow-rumps; Pines are more sluggish in foraging behavior, appear longer tailed, and the underparts with blurred streakes only on the sides of the breast. Immature female CAPE MAY WARBLERS are smaller, with more slender bills and shorter tails; their rumps are dull greenish, rather than yellow; the underparts show are more finely and uniformly streaked, and lack yellow on the sides of the breast (but may show a pale yellow wash in the center of the breast, which Myrtles lack).

PALM WARBLERS show yellowish rumps (but much duller, more greenish, and less contrasting). They are readily told by their constant, exaggerated tail-pumping habit and by their bright yellow undertail coverts. MAGNOLIA WARBLERS, also "yellow-rumped," are extensively yellow on the underparts in all plumages and have a different pattern of white in the tail.

♪ VOICE

SONGS of both groups are generally similar; songs are often given on winter grounds in early spring (these spring songs are often less structured, quieter than territorial songs on breeding grounds). CALL NOTES are diagnostic for each group, but FLIGHT NOTES similar. Quite vocal: chip notes given very frequently and often (when bird is excited) in series; "flight notes" also given when making short movements through foliage or on ground.

"MYRTLE" GROUP:
SONG is a variable and rather loosely structured trill, often difficult to identify. Most songs are two-parted: *chee-chee-chee-chee-cheedle-cheedle,* or *chew-chew-chew-chew-chew-chee-chee-chee.* CALL NOTE is a loud *tup, chup, tsup,* or *check,* flatter and softer than common chip note of Audubon's and with a weaker *ch* component. Very vocal, often giving many calls in rapid succession. FLIGHT NOTE is a clear high *sip,* lacking any buzzy quality and often given in a series.

"AUDUBON'S" GROUP:
SONG much like that of Myrtle, and similarly variable. Weaker, simpler songs may suggest a Grace's Warbler or a junco, whereas richer versions recall Painted Redstart. CALL NOTE a loud *chep, chip, chwit,* or *chent,* with *ch* quality usually evident. Like Myrtle, extremely vocal, giving chip calls in rapid succession when excited. FLIGHT NOTE a clear, high *sip,* identical to that of Myrtle.

Behavior

The two groups are generally similar. Foraging behavior is perhaps more varied than any other warbler. Aerial sallying and hover-gleaning are common in all but the coldest weather, augmenting more typical foliage-gleaning behavior. Foraging heights in trees range from lower branches to the tops of tall trees. It is extremely active, often twitching the tail. Birds often feed on the ground in winter and migration, sometimes in large flocks and often mixed with other species such as bluebirds, pipits, and Palm Warblers; even routinely feeds on flies on beaches. Often very tame. In fall and winter, feeds extensively on fruits of bayberries and wax myrtle *(Myrtica),* poison ivy *(Toxicodendron),* and many other plants; this especially true of Myrtle Warbler. This varied diet and emphasis on berries is an important factor in the abundance of this species at high latitudes during the winter; specializations in the digestive tract of Yellow-rumped Warblers allow them to exploit these waxy berries.

NEST usually placed along horizontal limb of a conifer or other evergreen at medium heights (usually 15–20 ft.); sometimes in deciduous trees or bushes. Nest relatively bulky, often lined with feathers.

Habitat

"MYRTLE" GROUP:

BREEDS in coniferous forest, often with a mixture of deciduous trees; preferred conifers include hemlocks, white pines, jack pines, spruces, and firs. Northwestern populations (Alaska) more partial to deciduous forests. Shuns deep, dense forests, preferring open woodlands, forest edges and openings, high-elevation stunted forests. In some areas, breeds in pine plantations (and even Christmas tree farms).

WINTERS in a wide variety of open, brushy, and forest-edge habitats, with abundance mainly determined by food availability (berries and insects); also within woodlands where berries are plentiful. Favored habitats include bayberry and wax myrtle thickets, juniper stands, beaches (where feeds on insects attracted to seaweed), palmettos, citrus groves, and gardens. In West, partial to riparian thickets (especially willows), but scattered through most brushy and lightly wooded habitats.

"AUDUBON'S" GROUP:

BREEDS in coniferous forests, including firs, spruces, Douglas-firs, often with a mixture of pines or aspens. Breeds in mountains to

timberline, and in coastal coniferous forests to sea level. Generally avoids deep, shady forests.

WINTERS in virtually all but the most heavily wooded habitats,
requiring only some brush or taller vegetation. Habitats include
parks and gardens, agricultural fields and pasturelands with
brush or tree-lined borders, riparian groves, open woodlands, chaparral, and beaches. Extremely abundant in groves of winter-flow-
ering eucalyptus trees planted commonly in urban and suburban
California. In Central American winter range, occurs mostly in
pine-oak forests of highlands. Both groups extremely widespread
in migration.

 ## DISTRIBUTION

"MYRTLE" GROUP:

BREEDS from interior Alaska (north to Brooks Range) eastward
across the taiga zone through Yukon, w. and cen. Dist. of Mack.,
n. Man., n. Ont., n. Que., Lab., and Nfld.; breeds south to nw.
B.C., n. and cen. Alta., s. Sask., s. Man., Minn. (locally to se.), n.

YELLOW-RUMPED WARBLER
(MYRTLE WARBLER)
Dendroica coronata

YELLOW-RUMPED WARBLER
(AUDUBON'S WARBLER)
Dendroica c. auduboni

Wisc., n. Mich., n. Pa., N.Y. (mainly Adirondacks and Catskills, but has nested to Long Island). Has nested recently in nw. Conn., high mountains of W. Va., and once each in N.J. and Md. Most of these southerly nestings in the eastern portion of the range are relatively recent. Scattered midsummer records of nonbreeders exist as far south as s. Fla. An early arrival on the breeding grounds, it appears even in the northern portions of the breeding range by late April.

WINTERS abundantly through the Atlantic Coast states (north to Mass.) and the Gulf states; among the commonest wintering passerines in many of these areas. Small numbers winter on the East Coast north to N.S., and a few remain as late as January in Nfld. Through the interior of the continent, where winter food supplies (berries) are less dependable, numbers vary. May be fairly common to common in some years north to Great Lakes; has wintered as far north as Wisc. and Minn. Rather common in winter in the s. Great Plains, occurring in small numbers north to Iowa, S.D. Generally rare to uncommon in the s. Rockies, s. intermountain West, and the desert Southwest. Uncommon to

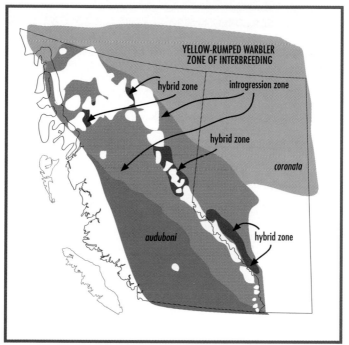

Zone of interbreeding between "Myrtle" and "Audubon's" warblers. In the dark blue areas, the average bird shows characters intermediate between the two forms. In the light blue areas, birds tend toward "Myrtle" (north and east) or toward "Audubon's" (west), but show some intermediacy. White areas are unoccupied. After Hubbard (1969).

common from n. Ore. to Baja Calif. along the West Coast, with greatest numbers from southern Ore. to cen. Calif. Winters south through Mexico (most numerous in east; scarce in northwestern states) and Central America (especially Caribbean slope), where it winters erratically south to Panama. Also winters commonly through the Greater Antilles. Unlike most other warblers, Yellow-rumps may move considerably through the winter season (facultative migration), probably in response to shifting food resources; this movement even involves nocturnal migration behavior more typical of spring and fall.

SPRING MIGRATION is early, but difficult to ascertain because of widespread abundance of wintering birds. A push of spring migrants begins in Fla. by early February and passes through the middle tier of eastern states by the second week of March, peaking in late April and diminishing after early May. Reaches the Great Lakes in late March or early April, peaking at the end of April and becoming scarce after mid-May. The earliest warbler to arrive in the interior of Canada, sometimes by late April; most individuals probably arrive at the northernmost breeding areas by end of May.

FALL MIGRATION is correspondingly late. The first birds arrive south of the breeding grounds in northern U.S. and Canadian prairie regions by mid-August, but numbers are not great in these regions until mid- to late September, peaking in early October. The first arrivals in southern U.S. are usually not until late September, with the main movement through southern states in October (late October in Fla.).

CASUAL north of breeding range in Alaska and Canada from May to October, and on Bering Sea islands in late spring (and once to e. Siberia in May 1879). In winter, casual in n. South America (recorded Colombia, Venezuela, Netherlands Antilles), Tobago, Lesser Antilles. Second most frequently recorded wood-warbler (after Blackpoll) in Europe, including 22 records for British Isles. Most British records for October, but also recorded May/June and once in winter.

"AUDUBON'S" GROUP:

BREEDS from coastal, cen. and se. B.C. (and southeasternmost Alaska), s. Alta., sw. Sask. (Cypress Hills) south through mountains of w. U.S. (and in coastal coniferous forests west of mountains from n. Calif. northward). Breeds east to w. S.D., sw. N.D., nw. Neb., and Guadalupe Mtns. of Texas (and has bred recently in Davis Mtns.). Breeding range extends south to n. Baja Calif. (Sierra San Pedro Martir), Chihuahua, and Durango, with an isolated and distinctive form in e. Chiapas and w. Guatemala (see under Subspecies).

WINTERS commonly from n. Calif., cen. Ariz., s. N.M., and w. Texas south through western and highland Mexico. Smaller numbers winter on the West Coast north to Washington (but are outnumbered by Myrtles from nw. Calif. northward), and through the interior West from Idaho, Ut., and Colo. south. Occurs sparingly southward to Honduras; recorded in Costa Rica and once in w. Panama. Significant "migratory" movements through the winter period are known.

SPRING MIGRATION not pronounced; withdraws from winter range in coastal lowlands by the first of May, but small numbers move north through the southwestern desert regions through much of May. Arrives in northernmost breeding areas as early as the end of April.

FALL MIGRATION relatively late, with migrants beginning to appear outside breeding areas in north by mid-August, and may reach southern interior early in September. Rare in coastal southern Calif. before mid-September, and not numerous there until early October.

CASUAL in most states and provinces of e. North America, north to N.S. and south to Fla. Most records are from October through May, with a peak in spring. Has wintered as far north as Minn., Nfld. Recorded once in Aleutians (Attu, May 1980).

A *zone of intergradation* between Myrtle and Audubon's warblers occurs in the n. Rockies in a roughly diagonal area from nw. B.C. to the s. B.C./Alta. boundary, with some degree of introgression noted more broadly from se. Alaska through much of cen. and e. B.C. and w. Alta. In these regions, Audubon's dominate in western montane forests of Douglas-fir, Engelmans spruce, and western white spruce, whereas Myrtles are typical of boreal forest dominated by white and black spruce; intergradation occurs where these habitats weave together and suitable nesting habitat is limited. These two forms show less genetic differentiation than do typical species pairs.

 ## STATUS AND CONSERVATION

This species' conspicuousness and abundance, along with annual variation in winter numbers, may mask any population changes. No marked population trends are evident in regions covered by the Breeding Bird Survey. This species appears thinly distributed on its breeding grounds compared with winter and migration densities. The boreal forest habitat of Myrtle is relatively unchanged. Frequent cowbird host in portions of range; some evidence of cowbird egg rejection. Overall, there is some indication of regional range expansion into regenerating coniferous forests and plantations.

SUBSPECIES

Relationships and distinctions between the "Myrtle" and "Audubon's" groups are discussed above. Within the "Myrtle" group there are two generally recognized but weakly differentiated subspecies. Nominate *coronata* occupies the majority of the breeding range, northwest to n.-cen. Alberta, and winters from cen. and e. North America south to the Greater Antilles and Central America. The breeding subspecies of Alaska, n. Yukon, and nw. District of Mackenzie south to n. British Columbia is *hooveri*; this race winters along the West Coast and in the w.-cen. states south through the Central American winter range of nominate *coronata*, and occurs sparingly to the Gulf Coast. The wings and tail of *hooveri* average longer than in *coronata*, but variation is largely clinal; breeding males show less black on the breast. Winter *hooveri* tend toward gray-brown rather than rich brown on the upperparts, and are whiter (less buffy) below.

Within the "Audubon's" group, variation is more complex, though it is clinal and rather minor within our area. The subspecies *auduboni* breeds essentially in the Pacific slope portion of the range of the "Audubon's" group. Many authorities recognize a Great Basin and Rocky Mountain subspecies, *memorabilis*, breeding from se. British Columbia southward (east of the Cascades and Sierra Nevada) to Arizona, New Mexico, and w. Texas. *D. c. memorabilis* averages larger than *auduboni* and southern populations show more extensive black below in spring males. Outside of our area, the race *nigrifrons* breeds in the mountains of Chihuahua and Durango in w. Mexico; it is recorded in non-breeding season farther south in Mexico. Breeding male *nigrifrons* average blacker than northern races, with solid black auriculars and forehead, extensively black back, and solid black of underparts extending farther through the flanks; overall *nigrifrons* is slightly larger and longer winged. Although *nigrifrons* breeds only south of the U.S., extremely black birds within the southernmost portion of the range of *memorabilis* may suggest intergradation. The distinctive subspecies *goldmani* ("Goldman's Warbler") is resident in the highlands of se. Chiapas (now rare) and Guatemala; adult males are solidly black above and extensively black below, with a white chin, white corners to the yellow throat patch, white behind the yellow crown patch, and reduced white in the wing coverts and tail. Seasonal plumage differences in *goldmani* are relatively minor; females are browner.

Taxonomic Relationships

Perhaps closest to Magnolia Warbler within *Dendroica*, although some consider Palm and, less closely, Blackpoll/Bay-breasted as closest relatives. The "Myrtle Warbler" has hybridized at least twice with Townsend's Warbler (one specimen), and once each with Northern Parula, and Palm (specimen), Cape May (specimen), Pine, and Bay-breasted warblers. A hybrid "Audubon's" × Grace's was collected in Colorado.

Plumages and Molts

Myrtle Warbler

SPRING ADULT MALE: Forehead, sides of crown, nape, and sides of neck gray, variably marked with black (especially on forehead and sides of crown) and setting off a bright yellow patch in the center of the crown. Lores and

Yellow-rumped "Myrtle" Warbler. Male in New York in May. (Photo: A. Morris/VIREO)

auricular patch jet black, bordered above by a small white supraloral spot and a short white postocular line. White arcs above and below eye. Chin and upper throat pure white, extending partway around the lower rear portion of the auricular patch. Breast with thick black streaks, often merging on the center of the breast to form a nearly solid black patch. On many individuals, this streaking extends anteriorly through the center of the lower throat. A bright yellow patch on upper sides is bordered below by a rearward extension of the black breast streaking. Flanks with thick black streaks; otherwise underparts white. Upperparts gray (nearly blue-gray) with black feather centers forming broad streaks on the back. Bright yellow patch across rump. Uppertail coverts black centered with narrow blue-gray fringes. Lesser wing coverts gray-brown. Median and greater coverts blackish with white tips, forming two bold white wing bars. Tertials and flight feathers dusky black with clear gray fringes. Rectrices dusky black with large white spots on outer three pairs. **FIRST SPRING MALE:** Closely resembles spring adult male, but primary coverts and flight feathers duller, browner (showing greater contrast against fresh greater secondary coverts); less white on outer three rectrices. On some birds, plumage may appear duller than that of adult males, with some brown wash on the scapulars and lower back and with dark gray lores. **SPRING ADULT FEMALE:** Forehead and sides of crown dull gray with short black streaks. Patch of yellow in center of crown, averages smaller than that of spring males. Lores and auriculars range from slaty brown to (occasionally) slaty black, but never jet black. Thin whitish supraloral streak and postocular streak (the two usually not joined). Chin and throat clear whitish, shaped as in spring males. Breast streaked with black but lacking solid patches. Yellow of upper sides averages duller and less extensive than that of spring males. Flanks streaked rather narrowly with dusky black. Remainder of underparts whitish with a buffy tinge to the flanks. Hindneck brownish; upperparts brownish to gray-brown with black streaks.

Patch of yellow across rump averages paler than male's. Uppertail coverts dull blackish with extensive gray-brown fringes. Wings and tail as in spring males, but wing bars average thinner, and tail usually with only a small white spot on r4. **FIRST SPRING FEMALE:** Much like spring adult female but flight feathers and primary coverts duller, very little if any white in fourth rectrix. Considerably duller birds observed in late spring and early summer are undoubtedly first spring females; these birds may have black streaking on breast lacking, have more obscure yellow crown and side patches, and show a more extensive wash of brown on the upperparts. **FALL ADULT MALE:** Forehead, crown, and hindneck brownish, often with a clear gray tinge. Patch in center of crown bright yellow, but partly obscured by brownish feather tips. Lores and auriculars brownish or brownish slate, some birds showing black in lores and anterior part of auriculars. Dull whitish supraloral streak and postocular line. Throat white, this color curving back around rear of auricular patch. Malar region and rear sides of throat often tinged buffy. Underparts whitish, streaked with black on sides of breast and flanks (this streaking somewhat veiled by whitish feather tips); center of chest usually unstreaked; yellow patch on sides. A thin band of buffy brown usually present across upper chest, setting off whitish throat. Back brownish with partially veiled thick black streaks; some clear gray ground color shows on upperparts, especially the lower back. Bright yellow rump patch; a tinge of olive just anterior to rump patch in many birds. Uppertail coverts with broad black chevrons, moderately fringed with clear gray. Wings much as spring adult; wing bars formed by white tips to median and greater secondary coverts are slightly tinged buffy. Rectrices as in spring adult male. Any fall or early winter bird showing much clear gray on the upperparts and thick black marks on the breast is likely an adult male. **FIRST FALL MALE:** Not always distinguishable from fall adult males, and virtually identical to fall adult females. Average differences from fall adult male include black streaking on breast thinner and more limited to sides of the breast; upperparts more strongly tinged with brown, with little if any gray tint showing; some brown tips to blue-gray fringing of uppertail coverts; black centers to back feathers and uppertail coverts less extensive. Usually with small white spot on fourth rectrix. Considerable variation, with dullest birds perhaps not separable from first fall females and brightest birds much like fall adult males. **FALL ADULT FEMALE:** Nearly identical to first fall male and similarly variable. Uppertail coverts often fringed with more dull gray-brown or brown, less blue-gray. **FIRST FALL FEMALE:** The brownest plumage, with upperparts varying from warm brown to dull brown and marked with fine dusky streaks. Yellow crown patch limited in extent, usually completely concealed by brown feather tips. Supraloral spot and postocular stripe buffy, inconspicuous. Auricular region brown, not contrastingly darker than crown or neck. Throat tinged buffy, especially along sides and at lower border; pale of throat wraps around behind lower rear of auricular area as in all age and sex classes. Sides and flanks with thin, indistinct brownish streaks on buffy background. Yellow patch on sides indistinct and tinged with buff or even absent. Yellow rump patch conspicuous, as in other age and sex classes. Uppertail coverts with relatively thin dusky chevrons along shaft and with broad brown fringes. Wings dusky brown, with wing bars relatively thin and tinged buffy or tan. White in rectrices most limited of all age and sex classes, very limited or sometimes absent on r4. **JUVENILE:** Underparts dull whitish, heavily streaked with dusky brown on breast, belly, and flanks. Upperparts gray-brown, streaked with dusky. Rump dull whitish with dusky streaks (yellow patch absent). **BARE PARTS:** Bill black in spring males, tinged brown along tomium and base of mandible in females and immatures. Legs and feet blackish. Eyes dark brown.

Yellow-rumped "Audubon's" Warbler. Male in California in April. (Photo: Herbert Clarke)

SPRING ADULT MALE: Forehead, sides of crown, hindneck, and sides of head dark gray to blue-gray with some indistinct black streaking. Bright yellow patch in center of crown. Auricular area gray, not set off from crown and sides of neck but often becoming darker gray or even blackish around the eye and lores. In a minority of birds there is a very indistinct yellowish supraloral spot. Chin and throat bright yellow, the throat patch not widening posteriorly around the rear of the auricular as in Myrtle group. Breast and sides heavily marked with black, forming a solid patch over much of these regions (often with some gray feather tips). The black of the breast surrounds a yellow patch on the sides and continues onto the flanks in the form of heavy streaks. Black of underparts appears more solid and extensive by summer because of wear of gray fringes. Belly and undertail coverts white. Back appears gray with thick black streaks or chevrons. Rump patch bright yellow. Uppertail coverts with broad black centers, narrow gray fringes. Wings as in spring adult male Myrtle, but greater coverts not only tipped but also broadly fringed with white, giving the appearance of a large white wing patch rather than distinct wing bars (but this feature is variable, and some birds appear wing-barred). Rectrices blackish, edged clear gray. Noticeable white spots in outer four pairs of rectrices, and usually with a small amount of white in the fifth pair (r2).
FIRST SPRING MALE: Essentially identical to spring adult males. Best told in hand by flight feather wear, as indicated under first spring male Myrtle. On average, first spring males show less white in the outer three pairs of rectrices, but there is much overlap in this character. **SPRING ADULT FEMALE:** Forehead, sides of crown, auricular region, sides of head, and hindneck gray to brownish gray. Yellow patch in center of crown smaller and duller than that of spring males. Throat varies from pale yellow to bright yellow (often white on chin and lower throat), but in many individuals throat is

Yellow-rumped "Audubon's" Warbler. Adult male in California in December. (Photo: Larry Sansone)

Yellow-rumped "Audubon's" Warbler. First fall female in California in November. (Photo: Brian E. Small)

whitish with only a slight tinge of yellow. Breast with muted dark gray streaks on a grayish background; this streaking becomes more evident as plumage wears by early summer. Yellow patch on sides paler and less distinct than on spring males. Dull gray streaking on buff-tinged flanks. Belly and undertail coverts dull white. Back strongly tinged with brown and with thin black streaks. Bright yellow rump patch. Uppertail coverts with black chevrons broadly fringed with gray. Wing coverts tipped white or buffy, forming wing bars but not solid white patch of males. Rectrices with white spots on outer three pairs, white spot on r3 usually small, and white spot in r2 usually absent. **FIRST SPRING FEMALE:** Like spring adult female; best told in hand by flight feather wear. **FALL ADULT MALE:** Forehead, crown, auricular region, sides of head, and hindneck gray with strong brown tinge. Yellow crown patch, often obscured. Throat bright yellow. Breast marked with black feather centers strongly veiled with buffy across the chest and whitish on the lower breast. Yellow patch on sides. Thick black streaks on flanks veiled with whitish. Belly and undertail coverts white. Back gray with a variable amount of brown tinge; black chevron-shaped feather centers partly veiled with gray or brown. Bright yellow rump patch. Uppertail coverts with large black chevrons fringed broadly with gray. Wing coverts blackish fringed with clear gray and tipped with pale whitish tan, forming two thin wing bars. Flight feathers blackish with clear gray edges. **FIRST FALL MALE:** Very similar to fall adult males but with stronger wash of brown and very little gray on upperparts, black streaking of back averaging thinner and more veiled with brown, less black underlying the grayish and buff on the breast, and yellow patches on crown and sides slightly duller and less distinct. Yellow of throat variable, from mostly white to extensively yellow. Uppertail coverts with thin gray-brown edges (rather than clear gray). Averages less white on rectrices 2 and 3 than adult male. **FALL ADULT FEMALE:** Probably not safely distinguishable in field from first fall males. Upperparts generally lack gray tinge, and streaking on back is indistinct. Breast has dull streaked appearance. Uppertail coverts extensively fringed with brownish, showing less clear blue-gray than in first fall male. **FIRST FALL FEMALE:** Brown on crown, neck, auriculars, and upperparts with no hint of gray. Back streaking thin and indistinct. Uppertail coverts with small dusky centers, broadly fringed with brown. Throat varies from pale yellow or buffy yellow to whitish; chin whitish. Breast buffy brown to gray-brown, with only very indistinct streaking. Indistinct brownish streaking on buff-tinged flanks. Buffy yellow patch on sides dull and indistinct, sometimes nearly absent. Wing bars pale tan. Rectrices show least white of any age or sex class, usually with no white on r2. **JUVENILE:** As in "Myrtle" group. **BARE PARTS:** As in "Myrtle" group.

The prebasic molt occurs on the breeding grounds (complete in adults, partial in hatching-year birds). The prealternate molt is rather extensive, resulting in considerable change in body plumage and secondary coverts through the late winter and spring; most birds are in alternate plumage by late April or early May.

 REFERENCES

DISTRIBUTION: Moore 1946.
ECOLOGY, BEHAVIOR, VOCALIZATIONS, AND CONSERVATION: Place and Stiles 1992, Terrill and Crawford 1988, Terrill and Ohmart 1984.
IDENTIFICATION: Kaufman 1979b.
PLUMAGES, MOLTS, AND MORPHOLOGY: Dwight 1899, Yunick 1989.
SYSTEMATICS: Barrowclough 1980, Godfrey 1951, Graves 1993, Hubbard 1969 and 1970, Moore 1946, Oberholser 1921.

BLACK-THROATED GRAY WARBLER PL. 15

Dendroica nigrescens

4.75 in. (12 cm). This and the following four species form a closely related group of species to which we refer collectively as the "*virens* group." All share the characteristics of a black throat patch (in male and some female plumages), bold white wing bars, a long tail with extensive white spots in the outer three rectrices (reduced in immature females), buzzy (often wheezy) songs, and arboreal habits. This striking black, gray, and white member of the complex is at home in a wide variety of semi-arid oak and conifer woodlands of the western U.S. and sw. British Columbia. It is patterned almost exactly like the Townsend's Warbler but is gray rather than green on the upperparts, the dark auricular is broadly connected to the dark hindneck, and the yellow is restricted to a small spot in front of the eye.

DESCRIPTION

Generally gray above and white below, with a bold face pattern. The lack of yellow (except the small supraloral spot) and green in the plumage is distinctive. There are two bold white wing bars and much white in the outer rectrices. The general plumage pattern of males is almost identical to Townsend's, with a partial or complete black throat, black cheek patch, black in the crown, broad black streaks on the sides, and some black streaking on the back. Females, with black reduced or lacking, also mirror the plumages of corresponding age Townsend's. In all plumages the dark cheek patch connects broadly to the gray hindneck.

SIMILAR SPECIES

This is a striking and easily identified warbler; only Black-and-white and Cerulean warblers are likely to cause confusion. All **BLACK-AND-WHITES** show a white median crown stripe, and all except adult males have white cheeks, bordered above by a black postocular stripe. The back of Black-and-whites is striped with white, the tertials are boldly fringed with white, and the undertail coverts are spotted with black. Black-and-whites always lack yellow on the lores. The distinctive nuthatchlike creeping behavior of Black-and-white is very different from the more typical warbler gleaning actions of Black-throated Gray.

Immature female Black-throated Grays could be confused with immature male **CERULEANS**. The Cerulean is smaller and much shorter-tailed; its upperparts are aqua blue to blue-gray, with some black streaking on the sides of the back. The young female Black-throated Gray has a slightly brown-tinted gray back, with streaking very faint or absent. The Cerulean shows a largely pale cheek and dark transocular line; the Black-throated Gray has a dark cheek.

Note the superficial similarity to **CHICKADEES** (Mountain Chickadee, *Parus gambeli*, is broadly sympatric) and **BRIDLED TITMOUSE** (*P. wollweberi*); those species lack white wing bars and tail spots, lack streaking on the sides, and have pale cheeks.

VOICE

The **SONG** is buzzy but lacks the high, wheezy quality of Townsend's. It is variable in pace and pattern but starts with several similar buzzy notes and has a crescendo effect with an inflected ending, e.g., *zee-zee-zee-zee-bzz-zee, zee-zee-zee-ee-chew,* or *buzz-see buzz-see buzz-see buzz-see wueeo.* These songs are given most frequently early in the breeding season and in response to the presence of a female or of another territorial male. An alternative song type consists of a series of similar complex (almost warbled) buzzy notes and may lack the inflected ending. Song differences have been found east and west of Cascades. **CALL NOTE** is a dull *tup,* or *tip,* lower and duller than Townsend's and somewhat duller than the "tip" note of Hermit and Black-throated Green. The call may suggest the call of Yellow-rumped ("Myrtle") Warbler more than the calls of other members of the *virens* complex. **FLIGHT NOTE** a high, clear *see,* similar to the flight notes of its close relatives.

BEHAVIOR

Foraging, which is generally similar among all members of the *virens* complex, consists of deliberate gleaning and reaching, with occasional hover-gleaning and short sallies. Most foraging is at mid-levels within the canopy, averaging lower than in Townsend's and Hermit, in part because of the Black-throated Gray's preference for shorter, more arid woodlands. On the breeding grounds, males forage somewhat higher on average than females (closer to their song perches). In winter and migration this species will join in mixed-species flocks of other insectivorous birds. The diet consists almost exclusively of insects, especially caterpillars gleaned from oaks. Some late fall and winter vagrants in eastern North America have used feeding stations.

The **NEST** is a deep, compact cup of plant fibers and grasses, bound with spider webs and lined with fir, feathers, and hair. Nests are often placed low (3–10 ft.) in bushes or low shrubby oaks, but frequently are placed at 20 ft. or more (exceptionally to 50 ft.) well out on conifer limbs. Double-brooding is known from parts of the breeding range; nests are occasionally parasitized by Brown-headed Cowbirds.

HABITAT

BREEDS in a great variety of semi-arid woodlands, particularly of conifers and live oaks. Through much of the species' range in the interior West, mixed woodlands of pinyon pines and junipers are the preferred habitat; pure stands of junipers are occupied locally, but pure pinyon pine woodlands are generally shunned. In the western part of the breeding range and in portions of e. and s. Arizona it typically occupies oak woodlands of canyons and slopes. Dominant oaks may be canyon live oak, interior live oak, Gambel oak, or California black oak; these oaks are often intermixed with conifers such as big-cone Douglas-firs, digger pines, or ponderosa pines. Stands of Sargent cypress are inhabited locally in the coast ranges of California. A brushy understory of ceanothus, manzanita, or mountain-mahogany typifies most breeding habitats. In the Pacific Northwest, breeding habitats are somewhat moister, including stands of Douglas-firs mixed with oaks, madrones, and other deciduous trees, and also lowland forests dominated by deciduous hardwoods. Stands of deciduous trees and conifers regenerating after burns or clear-cuts are used in some areas of the Northwest. Breeding elevations range from about 3,000 to 7,000 ft. in the Sierra Nevada and up to 9,500 ft. in the White Mtns., California. Breeding elevations are considerably lower in the Pacific Northwest.

Birds in the main **WINTER** range in Mexico occupy semi-arid open woodlands and tall scrub; on average they are found at lower elevations and in less forested situations than the related Townsend's and Hermit warblers. Wintering birds in California are partial to oaks, particularly coast live oaks, but are sometimes found in streamside associations of willows and cottonwoods. Elsewhere in the southwestern U.S., winter birds use bottomland associations of cottonwoods, willows, mesquite, and sycamores. **MIGRANTS** are found in arid woodlands (pinyons, junipers, oaks), riparian forests, and brushy associations such as chaparral. In late summer there is some upslope movement in the mountains into subalpine conifer associations and montane meadow edges. Fall migrants are frequently found in such habitats, although on average, fall migrants are found at lower elevations than Townsend's and Hermit warblers.

 DISTRIBUTION

BREEDS from sw. B.C. (including s. Vancouver Is.; summer records on west slope of Rocky Mtns. to cen. B.C.) and w. Wash. south through the Pacific Coast states to n. Baja Calif. (Sierra Juarez, Sierra San Pedro Martir); also breeds in the interior from e. Ore. (local), s. Idaho, s. and nw. Wyo., and w. and se. Colo. south to se. Ariz., s. N.M. (local in the se. and ne. highlands), and possibly the Guadalupe Mtns. of w. Texas (where breeding status needs clarification); also breeds in the mountains of extreme ne. Sonora.

WINTERS from coastal cen. and s. Calif. (rare) and s. Ariz. (very uncommon) and in Mexico from s. Baja Calif., s. Sonora, and Coahuila south to Oaxaca. South of there, there is a 1 November

BLACK-THROATED GRAY WARBLER
Dendroica nigrescens

1936 sight record from the highlands of Guatemala. It is also rare but regular along the Rio Grande in w. Texas and the lower Rio Grande Valley in s. Texas. It winters casually north to nw. Calif. and w. Ore.; there are two winter records for w. Wash. and two December records for Vancouver, B.C. Also casual in winter in the western interior (north to Mont.), along the Gulf Coast, and in e. North America (see under vagrancy below).

Migration is through much of w. North America, although it is generally rare in w. Texas and east of the Rocky Mtns. Spring migration is somewhat earlier than in Townsend's and Hermit, and fall migration is quite protracted.

In **SPRING MIGRATION**, the first arrivals are found in s. Ariz. and s. Calif. during the last 10 days of March (a few to mid-March in s. Ariz.). A few can arrive in cen. and n. Calif. and s. Ore. by the end of March, but most arrive there (Ore.) by the first or second weeks of April. For w. Wash. and sw. B.C. there are scattered records for the first week of April, but first arrivals are usually during the second week of April. Arrivals in the interior West vary from the second week of April (ne. Ariz.) and the latter half of April (w. Colo.) to early May (e. Ore.) and the second week of May in s. Wyo. Peak spring movements over much of the West are for the last 10 days of April and first few days of May. In s. Calif. there is a sharp drop-off in numbers of migrants after 10 May, but a few are noted on the northern deserts through about 20 May. Concentrations of migrants have been found in nw. Ore. as late as mid-May. Exceptionally late was one on the Farallon Is., Calif., on 3 June.

FALL MIGRATION is protracted; unlike most other western warblers it may be more numerous in the desert lowlands in fall than in spring. A few fall migrants are noted in early August (sometimes in late July in the interior). Peak fall movements are at the end of August and early September in w. Ore., and from early to mid-September through early October over much of Calif. There is still considerable movement through s. Calif. in mid-October, and small numbers of migrants are detected through the end of October as far north as Ore. There are scattered records of migrants through November, and some of the December records away from known wintering areas may pertain to late fall migrants.

CASUAL in the s. Great Plains, Mont., Alta. (mostly summer), and Sask. It is a very rare, but annual, late fall vagrant and winter visitant to the Gulf Coast states (mostly along or near the coast); there are 75+ records for Fla., 50+ for La., and multiple records for Miss. and Ala. In the Southeast also recorded in Ga., the Carolinas, and Tenn. There are about 35 records for the Midwest, with a slight majority pertaining to fall birds (as early as 31 August) or birds attempting to winter. The few records of spring VAGRANTS are from the last week of April through the first half of May; there is an unseasonal mid-June record for near Toronto, Ont. In the Northeast about two-thirds of the roughly 75 records through 1995 are for fall, eight are for winter, and 13 are for spring (21 April to mid-May); a singing male was present in R.I. during much of July 1979. Black-throated Gray Warblers have been recorded from all eastern states and provinces except Mo., Man., P.E.I., Vt., N.H., and W. Va. State totals include N.J. (21), N.Y. and Mass. (11), Ont. (10), Pa. (9), and Ohio (8). The numbers of vagrants to the Gulf Coast states have declined somewhat in recent years.

STATUS AND CONSERVATION

Little information, although local declines of breeding populations due to deforestation and forest management practices seem likely. The frequency of the occurrence of vagrant Black-throated Gray Warblers in eastern North America (particularly the Gulf Coast) appears to have declined in recent years. This species is at least an occasional Brown-headed Cowbird host.

 ## SUBSPECIES

Birds in the eastern part of the breeding range, from e. Oregon and e. Washington south through Arizona and New Mexico and adjacent Sonora, are weakly differentiated by larger size and greater extent of white in the tail; these have been recognized by some authors as a separate subspecies *halsei* (which is not recognized by AOU 1957). Some authors have restricted the range of *halsei* to Arizona, New Mexico, and adjacent Mexico. However, one author found that wing length is greater in populations east of the Cascades than those to the west and feels that this variation confirms the validity of *halsei* as the breeding subspecies north to Oregon and Washington (east of the Cascades). An analysis found that genetic differences between Black-throated Gray Warblers of Washington and Arizona were as great as those between Townsend's and Hermit Warblers.

 ## TAXONOMIC RELATIONSHIPS

Black-throated Gray is the sister group to the *virens* superspecies (Black-throated Green, Golden-cheeked, Townsend's, and Hermit) and is sometimes included within it. One author, without explanation, considered it most closely related to the Black-throated Green Warbler, a result that disagrees with other studies based on inferred speciation events during the Pleistocene epoch and on the analysis of mitochondrial DNA. A specimen of a hybrid with Townsend's Warbler has been taken in British Columbia and there was a sight record of this combination in nw. Washington. A female that was phenotypically intermediate between Black-throated Gray and Hermit Warbler nested with a male Black-throated Gray in the San Gabriel Mtns., s. California, in 1994, raising at least one young.

 ## PLUMAGES AND MOLTS

SPRING ADULT MALE: Forehead, center, and sides of crown, lores, and auriculars black, the black of the auriculars connecting with the dark hindneck. Supraloral spot yellow, connected to or slightly constricted from the white supercilium. Rear crown mottled gray and black. Upperparts gray, with broad black feather centers on the back forming loose back streaks. Rump gray; uppertail coverts black with gray fringes. Chin and throat solid black

Black-throated Gray Warbler. Adult male in California in April. (Photo: Brian E. Small)

(but thin white line in intramalar area). Broad white malar stripe separating the black cheek from the black throat. Remaining underparts white with broad black streaks on the sides and flanks. Wings blackish with gray fringes to lesser wing coverts and broad white tips to the median and greater coverts, forming two bold wing bars. Tail blackish, with the outer two pairs of rectrices nearly all white on the inner webs; r4 is white on the inner web for about the distal two-thirds; there is a long white spot on the inner web of r3 and a narrow white inner edge to r2. **FIRST SPRING MALE:** Similar to spring adult male but crown less solidly black, with more mixture of gray in the center of the crown; the black centers of the back feathers are smaller, yielding thinner back streaking. Many individuals show much white on the chin, and some show a mixture of white in the black of the throat. In the hand, the rectrices appear more tapered than those of adults, the white spot on r4 is smaller, and the flight feathers and primary coverts are duller. See below for distinctions from spring females, which can be very similar. **SPRING ADULT FEMALE:** Variable. Typically differ from spring adult males in the following ways: the black on the crown is limited to the sides of the crown and short black streaks through the forehead, forecrown, and center of the crown, with little or no solid black on the forehead and forecrown; the chin is always white, and most individuals have a white throat, with a band of black across the lower throat and a patch of black at the sides of the rear throat; the auricular patch is slate gray or dull slaty black, but never jet black; the yellow supraloral spot averages paler; the black streaks on the back and uppertail coverts are narrower and less evident in the field; the side and flank streaks are thinner and grayer (less black); and the white spot on r4 is smaller. Many individuals have much black coming up on the center of the throat, with just a small white area on the chin and some white mottling on the uppermost throat; these birds are very similar to first spring males but in the hand can be aged as adults by their blacker remiges and greater primary coverts

Black-throated Gray Warbler. First fall female in California in October. (Photo: Herbert Clarke)

and by their more truncate and less worn rectrices. **FIRST SPRING FEMALE:** Similar to spring adult female; in the hand may be aged by duller flight feathers and primary coverts and by more tapered rectrices with smaller white spots on r4. The amount of black on the throat of spring females does not appear to be related to age. **FALL ADULT MALE:** Closely similar to spring adult male, but with thin white feather tips on throat giving a slightly frosted appearance; feathers of center of crown with slight gray tips. Back streaks somewhat veiled with gray. **FIRST FALL MALE:** Similar to first spring male, but cheeks gray, heavily flecked with black; crown with little black in center; back streaks narrower and strongly veiled with gray or gray-brown; throat less solidly black, especially on chin; white stripes on face broader. Probably indistinguishable in the field from many fall adult females, but in the hand first fall males show more tapered rectrices. **FALL ADULT FEMALE:** Like spring adult female but with back streaking strongly veiled with gray, and the black on the throat more heavily veiled with whitish. **FIRST FALL FEMALE:** Crown gray with indistinct short black streaks and a variable blackish border. Hindneck and back gray with a slight brownish tinge; dusky shaft streaks on back feathers narrow and indistinct (back appears unstreaked in the field). Rump and uppertail coverts gray, the latter with narrow, indistinct blackish shaft streaks. Supraloral spot pale yellow; broad white supercilium. Cheeks gray, connected at the rear to the gray of the hindneck. Chin, throat, and malar region white, with a limited and variable slaty patch at the sides of the throat. Remaining underparts dull white, with blurred dark gray streaking on the sides and flanks. Wings gray with white tips to the median and greater coverts (with narrow blackish shaft streaks through the white). Tail with extensive white on the inner webs of the outer two pairs of rectrices, a small white spot on r4, and no white on r3. **JUVENILE:** Upperparts dull brownish, darker on the crown. Broad dull whitish supercilium.

Underparts dull gray, becoming whitish on the belly. Wings and tail as in first fall birds. **BARE PARTS:** Bill black in spring adults, tinted slightly brown in fall adults and more extensively brown in first fall birds; legs blackish; eye blackish brown; some dull yellow on soles of feet.

The prebasic molt takes place on the breeding grounds; it is complete in adults but does not involve flight feathers in hatching-year birds. There is a very limited prealternate molt in late winter (February to April).

 REFERENCES

DISTRIBUTION: Leck 1983, Sharpe 1993.
ECOLOGY, BEHAVIOR, VOCALIZATIONS, AND CONSERVATION: Morrison 1982 and 1990, Morrison and Hardy 1983b, Sharpe 1993, Stein 1962.
SYSTEMATICS: Bermingham et al. 1992, Mengel 1964, Morrison 1990, Oberholser 1930, Rohwer 1994.

GOLDEN-CHEEKED WARBLER PL. 13

Dendroica chrysoparia

4.75 in. (12 cm). The Golden-cheeked Warbler is a localized member of the Black-throated Green Warbler *(virens)* superspecies. It breeds only on and near the Edwards Plateau of cen. Texas in old-growth woodlands of oaks and other hardwoods; it requires the presence of at least some Ashe junipers (locally called "cedars"), which are important in its nesting biology. Its specialized breeding habitat has suffered considerable modification from urbanization and negative impacts of rural land management practices, and this species is considered endangered in the U.S. It winters in the highlands of southern Mexico and northern Central America. In appearance it suggests a melanistic Black-throated Green Warbler; adult males are characterized by extensively black upperparts; the strong eye line and unmarked yellow cheek are distinctive in all plumages.

 DESCRIPTION

Generally similar to the Black-throated Green Warbler, but the adult males have the upperparts black; the upperparts of females and immature males are olive streaked with black. There is no yellow on the underparts. The eye line is bold in all plumages, usually joining the dark hindneck. The cheeks are solidly yellow in all plumages, with no dark lower border. Structural characters and age and sex variations parallel the other members of *virens* complex.

SIMILAR SPECIES

First fall females are very similar to immature female **BLACK-THROATED GREEN WARBLERS**; any suspected Golden-cheeked out of its normal range should be identified with great caution. Note that migrant Black-throated Greens are scarce within the breeding habitat of Golden-cheeked and that Golden-cheeks are virtually never seen north of Mexico away from their breeding grounds. The key character of all Golden-cheeks is the unmarked yellow cheek, bordered only above with the dark eye line (darker and more distinct than the eye line of Black-throated Green and often continuous with the olive nape); there is no olive lower border to the yellow cheek. Dull Black-throated Green Warblers always show an olive shadow on the lower border of the auricular; most have extensive olive on the cheeks with yellow only in the center of the cheek. All Golden-cheeks lack yellow in the vent; Black-throated Greens always show some yellow in that area. Even the dullest female Golden-cheeks show a trace of blackish streaking on the back; young female Black-throated Greens show no hint of back streaking. The green of the upperparts is duller, more olive, in Goldencheeks. See also **HERMIT WARBLER**, which shares the unmarked yellow cheek. Hermit has a grayer back, is unstreaked below, and has no strong eye line.

VOICE

SONG is a series of about four notes, the second usually lowest in pitch; the quality is harsher and buzzier than the song of the Black-throated Green Warbler, but the general quality and pattern is typical of the *virens* complex. A typical song is *zee, zoo, zidee zee* or *dzeee dzweeee dzeezy zee*. Variation in the song may relate to context and function (e.g., advertising vs. territorial songs, as in many warblers); alternate songs include a simpler *zee, zee, zee, zee see,* rising slightly in pitch and ending with a high, sharp note. **CALL NOTE** is *tip* or *tsip,* very similar to the call note of Black-throated Green. **FLIGHT NOTE** is a high, thin *see* with no buzzy quality.

BEHAVIOR

Forages by gleaning foliage and branches, especially in oaks; it may hang acrobatically to glean but only rarely sallies for flying insects. Because of the relatively low stature of its breeding habitat, some foraging on the breeding grounds is within a few feet of the ground, although it more typically works the middle and upper levels of vegetation. On the wintering grounds and in migration it forages in the middle and upper layers of vegetation in woodlands; there it occurs in mixed flocks of warblers (including Wilson's, Townsend's, Hermit, and sometimes Black-throated Green), Solitary Vireos, flycatchers, and other insectivores. The diet is almost exclusively insects, especially caterpillars and small grasshoppers and crickets.

Males sing as soon as they arrive on the breeding grounds in mid-March. Most foraging takes place in canyon bottoms and lower slopes, but males often sing from ridgetops — either from within the canopy or from a high, exposed perch. Singing males often fly long distances between song perches. Singing declines by mid-May and has generally ceased by late June.

The **NEST** is a bulky cup made largely of strips of bark from the Ashe juniper (*Juniperus ashei*) but incorporating grass and rootlets and bound by spider webs. The nest is lined wth hair and feathers. It is placed in the fork or crotch of a tree branch, often in a juniper but also in an elm, live oak, or other hardwood. Nests are placed from 5 to 30 ft. but usually around 15 ft. Nest trees are frequently in canyon bottoms.

 HABITAT

The Golden-cheeked is among the most specialized of our warblers, **BREEDING** only in woodlands containing Ashe juniper but dominated by oaks (especially Texas oak, plateau live oak, Lacy oak) and variably intermixed with ash, bigtooth maple, walnut, sycamore, cedar elm, escarpment black cherry, etc. Ideal breeding habitat occurs only very locally within the breeding range, especially where the above tree associations occur in woodlands only 10–30 ft. tall. The woodlands must contain Ashe junipers ("cedars") that are relatively mature, with much loose, stripping bark which is used for nest material. Despite the importance of this tree to the biology of the Golden-cheeked Warbler, pure stands of mature juniper do not constitute good warbler habitat.

WINTER habitat generally consists of montane pine and pine-oak associations, from cloud forests down to the upper edges of lower montane tropical forests. This species shows far greater flexibility in its choice of winter habitat than on the breeding grounds. **MIGRANTS** in e. Mexico have mainly been noted above 3,000 ft. elevation, mainly in oaks.

BREEDING range is limited to the hill country of central Texas, specifically to the Balcones Escarpment and adjacent areas of the geologically similar Edwards Plateau; the species is very localized within its breeding range. Breeding sites are known from Palo Pinto Co. (formerly also Dallas Co.) south to Kinney Co. at the southwest corner of its range. The current breeding range encompasses parts of about 30 Texas counties (it formerly bred in more than 40 counties).

WINTERS in montane regions from s. Mexico (Chiapas) south through Guatemala and Honduras and possibly to n.-cen. Nicaragua (two September specimens). Males appear to predominate in Chiapas, so it is possible that females winter, on average, farther south. In Chiapas, Golden-cheeks are estimated to be only about 1 percent as numerous as Townsend's Warblers. Birds have been noted on the wintering grounds in Chiapas well into March and exceptionally as late as 13 April.

GOLDEN-CHEEKED WARBLER
Dendroica chrysoparia
(following C. Sexton *in litt.*)

SPRING ARRIVAL on the breeding grounds is typically between 10 and 15 March, with records as early as 2 March in Travis Co. The earliest arrivals are males, with females arriving several days later. The observations of spring migrants in ne. Mexico have been during the middle third of March; these have come from the eastern escarpment of the Sierra Madre Oriental in Nuevo Leon, Coahuila, Tamaulipas, Veracruz, and Queretaro. The only record of a spring migrant in Texas away from nesting areas is 22 March in Medina County.

FALL MIGRATION is poorly understood. There are records for ne. Mexico as early as 22 June and three s. Texas records (well away from breeding areas) in late June and early July. There is a 3 August record for Galveston Is. on the upper Texas coast. Most birds have departed the breeding grounds by the beginning of August, with several records during the second week of August and one record for as late as 18 August. The earliest fall arrivals in the wintering grounds in the highlands of Chiapas are 5 and 11 August.

VAGRANT to Pinellas Co., w. Florida (first fall male collected 24 August 1964), and to se. Farallon Is., California (first fall male collected 9 September 1971, the latest record north of Mexico). Possibly correct was a sight record of a male on St. Croix, U.S. Virgin Islands, 23 November 1939 and 8 January 1940.

▥ STATUS AND CONSERVATION

Along with Kirtland's Warbler, this is certainly the rarest and most endangered species of the wood-warbler of North America (assuming that Bachman's Warbler is extinct). This species has declined both in population size and geographical range in historical times. Current population estimates are between 5,000 and 15,000 pairs in 30,000 to 105,000 hectares of habitat scattered among 30+ counties. This species' decline is due mainly to the clearing of woodland habitat (and especially Ashe junipers) for fencepost material and fuel, grazing land, and (more recently) urbanization; much key habitat was destroyed by landowners in anticipation of the species' December 1990 Federal Endangered Species listing. The remaining habitat is beset with impacts from rural land management practices, one result of which is perhaps an increased rate of brood parasitism by Brown-headed Cowbirds; Golden-cheeked Warblers are, however, often successful in raising one of their own young in a parasitized nest. Urbanization has also led to increased populations of Blue Jays, whose predation on eggs and nestlings has been implicated in the warbler's absence from remaining habitat near suburban areas.

SUBSPECIES

As expected for a species so geographically restricted, no geographic variation is described.

 TAXONOMIC RELATIONSHIPS

The Golden-cheeked Warbler is probably the sister species of the Black-throated Green Warbler. Some consider it a subspecies of Black-throated Green, though nearly all current authors treat *chrys-oparia* as a distinct species.

 PLUMAGES AND MOLTS

SPRING ADULT MALE: Forehead, crown, hindneck, and back solid black; a short yellow median stripe on the forehead is more pronounced in adult males than in other plumages. Particularly in early spring, the upperparts may show limited olive feather edges, especially on the lower back. Face (supercilium, supraloral area, auricular region, malar region, and sides of the neck) bright yellow. Distinct black stripe through the lores and eyes, extending back to the rear of the auricular region and from there backwards to join the black nape. There is a short extension of the black eye line down along the rear of the auricular. The chin, throat, and breast are black, with the black continuing as broad streaking on the sides and flanks (a few show short black streaks on the undertail coverts). The wings are blackish with two bold white wing bars; the tips of the median coverts are pure white, with no black shaft streak. There is a long white patch on the inner webs of the outer three pairs of rectrices. **FIRST SPRING MALE:** Nearly identical to spring adult male, but most show considerable

Golden-cheeked Warbler. Adult male in Texas in April. (Photo: Steve and Dave Maslowski)

Golden-cheeked Warbler. Adult female in Texas in May. (Photo: Greg W. Lasley)

olive mixed into the black of the crown and back. Most also show some yellowish or white tips to the black throat feathers. In the hand, the flight feathers are browner than in adults; the inner secondaries show narrower and less contrasting white edges and tips in first spring birds. **SPRING ADULT FEMALE:** Upperparts, including crown, olive green with black spotting and streaking. The extreme upper chin is yellow in all females. The black of the remaining chin and throat shows some yellow stippling, but the lower throat and sides of the breast are solidly black; there is strong black streaking on the sides and flanks. The white tips to the median coverts show thin dark shaft streaks. **FIRST SPRING FEMALE:** Very similar to spring adult female but with a whitish chin and less extensive black on the throat, and fainter streaking on the sides and flanks. The upperparts appear mainly olive green with fainter black streaking than in the spring adult female. In the hand, the flight feathers are browner than in spring adults. **FALL ADULT MALE:** Very similar to the spring adult male, but the black feathers of the throat are narrowly margined with white or pale yellow and the black of the upperparts has more extensive olive fringing. **FIRST FALL MALE:** The crown and upperparts are extensively fringed with olive green, appearing in the field as strong black streaking and spotting on an olive background. The black of the chin (especially) and throat is heavily veiled with grayish white or even slightly washed with pale yellow. The eye line is not as black as in the fall adult male. The white tips to the median coverts have thin dark shaft streaks. **FALL ADULT FEMALE:** Very similar to spring adult female, but the throat is more extensively veiled with pale yellow or white. **FIRST FALL FEMALE:** Forehead, crown, back, and rump olive, with thin, diffuse black streaks. Cheeks unmarked clear yellow. Even in this dullest plumage, the dark olive eye line is distinct and usually appears to join the olive nape. Throat very pale yellow, grading to pale buffy white on the underparts. There is an area of slaty mottling on the sides of the breast but very little streaking on the sides and flanks; what streaking is present is duller and more slaty (less black). **JUVENILE:** Olive-brown above, spotted with dusky. Sides of the head dull buffy; throat and breast grayish, becoming dull whitish on the belly; faint dusky streaking on the underparts. Wings and tail as in first fall birds. **BARE PARTS:** Bill black in spring birds, tinged with brown in fall and winter (extensively pale brown in first fall birds); legs and feet brownish black; eyes dark brown.

Molts appear to be the same as in other members of the superspecies. The prebasic molt, complete in adults, is undertaken on the breeding grounds and commences as early as the latter half of June. A limited prealternate molt, which takes place in late winter and early spring, results in little discernible change in appearance.

 REFERENCES

GENERAL: Oberholser 1974, Pulich 1976, Pulich et al. 1989, Sexton 1992.
DISTRIBUTION: Beatty 1943, Braun et al. 1986, Johnson et al. 1988, Lewis et al. 1974, Vidal et al. 1994, Wahl et al. 1990, Woolfenden 1967.
ECOLOGY, BEHAVIOR, VOCALIZATIONS, AND CONSERVATION: Engels and Sexton 1994, Kroll 1980, Vidal et al. 1994, Wahl et al. 1990, U.S. Fish and Wildlife Service 1990.

BLACK-THROATED GREEN WARBLER   PL. 13

Dendroica virens

4.75 in. (12 cm). The very common and confiding Black-throated Green Warbler is the eastern representative of the *virens* species complex (Black-throated Gray through Hermit warblers); it nests in a wide variety of eastern coniferous, deciduous, and mixed forests, with the preferred habitat varying geographically. Its migrations are prolonged, with fall birds lingering later than most other warblers in eastern North America. The Black-throated Green Warbler shares many characters with the other members of its complex, being a medium-sized, long-tailed *Dendroica* with a long tail extension beyond the undertail coverts. There is much white in the outer three pairs of rectrices, bold white wing bars, and little seasonal change in plumage. This species is characterized by bright green upperparts, a yellow triangle outlining the indistinct olive auricular, and (in all but immature females) much black on the throat. Its songs are distinctive and easily learned.

DESCRIPTION

The upperparts are bright green in all plumages, with upperpart streaking relatively limited (visible streaking is present mainly in adult males). Yellow is primarily restricted to the face; there is also a yellow wash in the vent in all plumages, which is diagnostic within the *virens* group. The yellow auricular region is faintly to strongly outlined in green. All birds except immature females have black on the breast, and all plumages show streaks on the sides.

 ## SIMILAR SPECIES

Most likely to be confused with the Golden-cheeked Warbler and with Townsend's × Hermit hybrids. **GOLDEN-CHEEKED** and all other members of the *virens* complex except Black-throated Green lack yellow in the vent. There is some black streaking in the back of all Golden-cheeked plumages (coalescing into nearly solid black in adult males), and the ground color of the crown and back is a duller olive than in Black-throated Green. The eye line is stronger in Golden-cheeked and is connected to the dark color of the nape. All Black-throated Greens show a dark green lower border to the auriculars, whereas Golden-cheeked is clear yellow here, the eye line being the only dark area on the face. See **TOWNSEND'S WARBLER**; for distinctions from **TOWNSEND'S × HERMIT HYBRIDS** (which also lack yellow in the vent), see under **HERMIT WARBLER**.

 ## BEHAVIOR

This is a rather tame and confiding warbler; it can be quite aggressive toward other small passerines on the breeding grounds. Most foraging takes place at middle levels of vegetation, along twigs and within foliage but generally not at the tips of branches. Prey is mainly gleaned from leaves and small branches (less often twigs and larger branches); hover-gleaning and sallying for insects is seasonally common in some areas. Food is primarily insects, especially caterpillars and (during major outbreaks) spruce budworms; some berries (especially poison ivy) are taken in migration and winter.

The **NEST** is a deep cup of grasses, bark shreds, moss, fine twigs, and spider webs, lined with hair and feathers. Nests are usually placed from 3 to 10 ft. (often to 20 ft. and rarely to 40 ft.) in conifers such as white pines, hemlocks, and spruces, but sometimes in birches, maples, and other hardwoods. The nests are placed on a horizontal branch, often supported by adjacent branchlets and usually well away from the trunk. Ground nests have been recorded.

 ## Voice

SONGS of two distinct types are given in different contexts by a single individual. The first type, with an accented ending, is a deliberate, *zeee zeee zee-zoo zee!* or *see see see su-zee*, the last note highest; this song varies in the number of notes and exact pattern. The other song, also variable but with an unaccented ending, is *zoo zee zoo zoo zee* (often given as *trees, trees, murm'ring trees.* The songs are typical of the *virens* complex but are less raspy and more patterned than those of Townsend's. There has been much study by Morse and others on the contexts of Black-throated Green Warbler songs. Songs with an unaccented ending are usually given while advertising territory or are stimulated by another male; they are typically given from a fixed and usually prominent perch. Accented-ending songs predominate as pair bonds are established and again late in the breeding season; they tend to be given from lower perches or while the male is foraging. Prior to pair formation, unaccented songs predominate at dawn and dusk, and accented songs predominate otherwise. After pair formation, unaccented songs dominate through the early morning, but accented songs dominate later in the morning and in the afternoon.

The **CALL NOTE** is a soft, flat *tip* or *tsip* essentially identical to the call note of Hermit; it is not quite as high and sharp as the chip note of Townsend's. This call is also very similar to the chip note (relatively rarely given) of the Black-and-white Warbler. A double chip is frequently given between unaccented-ending songs. The **FLIGHT NOTE** is typical of the species complex, a high, sweet *see* without any buzzy tones.

 ## Habitat

BREEDS in a wide variety of coniferous and mixed forest habitats, and even in purely deciduous forests in parts of its range. A common characteristic of all breeding habitats is the multistoried layering of foliage, often best developed in fairly open forests or around edges or openings in denser forests. There is usually a well-developed shrub layer. A wide variety of conifers are chosen, with white pines being especially important in the northern parts of the breeding range, hemlocks in the Appalachian region. Other locally important conifers include spruces, balsam fir, red cedar, pitch pine (s. New England, Long Island), Virginia pine (Alabama), and Atlantic white cedar (cen. New Jersey pine barrens). Many species of deciduous trees may be intermixed with conifer breeding habitat, including birch, aspen, poplar, oak, maple, and hickory. In parts of the range (e.g., New Hampshire, West Virginia) greatest densities are reached in pure deciduous hardwood forests. The subspecies *waynei* of the southeast Atlantic coastal plain nests in swamps of cypress and Atlantic white cedar.

WINTERS in a variety of wooded habitats; in Mexico it occurs in lowland and highland habitats (usually below 7,000 ft.), but farther south it is primarily found in montane regions. It mixes with other members of the *virens* superspecies in winter but also occurs in their absence at lower elevations. It occupies tropical evergreen forest, cloud forest, oak woodlands, and pine-oak associations, often in semi-open areas and forest edges. This species has been found wintering in planted conifers in Jamaica. Within the main part of the U.S. winter range (s. Florida), it is found in mixed passerine flocks in tropical hammocks.

MIGRANTS are found in a great variety of woodland and scrub habitats.

 DISTRIBUTION

BREEDS across boreal forests of Canada, Great Lakes region, and New England, from e.-cen. B.C., n. and cen. Alta., cen. Sask., cen. and s. Man., most of Ont., s. Que. and Nfld. (including s. Lab.) south to cen. Minn., cen. and (locally) s. Wisc., n.-cen. Ill. (Ogle Co.), s. Mich., e. Ohio, cen. N.J., and s. N.Y. (including a few on Long Island). Also breeds in the Appalachian mountains and foothills south to nw. S.C., n. Ga., and cen. Ala. In recent years, isolated small populations have been found in the Ozark Mtns. of nw. Ark. Has bred in n. and s.-cen. Ind. and may occasionally breed in w. Ohio, Ky., and Ill. (outside regular nesting area in Ogle Co.). The subspecies *waynei* breeds on the immediate Atlantic coastal plain from se. Va. south to Charleston Co., S.C.

WINTERS mainly from ne. Mexico (north to s. Nuevo Leon) and w. Mexico (in small numbers north to Nayarit) south through Central America to cen. Panama. A few winter east to Darien, e. Panama, and it also winters rarely in n. South America (n. Colombia, n. Venezuela). Also winters in the Bahamas and Greater Antilles (especially Cuba and Jamaica), but rare in Puerto Rico and Virgin Is. and casual in the Lesser Antilles, Trinidad, and Netherlands Antilles. Within the U.S. it winters regularly only in s. Fla. (up to 11 on a single Christmas Bird Count in Ft. Lauderdale). It becomes very rare in n. Fla. (including the Panhandle) and westward along the Gulf Coast (it is annual in the Mississippi Delta region of s. La.). A very few winter regularly in the Rio Grande Valley of s. Texas. There are records for December and early January north to S.C., Ky., Kans., Ill., Ont., s. N.Y., Conn., Mass., and N.S., but few if any of these records represent successfully overwintering birds. There is a January record for se. Ariz., and some dozen winter records for Calif. (many of these are for December only, but a few involve overwintering birds).

MIGRATIONS of this species through e. North America are complex and extended, no doubt because of the species' extensive breeding and winter ranges. Much of the spring migration is trans-Gulf, but some migrate through Fla. and also well up the Rio Grande Valley of Texas (where most other eastern warblers are scarce). Apart from breeding *waynei*, this species is scarce in spring on the Atlantic coastal plain south of Del. and N.J.; conversely, it is more numerous in the Rio Grande Valley of Texas (away from the coast) and along the e. Great Plains (n.-cen. Texas to the e. Dakotas) than are most other eastern warblers. There is an eastward shift in fall migration, with decreased numbers in coastal Texas and increased numbers in Fla.; this shift is less pronounced, however, than in most trans-Gulf migrants.

The first **SPRING MIGRANTS** appear in Fla. and the Gulf Coast during the latter half of March, exceptionally to 11 March in n.-cen. Texas and 13 March in Tenn. There are scattered late March records throughout the East, even north to s. Ont. and Mass. The subspecies *waynei* arrives on breeding grounds in coastal S.C. by 20–25 March, and in se. Va. by the end of March. Returning breeders are widespread at the latitude of e. Tenn., Ky., se. Ohio, and W. Va. during the first half of April. Across much of the Midwest and Northeast, spring arrivals are typically in the last week of April; in the Great Lakes region and n. New England, birds arrive in the first few days of May, and at the northern end of the breeding range arrivals are around mid-May (exceptionally as early as 27 April in Man.). Peak spring movements on the Gulf Coast are in the last week of April and into the beginning of May. Over the Midwest and Mid-Atlantic region, numbers peak in the first half of May, and in the Great Lakes and New England they peak in the second and third weeks of May. On the Gulf Coast and across the Deep South, migration is mostly over by the middle of May, but stragglers have occurred into late May in Fla. and elsewhere. Exceptional are records for the Dry Tortugas Is., Fla., on 23–24 June and the s. Bahamas on 8 June. Migration continues through much of the Midwest to the fourth week of May; migrant counts of 100+ have been made as late as 25 May at Lake

BLACK-THROATED GREEN WARBLER
Dendroica virens

Ontario, N.Y. Stragglers occur in the Midwest and e. Great Plains into mid-June.

The earliest **FALL MIGRANTS** may occur as early as late July across much of e. North America (more typically the first half of August), but general arrivals across the Midwest and New England are not until late August. In Fla. and elsewhere in the Deep South, migrants are not noted until early September (exceptionally mid-August), and do not occur in numbers until the last third of September. Departure from the northernmost breeding grounds is mostly from mid-August to mid-September. Peak migrant counts in the Midwest and Northeast are in mid- and (especially) late September, but significant numbers still move through during the first week of October when nearly all other warblers have departed. A count of 17 in the New York City region on 20 October indicates how late this species' movements can be. Stragglers are widely recorded in the north through much of November. Peak fall movements in Fla. and the Deep South occur through most of October, and post-hurricane counts of 125 on 2 November and 20 on 12 November in coastal Mississippi are again indicative of this species' late migration.

Rare **VAGRANT** in w. North America, with multiple records in most states (but unrecorded in Idaho and perhaps Ut.). Records occur in spring and fall on the w. Great Plains, but farther west the great majority of the records are for fall. Of Calif.'s 288 records (through 1995) about 80 percent are for fall (mainly October and November) and 15 percent are for spring (mid-May to mid-June); most are for the immediate coast. There are mid-summer records for Calif., Wash., Ariz., and Colo. Late spring and summer vagrants have been recorded in coastal B.C., se. Alaska, and w. Northwest Territories. Recorded in winter in Baja Calif. and in spring on Isla Socorro off w. Mexico.

There are three old fall records for Greenland and a 19 November 1858 record for Heligoland, Germany. Also, a corpse was found on a ship off Iceland 19 September 1984.

ılıl STATUS AND CONSERVATION

Long-term population trends are unclear and confused by year-to-year population fluctuations. Greatest abundances are reached in spruce-hardwood associations in Maine, Nova Scotia and New Brunswick, and in the Adirondack Mtns. Breeding Bird Survey data show about equal numbers of regional declines and increases, but long-term declines have been reported for some areas. Range contraction has occurred with habitat loss in portions of the breeding range, e.g., Wisconsin, s. Michigan, s. Ontario, and s. New England. Annual averages of vagrants to California have declined from about 15 per year in 1975–1979 to about 10 per year since 1980, even with increased observer coverage. This species' ability to winter in forest edge and second-growth habitats make it less susceptible to the effects of winter habitat destruction than many warblers.

SUBSPECIES

A weakly differentiated subspecies, *waynei*, is isolated in cypress and other deciduous swamps of the Atlantic coastal plain; many authors consider this species monotypic. *D. v. waynei* is characterized by its slightly smaller size and especially its shorter and more delicate bill. A slight tendency toward duller, less yellowish plumage is reported, but such differences are weak. South coastal *waynei* arrives early on its nesting grounds, with nests recorded as early as early April. Its winter grounds are uncertain, but include at least w. Cuba.

Taxonomic Relationships

The Black-throated Green forms a superspecies with the closely related Townsend's, Hermit, and Golden-cheeked and perhaps Black-throated Gray warblers; it (along with Golden-cheeked) appears to be a sister group to the Townsend's/Hermit species pair. Isolation and speciation within this complex occurred during the Pleistocene glaciations, when suitable habitat was limited to certain refugia; the exact nature and timing of species formation is still debated. Genetic studies have uncovered one hybrid between Black-throated Green Warbler and Townsend's Warbler, although that individual was exactly like Townsend's in appearance.

Plumages and Molts

SPRING ADULT MALE: The forehead and crown are bright yellow-olive, nearly pure yellow on the sides of the forehead. The face (supercilium, malar region, cheeks, and sides of the neck) is bright yellow; there is an olive green outline to the auricular area formed by a line from the lores back through the eye and wrapping down around the rear of the cheek, as well as a faint olive lower border to the auricular. The chin, throat, and upper breast are black, with the black extending solidly onto the sides and as bold black streaks onto the lower sides. The remainder of the underparts is white, with a pale yellow wash sometimes present below the black of the breast, and with yellow on the sides of the vent that often meets to form a patch across the vent. The longer undertail coverts show thin but distinct black streaks in many individuals of this and other plumages. The back and rump are bright yellow-olive; there is variable but generally quite limited black spotting across the back, arranged as streaks. The uppertail

Black-throated Green Warbler. Male in Texas in May. (Photo: Rick and Nora Bowers)

Black-throated Green Warbler. First fall in Newfoundland in August. (Photo: Shawneen E. Finnegan)

coverts are dull gray with black shaft streaks. The wings are blackish, narrowly edged with pale gray. There are two bold white wing bars; the white tips to the median coverts lack dark shaft streaks. The outer three rectrices show long white spots on the inner webs. **FIRST SPRING MALE:** Much like spring adult male, and probably only reliably aged in the hand by rectrix shape and the degree of wear on the primary coverts and flight feathers. Many individuals have some whitish on the chin and some veiling of the black throat by whitish feather tips. White in r4 reduced compared with adult male. **SPRING ADULT FEMALE:** Much like spring adult male, but the chin is yellowish, and the black of the throat is strongly veiled with whitish feather tips. Some variants with extensive black coming up onto the chin may not be safely told from males. Back streaks are absent or, if present, very thin and faint. There is little if any yellowish wash on the lower breast, but yellow is present on the sides of the vent as in all plumages. **FIRST SPRING FEMALE:** Many are very similar to spring adult females. There is some slate color coalescing on the sides of the throat, but very little black or slate in the center of the throat. Some individuals have very little black on the throat and look very much like first fall females. Back streaking is absent. **FALL ADULT MALE:** Nearly identical to spring adult male, but the black on the throat and breast is heavily veiled with white tips, and the yellow wash on the lower breast is often stronger. The back streaking is less evident, being veiled with green. **FIRST FALL MALE:** The throat is even more veiled with whitish feather tips than in the basic adult; there is at least a small solid white area on the chin and upper throat. In general first basic males are very similar to basic adult females but have, on average, more black on the throat, coming farther up the chin. The back streaking is very thin and heavily veiled. **FALL ADULT FEMALE:** Essentially identical to the spring adult female, but the streaking on the sides is more blurred and the pale veiling of the black throat is more extensive (the center of the throat can appear extensively whitish). Most fall adult females cannot be safely told in the field from first fall males; in the hand, rectrix shape (less tapered in adults) and flight feather color (blacker in adults) may confirm age. The pattern of white on r4 differs subtly from that of first fall male, but rectrix shape is a better aging criterion. **FIRST FALL FEMALE:** Entire upperparts bright yellow-olive, with the faint and thin streaks on the back so veiled as to be invisible in the field. Supraloral area, supercilium, sides of neck, malar region, and broad, diffuse arc under the eye yellow. Lores, transocular line, and auricular outline olive. Chin pale yellowish; remainder of throat dull whitish with variable veiled slate color across the center of the throat and on the sides of the throat and chest. In dullest individuals this dark color is limited to a veiled slaty patch on the sides of the lower throat. Sides and flanks streaked with slaty, this streaking somewhat veiled by buffy white. There is a faint wash of yellow on the center of the breast and a yellow wash on the sides of the vent. The remaining underparts are dull whitish. Wings dull gray with two bold white wing bars. Long white spot on the inner webs of the outer two rectrices; little if any white on r4. **JUVENILE:** Grayish brown above, tinged with olive. Supercilium dull whitish; auriculars slaty. Dull buffy whitish below, obscurely spotted and streaked with slaty. **BARE PARTS:** Bill black in spring adults, becoming tinged with dark brown in winter; there is more extensive brown on mandible of first basic birds. Eye dark brown; legs blackish slate, tinged brown.

The prebasic molt (complete in adults, partial in hatching-year birds) occurs almost exclusively on the breeding grounds. There is a limited prealternate molt in late winter and early spring, resulting in a significant change in appearance only in many first-alternate males.

 REFERENCES

GENERAL: Morse 1968 and 1993.

ECOLOGY, BEHAVIOR, VOCALIZATIONS, AND CONSERVATION: Collins 1983, MacArthur 1958, Morse 1967c, Rabenold 1980, Stein 1962.

SYSTEMATICS: Bangs 1918, Bermingham et al. 1992, Mengel 1964, Rohwer 1994.

TOWNSEND'S WARBLER   PL. 14

Dendroica townsendi

4.75 in. (12 cm). This western member of the Black-throated Green Warbler superspecies breeds in shady, moist coniferous forests, where it spends much of its time high in the trees. Migrants and winter birds occur in a greater variety of wooded habitats and forage over a broader range of heights. This species' winter distribution shows an interesting division between the highlands of Mexico and northern Central America and the coastal woodlands of California. Townsend's is unique within this complex of closely related warblers in having extensive yellow on the breast and a dark cheek patch; the back is green in all plumages. Hybridization with the Hermit Warbler is frequent where the breeding ranges overlap, primarily in Washington State.

DESCRIPTION

Townsend's shows the general characters of the *virens* (Black-throated Green Warbler) complex, including extensive white in the rectrices, bold white wing bars, black throat patch (strongest in adult males; reduced in adult females and generally absent in first fall females). All Townsend's show a strongly contrasting face pattern with yellow framing a dark cheek patch, extensive yellow on the breast, and a bright yellow-olive back. This species lacks yellow in the vent area in all plumages. There is little seasonal change in appearance.

Structurally, all members of the *virens* complex are medium-sized, rather long-tailed warblers with rather small bills.

SIMILAR SPECIES

In all plumages, the dark cheek patch boldly outlined with yellow and the yellow breast identifies the Townsend's Warbler from other members of the *virens* complex (such as BLACK-THROATED GREEN, GOLDEN-CHEEKED and HERMIT WARBLERS). See under Hermit Warbler for problems with Townsend's × Hermit hybrids. BLACK-THROATED GRAY WARBLER is similar in pattern but is gray above and white underneath, rather than green and yellow. Most likely to be confused with first basic BLACKBURNIAN WARBLERS, especially females. Back color more brownish olive, less green, in Blackburnian, and the dark back streaks in Blackburnian result in more of a striped look. Blackburnian has pale streaks on the sides of the back, forming a pale V or brace; Townsend's lacks pale streaks on the back, which is patterned only with inconspicuous, fine blackish streaks in females. Most Blackburnians show a short yellowish median streak on forehead, lacking in Townsend's. Supercilium shape differs subtly: in Blackburnian it broadens slightly behind the eye. In Blackburnians the dark cheek is almost always completely framed by yellowish or orange, though this can depend on posture; in all Townsend's the dark cheek patch has at least a thin connection at the rear with the dark hindneck (difficult to see in some postures). First fall male Blackburnians have a strong orange tint to the throat and breast; first fall female Blackburnians have a buffy or ocher tint to the dull yellow of the throat and breast. Some are very pale below, paler than any Townsend's; the throat and breast are purer yellow in Townsend's. Call notes differ, with Blackburnian giving a thin, downslurred *chip*.

 ## VOICE

SONG is a high, raspy, wheezy, buzzy *weazy-weazy-weazy-dzeee, zhee-zhee-zhee-eee-zee, dzeer-dzeer-dzeer-tseetsee,* or *zwee zwee zwee zwee sweezit*. The song rises in pitch, but often drops at the end; the pattern is quite variable. An alternate song begins with a rapid series of short, slightly buzzy notes and concludes with more typical raspy notes: *zi-zi-zi-zi-zi-zi, zwee zwee*. Some song differences between eastern (Montana) and western (w. British Columbia) populations have been described. Songs generally resemble those of Black-throated Gray Warbler but are higher and wheezier. Rarely, Townsend's sings a clear *peeo peeo peeo peeo*. **CALL NOTE** is very similar to that of Black-throated Green or Hermit, but slightly sharper and higher: *tip* or *tsik*. This call is distinctly sharper and higher than the dull *tup* of Black-throated Gray. **FLIGHT NOTE** is a thin, sweet, very high *see*, which lacks any buzzy quality; flight notes of all members of *virens* superspecies are similar.

 ## BEHAVIOR

Foraging birds on the breeding grounds spend most of their time high in the crowns of tall conifers and are thus often difficult to observe. In migration and winter, foraging takes place at all levels, even near the ground, and in a broader variety of trees. During those seasons they often join mixed flocks of kinglets, chickadees, and other warblers (including other members of the *virens* superspecies). In much of the Mexican and n. Central American highlands, Townsend's is often the most numerous member of these mixed flocks. Most foraging is by rather deliberate gleaning, with some hover-gleaning and, more rarely, aerial sallying. Food is almost exclusively insects and spiders. Males on the breeding grounds may defend territories against Hermit Warblers as well as other Townsend's.

NESTS are built high in conifers, exceptionally as low as 8 ft. and as high as 100 ft. The nest is a bulky but shallow cup of plant fibers and bark, lined with moss, plant downs, and hairs; the nest is placed on a limb well out from the trunk and usually protected above by a spray of needles.

BREEDS in moist shaded coniferous forests of spruce, fir, Douglas-fir, lodgepole pine, and hemlock, with dominant tree species varying through the range. Favored forests are dense and often composed of towering old-growth trees. Undergrowth characteristics seem unimportant to these treetop foragers. Within their range they may be uncommon or patchy in dense rain forests (as on the west side of the Olympic Peninsula in Washington) and in more open and subalpine coniferous woodlands. Where Townsend's overlaps with the Hermit Warbler, the two species show some habitat separation; on the Olympic Peninsula, for example, Townsend's breeds below 1,600 ft. and above about 3,900 ft., with Hermit breeding at intermediate elevations. Within our area it **WINTERS** in heavily wooded coastal habitats of live oaks, conifers, laurels, and madrones, and also in riparian woodlands (sycamores, alders, and willows). They will utilize flowering eucalyptus and other exotic plantings, especially when mixed with any of the above habitats. The populations wintering from Mexico into Central America are found almost exclusively in humid montane pine-oak woodlands and cloud forests, but also locally down into tropical semi-deciduous forest and even tropical evergreen forest. In general, nonbreeders are less partial to conifers than is the Hermit Warbler. **MIGRANTS** occur in a variety of wooded and brushy habitats. Spring birds may be numerous in flowering live oaks and chaparral; in fall, migrants are especially numerous in montane coniferous forests.

🦅 DISTRIBUTION

BREEDS from south coastal and e.-cen. Alaska, s. Yukon, n. (but not ne.) B.C. (including Queen Charlotte Is. and Vancouver Is.), and sw. Alta. south to w. Wash., ne. and cen. Ore. (mainly on east side of Cascade Mtns.), cen. Idaho (has bred in Cassida Co., s.-cen. Idaho), and w. Mont. There are historical (and a few recent) nesting records for the Yellowstone region of nw. Wyo., and a breeding record for the Cypress Hills, Sask., in 1979. One nonbreeder was well south of the breeding range in Santa Cruz Co., Calif., 15 June to 3 July 1996.

WINTERS in two distinct geographical areas. The coastal population winters from w. Wash. (small numbers) and rarely sw. B.C. (and once on the Queen Charlotte Is.) south to s. Calif., with a few into Baja Calif. The largest numbers are found in cen. Calif. Winter populations north of Ore. fluctuate from year to year, and numbers may diminish in severe winters. Winter birds in these coastal populations may occur in small numbers in wooded valleys inland to the foothills of the Cascades and Sierra Nevada, as well as the mountains of s. Calif. The southern interior wintering population is found in the mountains from n. Mexico (Sonora and s. Coahuila) south to n. Nicaragua, and rarely but regularly to Costa Rica. It is recorded casually south to w. Panama (four records in w. Chiriqui) and there is an exceptional January specimen from the Guajira Peninsula of n. Colombia (the only South American record). Also a sparse winter visitor in se. Ariz. (with only a few remaining through the entire winter); a few regularly winter in the Chisos Mtns. of w. Texas. Casual in winter on the deserts of se. Calif., sw. Ariz., and s. N.M. There are winter records for s. Nev. and Ut. and one from east of the Cascades in Ore. (Bend).

MIGRATION in spring and fall is through the Pacific Coast states and the intermountain West, east to w. (rarely s.) Texas and the Rocky Mtns. region. Spring movements are concentrated along the border from w. Texas to s. Calif., then up through the Pacific states. In fall it is more widespread, moving regularly through the s. Rocky Mtn. states and in small numbers along the w. Great

TOWNSEND'S WARBLER
Dendroica townsendi

Plains from Alta. to e. N.M. (and very rarely but regularly east to the western parts of Neb., Kans., and Okla.). Movements and timing of this species are complicated by the existence of the two separate wintering populations.

SPRING MIGRATION of the populations wintering on the U.S. Pacific Coast is early, with most birds having departed coastal Calif. winter grounds in April. Farther north along the coast, spring movements peak from mid-April to early May, but migrants have been noted on the Wash. coast as early as late March. The breeding populations in nw. Wash. and coastal B.C. arrive between late April and mid-May. The populations wintering in Mexico and Central America generally do not arrive in the U.S. until the third week of April. The first arrivals in the interior Northwest are usually during the last week of April, with arrivals in the northernmost interior nesting areas (e.g., e.-cen. Alaska) being in mid-May. Peak movements of the southern winter population from s. Calif. to sw. Texas are in late April and early May, with some movement through mid-May and stragglers to the beginning of June. Migration peaks farther north (e.g., e. Ore., se. B.C.) are in mid-May. Late migrants have been noted in n. Calif. and e. Ore. as late as mid-June. There are several exceptional late June records for Ariz., N.M., and Colo. (once as late as 3 July). Records for 17 and 26 July in Yosemite, Calif., are hard to categorize but may pertain to early fall migrants.

FALL MIGRATION may begin as early as the first week of August in the interior, with an exceptional 24 July 1987 record from Arriba County, N.M. Interior fall arrivals are more typically in mid-August, with peak movements from late August to mid-September. These interior birds undoubtedly winter in Mexico and Central America. Coastal fall migrants may appear as early as mid-August, with more typical arrivals being in late August and peaks occurring from mid-September to early October. Coastal birds in fall probably represent a mix of coastal and southern wintering populations. A few migrants are found in the interior until mid-October, but the species is very rare or casual in the interior later in fall (apart from the southernmost interior where a few may winter). Records in the far north are as late as 19 November in Alaska, 3 November in interior B.C., and 20 November at Edmonton, Alta.

CASUAL over much of e. North America in fall, winter, and spring, with some 90 records east of the Great Plains states and Texas; there are records for well over half of the eastern states and provinces, with a remarkable 16 records for N.Y. State alone. In the Midwest region there are about 20 records, all for spring (April to mid-May) except one in late August and one in early winter. The nearly 50 records for the Northeast are divided almost evenly among spring (mid-April to mid-May), fall (early September to November), and winter (but very few successfully overwintering). There are six late fall and early winter records for Nfld. Of some 15 records for the Southeast, most are for fall (September–October); the others are divided between spring (late April) and winter. There are five records (four in fall, one in winter) for Bermuda and two (late January and late April) in the Bahamas. There are two records for Pt. Barrow in n. Alaska (16–17 September 1985 and 24 May 1993), and a 3 October 1977 record for Shemya Is. in the w. Aleutians.

 ## STATUS AND CONSERVATION

No clear trends are evident from the Breeding Bird Survey, although a slight overall increase is indicated. The breeding range of Townsend's has gradually extended southward in Washington and Oregon with changes in climate and forest composition in recent centuries; the hybrid zone with Hermit Warbler has likewise moved southward. Townsend's is possibly susceptible to forest fragmentation, as it is consistently most abundant in breeding season in extensive old growth. There are relatively few records of parasitism by Brown-headed Cowbirds, but this might be due in part to the difficulty of monitoring Townsend's nests high in conifers.

SUBSPECIES

There are no named subspecies, but birds wintering along the Pacific Coast of the U.S. are characterized by a shorter wing chord and marginally larger bill and tarsus. These birds are presumed to breed on the Queen Charlotte Is. and probably also Vancouver Is., British Columbia, and possibly also south coastal Alaska.

TAXONOMIC RELATIONSHIPS

Townsend's is very closely related to other members of the *virens* superspecies; it hybridizes frequently with the Hermit Warbler in the northern Cascades (see under Hermit Warbler for description and status of hybrids). One hybrid with Black-throated Gray Warbler is known from Vancouver Island, British Columbia; this bird sang like Townsend's but was intermediate in plumage between the two species. A bird apparently of Townsend's × Black-throated Gray parentage was seen in San Diego County, California, 4 May 1975. A specimen morphologically identical to Townsend's but showing genetic characters of Black-throated Green Warbler was collected in e. British Columbia. A hybrid with Yellow-rumped ("Myrtle") Warbler, was taken in Santa Barbara, California, 3 December 1983 (specimen in San Bernardino County Museum), and another presumed to be of this combination was seen on Pt. Reyes, California, 8–10 October 1988.

✒ PLUMAGES AND MOLTS

SPRING ADULT MALE: Crown, cheeks, chin, and throat solid black; thin black connecting stripe between the rear of the cheek and the hindneck. Remainder of head (outlining cheek patch) bright yellow, including small arc below eye. Back yellow-olive, boldly spotted with black; upper tail coverts black with gray fringes. Breast bright yellow, belly and undertail coverts white; strong black streaks on sides and flanks, black shaft streaks on the longest undertail coverts. Lesser upperwing coverts black-centered with yellow-olive fringes. Median and greater secondary coverts gray with broad pure white tips, forming bold white wing bars. Primaries, secondaries, and tertials slaty with pale gray edges. Rectrices slaty; inner webs of outer two rectrices almost entirely white, inner web of r4 with an elongate white wedge extending to the tip. **FIRST SPRING MALE:** Most are similar to spring adult males but with black spotting on back reduced; many individuals show some green mixed in on the crown. The extent of the black throat patch may be slightly reduced in some birds, with some yellow present on the chin; in a minority of birds there may be extensive yellow on the chin and upper throat. The median secondary coverts may be pure white (as in adult) or show a thin shaft streak (if retained from first basic plumage). The amount of white on r4 is reduced compared with the adult male. **SPRING ADULT FEMALE:** Generally similar to adult male, but crown olive with black streaking rather than solid black; cheeks dark olive. Black

Townsend's Warbler. Male in California in May. (Photo: Larry Sansone)

Townsend's Warbler. First fall female in California in September. (Photo: B. E. Small/VIREO)

markings on the back narrower, giving the appearance of fine streaks. Uppertail coverts gray with narrow black centers. Streaking on sides and flanks thinner than in males. Chin and throat solid yellow, or with variable black mottling up the center of the throat and a blackish band across the lower throat, often solid black on the sides of the lower throat. Wings as in adult male, but white tips to median coverts are bisected by a thin black shaft streak. Less white in rectrices than in adult male, with white on r4 limited to a thin streak on the inner web. **FIRST SPRING FEMALE:** Similar to spring adult female. On average birds there is less black on the throat; if present, this black is heavily veiled with pale yellow. Black streaking in the crown fine and inconspicuous. Yellow of underparts paler. Rectrices as in first fall female, but more worn. **FALL ADULT MALE:** Very similar to spring adult male, but black crown feathers have thin yellow-olive tips and the black of the back is strongly veiled with green; black streaking of throat and of side and flank slightly obscured by yellow feather tips. Fresh fall birds may show a slight hint of pale yellow in the vent area. **FIRST FALL MALE:** Most closely resembles fall adult female. Chin usually yellow, lower throat veiled black; cheeks olive (not black as in adult male). Scattered spots of black on back, smaller than in adult male but larger than the finer streaks of all female plumages. Thin black shaft streaks through white median covert tips. Rectrices more tapered than those of fall adult female; pattern of white in rectrices generally similar to adult female. **FALL ADULT FEMALE:** Very similar to spring adult female, but the thin black back streaks and any black present on the throat are more heavily obscured by yellow-olive feather tips. Very similar overall to first fall males. **FIRST FALL FEMALE:** Crown, back, and rump dull yellow-olive without streaking; rump brighter yellow-olive with inconspicuous dark shaft streaks. Uppertail coverts olive-gray with thin dark shaft streaks. Cheeks olive, framed by bright buffy yellow supercilium, malar region, chin, throat, and lower sides of the neck. Lower throat and breast pale yellow, with a smudge of grayish black across the lower throat in many birds. In some birds the center of the throat may be pale to yellowish white. Diffuse dusky olive streaks on the sides and flanks; flanks tinged buffy. White tips of median coverts clearly show a dark shaft streak. White in the rectrices usually limited to the outer two pairs. **JUVENILE:** Olive-brown above, dull whitish below, with a hint of the post-juvenal face pattern (dull buffy supercilium and malar area outlining a brownish olive cheek patch); throat smudged dusky, flanks streaked with dusky. **BARE PARTS:** As with other members of *virens* species group: bill black, with slight brown tint in young birds; legs and feet blackish brown, foot pads dull yellow-orange; eyes blackish brown.

The prebasic molt takes place from late June to early September on the breeding grounds, although it may not be completed in some individuals until they have migrated south in fall. This molt is complete in adults but does not involve the flight feathers in first-year birds. A partial prealternate molt occurs from late January to early April on the winter grounds; it is limited in adults but more extensive in first-year birds. Most of the change in appearance between winter and spring birds is due to the wearing of pale feather tips.

 REFERENCES

DISTRIBUTION: Garrett and Dunn 1981, Grinnell 1905, Jaramillo 1995, Mengel 1964.
ECOLOGY, BEHAVIOR, VOCALIZATIONS, AND CONSERVATION: Dobkin 1994, Sharpe 1993.
PLUMAGES, MOLTS, AND MORPHOLOGY: Jackson et al. 1992.
SYSTEMATICS: Jewett 1944, Morrison 1983, Morrison and Hardy 1983a, Mengel 1964, Rohwer 1994.

HERMIT WARBLER

PL. 14

Dendroica occidentalis

4.75 in. (12 cm). The Hermit Warbler is a Pacific Coast representative of the Black-throated Green Warbler (*virens*) superspecies that shows a strong preference for conifers throughout the year. Its breeding range extends from nw. Washington south to s. California. It is generally gray above and pure white below, with yellow limited to the head. There is some black on the throat of all birds except immature females. Like other members of this complex of closely related species (Black-throated Gray through Townsend's Warbler) it shows bold white wing bars and extensive white in the tail. The Hermit Warbler hybridizes regularly with the Townsend's Warbler in Washington and Oregon.

DESCRIPTION

Hermit Warblers show the general characters of the *virens* super-species, including white outer rectrices, two prominent white wing bars, a rather long-tailed shape, and black throat in the male. In all plumages the face is yellow, with the cheek patch absent or very weak. The back is gray to olive-gray, but never bright olive. The underparts are pure white, lacking yellow, and the flank streaking is limited or absent. There is little seasonal change in plumage.

SIMILAR SPECIES

Adult males with yellow cheeks, relatively small black throat patch, gray back, and white underparts are unmistakable. The main identification problem in other plumages is with Black-throated Green Warbler, and also with Hermit × Townsend's hybrids (see below). All **BLACK-THROATED GREEN WARBLERS** show yellow in the vent, which is never present on Hermit. Hermits are duller and grayer above, never showing strong green tones as in Black-throated Green. In immature female Hermits, the yellow in the face is clearer and extends farther up toward the crown; they lack the outline of a cheek patch and the dark stripe through the eye of Black-throated Green. Hermits are also somewhat similar to **TOWNSEND'S** and **GOLDEN-CHEEKED WARBLERS**. The strong dark eye line of Golden-cheeked, set off from the unmarked yellow cheek, distinguishes it from Hermit or any Hermit × Townsend's hybrid. Hermits are distinguished from Townsend's by the grayer back, lack of yellow on the breast, and lack of a strong dark auricular patch or dark forehead.

The female Hermit is superficially similar to the female **OLIVE WARBLER** but differs in many important characters. Olive has a longer bill, greenish yellow edges to flight feathers, a more sharply notched tail; it shows no hint of a throat patch but does have a darkish triangular outline to the auricular. Olives characteristically flick their wings. The *kew* and dry *pit* calls of Olive are unique among our warblers and very different from any calls of Hermit.

Beware of hybrid **HERMIT × TOWNSEND'S WARBLERS** (see Taxonomic Relationships). Females of this combination are similar to female Black-throated Green Warblers but differ in having less face pattern and showing some yellowish on the breast; these hybrids also show some flank streaking and lack yellow in the vent area. Out-of-range Hermit Warblers should be carefully checked for evidence of intergradation with Townsend's.

Voice

SONGS highly variable; each male has two or more songs in its repertoire. A wheezy *zeee-zeee-zeee-see-see-zee?* is a typical rendition, but alternative songs are clearer, some even suggesting a weak, subdued Yellow Warbler in quality and pattern. The songs are rapidly delivered, accelerating toward the end. The song usually ends with an abrupt change in pitch (one or two higher or lower notes). Many songs suggest those of Townsend's Warbler, but Townsend's songs are wheezier, hoarser, and more buzzy; songs may also be similar to those of Black-throated Gray Warbler. Hermit does not sing in spring migration as much as Townsend's or Black-throated Gray. Songs of Townsend's × Hermit hybrids are very similar to those of Hermit. **CALL NOTE** is a flat *chip* or *tip,* inseparable from call of Black-throated Green Warbler and very close to slightly higher and sharper call of Townsend's. The call is usually separable from slightly lower, duller *tup* note of Black-throated Gray Warbler. **FLIGHT NOTE** is a very high clear *sip,* with no buzzy quality; it is identical to the flight calls of other members of the *virens* complex.

Behavior

When foraging, partial to pines and other conifers, only rarely using other trees (except in spring migration). Most foraging is by gleaning along small twigs and needle clusters high in conifers; quick sallies and hover-gleans are also performed. Food consists mainly of insects and spiders. On the breeding grounds it sings from high in conifers. General postures and behaviors as in other member of *virens* complex.

The **NEST** is placed high in a conifer (20–120 ft., rarely lower); it is saddled on a main horizontal limb, often near the trunk. One ground nest has been recorded. The nest is a cup of fibers, stems, bark, and needles, decorated with moss and lichen and lined with plant down and fur.

Habitat

BREEDING birds occupy a variety of coniferous associations, especially montane forests. Douglas-fir is perhaps the most important conifer through most of the breeding range. At the northern end of its breeding range the Hermit occurs in Douglas-fir, western hemlock, Pacific silver fir, and other firs; it bred in oak-fir associations east of Puget Sound in nw. Washington but is now largely absent from this vanishing habitat. In coastal n. California it breeds in Douglas-fir/coast redwood associations. In the Sierra

Nevada it is found mainly in wetter associations of red and white firs, sugar and ponderosa pines and sequoias. In the mountains of s. California (where scarce) it is closely tied to sugar pines, Jeffrey pines, and white firs. This is the most abundant breeding warbler in coniferous forest habitats in montane Oregon and Washington. Although it occupies old-growth forests, it also succeeds locally in the Pacific Northwest in stands as young as 20–25 years old. In **WINTER** it is also partial to conifers, including native coastal pines (e.g., Monterey and Bishop pines) and mature planted pines intermixed with live oaks. Wintering birds in the highlands of Mexico occupy humid pine-oak associations but confine most of their activities to the pines. Winter habitats in Mexico and Central America are mainly from 5,000 ft. (rarely 1,500 ft.) up to 10,000 ft. **MIGRANTS** are still partial to conifers (including introduced conifers) where available, but utilize a wider variety of trees, such as live oaks and cottonwoods in spring, tamarisks in fall. Spring migrants also occur widely in brushy habitats such as chaparral and desert woodlands.

DISTRIBUTION

BREEDS in western coniferous forests from w. Wash. (s. Cascade Mtns. and locally to the cen. Cascades, the Olympic Peninsula east of the Olympic Mtns., and rarely around the southern end of Puget Sound; also formerly nested rarely to ne. counties of Wash., but in recent years no proven breeding east of Chelan Co.), w. Ore. (coast and both slopes of the Cascade Mtns.; possibly also breeds in the Blue and Wallowa mountains of ne. Ore.) south through the Sierra Nevada of Calif. (to Kern Co.) and in the coast ranges south to Marin County. There is a small breeding population in the Santa Cruz Mtns. (Santa Cruz and Santa Clara Co., Calif.). Small numbers also breed annually in the San Gabriel and San Bernardino mountains of s. Calif. Casual in sw. B.C.

WINTERS primarily in montane w. Mexico, from Sinaloa, Durango, and s. Nuevo Léon south through the highlands of n. Central America to Nicaragua. Recorded casually in winter south to Costa Rica, and there are two records for w. Chiriqui, Panama. Small numbers also winter in coastal central and southern Calif., most often in native coastal conifers and introduced pines from Marin Co. south to Santa Barbara Co.; a high count of 22 was recorded on a Monterey Peninsula Christmas Bird Count. Winters rarely but annually south in coastal regions to San Diego Co., and casually north to w. Ore. and inland in Calif. to the Central Valley and Transverse mountain ranges. Also recorded casually in winter in s. Ariz., with additional winter records for Texas (Big Bend

National Park; Goose Is., Aransas Co.), Mo., and N.S.

MIGRATION through our area is largely restricted to s. Ariz. and the Pacific states. Spring migrants move through desert and coastal lowlands as well as mountains; fall migration is mainly through the mountains east to s. Nev., Ariz. (except northeast), and sw. N.M.

In **SPRING MIGRATION** this species is numerous in s. Ariz. from the San Pedro R. west, being found only rarely in se. Ariz., N.M., and w. Texas. The first spring migrants may arrive in s. Ariz. in early April, but more typical arrivals are in mid-April both there and in s. and cen. Calif. There are several early April records from Calif. that are thought not to pertain to wintering birds. Earliest arrivals on the breeding grounds in n. Calif. are mainly during the last third of April, and arrivals at the northern end of the breeding range in Wash. are during the last few days of April. Peak spring movements in Ariz. and s. Calif. are from about 25 April to 10 May, with smaller numbers passing through in the middle third of May and stragglers to the beginning of June.

HERMIT WARBLER
Dendroica occidentalis

FALL MIGRATION through the montane West begins as early as mid-July, even well away from the breeding range (e.g., se. Ariz.). Fall migrants are not typically noted along the coast until early August. The bulk of the fall passage is from mid-August to early September, with smaller numbers passing through the mountains until about 20 September. Stragglers are noted in the mountains until mid-October, and along the coast (away from known wintering areas) casually into November. Fall migrants are regularly noted east to the mountains of w. Texas (rare there in spring).

CASUAL (mainly in spring) in cen. and e. North America. It is clearly rarer in the East than the related Townsend's and Black-throated Gray warblers. Recorded in Kans., Mo., Minn. (2), Conn., Mass. (2), e. and s. Texas, La., s. Ont. (4), Que., N.S. (3), and Nfld.

STATUS AND CONSERVATION

It has been suggested that the hybrid zone between Townsend's and Hermit warblers has moved south, which could mean that Townsend's are competitively superior to Hermits. It is thus possible that explanding Townsend's are pushing the breeding range of Hermit Warblers south, but this needs verification through long-term censuses. Otherwise there is little information on population trends. Small populations in mountains of s. California were unknown before the 1970s. Parasitism by Brown-headed Cowbirds has been recorded.

SUBSPECIES

No subspecies or geographic variation described.

TAXONOMIC RELATIONSHIPS

Closely related to other members of the *virens* superspecies, and especially close to the Townsend's Warbler; hybridization between these two species is frequent in the Cascade Mountains of Washington, at the northern end of the Hermit's range. Hybrids are noted rarely but regularly in migration elsewhere in the Pacific states and Southwest, and once in the East (23 May 1995 in Brig Bay, Newfoundland). Suspected Hermit Warblers in the East should be carefully checked for signs of hybridization with Townsend's. Hybrid Hermit × Townsend's warblers tend to show the face pattern of a Hermit but the underparts of a Townsend's (at least some yellow on the breast below the black throat patch, streaking on the sides). The back of hybrids is usually greener than in a pure Hermit; the black on the rear crown of males may extend farther forward on hybrids than on pure Townsend's. More rarely, hybrids may resemble Townsend's in face pattern and back color but lack yellow on the breast and show limited streaking on the sides. First fall hybrids may closely resemble Black-throated Green (see Similar Species). They are rather bright yellow-olive above with thin streaks (females) or thicker black spots (males) on the back. Males show black spotting on the crown, but the forehead is yellow; they also may show variable black in the center of the throat. The face, throat, and breast are yellow, with a grayish olive wash through the auriculars. The remaining underparts are whitish with thin dark streaking on the flanks; there is no yellow in the vent area. Backcrosses between hybrids and pure Townsend's or Hermit may show only subtle signs of intergradation. The songs of hybrids resemble those of Hermit, and hybrids respond to songs of both parents' species. A sight record exists of a female hybrid with Black-throated Gray Warbler from the San Gabriel Mountains of southern California; it nested with a male Black-throated Gray.

PLUMAGES AND MOLTS

SPRING ADULT MALE: Forecrown and entire face (including sides of neck) bright yellow, the yellow extending variably back through the crown. Nape black, with variable black mottling or spotting on the rear of the crown. The back is gray, tinged very slightly with olive in many birds. Extensive black feather centers form bold spotting on the back. The rump is clear gray, and the uppertail coverts have broad black centers. The chin and throat are solid black, the black of the lower throat being cut off sharply from the white breast. Remaining underparts white, with limited and

Hermit Warbler. Adult male in California in April. (Photo: Brian E. Small)

Hermit Warbler. Adult male in California in August. (Photo: Brian E. Small)

indistinct gray streaking on the flanks. Wings gray with bold white wing bars; tail dark gray with extensive white in the outer three pairs of rectrices. **FIRST SPRING MALE:** Rarely separable in the field from spring adult male. In some individuals the throat is less solidly black, with a little white or pale yellow mottling on the chin. Many show black feather tips on the crown (as do some adults). The flight feathers and primary coverts are duller than in adults, and the rectrices appear more worn and average more tapered; there is less extensive white in the rectrices (very little, if any, white shows in r4). **SPRING ADULT FEMALE:** Crown, face, and chin yellow, with some dusky mottling in the auriculars and variable blackish spotting on the forecrown and center of the crown. Rear crown and nape with blackish feather centers and olive fringes. Back gray with a slight tint of olive and indistinct narrow dusky streaks. Rump gray; upper tail coverts with narrow blackish feather centers. Throat is washed with yellow in some birds; the center and lower portions of the throat have black feather centers that are variably (and usually heavily) veiled by whitish feather tips. Remaining underparts dull whitish with a hint of blurred grayish streaking on the flanks. Tail with large white spots in r5–6 and a small white spot on r4. **FIRST SPRING FEMALE:** Similar to spring adult female, but flight feathers and primary coverts browner and more worn. The rectrices are more worn and average more tapered; white in the rectrices is limited to r5 and r6. **FALL ADULT MALE:** Very similar to spring adult male but with white tips to the black feathers of the chin and throat and a veil of olive-gray to the upperparts, somewhat obscuring the black streaking. The yellow of the forecrown and auriculars is slightly washed with olive. The underparts are very slightly tinged with buffy. **FIRST FALL MALE:** Like fall adult male, but back with a stronger olive cast; noticeable but somewhat veiled black spots on the back (not forming longer, more conspicuous streaks as in fall adult males); uppertail coverts with moderately large black centers. Some black feathering on the crown. Black throat patch

Hermit Warbler. First fall female in California in September. (Photo: Herbert Clarke)

strongly veiled with white, thus not appearing solid. Slight buff tinge to the underparts. This plumage is quite similar to fall adult female; first fall male shows larger black spots on the back and browner primary coverts. **FALL ADULT FEMALE:** Similar to spring adult female and difficult to separate from first fall males in the field. The amount of black on the throat and of black stippling on the crown is variable. The back is slightly veiled with olive, with some black spotting. **FIRST FALL FEMALE:** The crown is washed with olive, with only a hint of yellowish on the forehead. Any black spotting on the crown is limited and inconspicuous. The auriculars are dull yellowish, strongly washed with olive-gray. The back is strongly washed with olive-brown and appears unstreaked (the thin dusky back streaks are heavily veiled); the narrow dark shaft streaks on the uppertail coverts are inconspicuous. There is no black on the throat. The underparts are more strongly tinged buffy than in other fall age and sex classes; the flanks are washed with gray-buff but not streaked. **JUVENILE:** Head and upperparts olive-brown with a hint of streaking; auricular area darker. Throat and breast light grayish brown, becoming whitish on the belly. Wings and tail as in first fall birds. **BARE PARTS:** Bill blackish in adults; immature birds have variable dark brownish on the mandible. Eyes dark brown. Legs and feet blackish gray; soles of feet dull orange-yellow.

The complete prebasic molt is mostly completed on breeding grounds, in July and August; a few birds are molting as late as October, south of the breeding grounds. The first prebasic molt of immatures, which does not involve the flight feathers, may rarely extend as late as December. A limited prealternate molt takes place from February to April.

REFERENCES

DISTRIBUTION: Chappell and Ringer 1983, Jaramillo 1995, Sharpe 1993, Yocum 1968.

Townsend's × Hermit hybrid. First fall female in California in August. (Photo: Brian E. Small)

ECOLOGY, BEHAVIOR, VOCALIZATIONS, AND CONSERVATION: Airola and Barrett 1985, Barlow 1899, Morrison 1982, Munson and Adams 1984, Sharpe 1993.

PLUMAGES, MOLTS, AND MORPHOLOGY: Jackson et al. 1992.

SYSTEMATICS: Jewett 1944, Mactavish 1996, Morrison and Hardy 1983, Rohwer 1994.

YELLOW-THROATED WARBLER   PL. 17

Dendroica dominica

5 in. (12.7 cm). Named for its bright yellow throat, set off by a striking black and white face pattern, this warbler is especially common in southeastern and Mississippi and Ohio valley flood-plain woodlands of sycamores, cypresses, pines, or oaks. Its creeping foraging behavior is distinctive, though not as striking as in the Black-and-white Warbler. It is a rather hardy warbler and a very early spring migrant. There are three generally recognized subspecies in our area and another in the Bahamas that is a potential vagrant to Florida. These subspecies vary in overall size, bill length and shape, supraloral color, and color of the under-parts.

 ## DESCRIPTION

Generally similar in all plumages, with a bright yellow throat and upper breast framed by a black auricular patch that is continuous with the bold black stripes on the sides of the breast. Forehead black with variable black markings back through the center of the crown. White supercilium; supraloral area white or yellow; white patch on sides of neck. Unmarked gray (or slightly brown-tinged) upperparts, white underparts with black streaks on flanks. White wing bars and tail spots. A medium-sized warbler with a relatively long bill (exceptionally long in some populations).

SIMILAR SPECIES

Most similar to the GRACE'S WARBLER of southwestern coniferous forests; although breeding ranges do not overlap, vagrants may occur in the same area (in our area especially in coastal California, but also on wintering grounds in s. Mexico and n. Central America). See Grace's Warbler account for distinctions.

Fall immature male BLACKBURNIAN WARBLERS with clear yellow throats can be mistaken for Yellow-throated Warblers. Yellow-throated easily told by even gray or gray-brown upperparts (lacking pale lines of Blackburnian), the presence of a white patch on the sides of the neck, and clean white supercilium. TOWNSEND'S WARBLER female has olive back, yellow supercilium.

The resident Yellow-throated Warbler of Abaco and Grand Bahama (*flavescens*; see under Subspecies), with its more extensively yellow underparts and more obscure head pattern, has been confused with KIRTLAND'S WARBLER. Kirtland's (now very rarely detected on its winter grounds) has a different face pattern, vigorously pumps its tail, and forages low within dense thickets rather than creeping on trunks and branches of conifers.

VOICE

Distinctive SONG starts with a descending series of clear slurred notes, followed by two or more fainter, lower, and more rapid notes, and often ending in a sharply upslurred note. Song may be represented as *teedle-teedle-teedle-teedle-tew-tew-tew—tew-twee*. Some songs lack the terminal note(s). The clear slurred opening notes and weakening end of the song suggest the song of Louisiana Waterthrush. Some song renditions may suggest Indigo Bunting (*Passerina cyanea*).

CALL NOTE is a rather high, soft *chip* or *tsip*, nearly identical to call note of Grace's Warbler and very close to that of Pine Warbler. FLIGHT NOTE is a clear, high *see*.

BEHAVIOR

Frequently creeps along branches, suggesting a Pine or Black-and-white Warbler, but also engages in more typical warbler gleaning behavior and short sallies after flying insects. Often appears rather sluggish. Foraging often takes place high in tree-tops, especially on breeding grounds.

NEST is usually placed in a clump of Spanish moss (*Tillandsia usneoides*) but may also be in a clump of pine needles; usually out toward the tip of a branch, at a height of 15–100 ft., averaging around 30 ft. Nests are placed in sycamores in much of the species' range but also in pines and other tall trees. Nests are constructed of fine grasses, weed stems, and plant downs, as well as the Spanish moss in which it is often placed. The more westerly subspecies *albilora* often lines the nest with soft down from sycamores.

Habitat

BREEDING habitat varies throughout range; the species tends to frequent lowland forest, but the tree composition of the habitat varies regionally. In the southern states the presence of Spanish moss for nesting appears to be important. In the Deep South, essentially coincident with the range of the races *dominica* and *stoddardi*, the preferred habitat is tall woods within swampy bottomlands, often of cypress, oaks, and tupelo. Lowland pine forests are important breeding habitat in much of the range of the race *albilora*, and loblolly pines are important in the Delmarva peninsula population of *dominica*. Through much of the Midwest, and east to the Delaware River, *albilora* occupies woodlands of large sycamores along streams. Interestingly, sycamores are avoided in portions of this range (e. Kentucky, e. Oklahoma) where populations breed in pines or cypress swamps. Bahama birds inhabit pine forests.

In **WINTER**, found in pines, palms, *Casuarina*, and occasionally mangroves; often favors habitats with considerable epiphyte growth. Also in gardens and around human habitations.

Distribution

BREEDS from the s. Great Lakes region south through the Miss. and Ohio river valleys to the Gulf states, and along the Atlantic Coast from N.J. to Fla. Has expanded range northward in recent decades, through much of Pa., n. N.J., and (rarely, and perhaps not regularly) into s. N.Y. and nw. Conn. Has recolonized much of former breeding range in Ohio (mainly s. and cen. portion), s. Ind. Breeds in extreme sw. (and very locally s.-cen.) Mich. and formerly elsewhere in s. Mich. At western edge of range breeds to s. Ill. (locally in north, and may breed just into Wisc. (Rock Co. and extreme sw.), Iowa (rare; mainly se.), e. Kans. (rare, local), e. and cen. Okla., and the Edwards Plateau of Texas. Generally

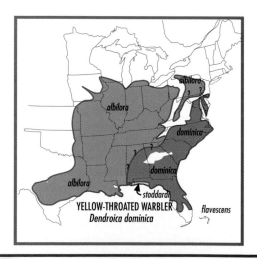

YELLOW-THROATED WARBLER
Dendroica dominica

absent from higher elevations such as the Appalachians. Breeding range in Fla. extends about halfway down the peninsula. Also breeds in Grand Bahama and Abaco in the Bahamas.

WINTERS in the southernmost portion of the breeding range; uncommon to fairly common from coastal S.C. through the Florida peninsula, uncommon in southernmost Texas, and generally rare elsewhere along the Gulf Coast. A few winter records extend north to nw. La., Ark., Tenn., and exceptionally to Ohio and N.Y. The majority of nominate *dominica* (see under Subspecies below) winters in the Bahamas and Greater Antilles and rarely also to Bermuda. The race *albilora* winters mainly from e. Mexico (a few in w. Mexico) south through Nicaragua and rarely to Costa Rica and Panama; there are two sight records for Colombia.

SPRING MIGRATION begins very early, with the first migrants noted in Fla. and s. La. by late February; birds may reach breeding grounds on the coastal plain of the Deep South by the second week of March. Tower kills in nw. Fla. suggest a prolonged spring peak from the beginning of March to around 10 April. Reaches the northern portion of the breeding range in the Midwest by mid- to late April. On Atlantic Coast, Delmarva birds arrive in late March and early April. Except for the immediate Gulf Coast, spring migrants are seldom noted away from known nesting areas. Spring overshoots are frequent from late April to mid-May in the Great Lakes region (*albilora*); overshoots from mid-April to late May in coastal N.Y. and Conn. mainly represent *dominica*. A few stragglers may linger in extreme s. Fla. as late as mid-May.

FALL MIGRATION is also early, with migrants noted south of the breeding range in Fla. routinely by late July (and even as early as late June). Fla. tower kills indicate a prolonged fall peak from the second week of August to the third week of October. This species becomes inconspicuous on the breeding grounds after singing ceases, and the timing of its migration is poorly understood in many areas. Departure from northern breeding areas is typically in early to mid-September. Stragglers are noted within the summer range well into October, with a few November records. As in spring, migrants are rarely noted away from known breeding areas.

VAGRANT, mostly in fall, north on Atlantic Coast to the Maritime Provinces and Nfld. There are some 100 records for Ont., most of which are for spring; three Ont. birds have shown the characters of nominate *dominica,* including one late fall bird at James Bay. Casual in Que. Casual on the n. Great Plains. Recorded in all western states except Wash. There are over 25 records for Colo., nearly 20 records for Ariz., and 75 records for Calif. Most western records are for spring (mid-April to early June), but there are many fall records, especially for Calif. coast. Has summered in

Calif. There are winter records for Calif. and Ariz. (and one bird remaining to December in Mont.). Most western records appear to be *albilora*, but at least four birds showing characters of *dominica* have been recorded in Calif. (three in late fall, one remaining through the winter).

📊 STATUS AND CONSERVATION

The subspecies *albilora* appears to be expanding its range northward and eastward, but much of this expansion may simply represent reclaiming range lost to deforestation during the 1800s. The race *stoddardi* of the Florida panhandle and adjacent Alabama appears to be declining and has been considered for endangered species listing by the U.S. Fish and Wildlife Service. There are no clear population trends for nominate *dominica*.

🦅 SUBSPECIES

Nominate *dominica* breeds along the Atlantic coastal plain from extreme s. New Jersey, s. Delaware, and e. Maryland south to cen. Florida. It winters from south coastal South Carolina, cen. Georgia, and Florida through the Greater Antilles and Bahamas. Within *dominica* there is variation in bill length, with pine-dwelling birds of the Delmarva Peninsula of the Mid-Atlantic Coast being the longest billed. The subspecies *stoddardi* is limited to the coastal portion of the Florida panhandle (from Gulf Co. west) and adjacent Alabama (Baldwin Co.); its winter range is unknown, and some birds may be resident. *D. d. stoddardi* is only very weakly differentiated from the nominate subspecies; the bill is longer and more slender than most populations of *dominica* (although its bill length is approached or exceeded by *dominica* on the Delmarva Peninsula).

The subspecies *albilora* ("Sycamore" Warbler) breeds over the western and northern portions of the range, breeding east to w. North Carolina, extreme nw. South Carolina, and n. Georgia, and south to cen. Alabama, s. Mississippi, s. Louisiana, and the Edwards Plateau of e.-cen. Texas. *D. d. albilora* now also breeds east to the Atlantic Coast in cen. and n. New Jersey and n. Delaware. Its northern limits have expanded in recent years. The subspecific identity of populations breeding in n. Delaware is uncertain, but birds there resemble *albilora* in habitat choice. In n. Georgia and n. and sw. Alabama, information on subspecies is fragmentary; it is likely that *albilora* is the widespread subspecies in these areas, but clarification is needed. *D. d. albilora* is distinguished from the nominate race by its smaller bill (bill size is con-

Yellow-throated Warbler. Adult male dominica *in Georgia in August. (Photo: Giff Beaton)*

sistent throughout its range), and by the white, rather than yellow, supraloral stripe (but many *albilora* have a yellow tinge to supraloral area, and some nominate *dominica* appear almost whitish there). Most, but not all, *albilora* show some white on the extreme upper chin (often extending back slightly toward the sides of the throat), an average difference from the yellow-chinned nominate race (some individual *dominica* show white on the uppermost chin). On average *albilora* also shows more white in the outer rectrices; from below the white usually appears to meet the white undertail coverts (see Pls. 17 and 31). In nominate *dominica* most show a narrow dark zone between the white tail spots and the white undertail coverts. Many male *albilora* show more extensive black on the crown than males of the nominate race.

Extralimitally, the subspecies *flavescens* of the Bahamas (resident locally on Grand Bahama, Little and Great Abaco) is quite distinct in plumage and song; it perhaps deserves specific rank and should be considered a potential vagrant to Florida. *D. d. flavescens* is a long-billed, yellow-"lored" subspecies best told by a wash of yellow from the lower breast through the belly, more strongly and consistently streaked undertail coverts, and a more subdued face pattern: a thinner and less conspicuous white patch behind the black facial markings, limited black on the forehead in adult males, and a thinner supercilium that is nearly broken above the eye. The back and flanks are tinged with buff in immature (and fresh adult) plumages. The lower wing bar, formed by the greater coverts, is thinner and dull white. The longer bill is also distinctively shaped, with a curved culmen and straight lower mandible (in mainland birds the lower mandible angles slightly upward at the gonys).

The closest relative appears to be the Grace's Warbler. Sutton's Warbler (*"Dendroica potomac"*) is considered a hybrid between Yellow-throated Warbler and Northern Parula. These birds generally resemble Yellow-throated, but face pattern is more subdued, sides and flanks are generally unstreaked, and the center of the back is tinged yellow-olive; males may have a tinge of reddish brown on the chest. The song is said to be similar to Northern Parula's, repeated twice. Most records are from West Virginia, but also reported in Indiana, South Carolina, Alabama, Florida, and Texas. There are very few documented reports of Sutton's Warblers since 1970.

PLUMAGES AND MOLTS

The following descriptions pertain to the nominate race. **SPRING ADULT MALE:** Forehead, auricular area, and lores solid black; black flecking extending back toward the rear of the crown. Remaining crown and hindneck clear gray. Supraloral stripe yellow (but see under Subspecies). Supercilium white from above eye. White arc under eye. Patch of white on side of neck behind the auricular and usually set off from the white supercilium by a dark eye line extending back from the upper auricular area. Chin, throat, and upper breast brilliant yellow. The black auricular extends down and rearward to frame the yellow throat, joining the bold black stripes on the sides of the breast. Back, rump, and uppertail coverts clear gray. A minority of birds show a few short black streaks on the back. Remaining underparts white, with bold black streaks on the sides and flanks. Wing coverts blackish with broad white tips, forming two bold wing bars. Primaries and secondaries dusky black with clear gray edgings.

Yellow-throated Warbler. First spring female showing characters of albilora. *In Florida in April. (Photo: Kevin T. Karlson)*

Yellow-throated Warbler. Subspecies flavescens *on Grand Bahama in October. (Photo: Bruce Hallett)*

Rectrices blackish, edged gray. Distal half of inner web of outermost rectrix white; progressively less white on fifth and fourth rectrices. On the folded tail, the white tail spots usually do not join the white of the undertail coverts in any plumage of nominate *dominica*. **FIRST SPRING MALE:** Nearly identical to spring adult male, but black of crown averages slightly less extensive, back may show slight brownish cast. The primaries and rectrices are browner and more worn than in adult. **SPRING ADULT FEMALE:** Similar to males; the following characters should distinguish spring females from most spring adult males and some first spring males. Solid black on crown usually limited to forehead and sides of forecrown; center of crown with black flecks, usually not extending posteriorly much past the eye. Black of auriculars slightly duller. Back sometimes with a slight brownish cast. Yellow of throat slightly less bright. Flank streaking slightly thinner. **FIRST SPRING FEMALE:** Much like spring adult female, but averaging slightly duller. The primaries and rectrices are browner and more worn than in adult. **FALL ADULT MALE:** Like spring adult male, but some thin white fringes to black streaking of sides of breast and flanks. May show a hint of brownish in the gray of the upperparts. **FIRST FALL MALE:** Differs from fall adult male in having a stronger (but still slight) hint of brownish on upperparts and a buff tinge on flanks; black of crown slightly less extensive; throat slightly duller yellow. Probably not distinguishable in field from fall adult female. **FALL ADULT FEMALE:** Like spring adult female, but some whitish veiling to streaking of underparts and with a slight buffy suffusion on the flanks. **FIRST FALL FEMALE:** Black of crown limited and broken, usually only on forehead and sides of forecrown, with some short black streaks through center of forecrown. Auricular patch dull black. Yellow of throat slightly paler than in other age and sex classes. Streaking on sides and flanks thinner, with much buffy white veiling. Strong brownish tint to upperparts and much buff on belly and flanks. **JUVENILE:** Mottled gray-brown on the head and upperparts, indistinctly streaked; whitish below

Yellow-throated Warbler. Subspecies flavescens *on Abaco, Bahamas, in October. (Photo: Bruce Hallett)*

with some dusky spotting on throat, breast, and sides. Only a hint of the distinctive head pattern of post-juvenal plumages is present. **BARE PARTS:** Bill of spring birds black; first fall birds have dull brown bills. Eyes dark brown. Legs and feet brownish, with a yellowish tint to soles of feet.

Prebasic molt takes place from June to August on the breeding grounds; it is complete in adults, partial in hatching-year birds. The prealternate molt is apparently absent; there is very little seasonal change in appearance.

 REFERENCES

GENERAL: Hall 1996.
DISTRIBUTION: Baird 1958, Parkes 1953.
ECOLOGY, BEHAVIOR, AND CONSERVATION: Ficken et al. 1968.
PLUMAGES, MOLTS, AND MORPHOLOGY: Hall 1983.
SYSTEMATICS: Baird 1958, Carlson 1981, Hall 1983, Parkes 1953, Ulrich and Ulrich 1981.

GRACE'S WARBLER   PL. 17

Dendroica graciae

4.75 in. (12 cm). This small *Dendroica* of coniferous forests from the southwestern border states to Central America is in many ways a southwestern counterpart of the Yellow-throated Warbler. It is extremely partial to pines. The yellow throat and supercilium are evident in all post-juvenal plumages; otherwise it is mainly gray above and white below, with white wing bars and extensive tail spots. This species is seldom seen in our area outside of its nesting habitat and is unrecorded in the East.

DESCRIPTION

Generally gray above, with black streaks on crown and back in adults; gray color and black streaking (when present) of upperparts veiled by a brown wash in fall and winter adults, and a strong brown wash in immatures (especially females). Supraloral area, supercilium (to rear of eye, with short white extension posterior to eye), throat, and breast are all yellow. Remaining underparts white, with black streaking on flanks (varying with age, sex). White wing bars and extensive white in the tail. Among the smallest *Dendroica*; tail of moderate length, with considerable extension beyond undertail coverts. Bill rather fine.

SIMILAR SPECIES

YELLOW-THROATED WARBLER is most similar, but is easily told by its bold face pattern (black auricular region bordered behind by a white patch, extensive white supercilium with yellow absent or limited to area forward of eye); back of Yellow-throated lacks black streaks (female Grace's, especially immatures, also lack these streaks, but back is brown-tinged); Yellow-throated is larger, more apt to creep along branches. Otherwise, compare with the same confusion species as for Yellow-throated, including **BLACKBURNIAN, TOWNSEND'S** (both of which show a much longer supercilium). **"AUDUBON'S" YELLOW-RUMPED WARBLER** superficially resembles Grace's and is common in same pine forest habitat, but is easily told by yellow rump and crown patches, more limited yellow throat (not extending to chest), larger size, and (when present) black areas on underparts.

BEHAVIOR

Mostly forages by probing pine needle clusters and gleaning along twigs and small branches, but does not habitually creep along branches as does Yellow-throated. Like many arboreal warblers, it frequently makes short sallies after flying insects. Most activities, including singing and foraging, take place in pines (including ponderosa, chihuahua, apache pines); only rarely does it forage in oaks and other nonconifers.

NESTS are placed high in pines (40–60 ft.), usually well out a horizontal branch within clumps of needles.

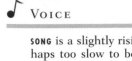

♪ Voice

SONG is a slightly rising and accelerating series of *chee* notes, perhaps too slow to be considered a trill, lasting about 2 seconds. The song consists of two (occasionally one or three) slightly differing phrases, e.g., *chew chew chew chew chew chew chee chee chee*. Each male has several variations of this song, singing these song variants in different combinations in different contexts. The song is suggestive of some songs of Cerulean Warbler but lacks the terminal buzz; it may also suggest certain songs of Pine Warbler. Some variations of the songs of Virginia's and "Audubon's" warblers (often common in the same habitats) can suggest Grace's, as can some Dark-eyed Junco (*Junco hyemalis*) songs. **CALL** a soft, slurred *chip,* very close to chip note of Yellow-throated and Pine. **FLIGHT NOTE** a very high, thin *sip.*

Habitat

BREEDS almost exclusively in open forests of tall pines. Ponderosa pines are occupied in most of the U.S. range of the species except along the Mexican border, where apache and chihuahua pines are also used. Breeding habitat may include a mixture of oaks, junipers, and firs, but pines are almost always an important element. At a few breeding sites near the edge of the species' range (such as in Nevada), white firs rather than pines are occupied. **WINTERS** in pine forests also. Rarely seen in winter and during migration in our area, but most records are of birds in pines (including exotic species, such as the Monterey pines planted in southern California). **MIGRANTS** and **VAGRANTS** have been noted in riparian woodlands, oaks, and tamarisks as well as pines.

Distribution

BREEDS uncommonly to fairly commonly in montane forests in s. Nev. (Mt. Charleston, Sheep Mtns., Mt. Irish; recorded on Potosi Mt.), s. Ut., and sw. Colo. (Uncompahgre Plateau and San Juan Mtns.; has nested in Custer and Pueblo counties), and commonly through appropriate habitat in Ariz. and w. and cen. N.M. Also fairly common in the Guadalupe and Davis Mtns. in w. Texas. There are summer records for e.-cen. and s. Calif. (Glass Mtn., Mono Co.; Clark Mtn. and the San Bernardino Mtns., San Bernardino Co.), but no confirmed breeding there. Recorded once in summer in Jawbridge, extreme n. Nev. Breeds southward to Nicaragua (with the northern, nominate race breeding south to se. Sonora, s. Chihuahua; see under Subspecies). Arrives on breeding grounds in April (exceptionally to late March in se. Ariz.)

or early May; recorded within breeding habitat in Ariz. as late as late September and, exceptionally, late October.

WINTERS primarily in highlands of Mexico. Winter specimens of the nominate race are known from Nayarit, Morelos, and the state of Mexico, but exact winter range is difficult to determine because of overlap with resident Mexican subspecies and lack of adequate specimen material. At least nine presumed nominate birds have wintered in coastal s. Calif. (including one bird in Santa Barbara Co. returning for 9 winters); there is one late-February record for lower Colorado River Valley in southernmost Nev. Scarce **MIGRANT** or **VAGRANT** in lowlands and foothills in or near breeding range, generally from mid-April to mid-May and mid-August to late September. Several records from cen. Colo. on edge of Front Range in late April, May, and September (exceptionally as late as 10 November). **CASUAL** migrant away from limited breeding area in w. Texas, in Big Bend region and El Paso. Casual in fall on the s. Calif. coast; the 15 records are mainly in September. Unrecorded in the U.S. east of Colo. and w. Texas.

GRACE'S WARBLER
Dendroica graciae

Generally common within appropriate pine habitat. No information on population trends.

 SUBSPECIES

Nominate *graciae* is the subspecies occurring in the U.S. Relative to other subspecies, *graciae* is characterized by longer wings and tail, paler (more yellow, less orange-yellow) throat, and more gray-brown (less blue-gray) upperparts with narrower streaking; the portion of the supercilium behind the eye is white. Variation in this species is minor and clinal. The northern, nominate birds are the most migratory. *D. g. yaegeri* (Durango and Sinaloa south to Jalisco) is generally intermediate in appearance between *graciae* and the two southerly subspecies. Sedentary subspecies of Central America are *remota* (*ornata* is a synonym) of the highlands of s. Mexico to n. Nicaragua, and *decora* of pine ridges of Belize and lowland pine savannas of e. Honduras and ne. Nicaragua. *D. g. decora* is purest gray (least brown) on the back, most orange-yellow on the throat, and shortest in wing and tail measurements; *remota* is a variable subspecies somewhat intermediate between *yaegeri* and *decora*.

 TAXONOMIC RELATIONSHIPS

Considered by most workers to be closely related to the Yellow-throated Warbler; these two species (along with Adelaide's Warbler of Puerto Rico and the Lesser Antilles) are considered to be a superspecies (AOU 1983), with the Olive-capped Warbler of Cuba and the Bahamas also closely related. Despite the apparent close relationship of *graciae* and *dominica*, the two species differ strongly in shape, foraging behavior, and songs. One hybrid with Yellow-rumped (Audubon's) Warbler known from Colorado.

 PLUMAGES AND MOLTS

SPRING ADULT MALE: Crown, nape, auricular region, and upperparts medium gray. Black streaks through the crown, concentrated at the front and sides of the crown, sparser across the top of the crown. Black of sides of crown forms black upper border to supercilium. Supraloral stripe and front part of supercilium (about to rear of eye) bright yellow; supercilium extends a short distance behind eye, where white. Yellowish white crescent below eye. Thick black streaks across entire back, black centers to upper tail coverts. (With wear through late spring and early summer, crown and

Grace's Warbler. Male in Arizona in June. (Photo: Herbert Clarke)

back streaks appear bolder and more extensive.) Chin, throat, and breast bright yellow, ending rather abruptly on lower breast. Hint of black moustachial line separating gray auriculars and yellow throat; some black extending into lores. Irregular border to sides of yellow breast formed by short black streaks. Remaining underparts white, with fairly bold black streaks on the flanks. Wings gray, remiges edged pale gray. White tips to median and greater coverts form two wing bars, the anterior one broader. Rectrices dark gray; inner web of r6 and r5 white, and extensive white on inner web of r4 and r3. **FIRST SPRING MALE:** Very similar to spring adult male, but black streaking on crown and back somewhat narrower and more limited. Primaries and greater primary coverts duller, browner. Differs from spring females in having thicker, more extensive black streaking on flanks. Rectrix pattern like that of first fall male. **SPRING ADULT FEMALE:** Similar to spring adult male, but black of crown less extensive; lores and moustachial line gray, lacking any black; black back and flank streaking thinner, less bold; black centers to upper tail coverts less evident. Spring females average very slightly browner on the upperparts and wings than spring males. White in fourth rectrix usually limited to a small spot, as in immature males. **FIRST SPRING FEMALE:** As in spring adult female, but primaries, primary coverts, and rectrices browner, more worn. White on r4 usually absent, as in first fall female. **FALL ADULT MALE:** Resembles spring adult male, but black streaks of back and crown are largely veiled with gray. Slight hint of yellowish buff on white of underparts. **FIRST FALL MALE:** Crown, hindneck, and upperparts mouse brown with thin black streaking almost entirely veiled. Short, indistinct black streaks along sides of crown above yellow supraloral area and yellow and white supercilium. Chin, throat, and breast yellow with slight buff tinge. White of underparts with buffy wash, strongest on flanks. Flank streaking black and rather bold (but less bold than in fall adult male). White in tail more limited than in adult male (usually only small white spot on r4). **FALL ADULT FEMALE:** Similar to first fall male, with thin black back streaking almost completely veiled by mouse brown; flank streaking thinner. **FIRST FALL FEMALE:** Similar to fall adult female, but back is solidly mouse brown with no gray, and back streaking is absent; streaking on sides of crown essentially absent; more extensive wash of buff on belly and flanks; dark flank streaks narrow and diffuse. White on r4 usually absent. **JUVENILE:** Much like first fall birds, but underparts buffy white, with breast spotted and streaked with dusky; yellow of throat and breast absent. **BARE PARTS:** Bill dull black in spring males; in females, winter males, and immatures there is brown at the base of the mandible and along the tomium (this brown most extensive in immature females). Eyes dark brown to hazel. Legs and feet dark brown.

The complete prebasic molt of adults is completed on the breeding grounds. Prebasic molt of hatching-year birds does not involve flight feathers or primary coverts; streaky juvenile plumage generally seen only in June, July. Prealternate molt has never been described.

REFERENCES

ECOLOGY, BEHAVIOR, VOCALIZATIONS, AND CONSERVATION: Staicer 1989.
SYSTEMATICS: Webster 1961.

PINE WARBLER PL. 19

Dendroica pinus

5.25 in. (13.3 cm). This large, long-tailed, rather heavy-billed *Dendroica* is aptly named, for it is found almost exclusively in pines during the breeding season. It is a widespread and common resident over much of the Southeast but is more local (and more migratory) in the North. The Pine Warbler is somewhat sluggish in its foraging behavior, employing much creeping and probing. In its drab immature plumages it may be confused with several other warbler species.

DESCRIPTION

Adults and immature males are unstreaked dull olive green to rather bright green above and range from dull yellow to bright yellow on the throat and breast. Females are browner above and paler below; drabber immature females are quite dull above and may almost completely lack yellow in the plumage. In all plumages the dark auricular area contrasts with the paler throat (which curves around slightly behind the auricular). There is variable broad dark streaking on the sides of the breast. The broad wing bars are bright white in adults, slightly duller in other plumages. The white tail spots are extensive and elongated. Aging and sexing generally difficult, partly because of variation within age and sex classes; it is possible to age and sex many individuals based on greenness (vs. brownness) of back, brightness and extent of yellow on underparts, details of ventral streaking, eye-ring color, and wing bar color.

Structurally this is a large, long-tailed *Dendroica*, showing considerable extension of the rectrices beyond the undertail coverts. Primary extension beyond the tertials is relatively short (15–20 mm). The bill is relatively heavy.

 ## SIMILAR SPECIES

Some plumages very similar to fall **BLACKPOLL** and **BAY-BREASTED WARBLERS** with olive upperparts, yellowish breast, pale vent and undertail coverts, and obvious whitish wing bars. In particular, many observers fail to appreciate how yellow fall Blackpoll Warblers can be ventrally. Pine may always be distinguished from both species by its shape characters: a longer tail showing considerably more extension beyond the undertail coverts, shorter primary extension beyond the tertials, and (from Blackpoll) by a somewhat longer and especially heavier bill. Additionally, Pines show considerably more white in the tail, with the white areas on the outer two rectrices about twice as long as those of Blackpoll and Bay-breasted; the tertial edges are not as cleanly edged white in Pine, and the white tips to the primaries are absent; the wing bars of Pine are less vividly white, often suffused with brownish on the inner greater secondary coverts; face patterns differ, with the olive to olive-gray auricular area of Pine distinctly set off from the yellow throat (face of Blackpoll and Bay-breasted more blended, with hint of dark transocular line and supercilium); the yellowish throat of Pine extends around the rear of the auricular, a pattern not shown in the other species; the upperparts of Pine are unstreaked (but beware of some Blackpolls and especially Bay-breasteds with subdued dorsal streaking); Pines (usually females) showing a strong brown or gray-brown wash to the upperparts are easily told from the more olive Blackpoll and Bay-breasted; male Pines are brighter yellow on the underparts, and the yellow is separated more sharply from the white lower belly. Leg color may be a useful distinction from Blackpoll (which has feet and usually at least the rear portion of the leg yellowish), but beware of some fall Pines with relatively pale (straw-brown) feet. Pines showing blurred streaks on the sides of the breast are easily told from the clearer-breasted Bay-breasted; that species does not approach male Pines in the intensity of the yellow of the underparts. The call note of Pine is somewhat softer than that of Bay-breasted and Blackpoll.

PRAIRIE WARBLERS are superficially similar to those adult male Pines which show black streaks on the sides of the breast. Prairies are much smaller and finer billed, show more extensive yellow on underparts (through the belly), have less conspicuous wing bars, streaking extending to the flanks, a different face pattern, and (usually) reddish spotting on the back. Prairies pump their tails more frequently. Fall **TENNESSEE WARBLERS**, suggestive of Pines in general color, lack broad wing bars and are much finer billed, shorter tailed, and smaller overall.

Very dull first fall and first spring female Pine Warblers show few distinctive markings and often confuse observers; compare these plumages with immature female **YELLOW-RUMPED** (which always shows a bright yellow rump) and **CAPE MAY** (which has slimmer bill, shorter tail, yellow-green rump, more streaking on underparts).

The **YELLOW-THROATED VIREO** (*Vireo flavifrons*) is superficially similar to a bright male Pine Warbler. These vireos show a much thicker, hooked bill and a somewhat shorter tail. The face of the Yellow-throated Vireo shows conspicuous yellow spectacles (supraloral stripe and complete eye-ring); it lacks the large white tail spots of Pine Warbler (but does show thin white edges to the rectrices); the yellow of the underparts does not extend as far onto the flanks and belly, and there are no streaks on the sides of the breast; the rump and uppertail coverts are grayish in the vireo, olive in the warbler. The vireo's actions are more sluggish; it gleans from foliage and is not likely to be seen creeping along branches or foraging in fields.

 ## VOICE

SONG is a simple, rapid, musical trill, suggestive of Chipping Sparrow (*Spizella passerina*) song but considerably more musical. Notes are of an even pitch, pace, and strength, and are delivered at rates of about 10 to 25 notes per second. Songs also recall those of Worm-eating and some Orange-crowned warblers, but with different tone and quality. An individual may sing two song types, a faster trill and a slower one with more inflected notes. Resident southeastern birds sing virtually all year, with songs least frequent during late summer molting period. Northern migrants sing into early fall before departing the breeding grounds. Except for many spring migrants, songs are almost always delivered from pines. **CALL NOTE** is a slurred *chip* or *tsup* recalling calls of Yellow-throated and Grace's warblers. **FLIGHT NOTE** is a slightly buzzy *zeet*.

BEHAVIOR

Pine Warblers frequently pump their tails, although not as forcefully or constantly as Palm and Prairie warblers.

Overwhelmingly a bird of pines, this species forages by slowly and methodically creeping along trunks and branches and probing into needle clusters and cones. Occasionally sallies for insects. Normally feeds rather high in pines, but they will feed lower, and even on the ground, in migration and winter. Quite gregarious in winter, with flocks often joining other species such as Chipping Sparrows and Eastern Bluebirds (*Sialia sialis*). Often acts aggressively toward congeners and ecologically similar sympatric species, such as Yellow-throated Warblers and Brown-headed Nuthatches (*Sitta pusilla*). Although mainly insectivorous, winter birds also feed on berries and will readily come to feeders for suet, bread, or sunflower seeds.

NESTS almost exclusively in pines, occasionally in other conifers. Nest is placed high (25 to 40 ft., sometimes over 100 ft.), well out on a horizontal branch but hidden by needle clusters.

HABITAT

Throughout its **BREEDING** range, pines are the key component of the habitat. Important pine species vary geographically: loblolly, longleaf, and shortleaf pines in the South, Virginia pine in s. Midwest, pitch pine on the coast from New Jersey to New England, white and red pines in much of the North. In the South, preferred pine forests are rather open, even savanna-like, but contain numerous tall, mature trees; especially in the North, denser mature pine or mixed pine and hardwood forests are also occupied. In **WINTER** *and* **MIGRATION** there is still a strong preference for pines, but birds are regularly also found in hardwood forests, cypress swamps, and even in rather open fields and pastures adjacent to woodland.

DISTRIBUTION

RESIDENT in pine woodlands over much of the South, from e. Texas, e. Okla., Ark., and La. east to S.C. and coastal N.C., and south to the Gulf Coast and throughout the Fla. peninsula. Also resident on the coast of Va., Md., and s. Del., although a large portion of this population is migratory. Generally absent from the mountain and upper Piedmont regions of the southeastern states. **SUMMERS** locally in the s. Midwest in Ky. and Tenn. (mainly eastern regions of those states), the Ozark region of Mo., southernmost Ill., s.

Ind., and se. Ohio. Inland breeding populations in the Mid-Atlantic states are almost entirely migratory. Scarce breeder or only a migrant in the remaining areas of the Midwest. Also breeds locally, where habitat remains, in se. Man. (and possibly e. Sask.), cen. and n. Minn., Wisc., Mich., w. and s. Ont., and s. Que. On the Atlantic Coast, summers in pitch pine habitat north through New England very locally to sw. N.B. and into s. Que.

In **WINTER**, among our hardiest warblers, occurring commonly throughout the resident range outlined above (where numbers are augmented by northern migrants), less commonly along the Atlantic Coast to Va., Md., and s. Del., and in very small numbers north to Mass. and even Nfld.; a few often winter in Bermuda. Small numbers also winter inland to e. Okla., the Ozark region, the s. midwestern states, and through much of the Northeast; numbers in inland regions vary from year to year, depending on the severity of the winter. Many of these far northern birds are noted only in early winter and are associated with feeding stations; they often do not successfully overwinter. A few winter south of the normal resident range, to south coastal Texas (rarely n. Tamaulipas, Nuevo Léon) and the Fla. Keys.

MIGRATION patterns and timing are difficult to determine accurately because of this species' tendency to overwinter in northern regions. Pure transients are not frequently encountered anywhere in spring or fall.

SPRING MIGRATION is early, with only "Myrtle" Warblers moving into the north as early. The earliest returning breeders appear just north of the range of resident birds by late February; the great majority arrive in these areas during March. The main arrival of breeding birds in the southern Great Lakes states is in the latter half of March and early April, but pure transients through that region are most numerous in late April. New England and upper Midwest arrivals are generally in mid-April. Birds arrive at the northern end of the breeding range in late April (early May at the extreme nw. edge of the range in Manitoba). Late migrants, usually dull immature females, occur around the Great Lakes into mid-May, with strays to the end of May. A rare spring migrant along the e. Great Plains.

FALL MIGRATION is relatively late; the earliest birds may be found away from breeding areas by late August (exceptionally to late July), but the bulk of the poorly defined fall migration occurs from late September through the first half of October (with a few into late October). Generally uncommon in fall, but may be locally more frequent on the coast of s. New England. The nature of early fall movement is obscured by frequent misidentifications (especially with Bay-breasted and Blackpoll warblers); late fall passage (November) is difficult to determine because of the fre-

PINE WARBLER
Dendroica pinus

quency with which birds attempt to overwinter well north of the normal winter range.

Rare but regular **VAGRANT** north of regular range in the Canadian Maritimes to Nfld., P.E.I., and Grand Manan Is., mainly in fall. Very rare or casual on the n. Great Plains and Prairie Provinces. In the w. U.S. has occurred in Colo. (about a dozen records, mainly in fall in east), Wyo., Mont., N.M., Ariz., and Ore.; the great majority of western records are from coastal s. Calif. Of about 52 Calif. records, most are for late fall (mid-October to November), with 17 records of wintering birds (mostly in planted pines); there are three late spring records. There is one record for Greenland (1 October 1899); also recorded once on Mona Is. (off Puerto Rico), and there are a few records for the Bahamas south of the resident range of the race *achrustera*. August and September sight records for Costa Rica defy any established pattern of movements of this species and require verification.

Populations appear to be stable over the southern portion of the range. Some local increases noted in recent decades in the north (including Ohio, Ontario) with maturation of pine plantations. Loss or fragmentation of pitch pines in coastal Massachusetts, Connecticut, and Long Island has resulted in declines; local declines also caused by clearing of pines in n. Michigan, the Ozarks, and parts of the Great Lakes region. Cowbird parasitism of this species does not appear to be severe. This species is prone to suffer population declines after severely cold winters, with population reductions reflected in lower breeding densities for several years.

 SUBSPECIES

There are four weakly marked subspecies. The nominate sub-species occupies most of the continental distribution of the species. The race *florida* is resident in peninsular Florida. It is characterized by a longer bill, somewhat duller plumage, and reduced ventral streaking. Two extralimital subspecies are very similar to mainland birds: *achrustera* on the Bahamas and *chrysoleuca* on Hispaniola. *D. p. chrysoleuca* is characterized as being slightly brighter yellow and clearer white below, and with narrower wing bars. *D. p. achrustera* is duller, paler yellow below, chunkier and shorter winged than mainland birds.

TAXONOMIC RELATIONSHIPS

Has hybridized once with Yellow-rumped Warbler (specimen taken in New Mexico). Relationships within *Dendroica* have been postulated with Prairie and perhaps Palm warblers.

 PLUMAGES AND MOLTS

SPRING ADULT MALE: Entire upperparts bright olive green, strongly washed with yellow. Supraloral streak and split eye-ring bright yellow. Lores dusky olive. Auricular region olive green, darkest in the transocular area and the lower border (rarely blackish in latter area). Chin, throat, and breast bright yellow, with some yellow wash extending onto the upper belly and often a hint of pale yellow in the vent area. The yellow of the throat shows an ill-defined extension around the rear of the auricular patch. The sides of the breast have short, broad, poorly defined dark olive to blackish streaks. The flanks are yellow-olive with faint, dull olive streaks. Lesser wing coverts olive; median and greater coverts dull blackish and broadly

Pine Warbler. Male in New Jersey in May. (Photo: Mike Danzenbaker)

edged with white, forming two broad wing bars. The inner greater coverts and tertials are edged grayish. Remiges dull blackish, indistinctly edged with gray. Rectrices dull blackish with the distal ⅔ of the inner web white on r6 and distal half white on r5. **FIRST SPRING MALE:** Very similar to spring adult male, and rarely distinguishable. Some may retain a brownish tinge to the upperparts, not shown in spring adult males. Flight feathers and primary coverts average duller. On a few first spring males the yellow below is somewhat paler and less extensive; these birds may not be safely distinguishable from adult females. **SPRING ADULT FEMALE:** Upperparts dull olive green with a slight brownish wash. Supraloral streak pale yellow; split eye-ring whitish to pale yellow. Auricular area dusky olive, lacking any dark lower border. Chin, throat, and breast yellow, duller, and greener than in males. Yellow of breast does not extend onto upper belly or vent. Sides may show a hint of faint olive streaking, but most appear generally unstreaked in the field. Wing bars average slightly duller and grayer than in spring males. White in rectrices averages less than in adult male, but this is not a dependable sexing character. **FIRST SPRING FEMALE:** Easily the dullest plumage. Upperparts dull olive-brown to gray-brown. Faint supraloral streak and split eye-ring whitish. Grayish auricular, somewhat set off from throat color. Chin, throat, and breast dull grayish white, with a slight wash of pale yellow on the breast. Flanks dull, pale grayish brown. Underparts unstreaked. Wing bars relatively thin and tinged grayish. Flight feathers and primary coverts duller than in adult. White in rectrices more limited, often only faintly white on r5. **FALL ADULT MALE:** In fresh plumage shows a wash of brown on the olive green upperparts and a tinge of brownish on the flanks. Streaking on the sides of the breast generally more veiled. Otherwise identical to spring male, and spring appearance is acquired mainly through wear. **FIRST FALL MALE:** Like first spring male, but fresher plumage is more strongly washed with brown above and tinged

Pine Warbler. First fall female in Florida in December. (Photo: Jon L. Dunn)

brownish on the flanks. Yellow of underparts averages less bright than adult males. On average there is less white in the rectrices, but this is not a dependable aging character. **FALL ADULT FEMALE:** Like first spring female, but fresher plumage is browner, less gray, and buffier on the flanks. **FIRST FALL FEMALE:** Like first spring female, but fresher plumage may be tinged more strongly brown above and buffy on the belly and flanks. White in rectrices averages least extensive. **JUVENILE:** Upperparts uniformly brown, underparts grayish buff, heavily marked with dull brownish spots on the throat, breast, and flanks. Wings and tail as in first fall birds, but wing bars buffier. **BARE PARTS:** Bill blackish in spring adults, but strongly tinged brown on tomium and mandible in fall birds (especially females). First fall birds show much pinkish gray color on the basal half of the mandible and sides of maxilla. Legs and feet dull blackish brown, with soles paler, yellower. In fall and winter, foot color may be paler, more straw-brown. Eyes dark brown.

The prebasic molt occurs from June to August (on the breeding grounds for migratory populations); it is complete in adults but does not involve remiges in hatching-year birds. In some hatching-year birds the first prebasic molt may include some or all rectrices, which is unusual among warblers. The prealternate molt is absent or very slight (perhaps more extensive in hatching-year birds).

 REFERENCES

ECOLOGY, BEHAVIOR, VOCALIZATIONS, AND CONSERVATION: Ficken et al. 1968, Morse 1967b and 1974.
IDENTIFICATION: Kaufman 1990a, Whitney 1983.
PLUMAGES, MOLTS, AND MORPHOLOGY: Norris 1952.
SYSTEMATICS: Wetmore and Swales 1931.

Dendroica kirtlandii

5.5 in. (14 cm). Apart from the probably extinct Bachman's Warbler, this large *Dendroica* is our rarest warbler, with an estimated 1,400 breeding individuals remaining in 1996. It is limited in the breeding season to a highly specialized habitat of brushy young jack pines, mainly in the north-central part of Michigan's lower peninsula. Intensive habitat management and cowbird control have been instrumental in preventing or delaying extinction of this species. It is known to winter only in the Bahama Islands and is rarely encountered in migration. In plumage, the Kirtland's Warbler is mainly gray to gray-brown above, with a streaked back, and yellow below; it vigorously pumps the tail down and up. Beware confusion with first spring female Magnolia Warblers

DESCRIPTION

Generally gray above, but fall birds variably suffused with brown on the back and head; back boldly streaked with black. The lores are black in spring males, at least darker than the rest of the face in other plumages; there is a thin whitish eye-ring in all plumages, split in front and behind. The throat, breast, and belly vary from clear yellow to pale buffy yellow, becoming white on the undertail coverts. The sides are streaked with black, boldest in adults. The wing bars are thin and inconspicuous; white tail spots, boldest in adult males, are concentrated near the corners of the tail.

Structurally, it is a large and relatively long-tailed, heavy-billed *Dendroica*.

SIMILAR SPECIES

The vigorous tail-pumping habit is shared with a few other *Dendroica*, notably Palm and Prairie warblers. PRAIRIE WARBLER is much smaller, with greenish upperparts and a more complex face pattern. PALM is quickly told by contrasting greenish yellow rump (grayish in Kirtland's) and bright yellow undertail coverts (white in Kirtland's). Some first spring female MAGNOLIA WARBLERS have been mistaken for Kirtland's because of their rather plain gray heads with white eye-rings, indistinct superciliums, and limited streaking on the breast. Magnolias in this plumage, however, show a greenish back, yellowish rump, bolder wing bars, and a very different pattern of white on the tail; Magnolias do not pump their tails. Compare also with PINE and CANADA WARBLERS.

On the wintering grounds, the *flavescens* subspecies of YELLOW-THROATED WARBLER in the Bahamas has been mistaken for this species. Although *flavescens* has a more subdued facial pattern and more extensive yellow on the underparts than mainland races of Yellow-throated, it should still be readily told by the bold super-cilium, longer bill, more extensive white in the tail, and bolder wing bars. Yellow-throateds feed at medium to high levels, often by creeping along branches and tree trunks like a Black-and-white Warbler, whereas Kirtland's feed low (often even on the ground).

Since a large number of Kirtland's Warblers have been fitted with combinations of color leg bands, we note that one clue for identifying migrants is the presence of such bands.

♪ VOICE

SONG is loud and distinctive, often broadcast from the top of a small jack pine; singing peaks through the month of June and into early July, and may sometimes be heard into early August. One male was observed to sing 2,212 songs in one day. The lively, bubbly song is relatively low-pitched, rising in pitch, tempo, and volume as it progresses; it lacks any buzzy notes. Normal songs have been described as *chip-chip-che-way-o* and *chip chip chip-chip-chip tew tew weet weet*. Resemblance to songs of Northern Waterthrush and even House Wren (*Troglodytes aedon*) and Indigo Bunting (*Passerina cyanea*) have been noted. A simple chatter song is often given late in the summer season; interacting males may also give a soft, bubbly, wrenlike whisper song.

CALL NOTE is a low, forceful *chip,* lower than somewhat similar note of Prairie or Palm warblers and even suggesting the rich, low call note of a Kentucky Warbler or Ovenbird. **FLIGHT NOTE** is a thin, high *zeet.*

BEHAVIOR

An extremely tame warbler with deliberate movements and a distinctive tail-pumping behavior (jerking the tail downward, then slowly back upward). Although most birders encounter Kirtland's Warblers as singing males at or near the tops of jack pines, most activities of the species are concentrated low in the pines or near or on the ground. Forages by gleaning pine needles, leaves, and ground cover; will occasionally make short sallies or hover-glean at terminal needle clusters. The dense structure of its breeding and winter habitat makes observation difficult (except of singing males). Territories (mean size in various studies range from 3.4 to 8.4 hectares) are often clustered in loose colonies.

The **NEST** is located on the ground, concealed by grasses and other low vegetation. It is a cup of grasses, leaves, moss, and hair nestled into a pit in the sandy soil.

Habitat

The specialized **BREEDING** habitat consists of large stands of young jack pines (*Pinus banksiana*) on loose, sandy soil; these stands must be dense, with interconnected low branches and a ground cover of grasses, sedges, ferns, and berry brambles. Occupied stands characteristically have small openings. Stands are first occupied when five to six years old, with trees 3–6 ft. tall; they are abandoned after about 15 years when the trees are 10–15 ft. or taller, and when lower branches begin dying back. The most suitable young jack pine stands are the result of fires that burn mature growth and stimulate germination of seeds and the formation of patchy new seedling growth. The creation of suitable habitat with dense plantations of jack pine, and rarely even red pines (*P. resinosa*), has shown some recent success; by 1994, more breeding pairs were found in plantations than in burns.

The habitat of breeding Kirtland's Warblers is in the southernmost range of the jack pine, a tree that occurs through most of sub-Arctic Canada. Suitable habitat has probably only been available in Michigan for 6,000–8,000 years, following the retreat of the Wisconsin glaciation.

WINTER habitat consists of dense broadleaf scrub thickets less than 6 ft. high, with scattered taller trees. Wintering birds are generally solitary, secretive, and rarely encountered within this preferred habitat.

Distribution

BREEDS in loose "colonies" locally in the northern part of the lower peninsula of Mich., with the majority of birds in a roughly 80-by-115-mile area lying mostly within the Au Sable River drainage. The largest recent breeding populations are in Crawford, Oscoda, and Ogemaw cos., with smaller populations in seven additional counties. Occasional summering birds, usually unmated males, are found on the upper peninsula of Mich. (where breeding recently confirmed), in w.-ccn. and nw. Wisc., and in s. Ont. (one confirmed breeding in 1945; probably nested near Petawawa and perhaps elsewhere early this century). One territorial bird was

KIRTLAND'S WARBLER
Dendroica kirtlandii

✳ indicates additional counties
where there has been breeding
within the last few years

found in s. Que. in 1978. Most birds arrive on the breeding grounds during or soon after the second week of May.

WINTERS, as far as known, only in the Bahama Islands, with records from late August to early May. Records are from the larger northern islands, with most specimens from New Providence and Eleuthera, south to Caicos. There is a questionable sight record from Hispaniola; another sight record from Veracruz, Mexico, is almost certainly incorrect.

Now rarely recorded in **MIGRATION.** All migration records should be carefully documented; our understanding of migration status is obscured by numerous questionable sight records. Spring migration records are much more numerous than fall, probably because loudly singing males are more readily encountered. Migrants are most often encountered near the breeding grounds. For example, in the Midwest there are about 45 records each for Ohio and Ont., 14 from Ill., 12 from Ind., 8 from s. and cen. Wisc., and several from s. Mich. (away from breeding areas). Most of these records are for spring. In the South recorded most frequently in Fla. (about 15 reports; specimen), Ga. (10 reports; several specimens), and S.C. (about 10 reports). There are also specimen records or photographs for Va., Mo., Minn., and Pa.; sight records exist for Ala., Tenn., N.C. (one spring, two fall), and W. Va. Spring records in the southern states are mostly from mid- to late April, whereas most spring records from the upper Mid-west are from 10 to 25 May (as late as 1 June in Ont.). Hatching-year birds may begin to migrate south in late August (earlier than adults); adults have been trapped on the breeding grounds as late as the first week of October. Many fall migration records are dur-ing October, and the species has been recorded as late as the first week of November in Fla.

 STATUS AND CONSERVATION

A federally listed endangered species. Latest population censuses revealed 766 singing males in 1995 and 692 in 1996; the popula-tion low of 167 singing males was reached in 1974 and 1987. This species has probably always been uncommon and local, but populations have been further limited by habitat loss and modifi-cation and by brood parasitism by Brown-headed Cowbirds. Pop-ulations may have peaked late in the 19th century with the felling and burning of forests, prior to the main invasions of cowbirds. Fire suppression has been the main factor leading to loss of quali-ty habitat. Cowbirds appear to have reached Kirtland's Warbler breeding habitat in Michigan in the 1880s, with disastrous effects on breeding success by the 1950s and 1960s. Intensive cowbird control programs begun in the early 1970s have been very suc-cessful; some 4,000 cowbirds have been removed annually, reduc-ing parasitism rates from as high as 70 percent down to 3 percent or less and tripling warbler productivity. Despite successful cow-bird control, the lack of suitable breeding habitat led to continued low populations through the early 1980s. Controlled burns (espe-cially) and, more recently, plantations have been successful in maintaining adequate habitat; 60 percent of the Kirtland's War-bler population in 1993 was concentrated in the 1980 Mack Lake burn area (a management burn that got out of control). Even in suitable burn areas, habitat fragmentation, recreational cabins, and predators such as domestic cats are all increasing problems.

SUBSPECIES

None reported, nor would any significant variation be expected from a bird with so limited a nesting range.

TAXONOMIC RELATIONSHIPS

Although usually placed next to Pine and Prairie warblers in taxonomic lists, its relationships within *Dendroica* are unstudied; a postulated relationship with the Yellow-throated Warbler seems unconvincing.

PLUMAGES AND MOLTS

SPRING ADULT MALE: Crown, hindneck, and sides of face clear deep gray, tinged bluish. Lores and a narrow strip across the forehead (just above the bill) black; this black extends to just behind the eye and down through the anterior cheek and malar area (black is less extensive in cheek area on some individuals). Narrow white eye-ring, interrupted by black in front and back. Remaining upperparts gray, boldly streaked across the back with black; black centers to gray uppertail coverts. Chin pale yellowish white; throat, breast, and belly clear yellow; undertail coverts white. Short but bold black streaks on the sides of the breast and flanks. In some individuals there is also some black stippling across the center of the breast. Lesser wing coverts clear gray; median and greater coverts black-centered with grayish white fringes, forming two thin and rather indistinct pale wing bars. Rectrices blackish, with white spots on the distal portion of the inner webs of r5 and r6 and a tiny amount of white on r4. **FIRST SPRING MALE:** Not reliably separated in the field from very similar spring adult male, but unlike that plumage often faintly washed with brownish on the back; on average there is less black in the cheek area. First spring males may be more likely than adults to show small black stippling on the center of the breast, but this character is not reliable for aging. Primaries and rectrices browner and more worn than in adult. **SPRING ADULT FEMALE:**

Kirtland's Warbler. Adult male in Oscoda Co., Michigan, in June 1996. (Photo: Ron Austing)

Kirtland's Warbler. Male (L.), female (R) in Crawford Co., Michigan, in June 1969. (Photo: Ron Austing)

Crown, neck, and face gray, with no black in the lore and cheek region. Thin, broken, dull white eye-ring. Remaining upperparts gray with brown wash across the back; bold black streaking on back as in male. Chin whitish; throat, breast, and belly pale yellow; undertail coverts whitish. Bold black streaking on sides and flanks. Variable dark stippling across the center of the breast present in most individuals. Dull whitish wing bars thin and inconspicuous. White in tail limited to spots near tips of outer two pairs of rectrices. **FIRST SPRING FEMALE:** Not reliably told in field from spring adult female, but may average slightly duller, browner above. Primaries and rectrices browner and more worn than in adult. **FALL ADULT MALE:** Resembles spring adult male, but crown slightly suffused and back strongly suffused with brown; the black in the lores and cheeks is much reduced or absent. Yellow of underparts slightly paler and buffier; black streaks on sides and flanks partly veiled with yellowish white. Aging and sexing of all plumage classes in fall cannot be safely done in the field; however, if a bird shows some black in loral area at this season, it is almost certainly an adult male. **FIRST FALL MALE:** Similar to fall adult male, but black is never present in lores; head washed slightly browner; streaks on sides and flanks less bold. Closely resembles fall adult female. **FALL ADULT FEMALE:** Probably indistinguishable from many fall adult males and from first fall birds of both sexes. Head and upperparts average slightly browner, breast slightly buffier and more stippled than fall adult males, and black never present in the lores. **FIRST FALL FEMALE:** Generally the brownest plumage; upperparts and face strongly washed with brown. Yellow of underparts pale and with buffy tint. Streaks on sides and flanks thin, not much bolder than stippling across breast. Inconspicuous wing bars are tinged buffy. White in rectrices of first fall/first spring females averages least of any age or sex class. **JUVENILE:** Grayish brown above, paler below with sooty brown splotching. Yellow begins to appear on sides of breast about two weeks after fledging. **BARE PARTS:** Bill black in spring; fall birds of both sexes show much brown at base of mandible and along cutting edge of bill. Eyes dark brown. Legs and feet blackish.

The prebasic molt is mostly completed from July into September, on the breeding grounds; this molt is complete in adults but does not involve remiges and rectrices in hatching-year birds. Hatching-year birds generally complete the prebasic molt by early September. Prealternate molt occurs from February to April, involving only the body feathers.

 REFERENCES

GENERAL: Mich. D.N.R. 1992, Mayfield 1960 and 1992, Walkinshaw 1983.
DISTRIBUTION: Austen et al. 1994, Brewer et al. 1991, Clench 1973, Radabugh 1974.
ECOLOGY, BEHAVIOR, VOCALIZATIONS, AND CONSERVATION: Brewer et al. 1991, Mayfield 1972, Sykes 1997, Sykes et al. 1989.
PLUMAGES, MOLTS, AND MORPHOLOGY: Mich. D.N.R. 1992, Goodman 1982.

PRAIRIE WARBLER PL. 19

Dendroica discolor

4.5 in. (11.5 cm). This tail-bobbing warbler is most abundant in the southeastern U.S. and the Atlantic coastal region. The Prairie Warbler is a successful species whose range has expanded greatly during the 20th century, although it has recently experienced declines in parts of its range. A thorough monograph of this species by Val Nolan Jr., published in 1978, makes this one of the best studied of all the wood-warblers. All plumages show a distinctive facial pattern, with a yellow supercilium (whitish in some plumages), dark transocular line, broad pale crescent below the eye, and dark lower border to the cheek; this, combined with the almost entirely yellow underparts, streaked sides, pale wing bars, and frequent tail-bobbing, make field identification straightforward.

 DESCRIPTION

The facial pattern is distinctive in all plumages, although rather subtle in immature females. There is a broad, pale subocular crescent (yellow except in immature females, where whitish) that is bordered below by a dark (black, olive, or dark gray) moustachial stripe. This curving, dark moustachial stripe forms the lower border of the auriculars. All plumages also show a spot of dark on the lower sides of the neck. Generally olive above with variable chestnut spotting on the back. Mostly yellow below with streaks or spots on the sides, paler (almost whitish) undertail coverts. The two wing bars, usually tinged yellow, are not especially distinct. There are long white spots in the tail.

This is a small, small-billed *Dendroica* with a rather long tail.

 SIMILAR SPECIES

Most likely to be confused with bright male PINE WARBLER, which shares a somewhat similar (but more subdued) facial pattern, extensively yellow underparts, streaks on the sides, wing bars, extensive white tail spots, and a similar call note. Pine Warblers are also tail-bobbers, though they do not bob as strongly as Prairie or Palm warblers. Pine Warblers are larger and heavier-billed than Prairies, a difference that is clear in the field; their facial pattern lacks the bold crescent forming the lower border of the auriculars as well as the dark spot on the side of the throat. Bright male Pines have bolder, whiter wing bars; they are more extensively white on the posterior underparts, and their backs are plain green (never with any chestnut spotting).

Fall MAGNOLIA WARBLER is somewhat similar in general plumage pattern. Note the grayish head and complete, distinct eye-ring of Magnolia, along with the extensive white in the undertail coverts and the yellowish (not olive) rump. The tail pattern of Magnolia is distinctive, with a broad white band across all but the central rectrices; unlike Prairie, the tail is not bobbed. PALM WARBLERS share the habitual tail-bobbing, and bright "Yellow" Palms (*hypochrysea*) suggest Prairie in plumage. Breeding adult Palms have distinctive chestnut crowns. In winter, the bright yellow undertail coverts, yellow-green rump, long supercilium, and less extensive white in the tail should easily tell Palms. Immature and fall female KIRTLAND'S WARBLERS, also tail bobbers, are much larger than Prairies, lack the pale subocular crescent, and are extensively white on the undertail coverts.

 VOICE

The SONG is distinctive, a high, quick series of thin, buzzy notes that starts out on one pitch, then rises rather sharply over the last half or two-thirds of the song. The notes are usually delivered rapidly (too fast to count), but slower versions may have only 3–4 notes per second. Alternate songs are quieter, more variable, and less structured, often with an opening series of longer notes followed by a series of short notes; note quality ranges from clear to raspy. Simple songs have rarely been noted from females. Males may begin singing in March on the winter grounds, and resident *paludicola* of coastal Florida peninsula sings as early as mid-January. There is some resurgence of singing in late summer. Several instances of Prairies singing songs typical of Black-throated Green Warblers have been described.

The **CALL NOTE** is a smacking *tsip* or *tchick,* quite similar to the call of Palm Warbler. Also gives a drier *chip* note suggestive of that of a Canada Warbler or Lincoln's Sparrow. **FLIGHT NOTE** is a thin *seep* with no buzzy tones. Several other call notes have been described.

Behavior

After the Palm Warbler and the waterthrushes, the Prairie is more of a tail bobber than any other warbler. The tail bobbing is actually a quick downward movement followed by a slower return to the original position. There is only a slight lateral movement of the tail during the bob, and the tail is not normally cocked above the normal horizontal position. As with most or all tail-bobbing warblers, both sexes bob the tail, and tail bobbing becomes more frequent when the bird is alarmed. Males do not normally bob their tails when singing from a song perch. In general this is an active and rather restless warbler; it is usually quite responsive to pishing.

Territorial males choose high song perches, often on an exposed snag. They often sing well into the heat of the day. Males on the breeding grounds may give "butterfly" or "moth" flights with exaggerated wingbeats.

Prairie Warblers forage from shrub height well up into the trees, and occasionally on or near the ground. Most foraging is by gleaning, including quick hover-gleans and acrobatic hanging. Some sallying is noted in summer. Winter birds and migrants often join mixed flocks of other warblers, gnatcatchers, and chickadees. Food mainly consists of insects (especially caterpillars) and spiders; winter birds will also take nectar.

The **NEST** is a compact cup of plant down, grasses, pine needles, and bark shreds, bound with spider webs. It is usually placed in the crotch of a sapling but sometimes well out onto small branches; nests are usually placed in young hardwoods, junipers, or spruces, but some are placed in shrubs or brambles. Birds of coastal peninsular Florida place their nests in mangroves. Nests are usually within 1 0 ft. of the ground, but nest heights range from less than one foot to over 4 0 ft. Nests of Prairie Warblers are hard hit by Brown-headed Cowbirds; parasitism rates of up to one-third are recorded in some regions. Double broods are frequent, at least in Indiana; polygyny is regularly recorded. A sum-

mering male in Inyo Co., California, was observed feeding Lesser
Goldfinch (*Carduelis psaltria*) fledglings.

HABITAT

These are birds of successional habitats such as regenerating old
fields, pastures, clear-cuts, power line right-of-ways, abandoned
orchards, and reclaimed strip mine sites; they may occupy small
patches of habitat and are among the earliest warblers to colonize
scrubby successional habitats. The vegetation may be deciduous
or mixed deciduous-coniferous. Christmas tree plantations are
used in some areas. Natural successional habitats used by Prairie
Warblers include dune vegetation on the Atlantic Coast and
Great Lakes, ridgetops, cliff edges, and open pine and oak barrens. All of these habitats allow much light penetration, and most
are on poor (often sandy) soil; preferred habitats are usually on
dry upland slopes. Pines are an important habitat component
over much of the South and the Atlantic Coast, including pitch
pines, slash pines. In portions of the Midwest and Appalachian
region, red cedars and deciduous shrubs are important, while in
parts of Ontario, stunted pine-oak-juniper scrub on rocky substrates is preferred. Prairie Warblers formerly bred in jack pine
plains of n.-cen. Michigan, but birds in that state are now mainly
restricted to lakeshore dune vegetation. Close-canopied forest
interiors are usually avoided, although this species does breed in
Smilax understory of mixed hardwood forest in the Great Dismal
Swamp, Virginia. This species is absent from most of the higher,
forested parts of the Appalachian Mountains, but is found locally
on ridgetops as high as 3,000 ft. to nearly 3,800 ft. in West Virginia and Virginia. The subspecies *paludicola* of the Florida
peninsula is resident in mangroves (especially red mangrove, *Rhi-
zophora mangle*, but also in black and white mangroves); less
commonly they occur in stands of Virginia live oak on coastal
strands.

WINTER habitats are varied but generally open and scrubby,
including forest edges and clearings, coastal scrub, mangroves,
dry scrub, overgrown fields, citrus groves, and coffee plantations.
This species has probably benefited from deforestation on the
wintering grounds. MIGRANTS occur in a variety of open habitats
from open woodlands and woodland edges to brushy or weedy
fields.

DISTRIBUTION

BREEDS from e. Okla., ne. Kans. (local), s. Mo., s. (locally cen.) Ill.,
Ind., Mich. (only in nw., local), Ohio (mainly s. and e.), s. Ont.

(north to se. Georgian Bay and, recently, Manitoulin Is.), N.Y. (mainly s.), se. and sw. Vt., s. N.H. and sw. Me., south throughout the eastern U.S. to e. Texas, the southern portions of the Gulf states, and s. Fla. There are old nesting records for Neb., and a probable old nesting record for se. Iowa. Extirpated from former breeding range in n.-cen. Mich. Summer males turn up rarely but regularly north of the breeding range, e.g., Wisc., parts of Mich., and exceptionally N.D. and sw. Man.

WINTERS primarily in the West Indies. Abundant on the Bahamas and most of the Greater Antilles, with smaller numbers wintering into the w. Caribbean (e.g., Bay Is. off n. Honduras). A few also winter in the Lesser Antilles, especially in the north; there are single records as far south as Barbados and Grenada. Up to 10 per winter have been recorded on Bermuda. Uncommon to rare along the east coast of the Yucatán peninsula, Belize, and n. Honduras. Casual in s. Veracruz, along the Pacific Coast from Nayarit, Mexico, south to El Salvador, and south to Costa Rica, Panama, and the Netherlands Antilles. There are single records for Colombia (Cordova) and Trinidad.

Within the U.S. the Prairie Warbler winters mainly in Fla., where it is numerous only in the southern part of the state, where the subspecies *paludicola* is resident; it is rare in n. Fla. and very rare in the Fla. Panhandle. Also winters rarely in coastal Ga. and S.C., with a few noted regularly as far north as se. N.C.; it is very rare or casual in winter along the Gulf Coast west to e. Texas. There are multiple early winter records along the coast north to Mass. Recorded exceptionally in early winter in N.S. and, inland, in Ky. Some of the records of vagrants in the west pertain to early winter or overwintering birds, including three for Ariz. and nearly 20 for Calif. (at least two of which have returned for consecutive winters).

MIGRATION is primarily between the West Indies and se. U.S., with little trans-Gulf migration; fall migration routes largely retrace those of spring. The moderate number of breeding birds noted in La. and e. Texas are believed to have arrived from points further east. This species is very rare on the upper Texas coast in spring, and only slightly more numerous in fall. Except in Fla., the eastern Gulf Coast, and the Atlantic states, this species is encountered only uncommonly away from known breeding areas.

SPRING MIGRATION begins in s. Fla. in March, although migrants are not regular until late in the month; information on early arrivals is confused in coastal s. Fla. by the presence of resident *paludicola*. There are a few March sightings for Ga., but there, as well as the coast of the Carolinas and the Gulf states, arrivals in early April are more typical. Inland through most of the southern states the earliest arrivals may be during the first week of April

PRAIRIE WARBLER
Dendroica discolor

discolor

paludicola

paludicola

but are more typically in mid-April. In the Midwest, typical arrivals are in the third week of April; in s. New England birds arrive at the end of April or beginning of May, and in Me. and Vt. they arrive in mid-May. The few birds still breeding in Mich. arrive during the first half of May; those in Ont. arrive in the second week of May, although records extend back to early April. Peak spring movements in Fla. occur in April; those along the Mid-Atlantic Coast are in early May. The small numbers noted at migrant traps around the Great Lakes peak in early May. The latest spring dates are in mid-May in Fla. (away from nesting areas) and in late May in the Great Lakes region (exceptionally to early June in all regions).

FALL MIGRATION is detected earlier in the Deep South and Gulf Coast than farther north, no doubt because breeding is earlier in the south. Migrants are noted in Fla. as early as the second week of July, and a concentration of 200 was found in coastal Ala. on 27 July. Migrants first appear in the Mid-Atlantic region and Midwest by early August, but more typical arrivals are in mid-August. Fall migrant Prairie Warblers are found in numbers only in Fla.

and along the Atlantic Coast. Peak fall movements in the Mid-Atlantic region are from the last third of August to mid-September; the extended peak in Fla. is from about 10 August to 10 October. Most birds have departed the northern breeding areas from the latter half of September (Midwest) to mid-October (Atlantic region). A few migrants are routinely noted through October in Mass. and coastal N.Y., and records extend into November in the Midwest and Great Lakes regions. For later records, see under Winter.

CASUAL on the s. Great Plains from n.-cen. Texas to S.D. (and once in N.D.). Also casual in Minn., Iowa, n. Mo., and Que., mainly in spring. Rare but regular in spring and summer in Wisc., but casual there in fall. Regular in fall (mid-August through October) on the northern Atlantic Coast from Me. through the Canadian Maritime Provinces, and in Nfld. Away from Calif., casual in the West; recorded in Colo. (about 10 records, mostly in spring), Ariz. (one in September, three in winter), Ore. (six coastal fall records), and once each in sw. Man. (summer), N.D. (summer), Mont. (early September), Wyo. (spring), N.M. (late November and January), Nev. (May), and n. Baja Calif. (one sight record). In Calif., about 90 percent of the 355 records (through 1995) are from fall (mid-August to November) on the coast; there are eight spring/summer records and 17 during the winter period. Nearly two-thirds of the Calif. records are from the northern part of the state, and only about 5 percent are from the interior. Exceptional records are for Cocos Is. off w. Costa Rica (February specimen), off s. Guatemala, in the n. Atlantic some 300 miles south of Nfld. in September, on the Queen Charlotte Is. and Triangle Is. off B.C. in fall, and twice in September in s. coastal Alaska. There is a 20 June specimen from Chihuahua, Mexico.

⅄ STATUS AND CONSERVATION

This species has dramatically increased its range and abundance through the present century, benefiting from the clearing of forests and the creation of edge and second-growth habitats. This expansion has occurred northward, but also southward (into northernmost Florida) and westward (into e. Texas). The breeding range expansion has largely stabilized, and there have been some declines and range contractions in e. Oklahoma, e. Kansas, s. Ontario, and Michigan. In s. Ontario declines are related to habitat destruction, particularly of lakeshore dune scrub. Catastrophic declines in Michigan are hard to explain; the species is now absent from jack pine plains of n.-cen. Michigan, and largely restricted to dune habitats on the shore of Lake Michigan. Breeding Bird Survey data show recent declines over most of the species' range. The sharp declines in Florida since 1971 involve the endemic subspecies *paludicola*; they are on the state's Species of Special Concern list. Causes of the declines in Florida include destruction of mangrove habitats and possibly cowbird parasitism (mainly Brown-headed Cowbird, but the Shiny Cowbird has increasing potential as a problem).

SUBSPECIES

The nominate subspecies, described above, is widespread. The weakly differentiated subspecies *paludicola* (*collinsi* is a synonym) is restricted to mangrove and adjacent habitats along the coasts of peninsular Florida, north to Pasco Co. in the west and Volusia Co. on the East Coast; it is recorded as a vagrant on Cuba. This resident subspecies is not separable from nominate birds in the field. It averages slightly more grayish (less greenish) above, slightly paler yellow below (may be almost white on the chin) with the streaking less distinct, and has the chestnut markings on the back more restricted. It averages slightly larger than nominate birds in bill, tail, and tarsus measurements.

TAXONOMIC RELATIONSHIPS

The closely related Vitelline Warbler (*Dendroica vitellina*) is resident on the Cayman and Swan Islands in the Caribbean; the two form a superspecies and have sometimes been considered conspecific. Relationships within *Dendroica* not certain, although the possibility of a relationship with Pine and Palm warblers seems reasonable; all share the habit of tail-bobbing and rather simple songs of rapidly repeated notes.

Prairie Warbler. Male in Ohio in May. (Photo: Steve and Dave Maslowski)

SPRING ADULT MALE: Forehead, crown, and hindneck olive-yellow. Broad bright yellow supraloral stripe, extending back as a narrower supercilium. Narrow streak through lores dull black, extending just behind the eye. Broad yellow arc below eye, bordered below by a black moustachial stripe that curves down from the loral area and back along the lower border of the auricular, merging into the olive-yellow rear portion of the auricular. Remaining upperparts olive-yellow, slightly brighter on the rump; back variably marked with chestnut feather centers forming broad streaks or, in some individuals, a nearly complete patch on the upper back (more evident with wear through the spring and early summer). Uppertail coverts grayish olive with indistinct black centers. Chin, throat, lower sides of the neck, breast, and belly bright yellow, becoming paler yellow on the lower belly and undertail coverts. Sides and flanks boldly streaked with black, with the thickest black streaks on the sides of the breast. There is an isolated black spot on the side of the throat below the rear portion of the auricular. Wings slate-gray, edged pale grayish olive. Anterior wing bar (tips of median coverts) pale yellow; indistinct posterior wing bar (tips of greater coverts). Tail slaty, edged grayish olive. Outer rectrix mostly white on inner web; r4–5 with large white spots extending to the tip; r3 with a variable small white spot on the inner web. **FIRST SPRING MALE:** Similar to spring adult male, but eye line and dark moustachial crescent may be partly gray rather than solid black, and the chestnut on the back is reduced. Wings and wing bars duller than in adult. Rectrices duller and more tapered, with a smaller white patch on r4, small white spot on r3 usually absent. **SPRING ADULT FEMALE:** Head pattern resembles that of spring adult male, but the loral streak and short extension of the eye line beyond the eye are olive, rather than black, as is the dark spot on the lower neck and the moustachial stripe along the lower border of the auriculars (the

Prairie Warbler. First fall male in New York in October. (Photo: Arthur Morris/Birds as Art)

Prairie Warbler. First fall female in New York in September. (Photo: Tom Vezo)

latter may show some black feathering in some individuals). The olive of the upperparts is slightly duller, and the chestnut on the back is reduced to small feather centers that are inconspicuous in the field. The yellow of the underparts averages slightly paler; the black streaking on the sides is thinner than that of all spring males, and becomes blurred and inconspicuous on the flanks. The rectrices show a moderately large patch of white on r4. **FIRST SPRING FEMALE:** Similar to spring adult female, but the auriculars are tinged gray, and the supercilium and crescent below the eye average paler yellow; some individuals show some whitish intermixed with the pale yellow of the chin and throat. The wing bars are thinner and grayer than in adults, and the rectrices are duller and more tapered. **FALL ADULT MALE:** Nearly identical to spring adult male, but in fresher plumage there is slight yellow veiling to the black areas and the chestnut of the back is much obscured by olive-yellow. Wing bars are more strongly tinged yellowish. **FIRST FALL MALE:** Variable; some individuals closely resemble fall adult males, but others are considerably duller. Consistently differs from adult male in having some gray in the auriculars, some (sometimes extensive) grayish or yellow-olive flecking in the black moustachial crescent, and whitish or yellowish white eyelids (the narrow ring of feathers around the eye; the broader supercilium and crescent below the eye are slightly or strongly tinged yellow in first fall males and bright yellow in adult males). The anterior wing bar formed by the tips of the median coverts is only slightly tinged with yellow. The upperparts are slightly duller olive than in adult male. There is a moderate amount of veiled chestnut on the back, usually less than in fall adult male but more than in fall females. In the hand, the rectrices are narrower and more tapered. **FALL ADULT FEMALE:** Nearly identical to spring adult female, but facial pattern, side streaking, and chestnut back spots somewhat more veiled with yellow-olive feather tips. **FIRST FALL FEMALE:** The dullest plumage, with the olive of the upperparts relatively dull and the yellow below paler, often nearly whitish on the chin and throat. The back lacks chestnut. The face pattern is muted, with the olive-gray eye line and moustachial crescent lacking any black. There is a variable amount of gray in the auriculars, and the supercilium is dull whitish; the narrow eyelids are white. The streaking on the sides and flanks is thin and blurred, and the spot on the lower neck is an indistinct olive-gray; many show a tinge of buff on the rear flanks. The pale grayish olive wing bars are narrow and indistinct. Rectrices relatively narrow and tapered; white in r4 very limited. **JUVENILE:** Head and upperparts dull brownish olive, with dull whitish supercilium area and crescent under eye. Underparts dull buffy, lightly streaked with olive. Wings and tail as in first fall birds, but wing bars buffy. **BARE PARTS:** Bill blackish, with some yellowish brown along the cutting edge and the base of the lower mandible; first fall birds have dusky brown bills, paler at the base of the lower mandible. Legs blackish brown, dull yellow on the soles. Eyes dark brown.

The prebasic molt takes place primarily on the breeding grounds from June (it may begin in May in the southernmost populations) to August. This molt is complete in adults but does not involve the remiges or rectrices in hatching-year birds. The prealternate molt involves mostly the feathers of the head; it occurs through the winter and early spring (until April).

 REFERENCES

GENERAL: Nolan 1978.
DISTRIBUTION: Austen et al. 1994, Lambert and Smith 1984.
ECOLOGY, BEHAVIOR, VOCALIZATIONS, AND CONSERVATION: Walkinshaw 1959.
PLUMAGES, MOLTS, AND MORPHOLOGY: Nolan and Mumford 1965.
SYSTEMATICS: Howell 1930, Lambert and Smith 1984.

PALM WARBLER   PL. 20

Dendroica palmarum

5 in. (12.7 cm). This species is a habitual tail-pumper — more so than any other warbler. It also shows a greater preference for open, unwooded habitats than most other warblers. "Palm Warbler" is a misnomer, because this species shows no inclination to use palms and only occurs in habitats dominated by them in portions of its wintering grounds. It is a hardy warbler, moving north early in spring and returning south late in the fall. The bright yellow undertail coverts, often contrasting with the whitish underparts, are distinctive in all plumages. The two distinct subspecies are separable in the field.

Description

The whitish or yellow supercilium and dark eye line give a strong face pattern in all plumages. The undertail coverts are always bright yellow, but the ground color of the remaining underparts varies from dull whitish to yellow, depending on age, season, and subspecies. The breast is finely streaked with dusky or chestnut. The upperpart color varies from yellowish brown to grayish, with dull streaks; the rump is brighter greenish yellow. Adults begin molting in a chestnut crown in midwinter. The tail corners show white spots. The two subspecies, "Western" Palm Warbler (*D. p. palmarum*) and "Yellow" Palm Warbler (*D. p. hypochrysea*) are separable in the field in all plumages. The "Yellow" Palm is slightly larger and always strongly washed with yellow through the entire underparts. Aging and sexing of Palm Warblers is very difficult, although males tend to show more chestnut on the crown than females within an age group.

Similar Species

The tail-pumping habit and bright yellow undertail coverts make this a very distinctive warbler. It prefers open habitats and has a strong tendency to remain on or very near the ground. PRAIRIE and KIRTLAND'S WARBLERS, also habitual tail-pumpers, lack the strong supercilium and transocular line. The undertail coverts of Kirtland's are whitish. Prairie is nearly uniformly yellow on the underparts (unlike any nominate Palm), and lacks the contrasting yellow green rump. Dull fall and winter nominate birds might be confused with "MYRTLE" WARBLERS; the latter species has a bright yellow (not dull yellow-green) rump and a different face pattern, and is not a tail-wagger. Compare yellower individuals with CAPE MAY WARBLER, which does not pump its relatively short tail. WATERTHRUSHES also have a strong supercilium and transocular line, and they frequently bob the rear portions of their bodies (suggestive of the Palm's tail-pumping); they are heavier birds with more distinctly streaked underparts and white, not yellow, undertail coverts. Beware of the superficial similarity in plumage and behavior to some *Anthus* PIPITS and *Motacilla* WAGTAILS.

Voice

SONG is a series of somewhat musical yet buzzy notes with little change in pitch, delivered at about five notes per second. May be represented as *zwee zwee zwee zwee zwee zwee zwee* or *sawee sawee sawee sawee sawee*. The song is not particularly strong and sounds somewhat hesitantly delivered; it is often most forceful in the middle. There are many variations in the nature of the individual buzzy notes, but they are generally consistent throughout the song. Song is not often heard in migration, and even on the breeding grounds this species does not sing as persistently as most warblers. **CALL NOTE** is a sharp, slurred *tsik* or *tsup,* quite distinctive once learned (but does recall note of Prairie). The call of the "Yellow" Palm is slightly higher and sharper than that of nominate birds. The **FLIGHT NOTE** is a high, light *seet* or *see-seet*.

BEHAVIOR

Behavior is distinctive at all times, with the tail constantly pumped in a down-and-up or slightly circular motion. Runs as well as hops on the ground. Despite its generally terrestrial behavior, it will spend some time in trees, especially budding trees in spring and singing perches on the breeding grounds. Quite gregarious in migration and winter, often flocking with Yellow-rumped Warblers, Pine Warblers, Chipping Sparrows (*Spizella passerina*), and Eastern Bluebirds (*Sialia sialis*).

The **NEST** is placed on or very near the ground in sphagnum moss, grasses, or at the base of a shrub, either at the edge of a spruce bog or in other open, barren areas adjacent to woodland. The nest is well concealed and built mainly of grasses and weed stems. Feathers are often incorporated into the nest lining. Among *Dendroica*, only the Kirtland's Warbler is also a habitual ground-nester. Occasionally two broods are successfully raised.

HABITAT

BREEDING habitat is quite specialized and often localized. Preferred sites are open bogs with a wooded margin of spruces or tamaracks, which provide singing perches. The bog cover may be sphagnum moss, sedges, or other plants of damp ground. Heavily shaded bogs are avoided, as are bogs overgrown with shrubs. Palm Warblers also nest in open or cutover woodlands of jack pine with clearings of low ground cover, and in bogs between sand ridges with red and white pines. In **WINTER,** Palm Warblers are generalists in open habitats, occurring in cultivated fields, marshes, prairies, cheniers, pastures, parks, and gardens. Wintering "Yellow" Palm Warblers show an average preference for more wooded habitats, especially pinelands (often recently burned) with wet grass or sedge ground cover; they also inhabit the edges of forests along streams. **MIGRANTS** are found in a variety of open and semi-open habitats, including fencerows, hedges, weedy fields, shrubby areas, and dune vegetation. The habitats are often near water.

Spring migrants, particularly, will feed well up into trees at woodland edges.

DISTRIBUTION

BREEDS locally in suitable habitat from extreme se. Yukon, Dist. of Mack. and ne. B.C. east through the northern portions of the Canadian Prairie Provinces, n. Ont., cen. Que., s. Lab., Nfld., and the Maritime Provinces; breeds south to n.-cen. and ne. Minn., n. Wisc., n. Mich., n. N.Y. (rare), ne. N.H. (rare), Vt. (rare, recent), and Me. The "Yellow" Palm Warbler (*hypochrysea*; see below) occupies the eastern portion of the breeding range from cen. Que., Lab., and the Maritime Provinces south to se. Ontario andNew England.

WINTERS mainly in the se. U.S. and the Caribbean region. Primarily occurs from coastal N.C. south through Fla., and west along the Gulf Coast to La. (and a few on the upper Texas coast); also winters on Bermuda, through the Bahamas and Greater Antilles to the Virgin Is., in the islands of the w. Caribbean, and from coastal Yucatán south along the Caribbean coast to Costa Rica. Recorded rarely on the Pacific slope of Costa Rica and in Panama. Casual south to the Netherlands Antilles, and recorded once in Colombia. Exceptional was an alternate-plumaged adult photographed at Lago Mucubají, Sierra Nevada National Park, in nw. Venezuela on 29 June 1995. Small numbers winter on the Pacific Coast from sw. B.C. south to Oaxaca. The northern limits of the winter range along the Atlantic Coast vary from year to year, with birds wintering farther north (including Md.) in mild winters. The limits of the winter range are confused by the frequent occurrence of stragglers into early winter well north of the normal range in the eastern U.S., especially along the coast. The subspecies *hypochrysea* winters primarily from n. Fla. across the southern portions of the Gulf states to se. La., a region also occupied by small numbers of nominate birds; also rarely in e. Texas, s. Fla., and n. Bahamas. One reported in Quintana Roo, Mexico.

SPRING MIGRATION of nominate *palmarum* proceeds through the se. U.S., then northward up the west side of the Appalachians through the Mississippi and Ohio valleys. Usually only very small numbers move up the Atlantic Coast north to the Mid-Atlantic region; Palm Warbler is casual in spring in New England. Small numbers also move through the southern Great Plains, and rather larger numbers through the northern Great Plains. Spring migrants begin to appear in the Mississippi Valley north of the winter grounds around 10–20 April (but timing is confused by occasional wintering birds); they generally arrive in the upper

Midwest during the last third of April, and on the southern breeding grounds during the first week of May (occasionally late April). The peak spring movement through the Midwest is from the last few days of April through the first week of May. Migration drops off rapidly after mid-May, with only a few records into early June. The "Yellow" Palm migrates northeastward along the Atlantic Coast; it moves relatively early in spring, departing the winter grounds earlier than nominate *palmarum*, with most birds gone from the winter range by early April. It arrives in the Northeast in early April, with the spring movement peaking there during the latter half of April; arrives on the breeding grounds in N.S. around 20 April (but recorded as early as 7 April). Its early May arrival in Nfld. is among the earliest of that region's wood-warblers.

FALL MIGRATION of nominate *palmarum* is more easterly than spring migration; it is generally scarcer in fall than spring in the interior U.S. south of the Great Lakes. The first migrants south of the breeding range are noted in the first half of August, but the main arrival is not until the second week of September, and peak

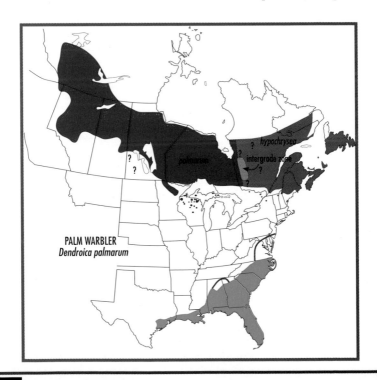

PALM WARBLER
Dendroica palmarum

Palm Warbler. Subspecies hypochrysea *in New York in May. (Photo: Arthur Morris/Birds as Art)*

fall movements are in late September and early October in most regions. It remains numerous until mid-October. Nearly all depart the Midwest and Northeast by early November, but there are numerous early winter records from the eastern Midwest (Tenn., Ky., Ohio) and the coast north to Mass. A few of these birds may successfully overwinter. "Yellow" Palm is a late fall migrant, with the earliest records of migrants in the Northeast in mid-September and most not occurring until the end of September and especially early October. The first birds generally do not reach the wintering grounds in the Gulf states until mid-October. Birds of this subspecies move southwesterly along the coastal plain east of the Appalachians and in small numbers along the outer Atlantic Coast. In New England, most fall Palms occurring along the coast are nominate birds; "Yellow" Palms are more likely to be found inland. A few nominate birds appear each fall in e. Nfld. and s. Lab. Farther south along the Atlantic Coast in fall, *palmarum* also greatly outnumbers *hypochrysea*.

Nominate *palmarum* Palm Warblers are generally very rare fall migrants through the western states, except along the West Coast (especially Calif.) where they are among the most numerous "eastern" warblers from mid-September to mid-November, with a total of over 6,000 records (an exceptional total of 1,000 in fall 1993). Palm Warblers may go undetected over much of the interior West because their preference for open, scrubby habitats makes them less likely to concentrate at traditional "vagrant traps." They are recorded in every western state and province. There are about 20 Alaska records (west to Nunivak Is., north to Barrow), mostly from mid-September through October. Nominate birds are recorded casually in spring in the West; many April records may pertain to individuals that wintered locally.

D. p. hypochrysea is a rare migrant west of the Appalachians to Lake Erie, and **CASUAL**, mainly in late fall and early winter, west to Ind., Mo., N.D., Okla., Colo., N.M., Ariz., and Calif. (about 20 records for Calif., including at least four in spring). One Great Britain record (subspecies not determined), a beached corpse in mid-May.

STATUS AND CONSERVATION

Populations appear to be relatively stable, although a downward trend in the numbers of migrants and wintering birds has been noted in some areas, such as Florida. Breeding habitats, although locally distributed, do not appear to be severely threatened.

SUBSPECIES

The nominate subspecies ("Western" Palm Warbler) occupies most of the breeding range of the species and is described above. The race *hypochrysea* ("Yellow" Palm Warbler) breeds from s. Labrador, Newfoundland, and the Canadian Maritime Provinces south into New England and locally west to cen. Quebec and (possibly) the Ottawa region of e. Ontario. The range of the nominate subspecies extends east to James Bay. Intergrades have been collected in the Amos region of w. Quebec; the eastern limits of nominate *palmarum* in w. Quebec are unknown.

"Yellow" Palm Warblers are distinctive in alternate plumage, with the plumage solidly yellow below, from the throat through the undertail coverts. In the nominate race the yellow throat and undertail coverts contrast with a pale midsection (which may be slightly washed with yellow). "Yellow" Palms also show broad

Palm Warbler. Subspecies hypochrysea *in New York in late October or early November. (Photo: J. Schumacher/VIREO)*

chestnut-red streaks down the underparts and flanks (streaks in these areas are finer and darker in nominate birds), and a distinctive greenish tint to the sides of the face and the upperparts. *D. p. hypochrysea* shows a yellow eye-ring (whitish in nominate birds). In basic plumages the differences between the two subspecies are more subdued, but most birds are still identifiable. In fall, many individuals of nominate *palmarum* get a suffusion of pale yellow through the belly; these are often incorrectly identified as intergrades or as *hypochrysea*. Nominate birds at the yellowish extreme differ from *hypochrysea* in that the yellow of the belly still contrasts with the bright yellow undertail coverts; the upperparts are more grayish brown, with less of a yellow-green tint; the tips and edges to the wing coverts are more buffy, less reddish brown; the supercilium is whitish (yellow in *hypochrysea*); and the rump is duller green (yellower in *hypochrysea*). Intergrades show intermediacy in the extent of yellow on the underparts.

TAXONOMIC RELATIONSHIPS

Within *Dendroica* the Palm Warbler has been considered possibly allied to a group including Prairie and Pine warblers, but further study is needed. One hybrid with Yellow-rumped ("Myrtle") Warbler was found in Illinois.

PLUMAGES AND MOLTS

The following descriptions pertain to nominate *palmarum*; see Subspecies for comparison with *hypochrysea*. **SPRING ADULT MALE:** Forehead and crown chestnut, except for a very inconspicuous short median streak of yellow on the forehead in most birds. Supercilium yel-

Palm Warbler. Subspecies palmarum *in Florida in May. (Photo: Brian E. Small)*

low, bordered below by a dusky eye line. Auriculars gray-brown, sometimes with a slight rusty wash. Submoustachial region, chin, throat, and breast clear yellow; short brown streaks form an inconspicuous malar stripe. Remaining underparts whitish, variably washed with pale yellow on the belly and flanks. Breast and flanks with thin brown streaks, the streaking on sides of breast often strongly rusty. Undertail coverts bright yellow. Hindneck and back gray-brown (slightly tinged yellow-brown in many birds), with dull dusky streaks. Rump and uppertail coverts yellow-olive. Wing coverts and remiges dusky with paler buffy tips to the median and greater coverts forming two thin and indistinct wing bars. Rectrices dusky black, edged yellow-olive. White spots on the distal ends of the inner webs of the outer two rectrices, appearing in the field as a small white patch in the tail corners. **FIRST SPRING MALE:** Very similar to spring adult male, though on average may show less chestnut in crown and less yellow on breast. The primaries and rectrices are browner and more worn than in adults. **SPRING ADULT FEMALE:** Almost identical to spring adult male but averaging slightly duller, often with less chestnut on the crown and ear coverts and less yellow on the breast. **FIRST SPRING FEMALE:** Generally indistinguishable from spring adult females, though averaging slightly duller still, sometimes lacking chestnut in the cap and with little yellow on the throat and breast. The primaries and rectrices are browner and more worn than in adults. **FALL ADULT MALE:** Crown brownish, with a few (or many) chestnut feathers that are mostly obscured by brown feather tips. Supercilium whitish or pale buffy yellow. Underparts dull whitish to very pale yellow; the brighter yellow on throat and breast of spring birds is absent. Ventral streaking usually lacks reddish tint. Upperparts slightly more brownish than in spring birds, with dusky streaking largely veiled with brown. Wing bars and tertial edges tinged rich buffy brown. **FIRST FALL MALE:** Like fall adult male but with very little if any chestnut evident in the crown. **FALL ADULT FEMALE:** Not safely distinguishable in the field from fall males; some birds may completely lack chestnut in the crown. **FIRST FALL FEMALE:** Very

Palm Warbler. Subspecies palmarum *in New Jersey in September. (Photo: A. & E. Morris/VIREO)*

similar to other fall plumages, but chestnut completely lacking in the crown. On average, this plumage appears brownest above and buffiest below. **JUVENILE:** Brownish olive above and pale yellowish below, marked throughout with indistinct spots and streaks; uppertail coverts yellowish olive. **BARE PARTS:** Bill mostly blackish in spring adults, with brown along the cutting edge and the base of the mandible. Fall and winter birds have more brown on the mandible. Eyes dark brown. Legs and feet dark brown; soles slightly paler.

The prebasic molt occurs from July to September on the breeding grounds; it is complete in adults but does not include the flight feathers in hatching-year birds. The prealternate molt can begin as early as January on the wintering grounds (when many birds begin showing much chestnut in the crown), and is usually complete by April.

 REFERENCES

GENERAL: Wilson 1996.
DISTRIBUTION: Pittaway 1995, Walkinshaw 1957.
ECOLOGY, BEHAVIOR, VOCALIZATIONS, AND CONSERVATION: Harris 1990, Welsh 1971, Wunderle 1978.
IDENTIFICATION: Pittaway 1995.
SYSTEMATICS: Johnston 1976, Pittaway 1995.

BAY-BREASTED WARBLER PL. 18

Dendroica castanea

5.25 in. (13.3 cm). This large, chunky, short-tailed *Dendroica* is very similar to the Blackpoll Warbler in structure and in its fall plumages. It is another species that exploits spruce budworms, and its numbers fluctuate greatly from year to year depending on prey availability. It is a trans-Gulf migrant that breeds across the boreal regions of Canada. The extensive chestnut color and lack of yellow in the plumage of spring birds is distinctive, but basic-plumaged birds are much plainer and may be confused with Blackpoll and Pine warblers.

 DESCRIPTION

Considerable seasonal change in plumage, with rich bay colors of face and sides and streaked grayish backs replaced by a fall plumage with greenish upperparts and buffy yellow to whitish underparts, variably suffused with bay or pinkish on the flanks. Bold white wing bars, white spots in the tail corners (outer two rectrices) in all plumages; fall birds show bold white tertial edges and white tips to primaries and secondaries. A small minority of birds, most often in first fall plumage, show indistinct dark stippling on the underparts. The legs and feet are usually entirely dark, an important distinction from most Blackpoll Warblers.

A large and heavy *Dendroica* with a relatively short tail (extending only a short distance beyond the tips of the longest undertail coverts). Like Blackpoll Warbler, appears long-winged, with primary tips extending well beyond the secondaries and tertials.

 ## SIMILAR SPECIES

Fall birds, especially females, can be very similar to fall **BLACKPOLL WARBLERS**, and must be distinguished with care (see p. 384). **PINE WARBLERS**, especially immatures, are similar to fall Bay-breasteds, but should be readily separable by the following criteria (most of which also hold for separating Blackpoll from Pine): Pine has a proportionately longer tail (showing much more extension of the rectrices beyond the longest undertail coverts), and shorter primary extension. The wing bars of immature Pines are less distinct, and Pines lack the distinct white tips to the tertials and primaries. Pines have unstreaked backs, but the back streaking of some fall Bay-breasts can be faint and diffuse; the presence of streaking on the back should eliminate Pines. Pines tend to have darker olive auriculars showing more contrast with the yellowish throat, differing from the plainer face of Bay-breasted. Finally, the white spots in the tail of Pine are more elongated, whereas those of Bay-breasted give the impression of round spots near the tail corners. Fall **CHESTNUT-SIDED WARBLERS** showing some chestnut on the sides may suggest Bay-breasted, but Chestnut-sided has yellowish wing bars, a very different face pattern, and more white in the tail. Immature female **BLACKBURNIAN** vaguely similar, but note more distinct auricular and supercilium, pale lines on back, and more white in tail.

 ## VOICE

SONG is a very high-pitched and somewhat lisping series of 3 to 10 *see* or *see-se* notes, sometimes dropping slightly in pitch at the end. The number and pattern of single and double notes in the song varies among individuals. One representation is *see see-se see-se see.*

CALL NOTE is a loud slurred *chip* essentially identical to chip note of Blackpoll Warbler. Also gives a thin, high-pitched *tseet* note. **FLIGHT NOTE** is a buzzy *zeet,* also very similar to flight note of Blackpoll.

BEHAVIOR

Bay-breasted Warblers are sluggish and deliberate in their movements; the tail is frequently pumped in subdued fashion. They feed at medium levels in dense coniferous forest during the breeding season. They methodically glean needle clusters and twigs, and only rarely employ more active foraging techniques such as hover-gleaning or sallying after flying insects. In fall migration, they often forage lower, even in shrubs and weedy growth. Winter birds forage at middle to high levels in vegetation. They take considerable amounts of fruit from midwinter to spring, at which time they are more likely to be encountered in mixed species flocks.

The **NEST** is saddled on a horizontal limb at medium heights (averaging about 20 ft. off the ground in some studies), usually in a conifer. The nest is a fragile-appearing cup made of conifer twigs, bark shreds, grasses, and plant downs, and lined with fine grasses and rootlets. Larger clutches are noted in response to spruce budworm outbreaks.

HABITAT

BREEDS in boreal forests where cool, dense coniferous growth is interrupted by small openings such as bogs or clearings. Preferred conifers include balsam fir and spruces, mixed with (or, less often, dominated by) tamaracks, white pines, birches, or aspens. More exceptionally may nest in pure deciduous growth (such as aspens) in response to outbreaks of caterpillars.

WINTERS in forest edges and clearings, semi-open woodlands, and second growth; winter habitats quite broad in n. South America and may include mangroves, riverbank growth, thorn scrub, cloud forests, and stunted scrub near highland paramo zone. **MIGRANTS** are widely distributed through brushy and wooded habitats; fall migrants often move along mountain ridges.

DISTRIBUTION

BREEDS in boreal forests of Canada and n. New England, with the bulk of the population in Ont., Que., and the Maritime Provinces. The breeding range extends from e.-cen. and ne. B.C., extreme se. Yukon, ne. Alta., and sw. Dist. of Mack. across n. Sask., cen. Man. (scarce in s. Man.), n. Ont., cen. Que., and w. Nfld., and south to n.-cen. and ne. Minn., the upper peninsula of Mich., ne. N.Y., ne. Vt. (rare), n. N.H., and Me. Except in Me., it is generally uncommon to rare in the U.S. portion of its breeding range. Has summered in n. Wisc., but no breeding evidence.

Once summered in W. Va., well south of breeding range, apparently mated with a Blackburnian. Several summer records for Colo., with nesting of one pair documented in 1978 in Douglas Co. Like the Cape May and other "spruce-woods warblers," Bay-breasted populations are cyclic, with large numbers inhabiting a given area during a budworm epidemic but largely or completely abandoning the area in subsequent years.

WINTERS primarily from Costa Rica (where uncommon) and Panama to nw. South America (primarily west of the Andes) in w. Colombia and n. and w. Venezuela. Recorded casually in winter in Trinidad, e. Venezuela, and n. Ecuador. There are a number of early winter records from the s. U.S., but the only records of over-wintering birds are two or three from coastal s. Calif. and a late January specimen from Ga. Numerous winter reports from Fla. lack convincing documentation.

A trans-Gulf **SPRING MIGRANT,** with the great majority of spring birds passing through the Gulf Coast of e. Texas and La. Large numbers are encountered in these coastal areas during storms out of the north ("northers"); in the absence of these storms migrants pass directly inland where they are less easily detected. Generally found in much smaller numbers along the s. Texas coast and from Miss. east to w. Fla. These trans-Gulf migrants presumably originate from the Yucatán peninsula, and this species is a fairly common spring migrant in se. Mexico. The spring arrival along the Gulf Coast is typically around 20 April, with peak numbers recorded during the last few days of April or first week of May (depending on weather patterns). The spring passage is rather concentrated, with very few birds passing through the Gulf Coast by late May. Most spring birds move north through the Midwest, west of the Appalachians; only very small numbers pass up the Atlantic Coast south of N.J. and n. Md. Spring arrival in the s. Midwest (Tenn., Ark., Mo.) is usually in late April or early May, more rarely as early as the third week of April; migration peaks in these areas around 10 May. Farther north, upper Midwest and Great Lakes region arrivals are generally during the second week of May, with migration peaking during the third week of May and stragglers occurring into early June. Birds typically begin to arrive on the breeding grounds in mid-May (occasionally the second week of May), with main arrival around 20–25 May. Rare to uncommon migrant through the e. Great Plains.

FALL MIGRATION is quite protracted, with a few birds noted away from breeding areas in late July and some still passing through the southern states in early November. The general fall passage is more easterly than in spring, with the species much more numerous along the Atlantic Coast. The earliest southbound migrants

BAY-BREASTED WARBLER
Dendroica castanea

usually arrive in the upper Midwest during the third week of August and are most numerous from late August through mid-September. Birds do not normally arrive on the Gulf Coast and in Fla. until mid- to late September, peaking in mid-October (and with significant numbers sometimes still passing through in early November). Most have departed the northern states by the first half of October, with a few stragglers to the end of the month. Recorded casually in the northern states in November, and exceptionally to December (including Ill., N.Y.). Uncommon fall transient in Bermuda, and very scarce in fall in the West Indies (mainly Bahamas and Greater Antilles; also recorded St. Vincent, Barbardos, possibly Antigua). Uncommon to fairly common in fall in e. Mexico.

VAGRANT in all the western states except Wash.; 255 records for Calif., with about one-third in spring (mostly late May and June, especially early June) and two-thirds in fall (early September to late November, exceptionally to December, plus winter records noted above). One late spring sight record from near Fairbanks,

Alaska. Vagrant to Sonora, Mexico, and to Revillagigedo and Clipperton Is. Recorded casually in Lab., and once in October in Greenland. One record for the United Kingdom, a bird at Land's End, Cornwall, on 1 October 1995.

 ## STATUS AND CONSERVATION

Like other species that exploit spruce budworms, populations fluctuate considerably from year to year. Some declines noted or anticipated where mature forests are replaced with second-growth plantations of trees resistant to budworm infestations. Annual spraying for budworms in e. Canada has undoubtedly reduced populations of this and other spruce-woods warblers. In suitable habitat during budworm outbreaks, populations may be extremely high, with densities up to 596 pairs per square mile noted in Ontario.

 ## SUBSPECIES

None described.

 ## TAXONOMIC RELATIONSHIPS

Has hybridized with Blackpoll Warbler, its presumed closest relative; three specimens of this combination exist (two spring males and a spring female). Has also hybridized with Yellow-rumped ("Myrtle") Warbler. Apparently paired once with Blackburnian Warbler in West Virginia; there is a May sight record of a female Blackburnian × Bay-breasted hybrid in Louisiana.

PLUMAGES AND MOLTS

SPRING ADULT MALE: Forehead, sides of forecrown, lores, auricular and malar regions dull black, with black extending through center of forecrown on some birds and onto chin in extreme individuals. Remainder of crown and nape, chin, throat, upper breast, sides, and flanks deep rich chestnut (bay) color. Creamy white patch on the sides of the neck behind the auricular patch, extending onto the extreme upper sides under the bend of the wing. Hindneck and back light grayish olive to grayish buff, boldly streaked with black. Rump gray with more limited black streaking; uppertail coverts with broad black centers, gray fringes. Lower breast, belly, and undertail coverts dull whitish. Wing coverts blackish, with broad white tips to median and greater coverts forming two bold white wing bars. Remiges dusky blackish, with secondaries narrowly edged grayish olive. Rectrices blackish, with white spots near tips of inner webs of outer two pairs. **FIRST SPRING MALE:** Generally duller than spring adult males.

Bay-breasted Warbler. Adult male in Texas in May. (Photo: Brian E. Small)

Lores and auricular area mottled with grayish. Bay of crown as rich as in adults, but color on throat, sides, and flanks somewhat paler, variably mottled with whitish (especially on sides, flanks). The primaries and rectrices are browner and more worn than in adults. **SPRING ADULT FEMALE:** Quite variable in plumage, with brighter individuals almost resembling first spring males and duller birds having very limited chestnut. Forehead olive-gray with thin black streaks. Crown moderately to extensively chestnut. Lores and auriculars mottled grayish buff and slaty. Supraloral area and eye-arcs creamy. Creamy patch on sides of neck behind auriculars. Upperparts olive-gray streaked with black. Rump unstreaked olive-gray; uppertail coverts gray with thin black feather centers. Chin, throat, upper breast, sides, and flanks pale chestnut, mottled with creamy white; in many individuals these areas mostly buffy, with pale chestnut restricted to sides of throat and chest, sides, and flanks. Wings with two bold white wing bars. White spots near tips of outer two pairs of rectrices. **FIRST SPRING FEMALE:** Much like spring adult female but averaging duller, with more restricted chestnut on crown and underparts. On dullest birds crown is grayish to olive, finely streaked with black; others have as much chestnut on crown as spring adult females. Chestnut on underparts mottled with creamy white and usually restricted to sides of throat and chest and to sides, flanks; on some birds chestnut is lacking altogether, with throat, chest, sides, and flanks buffy. Auriculars mottled grayish. Back streaking averages finer than on males and spring adult females. The primaries and rectrices are browner and more worn than in adults. **FALL ADULT MALE:** Crown bright yellow-green, often with a few inconspicuous chestnut feathers; hindneck and back bright yellow-green, finely to moderately streaked with black. Lores and ocular stripe grayish; indistinct pale yellowish superciliary and eye-arcs. Auriculars yellow-green. Throat varying from whitish to pale yellowish buff, occasionally with a few chestnut feathers; breast and sides yellowish buff to buffy olive. Sides and especially flanks strongly washed with chestnut, but this color is partly veiled by creamy feather tips. Belly whitish to buffy; undertail coverts buffy. Rump grayish olive, mostly unstreaked. Uppertail coverts grayish, with black feather centers largely obscured. Wing coverts blackish with two bold white wing bars. Tertials blackish, boldly edged whitish. Secondaries and primaries narrowly tipped with white. **FIRST FALL MALE:** Similar to fall adult male, but chestnut of sides and flanks paler and more restricted, often entirely replaced by rich buff. Crown and throat always lacking chestnut feathers. Back streaks average finer than in fall adult male, and rump more tinged with olive. Occasional individuals are lightly stippled with fine blackish markings on the breast and/or sides. **FALL ADULT FEMALE:** Similar to fall males, and rarely separable in field from duller examples, especially first fall males. On average rump is greener, and back streaking is finer. Chestnut is lacking in plumage, but flanks may be tinged with rich buff (matching many first fall males). **FIRST FALL FEMALE:** Upperparts entirely olive-yellow, very finely streaked with black on the back and with extremely faint and fine spotting on the crown. In the field, some individuals may appear to lack streaks on back. Uppertail coverts greenish, with no evident dark centers. Indistinct face pattern with pale supercilium, olive line through the eye, pale eye-arcs, yellowish olive auriculars. Throat whitish; breast, sides, and flanks yellowish buff, variably tinged pinkish buff on the flanks and vent area. Undertail coverts buff to whitish buff. Occasional individuals show dusky stippling on the breast and sides. Bold

white wing bars and tertial edges; thin white tips to flight feathers. **JUVENILE:** Generally dull olive-gray above and buffy white below, strongly streaked above and spotted below with dusky; yellowish tinge to sides of head. **BARE PARTS:** Bill blackish brown in spring males; extensive pale brown at base of mandible in spring females and fall adults, most of mandible pinkish brown in first fall birds. Legs and feet dull slaty gray to

Bay-breasted Warbler. Adult male in New York in September. (Photo: Kevin T. Karlson)

Bay-breasted Warbler. First fall female in Ontario in September. (Photo: Tony Beck)

dark brown, soles can be slightly tinged yellowish gray. Some individuals have paler, pinkish brown legs. Eyes dark brown.

Prebasic molt occurs on the breeding grounds, complete in adults but not involving remiges and rectrices in hatching-year birds. An extensive prealternate molt, involving body feathers, takes place on the winter grounds from February through April.

 ## References

GENERAL: McWilliams 1996.

DISTRIBUTION: Andrews and Righter 1992.

ECOLOGY, BEHAVIOR, VOCALIZATIONS, AND CONSERVATION: Greenberg 1984, MacArthur 1958, Morse 1978, Morton 1980, Sealy 1979.

IDENTIFICATION: Whitney 1983.

PLUMAGES, MOLTS, AND MORPHOLOGY: Howard 1968.

SYSTEMATICS: Banks and Baird 1978, Brodkorb 1934 (Bay-breasted × Blackpoll hybrid), Graves 1996b, Hurley and Jones 1983.

BLACKPOLL WARBLER   PL. 18

Dendroica striata

5.25 in. (13.3 cm). The most highly migratory wood-warbler, the Blackpoll breeds across the boreal forests as far north as northwest Alaska and winters mainly east of the Andes in northern South America. In spring its migration is mainly north through peninsular Florida or across the Gulf of Mexico, but the fall migration is quite easterly, with many birds apparently flying well out over the Atlantic from the northeastern states and provinces. The Blackpoll is similar to the closely related Bay-breasted Warbler in proportions (though smaller billed) and fall plumages. The black and white alternate plumage of males is distinctive, but this species undergoes a strong seasonal plumage change, fall birds becoming very difficult to age and sex.

 ## DESCRIPTION

The spring male is one of only three "black and white" warblers in North America; the white cheek, framed by a black cap and black moustachial stripe, is distinctive. Spring females are quite variable, but generally olive with dark streaks above and white with a yellowish wash below, with some streaking. Fall birds are generally olive above with dark streaks, yellowish on the throat and breast, and white on the lower belly and undertail coverts; adult males generally show the most ventral streaking in fall, and first fall females the least, but most birds cannot be confidently aged or sexed in the field. In proportions a rather large, stocky *Dendroica* with a relatively short tail (and correspondingly short projection of the rectrices beyond the longest undertail coverts). The wings are quite long, with considerable primary projection (18–26 mm) beyond the secondaries and tertials. The bill is slightly thinner than that of Bay-breasteds.

 ## SIMILAR SPECIES

The main confusion species is BAY-BREASTED; fall plumages of Blackpolls can be exceedingly similar to those of first fall Bay-breasts, and these species must be distinguished with care. These two species are similar in behavior, calls, and shape, although Bay-breasteds often appear somewhat bulkier and more sluggish. Most Bay-breasts show bay or rich buff on the sides and flanks and are readily told from fall Blackpolls, which have a ground color of yellow or pale yellow-olive in this area. Some Bay-breasts, however, are yellowish buff there. These, mainly first fall females, are best told by a combination of the following characters. The vent area (especially) and undertail coverts are buffy or creamy in Bay-breasted, white in most Blackpolls (a few Blackpolls are washed with pale lemon yellow in these areas). The crown, nape, and back of Bay-breasted average brighter, more lime green (less olive), though some individuals are quite dull. The face pattern of Bay-breasted is more subdued, with a less distinct transocular line than in Blackpoll. Blackpolls tend to be streaked on the sides of the breast and flanks; Bay-breasts generally lack distinct streaking below but may show some suffused streaks (and rare individuals of both species may show fine dark stippling on the breast). The white primary tips tend to be more distinct in Blackpoll. The bill of Bay-breasted is slightly longer and thicker than that of Blackpoll. Finally, the pale, yellowish legs and feet of Blackpoll are distinctive, but many fall Blackpolls (especially young birds) show mostly dark legs; the key feature is the soles of the toes and feet, which are always yellow in Blackpoll and range from pale yellowish gray to dark gray in Bay-breasted. Note that some Bay-breasteds do have pinkish (but never yellow) legs.

Compare spring females, some of which show little yellow, to female CERULEAN WARBLER; Cerulean is smaller, unstreaked above, and shows a more prominent supercilium. See PINE WARBLER, which can be very similar to fall Blackpolls.

♪ VOICE

SONG is extremely high-pitched (at 8–10 kHz, as high as any warbler's song, along with Blackburnian, Cape May, Bay-breasted, and Black-and-White); it is delivered as a repetitious series of several (up to 20 or more) single or double notes. The rate of delivery is highly variable among individuals, from about 5 to about 12 notes per second, but consistent within a single song. Songs often build up in intensity in the middle.

CALL NOTE is a loud, sharp *chip,* somewhat reminiscent of the common note of a Yellow Warbler and indistinguishable from the call note of Bay-breasted. Calls rather infrequently. FLIGHT NOTE is a loud, sharp buzzy *zeet,* again exactly like note of Bay-breasted.

🦅 BEHAVIOR

A rather sluggish and deliberate warbler, feeding most often by gleaning. In spring and on the breeding grounds, Blackpolls tend to feed in middle and upper levels and stay within the canopy. Foraging is often much lower in the fall.

NESTS are placed low in young conifers, only 2–6 ft. off the ground, or occasionally on ground, and rarely several meters high. They are usually placed against a trunk and well concealed by hanging foliage; built of twigs, grasses, lichens, and fibers.

🏞 HABITAT

BREEDS in cool, wet forests of low conifers, particularly stunted red spruce, black spruce, and balsam fir. This stunted habitat is found along the northern edge of the boreal forest, on mountaintops in the southeastern part of the breeding range (New York, New England), and in windblown maritime regions. Breeding habitat is also found at the edges of bogs and burned areas within taller coniferous forest. Locally, Blackpolls may breed in taller forests along mountain slopes, as in the Adirondacks (where, more typically, they occur up to the highest summits). In the western boreal regions (such as Alta., Alaska) Blackpolls breed in habitats dominated by deciduous trees as well as black spruces, including willows, alders, and balsam poplars.

WINTERS in light woodlands, forest borders and clearings, mangroves, cloud forests, deciduous forests, and rain forests.

MIGRANTS use both deciduous and coniferous wooded habitats in spring; in fall they are quite generalized, often feeding in low brushy areas and weed patches.

 DISTRIBUTION

BREEDS across the northern boreal forests from nw. Alaska, Yukon, and the Northwest Territories to n. Ont., n. Que., and Nfld.; breeding range extends south to s.-cen. B.C., sw. and cen. Alta., n. Sask., cen. Man., n. Ont., s.-cen. Que., N.B., N.S., Me., Vt., N.H., Mass. (Mt. Graylock), and N.Y. (south to Ulster Co.). Bred recently in Wyoming Co., ne. Pa. In southernmost portion of breeding range breeds mainly above 3,000 ft., but in a few sites in N.Y. as low as 900 ft.

WINTERS almost exclusively in South America, mainly east of the Andes. Found in Colombia, Venezuela (especially in south), Guyana, Surinam, e. Ecuador, e. Peru, and the w. Amazon basin of Brazil. Smaller numbers recorded farther south, and overshoots have been found as far as 40° S in Chile and Argentina (the southernmost records of a North American migrant warbler). A very few winter north to Panama, Costa Rica, and Trinidad. Has wintered north to the Lesser Antilles and Bermuda.

SPRING MIGRATION from South America is mainly over the w. Caribbean; most birds appear to overfly the islands (the species is casual in Jamaica, for example, and recorded in small numbers in the Caymans; it is numerous only in the Bahamas). Most birds move into North America through Fla., but the migration front also includes the Gulf Coast west to e. Texas (with small numbers on the cen. and s. Texas coast). Migrants then move north up the East Coast of the U.S. and through the Mississippi and Ohio valleys. Small numbers also move north through the Great Plains, west to e. Colo., e. Wyo., and e. Mont. This species is one of the few warblers to move up the Atlantic Coast in spring in large numbers. Normally it is one of the later warblers to arrive, but there are scattered records along the Gulf Coast in early April. Arrivals normally begin in mid-April, with peak movements through the Gulf Coast and Fla. from the end of April to about 10 May. Spring arrival dates in the Midwest and Mid-Atlantic states are rarely as early as the third week of April, but most birds arrive in the second week of May and peak from mid- to late May. Birds may arrive in New England as early as the end of April, with the passage peaking in late May. Straggling spring migrants may occur well into June on the Gulf Coast, and to the end of June in New England and the northern Midwest.

FALL MIGRATION is much more easterly than spring migration. These warblers are quite uncommon in the midwestern states south of the Great Lakes, in fall, and rare south of there to the Gulf. They are more common around the Great Lakes and abundant in New England and N.Y. Uncommon to rare in fall in the central and southern Atlantic states. Banding and tower kill data suggest that at least a proportion of individuals take off from the Atlantic Coast north of Cape Hatteras on a nonstop overwater

BLACKPOLL WARBLER
Dendroica striata

flight to n. South America; their heading is toward the southeast, but prevailing winds on the latter half of their journey push them southwestward toward the n. South American mainland. Fall migrant Blackpolls arrive in the northern states during the last week of August (occasionally to mid-August, but this species' similarity in fall to Bay-breasted Warbler makes many early sight records suspect); fall arrivals in the Great Lakes region are slightly earlier than along the Atlantic Coast. The peak fall movement for most northern states is in mid- to late September; birds have almost completely departed the Great Lakes region by the second week of October, but numbers are present in the coastal Northeast to mid-October. A few late stragglers occur into November (and exceptionally to December) in New England and Nfld.

Blackpolls are among the most numerous "eastern" warblers in fall in the western U.S.; they are recorded in all western states except Idaho. Well over 3,000 individuals recorded in Calif. (mainly along the coast) where they average about 120 birds per year, though more recent averages have dropped to about 105 per year. The maximum daily count is 23 on se. Farallon Is., on 27 September 1974. Well over 90 percent of the records are for fall; peak fall passage on the West Coast is from the end of September to early October; there are a few November records.

CASUAL in spring (mainly May and June) west of the Great Plains, with a few records from western states into July and even early August. Casual migrant in Mexico, though undoubtedly regular in fall in Baja Calif.

VAGRANT to Greenland (seven records), Iceland (six), the British Isles (35 records, mostly in September and October), and France (two). Recorded on Clipperton Is. and once in May on the Galapagos Is.

Blackpoll Warbler. Male in Florida in May. (Photo: Brian E. Small)

In general quite abundant; often one of the most numerous fall migrant warblers in the Northeast. Populations fluctuate less widely than those of the "spruce budworm" warblers, including the Bay-breasted. This species is perhaps less susceptible to human effects on breeding habitats because of its far northern breeding range, yet some declines in the number of migrants at well-studied sites has been noted.

▶ Subspecies

No significant variation. A breeding race from Alaska east to James Bay, *lurida* (not recognized by most authorities) is said to be darker (less olive) and less broadly streaked above.

⚘ Taxonomic Relationships

Has hybridized with Bay-breasted Warbler (three specimens; Graves 1996), and these two species are clearly closely related. Has possibly also hybridized with Northern Waterthrush but the hybrid in question may be Cape May × Northern Waterthrush.

✐ Plumages and Molts

SPRING ADULT MALE: Crown, forehead, lores, and nape black; olive tips to a few crown feathers on some birds. Hindneck often with a narrow collar of black and white streaks. Back with heavy black stripes on a gray, olive-gray, or olive-brown background; narrower and sparser black streaks through the olive-gray rump. Uppertail coverts olive-gray with black shaft

Blackpoll Warbler. Female in Florida in April. (Photo: Kevin T. Karlson)

streaks. Auricular area and adjacent sides of the neck white. Bold black malar stripe below the auriculars, and often a few black feathers on the chin. Throat and remaining underparts white, with broad black streaks on the sides of the breast (continuous with the black malar stripe), sides, and flanks. Median and greater wing coverts broadly tipped white, forming two bold wing bars. Tertials dusky black, broadly edged whitish. Primaries and secondaries edged yellowish olive. Rectrices dusky black with white spots on the distal parts of the inner webs of the outer two pairs, forming white tail corners. There is some variation among adult males in the width of the black malar stripe and the streaking on the sides of the breast, as well as the amount of olive color showing on the upperparts. **FIRST SPRING MALE:** Essentially identical to spring adult male, but flight feathers are browner, more worn, and contrast more with the black body feathers and coverts. On average the malar stripe is thinner on first spring male, but it is not a reliable aging character. **SPRING ADULT FEMALE:** Quite variable in color of underparts (ranging from whitish to yellowish), amount of streaking on underparts, and background color of upperparts (grayish to olive green). An "average" bird is described below, with variations noted. Crown olive-gray to olive green, densely streaked with black; on a few birds the heavy black crown streaks suggest a black cap (like male), but close inspection shows some olive-gray streaking. Auricular area grayish white to pale olive, mottled with dusky. Whitish or pale yellowish supercilium, contrasting with a dark transocular line. Remainder of upperparts grayish olive (but ranging from gray to rather bright olive green), strongly streaked on the back with black; rump and uppertail coverts less prominently streaked. A few short dark streaks on malar area usually present, but these do not form a malar stripe. Underparts whitish, tinged pale yellow on the throat, breast, and flanks on most birds and strongly washed yellowish on some birds. A minority show almost no yellow below. There are a few short

Blackpoll Warbler. In California in October. (Photo: Brian E. Small)

Blackpoll Warbler. In New York in September. (Photo: Dominic F. Sherony)

blackish streaks on the sides of the throat and breast and on the flanks. Some birds have streaking restricted to the sides of the breast, whereas others are more prominently streaked across the breast and through the flanks. **FIRST SPRING FEMALE:** Not reliably told from spring adult females, and similarly variable. On average, first spring females show thinner and more restricted streaking above and below. Flight feathers somewhat browner and more worn than in adult. **FALL ADULT MALE:** Crown and upperparts olive green to grayish olive, with sparse to rather dense black streaks throughout. Pale yellowish supercilium and dusky olive transocular line on an otherwise unmarked olive face. Some birds show a few blackish spots in the malar area. Underparts whitish, washed with pale yellow on the throat, breast, and flanks (a few birds lack yellow below). Thin blackish streaks on sides of throat, sides of breast, and flanks. Undertail coverts white. Bold white wing bars; conspicuous white edges to the tertials, and white tips to the primaries. **FIRST FALL MALE:** Closely resembles fall adult male, and not safely told in the field. Averages more olive green (less gray) above and more yellow below; streaking never as extensive along the sides of the breast and flanks as in some fall adult males, and malar spotting lacking. A small minority show some fine black stippling across the breast. **FALL ADULT FEMALE:** Generally olive green above, with thin dark streaking on the back but little or no streaking on the crown. Indistinct yellowish supercilium and dark transocular line, as in other fall plumages. Throat, breast, and flanks yellowish to pale yellow-olive, with indistinct streaks on the sides of the breast and flanks. Belly variably washed with pale yellow, but undertail coverts usually white (may be very faintly washed with pale yellow). **FIRST FALL FEMALE:** Not safely told from fall adult female or first fall males, but streaking relatively sparse and indistinct; averages slightly brighter yellow below. A small minority show some fine black stippling across the breast. **JUVENILE:** Dull brownish olive on upperparts and grayish white below, extensively spotted and barred with dusky black throughout. **BARE PARTS:** Bill of adult male dusky black along culmen but yellowish along tomium and on mandible; females and first fall birds show less contrast between the upper and lower mandibles. Legs and feet yellowish in spring birds, including toes and soles; fall birds, especially immatures, have duller, darker legs, but soles always distinctly yellow; the back of the tarsus is often yellow in these immatures as well. Eyes dark brown.

Prebasic molt completed on the breeding grounds, complete in adults but not involving flight feathers in hatching-year birds. The extensive prealternate molt takes place from February to April.

 REFERENCES

DISTRIBUTION: McNair and Post 1993, Murray 1965, Nisbet 1970, Stiles and Campos 1983, Williams 1985.
IDENTIFICATION: Stiles and Campos 1983, Whitney 1983.
PLUMAGES, MOLTS, AND MORPHOLOGY: Blake 1954.
SYSTEMATICS: Burleigh and Peters 1948 (describes subspecies *D. s. lurida*), Graves 1996, Parkes 1978 (advocates Cape May rather than Blackpoll as "Carbonated Warbler" parent), Short and Robbins 1967.

BLACKBURNIAN WARBLER PL. 16

Dendroica fusca

4.75 in. (12 cm). The Blackburnian Warbler is a common breeding bird of hemlock and other coniferous forests in the boreal regions and Appalachians. The bright orange, black, and white colors of the adult male are distinctive; in other plumages the orange areas are more yellow or ocher. In some aspects of plumage Blackburnians resemble Townsend's Warblers in the Black-throated Green Warbler (*virens*) complex, although they differ in vocalizations and posture and may not be particularly closely related to that group. We believe its affinities lie closer to the Cerulean Warbler; the primary identification problem concerns dull Blackburnians and female Ceruleans.

 DESCRIPTION

The bright orange plumage of adult males and pale orange or ocher of females is distinctive. Within *Dendroica* the pale stripes or "braces" on the back are diagnostic. The auricular patch is distinctive in shape, appearing triangular (pointed at the rear and bottom). All ages show a pale median forehead stripe of varying color, although in some individuals (especially immature females) it may be very inconspicuous. Structurally, Blackburnians are moderate in size and fairly long tailed.

SIMILAR SPECIES

Dull first fall females can be mistaken for **CERULEAN WARBLERS** (distinctions noted under that species' account) and immature female **TOWNSEND'S WARBLERS.** In Townsend's the upperparts are strongly tinted with olive green and the pale mantle stripes are lacking. Note differences in the shape of cheek patch, which is more pointed at bottom in Blackburnian. Only first fall male Blackburnians have a yellow throat color that might be mistaken for Townsend's — in other plumages it is either brighter orange (adults) or paler buff-ocher (immature females). Even winter and immature Townsend's have an all dark bill; bills of winter Blackburnians are extensively pale on the lower mandible. The **YELLOW-THROATED WARBLER** is readily told by its mostly unstreaked gray upperparts (many show black spotting) and the white patch on sides of neck bordered by black; again, only first winter male Blackburnian will have a yellow throat. Creeping behavior of Yellow-throated unlike more typical warbler gleaning behavior of Blackburnian. Immature female could be confused with **BLACKPOLL** and **BAY-BREASTED WARBLERS;** these latter two lack strong supercilium, dusky auricular patch, and pale mantle streaks, and are plumper and slightly shorter tailed; unlike Blackburnian, these two species frequently bob their tails. The white in the tail forms spots near the tail corners in Blackpoll and Bay-breasted, and is more extensive in Blackburnian. First fall Bay-breasteds are less streaked on the underparts than Blackburnians.

VOICE

SONG is very high-pitched and wiry, consisting of one or two series of thin, high notes followed by an even higher, upslurred note. Some songs rise to a very high pitch in the middle rather than at the end. These unaccented-ending songs may be represented as *seep seep seep seep zeee!* or *wee-see-see-see-see-zi-zi-zi-zeee!* The highest notes in the song are inaudible to many birders' ears. We liken it to a very high-pitched Cerulean Warbler song. It may be confused with the high-pitched songs of Golden-crowned Kinglets (*Regulus satrapa*). *Chip* calls are often given between unaccented-ending songs. Accented-ending songs are given mainly by unmated males and when males are in the vicinity of females; these consist of a series of high, two-parted phrases, each phrase containing alternating high and very high notes; these songs may be mistaken for songs of Black-and-white, Bay-breasted, and Cape May warblers. The **CALL NOTE** is a rich *chip* or *tsip*. The **FLIGHT NOTE** is a buzzy *zzee*.

BEHAVIOR

When foraging, the Blackburnian frequently cocks its tail slightly and droops the wings, in a manner suggesting a Chestnut-sided Warbler. It generally forages high in conifers and hardwoods; it is often found lower in foliage in migration, especially in fall. Most foraging is by gleaning of foliage and needles, with occasional hover-gleaning and sallying. The Blackburnian is one of several boreal warblers that exploits outbreaks of spruce budworms, with population size and reproductive output increasing during outbreaks of the caterpillar. Blackburnians are subordinate in interactions with other "spruce-woods warblers," but do dominate the small Northern Parula. In winter they often join mixed-species flocks of other migrant warblers and Neotropical passerines; wintering birds forage over a wide range of heights but concentrate especially in upper levels.

The **NEST** is usually placed in a conifer at moderate to high levels (averaging about 30 ft., but sometimes as high as 75 ft.), but occasionally as low as 5 ft. The nest is generally placed on a horizontal branch well away from the trunk. It is made of conifer twigs and needles, bark strips, and other fine materials and lined with rootlets and grasses. *Usnea* lichen, when available, is often used in nest construction and for concealment.

HABITAT

BREEDS in tall, mature coniferous or mixed woodlands, especially of hemlock, spruce, and fir, but locally in pines and sometimes in mature hardwood forests. Within mixed forests Blackburnians still concentrate their activity in conifers. Tall timber (especially hemlocks) is important, along with, in many northern areas, the presence of *Usnea* lichen. In the Appalachians, Blackburnians breed mainly in spruces at higher elevations, but locally are found lower in oak-hickory-pine associations and mature deciduous forest. White pines and balsam firs are important habitat components in parts of the range.

In **WINTER** the species is most numerous in humid montane evergreen forest from about 3,000 to 7,000 ft.; they occur both within mature forests and at forest edges, and also in second growth, coffee plantations, and dwarf forest.

MIGRANTS are found in a variety of wooded habitats and are more partial to mature woodlands in migration than are most wood-warblers.

 ## DISTRIBUTION

BREEDS from e.-cen. Alta. (sporadic and local), cen. Sask. eastward through the boreal regions of s. Canada to the Maritime Provinces and sw. Nfld. Breeds south to n. Minn., n. and s.-cen. (Baraboo Hills) Wisc., extreme nw. Ind. (probable), Mich., e. Ohio (local; summer records but few proven breeding records), and in the higher elevations of Pa., N.Y., and New England. It is also found south through the Appalachian Mountains locally to e. Ky. (Black Mtn.), e. Tenn., w. N.C., extreme sw. S.C. (summer records but no breeding evidence), and n. Ga. Exceptional summer records in appropriate breeding habitat exist west to the Black Hills (S.D.) and cen. Colo.

WINTERS mainly in the Andes of South America from Venezuela and Colombia south through Ecuador to Peru; also winters in the Tepui region of s. Venezuela. It is especially numerous in the n. Andes of Colombia and Ecuador. It has also been recorded rarely or casually from nw. Bolivia, Surinam, and n. Brazil (Espiritu Santo and Manaus). Small numbers winter in s. Central America in Costa Rica and Panama (more numerous in Darien region of e. Panama).

Casual as late as December in eastern North America (N.S., Gulf Coast) and the Pacific Coast (Wash., Calif.). Later in the winter recorded three times in Calif., once in w. Ore., and once (a bird present for two days in January) in Kingston, Ont. Of some 25 winter reports from Florida, none is fully substantiated; the validity of several winter reports from Puerto Rico and the Virgin Is. is also uncertain. There are four winter and spring sight records for Trinidad.

This is a classic trans-Gulf migrant, with the fall route being more easterly than that of spring. This easterly shift is illustrated by tower kill data in Leon Co., Fla., with up to 374 casualties in a fall, and none in spring; this species is much more numerous in spring than fall in coastal Texas and La. It is rare along the Atlantic Coast from the Mid-Atlantic states south in spring, but more numerous in those regions in fall.

SPRING MIGRATION begins in early April (rarely late March) along the Gulf Coast. In the s. Midwest, cen. Appalachians and Mid-Atlantic region spring arrivals are at the end of April (casually mid-April, regularly so in the s. Appalachians), and around the Great Lakes and New England they are first recorded in early May (exceptionally back to the third week of April). Birds arrive at the northern end of the breeding grounds in mid- to late May. The spring peak is late, even along the Gulf Coast (where peaks are during the second week of May). From the s. Midwest to the Mid-Atlantic region peaks are in mid-May; from the n. Great Lakes to New England peak numbers are in the last third of May. Small numbers pass through to the end of May (even in the Deep South) and first few days of June (with an exceptional count of 100 at Pt. Pelee, Ont., on 1 June). Stragglers are recorded casually well away from the breeding grounds to mid-June and exceptionally late June.

FALL MIGRATION is more easterly than in spring, and relatively early for a boreal warbler; the earliest migrants are often reported in the Midwest and Great Lakes area, away from the breeding grounds, by the end of July (exceptionally as early as the second week of July) or early August; it is recorded casually along the Gulf Coast as early as late July. By mid-August this species is

BLACKBURNIAN WARBLER
Dendroica fusca

numerous across much of the East, with the peak passage during the last week of August and the first third of September; the peak in the Deep South (including Fla.) extends through September into the beginning of October. Across most of North America it is only rarely noted after the first week of October, and only casually after the third week of October. There are many November records in the East, in addition to the December records noted above. This species is an uncommon fall migrant in Bermuda (only one spring record there), and rare in the Bahamas. It is a rare to uncommon migrant through the western Greater Antilles, but casual east of there.

VAGRANT to the Lesser Antilles (Grenada). North of the breeding range recorded once at Ft. Severn on Hudson Bay in nw. Ont. In w. North America this species is noted very rarely on the w. Great Plains from Mont. south to N.M., mostly in spring (it is uncommon on the e. Plains). Recorded in all western states except Idaho, with most records west of the Great Plains being in fall; casual in w. Alta. and B.C., mainly in spring and summer. Calif. had nearly 475 records through 1995, evenly divided between north and south and with most records from along the coast; over 90 percent of Calif. records are for fall (the three winter records are noted above). Fall records for Calif. are mainly from late September and early October (with extremes from 31 August into December); the few spring records are mainly from June. Recorded in fall in n. Baja Calif.

There are two fall records for Greenland, an October record at sea off Iceland, and two October records for Great Britain (Dyfed and Fair Isle).

🔊 STATUS AND CONSERVATION

Although no serious declines of this species have been noted, its preference for mature forests perhaps makes it vulnerable to habitat changes from forestry practices on the breeding grounds. A more direct threat is the growing infestation by introduced insect pests of hemlocks (*Tsuga canadensis*) in the Northeast; large-scale loss of hemlocks could seriously affect this and other wood-warbler species. The loss of humid evergreen forests on the wintering grounds may also affect this species adversely. As noted above, populations of Blackburnian Warblers do show fluctuations in response to fluctuations of spruce budworm populations.

🦇 SUBSPECIES

No subspecies; no geographical variation described.

Suggested as a possible relative of the *virens* complex (Black-throated Green/Hermit/Townsend's/Golden-cheeked) by several workers, and by its placement next to that group in the 1957 AOU Check-list, but this treatment appears to be based on superficial plumage characters. Many features suggest a relationship with Cerulean Warbler. These include postures, songs (unaccented-ending version of Blackburnian song suggests high-pitched version of Cerulean song), both "chip" notes and flight notes, and the preference for mature forest habitats on both the breeding and wintering grounds; some aspects of immature plumage are quite similar as well. Our placement of Blackburnian next to Cerulean restores the treatment in the 1931 AOU Check-list.

A hybrid photographed in Ontario is considered by some authorities to be a Blackburnian × Black-and-white Warbler (although some feel it may be a Blackburnian × Chestnut-sided). One Blackburnian paired and nested with a Bay-breasted Warbler in West Virginia; there is a sight record of a Bay-breasted × Blackburnian hybrid in May in coastal Louisiana.

✒ Plumages and Molts

SPRING ADULT MALE: Throat, breast, broad supercilium, forecrown patch, thin central stripe on forehead, sides of neck, and arc under eye are bright yellow-orange, brightening to vivid deep orange (even red-orange) on the throat and upper breast. Remainder of forehead and crown, hindneck, lores, and auricular patch black; black of the rear of the auriculars extending backward toward (but not meeting) black hindneck, and a black spur from the lower rear auriculars connecting (or nearly connecting) to the black streaks on the sides of the breast. Lower breast yellow, with a hint of yellow suffusion on the belly and flanks in many birds. Bold black streaks on the sides of the breast and (more sparsely) on the flanks. Upperparts black, with a creamy white stripe or "brace" down each side of the back — disarrangement of feathers may cause these pale braces to appear as several shorter pale streaks. Median and greater coverts largely white, forming a large and conspicuous wing patch; tertials black with conspicuous white fringes; primaries and secondaries dusky blackish, narrowly edged with olive-gray. Rectrices dusky blackish with narrow olive-gray edges; the inner webs of the outer four pairs extensively white. **FIRST SPRING MALE:** Like spring adult male, but primaries and secondaries duller and browner, contrasting with the fresh black back feathers and black and white wing coverts; white on greater coverts averages less extensive, often breaking up the white wing patch into two wide white wing bars; belly whiter **SPRING ADULT FEMALE:** Throat, upper breast, and broad supercilium pale or medium orange to deep ocher-yellow, becoming pale orange-buff on rear of super-

Blackburnian Warbler. Male in Ohio in May. (Photo: Steve and Dave Maslowski)

cilium, sides of head (behind auriculars), and patch on forecrown. Lower underparts dull creamy whitish, often with a faint yellow suffusion. Sides and flanks marked with thin blackish streaks. Auricular patch unmarked gray-brown to olive-brown. Crown (apart from pale crown patch), hindneck, and upperparts olive to olive-gray, with variable black flecking or spotting in the crown and hindneck. Black feather centers on the back give a streaked appearance, with at least one pale creamy "brace" or diagonal stripe on each side of the back (as in male, rearrangement of back feathers can produce appearance of two or three short pale streaks rather than one long brace). Broad white wing bars, formed by tips of median and greater coverts, in some birds extensive enough to produce a large patch on at least the inner greater coverts. White spots in rectrices average smaller than in adult male, and are restricted to the outer three rectrices. **FIRST SPRING FEMALE:** Basically identical to spring adult female, with color of face and throat averaging slightly yellower, less orange. Wings and tail browner and more worn than in adult. **FALL ADULT MALE:** Resembles spring adult male but orange colors much less intense, more yellow. Fresh fall and early winter birds show olive fringes to black feathers of head and upperparts, and may show a few dark feather tips in the yellow-orange forecrown patch. A few birds may be all black on the upperparts. Median and greater wing coverts broadly tipped white, forming two wide wing bars, but white less extensive than in spring adult male and does not form a solid patch. Black streaks on sides of breast and flanks rather bold, but slightly veiled with yellowish. A variable yellow wash through the lower breast, belly, and flanks, faint in some birds but rather bright in others; in general this yellow wash is more extensive than on spring adult males. **FIRST FALL MALE:** Resembles fall adult male, but more extensively olive above because of broader olive fringes and narrower black centers to feathers of crown, hindneck, and back; yellow forecrown patch more diffuse, olive-tinged. Auriculars brownish olive, bordered on top with a

blackish eye line. Bright areas of face, throat, and upper breast purer yellow, with little or no orange tint. Streaking on sides and flanks less bold. This plumage is similar to fall adult female, but immature males tend to be more pure yellow (less orange or ocher) on the throat, with the yellow extending farther down the breast. **FALL ADULT FEMALE:** Similar to spring adult female, but more olive-brown above and with less white in the greater wing covert bar. Streaking on sides and flanks is more blurred. Also similar to first fall male, but lacks black in the eye line, and the yellow throat is more orange or ocher in tint. The bright yellow-ocher on the throat does not extend as far down on the lower breast and flanks, although a pale yellow wash is usually present in those regions. **FIRST FALL FEMALE:** Color of chin, throat, and upper breast varies from very pale yellow-buff (almost whitish on chin and supercilium) to slightly brighter yellow-ocher. In a minority of individuals, especially by midwinter, the underpart color is restricted to a faint wash of pale ocher across the lower throat and in the malar region. Streaking on the sides and flanks is blurred and dusky or grayish, not black. The auricular patch is unmarked gray-brown. The forecrown patch is indistinct or absent. The ground color of the upperparts may vary, with duller individuals appearing dull grayish brown above and brighter birds with more of a buffy cast. The back is marked with diffuse dusky streaking; the pale braces are present but indistinct. There is no black flecking on the crown or elsewhere on the upperparts. Wing bars are distinct and white, but average narrower than in other age and sex classes. **JUVENILE:** Upperparts dull gray-brown, streaked with dusky and buff. Throat and breast dull, pale gray-brown; remaining underparts dull buffy, lightly spotted with dusky on breast, flanks. Gray-brown auricular patch, with buffy supercilium and sides of neck. **BARE PARTS:** Bill of spring males blackish, with brown along the tomium and at the base of the mandible; more extensive fleshy-brown on mandible of winter males, all females. Eyes dark brown. Legs and feet dusky brown.

A complete prebasic molt takes place on the breeding grounds. The first prebasic molt is incomplete, with juvenal flight feathers retained. A partial prealternate molt occurs on the wintering grounds, involving at least the head and chest feathers and wing coverts.

 ## REFERENCES

GENERAL: Morse 1994.
DISTRIBUTION: Whitney 1994.
ECOLOGY, BEHAVIOR, VOCALIZATIONS, AND CONSERVATION: Benzinger 1994a, b, Chipley 1980, Doepker et al. 1992, Lawrence 1953, Morse 1967, Nice 1932.
IDENTIFICATION: Lehman 1987.
SYSTEMATICS: Bain 1996, Hurley and Jones 1983, Parkes 1983.

CERULEAN WARBLER

Dendroica cerulea

4.5 in. (11.5 cm). This small, short-tailed *Dendroica* is a specialist of the upper canopy of extensive mature deciduous woods. The unique blue or aqua upperparts found in most plumages can be hard to see as this species forages high in the trees. All plumages show bold white wing bars, and females and immatures have a broad supercilium. Young females in fall should be distinguished with care from drab young female Blackburnian Warblers. Highly migratory, the Cerulean Warbler breeds most commonly in the upper Ohio River Valley and Allegheny region, but has expanded its range somewhat this century into the Northeast. This range expansion has been more than offset by severe declines in the core of its Midwest breeding range. These declines are no doubt due to specialized breeding habitat requirements as well as increasing threats to the mature woods required on the wintering grounds, which lie almost exclusively in South America.

 ## DESCRIPTION

All Ceruleans are distinctive, with their short-tailed appearance and small size; this is the smallest *Dendroica* and among the smallest of all our warblers. The body appears plump, and the tail extension beyond the undertail coverts is the shortest of all *Dendroica*s. Primary projection is long, as is typical of such long-distance migrants. The bill is rather short and thick for a *Dendroica*.

Adults show strong sexual dimorphism but little seasonal variation in plumage. The upperparts of all but the immature females have distinctive bluish or aqua tones. White tail spots and broad white wing bars show prominently in all plumages. There is a prominent supercilium that broadens behind the eye in all but adult male plumage.

 ## SIMILAR SPECIES

Adult and first spring males are striking and distinctive with their bluish upperparts, white underparts, and the thin dark breast-band that is usually present. In all plumages, Ceruleans are distinctive with their short-tailed appearance and small size, but females and immature males can be confused especially with Blackburnian and Black-throated Gray warblers.

Females and first fall male Ceruleans are frequently confused with drab first fall female **BLACKBURNIAN WARBLERS**. In both species the supercilium broadens slightly behind the eye (our only *Dendroica*s so marked), and especially late in the fall young female Blackburnians may appear very white or pale buff below, thus resembling Ceruleans (which, however, are lightly washed with lemon yellow below). In Blackburnian, which is slightly larger and much longer tailed, look for a different head pattern: a darker and more triangular cheek patch, with the supercilium joining the pale area on the side of the neck. Most Blackburnians, if seen well, show a hint of a pale median stripe on the forecrown. The back pattern on Blackburnian is diagnostic but can be difficult to observe on birds foraging high in the trees; Blackburnians show pale lines on the sides of the back and some dark streaks across the back. There is a subtle difference in the color of the underparts between the first basic females: on Cerulean it is clear pale yellow, and on Blackburnian it is pale buff, even fading to whitish. Blackburnians are longer tailed and slightly larger in body size than Ceruleans. Both species can frequent the same wooded habitats in migration, and both tend to be rather silent. Flight and chip notes of the two species are similar.

First fall males could be confused with first fall female **BLACK-THROATED GRAY WARBLERS**; in the latter look for a broader dark cheek patch, gray (not bluish) upperparts, and a much longer tail with extensive white in the outer rectrices. Among other *Dendroica*, see also drab fall **PINE, BLACKPOLL,** and **BAY-BREASTED WARBLERS**.

The **TENNESSEE WARBLER** is similar to Cerulean in shape, but is always told by the lack of bold wing bars, the thinner and more sharply pointed bill, less prominent supercilium, much more limited white tail spots, and lack of any streaking on the underparts.

VOICE

SONG is a series of buzzy *chee* or *zeep* notes, shifting to an ascending and accelerating buzzy series and ending in a high, prolonged buzz. The effect is of a buzzy song rising in three stages: *zeep zeep zeep zeep zizizizi zeee! zray zray zray zray-zray zreeee!* or *burr-burr-br-br-br-br-bree?* The song is easily confused with some songs of Northern Parula, but the terminal high-pitched buzz of Cerulean is diagnostic. Some songs may also resemble some rarely heard alternate songs of Blue-winged and Golden-winged warblers. Compare also with songs of Black-throated Blue Warbler (which is slower, with fewer notes) and Blackburnian Warbler (which is higher in pitch than Cerulean's). Simpler song variants may occasionally lack the high terminal buzz. One singing bird collected by Ridgway (specimen at USNM) proved to be a female. Singing on the breeding grounds diminishes after early July, with some resurgence in August (even in southbound migrant males). Singing is frequent on the wintering grounds. The **CALL NOTE** is a full, slurred *chip*; this species calls relatively infrequently. **FLIGHT NOTE** is a buzzy *zzee*, similar to that of Blackpoll, Bay-breasted, Blackburnian, and Yellow warblers.

 # BEHAVIOR

Birds typically forage in the upper canopy of tall deciduous trees well within woodlands, working methodically and relatively sluggishly outward along thin branches. Feeding movements mainly involve gleaning the undersides of leaves, with occasional short upward sallies. Migrants sometimes forage lower, especially early in the spring and during cold fronts, but foraging high in the foliage is the rule on the wintering grounds. The diet consists almost entirely of insects and spiders. Territorial males on the breeding grounds are vigorous and persistent singers, usually singing from the highest available foliage. In winter, one or two Ceruleans are often noted in mixed-species foraging flocks.

The **NEST** is located well off the ground in a deciduous tree, usually at 30–50 ft. but as low as 15 ft. and as high as 80 ft. It is placed on a horizontal branch, usually at a fork, well away from the trunk. It is a shallow, compact, silvery cup of bark strips, weed stems, lichens, and spider webs, lined with grasses, moss, and hair. Late broods (July) are sometimes noted, but it is uncertain whether this species can be double-brooded. Cowbird parasitism is at least moderate.

For **BREEDING**, Cerulean Warblers require large tracts of old growth deciduous forest, primarily along rivers, streams, and swamps. They also breed in upland habitats (generally below about 3,000 ft.) as long as the requisite extensive mature broadleaf forest is present. At the northern edge of the range (Ontario, ne. Ohio) they breed in mixed deciduous-coniferous forests. Key tree species vary through the range but include sycamore, silver maple, ash, sweet gum, red maple, and cottonwood. In upland areas they occur locally in oaks, oak-hickory associations, black walnut, black birch, and black locust. All of the above habitats must have largely closed canopies and subcanopies with little undergrowth. Ideal woodlands are of at least 7,500 acres in area. Even within appropriate habitat, this species is localized and often appears somewhat colonial.

WINTER birds are largely restricted to mature, tall evergreen forests within a fairly narrow elevational range of 1,800–4,400 ft. Some sources indicate that birds may winter in second-growth woodlands and shaded coffee plantations, but such habitats are certainly less important than mature, virgin forests. In **MIGRATION** in Belize, birds again used mature foothill evergreen forests. Migrants encountered along the Gulf Coast may use any available clumps of trees, but farther north they are only rarely encountered outside of typical breeding habitat.

DISTRIBUTION

BREEDS mainly from cen. Minn., n. Wisc., sw. and s.-cen. Mich. (and very locally in w. portion of upper peninsula of Mich.), s. Ont., N.Y., Conn. and R.I. south to Ark., cen. Miss., cen. Ala. and e. N.C. (Roanoke River basin). Very small numbers breed, or have bred, west to e. S.D., e. Neb., e. Kans., and e. Okla. (with former breeding in ne. Texas) and north to sw. Que., nw. Vt., and w. Mass. Possibly breeds south to extreme nw. S.C. and La. The bulk of the breeding population is in the Mississippi and Ohio river valleys, west of the Appalachian Mtns. There has been some extension of the breeding range north and northeastward in recent decades, as well as onto the Piedmont plateau and the Atlantic coastal plain.

WINTERS almost exclusively in n. South America, from Venezuela and Colombia south to s. Peru and n. Bolivia. It winters on the west slope of the Andes in Colombia, but the main winter range is in the eastern foothills of the Andes from Venezuela south. It winters also at middle elevations in the tablelands of e. Venezuela and has been recorded very locally in forested foothills south to se. Brazil. Very small numbers may winter in the foothills of Costa Rica and Panama.

Primarily a trans-Gulf **MIGRANT**, with the fall migration route somewhat more easterly than that of spring. Spring migrants moving out of South America appear to cross the s. Caribbean in a northwesterly direction, staging in the foothills and mountains from Nicaragua and Honduras north to Belize and se. Chiapas. The majority of spring migrants are noted from the upper Texas coast to sw. La., with smaller numbers encountered east to the Panhandle; considered rare in spring on the Fla. Gulf Coast and Keys. Also rare in s. Texas and the Texas hill country. Most of the spring migration proceeds north through the Mississippi and Ohio river valleys, east to the Appalachians. This species is a rare or casual spring migrant on the s. Atlantic coastal plain. The fall migration route lies well to the east of the spring route. It is casual in fall in Texas and sw. La., but more numerous from se. La. to Fla. (including the entire peninsula); all of the Fla. tower kills of Ceruleans have been in fall. It is more frequently recorded in fall than in spring in the Atlantic coastal states, and all records for Bermuda and the Bahamas are for fall.

SPRING MIGRATION is fairly early, with the first migrants appearing on the Gulf Coast around 5–10 April; there are a few records in late March, even as far north as Okla., Ark., Tenn., and Ga. Usual spring arrivals in s. Mo., Tenn., and Ky. are in mid-April, and arrivals through much of the remaining Midwest as well as on the mid-Atlantic coast are usually during the last week of April. In the Great Lakes region, birds arrive during the first week of May, and the earliest arrivals at the northern end of the breeding range are during the second week of May. Peak spring counts on the Gulf Coast (only rarely in double figures) occur around 15–25 April, and very few are noted in the South after the first week of May. A few migrants are noted in the Great Lakes region as late as the end of May (and exceptionally to early June). Spring migration is not very pronounced away from migrant traps on the western Gulf Coast, n. Ga., and very locally elsewhere; migrant traps along the Great Lakes shore rarely produce more than 2–3 birds per day.

In **FALL MIGRATION**, Cerulean is one of our earliest warblers, although details of timing and routes are poorly understood. Most singing ceases on the breeding grounds after early July, and Ceruleans are rarely detected after that, although there may be some resurgence of song in August. Few fall migrants are recorded away from Fla., the e. Gulf Coast, and locally in inland regions of the southeastern states (including n. Ga.). This species is very rare in fall in the northern Midwest and also in New England (where primarily coastal). Fall migrants have been noted in the southeastern states as early as the second week of July, and peak passage through the South extends from late July to early September. Records of fall migrants in the East extend through September; away from the Southeast this species is strictly casual after mid-September, with only a few well-documented October records. A handful of records in the southern states extend to mid-October. Many late fall reports may pertain to misidentified Blackburnian Warblers. This is one of the earliest North American migrants to arrive on South American wintering grounds, arriving as early as August.

Very rare or **CASUAL** west to N.D. and sw. Man. and north to s.-cen. Ont. (North Bay), N.H., Me., N.B., N.S. (mid-May to mid-June and mid-August to mid-October), and Nfld. (two September records and an exceptional record to 2 December 1995, the latest for North America). Among the rarest of the "regular" warbler

CERULEAN WARBLER
Dendroica cerulea

migrants on Bermuda, where all records are for fall. Casual (mainly in fall) in the Bahamas and Greater Antilles; unrecorded in the Lesser Antilles.

VAGRANT to w. North America, where it is one of the rarest "eastern" warblers to occur. These records are mainly in fall (2 September to 27 October), but there are also seven late spring records (17 May to 6 June). Records exist for Colo. (2), N.M. (1), Ariz. (2), Nev. (1), Calif. (13), and n. Baja Calif. (1). This is perhaps the only "eastern" warbler for which w. North American records have actually declined in the past two decades (despite ever more thorough observation).

STATUS AND CONSERVATION

This species is now uncommon over most of its range; accounts from early in the 20th century indicate that it was formerly much more common. Currently the highest densities are in the Cumberland Plateau region of e. Kentucky, e. Tennessee, and s. West Virginia. There has been some expansion of the breeding range in the Northeast in recent decades. Some of this expansion involves reoccupation of former breeding range (as in Delaware), and some may in fact be an artifact of increased coverage in connection with state Breeding Bird Atlas projects. Breeding was established in New Jersey in 1947, in Connecticut in 1972, in Rhode Island in 1986, and in Massachusetts in 1989; colonization of sw. Quebec began in the 1950s.

Through most of its breeding range, the Cerulean Warbler has declined precipitously. Breeding Bird Surveys from 1966 to 1987 show an annual decline of 3.4 percent, the highest for any of our warblers. The greatest declines have been in the Ohio, Mississippi, and lower Missouri river valleys due to large-scale conversion of forests to farmland. Besides deforestation, important causes of this species' decline in the breeding range include management of hardwood forests for even-aged stands, fragmentation and isolation of forest habitat, loss of key tree species (oaks, elms, American chestnuts, sycamores) through disease, and cowbird parasitism. This species' requirement for mature humid foothill forests in winter and even migration has put it at great risk because of the extensive loss of such habitats.

SUBSPECIES

No subspecies recognized; no geographical variation described.

Perhaps most closely related to Blackburnian Warbler (see p. 398). An alliance with the Black-throated Blue Warbler has been postulated, but this would appear to be based on little other than bluish dorsal coloration of the males. Cerulean has once hybridized with Black-and-white Warbler.

PLUMAGES AND MOLTS

SPRING ADULT MALE: Forehead and crown bright "cerulean" blue; remaining upperparts similar but tinged grayish, especially on the rump. There is considerable individual variation in the depth and brightness of the blue on the crown and upperparts. Back heavily streaked with black; uppertail coverts with broad black centers. The sides of the crown are indistinctly and variably streaked with black; there is sometimes a hint of blackish streaking in the center of the crown. Supercilium light blue, sometimes showing a hint of white in the rearmost portion. Lores and ocular stripe slaty; auriculars gray with a slight bluish tint. Chin and throat white. There is a thin band of black across the upper breast; this band is variable in width and may be slightly veiled with whitish. The sides and flanks are strongly streaked with deep blue-gray or blackish, with some whitish veiling. Remaining underparts white. Lesser wing coverts bluish; median and greater secondary coverts and primary coverts black with blue-gray edging and broad white tips forming broad and conspicuous wing bars. Tertials blackish, edged with blue-gray and narrowly with white; flight feathers blackish, edged with blue-gray. Rectrices blackish, edged with blue-gray. White spots on the inner webs of the outer five pairs of rectrices. **FIRST SPRING MALE:** Similar to spring adult male, with the following differences:

Cerulean Warbler. Adult male in Texas in May. (Photo: Brian E. Small)

Cerulean Warbler. First fall female on Farallon Islands, California on 23 October 1981. (Photo: R. Stone/VIREO)

The upperparts are more strongly washed with gray-brown, and the blue of the crown is not as bright; the black markings on the back and uppertail coverts average thinner; there is an evident white supercilium behind the eye. Many individuals show a thinner breast-band than in the adult male, but breast-band width is variable (occasionally broken). The edgings to the remiges are dull (more gray-green), and the primary coverts are dull brownish slate without blue edgings. The white spot on r2 is reduced or absent. **SPRING ADULT FEMALE:** This plumage is somewhat similar to that of first spring males, but there is no hint of a breast-band, the back is unstreaked, and the supercilium is bolder and more complete. The crown is light blue, only slightly tinged with greenish. Remaining upperparts plain blue-gray with a slight greenish tint. Complete supercilium whitish or very slightly tinged yellow; whitish arc under the eye. Lores and indistinct transocular stripe gray; cheeks pale blue-gray. Underparts dull whitish, with a variable yellow wash on the sides of the throat and upper breast. Diffuse grayish or gray-green streaking on the sides and flanks. Flight feathers and wing coverts blackish brown, edged blue-green; median and greater coverts tipped white. Rectrices dull blackish, narrowly edged blue-green, and with white spots on the inner webs of the outer four pairs. **FIRST SPRING FEMALE:** Very similar to spring adult female, but on average the upperparts and crown are more strongly washed with green, and the breast is more strongly washed with yellow; there is considerable variation, however, and some birds are as bluish as spring adult females. Best distinguished by duller, more worn flight feathers and primary coverts that lack blue-green edging. **FALL ADULT MALE:** Very similar to spring adult male. The breast-band may be partly veiled (in a few birds almost obscured) with whitish feather tips, and most individuals show some white in the rear portion of the supercilium. **FIRST FALL MALE:** The crown and upperparts are generally bluish to blue-gray, but noticeably washed with green. Streaking is present on the upperparts, but may be limited to the sides of the back. The uppertail coverts are bluish, with small black centers. The sides of the crown show a hint of dark streaking. There is a striking whitish supercilium, broadening behind the eye; it is sometimes tinged yellowish in the rear. A dark postocular line contrasts with the supercilium and forms an upper border to the grayish cheeks. The underparts are whitish, variably tinged yellowish on the sides of the throat, upper breast, and rear flanks. The breast-band is absent or limited to the sides of the breast. The sides and flanks show moderate, blurred grayish olive streaks. The wing coverts and flight feathers are edged with blue-gray; two white wing bars. **FALL ADULT FEMALE:** Essentially identical to spring adult female, but often washed more strongly with yellow below and greenish above. **FIRST FALL FEMALE:** The most "green and yellow" plumage, with little if any hint of bluish. The crown and upperparts are uniformly gray-green to olive, with no streaking. The face is marked with a striking pale supercilium (whitish but tinged with yellow) which broadens behind the eye. Postocular stripe grayish; auriculars pale grayish, washed with yellow. Underparts dull whitish but extensively washed with pale yellowish, especially on the sides of the throat, across the breast, and on the flanks. Some individuals are more uniformly yellowish below, showing whitish only on the chin and undertail coverts. Flanks diffusely streaked with grayish olive. Coverts and flight feathers dusky gray, narrowly edged with pale gray-green. Wing bars whitish. Rectrices grayish with white spots on the inner webs of the outer three pairs. **JUVENILE:** Crown and upperparts brownish; underparts dull buffy white. Buffy white supercilium and brownish postocular stripe. Wings and tail resemble those of first fall birds. **BARE PARTS:** Bill dull blackish in adult male; lower mandible with some brown in adult female, and extensively pale brownish in immatures. Legs and feet slaty; soles of feet paler. Eyes dark brown.

Cerulean Warbler. Female in Texas in May. (Photo: Brian E. Small)

The prebasic molt takes place in late summer on the breeding grounds; it is complete in adults but partial in hatching-year birds (not involving flight feathers or rectrices). The partial prealternate molt takes place in late winter and early spring; it appears to be rather extensive in first-year birds.

 ## REFERENCES

DISTRIBUTION: Austen et al. 1994, Lynch 1981, Ouellet 1967, Parker 1994.
ECOLOGY, BEHAVIOR, VOCALIZATIONS, AND CONSERVATION: Ambuel and Temple 1982, Kahl et al. 1985, Lynch 1981, Oliarnyk and Robertson 1996, Parker 1994, Robbins et al. 1989 and 1992.
IDENTIFICATION: Lehman 1987.
SYSTEMATICS: Parkes 1978.

BLACK-AND-WHITE WARBLER PL. 15

Mniotilta varia

5 in. (12.7 cm). The distinctively striped Black-and-white Warbler is unique among our warblers in the extent to which it employs a nuthatchlike vertical creeping behavior. Although closely allied with *Dendroica*, it shows certain structural modifications related to its creeping habits and bark-probing foraging behavior: an elongated hind claw, shortened tarsi, and a long thin bill with a slightly curved culmen. The black-and-white-striped crown and back are distinctive in all plumages. This species is a widespread breeder in a variety of deciduous and mixed woodlands across the boreal regions and through much of the eastern U.S. Its migration begins early and is prolonged; it is one of the more frequently occurring "eastern" warblers in the western states. One banded individual was recovered at an age of over 11 years, a longevity record for the Parulidae.

 ## DESCRIPTION

Entirely black and white in all plumages, except for a creamy wash on the face and flanks in many females. This is our only warbler with a white median crown stripe bordered by black (conspicuous in all plumages). The bold white border to the tertials is distinctive in all plumages, as are the black uppertail coverts with white fringes.

Like a moderately short-tailed *Dendroica* in shape, but the bill is relatively slender and slightly curved on the culmen. The feet are relatively large, with an elongated hind claw; the tarsi are short.

SIMILAR SPECIES

BLACK-THROATED GRAY WARBLER is always distinguished by the dark (gray or black) median crown and by the lack of white stripes on the back. **BLACKPOLL WARBLERS** in alternate plumage, particularly males, have solid dark crowns and an olive tinge to the upperparts (which lack white stripes). Neither of these species regularly "creeps." Among our warblers only the **YELLOW-THROATED** routinely "creeps" along branches; it is easily distinguished by the bright yellow throat and upper breast. **PINE WARBLERS** occasionally "creep" but are entirely different in color and pattern. Black-and-white Warbler is superficially similar to **NUTHATCHES** (*Sitta*) because of creeping behavior but differs strongly from all New World nuthatches in having striped upperparts and strong wing pattern, as well as a longer tail and thinner bill.

VOICE

SONG is a lengthy (to 3 seconds) series of thin, squeaky, very high-pitched notes, being a rhythmic cadence of *wee-see* phrases (second note lower). Usually at least 6, often 10 or more phrases in song. In some individuals 2–3 series of slightly different phrases will be incorporated into song. Song distinguished from other "high-pitched" warbler songs by the chanting rhythm and the absence of a complex ending. A second, less frequently heard song is longer, faster, and often more varied in pitch; this song is sometimes given in flight. **CALLS** include a dull *chip* or *tik,* suggestive of a Black-throated Gray Warbler; also a doubled *seet-seet* or *zeet-zeet* (sometimes a single *zeet*), which is also given as a **FLIGHT NOTE.**

BEHAVIOR

The predominant foraging behavior involves creeping along branches and trunks, picking and probing with the thin bill. Often creeps upside-down along undersides of branches, and may creep downward, headfirst. Like nuthatches (but unlike creepers and woodpeckers), the tail is not used as a prop when creeping. The creeper or nuthatchlike probing behavior allows access to subsurface insects, a food source that can be exploited earlier in the spring than most surface or aerial insects; this foraging behavior is certainly a factor in the species' early spring arrival. Other foraging behaviors include occasional flycatching, hover-gleaning, and typical warbler gleaning. Rather solitary, although it sometimes joins mixed-species flocks in winter and migration. May sing upon arrival on winter territories.

NEST is a stout cup usually placed on ground, often at foot of log or stump, among roots, or in a depression. Nests placed aboveground are usually in stumps, crevices.

Habitat

BREEDS in mature and second-growth woodlands, either pure deciduous or mixed, with large trees being a critical component of the habitat. Understory and ground cover may vary from dense to rather open, but always with some tangles, dead leaves for nest concealment. Pure coniferous forests generally avoided. Riparian corridors, swamp hardwoods, and oak-hickory thickets used in portions of range.

WINTERS in a variety of forests from high-elevation cloud forests to lowland evergreen and deciduous forests, woodland borders, gardens, coffee plantations. More numerous at lower elevations.

MIGRANTS widespread, but generally in areas with at least a few tall trees.

Distribution

Boreal **BREEDING** range extends from extreme se. Yukon, sw. Dist. of Mack., ne. B.C., n. and cen. Alta. east across the boreal forests to s. Que., Maritime Provinces, Nfld., and Lab. (Goose Bay); generally common in these regions. Breeds commonly south to ne. Minn., n. Wisc., Mich., s. Ont. (except extreme south near Lake Erie), N.Y., New England states. Generally less common and more local around s. Great Lakes. Also a generally common breeder through Atlantic and Appalachian states south to the Carolinas (generally inland from coastal plain), n. Ga., n. Ala. Generally uncommon to rare and somewhat local as a breeder in the Midwest and Mississippi River Valley, and westward to cen. Texas (locally west to Edwards Plateau), cen. Okla., e. Kans., Missouri River Valley west to the Dakotas and e. Mont.; also east to n. La., s. Miss., and s. Ala. Arrives and departs relatively early from breeding grounds. Birds in southernmost part of range may fledge young by late May when migrants from northernmost populations are still passing through. There are a number of summer records for the western states, although many of these may pertain to late spring vagrants or very early fall migrants.

WINTERS uncommonly along the southern Atlantic Coast (S.C. to Fla.) and the Gulf Coast, but fairly common in winter in peninsular Fla. Very scarce in these regions well inland from the coast. Very small numbers winter annually in coastal Calif., with winter records scattered elsewhere through the Southwest. Casual into early winter in the northern states and s. Canada, with an exceptional record from Duluth, Minn., 15 February to 21 March 1975. The majority of birds winter in the Bahamas and Greater Antilles and on the mainland from coastal Mexico (except the far northwest) south through Central America to n. Venezuela, Colombia, and Ecuador (casual to n. Peru, e. Venezuela). Rare in winter in Lesser Antilles; several records for Trinidad.

MIGRATION is on a broad front in e. North America in both spring and fall, and is prolonged.

SPRING MIGRATION begins very early — a few birds appear by the first of March, and the species is regular by the second week of March on a broad front along the Gulf Coast. A common migrant through the Gulf Coast states, west through coastal and eastern Texas, peaking from late March to early May (later birds are the more northerly nesters). A few arrive in Midwest and Mid-Atlantic states by early April (most of these are returning breeders), but peak movement through Great Lakes region is during the first third of May (occasional April flights at Great Lakes are associated with strong southerly winds). Arrives on northernmost breeding grounds in mid-May, although there are numerous late April records well into the northern part of the species' range. Through most of the East small numbers are still moving through in late May, with a few into early June in the Midwest and Northeast.

FALL MIGRATION is similarly very early; in the southern states fall movement consists of a wave of early southerly breeders beginning in early July, and a later peak from late August through September and into mid-October, probably consisting of breeders from more northerly populations. A few migrants are regularly noted in July (especially late in the month) in the northern states, but they do not begin to appear in any numbers until early August. The peak fall movement through the Great Lakes, midwestern, and Atlantic states is in late August and September, with numbers dropping rapidly after early October. A few stragglers occur in the northern states and southern Canadian provinces into late October and early November (exceptionally into December, and even a few overwintering attempts).

Scarce but regular transient through the western states in both spring and fall; one of the most numerous "eastern" warblers in much of the West. There are about 2,500 records for Calif.; near-ly two-thirds are for fall, but there are over 600 spring and 300 winter records. More early spring (March, April) and early fall (August) records in West than for most "eastern" vagrants. Recorded frequently in Bermuda (mostly late September and October; many also winter).

CASUAL north to Alaska (recorded in June in Hyder in the south-east, October on n. slope). VAGRANT to Iceland, Faeroes, Ireland, Great Britain (where one of the most frequent American war-blers; fourteen records, mainly September to December, once through winter).

⊞ STATUS AND CONSERVATION

In many regions that suffered extensive deforestation in 19th cen-tury, populations increased during the current century with forest regeneration. Regional declines have occurred, however, where such forests have undergone fragmentation. Heavy parasitism of this ground-nester by Brown-headed Cowbirds may have con-

BLACK-AND-WHITE WARBLER
Mniotilta varia

tributed to these declines. Local population declines in the Great Lakes region and Midwest have resulted from the clearing of the bottomland forests.

 ## SUBSPECIES

None described.

 ## TAXONOMIC RELATIONSHIPS

Mniotilta is clearly allied with *Dendroica,* with its distinguishing characters mainly related to morphological adaptations for its creeping habits. Many taxonomists agree that these genera should probably be merged, although the nomenclatural rules of priority would then dictate that the resulting genus be named *Mniotilta*. The Black-and-white Warbler has hybridized with Cerulean Warbler and Blackburnian Warbler.

 ## PLUMAGES AND MOLTS

SPRING ADULT MALE: Strongly patterned head consisting of broad black lateral crown stripes, a white median crown stripe (extending all the way down the hindneck and nape), bold white supercilium, thin white supraloral stripe, black auricular patch, black lores, and a small white crescent under the eye. Center of upper throat marked with black, either a solid black patch (or with variably white fringing) or a few large black spots on a white background. Some white may be present on the extreme anterior chin even in the blackest-throated birds. Broad, bold black spots on the remainder of the throat and upper breast, extending back conspicuously along the sides and flanks. Ground color of underparts pure white. Black

Black-and-White Warbler. Adult male in Ontario in May. (Photo: Jim Flynn)

Black-and-White Warbler. Female in New Jersey in September. (Photo: Brian E. Small)

arrowlike marks on the undertail coverts. Back strongly striped black and white; rump and uppertail coverts black, the latter strongly fringed with white. Wing coverts black, with broad white tips to median and greater coverts forming two bold white wing bars. Black tertials boldly fringed with white, forming a horizontal white streak that appears to extend back from the dorsal edge of the rear wing bar. Primaries and secondaries dusky black (not contrasting markedly with the black of the body), edged with clear pale gray. Central rectrices gray with black shaft streaks. Remaining rectrices slaty; distal half of the inner webs of the outer two rectrices white. **FIRST SPRING MALE:** Closely resembles spring adult male, but flight feathers and primary coverts duller, less black (showing more contrast with black of the body plumage than in adults). Extent of black on the chin and throat averages less, often reduced to black spotting on a white background. Black auricular patch may be mottled with white. **FALL ADULT MALE:** Differs from spring adult male in usually having completely white chin and less extensive black on the throat; throat color is variable — may completely lack black, be spotted with black (typically), or be nearly solid black. In extreme individuals, chin and throat are black, with a hint of white veiling; these birds are essentially identical to spring adult males. Auriculars are black, as in spring males. **FIRST FALL MALE:** Differs from fall adult male in having grayish or mottled gray and white rather than black auriculars. Thin postocular stripe black. Chin white; throat white, sometimes with a few black spots on the upper throat. Sides and flanks broadly streaked with black, nearly as boldly as in fall adult male. In early-breeding southerly populations, birds in first basic plumage may be noted by late May. **SPRING ADULT FEMALE:** Differs from spring males of all ages by having black in the lores and auriculars replaced by pale gray or grayish tan, and in having a completely unmarked creamy whitish chin and throat. Streaking across breast duller and more reduced than in males (may be lacking in center of breast). Sides, flanks, and undertail coverts with narrower and duller streaks than in males, the black being rather veiled. Background color of flanks slightly buffy. **FIRST SPRING FEMALE:** Not easily distinguishable from spring adult female. Flight feathers and primary coverts appear duller, more worn, contrasting more with the black body plumage than in adults. **FALL ADULT FEMALE:** Nearly identical to spring adult female, but streaking of sides, flanks, and undertail coverts more veiled, with stronger buff tint to background color. **FIRST FALL FEMALE:** Closely resembles fall adult female, perhaps averaging even less distinctly streaked on underparts and buffier on flanks. **JUVENILE:** This plumage held only briefly; resembles first fall plumage but head and underparts with extensive spotting, streaking on buffy background. **BARE PARTS:** Bill blackish to dark slaty brown, paler (pale gray, brown, or dull white) on basal half of mandible. Eyes blackish brown. Short legs and large feet slate gray to olive-gray, soles and claws paler.

Prebasic molt occurs on the breeding grounds (as early as late May in southerly populations); complete in adults, but first prebasic molt does not involve flight feathers, primary coverts. A partial prealternate molt occurs from February to April.

 REFERENCES

GENERAL: Kricher 1995.
ECOLOGY, BEHAVIOR, VOCALIZATIONS, AND CONSERVATION: Blake and Cadbury 1969.
PLUMAGES, MOLTS, AND MORPHOLOGY: Osterhaus 1962.
SYSTEMATICS: Parkes 1978.

AMERICAN REDSTART   PL. 27

Setophaga ruticilla

5 in. (12.7 cm). The distinctive and generally abundant American Redstart is a flashy and active warbler, easily told by the orange or yellow patches at the base of its flight feathers and rectrices. The wings are often drooped and partly spread, and the tail is frequently fanned. In these actions it is superficially similar to the distantly related Neotropical *Myioborus* warblers, which are also known as redstarts. The American Redstart is sexually dimorphic, and males wear a femalelike plumage until their second prebasic molt, after which they attain the unique orange and black adult male plumage. This is one of our best-studied warblers.

Description

The black, orange, and white plumage of adult males is distinctive and should not be confused with any other north American birds. The large yellow or orange (adult males) patch at the base of the primaries and secondaries is also unique among the wood-warblers; this patch is often readily apparent in flight. The yellow or orange patches on the basal ⅔ of the tail are easily seen from below. From above the spread tail shows this color on the outer four pairs of rectrices (and on parts of the pair adjacent to the gray or black central rectrices).

Sexual differences in plumage are strong, with immature males resembling females until their second prebasic molt. Seasonal variation is slight, as is geographical variation. American Redstarts are moderate-sized warblers with rather long tails, wide bills, and extensive rictal bristles.

 ## Similar Species

Visually, the American Redstart is not likely to be confused with any other species. The combination of the wing- and tail-fanning behavior, yellow or orange flight feather patches, and generally gray or black upperparts is distinctive within the wood-warblers. **PAINTED** and **SLATE-THROATED REDSTARTS**, similar in some behaviors, lack yellow or orange in the wing and tail but instead show extensive white in the tail. Note that many songs of American Redstarts are quite similar to those of several other warblers, including Yellow, Chestnut-sided, Magnolia, and Black-and-white.

 ## Voice

SONG is quite variable, both within and between individuals; it generally consists of a short series of 4–7 similar high, somewhat buzzy notes, with or without an accented ending. Accented-ending songs, the most commonly heard song type, conclude with a lower (or occasionally higher) note. The general quality can be clear and strident, or slightly buzzy. Notes are not delivered especially rapidly — usually slowly enough to count. Some renditions include *see-see-see-see-seeoo, zee-zee-zee-zee-zweeah,* or *teetsa-teetsa-teetsa-tee.* Some variations recall other species such as Yellow, Magnolia, Chestnut-sided, Bay-breasted, and Black-and-white warblers. Individual males have a repertoire of four or more different songs, and often alternate between songs during a singing bout. Unaccented songs, lacking the distinctive slurred (or higher) ending, are given more often late in the summer. Redstarts are relentless singers, often in full song in the heat of mid-day when other warblers have ceased singing. Female song is known, but rare.

CALL is a thin, slurred *chip* or *tsip*, recalling the chip of Yellow Warbler but thinner and more sibilant, often with an almost hissing quality. **FLIGHT NOTE** is a penetrating, clear *seep*; this note sometimes also given as a contact call.

 ## BEHAVIOR

A tame and inquisitive warbler, quite responsive to pishing and squeaking. The partial spreading and drooping of the wings, along with the fanning of the tail, are conspicuous and characteristic behaviors unlikely to be missed when observing birds for prolonged periods. The tail is held fanned out for a second or two, or continuously for longer periods; this is quite different from the quick flicking open of the tail of warblers such as the Hooded. Wing and tail spreading is also used in various displays. Often foraging birds will quickly flick the wings and tail with little accompanying tail fanning, but eventually the fanning behavior will be apparent.

The foraging repertoire of this species is quite varied. It does more sallying for flying insects than do most wood-warblers; sallies are sometimes long and acrobatic. During the breeding season it is quite similar in foraging behavior to small flycatchers of the genus *Empidonax*, especially the Least Flycatcher (*E. minimus*). Aggressive interactions between redstarts and Least Flycatchers are frequent; the flycatchers dominate interactions, but the redstarts show more ecological flexibility. It also hover-gleans, gleans from foliage, and creeps along trunks and branches. Most foraging is at low to mid-levels of the forest, but this species will often forage high in trees as well. Food consists mainly of insects (beetles, caterpillars, hymenoptera), but also berries and occasionally even seeds.

The **NEST** is a neat cup of grasses, plant fibers, and spider webs, lined with fine grasses and hairs. It is usually placed in a fork or near the trunk of a deciduous tree, often a sapling; most nests are placed at heights less than 15 ft., but exceptionally to 80 ft. In some parts of the range, nests are placed within grapevine tangles. May be double-brooded in some regions.

 ## HABITAT

BREEDS in wet deciduous or mixed deciduous-coniferous forests, where there is an understory of young trees. Often found near ponds, streams, or swamps. In the boreal regions and Appalachians they are especially common at the edges of forests or in second-growth habitats, and may proliferate following clearing, burns, and windfalls. Locally they may nest in orchards, towns, and old pastures. Over much of the Midwest and South they are primarily restricted to riverbottom woods and are thus local in distribution. In the West, where scarcer, breeds in deciduous woods (such as willows or alders) near water at lower elevations, and in birches and aspens at higher elevations.

WINTERS over most of its range in mangroves and in lowland evergreen and semi-deciduous woodlands and forest borders, including second growth and towns. Also at higher elevations in cloud forest, shrubby growth, and gardens. In the northernmost part of the winter range often found in mangroves (Florida, Baja California) or exotic tamarisks (southeastern California).

MIGRANTS are widespread in wooded and shrubby habitats, but still demonstrate a preference for deciduous trees.

 ## DISTRIBUTION

BREEDS from se. Alaska, s. Yukon, w.-cen. and s.-cen. Dist. of Mack., n.-cen. Sask., n.-cen. Man., n.-cen. Ont., cen. Que., s. Lab. and Nfld. south to cen. Ore. (very local), nw. Calif. (rarely), s. Idaho, ne. Ut., Colo., e. Texas and through the Gulf Coast states to sw. Ga., nw. Fla., and S.C.. Scarce or absent over the s. Great Plains, breeding mainly in easternmost Neb., Kans., and Okla. Uncommon to rare over the westernmost part of the range outlined above, from Alaska to n. Calif. and east through Ut.; has bred intermittently in e.-cen. Ariz. (near Eagar). Quite common in the remaining eastern and northern part of the breeding range, except on se. coastal plain, where uncommon and local. Bred once recently in Cuba.

WINTERS from nw. Mexico (cen. and s. Baja Calif., Sinaloa) and e. Mexico (Veracruz) south through Central America into n. South America, south to Peru (rarely sw. Peru), Venezuela, Guyana, Trinidad and Tobago, and rarely n. Brazil. Also winters in Bermuda and throughout the West Indies (more common in the Greater Antilles than Lesser Antilles). Within the U.S. most numerous in winter in s. Fla., where daily high counts have exceeded 30 individuals. Small numbers winter annually in se. Calif. (Salton Sea, lower Colorado R.) and very rarely elsewhere in the state; casual in winter in s. Ariz. Rare but regular in winter in Texas (lower Rio Grande Valley and coast) and s. La. There are a few early winter records north to Ore., Ill., Ohio, W. Va., N.Y., and N.S., but many of these may pertain to late fall migrants.

MIGRATION through e. North America is on a broad front from the Gulf Coast and Mississippi Valley east to the Atlantic Coast; this is one of the few wood-warblers that is common in spring along the entire Atlantic Coast. As with most warblers in e. North America, there is a slight easterly shift in fall movements.

SPRING MIGRATION is relatively late. The first birds may arrive in the Deep South by late March, but early arrivals are more typically in early April. In Ky., Tenn., Va., and Md., typical arrivals are just after mid-April; first arrivals in the s. Great Lakes region and s. New England can be as early as the last third of April (recorded exceptionally as early as 20 March in Wisc.), but are more typically at the end of April or beginning of May. Earliest arrivals at the northern edge of the breeding range are around 25–30 May. Peak movements on the upper Gulf Coast and in Fla. are in the last week of April and first third of May. Peaks in the southern Midwest are around 10–20 May, and those in the n. Midwest and most of New England are during the last third of May. Spring migration is protracted, with northerly-breeding migrants still

AMERICAN REDSTART
Setophaga ruticilla

moving north through the first third of June; first spring males constitute much of these late spring movements. In the West, where relatively small numbers breed, arrivals on the breeding grounds are usually at the end of May; even in the Southwest, migrants peak during the last week of May and first week of June.

FALL MIGRATION is protracted, and the first migrants may be noted well south of the breeding range by mid-July (but more typically in late July or early August). Numbers increase by mid-August, and across much of the n. U.S. and s. Canada peak fall movements are from late August to mid-September; at this time this is one of the most abundant migrants along the Atlantic Coast. Small numbers are still moving through these northern regions to the end of September, with a few into the first week of October. Farther south (as in Fla.), peak movements are from mid-September into the second week of October; smaller numbers pass through into late October, with stragglers noted into November. Exceptional was a count of 50+ on the Miss. coast on 2 November 1985 after a hurricane. There are scattered records through e. North America during November (Mass., N.S.), with a handful of records into December. In the West (north to sw. B.C.) this is a regular fall migrant in small numbers. The peak in the interior Southwest (including the Calif. deserts) is during the first half of September; peak movement along the Calif. coast is through the month of September, with a few passing through in October and stragglers noted into November.

CASUAL in migration north to n., cen., and s. coastal Alaska. Exceptional northerly records come from Northwest Territories (Banks Is.), n. Man. (Churchill), and off the n. tip of the Labrador Peninsula. Also recorded from Greenland (five records), Ireland (once), Britain (five records, October to December), France (once, October), and near the Azores (twice, October).

STATUS AND CONSERVATION

Declines have been noted in parts of the breeding range in the Midwest (where there has been large-scale conversion of forest to agricultural fields) and South (where suitable breeding habitat is largely limited to riparian corridors). Populations appear to be stable over most of the boreal and Appalachian regions, where this species uses a broader range of habitats including second-growth forests, but some declines have been noted in New England, perhaps as a result of maturation of preferred successional habitats. Breeding Bird Survey data show no significant overall population changes in North America, but significant declines were recorded from the Great Lakes south to Arkansas and Alabama and increases in the Northeast and Canadian Maritime Provinces. American Redstarts breed commonly and successfully in second-growth woodlands and are thus somewhat resistant to the effects of deforestation. In many regions their populations may have peaked in the early to middle 20th century as extensively lumbered areas became reforested; some recent local declines may be due to the maturation of these forests. This species is a frequent host of the Brown-headed Cowbird.

 ## SUBSPECIES

The subspecies *tricolora* has been described from the northern and northwestern part of the breeding range (essentially the Canadian portion of the breeding range, plus the western states and portions of the Canadian border states). *S. r. tricolora* is characterized as averaging smaller but with a longer tail; the upperparts of females are said to be grayer (less olivaceous), and the yellow wing patches smaller. These differences are inconsistent, and most current workers consider the species to be monotypic. Any patterns of geographical variation in male plumage that may exist are overridden by extensive individual variation.

 ## TAXONOMIC RELATIONSHIPS

The monotypic genus *Setophaga* is thought to be closely allied with *Dendroica*. Similarities in behavior and plumage with the redstarts of the genus *Myioborus* result from convergence, although the northernmost *Myioborus*, the Painted Redstart, was erroneously considered part of *Setophaga* as late as the 5th edi-

American Redstart. Adult male in Texas in May. (Photo: Brian E. Small)

tion of the AOU Check-list. *Setophaga* differs from *Myioborus* in many details: the juvenal plumage is fleeting in *Setophaga* but held well after fledging in *Myioborus*; vocalizations and displays of *Setophaga* fit well within the diversity found in *Dendroica* and differ strongly from those of *Myioborus*; finally, *Setophaga* is strongly sexually dimorphic, whereas dimorphism is very weak in *Myioborus*.

The American Redstart has hybridized with the Northern Parula; probable hybrids with Nashville Warbler have been reported in California and Missouri.

PLUMAGES AND MOLTS

SPRING ADULT MALE: Head, neck, upperparts, and upper breast black. Central rectrices black; the remaining rectrices are orange to salmon on the basal ½ to ⅔, and black on the distal portion. The wings are black with an orange to salmon pink patch at the base of the flight feathers. The sides of the breast and the underwing coverts are orange. The belly is white, variously tinged with pale orange on the sides. Variants can show a more extensive wash of orange on the belly. Also, some variants have the black of the breast extending well down to the belly. Still other variants show extensive orangish scaling on the black of the back, contrasting with the solid black nape and crown. **FIRST SPRING MALE:** Similar to adult female (see below), but the upperparts are darker, more strongly washed with olivaceous or brown, and marked with few to many scattered black feathers. The uppertail coverts are darker, and often solidly black. The yellow areas of the wing and tail average richer than in the female; the yellow patch on the side of the breast is often strongly tinted orange or salmon. The breast usually has at least a few black feathers. The lores are consistently black

American Redstart. Female in New Jersey in September. (Photo: Brian E. Small)

*American Redstart.
First spring male in
Ohio in May. (Photo:
Giff Beaton)*

in this plumage, even if there is virtually no black elsewhere in the plumage; on many birds this black extends back into the auricular area and as flecks on the throat and breast. In general, first alternate males can be difficult to distinguish from adult females; look especially for black in the lores and uppertail coverts of males. The singing behavior of immature males also distinguishes them from females. **SPRING ADULT FEMALE:** Crown, hindneck, and sides of head gray, tinged with olive on the back and rump. Narrow, incomplete white eye-ring. Wings and tail as in adult male, but the patches are pale yellow to pale yellow-orange instead of deep orange; variation in the color of the wing and tail patches in females appears to be independent of age. Remainder of the underparts white, with a patch of yellow on each side of the breast; the center of the breast, sides, and flanks are often tinged yellowish. **FIRST SPRING FEMALE:** Like adult female but with yellow wing patch averaging smaller (often entirely concealed on the folded wing), and yellow on rectrices averaging slightly less extensive. **FALL ADULT MALE:** Very similar to spring adult male, but with indistinct buffy edges to the black body feathers. **FIRST FALL MALE:** Similar to fall adult female, but the upperparts are slightly darker, more greenish or olive, and the yellow of the sides of the breast is often tinged with orange. **FALL ADULT FEMALE:** Virtually identical to alternate adult female, but the upperparts are more brownish, with somewhat less contrast between the head and back. The throat and breast are tinged with dull buff. **FIRST FALL FEMALE:** Like first spring female, but the upperparts are darker, and more strongly olive green. The throat is even more strongly tinged with buff (less whitish). The patches on the sides of the breast are paler yellow than in any other plumage. **JUVENILE:** Head, breast, and upperparts olive-brown; throat and remaining underparts dull whitish. Two indistinct buffy wing bars. Wings and tail as in first fall birds. There is a rapid molt out of the juvenal plumage, which is often largely completed within the nest.

BARE PARTS: Bill black to dark blackish brown (appearing essentially black in the field) in adult males. Bill of females tinged with slate and brown, but still appearing dark; that of juveniles extensively pinkish. Legs and feet dull blackish brown. Eyes very dark brown.

Juvenal body plumage is replaced through a partial first prebasic molt around the time of fledging; adults undergo a complete prebasic molt on the breeding grounds. First-year males undergo a prealternate molt that appears to be limited to the rictal bristles and facial area and to the appearance of occasional black spots elsewhere; this molt occurs on the wintering grounds, beginning as early as December. Much remains to be learned of the exact nature of prealternate molt in this species, but it is clearly limited.

 REFERENCES

ECOLOGY, BEHAVIOR, VOCALIZATIONS, AND CONSERVATION: Bennett 1980, Ficken 1962 and 1963, Ficken and Ficken 1965 and 1967, Holmes et al. 1978, Hunt 1996, Lemon et al. 1985, Proctor-Gray and Holmes 1981, Seidel and Whitmore 1982, Sherry 1979, Sturm 1945.

DISTRIBUTION: Kirkconnell and Garrido 1996.

PLUMAGES, MOLTS, AND MORPHOLOGY: Foy 1974a, b, Gray 1973, Proctor-Gray and Holmes 1981, Rohwer et al. 1983, Spellman et al. 1987.

SYSTEMATICS: Burleigh 1944 (American Redstart × Northern Parula), Mayr and Short 1970, Parkes 1961, Sibley 1994 (illustration of bird believed to be an American Redstart × Nashville Warbler), Wetmore 1949.

PROTHONOTARY WARBLER   PL. 1

Protonotaria citrea

5.25 in. (13.3 cm). Among the most stunning of the wood-warblers, the Prothonotary Warbler has been given the appropriate nickname "Golden Swamp Warbler" because of its brilliant coloration and preference for dark, damp lowland woods. Even in migration the Prothonotary usually seeks out wet, shady areas. This species is a rather large, chunky warbler with a long spikelike bill. It is one of only two North American warblers that habitually nests in cavities.

 DESCRIPTION

The head and most of the underparts vary with age and sex from brilliant golden with an orange tint to yellow tinged with olive.

The undertail coverts and a variable portion of the lower belly and vent area are white. The upperparts are greenish, and the flight feathers are contrastingly gray. The wings appear unmarked in the field, although there is a white line along the inner edges of the tertials and secondaries, and a white outer edge to the outermost greater secondary covert that may sometimes be visible. The mostly gray tail has extensive white spots in all plumages; from below the tail appears largely white, with a blackish tip. Males are brighter than females, and adults are brighter than first-year birds; there is little seasonal change in plumage, although bill color changes significantly with season.

This heavy-bodied warbler has a heavy, long spikelike bill. The tail is relatively short. The dark, beady eye stands out boldly on the plain face.

SIMILAR SPECIES

The bright golden yellow coloration of the head and underparts, combined with the greenish back, grayish wings, and large white tail spots should make identification straightforward. The Prothonotary's shape is quite different from other largely yellow warblers; note the long spikelike bill, overall heavy appearance, and relatively short tail. Compare especially with **BLUE-WINGED WARBLER** (which always shows a dark eye line and whitish wing bars) and **YELLOW WARBLER** (which has yellow, not white, tail spots, yellow edges to wing coverts and flight feathers, and a smaller bill). Female **HOODED WARBLER** may vaguely suggest Prothonotary, but has a much longer tail and a suggestion of a dark frame around the yellow face.

VOICE

SONG is ringing and clear with repetitious, slightly upslurred notes, such as *sweet-sweet-sweet-sweet-sweet* or *tweet-tweet-tweet-tweet-tweet-tweet-tweet*. An individual usually sings the same song but may vary the number of notes from about 5 to 12. Different individuals have slightly differing note qualities. This is one of the easiest warbler songs to learn. Rarely given is a flight song, delivered with fluttering flight and wing and tail raised; it resembles the typical song but ends with a warbling phrase. The **CALL NOTE** is a dry, loud *chip,* suggestive of Hooded Warbler or Swainson's Warbler, or a softer version of a Louisiana Waterthrush note. The **FLIGHT NOTE** is a loud *seeep* without any buzzy tones. This note is also given by perched birds.

Foraging is rather deliberate and usually low; no tail-wagging behavior is shown. Much time is spent probing around trunks and branches, rotten timber, and around the edges of pools. Sometimes forages higher in trees; on average, males forage higher than females. Males habitually sing motionlessly from a high but inconspicuous perch. The flight is direct and rapid, often just over the water's surface. Feeds mainly on insects, especially aquatic forms. Occasionally takes small crustaceans and snails. Nectar and fruit are important components of the winter diet, including fruit such as oranges that have initially been sliced open by parrots; it occasionally visits hummingbird feeders.

The **NEST** is usually in a tree cavity over or near water; in some habitats nests may be up to several hundred meters away from water. Most nests are in natural cavities or crevices, but woodpecker holes and man-made objects such as nest boxes (including those made from milk cartons, old cans, or pails, etc.) are also readily used. Most nests less than about 6 ft. off the ground, but nests may be 25 ft. or higher. Moss is important in nest construction. The clutch size is relatively large for a warbler, with up to eight eggs; Prothonotaries are frequently double-brooded in the southern portions of the breeding range.

In winter they may form male-female pairs and may roost in groups, often staging in trees late in the afternoon before flying to roost. There is circumstantial evidence that trans-Gulf migrants may migrate together in monospecific flocks, maintaining flock cohesion through call notes.

Habitat

BREEDING habitat consists of wooded swamps, flooded bottomland forests, and riparian corridors along streams. Slow-moving water, pools, or ponds are typical habitat components. The presence of dead snags or stumps (or man-made nest cavities) is essential. In southeastern forests dominant trees include cypress, gum, and tupelo. Farther north, a variety of tree associations are used, all of which are associated with ponds, pools, or slow-moving streams. Willows, maples, ash, cottonwoods, American elms, black oak, and black gum may be locally important.

WINTERS in wet lowland woods around streams, ponds, and swamps, including mangroves; also frequently found in drier scrub well away from water.

MIGRANTS may occur in a variety of well-vegetated habitats; transients in Central America are sometimes noted in foothills and highlands, although most occur in the lowlands. Migrants show a preference for wet wooded habitats.

▼ DISTRIBUTION

BREEDS locally within appropriate lowland habitat over most of the e. U.S. except the northern tier of states and New England. Much more abundant and widespread in the lowlands of the southeastern states; very local within the northern part of the breeding range. Breeds locally north to se. and s.-cen. Minn., cen. Wisc., cen. Mich., n. Ohio, nw. Pa. (rare and local elsewhere in Pa.), s. Ont. (a few localities, mostly along north shore of Lake Erie), n. N.J., and N.Y. (very rare and local, including recent nestings on Long Island). Rare nestings have been recorded north of this range, in R.I., Conn., and Mass. The breeding range extends west in river floodplains to Iowa, se. Neb. (rare and local), e. Kans., cen. Okla., and through the e. third of Texas; there are old possible breeding records from se. S.D. Breeds south to the Gulf Coast from the upper Texas coast east to cen. Fla., and along the Atlantic Coast to cen. Fla.; also breeds very locally in s. Fla. (Big Cypress Swamp). Absent from the higher Appalachian Mtns. Individual singing males often appear beyond the northern edge of the breeding range, and there are scattered breeding records north of the range indicated above. This frequent spring overshooting combined with the males' habit of building "dummy nests" makes determination of the northern limits of the breeding range difficult.

WINTERS mainly from s. Mexico (rare, from s. Veracruz south, but mainly on Yucatán peninsula) and n. Honduras (scarce) south to Panama, Colombia, and n. Venezuela. A few also winter east to Trinidad and Tobago, Guyana, and Suriname, and south to nw. Ecuador. Recorded once in Brazil and once on the Galápagos Is. Rare to uncommon winter visitor throughout the Greater and Lesser Antilles; it is casual in winter on Bermuda, where it is a regular spring and fall migrant. North of the main wintering range there are winter records for Fla. (especially in early winter) and coastal Texas. There are December records for coastal Miss. and La., and exceptional midwinter records for Ill. (Chicago, December to January) and Ga. (January). There are three records of wintering birds in coastal Calif.

SPRING MIGRATION is mainly trans-Gulf; typical spring arrival on the Gulf Coast is after about 15 March, but there are a few records back to the first week of March (exceptionally to 23 February in S.C.). At least in Panama, this species is the earliest of the North American warblers to depart in spring, so these early

Gulf Coast arrivals are not surprising. Migration peaks on the Gulf Coast in the second week of April, with a few birds still passing through in early May (exceptional records of migrants to about 20 May in Fla.). Migration is not very evident north of the immediate Gulf Coast since the species is so widespread in the Southeast as a breeder, and birds are only rarely noted away from breeding habitat. Birds at the latitude of s. Ark., s. Mo., Tenn., and s. Ky. usually arrive on nesting territories in early April (a few in late March). In Kans., n. Ky., s. Ill., and s. Ind., arrivals are typically around 15–20 April, and most arrive in s. Ohio and cen. Ill. in late April. At the northern edge of the breeding range they arrive in early May, with a few earlier records. In the Mid-Atlantic states birds generally arrive during the second week of April on the coastal plain, and about 10 days later in inland regions. Overshoots north of the mapped breeding range in spring are frequent, and usually occur in May. There are a number of early spring records (late March and early April) along the Atlantic Coast from N.Y. to N.S.; these may represent storm-blown birds.

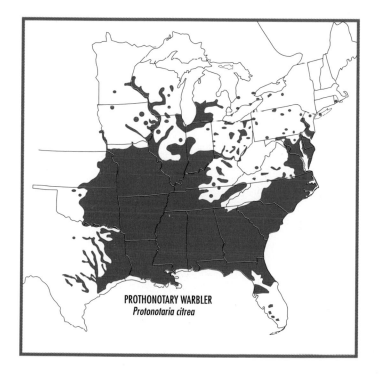

PROTHONOTARY WARBLER
Protonotaria citrea

FALL MIGRATION is not pronounced, but rather is marked by the disappearance of birds from the breeding grounds by late August or early September. There are scattered records in the Midwest and on the Atlantic Coast into October (exceptionally to late November in Ill., Ind., and Conn.). In Fla. and along the Gulf Coast birds are noted away from breeding areas by early August. Peak tower kills at n. Fla. stations are from about 10 August to 20 September, and the latest migrants in these areas are usually noted in early October. May be numerous well off Atlantic Coast in fall, with maximum of 23 per day noted in August in Bermuda.

Regular **VAGRANT** in western North America. On the Great Plains it is a rare spring and casual fall vagrant; there are about 40 records for Colo. (about ⅔ for spring, in May and early June). Casual on the n. Great Plains and Prairie Provinces. There are 158 records for Calif. (about 80 percent in fall, mainly late August to late October; most spring records are from late May and early June); recorded from all western states except Idaho; there are 40 records for Ariz. Regular spring overshooting north of normal breeding range in Midwest and Atlantic Coast noted above. Vagrant well north of breeding range in spring and fall (Que., Canadian Maritimes, Nfld., Lab., James Bay in n. Ont.). Vagrants noted in Baja Calif. (Los Coronados Is.), Sonora (Alamos in April), Jalisco, and Clipperton Is. (several fall records).

▥ STATUS AND CONSERVATION

Although populations are largely stable, this species is probably limited by nest site availability, and reproduction is often severely curtailed by heavy spring floods. The destruction of floodplain

Prothonotary Warbler. Adult male in Ohio in May. (Photo: Steve and Dave Maslowski)

forests has caused important local declines in the Mississippi River Valley; wetland drainage has probably reduced populations in the Southeast, but reservoir construction may have locally benefited populations. Some cowbird parasitism has been noted, with rates as high as 20 percent recorded, but as a cavity nester this species is perhaps immune to heavy parasitism. House Wrens often destroy eggs and usurp nest cavities; the southward spread of breeding House Wrens has perhaps had local effects on this warbler.

SUBSPECIES

No variation described; no subspecies recognized.

TAXONOMIC RELATIONSHIPS

Although generally considered to be related to the genus *Dendroica*, the monotypic genus *Protonotaria* has no certain affinities.

PLUMAGES AND MOLTS

SPRING ADULT MALE: The brightest plumage. Head (including nape), breast, belly, and sides are bright golden yellow with a variable orange tint. The golden head and nape contrast sharply with the green back; the green upperparts have a mustard yellow tint to them. The rump and uppertail coverts are gray. The undertail coverts are clean white; the lower belly and vent area are usually lightly washed with yellow, but may be bright yellow in some individuals. There is a slight grayish tint to the rear flanks. The

Prothonotary Warbler. Adult female in Florida in April. (Photo: Kevin T. Karlson)

lesser and median coverts are broadly edged green, contrasting with the blue-gray greater coverts and flight feathers. The rectrices are mostly gray with large white spots on the inner webs of all but the central pair; the upper sides of the rectrices show blackish shaft streaks, broadening slightly toward the tip. **FIRST SPRING MALE:** Similar to spring adult male and often not separable in the field. The hindneck shows a suffusion of olive green, contrasting with the yellow crown, but is still yellower than the green back. The flight feathers of the wing are slightly tinged brownish, showing more contrast with the gray greater coverts than in adults. **SPRING ADULT FEMALE:** Generally similar to spring adult male, but the crown and nape are extensively washed greenish yellow, contrasting only slightly with the green back. The yellow of the underparts is bright, but lacks the deep golden or orange tint shown by most spring males. The yellow of females averages less extensive in the lower belly and vent region than in males. There is less white in the rectrices than in males, usually confined to the outer three pairs. **FIRST SPRING FEMALE:** Crown and nape are olive, showing little or no contrast with the green upperparts. The cheeks and sides of the neck are also washed with olive. The olive of the upperparts is washed with a slight mustard-brown tint. The yellow of the underparts is relatively dull, with a very slight olive tinge on the face, flanks, and belly. The yellow is the least extensive in the lower belly region of all plumages. The flight feathers have a slight brownish tinge, contrasting with the gray greater coverts. This plumage (including first fall birds) shows the least extensive white in the tail. **FALL ADULT MALE:** Virtually identical to spring adult male, but with slight olive tips to the rear crown and nape. Note seasonal changes in bill color (see Bare Parts, below). **FIRST FALL MALE:** Like first spring male, but plumage fresher; a few young males (fall and spring) may show a strong olive wash through the crown and auriculars, with little contrast between nape and back. These birds cannot be distinguished from females. **FALL ADULT FEMALE:** Like spring adult female, but with slightly

Prothonotary Warbler. First spring female in California in May. (Photo: Brian E. Small)

more extensive olive tipping to yellow feathers. **FIRST FALL FEMALE:** Similar to first spring female, but plumage fresher. **JUVENILE:** Generally dull brownish olive above and dull yellowish olive below, becoming paler on the belly and undertail coverts. **BARE PARTS:** The bills of males are entirely black from about March to June; in spring females the bill is blackish on the maxilla but shows some brown on the mandible. Immatures and winter birds show much brown on the maxilla and light pinkish brown on the mandible. Eyes are dark brown. The legs and feet of adults are dark gray; immatures show paler, browner legs.

The prebasic molt takes place on the breeding grounds from June to August; it is complete in adults but in birds of the year does not involve the flight feathers. No prealternate molt has been described; the very slight seasonal change in appearance may be due mainly to feather wear.

 REFERENCES

GENERAL: Walkinshaw 1953.

DISTRIBUTION: Austen et al. 1994, Petit and Tarvin 1990.

ECOLOGY, BEHAVIOR, VOCALIZATIONS, AND CONSERVATION: Bohlen 1989 (local declines of Prothonotary Warbler), Lefebvre et al. 1992, Moore 1990, Peterjohn and Rice 1991 (local declines of Prothonotary Warbler), Petit 1989, Petit et al. 1990, Walkinshaw 1938 and 1941.

PLUMAGES, MOLTS, AND MORPHOLOGY: Kowalski 1986.

WORM-EATING WARBLER PL. 21

Helmitheros vermivorus

5.25 in. (13.3 cm). The outstanding plumage feature of this olive-brown and rich buff-colored warbler is the presence of two pairs of distinct blackish stripes on the head. This stocky, long-billed warbler has a distinctive preference for foraging by probing into clusters of dead leaves. It usually remains at low or intermediate heights within shaded woodlands, only rarely descending to the ground (where it hops, instead of walking like the other "brown" warbler species). The Worm-eating Warbler breeds mainly on heavily wooded deciduous slopes in the Appalachian region, and locally in hilly areas of the southern states.

 DESCRIPTION

Males and females are identical in plumage. All individuals share the following features: The upperparts, wings, and tail are uniform olive-brown; the underparts are buffy, often deepening to a rich pumpkin-buff on the breast. Distinct blackish stripes extend from just in front of the eye back along the upper border of the auricular, and from the bill back along the sides of the crown. The crown and supercilium are buffy. The undertail coverts have dark dusky centers often visible in the field. Plumage variation is not easily correlated with age, sex, or season, although first-year birds can often be told by the presence of cinnamon tips to the tertials (and in the hand by their more pointed rectrices).

Structurally, this is a heavy-bodied warbler with a relatively short tail. The bill is heavy at the base, long, and spikelike; there is a very slight decurvature to the culmen. As with many warblers, males average slightly larger than the females, but this difference is not detectable in the field.

 ## SIMILAR SPECIES

A very distinctive species, not likely to be confused with any other North American warbler. The SWAINSON'S WARBLER is generally similar in body plumage, though browner (less olive) above; it lacks the bold head stripes, showing instead an unmarked rich brown crown. Swainson's is a larger and even longer-billed bird that feeds mostly on or near the ground. Superficially similar in plumage to the Worm-eating are some of the duller *Basileuterus* warblers of the Neotropics, especially the THREE-STRIPED WARBLER (*B. tristriatus*), which it marginally overlaps in winter in Costa Rica and Panama. Northernmost populations of Three-striped, which overlap Worm-eating, show black in the cheeks and are more yellowish, less buffy, on the underparts. GOLDEN-CROWNED WARBLER is much more yellowish on the underparts.

Behavior and bill shape easily distinguish the Worm-eating Warbler from various sparrows (Emberizidae), such as the OLIVE SPARROW (*Arremonops rufivirgatus*), that are superficially similar in plumage.

 ## VOICE

The SONG is a loud, rapid, dry trill very suggestive of the song of a Chipping Sparrow (*Spizella passerina*), but perhaps a bit drier. Song is perhaps best distinguished from Chipping Sparrow's by habitat of singer, with Worm-eating singing in dense shaded woodlands and Chipping in open woods, orchards, or field borders. The song is mechanical in quality, consisting of up to 27 notes per second; the length of the song varies considerably, but the pitch of the trill does not change noticeably through the song. A rarely given flight song is softer but more varied in pitch than the standard song; it is given as the singer flies through the woods in level flight below the canopy. Worm-eating Warblers do very little singing in spring migration, and may reduce singing on the breeding grounds earlier in summer than most other warblers. Compare the song also with that of Pine Warbler; Pine's trill is more musical.

The most frequently heard **CALL NOTE** is also the **FLIGHT NOTE**, a double *zeep-zeep* or *zeet-zeet*, or *zit-zit*, sometimes given in a series. The chip note is dull but rather loud, and slightly slurred; it is suggestive of chip notes of Black-and-white and Black-throated Gray Warblers. This call is infrequently heard away from the breeding grounds.

Behavior

While foraging, this species specializes on dead leaves, especially but not exclusively during the nonbreeding season. It uses the long spikelike bill to probe into clusters of dead leaves for caterpillars and other insect larvae, spiders, and other arthropod prey. They typically seek out hanging clusters of dead leaves to the exclusion of other foliage within their wooded habitats, and can be quite acrobatic when feeding at such clusters. Occasionally they will creep along branches and trunks in a manner suggestive of the Black-and-white Warbler. Most foraging is performed around 3–15 ft., but occasionally higher and rarely also in leaf litter on the ground. Foraging averages higher in spring, but is increasingly limited to the understory as the breeding season progresses. Although many sources refer to this species' habit of walking on the ground with the tail partly cocked, we see no evidence that this species ever walks. On the rare occasions when Worm-eating Warblers forage on the ground, they hop rather than walk. Singing birds may perch motionless high in the foliage, often well above their normal foraging sites.

The **NEST** is located on the ground, well hidden among piles of leaf litter at the base of a shrub or sapling, usually on a hillside. The nest is constructed mainly of dead leaves and lined with finer fibers, grasses, hairs, and hair moss stalks.

Habitat

BREEDING habitat consists of deciduous or mixed woodlands on gentle or steep slopes, along ravines, and less commonly in swampy and drier mixed lowland woods. A dense, junglelike understory is typical of most breeding habitats. The preferred tree associations vary through the species' range and include oak, beech, maple, hickory, chestnut, magnolia, hemlock, and pine. Densities are higher in wetter woodlands, but in some areas Worm-eating Warblers breed on drier slopes of oak-pine or oak-chestnut, and in dune forests of beech and hemlock. This species appears to require extensive tracts of forest and is adversely affected by forest fragmentation.

On the WINTERING grounds, a variety of deciduous and evergreen forests are occupied, with the species showing a strong preference for dead leaf clusters and tangled vines when searching for insect prey. Winters mostly in lowland and foothill regions. Habitat choice is less specialized during MIGRATION, but fairly dense woodlands with a well-developed understory and a plentiful supply of dead leaves are favored.

◆ DISTRIBUTION

BREEDS primarily in the Appalachian states and adjacent regions from Pa., s. N.Y., sw. and e. Mass., and R.I. south through Md. and Va. locally to S.C., cen. Ga., sw. Ala., Miss., and cen. La. Breeds west locally through unglaciated portions of the Midwest to cen. Ohio, s. Ind., n. Ill., cen. (locally n.) Mo., se. Iowa, and Ark. To the north there are isolated small breeding populations in sw. Mich. and sw. Wisc., and in the South it has nested in e. Texas, se. La., and the Fla. Panhandle.

WINTERS from e. and s. Mexico south to Panama, and in the West Indies. In Mexico occurs mainly from s. Tamaulipas and Veracruz south through the Yucatán peninsula, and on the Pacific slope north to Oaxaca (rarely to Nayarit); winters southward in lowland and foothill regions through Central America to w. and cen. Panama. Also winters from the Bahamas south and east through the Greater Antilles to the Virgin Is.; winters regularly in small numbers on Bermuda. Recorded twice in the n. Lesser Antilles (St. Martin, Antigua). There is one recent winter record from Venezuela. Winters rarely in Fla. (mainly in south), and casually along the Texas coast and Rio Grande Valley; there are three December records for La. There are several winter records for Calif., north to Humboldt Co.

In SPRING MIGRATION, travels on a rather broad front from the Texas coast to Fla. The first migrants are noted along the Gulf Coast by late March, with a few records as early as mid-March; birds have also been noted on the southernmost breeding grounds (La., Ala.) in mid-March. The peak spring migration on the Gulf Coast is during the first three weeks of April, with stragglers noted to mid-May. Arrives in the southern Midwest region during the latter half of April; in the more northerly parts of the Midwest breeding range usually arrives in late April or early May (exceptionally in early April). Arrivals in the Northeast (N.Y., s. New England) are typically in late April or early May, rarely as early as mid-April. There is a regular late spring pattern (mostly late April to mid-May) of overshoots north of the breeding range in the Great Lakes region (north to Minn., s. Ont.). Casual in spring north to N.S. and Que.

FALL MIGRATION is rather early, and numbers are usually small; on average, the fall movement is slightly more easterly than that of spring. Fall migrants have been noted away from breeding grounds as early as the beginning of July, with a more substantial movement starting late in July. Peak numbers are seen on the mid-Atlantic Coast in the latter half of August; the fall peak along the Gulf Coast is in mid- to late September, with a few occurring to mid-October. In contrast to spring, there are few fall records from north of the breeding range. In most regions north of the Gulf Coast this species is casual after mid-September. Late fall stragglers have been noted rarely in the Midwest into early

WORM-EATING WARBLER
Helmitheros vermivorus

November (there are three exceptional mid-November records for Minn.).

Casual or very rare in Que., the Canadian Maritimes, Nfld., and Saint-Pierre.

A rare but regular **VAGRANT** in the West from Colo. to w. Texas. Very rare in Calif. (where there are 86 records, with over half from late August to late November); also very rare in Ariz. (33 records) and N.M. (30 records). Casual elsewhere in the West, but unrecorded in Wash., Idaho, Mont., the western Canadian provinces, and Alaska. One fall record for northern Baja Calif.

STATUS AND CONSERVATION

This species can be quite common during the breeding season in appropriate habitat. Densities in deciduous forests of wooded slopes in Maryland have been reported to be as high as 40–60 pairs per 100 acres. Regional declines have been noted, almost certainly as a result of forest fragmentation. This species is a frequent cowbird host.

SUBSPECIES

None recognized.

TAXONOMIC RELATIONSHIPS

The Worm-eating is superficially suggestive of Swainson's Warbler in plumage and shape. Some experts have actually merged the Swainson's Warbler's monotypic genus *Limnothlypis* into *Helmitheros* based on some structural similarities, but there is no good evidence for the close affinities of Worm-eating to Swainson's. In many aspects of shape, foraging behavior, nest site, and vocalizations, Worm-eating suggests a heavy-billed *Vermivora* and is probably best placed near that genus. It is argued that the name *Vermivora americ* should apply to the Worm-eating Warbler, necessitating the use of *Helminthophila* for those species usually placed in the genus *Vermivora*; this course has not been adopted by the AOU.

PLUMAGES AND MOLTS

SPRING ADULT: Forehead, crown, lores, supercilium, and underparts rich buff, brightest on the sides of the throat and on the breast. Buff of crown and auricular slightly tinged with olive. Chin and upper throat pale buff or nearly whitish. Flanks strongly tinged with dull olive. Undertail coverts

Worm-eating Warbler. In Florida in April. (Photo: Kevin T. Karlson)

with dusky centers and broad buffy white tips. The color of the underparts varies among individuals from pale buff to a very rich buff, sometimes deepening to a bright orange-buff on the breast. Conspicuous dull blackish lateral crown stripes extend well back on the hindneck. A dull blackish transocular stripe begins just in front of the eye and extends back beyond the rear border of the auricular. The upperparts, wings, and tail are uniformly dull olive green with a slight gray tinge. The bend of the wing is pale buffy yellow. **FIRST SPRING:** Indistinguishable from spring adults, as cinnamon tips to the tertials shown in first fall and winter have worn away by early spring. In the hand, shows more tapered and worn rectrices than spring adults. **FALL ADULT:** Nearly identical to spring adults, but in this fresher plumage averages somewhat brighter olive above and richer buff below. **FIRST FALL:** Nearly identical to fall adults, but the tertials show inconspicuous cinnamon tips that may be retained as late as February or March; in the hand, the rectrices appear more tapered. **JUVENILE:** Generally brown above and buffy below, with postocular and crown stripes brownish. Strong cinnamon tips to the tertials and median and greater wing coverts. **BARE PARTS:** Bill blackish brown on upper mandible, pale pinkish gray on lower mandible and cutting edge of upper mandible. Eyes dark brown. Legs and feet pinkish.

The prebasic molt takes place on the breeding grounds, from June to August; it is complete in adults but does not involve flight feathers in hatching-year birds. There is no prealternate molt.

 REFERENCES

ECOLOGY, BEHAVIOR, VOCALIZATIONS, AND CONSERVATION: Greenberg 1987a, b, Whitcomb et al. 1981.

Limnothlypis swainsonii

5.25 in. (13.3 cm). This is a subtly marked but distinctively shaped brown warbler of wooded swamplands and canebrakes of the southeastern lowlands and rhododendron thickets and other heavily wooded areas of the central and southern Appalachian Mountains. The exceptionally long bill is straight along the culmen and angled slightly upward on the lower mandible. This uncommon and furtive species often remains within dense underbrush; it is most easily detected by its ringing song. Perhaps best observed during spring migration at migrant traps in Florida and along the Gulf Coast.

 ## DESCRIPTION

Generally brown above, with a rich brown crown and hindneck. A long, distinct supercilium is dull whitish or very pale yellowish white; there is a dark brown transocular line. The underparts vary from dull whitish to very pale yellowish, with a suffusion of gray-brown on the sides and flanks. The wings and tail are unmarked brown. The sexes are identical in plumage, and aging is not possible in the field and difficult in the hand. There is no significant seasonal change in plumage. Individual variation in plumage mainly involves the extent and depth of yellow on the underparts, richness of the crown color, and richness of the olive-gray wash on the breast and flanks.

Quite distinctive in structure, being rather large and heavy bodied with a rather short tail. Notable is the long, spikelike bill that is straight along the culmen; the culmen meets the uniquely flattened forehead to yield a head silhouette quite different from that of other warblers. The lower mandible angles slightly upward about a third of the way toward the tip.

 ## SIMILAR SPECIES

Not likely to be confused with any other warbler given reasonable views, but the species' furtive habits make observation difficult. With poor views might be mistaken for **WORM-EATING WARBLER** (which shows bold head stripes and richer, buffier underparts) or waterthrushes (which are heavily spotted on the underparts). The **LOUISIANA WATERTHRUSH**, in addition to superficial similarity of the upperparts, has a song that may closely resemble that of Swainson's. The brown upperparts and prominent supercilium may suggest **CAROLINA** or **BEWICK'S WREN** (the latter rare within Swainson's range) to beginning birders.

♪ Voice

The **SONG** is loud and distinctive, being by far the best way to locate this species in spring and summer. The 2–4 clear, downslurred opening notes strongly suggest the beginning of the song of the Louisiana Waterthrush. These introductory notes are followed in Swainson's by several (usually three) more rapid, descending notes. The song is sometimes represented *whee whee whip-poor-will* or *teo teo teo teo teedle-de teo*. In contrast, the latter part of the Louisiana Waterthrush song typically consists of short, weak sputtering notes. Swainson's song is rather ventriloquial, and the singer can be hard to locate. A whisper song is also periodically heard throughout the breeding season.

The **CALL NOTE** is a distinctive *chip*, somewhat louder and sweeter than the note of Prothonotary (which often shares the same habitat). Some notes are flatter (*tshup*), suggestive of a Kentucky Warbler or a soft Northern Waterthrush. The **FLIGHT NOTE** is a very high, thin, slightly buzzy *swees*, sometimes doubled.

Behavior

This is a skulking and rather lethargic warbler that is usually very difficult to observe. When foraging, it is usually on the ground, shuffling (not clearly hopping) through the leaf litter and among fallen branches and the bases of tree trunks, often with a quivering movement of the rear parts. Foraging birds frequently pick up and overturn fallen leaves, inspecting the underside for insect larvae, spiders, millipedes, or other prey. Often they may almost become buried in the leaf litter, and they are sometimes detected by the sound of rustling leaves. Rarely they may forage in shallow, slow-moving water. When flushed, birds may sit motionlessly, thrushlike, for long periods. The flight is swift and strong, but flights are usually short. Singing birds often sit fairly high in trees, remaining on a song perch for a considerable time; they may also sing from on or near the ground or in flight, where songs typically run together. Singing perches are usually well concealed by foliage. Wintering birds will respond to playbacks of tape-recorded songs by approaching and calling, but only rarely by singing.

The **NEST** is located from just above ground level to about 10 ft. in dense forest understory. Lowland birds often build in cane or palmettos, whereas highland birds use a variety of shrubs, tangles, or vines. The nest is a bulky mass of leaves, needles, mosses, and grasses. The eggs are often unmarked whitish (unusual among warblers). This species may occasionally be double-brooded; one case of probable polygyny has been recorded.

BREEDS in two very different habitat types. Lowland populations are found in wet deciduous woods of the Southeast, particularly around swamp edges and along stream systems where the ground is muddy or with small pools; they avoid extensively flooded swamps. Although this bird is generally considered a canebrake specialist and is characteristically found in patches of the giant cane *Arundinaria tecta* and *A. gigantea*, it also breeds in areas lacking cane as long as there is appropriate dense undergrowth such as palmetto or sweet pepperbush. Its lowland habitat is locally distributed. Highland populations occur up to about 3,000 ft. in along brooks and streams in well-shaded, damp ravines and canyons where rhododendron (*Rhododendron catawbiense*) is the key understory plant species. These montane habitats have a moderately dense understory but a sparse ground cover. Dominant taller trees include hemlock and various hardwoods.

WINTERS in the dense undergrowth of humid or swampy forests, montane forests, requiring extensive leaf litter; also winters locally in wooded gardens and mangroves.

MIGRANTS prefer fairly dense woods where they shuffle about in the leaf litter. Coastal cheniers, such as at High Is., Texas, provide habitat in which migrants are most frequently noted.

 Distribution

BREEDS locally in appropriate habitat from se. Okla., s. Mo., extreme s. Ill. (nearly extirpated), Ky. (mainly e.), Tenn. (except cen.), W. Va., and se. Md. (Pocomoke Swamp) south to se. Texas, the Gulf Coast, Fla. Panhandle, and the Fla. peninsula south to about Gainesville. Has summered in appropriate habitat north to Fayette Co., sw. Pa. Populations in the Appalachians from W. Va. through e. Ky., e. Tenn., w. portions of N.C. and S.C., and n. Ga. are somewhat isolated from lowland populations of lower Mississippi Valley and Gulf and s. Atlantic coasts. Birds remain and sing on the breeding grounds well into August, and some may remain into early September.

WINTERS primarily in the West Indies, especially the Greater Antilles; the largest known wintering populations are on Jamaica. Small numbers winter east to the Virgin Is., and the species has wintered several times on Bermuda. Casual in winter in the Bahamas, where it is a rare migrant. In Mexico, winters on the Yucatán peninsula, and has also been recorded in Veracruz; also winters in Belize, and recorded in late winter on Swan Is. off Honduras.

Swainson's is a broad front **MIGRANT**, but its true patterns are difficult to determine since migrants are seldom detected away from a handful of sites where they tend to concentrate.

SPRING MIGRATION typically begins on the Gulf Coast in late March, but records extend back to mid-March in Fla. and, exceptionally, early March in Texas. Migrants are noted along the entire Gulf Coast (though scarce on the Louisiana coast) and throughout Fla., as well as in coastal e. Mexico. The spring migration peak in this region is during the second and third weeks of April; migrants are noted routinely to the end of April, rarely in early May, and exceptionally to the middle of May. Birds arrive on the southern breeding grounds around mid-April and on the northern breeding grounds around the third week of April or later. **FALL MIGRATION** is largely unnoticed away from migrant traps (and tower kills) in Fla. and the Gulf Coast. The southward movement is relatively late for a southerly-breeding warbler. The first birds are found away from breeding habitat on the Gulf Coast in August, but tower kills suggest that the fall peak is from around 10

SWAINSON'S WARBLER
Limnothlypis swainsonii

September to 10 October, with records to late October and, exceptionally, early November. There is a 6 December specimen from the Florida Keys.

VAGRANT north and west of the breeding range in spring, with overshoots casually noted mainly from late April through May north and west to Ill., Wisc. (once), Ohio, N.J., N.Y., Mass., Ont., Kans., and Neb. This species is recorded as a vagrant north of the breeding range far less frequently than other southern-breeding warblers. There are three to four convincing late spring reports for Colo. (one of which is supported by a specimen), two spring records for e. N.M., and a 12 June 1981 record near Springerville in e.-cen. Ariz. **CASUAL** in fall in the Northeast, with September and October records for N.J. and a 9 October 1972 record for Seal Is., N.S. It is unrecorded in Calif.

STATUS AND CONSERVATION

Generally uncommon, but in optimal habitat densities of up to 44 singing males per square mile have been reported. The breeding range has contracted in some areas, as in Illinois (where nearly extirpated), s. Missouri, and ne. Oklahoma. Habitat degradation is the most important cause of such declines; the clearing of cane from the forest understory can cause this species to disappear. Brood parasitism pressure from cowbirds is increasing because of habitat fragmentation and the continued spread of Brown-headed and Shiny cowbirds; cowbird parasitism may be a factor in local declines. On the winter grounds considered widespread and reltively common in the Blue Mountains of Jamaica. Up to 25,000 birds estimated to winter in the Blue and John Crow Mtns. National Park there.

SUBSPECIES

The highland nesting population in the Appalachian Mtns. has been described as a separate subspecies, *alta*, based on the slightly whiter (less yellow) underparts and duller, more brownish upperparts. The Appalachian breeders are quite distinct in habitat preference and geography, but the characters of *alta* are also shown through the remainder of the species' range, and most current workers do not recognize it.

TAXONOMIC RELATIONSHIPS

Some authors merge *Limnothlypis* into *Helmitheros* (the genus containing Worm-eating Warbler); these two warblers are characterized by a heavy, long spikelike bill, but details of bill shape differ, and foraging behavior, nest site selection, and vocalizations are strikingly different. We see no justification for this generic merger.

PLUMAGES AND MOLTS

SPRING ADULT: Forehead, crown, and hindneck warm brown to russet brown. Most individuals show an inconspicuous pale buffy median streak on the forehead just above the bill, visible at close range in the field. A long and fairly distinct pale creamy yellow to creamy white supercilium extends from the bill to well beyond the eye. This supercilium is set off by a gray-brown transocular line that begins at the bill. The entire upperparts are medium brown with a slight olive tint; the color of the upperparts contrasts little with the crown and hindneck. The chin and throat vary from pale creamy yellow to dull whitish. This color continues down through the remainder of the underparts but is interrupted by a variable wash of gray-brown, which is most extensive on the sides of the breast but may continue across the breast as indistinct mottling. The sides and flanks are also washed with gray-brown. The wings and tail are unmarked brown. **FIRST SPRING:** Indistinguishable in the field from spring adults. In the hand, rectrices and primaries may appear more worn and tapered, but this distinction is seldom reliable. **FALL ADULT:** Essentially identical to spring adults. There is a tendency for fresh fall birds to average yellower on the underparts and show more of a dark wash on the breast, sides, and flanks, but individual variation largely obscures this difference. **FIRST FALL:** Distinctions from adults as for first spring birds. **JUVENILE:** Like a laxly plumaged adult but with face pattern obscured and with buffy wing bars. **BARE PARTS:** Bill pale flesh on the lower mandible and sides of the upper mandible;

Swainson's Warbler. In Texas in April. (Photo: Larry Sansone)

somewhat darker brown along the culmen. Iris dark brown. Legs and feet fleshy.

The prebasic molt occurs on the breeding grounds from June to August; it is complete in adults but does not involve the flight feathers in hatching-year birds. There is apparently no prealternate molt.

REFERENCES

GENERAL: Brown and Dickson 1994, Meanley 1971.
DISTRIBUTION: Graves 1996a.
ECOLOGY, BEHAVIOR, VOCALIZATIONS, AND CONSERVATION: Graves 1992 and 1996a, Kirkconnell et al. 1996, Meanley 1966, Thomas et al. 1996.
SYSTEMATICS: Meanley and Bond 1950.

OVENBIRD PL. 21

Seiurus aurocapillus

5.75 in. (14.6 cm). This well-studied, thrushlike warbler is common and widespread in deciduous and mixed forests of boreal and eastern North America. It spends much of its time walking on the shady forest floor among the leaf litter and fallen logs. Its loud, repetitious *tea-cher!* song is one of the most characteristic sounds of its forested breeding grounds, and the species is far more often heard than seen. The olive upperparts and black-spotted white underparts are distinctive, as is the head pattern of a conspicuous white eye-ring and blackish lateral crown stripes. The orangish median crown stripe can be hard to see. The common name comes from the domed nest, which bears a resemblance to a Dutch oven. Several lines of evidence suggest that the Ovenbird may not be especially closely related to the waterthrushes, although it is usually placed in the same genus.

 DESCRIPTION

Generally olive to olive-gray above and white below, with bold black spotting on the underparts aligned into rows. All post-juvenal plumages show a conspicuous white eye-ring, thin blackish malar stripe, and blackish lateral crown stripes enclosing a dull orange central crown stripe. There very little variation in plumage due to age or season. The sexes are essentially identical, and the plumage accounts below apply to both males and females; females may average slightly paler orange on the median crown stripe, and white markings at the tips of the outer tail feathers may be more extensive in males. Minor geographical variation primarily involves the color of the upperparts. At least three melanistic specimens have been taken, each showing excessive blackish pigment. These birds have, to varying degrees, black or blackish blotches on the face, breast, sides, back, and flight feathers.

This is a robust, almost "pot-bellied" warbler with a moderately short tail. The eye is large and thrushlike, and the legs are stout and long.

SIMILAR SPECIES

Ovenbirds are unlikely to be confused with any other warblers except perhaps **NORTHERN** and **LOUISIANA WATERTHRUSHES**. The two waterthrushes are similar to the Ovenbird in their walking behavior (although their gait is less "high-stepping"), but they habitually bob their tail rather than cocking it upward as the Ovenbird does. Ovenbirds prefer the leaf litter of deep forest floors rather than the aquatic situations preferred by waterthrushes. Both waterthrushes show conspicuous superciliums and lack eye-rings. The black lateral crown stripes are absent on waterthrushes, and the dorsal coloration is brownish in waterthrushes and olive or olive-gray in the Ovenbird. From below, the Ovenbird is more heavily marked with blackish spots, whereas the waterthrushes have less organized brownish spotting or thinner striping. **THRUSHES** of the genus *Catharus* are superficially similar but run or hop rather than walk and lack the bold crown pattern of the Ovenbird. Note also the remote similarity of **PIPITS** *(Anthus)*, which are unlikely to be seen in the interior of forests.

VOICE

The distinctive and frequently heard **SONG** is a repetitive series of about 8–10 two-parted notes, best represented as *TEA-cher TEA-cher TEA-cher*... or (more rarely) *cher-TEE cher-TEE cher-TEE*... The song is loud and ringing, building to a crescendo. There is some individual and geographical variation in song pattern, and some birds give a simpler *teach! teach! teach! teach!*... Females are rarely known to sing. The song is usually delivered from a fixed perch, from just above the ground to 30 ft. or more up in the canopy. Occasionally birds will sing from the ground (at least in spring migration). Territorial males persistently counter-sing, one bird singing immediately upon the completion of its neighbor's song. Songs are occasionally heard after dark.

A flight song is often delivered during the breeding season; the male ascends 10–60 ft. above treetop level and hovers and flutters with spread wings and tail while singing; a similar song, the "attenuated song," is given from a perch as well; it is much more varied and rambling than the primary song, usually introduced by *whink* and *ple-bleep* notes and including typical song phrases as well as *tsick* notes and other phrases.

The **CALL NOTE** is a loud and rather sharp *tsick, chut* or *tsuck*; it is reminiscent of a soft version of the call of a Brown Thrasher (*Toxostoma rufum*) and may also suggest the *tik* note of boreal/northwestern Fox Sparrows (*Passerella iliaca*). The call is not quite as sharp and metallic as the *chink* call of the waterthrushes or of Hooded Warbler (often in same habitats). Often delivered in a rapid series in alarm, or in response to pishing. A number of other, softer calls are known, with the repertoire of males and females showing little overlap. **FLIGHT NOTE**, not often heard, is a thin, high *see*.

 ## Behavior

The Ovenbird is distinctive in its walking behavior, and its walking gait and carriage differ from those of other warblers (except perhaps Connecticut Warbler). The tail is tilted upward, and the wings may be slightly drooped. Sometimes the tail is quickly cocked upward then slowly brought back down to horizontal. The head often appears to bob while the bird is walking. Ovenbirds can be very tame, often approaching within a few feet of the observer while walking on the forest floor. When agitated (often in response to pishing) they will raise the crest slightly, showing the orangish color of the median crown conspicuously. When flushed they usually fly upward to a branch.

Foraging takes place almost entirely on the ground, in dense leaf litter and on fallen logs; they glean insect prey from the leaf litter, sometimes turning over leaves. Very little prey is gleaned from live vegetation, but occasionally (as in response to spruce budworm outbreaks) they will forage well up into trees. Besides insect prey, Ovenbirds are known to take snails, earthworms, spiders, and (very rarely) small lizards and frogs. Fruit and other vegetable matter may be consumed in fall and winter; a good deal of grit is also ingested. Prey selection by Ovenbirds has been intensively studied in the field and laboratory.

The Ovenbird's distinctive **NEST** is a domed structure with a side entrance, placed on or very near the ground in a clump of ferns, grasses, or other low plants, or at the base of a shrub, sapling, or stump. Often the nest is placed next to a path, road, or other forest opening. The nest is largely constructed of dead leaves but also may incorporate plant stems, grasses, hair, and pine needles.

Habitat

BREEDS in mature deciduous or mixed broadleaf-conifer forests without a moderate amount of undergrowth. Most breeding habitats are relatively dry, as they are in uplands or on slopes; however, in some areas Ovenbirds also breed in bottomland forests and swampy areas. They can be very abundant in mixed pine-deciduous forests. Although they generally avoid pure coniferous forests, they do breed in jack pine woodlands in the Great Lakes region and spruce-fir forests with limited deciduous growth at higher elevations in New England. In all breeding habitats, an abundance of dead leaf material on the forest floor is essential; this litter forms the preferred foraging substrate, and dead leaves are also an important component in nest construction. At the northern edge of their range they breed in aspen woodlands along well-drained river banks. Birds at the southwestern edge of the breeding range (*S. a. cinereus*) often breed in the deciduous growth of canyons and gulches and in mixed deciduous-conifer woods on lower mountain slopes; locally they may occupy scrub oak thickets or ponderosa pine forests with an understory of Gambel oaks and other shrubs. Ovenbirds require relatively large contiguous forest areas for breeding and may be absent or occur in very low densities in small fragments of otherwise suitable forest habitat.

WINTERS within Neotropical forests, but generally avoids wet lowland forests. As in other seasons, Ovenbirds seek shade and leaf litter, where there is moderate to extensive undergrowth. Locally they may be found in mangroves, second-growth woodlands, and shady coffee plantations.

In **MIGRATION** found in a variety of habitats, but prefers forests or thickets with much leaf litter.

 Distribution

BREEDS from ne. B.C., extreme se. Yukon, and sw. Dist. of Mack., across n. and cen. Alta., cen. Sask., cen. Man., Ont., and s. Que. through the Canadian Maritime Provinces and Nfld. The breeding range extends south to s. Alta. (local; including Cypress Hills of e. Alta. and adjacent Sask.), all but westernmost Mont., cen. Wyo., s.-cen. Colo. (locally along front range of Rockies), n. and e. Neb., ne. Kans., e. Okla., and n. Ark. (sparingly in south), and through the Ohio and Tenn. river valleys south to ne. Miss. and n. Ala. They also breed south through the Appalachian region to n. Ga. and w. S.C., and south along the Atlantic coastal plain to N.C. (recently also to cen. S.C.).

WINTERS primarily in Mexico, Central America, and the Caribbean region. In Mexico found from s. Sinaloa, s. Tamaulipas, and (in the interior) Jalisco and San Luis Potosi southward, including the Yucatán peninsula and adjacent islands. Winters through Central America to cen. Panama, and in the Caribbean region from cen. Fla., the Bahamas, Bermuda, through the Greater Antilles, and in small numbers through the Lesser Antilles (especially in north). Winters rarely or casually to e. Panama, n. Colombia, n. Venezuela, Trinidad and Tobago, and the Netherlands Antilles; recorded twice in s. Ecuador (Pichincha and Loja provinces).

Ovenbirds are noted rarely but annually in winter in s. Texas, and very rarely along the Atlantic Coast north to the Outer Banks of N.C., and along the coast of La. They are casual elsewhere along the Gulf Coast and in the interior of Texas. They may linger late into the fall, and most eastern states have multiple records in December. A few birds have overwintered in the Northeast (e.g., Ont., Mass., N.Y.), especially at feeding stations. There is one record into early January in Minn., and a mid-December record for N.S. In the West, several have overwintered in Calif.

SPRING MIGRATION occurs on a broad front through e. North America. Large numbers pass through the Gulf Coast from the upper Texas coast east through all of Fla.; some also move north through the Rio Grande Valley and hill country of Texas. The first spring migrants appear in the last third of March, though it can be difficult to separate spring arrivals from overwintering birds. More general arrivals are in early April over much of the South. Over much of the Midwest the earliest spring arrivals are in mid-April, with a few records as early as late March; birds are more generally encountered in the Midwest, Mid-Atlantic Coast, and s. New England at the end of April and beginning of May. Farther north, arrivals in N.S. are usually during the second week of May (exceptionally to mid-April), and in the northernmost parts of the breeding range around 20–25 May. Western *cinereus* is noted as arriving on the breeding grounds in S.D. during the third week of May. The peak of spring migration through the South extends from mid-April to early May. Peak counts in the southern Midwest and Mid-Atlantic states are usually in early May, and those in the n. Midwest and New England are around 10–20 May. In most of the e. U.S. migration has largely ended by late May, with a few stragglers noted into early June. Spring migration and breeding ground arrival of males is about 1–2 weeks earlier than females, a common phenomenon in wood-warblers.

FALL MIGRATION is prolonged, because of the broad latitudinal breeding range. There are several records for Fla. prior to mid-August (as early as 26 July), and earliest fall arrivals for most southern states are around 10 August. There are a number of records of migrants at Pt. Pelee, Ont., in July. Typical fall arrivals over much of the East are at the end of August, and peak fall counts generally occur during early and mid-September; significant movements may still occur in late September and very early October, and even later in the southern states. Large-scale late tower kills include 327 in Wisc. on 1 October, 625 in Tenn. on 28 September, 220 in Tenn. on 14 October, and (exceptionally late) 80 in s. Fla. on 16 November. Most birds have departed the northern breeding areas after early September. Stragglers are widely noted well into earlier winter, as noted above.

Rare but regular through most of w. North America; recorded in all western states. Calif. alone has 814 records, peaking in late May and early June, and late September and early October. A slight majority of the records in the West are for spring. Also recorded in spring in Sonora and Baja Calif. (Guadalupe Is.), Mexico; there are also fall records for Clipperton Is. One spring overshoot was recorded at Churchill, n. Man. Also a casual

OVENBIRD
Seiurus aurocapillus

VAGRANT well outside normal range. Recorded three times in Alaska, including a 10 September record for the Beaufort Sea coast at Prudhoe Bay. There are four records for Greenland, and five fall and early winter records for Britain and Ireland (some were birds found dead).

▥ STATUS AND CONSERVATION

This species has a well-documented requirement for relatively large forest tracts, and would thus appear to be quite vulnerable to the increases in predation and cowbird parasitism associated with forest fragmentation. In larger forest tracts (in excess of about 2,500 acres) this species can be quite abundant, but it is rare or absent from areas with only small forest patches (250–2,250 acres, depending on habitat and geographical locality). Breeding Bird Survey data showed general population increases from 1965 to 1979 but significant declines thereafter. The Ovenbird's preference for forested habitats in winter (both wet and dry) also suggests vulnerability to deforestation within the Neotropics. Towers, windows, and other human-built structures take a very large toll on migrants of this species.

SUBSPECIES

Three subspecies are generally recognized, reflecting minor variation in the color of the upperparts. As is so often the case, subspecific differences become less clear and often confused when the plumage is worn; assignment of specimens away from the breeding range, especially in late winter and spring, is often dubious. None of the subspecific characters are evident in the field.

Nominate *aurocapillus* (described above) occupies most of the breeding range of the species; birds from s. Appalachia have been separated as *canivirens* (characterized as somewhat paler than nominate birds), but few authorities recognized that race. Breeding birds of Newfoundland, *furvior*, are slightly darker than nominate *aurocapillus*, and their lateral crown stripes average heavier (this greater pigment saturation is typical of Newfoundland races of many species); differences are slight, however, and this race is not recognized by some workers. S. a. *furvior* appears to winter mainly in Cuba, the Bahamas, and the Caribbean regions of Central America. The most distinctive race — but again based only on average differences and not identifiable in the field — is western *cinereus*. It is paler and grayer on the upperparts and tail than nominate birds (usually grayish olive rather than olive green in fresh plumage); there is little if any hint of a tawny wash on the sides of the face and neck. This race breeds in s. Alberta, the Cypress Hills (se. Alberta and adjacent Saskatchewan), and the lower east slope of the Rocky Mtns. and adjacent Great Plains from e. Montana and w. South Dakota south to w. Nebraska and e.-cen. Colorado. It winters from w. Mexico (Sinaloa) to Honduras, mainly on the Pacific slope; some specimens from se. U.S. have been attributed to *cinereus*, but these could represent variants within eastern subspecies.

Taxonomic Relationships

A close relationship with the two waterthrushes has recently been questioned by K. C. Parkes, based in part on differences in juvenal plumage and the length of retention of that plumage. Ovenbirds and the waterthrushes differ also in many aspects of locomotion, behavior, and vocalizations; plumage similarities may represent convergence. If the genus were split, the generic name *Seiurus* would apply only to the Ovenbird. This species (and all wood-warblers) are not closely related to the Neotropical "ovenbirds" of the family Furnariidae.

Plumages and Molts

SPRING ADULT: Upperparts uniformly olive, interrupted only by the distinctive crown pattern. A blackish lateral crown stripe extends from the bill back to the sides of the nape (becoming somewhat diffuse from the rear of the crown back). The forehead, between the blackish stripes, is pale olive-gray, but the remaining median crown area between the stripes is tawny orange, variably tipped and obscured with olive. This orange color is most

Ovenbird. In Connecticut in May. (Photo: J. Dunning/VIREO)

Ovenbird. In New Jersey in September. (Photo: Kevin T. Karlson)

evident when the crown feathers are raised during encounters or in response to pishing, and it may be difficult to see from many angles when these feathers are flattened. The sides of the head, including the superciliary region and most of the auriculars, are olive-gray. The lower and anterior auriculars may be slightly mottled with whitish. There is a bold and complete white-to-creamy-white ring around the eye. The lores are pale grayish olive (to nearly dirty white). A broad submoustachial stripe is whitish, bordered below by a thin but distinct black malar streak that usually reaches the bill. The chin and throat are immaculate white. The whitish breast and sides are boldly marked with blackish spots that are loosely aligned into broken rows. This patterning extends to the lower breast and onto the flanks. The flanks are tinged with olive. The belly and undertail coverts are white. The wing coverts and tertials are unmarked olive; the flight feathers are dusky, edged with olive. The rectrices are unmarked olive; a thin whitish edge may be present on the tip of the outermost rectrix, occasionally (especially in males) expanded into a white spot. **FIRST SPRING:** Not distinguishable in the field from spring adults. The indistinct rusty tips to the tertials that are shown in the first fall have generally worn away by midwinter or early spring. In the hand, the rectrices may appear more tapered and worn in first spring birds. **FALL ADULT:** Very similar to spring adult, but plumage fresher, with a stronger olive tinge to the upperparts and often an evident wash of buffy or tawny on the auriculars, sides of the neck, and flanks (this wash is absent in many fall birds, however). In fresh fall birds the orange of the median crown stripe is somewhat obscured by gray feather tips, as are the blackish lateral crown stripes. The black markings on the underparts may appear broader but blurrier in fresh plumage, wearing to finer but more distinct spots by spring. **FIRST FALL:** Closely resembles fall adult, and often not distinguishable in the field. Most individuals show distinct rusty tips to the tertials at least through the fall. The rectrices are more tapered than those of adults, and the outer rectrices usually lack any whitish edge at the tip. **JUVENILE:** Head, neck, and upperparts brown, with indistinct blackish streaking and mottling on the scapulars and back. Lateral crown stripes only faintly visible. Underparts buffy with faint olive-brown streaking in the malar region and on the breast, sides, and flanks. Remaining underparts dull yellowish white. Median and greater secondary coverts tipped with cinnamon, forming wing bars on the otherwise dusky olive wings. Rectrices unmarked olive. **BARE PARTS:** Bill dark brown on the upper mandible and tip, pinkish or creamy on the tomium and lower mandible. Legs and feet rather bright pinkish, reddish pink, or fleshy. Eyes dark brown.

The prebasic molt takes place on the breeding grounds; it is complete in adults but partial in hatching-year birds (not including the flight feathers, although some or all rectrices may be replaced). The prealternate molt is quite limited and possibly lacking in many or most adults.

 REFERENCES

GENERAL: Eaton 1957, Van Horn and Donavan 1994.
ECOLOGY, BEHAVIOR, VOCALIZATIONS, AND CONSERVATION: Hann 1937, Lein 1980 and 1981, Porneluzi et al. 1993, Smith and Shugert 1987, Stenger 1958, Zach and Falls 1977, 1978, and 1979.
PLUMAGES, MOLTS, AND MORPHOLOGY: Lanyon 1966, Taylor 1970, Taylor 1973.
SYSTEMATICS: Miller 1942, Short and Robbins 1967.

NORTHERN WATERTHRUSH PL. 21

Seiurus noveboracensis

5.75 in. (14.6 cm). The two species of waterthrushes are easily told from other warblers, but they can be quite difficult to distinguish from each other. Both are terrestrial warblers somewhat suggestive of pipits *(Anthus)* or Spotted Sandpipers *(Actitis macularia),* with brownish upperparts, heavily streaked whitish underparts, and distinct pale superciliums. The tail and rear portion of the body are almost constantly bobbed up and down, both when perched and when walking on the ground. Both waterthrushes are usually associated with water, with the Northern preferring slow streams, the edges of wooded ponds, bogs, and swampy areas. Key identification criteria for the two waterthrushes involve bill size, supercilium shape and color, underpart pattern, flank color, leg color, tail-bobbing action, and vocalizations. The Northern Waterthrush has a broad breeding range over much of northern North America. Although it is a rather early migrant, especially in fall, its migrations are distinctly later than those of the Louisiana Waterthrush.

DESCRIPTION

Generally dark brown above (varying in shade from cold gray-brown to warmer olive-brown) and whitish to pale yellowish below and on the supercilium. Underparts distinctly marked with blackish streaks. Wings and tail unmarked dark brown. Males and females are identical in plumage, and there is no significant seasonal variation; first fall birds are very similar to adults but sometimes can be distinguished in the field with close study. Geographical variation is subtle, and largely masked by individual variation within populations. Typical nominate *noveboracensis* are described below.

Waterthrushes are rather heavy-bodied, short-tailed warblers; this species is relatively longer tailed than the Louisiana. The bill is fairly long and heavy, with a slightly decurved culmen and noticeable gonydeal angle. The legs are relatively stout.

SIMILAR SPECIES

Quite similar to the LOUISIANA WATERTHRUSH; out of range and unseasonal waterthrushes should be identified with extreme caution. Northerns showing a strong yellowish cast to the supercilium and underparts are easily told from all Louisianas, with identification confusion centered on the paler, whiter Northerns (which can be encountered throughout the species' range). Thus, though Louisianas are whiter on the supercilium and background color of the breast than are most Northerns, identification should be based on other characters treated below. The most important of these are supercilium shape and color, bill size, flank color, and bobbing behavior (along with vocalizations).

Head pattern: The supercilium of Northern is rather even in width, but gradually tapers behind the eye; it is set off below by a distinct and dark transocular line. Color of the supercilium of Northern may vary from yellowish to white but is usually uniform along the length of the supercilium. The supercilium of Louisiana is bolder, longer, and broader behind the eye than that of Northern; the two supercilia appear to almost meet on the nape in some individuals. The transocular line of Louisiana is browner and less distinct, and the supercilium is somewhat bicolored (washed with grayish buff in front of the eye but gleaming white behind the eye). Most Northerns have at least some dusky spotting on the throat, whereas nearly all Louisianas have unmarked, white throats. Throat pattern is not a diagnostic character, however; some Northerns show unspotted throats, especially with wear in late spring and early summer, and occasional Lousianas will show limited spotting on the throat. On average, the white lower eye-arc is broader and more conspicuous in Louisiana.

Underpart coloration and pattern: Most Louisianas show a wash of pinkish buff on the flanks; this color sometimes extends into the vent region and sometimes undertail coverts, especially in fresh fall plumage. This color contrasts with the clean white background color of the remaining underparts. Northerns may have a strong yellowish or yellow-buff wash below, but this color is uniform throughout the underparts rather than being concentrated in the flank region; note that Northerns showing strong yellow or buff on the underparts will also show that color on the supercilium. The dark spotting on the underparts differs subtly between the species. In Northerns the spotting is darker and more sharply defined, and more apt to be organized into lengthwise rows. Louisianas show somewhat sparser, browner, broader, and more blurred spotting below. In the hand, Northerns show extensive gray-brown on the basal halves of the five longest greater undertail covert feathers; in Louisianas these dark markings, if present, are more limited and restricted to the three longest coverts.

Other plumage characters: On average, the upperparts of unworn Northerns are darker brown, sometimes even tinged with olive; Louisianas average slightly grayer on the upperparts, but this difference is minor and not diagnostic.

Shape: The bill of Louisiana is longer and heavier than that of Northern, a difference that is usually evident in the field; there is some overlap in this character, however. The tail of Louisiana is relatively shorter than that of Northern; extension of the rectrices beyond the longest undertail coverts averages 11 mm in Louisiana (range 9–14) and 14 mm in Northern (range 12–23).

Legs: The legs of the Northern are generally duller, more dusky pink than those of Louisiana (which has brighter, "bubble gum" pink legs).

Behavior: One important behavioral distinction between the two species is the more deliberate and exaggerated tail-bobbing behavior of Louisiana; that species' tail bobbing is more circular and involves more body motion than in the Northern, which has a faster, more up-and-down tail bobbing.

Voice: Call notes differ subtly between the two species of waterthrushes, and songs are strikingly different; see Voice below.

Compare also with the **OVENBIRD**, which has a different head pattern (white eye-ring, blackish lateral crown stripes), is more heavily spotted with black below and more olive above, and cocks (but does not bob) its tail. The dullest fall and winter **PALM WARBLERS** superficially resemble waterthrushes in being brownish above, indistinctly streaked below, showing a pale supercilium, and bobbing their tails; they are easily told from waterthrushes by their yellow undertail coverts, smaller size, and hopping (not walking) behavior. Finally, compare with **AMERICAN PIPITS** (*Anthus rubescens*), which generally occur in more open habitats and show conspicuous white in the outer tail feathers.

 ## Voice

The **SONG** is a series of short, emphatic notes with a rich, ringing quality; most songs drop irregularly in pitch and speed in tempo toward the end. The notes are usually grouped into 3–4 series: *twit twit twit sweet sweet sweet chew chew chew,* or *sweet sweet sweet chit chit twit twit chew.* The song lacks the clear, ringing introductory notes and weak, jumbled ending of songs of Louisiana Waterthrush. A flight song is frequently given on the breeding grounds, most frequently just before dark. This song is a longer and quicker rendition of the typical song, interspersed with *chink* call notes, and is given with a labored wingbeat slightly (sometimes considerably) above treetop level.

The **CALL NOTE** is a ringing, metallic *chink;* excited birds may give this note in a series (2–3 per second); it is certainly one of our loudest warbler call notes. It is similar to but even sharper and more metallic than the call of Lousiana. The **FLIGHT NOTE** is a buzzy *zeet,* becoming somewhat louder and buzzier at the end.

 ## Behavior

Waterthrushes differ from our other warblers by combining a distinctive walking gait with obvious bobbing of the tail and rear portion of the body. Waterthrushes spend most of their time walking on the ground, although they will walk along tree limbs. They continue to bob when flushed up onto a limb. As noted above, the bobbing behavior of Northern Waterthrush differs somewhat from that of Louisiana. Northerns bob the tail almost continually in an up-and-down motion; this bobbing appears to involve only rear of the body. Flight is swift and low. Singing birds will perch well above the ground on horizontal limbs, and even from treetops in stunted forests in the northernmost parts of their breeding range. They forage deliberately on the ground, usually where there is damp leaf litter or even shallow water. They frequently turn over leaves with the bill, gleaning invertebrate prey from the undersides of the leaves or the ground under them. They may walk into shallow water or out onto partly submerged logs or on floating debris. On some occasions they have even been noted fluttering over the surface of a pond or slow-moving stream and picking prey from the surface; swimming behavior has also been noted but is certainly rare. Northerns also forage in drier situations from leaf litter, rocks, moss, or the surfaces of large limbs. Prey items include insects and other invertebrates (including worms, small snails, and crustaceans); small fish are also occasionally eaten. On average, prey items are smaller than those taken by the Louisiana Waterthrush. Northern and Louisiana waterthrushes are generally segregated by habitat, even in winter, but where territories overlap few interactions are noted. Small territories are held on the winter grounds and even for brief periods in migration.

NESTS are located on or near the ground, often among the root system of a fallen tree, at the base of a standing tree, or set into a streambank. The nest is a cup composed of stems, pine needles, and leaves and lined with moss stalks, rootlets, and fibers.

 # Habitat

BREEDS in wooded areas with slow-moving water, including swamps, bogs, streamsides, pond margins, and beaver flowages. Tree composition varies greatly throughout the species' range but typically includes deciduous growth such as alders within or adjacent to coniferous or mixed forests. Often Northern Waterthrushes will inhabit shrubby alder or willow thickets in the zone between coniferous (or mixed) forests and streams or ponds. Swamp associations occupied include various mixtures of red maple, white cedar, birch, spruce, balsam, and fir. Riparian associations of alder, willow, and balsam poplar are inhabited. In the northern Rockies, occupies deciduous growth within subalpine woodlands and the borders of montane lakes and willow-lined streams. In the northernmost parts of the breeding range (as at Seward Peninsula, Alaska) woodland canopy may be as low as 8 ft., provided there is dense vegetation near the ground and some standing or slowly moving water. Where Northerns overlap Louisiana Waterthrushes, Northerns tend to occupy areas with denser shrub cover and slower moving water.

In **WINTER**, they are especially numerous in mangrove associations but also occupy a variety of swampy woodlands and lake and stream margins. **MIGRANTS** prefer habitats with the characteristics of breeding and winter habitats but may occur around any small pool or damp, shaded area and are sometimes found well away from water.

 ## DISTRIBUTION

BREEDS from much of cen. and w. Alaska (but uncommon in south and rare in southeast), Yukon, and Northwest Territories east across the boreal regions to Lab. and Nfld. The breeding range extends south to ne. Wash. (and very locally in Cascade Mtns. south to cen. Ore.), n. Idaho (and possibly nw. Wyo.), w. Mont., N.D., ne. (and locally e.-cen.) Minn., n. and e.-cen. Wisc., s. Mich., ne. Ohio, and n. N.J. Also breeds south in the Appalachian Mtns. to W. Va. and w. Va. (possibly to w. N.C.). There are scattered midsummer records from well outside of the breeding range, including Colo. (has bred in Jackson Co.), Ariz., and Calif.

WINTERS primarily from Mexico to n. South America and in the West Indies. It occurs from the northern limits of mangrove associations in s. Baja Calif., Sonora, and Tamaulipas south through Mexico (mainly in the lowlands, especially coastal regions) and Central America to n. South America (Colombia, Venezuela, and the Guianas, and recorded south to n. Ecuador, ne. Peru, and nw. Brazil). It also winters on Bermuda and throughout the West Indies (most numerous in Greater Antilles, but also found throughout the Lesser Antilles and commonly on Trinidad and Tobago).

Within the U.S. it is most regular in winter in s. Fla., where it is uncommon. It is annual, or nearly so, in s. La., s. Texas, and Calif. (especially s. coast). Otherwise it is casual in winter north of Mexico, with widely scattered records of overwintering birds as far north as Ill., Ind., Ohio, Wisc., N.Y., s. Ont., s. New England, and B.C.; there are several winter records for the interior Southwest.

SPRING MIGRATION occurs on a broad front from s. Texas and the Gulf Coast to peninsular Fla. The first spring migrants are typically noted in the South in early April; a few may appear in very late March, but the situation is clouded by overwintering birds as well as confusion with the Louisiana Waterthrush, a much earlier migrant. First arrivals in Mo. and elsewhere in the s. Midwest are usually during the second week of April, and there are a few records as far north as the Great Lakes region at this time. For most of the Midwest and Northeast the first arrivals are not normally until the last week of April. Arrivals in much of the Canadian portion of the breeding range are in mid-May, and in the northernmost portions of the breeding range around 20 May. The peak of spring migration is in the last week of April and first week of May over much of the South and the second week of May in the Midwest. Only a few migrants still occur south of the breeding range after the last week of May (recorded exceptionally in Fla. as late as 3 June). Small numbers pass through the West regularly in spring, from late April through early June; it is more numerous in the interior West in spring than along the immediate Pacific Coast.

FALL MIGRATION routes are similar to those of spring, with a slight easterly shift (more numerous in fall than in spring along the Mid-Atlantic Coast). Fall migration begins rather early but is still later than that of the Louisiana Waterthrush. Early fall migrants are recorded in the Northeast and Mid-Atlantic states as early as 15 July, and small numbers are widely present by the end of July. During the period from late July to early August there is much overlap with Louisiana, but after about 20 August nearly all waterthrushes recorded in the U.S. are Northerns. For most east-

NORTHERN WATERTHRUSH
Seiurus noveboracensis

ern states, the earliest fall Northerns arrive in early August, and the species is not regular in any numbers until after mid-August. Fall migration peaks are in late August and early September in the Great Lakes region, and into mid-September in the Northeast and most of the Midwest. Small numbers continue to pass through into early October (exceptionally 38 in a tower kill in New York on 5 October). Peak fall migration extends through early October in the Gulf states. Over much of eastern North America, this species is rare but regular through the second week of October but casual after that; records of stragglers extend through October and into early November (a 4 November record for Yukon is exceptional, and there are two mid-December records for Nfld.). This species is somewhat more numerous in the fall in western North America than in spring. Most of the passage through the West in fall is from late August to early September, with scattered records as late as November (and winter records noted above).

VAGRANT in late spring on the north slope of Alaska and on St. Lawrence Is.; also recorded in mid-June on Chukotski Peninsula, Russia. Recorded once in September on Banks Is. in arctic Canada. Also vagrant in fall to Greenland and Europe (six records for the British Isles, two for France, and one for the Canary Is.).

STATUS AND CONSERVATION

Generally quite common. Some population declines have been reported from at least the southern portions of the breeding range, these perhaps due to a combination of cowbird parasitism (moderate in this species) and the filling or draining of wooded wetlands. Nevertheless, this species has a vast breeding range, much of it well away from human settlement. Some recent range expansions (portions of New England and Michigan) may represent the recovery of breeding habitat lost with earlier deforestation. The degree of degradation of wintering habitats is uncertain.

SUBSPECIES

Geographic variation is minor and largely obscured by variation within populations. Four races have been described, based on size, upperpart coloration, and the background color of the underparts (yellowish vs. whitish). Although most workers agree on the basic patterns of geographical variation in this species, there is disagreement as to whether this variation warrants the recognition of subspecies.

Geographic variation as recognized by AOU (1957) is outlined below. The nominate race occupies the easternmost portion of the breeding range from e. Quebec and Labrador south through the n. Appalachian region to West Virginia. Birds from New-foundland have been given the name *uliginosus*, though the race is not recognized by most authors; their relatively long wings, short bills, and yellow underparts simply represent the northeast-ernmost segment of a broad cline within eastern North America. Across the main boreal portion of the breeding range there is a trend toward birds with whiter underparts, duller (more gray-brown, less olive) upperparts, and longer bills from cen. Quebec (and w. Labrador) westward; birds from this entire region have been named *notabilis*. However, Alaskan birds, included within "*notabilis*," are as yellow as any eastern nominate birds and are longer-winged than "*notabilis*" from the n. Rocky Mt. region. Fur-thermore, the type specimen of *notabilis*, from Carbon Co. in se. Wyoming, is atypically long billed. It is not strictly correct, there-fore, to characterize western birds as whiter and longer billed, both because these characters extend as far east as cen. Quebec and because many western populations are as yellow as any from the East. Finally, birds from cen. British Columbia have been described as *limnaeus*, characterized by darker upperparts than *notabilis* and with underpart color intermediate between *notabilis* and nominate *noveboracensis*; the characters of "*limnaeus*" can be matched by individuals from throughout the northern and east-ern parts of the species' range.

TAXONOMIC RELATIONSHIPS

Closely related to the Louisiana Waterthrush (the two have been considered to possibly represent a superspecies). The two water-thrushes, on the other hand, are probably not closely related to the Ovenbird and perhaps deserve generic rank. One hybrid between the Northern Waterthrush and Blackpoll Warbler has been reported; however, the possibility has been raised that the *Dendroica* parent of this combination may have been a Cape May Warbler. In either case, a close relationship between the water-thrushes and *Dendroica* is suggested.

PLUMAGES AND MOLTS

SPRING ADULT: Entire upperparts, from forehead and crown to rump, dark brown with a slight olive tint (in some individuals a colder dark brown, lacking olive tones). The bases of the feathers of the median portion of the forehead are dull buffy whitish, sometimes giving the appearance in the field of a short pale streak. Complete transocular line, including lores, dark dusky brown; auriculars dark brown, indistinctly mottled with whitish or pale yellowish. Complete supercilium, roughly even in width throughout its length, pale buffy yellow to dull whitish. Submoustachial area dull whitish, bordered below by a thin dark brown malar streak (either solid or formed by a series of spots). The chin is whitish, and the throat is whitish with variable fine dark brown spotting; less than 5 percent of individuals have throat spotting so reduced that it might not be evident in the field. The breast, sides, and flanks are prominently streaked with dark blackish brown; these streaks are fairly distinct and are actually elongated spots that are aligned into long rows. The background color of the breast and belly varies from pale yellowish buff (sometimes strongly yellow) to dull whitish; yellowish color, if present, does not usually extend onto the throat. In general, degree of yellow tint on the underparts matches that of the supercilium; those individuals with a stronger yellow tint below also are usually warmer, more olive-brown on the upperparts. The flanks are slightly washed with buffy brown. The undertail coverts are dull whitish or very pale yellow; the dusky basal coloration of the undertail coverts sometimes shows in the field as blurred streaks. The wings and tail are unmarked dark brown; on a minority of individuals the outer 2–3 pairs of rectrices are narrowly tipped on the inner webs with dull whitish. **FIRST SPRING:** Indistinguishable in the field from spring adults, but in the hand, the rectrices appear more worn and tapered. The indistinct rusty tips to the tertial feathers in first fall birds have generally worn away by the first spring and summer. **FALL ADULT:** Virtually identical to spring adult, but in fresher plumage there is often a stronger buffy or yellowish tint to the supercilium and underparts, and the spotting on the throat averages slightly more evident (the dark spots are on the tips of the throat feathers

Northern Waterthrush. Typical bird in Ohio in September. (Photo: Steve and Dave Maslowski)

Northern Waterthrush. Pale extreme in Texas in May. (Photo: B. Schorre/VIREO)

and are therefore more prominent in fresh than in worn plumage). Fresh fall birds also average slightly darker on the upperparts than worn late spring and summer birds. **FIRST FALL:** Very similar to fall adult, but the tertials are indistinctly tipped with rusty or buff. Very few birds in their first year show whitish tips on the inner webs of the outer pairs of rectrices (this feature is shown more often in adults). **JUVENILE:** Dark olive-brown above, appearing finely spotted or barred with buff. Sides of the head olive-brown, with a buffy supercilium and indistinct pale mottling on the auriculars and sides of the neck. Underparts dull buffy white, rather strongly streaked and mottled with dusky on the throat, breast, and sides. Wing coverts and tertial edges with rusty or deep buff. **BARE PARTS:** Bill dusky black, paler grayish pink on the basal half or ⅔ of the mandible. Legs and feet range from fairly bright pinkish to duller yellowish brown. Eyes dark brown.

The prebasic molt takes place on the breeding grounds, beginning as early as mid-June. It is complete in adults and partial in hatching-year birds (involving the body feathers, wing coverts, and occasionally some of the rectrices). The prealternate molt is absent or limited to some feathers of the head.

 REFERENCES

GENERAL: Eaton 1957a, Kaufman 1990a, Lowery et al. 1968.

ECOLOGY, BEHAVIOR, VOCALIZATIONS, AND CONSERVATION: Craig 1984, 1985, and 1987, Schwartz 1964, Winker et al. 1992.

IDENTIFICATION: Binford 1971, Curson 1993, Wallace 1980, Zimmer 1985.

SYSTEMATICS: Behle 1985, Burleigh and Peters 1948 (describes subspecies *S. n. uliginosus*), Eaton 1957b, McCabe and Miller 1933, Parkes 1978 (Northern Waterthrush × Blackpoll or Cape May), Short and Robbins 1967.

Seiurus motacilla

6 in. (15.2 cm). The Louisiana Waterthrush is typically a bird of fast-flowing forested streams, with a more southeasterly breeding distribution than that of the Northern Waterthrush. It is one of our earliest spring migrants and also among our earliest warblers to depart in fall, rarely being recorded in our area after early September. In appearance it is closely similar to the Northern Waterthrush, with differences including the more prominent white supercilium (flaring behind the eye), the contrasting wash of pinkish or buff on the flanks of most birds, and the larger bill. The tail bobbing, characteristic of the waterthrushes, is slower and more exaggerated in the Louisiana. The two species are also easily told by their songs.

 ## DESCRIPTION

The sexes are identical, and there is very little age or seasonal variation in plumage. There is some individual variation in flank color and ventral spotting, but overall there is less variation in plumage than is the Northern Waterthrush.

This is a large, heavy-bodied warbler with a relatively short tail; extension of the rectrices beyond the undertail coverts averages about 3 mm less than in Northern. The long and heavy bill may appear slightly upturned because of the rather straight culmen and noticeable gonydeal angle. The legs are long and stout.

 ## SIMILAR SPECIES

Not likely to be confused with any warbler other than the **NORTHERN WATERTHRUSH.** For a detailed discussion of distinctions see under that species, p. 458. Briefly, Northern Waterthrush averages smaller-billed and bobs its tail more rapidly in an up-and-down motion. In plumage, Northern is often washed with yellow on the supercilium and underparts. Those Northerns with a whiter supercilium and background color to the underparts are told from Louisianas by fine spotting on throat (absent in a few Northerns and present on about 10 percent of Lousianas), narrower supercilium that is uniform in color in front and back of eye and does not widen behind the eye, lack of a well-defined buffy or salmon wash on the flanks and vent, and sharper ventral streaking that is more neatly aligned into long rows. The legs of Northern average duller (rarely if ever bright pinkish as in typical Louisiana).

VOICE

SONG is loud and distinctive, opening with 3–4 clear slurred whistles but quickly shifting to a fading series of jumbled, twittering notes. The effect is of a song that starts out strong and musical but ends up weak and disjointed. Often there is a middle series of quicker, lower slurred notes between the clear opening and jumbled closing series. One rendition might be *SWEEU SWEEU SWEEU chee ch-wit-it chit swee-you*. The opening slurred phrases often descend in pitch, and are thus suggestive of the opening of a Yellow-throated Warbler song, but the remainder of the song is quite different. The song is very suggestive of that of Swainson's Warbler (which will often respond vigorously to playbacks of Louisiana Waterthrush songs); the opening phrases are similar, but Swainson's song has an emphatic, musical ending, unlike Lousiana's weak, jumbled ending. A more complex song with a longer sputtering ending is given by Louisiana Waterthrush in territorial defense (as in response to tape playback). Flight song is given less frequently than in Northern Waterthrush and Ovenbird. It consists of labored horizontal flight above treetop level, accompanied by song phrases including loud slurred notes and lengthy twittering, followed by a plunge back to the stream border some distance from the origin of the flight. One record of female song.

CALL NOTE is a loud, rich *chik* or *chich* similar to the *chink* call of Northern Waterthrush but separable with practice. It lacks the metallic sharpness of Northern's call, and the quality is somewhat hollow, mildly suggestive of calls of Hooded or Kentucky warblers. **FLIGHT NOTE** is a high *zeet*.

BEHAVIOR

Like the Northern Waterthrush, this species spends much of its time on the ground, walking along streambanks, emergent rocks and logs within streams, and damp shaded ground. The characteristic tail-bobbing behavior of waterthrushes is even more extreme in Louisiana, with the bobbing motion slower and more deliberate, and more circular (less up-and-down) in motion. The tail bobbing appears to involve more of the entire body. Louisianas are usually somewhat shyer and less approachable than Northerns, and may flush for considerable distances along a stream course. Singing birds perch on a horizontal branch, usually a few meters off the ground; they will occasionally sing from the ground. The tail is not bobbed during singing bouts. There is a reduction in singing frequency of males after the females arrive on the breeding grounds, with only limited singing until completion of the prebasic molt (late July, early August) when much singing is again heard. Foraging behavior is much as in Northern, but perhaps more closely tied to flowing water, where the Louisiana often probes into crannies in streamside rocks and root systems. Prey items average larger than those taken by Northern, and in addition to insects include mollusks, earthworms, crustaceans, and even small fish and amphibians. This species is strongly territorial on the winter grounds as well as the breeding grounds.

The **NEST** (built by the female and male) is typically on a steep bank overhanging a stream but may also be located in the root system of a fallen streamside tree or rarely even in the crevice of a streamside rock or natural cavity in a stump surrounded by water. The nest is a rather large, bulky mass of leaves, moss, and twigs, lined with finer material. There is a platform or "walkway" of dead leaves leading to the nest. Nests are within 3–6 ft. of the water's surface.

 HABITAT

BREEDS along fast-flowing, rocky streams within woodlands. This species' preference for high-gradient streams of clear water makes it most numerous in montane and foothill areas. Occupied streams have a broad border of mature woodland providing much shade. Woodland tree species vary, with deciduous trees preferred in most of the range but woodlands of hemlock and other conifers also occupied. In the Appalachian region, they are commonly found along streams bordered by rhododendrons. In flatter terrain from s. New England to n. North Carolina this species also breeds in floodplain forests and swamps, but again prefers areas with clear, flowing water. One study comparing waterthrush habitat preferences in Connecticut showed that Louisianas chose habitats with sparser shrub cover than Northerns did.

In **WINTER**, Louisianas choose habitats similar to those used in the breeding season: clear, fast-flowing mountain and foothill streams with forested margins. They also winter around wooded montane lakes, and locally in lowland lakes and streams. They do not normally occur in mangroves and other swampy coastal habitats where Northerns are common. In **MIGRATION**, usually found around flowing or standing water with good cover.

 DISTRIBUTION

BREEDS from e. Neb. (formerly), Iowa, cen. Minn., n. Wisc., cen. Mich., s. Ont., possibly s. Que. (summer records in Gatineau

Park), n. N.Y., cen. (locally n.) Vt., cen. N.H. and extreme s. Me. south to e. Texas, cen. La., and n. (mainly nw.) Fla. It is absent as a breeding bird on the Atlantic coastal plain south of n. N.C. Rather local within the breeding range described above, and absent from extensive lowland areas.

WINTERS from nw. Mexico (to n. Sonora) and ne. Mexico (s. Nuevo Leon, sw. Tamaulipas) south mainly in mountains and foothills (but not in Mexican plateau) to Panama and rarely Colombia (mainly Santa Marta region). Also winters in the Bahamas and Greater Antilles. Winters rarely or casually south to the Lesser Antilles, Netherlands Antilles, w. Venezuela. Birds may appear in their Neotropical wintering range as early as the middle of July. Within the U.S. it winters rarely but nearly annually in Fla. (mainly s.; two specimens) and in se. Ariz. (an extension of w. Mexican wintering range). There are a few winter reports in the East for La., Texas, e. Okla., Tenn., Ga., Mich., and Md. (29 December, Bowie), but only the last is supported by a specimen. One winter record for Calif. The Northern Waterthrush is far more likely to be encountered in late fall and winter north of Mexico than is the Louisiana.

SPRING MIGRATION is along a broad front through eastern North America, and is among the earliest of all warblers; birds presumed to be migrants have been recorded in Fla. as early as mid-February. More typically, the earliest arrivals along the Gulf Coast from Texas to Fla. are during the second and third weeks of March. Through the remainder of the southern states, spring arrivals are usually during the latter half of March, and in the s. Midwest and the Mid-Atlantic states, birds arrive in late March and early April. Arrivals at the extreme northern end of the breeding grounds are during the latter half of April. Late March records exist as far north as Mich., s. Ont., and Mass. Away from the Gulf Coast there is little evidence of spring migration except at favored migration stopovers such as Pt. Pelee, Ont. The peak movement through the Gulf Coast is from the last week of March to mid-April, with a few stragglers as late as early May (there is a late May specimen from Cameron Parish, La.). Known spring migrants have been seen into the last third of May in the s. Great Lakes region, but the species is casual away from breeding areas that late in the spring. Suspected Louisianas found late in spring should be distinguished carefully from Northern Waterthrushes, which are still commonly moving through then.

FALL MIGRATION is the earliest of all eastern wood-warblers, with perhaps only a few Yellow and Tennessee warblers appearing as early. Birds believed to be fall migrants have been recorded in Fla. as early as 9 June, and migrants are widely recorded by early (and especially mid-)July. The peak of fall records at Cape May, N.J., is

LOUISIANA WATERTHRUSH
Seiurus motacilla

during the first week of August, and the peak in Fla. is during the last third of July and first third of August. Nearly all birds have departed the breeding grounds by the end of August, and nearly all fall migrants are also gone by that time. Numerous reports from mid-September into October likely pertain to misidentified Northerns; any claimed Louisiana after early September requires thorough documentation. Fall migration routes roughly retrace those of spring, with a slight eastward shift (this species is far more common on the upper Texas coast in spring than in fall).

CASUAL migrant on the Great Plains, and vagrant north to ne. Minn., the upper peninsula of Mich., Me. (away from the few known breeding areas to the south), and N.S. (mainly Sable Is.). Rare but regular vagrant to Bermuda in spring and fall. This is one of the rarest "eastern" warblers to appear as a VAGRANT in western North America (away from se. Ariz., where there are numerous winter records). There are several records (mainly spring) for Colo. and N.M., one spring record for Nev., nearly 40 records for

Ariz. (mainly late summer and winter), and eight records for Calif. (three in fall from 7 August to 18 September, four in spring from 3 May to 3 June, and one wintering bird). Unrecorded in the western provinces of Canada. Recorded twice in Baja Calif. (late April, November). There is a single **EXCEPTIONAL** record for w. Greenland (1949 specimen).

 ## STATUS AND CONSERVATION

As a specialist of restricted and linear habitats, this species occurs in rather low densities and is nowhere abundant. No strong population trends have been identified. Local declines, as in se. Michigan, are perhaps attributable to heavy lumbering along streams, which results in clouded water and inappropriate dry, open habitat. Deforestation and siltation of streams might also adversely impact wintering habitat. This species is a frequent cowbird host, and some populations have undoubtedly suffered from the effects of cowbird parasitism, but data are lacking.

SUBSPECIES

No variation described; no subspecies recognized.

TAXONOMIC RELATIONSHIPS

Closely related to the Northern Waterthrush; the two perhaps constituting a superspecies. Relationship to the Ovenbird is far more distant (the latter is perhaps best not treated as congeneric). No hybridization recorded.

Louisiana Waterthrush. In Texas in March. (Photo: Steve Bentsen)

SPRING ADULT: Forehead, crown, and entire upperparts uniformly gray-brown to olive-brown. An indistinct whitish median forehead streak is present, though largely obscured, on some birds. The supercilium is pale grayish to creamy white from the supraloral region to the eye, becoming white where constricted above the eye, then broadening into a bold white stripe extending well back to the side of the neck. The lores and a broad postocular stripe are dark brown. There is a white arc under the eye. The auriculars are dark gray-brown mottled with whitish. The submoustachial region is white, bordered below by a gray-brown malar streak (usually solid, but in some birds appearing as a row of spots). The chin is unmarked white; the throat is also white, marked in about 10 percent of individuals by small, inconspicuous dusky spots. The breast, sides, and belly are white (to creamy white), strongly marked with gray-brown spots or chevrons that are loosely aligned into rows. This spotting extends back through the flanks, which are variably (but often strongly) tinged with a salmon-buff to yellow-buff wash. The undertail coverts are creamy white. The wings are unmarked and similar in color to the upperparts. The dusky brown tail shows an indistinct whitish tip to the inner web of the outer rectrix in many individuals. **FIRST SPRING:** Not distinguishable in the field from adult; some individuals retain traces of cinnamon on the edges of the tertials (see First Fall) into spring. In the hand, the rectrices may appear more tapered and worn than in spring adults; there is no trace of white on the tips of the outer rectrices. **FALL ADULT:** Very similar to spring adults, but plumage fresher, often showing a richer and more extensive wash of salmon or buff color on the flanks (washing into the vent region and sometimes the sides and belly). There is much individual variation, however, in the extent of color on the flanks, and some fresh fall individuals

Louisiana Waterthrush. In Florida in April. (Photo: Kevin T. Karlson)

have very little such color. In fresh birds, the upperparts have more of an olive tint (not as cold brown or gray-brown as in spring birds). **FIRST FALL:** Very similar to fall adult, but with indistinct rusty or cinnamon edges to the tertials, visible in the field at close range. Outer rectrices lack white tips (which are often indistinctly present in adults). **JUVENILE:** Dark brown above, with buffy feather tips on the back and rump. Sides of head mottled pale buff and olive-brown, with a whitish supercilium behind the eye bordered by a dark brown postocular stripe. Dull whitish buff below with olive-brown streaking on the buffy throat, breast, and flanks. Rusty or deep buff edges to the wing coverts (forming wing bars) and tertials. **BARE PARTS:** Bill dusky on the upper mandible, pale brown or pinkish on the tomium and the lower mandible. Eyes dark brown. Legs and feet pinkish flesh, almost always appearing rather bright ("bubble gum") pink.

The prebasic molt occurs on the breeding grounds, beginning as early as late June. It is complete in adults; in hatching-year birds it involves body feathers, wing and tail coverts, and (in some individuals) one or more pairs of rectrices. There is no prealternate molt.

 REFERENCES

GENERAL: Eaton 1958, Robinson 1995.
DISTRIBUTION: Austen et al. 1994, McCracken 1991.
ECOLOGY, BEHAVIOR, VOCALIZATIONS, AND CONSERVATION: Craig 1984, 1985, and 1987, Hix 1916, McCracken 1991.
IDENTIFICATION: Binford 1971, Curson 1993, Wallace 1980, Zimmer 1985.
PLUMAGES, MOLTS, AND MORPHOLOGY: Schaeffer 1974.

KENTUCKY WARBLER   PL. 22

Oporornis formosus

5.25 in. (13.3 cm). An inhabitant of shaded deciduous forests, primarily in the south, the Kentucky Warbler spends most of its time on or near the ground. It is a rather chunky and short-tailed warbler with uniformly olive green upperparts and bright yellow underparts. All post-juvenal plumages show distinct yellow spectacles, and most plumages sport a thick black mark on the side of the face. During the breeding season this species is easily located by its loud, rolling song, which suggests a Carolina Wren (*Thryothorus ludovicianus*) or an Ovenbird. Aging and sexing many individuals can be difficult.

DESCRIPTION

All individuals show entirely olive upperparts and bright yellow underparts. The yellow supercilium broadens behind the eye and extends downward, curling under the eye and terminating without forming a complete eye-ring. All plumages except some immature females show at least some black on the sides of the face, and there may be a variable amount of black on the forehead. Occasional exceptionally orange individuals may have derived this color from the consumption of berries of honeysuckle (*Lonicera*) at the time of the prebasic molt.

This moderate-sized, chunky warbler has a fairly short tail; the undertail coverts extend within 10–12 mm of the tail tip. The typical *Oporornis* bill is rather heavy and somewhat bicolored; all birds show rather bright fleshy pink legs and feet.

SIMILAR SPECIES

The combination of the uniformly olive upperparts, entirely bright yellow underparts, and yellow spectacles is distinctive. The most frequent confusion species is the **COMMON YELLOWTHROAT**, particularly first fall males which show some black on the sides of the face. All Common Yellowthroats are duller (more olive-gray or olive-brown) on the upperparts, and nearly all show whitish on the belly and extensive brownish on the flanks. Even the most extensively yellow Common Yellowthroats, such as *chryseola* of the southwestern border, are not as uniformly bright yellow below as Kentuckies. Except for extremely rare variant males, Common Yellowthroats lack a distinct yellow stripe in the supraloral area or yellow around the eye. Yellowthroats are longer tailed, with twice as much tail extension beyond the longest undertail coverts as in Kentucky. In the Bahamas, where Kentucky is a rare migrant, compare with **BAHAMA YELLOWTHROAT**, also a woodland understory bird.

With poor views, the **HOODED WARBLER** (often common in the same habitats) may be mistaken for Kentucky, especially female Hoodeds with more restricted black. All Hoodeds are extensively yellow or yellow-olive on the face, and flash white in the relatively long tail. Compare with the **CANADA WARBLER**, which is also spectacled but is grayish above, has white undertail coverts, usually shows at least a hint of streaking on the breast, and has a long, expressive tail. Compare also with other *Oporornis*, particularly female and immature **MOURNING WARBLERS**.

VOICE

The **SONG** is a rich and loud rolling series of 5–8 (occasionally more) notes, each being two, or sometimes three, syllables: *churree churree churree...*, *tory-tory-tory-tory...*, or *ter-wheeter, ter-wheeter, ter-wheeter....* The song is usually delivered from a low perch, but the singer may move higher (30 ft. or more), especially in response to song playbacks. The song suggests a Carolina Wren, although the wren tends to give a series of four three-syllable notes and usually delivers songs 2–3 times more frequently; wren pairs routinely duet, a behavior unknown in Kentucky and nearly all other North American warblers. The Kentucky's song also suggests an Ovenbird's in general pattern, but the former's is more rolling, less mechanical, and tends to have an upward inflection at the end of each phrase.

CALL NOTE is a low, distinctive *chup* or *chuck*, given persistently when the bird is agitated or alarmed. The call has been likened to the *chup* note of a Hermit Thrush (*Catharus guttatus*) and strongly suggests the *chip* portion of the typical *chip-burr* note of the Scarlet Tanager (*Piranga olivacea*), as well as the *chuck* note of a Hepatic Tanager (*P. [flava] hepatica*); among wood-warblers it is most similar to the call of Swainson's. Deep in its understory habitat, the Kentucky Warbler is most easily located by its song and call. The **FLIGHT NOTE** is said to be a loud buzzy *zeep*.

BEHAVIOR

This species is rather secretive and usually stays very low, where it hops or briefly runs on the ground, fallen logs, or among the leaf litter. Numerous references in the literature to walking behavior appear to be incorrect. Kentuckies forage by gleaning for insects in the leaf litter (where they will often overturn leaves), along low twigs, and especially from the undersides of leaves by reaching up from the ground or a low perch. The tail is often held partly cocked upward and is sometimes flicked nervously. The crown feathers are raised when the bird is agitated. Singing birds usually choose a perch within a few feet of the ground but song perches are sometimes well off the ground, even near the tops of mid-level trees. Winter birds are territorial, but sometimes associate with other bird species exploiting ant swarms. In addition to insect food, Kentucky Warblers occasionally take small berries.

The **NEST** is rather bulky but well concealed, on the ground or, more frequently, just off the ground at the base of a small shrub. It consists of layers of dead leaves on the ouside and fine fibers and rootlets lining the open cup. The clutch size (averaging 4.5) is somewhat larger than that of most other southeastern U.S. warblers.

 HABITAT

BREEDS in deep deciduous woodlands and less commonly in mixed deciduous-conifer woodlands with extensive shade and considerable shrubby growth and ground cover. Occupied woodlands may be in bottomlands or uplands but always have a dense understory and are rather moist. Tree associations of occupied lowland habitats are varied, but hardwoods always dominate; frequently flooded swamp forests are usually avoided. In upland areas (to 3,000 ft. in the Appalachians, 2,400 ft. in Arkansas) the Kentucky is found in the thickly vegetated bottoms of ravines and on shaded north slopes.

WINTERS in humid forested lowland habitats and second growth. As on the breeding grounds, a dense shrub layer within the shaded forest is required. In **MIGRATION**, occupies a wider variety of habitats, but is still generally a skulker in dense, shady understory growth.

 DISTRIBUTION

BREEDS from e. Neb., w. and s.-cen. and e. Iowa, s. Wisc., se. Mich. (rare), n. Ill., n. Ind., n. Ohio, n. Pa., se. and s.-cen. N.Y. (mainly the lower Hudson River Valley), and Conn. (nesting not confirmed) south to the eastern hill country of e.-cen. Texas, the Gulf states, nw. Fla., Ga. (except se.), and S.C. Has nested once recently in s. Minn. (Nicollet Co.); there are old nesting records in s.-cen. N.Y. (Cortland Co.). Summer records of singing (and presumably unpaired) males extend north to s. Ont., the Niagara Frontier region, and Mass. The recent occurrence of breeding birds in the northeastern part of the range (se. N.Y., Conn.) represents a recolonization of formerly occupied breeding grounds. At the northwest limit of the range in nw. Mo., sw. Iowa, and se. Neb., Kentuckies are restricted to hills with fine loess soil (a situation in which several southern bird species reach their northwestern limits).

WINTERS from the lowlands of e. Mexico from Veracruz south through the Yucatán peninsula (and less commonly on the west coast north to San Blas, Nayarit), and south through Central America to Honduras (mainly Caribbean lowlands, rare on Pacific coast), Costa Rica, and Panama (mainly in the west). A few winter through e. Panama, in nw. Venezuela, and in the Santa

Marta region of Colombia. Recorded in winter in the Netherlands Antilles and the Lesser Antilles. North of the normal wintering range, Kentucky Warblers have wintered casually in s. Florida (one specimen), coastal and s. Texas, se. and nw. Louisiana, and s. California (at least five records).

SPRING MIGRATION is trans-Gulf, with the earliest spring arrivals on the Gulf Coast in late March (very rarely mid-March) and early April. Only on the Gulf Coast at traditional migrant traps (as on the upper Texas coast) are any significant concentrations noted, and these are usually in mid-April. Away from these areas it is quite uncommon as a spring migrant, with most spring arrivals being birds which have returned to their nesting grounds. Typically arrives in s. Ark. and n. Ala. in very late March or early April, whereas arrivals in s. Mo., Tenn., and Ky. are usually in the second or third week of April. Arrives at the northern end of the breeding range (n. Ohio, Pa., N.Y.) around 5–10 May, with some records of early overshoots, such as 4 April in Chicago and 17 April in Mass. Spring migration continues in Fla. and along the Gulf Coast to early May (rarely mid-May), and into early June in the more northern regions.

Occurs annually in spring north of the mapped breeding range, to n. Minn., Wisc. (St. Croix Co.), the northern Lower Peninsula of Mich., Ont. (Manitoulin District), upstate N.Y., and Mass. (up to 10 birds per spring). Vagrant even farther north (see below).

FALL MIGRATION is also primarily trans-Gulf but is somewhat more easterly than in spring. The species is not often noted in fall, because of its secretive nature, except at southern migration traps. Departure from the breeding grounds takes place from late July to mid-September. The fall peak in Fla., the state with the best published data, is from about 10–20 September (with the earliest fall migrants noted there in late July). It is casual in most of its range after late September, but there are numerous records through October from the Gulf states and a few farther north. Exceptionally, it is recorded into November in Ky., upstate N.Y., Mass., and N.S.

VAGRANT north of the normal range. Away from New England and the Canadian Maritimes, these overshoots are almost exclusively in spring. Mass. records are evenly divided between spring (mainly May and early June) and fall. Spring and fall records exist for N.S. and N.B., and there are about ten fall records from Nfld. Recorded in s. Que. and along the n. shore of Lake Ontario. There are sight records for Man. (late September, May), Sask. (late September), and Alta. (June), and the species is noted casually in spring and fall in N.D. and S.D.

In the West, it is of annual occurrence in Calif., with 115

KENTUCKY WARBLER
Oporornis formosus

records through 1995, mostly in spring; the Calif. total increased by some 30 percent in the spring of 1992, and numerous birds summered that year, especially in interior Santa Barbara Co. (This unprecedented invasion in the West also involved other southeastern warblers, such as Hooded and Northern Parula, and vireos; it may have been due to a spring of abnormal easterly winds over the Gulf of Mexico which affected trans-Gulf migrants.) Also regular in Ariz. (some 50 records, mostly spring). Casual in spring in N.M. and Colo., with a few summer and fall records. There are records for all remaining western states (except Idaho) and for Sonora, Mexico.

EXCEPTIONAL was a sight record for northern Alaska (Beaufort Lagoon) on 19 September 1982.

STATUS AND CONSERVATION

Although populations appear to be stable through most of the range, this species is a frequent cowbird host and is potentially sensitive to forest fragmentation. Their highest densities occur in large forest tracts. Forest clearing has resulted in some recent local declines (including Missouri). Locally, overbrowsing by deer has adversely impacted their required dense understory habitat. Population and range increases in Ohio and s. New England may represent recolonization of formerly occupied habitats following reforestation. Dense understory growth of introduced honeysuckles might locally benefit the Kentucky Warbler, but the long-term effects of these exotics may be negative if tree regeneration is adversely affected.

 ## SUBSPECIES

The more northerly breeding populations (from n. Missouri, s. Ohio, and Virginia north) have been considered to be separable as *O. f. umbraticus*, but most authors reject this treatment. *O. f. umbraticus* is supposedly characterized by lighter, more yellowish upperparts and paler yellow on the underparts.

 ## TAXONOMIC RELATIONSHIPS

Relationships within the genus *Oporornis* are unclear; the Kentucky Warbler does not seem closely related to any of the other three species of that genus as currently constituted. Apparent genetic similarity between the Kentucky Warbler and the Central American yellowthroat *Geothlypis semiflava* needs further investigation but certainly implies a close relationship between at least some members of the genus *Oporornis* and the yellowthroats. Two intergeneric hybrids with the Blue-winged Warbler are known, one the type specimen of the "Cincinnati Warbler," *Helminthophaga cincinnatiensis*.

 ## PLUMAGES AND MOLTS

SPRING ADULT MALE: Forehead black. Crown consists of black feathers with dark gray tips, these tips being broader in the center and rear of the crown; on many individuals the front half and sides of the crown appear solid black, with the appearance of a gray patch at the rear of the crown. Remaining upperparts deep olive green, slightly brighter and paler on the rump and uppertail coverts. Supraloral area and supercilium bright yellow, extending a few millimeters behind the eye. Bright yellow ring around the rear half of the eye connects with the yellow supercilium. Lores black. Cheeks solidly black, forming an elongated, downward-pointing mark from the auriculars to the rear border of the throat. Chin, throat, and entire underparts bright yellow, tinged with olive on the sides and flanks. Wing coverts and edges to the dusky flight feathers olive green like the upperparts. Rectrices unmarked dull olive green and relatively broad. In rare variants the black mark on the side of the face extends down to the sides of the breast, occasionally even with a few black feathers on the center of the chest. **FIRST SPRING MALE:** Very similar to spring adult male, but on average the gray tipping to the black crown feathers is more extensive, extending farther forward. The gray of the rear crown is tinged with olive. The black cheek patch may be less extensive in many individuals than spring adult males, and there is more of a tendency to have olive tips to the black auricular feathers. The rectrices average narrower, more tapered, and more worn than spring adults. **SPRING ADULT FEMALE:** Overall pattern similar to spring males, with variable amounts of black on the face and crown; this black averages less than spring males, but there is considerable individual variation. The tips to the black crown feathers are not clear dark gray but rather suffused with brownish olive. These tips extend farther forward on the crown than spring adult males, often through the forehead. The black cheek patch averages slightly less extensive and duller black than spring males, often with faint olive tips on the auricular feathers (as in first spring males). The brightness of the underparts is similar to spring males. The rectrices are similar to spring adult males. **FIRST SPRING FEMALE:** Very similar to spring adult female, but some individuals may have the black of the forehead entirely concealed by brownish olive feather tips, and may have even less black in the cheek patch. Rectrices as in first spring male. **FALL ADULT MALE:** Much like spring adult male, but gray tipping to crown feathers extends somewhat farther forward onto the forehead, and the black cheek patch has scattered, inconspicuous olive tips, especially on the lower portion. The fresh rectrices are relatively broad and truncate, with a small point at the very tip. **FIRST FALL MALE:** Differs from fall adult male in having the black of the forehead and crown much more heavily veiled with gray and olive-brown feather tips. On individual

Kentucky Warbler.
Female (L), male (R)
in Ohio in June.
(Photo: Steve and
Dave Maslowski)

*Kentucky Warbler.
Male in Texas in May.
(Photo: Brian E.
Small)*

crown feathers, a narrow band of dark gray is present between the black base and the olive-brown tip. The black cheek patch is duller and less extensive, with narrow olive tipping to the individual feathers. The yellow of the underparts may be slightly more tinged with olive than fall adults. The rectrices average narrower than fall adults and are more tapered to the tip. In general, this plumage is very similar to that of the fall adult female. **FALL ADULT FEMALE:** Much like first fall male, but on average there is slightly less black visible on the crown, and the black of the cheek patch is duller. Individual crown feathers are tipped with olive-brown, with little or no dark gray present on most birds. The broad, truncate rectrices are like the fall adult male. **FIRST FALL FEMALE:** The forehead and crown are strongly washed with olive-brown, obscuring most or all of the black. The cheek patch is variable, but any black present is always dull. Many individuals show only a small, dull black or dusky patch extending from the lores to just below the eye, with olive tips to the individual black feathers. The yellow of the underparts is somewhat tinged with olive, especially on the sides of the breast. Rectrices narrow, tapered at the tip. **JUVENILE:** Generally olive-brown above; wings olive with two brownish wing bars. Head and neck unmarked olive-brown. Underparts yellowish brown, becoming yellower on the flanks, belly, and undertail coverts. **BARE PARTS:** Bill blackish brown on the upper mandible, pale brown on the lower mandible, which is fleshy at the base. Bills of spring adult males, at least, may be more uniformly dark, with some pinkish at the base of the lower mandible. Eyes dark brown. Legs and feet rather bright pinkish. Little seasonal or age and sex variation in bare-part color.

The prebasic molt occurs from June to August on the breeding grounds; it is complete in adults but does not involve the flight feathers in hatching-year birds. The prealternate molt (February to April) is very limited in adults but probably more extensive in immatures, especially immature males.

 **REFERENCES**

DISTRIBUTION: Terrill et al. 1992.
ECOLOGY, BEHAVIOR, VOCALIZATIONS, AND CONSERVATION: Rappole and Warner 1980, Whitcomb et al. 1981.
PLUMAGES, MOLTS, AND MORPHOLOGY: Mulvihill et al. 1992.
SYSTEMATICS: Browning 1978, Graves 1988.

CONNECTICUT WARBLER

Oporornis agilis

5.5 in. (14 cm). The large, chunky, short-tailed Connecticut Warbler has a hooded appearance, olive upperparts, and dull yellow underparts; a distinct, complete white or buffy eye-ring is present in all plumages. The overall behavior, especially the walking gait, is reminiscent of that of an Ovenbird and quite different from the behavior of other *Oporornis*. This is one of our most highly migratory warblers, and the migration routes taken in spring and fall are distinctly different; it is our latest warbler to appear in spring and also one of the latest fall migrants. Because of its secretive habits it is poorly known in general, especially outside its rather limited breeding range; most or all individuals presumably winter in Amazonian South America.

 DESCRIPTION

Generally olive above and rather pale and dull yellow below, with a gray or brown "hood" and a conspicuous white or off-white eye-ring that is complete or nearly so. Age and sex variation primarily involves the color of the hood, throat, and eye-ring; fall immatures cannot reliably be sexed. Seasonal variation in plumage is slight.

This is a large, chunky warbler with a rather short tail and long undertail coverts that reach to within about 10 mm of the tail tip. The wing-minus-tail measurement is greater than 19 mm, and usually greater than 22 mm. The bill is fairly large and heavy, and the long legs and large feet are pale pinkish.

 SIMILAR SPECIES

This species is not too difficult to identify, given good views — but getting reasonable views is a difficult task. Behavioral clues are very important in identification. Critical aspects of the appearance include the chunky shape, long undertail coverts and short tail, large bill, long-legged and long-toed appearance, and the walking gait. This Ovenbird-like walking behavior is entirely different from the hopping behavior of other *Oporornis* and of *Geothlypis* yellowthroats. When Connecticut Warblers flush, they appear thrushlike, often sitting on a branch for an extended period. The yellow of the underparts is rather pale and dull in all plumages (even the relatively bright adult males are duller yellow than Mourning or MacGillivray's Warblers). The complete gray or brown hood and the bold and usually complete whitish eye-ring are outstanding plumage characters.

The Connecticut is most easily confused with **MOURNING WARBLER**. In addition to the important behavioral characters noted above (and different vocalizations, described below), a number of appearance characters are important, but all should be used with caution. The classic mark of Connecticut, the thick, complete eye-ring, is a useful distinction from most Mournings. Many Connecticuts, at least in fall, can show a small break at the rear of the eye-ring. Mourning Warblers often show a thin and essentially complete whitish eye-ring, but close inspection usually reveals a small break at both the front and the rear. In any case, the two species approach each other closely in the eye-ring character, so additional characters should always be used. Connecticuts lack the indistinct pale supraloral line present on at least some immatures of Mourning and MacGillivray's. Connecticuts also lack black on the head and throat in all plumages. The hooded appearance is a useful feature in separating Connecticuts from fall immature Mournings; the latter typically (though not always) have the yellow of the underparts continuing up through the throat. Even those Mournings with whitish or buffy throats (some immatures and adult females) lack the prominent hood (complete breast-band) of Connecticuts. All Connecticuts lack yellow in the throat, although some immatures are pale tawny on the chin and throat and in some lighting might appear to have a dull yellow wash there. Connecticut is slightly bigger billed and longer winged than Mourning. In the hand, the wing-minus-tail measurement of over 19 mm (usually over 22 mm) is diagnostic from the Mourning.

Most of the above characters also distinguish Connecticut from **MACGILLIVRAY'S WARBLER**. MacGillivray's prominent eye-arcs are always broken in front and rear. The underparts are considerably brighter yellow in MacGillivray's, and the shorter undertail coverts of MacGillivray's do not come close to the tip of the relatively long tail (tail extension beyond the undertail coverts averages about 10–12 mm longer in MacGillivray's than in Connecticut; Mourning is intermediate).

Confusion with the dull female **COMMON YELLOWTHROAT** is possible, especially those that have evident pale eye-rings and pale buffy throats. Yellowthroats are considerably smaller, slimmer, and longer tailed; note also the dull olive-brown flanks contrasting with the whitish belly and yellow undertail coverts. **NASHVILLE WARBLERS**, particularly dull fall immatures, are frequently confused with Connecticuts because of the bold, complete eye-ring. Nashville is a much smaller bird with a fine, sharp bill and very different behavior (active and acrobatic, feeding at fine branches, leaf clusters, and weed stems). Dull immature **YELLOW WARBLERS** have sometimes been confused with Connecticuts because of their eye-ringed appearance; note the yellow tail spots and yellow wing covert and tertial fringes in the Yellow Warbler, which is a much more active, arboreal, and easily seen bird than the Connecticut.

 ## VOICE

SONG is a loud, rocking *chuppa-cheepa chuppa-cheepa chuppa-cheep* or *chip-chuppy chip-chuppy chip-chuppy* with a distinctive jerking rhythm. Phrases may sometimes be simplified to a disyllabic *beecher* or *chuppy.* The song differs from those of other *Oporornis* and may recall songs of Ovenbird, Common Yellowthroat, or the terminal part of the Northern Waterthrush's song.

The rarely heard **CALL NOTE** is a loud, nasal *chimp* or *poitch,* lacking the raspy quality of the call of Mourning. This call appears to be given most often by agitated birds on the breeding grounds; it is occasionally heard in migration. Mourning and MacGillivray's warblers, in contrast, give call notes frequently at all seasons. **FLIGHT NOTE,** often heard in migration, is a buzzy *zeet,* suggesting the flight call of a Yellow or Blackpoll warbler. This is quite different from the flight notes of Mourning and MacGillivray's. This *zeet* note is also given by perched birds.

 ## BEHAVIOR

This is a retiring species that can be very difficult to observe. It does not often respond to pishing. It usually stays quite low, except in the case of singing males. The outstanding behavioral feature is the deliberate walking gait, very distinct from other *Oporornis.* The tail is bobbed slightly while the bird is walking but is not held cocked upward as in the Ovenbird. It may sometimes hop, as when moving up onto a low branch, but it typically walks when on the ground or along logs or tree limbs. When flushed off the ground it will often fly up and sit motionless on a branch for long periods, suggesting a thrush. This tendency to sit motionless can produce excellent views if the observer is patient and persistent.

When foraging it walks along the ground, bobbing its head back and forth or from side to side, and often peering upward. It gleans much of its food of insects, spiders, small snails, etc., from the undersides of low foliage; it often stretches or jumps vertically to grab prey. Prey is taken directly off the ground as well, and this species also forages along limbs well up into trees.

Males on territory usually sing from high perches (15 ft. or more); they may remain perched while singing for long periods. The singing perch is usually fairly well concealed within the canopy. While the bird is singing, the tail and body appear to shake. If the singing bird is approached, it will often walk out of view. Spring migrant males will frequently sing, often from lower perches than males on the breeding grounds; nonsinging birds are extremely difficult to detect in migration.

The **NEST** is a deep cup built on or very near the ground; it is well concealed, often nestled well into a mound of moss or a clump of grass. It is made of grasses, leaves, rootlets, and other fine material.

 ## Habitat

BREEDING habitat varies through the species' range from wet coniferous bogs to well-drained deciduous woodlands. Occupied woodlands are relatively open, with only moderate understory and ground cover; they vary greatly in moistness. Through much of the range the preferred habitat is tamarack or spruce bogs with an understory or ground cover of Labrador tea, pitcher plant, swamp laurel, and thick layers of sphagnum moss. Elsewhere, especially from Minnesota and Manitoba west, they occupy well-drained ridges and bluffs dominated by poplar and aspen. Other associations include mixed forests with balsam fir, white pine and various deciduous trees, and (in portions of the Great Lakes region) jack pine barrens.

WINTER habitat preferences are poorly known, but the Connecticut appears to occupy woodland areas and forest borders and clearings. In **MIGRATION** it can occur in a variety of habitats but usually seeks dense, low, and often moist tangles. Fall migrants in New England are usually found away from the outer coast in wet thickets under swamp maples; also in dense berry brambles, dense weedy areas (such as patches of ragweed), and even occasionally cornfields. Some of the largest numbers noted in fall on the East Coast are seen in flight near Cape May in the early morning. Not surprisingly, considering the species' secretive habits, more are detected in migration by banders than by birders.

◣ DISTRIBUTION

BREEDS in a rather narrow band through the boreal region from ne. and e.-cen. B.C. (where scarce and local) across cen. Alta., cen. Sask., cen. and se. Man., n. Minn., n. Wisc., n. Mich. (upper peninsula and northernmost lower peninsula), and Ont. (except south) to cen. Que. It is uncommon and local over much of this breeding range, although it can be numerous and almost loosely colonial in a few regions.

The Connecticut's **WINTER** range is the most poorly understood of our warblers, because of the species' retiring habits. There are no documented winter records north of South America. It perhaps winters largely within the Amazonian region and is thus among our most southerly wintering warblers. It has been recorded in w. and cen. Venezuela, n. and e. Colombia, w. and cen. Brazil (south to n. Mato Grosso), and in se. Peru. Many of the records outside of the Amazon basin may pertain to migrants. Most winter records are from below 6,000 ft., but migrants have been noted up to 13,000 ft. in Venezuela.

MIGRATION routes of this species are rather direct and well-defined. Fall migration is considerably more easterly than that of spring. In **SPRING MIGRATION,** birds presumably move over the Caribbean region; they then move through Fla. and then northwestward, west of the Appalachians, through the Miss. and Ohio valleys to the breeding grounds. The lack of records through the Greater Antilles may reflect lack of coverage combined with the difficulty of finding silent migrants of this species, but may also suggest long overwater flights (as in Fall Migration; see below).

Spring migrants arrive in Fla. as early as very late April, but more typical arrival dates are in early May. The spring peak in Fla. is during the second and third weeks of May, with the last birds recorded at the end of May. Arrivals in the upper Mississippi Valley, Ohio Valley and southern Great Lakes are generally in mid-May, with a few records back to early May; April records in these northern areas are suspect. Peak numbers pass through about 20–25 May, with a few still moving in early June; very late migrants may pass through as late as mid-June. This is one of the latest warblers to arrive on the breeding grounds; birds usually do not arrive at the northern and western end of the breeding range until around the first of June. The spring migration route does not include the western Gulf Coast — there is only one documented record for La., and only about five for Texas. It is casual or very rare in the s. Great Plains, but somewhat more numerous in the n. Great Plains, especially N.D. It is strictly casual in spring east of the Appalachians, with just a few spring records from Md. north to N.S.

FALL MIGRATION is more easterly than the spring movement, with migrants mainly detected from the Great Lakes east to New England, and from there south to Va. and the Outer Banks of N.C. It is extremely rare in the Midwest south of the Great Lakes; it is very rare but perhaps regular in N.S. and N.B. (and recorded once in September in se. Nfld.) and along the Atlantic Coast south of the Outer Banks. It appears that most birds depart the Atlantic Coast when weather conditions are favorable and head on a long overwater flight to South America, much as Blackpoll Warblers may do. This is suggested by the species' regularity on Bermuda in fall, with the notable concentration of 75 recorded there during Hurricane Emily on 26 September 1987. It is a very rare fall migrant in the West Indies, again suggesting that most birds overfly this region.

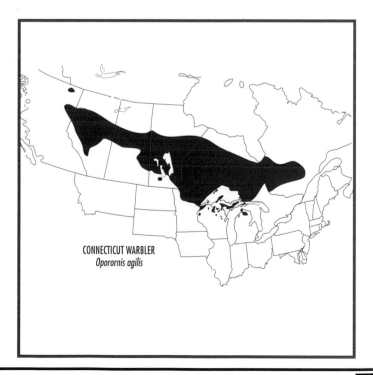

CONNECTICUT WARBLER
Oporornis agilis

Fall migration begins in the last week of August (exceptionally from mid-August), but the first birds are not noted in most areas until early September. The majority pass through from mid-September to early October, with the peak on the Atlantic Coast being about a week later than that in the Great Lakes area. Small numbers continue on the coast until mid-October, with a few until the end of the month. There is a 4–5 November record for Texas. Exceptional, if correct, was a sight record from s. Fla. on 28 December.

VAGRANT to w. North America, primarily in Calif., where there are 77 records (five in June, the remainder from early September to late October with most in mid- to late September). The fall records are coastal except for four from late September in the Death Valley region. Over half of the Calif. records are from the Farallon Is., where this secretive species can easily be detected. Elsewhere in the West it is extremely rare; recorded in Mont. (fewer than ten records), Nev., Colo., Ariz., Ut., and w. Okla. Recorded once in May in Belize, and on 1 November on Clipperton Is. off sw. Mexico. There are three fall specimens from w. Panama. Reported also from Honduras and Costa Rica.

STATUS AND CONSERVATION

Historical accounts suggest that this species was considerably more numerous in the 19th century than at present, at least as a fall migrant in New England. There are no clear reasons for a decline, as both breeding and presumed wintering habitats have remained relatively intact. This species is common nowhere.

SUBSPECIES

No geographical variation reported; no subspecies described.

TAXONOMIC RELATIONSHIPS

This species does not appear to be particularly closely related to the other *Oporornis*, particularly in behavior, vocalizations, and nest structure. It may well deserve generic rank. A possible hybrid with Mourning Warbler was taken in spring in Oklahoma.

PLUMAGES AND MOLTS

SPRING ADULT MALE: Entire head gray, forming a distinct hood; the gray is deepest and bluest on the crown, auriculars, and chest. The throat is slightly paler than the rest of the head, and there is a slight hint of olive on the rear of the crown that blends into the olive back. A conspicuous and complete ring of white encircles the eye. Remaining upperparts olive. Wings and tail olive-brown. The chest is darker gray than the throat, with a sharp border against the yellow of the underparts. The remaining underparts are generally light yellow, deepest and brightest on the center of the breast and belly. The sides and flanks are washed with olive-gray. **FIRST SPRING MALE:** Similar to spring adult male but slightly duller and browner above, with less contrast between the crown and the upperparts and with less of a sharp demarcation between the gray chest and yellow underparts. Rectrices more worn and tapered than in adults. **SPRING ADULT FEMALE:** Forehead and crown brownish olive, with only a slight gray tint and showing little or no contrast with the upperparts. Wings and tail as in spring adult male. Face and chest grayish, washed slightly with olive-brown. No sharp contrast between the gray chest and the light yellow underparts. Chin and throat dull whitish or pale gray-buff. Eye-ring complete (or very slightly broken at rear), white or slightly buffy. **FIRST SPRING FEMALE:** Not distinguishable from spring adult female, although averages slightly duller and brown, with buffier throat. In the hand, the rectrices appear more worn and tapered. **FALL ADULT MALE:** Very similar to spring adult male, but the feathers of the crown and hindneck are tipped with olive-brown, and the olive of the upperparts is more strongly washed with brown. There may be a hint of a brown wash to the gray of the chest. **FIRST FALL MALE:** Uniformly olive-brown on the forehead, crown, upperparts, sides of neck, and chest; often with a tinge of gray on the forecrown and chest. Chin and throat whitish or very pale gray-buff. Eye-ring buffy white, sometimes slightly broken at the rear. Underparts rather dull, pale yellow, washed with olive-gray on the sides and flanks. Rectrices tapered. **FALL ADULT**

Connecticut Warbler. Adult male in Illinois in September. (Photo: Rob Curtis/The Early Birder)

Connecticut Warbler. First fall from mouth of Big Sycamore Canyon, Pt. Mugu State Park, Ventura Co., California on 27 September 1987. (Photo: Larry Sansone).

FEMALE: Similar to spring adult female but more strongly washed with brown on the crown, upperparts, and chest. **FIRST FALL FEMALE:** Not distinguishable from first fall male, but on average more olive-brown (less gray-brown) on throat and forecrown and buffier (less whitish) on the throat. A few individuals appear dull yellowish buff on the chin and throat. Rectrices tapered. **JUVENILE:** Generally brown above and on the chest, sides, and flanks; buffy on the throat and light yellow on the lower breast and belly. Buffy eye-ring. **BARE PARTS:** Culmen and tip of lower mandible dusky brown; sides of upper mandible and most of lower mandible pinkish. Eyes dark brown. Legs and feet bright pinkish.

The prebasic molt takes place on the breeding grounds; it is complete in adults but does not involve the flight feathers in hatching-year birds. The limited prealternate molt takes place from February to April and may be more extensive in second-year birds than in older birds.

 REFERENCES

DISTRIBUTION: Robbins 1974, Sutton 1967 (supposed Connecticut × Mourning Warbler hybrid), Veit and Petersen 1993 (details declines of migrants from more than a century ago).

ECOLOGY, BEHAVIOR, VOCALIZATIONS, AND CONSERVATION: Elder 1991, Robbins 1974, Shanahan 1992, Veit and Petersen 1993 (describes habitats for migrants).

IDENTIFICATION: Curson 1992, Lanyon and Bull 1967, Pyle and Henderson 1990.

Oporornis philadelphia

5.25 in. (13.3 cm). The Mourning Warbler is a skulking bird of dense undergrowth, best located by its distinctive *chip* call or when males are singing in spring migration and on the breeding grounds. It is a boreal and eastern species that is very closely related to the western MacGillivray's Warbler; most purported instances of hybridization between the two, however, probably pertain to variant Mournings. The separation of Mourning and MacGillivray's warblers is perhaps the most difficult field identification problem among North American warblers, and much has been written on the subject. Mournings can also be easily confused with Connecticut Warblers and Common Yellowthroats. Individual variation is considerable in Mourning Warblers within all age and sex classes. This species is a circum-Gulf migrant, which is fairly unusual considering that it is a boreal breeder that winters well to the south — from Nicaragua to nw. South America. It has perhaps the latest spring migration peak of all our warblers, from mid-May through early June.

DESCRIPTION

Generally olive green above and yellow below. Adult males have a gray hood and black throat patch, and usually lack any white eye-arcs. In females and immatures the hood is less distinct or lacking, the throat varies from dull whitish to yellowish, and there is a variable thin broken eye-ring or eye-arcs. Seasonal variation in plumage is slight. Adults are easily sexed by plumage; some immatures can also be sexed by plumage. Individual variation within age and sex classes is considerable; such variation follows no clear geographical trends.

This is a moderately heavy, short-tailed warbler with long undertail coverts.

SIMILAR SPECIES

Separation from the closely related **MACGILLIVRAY'S WARBLER** can be difficult in all plumages. Adult males of the two are generally readily distinguished, but considerable individual variation in Mourning complicates this. The absence of white eye-arcs is diagnostic for Mourning, but some adult male Mournings do show traces of thin white eye-arcs; these are much thinner and less distinct than those of MacGillivray's. An adult male lacking blackish lores is a Mourning, but some Mournings have black lores similar to those of MacGillivray's. Adult male Mournings typically show a more solid and distinct black breast patch; this black area in MacGillivray's is more blended into the gray throat. Mournings may show some pale scaling on the black of the throat; the pale markings within the black of MacGillivray's are usually arranged into indistinct vertical stripes. Although not visible in the field, there is a tiny spot of white feathering on the extreme upper chin in spring male MacGillivray's; this area is deep gray in Mournings. Separation of female and immature Mournings and MacGillivray's is more difficult, and some birds may not be identifiable in the field. The lack of eye-arcs indicates Mourning (many adult females). In female and immature Mournings that do show eye-arcs, these arcs vary from white to buffy or even pale yellow and are thin but extensive, often forming a complete but very narrow ring. All MacGillivray's show evident white or whitish eye-arcs that are relatively thick and blunt, never forming a complete ring. In immature Mournings the throat is typically yellow to yellow-buff, whether slightly washed with that color or nearly the same color as the bright yellow underparts. Only a very small minority of female and immature MacGillivray's Warblers show a hint of dull yellow in the throat; these should be carefully separated from Mourning by the thicker eye-arcs, longer tail extension, and, ideally, call note. The yellow throat of Mourning typically continues into the yellow of the lower breast and belly without interruption by a grayish or olive breast-band; such a complete breast-band is present on adult female and immature MacGillivray's. Adult female Mournings may show a slight breast-band and lack yellow in the throat; again, such birds should be distinguished by eye-arc, tail extension, and call note characters. Immature Mournings typically show a yellow wash in the supraloral line, a region that is purer white in MacGillivray's. On average, Mournings show less olive on the flanks than MacGillivray's. In immature male Mournings, the presence of black spots on the center or sides of the breast is diagnostic versus MacGillivray's; however, many immature males may lack such markings.

Structurally, Mourning and MacGillivray's warblers are similar, although MacGillivray's typically has a longer tail extension beyond the undertail coverts (about 22 mm in MacGillivray's, 15 mm in Mourning). However, there is geographical variation in tail length in MacGillivray's, and shorter-tailed northern birds may overlap in tail extension with Mourning. A key in-hand character for nonmolting birds is the difference between the flattened wing measurement and the tail length measurement, with Mournings measuring 10 mm or more, and MacGillivray's measuring less than 12 mm (usually 2–9 mm, but exceptionally to 14.6 mm). Birds with a wing-minus-tail measurement in the range of 9–15 mm should be identified with additional corroborating characters.

Vocalizations are very helpful with problematic birds. Call notes, especially, are distinctive, with the flatter note of Mourning outside the range of MacGillivray's *chips* (which tend to be sharper and more metallic). Songs also differ, with those of MacGillivray's more complex and more variable. Both species give a similar flight note.

See **CONNECTICUT WARBLER**, which can be quite similar in plumage to some female and immature Mournings. Connecticut is best told by its fuller, more thrushlike shape, even shorter tail extension past the undertail coverts, different vocalizations, and walking gait. The bold and complete (or nearly complete) eye-ring of Connecticut separates it from Mournings, but beware of Mournings with thin but essentially complete eye-rings. The underparts of Connecticut are paler and duller than those of Mourning. All Connecticuts other than adult males show a broad olive or brownish breast-band separating the yellow of the posterior underparts from the whitish or pale tawny throat; the throat of Connecticut is only rarely tinged pale yellow, whereas it is often strongly tinged yellow in female and immature Mournings.

Beware of confusion between immature Mournings and female **COMMON YELLOWTHROATS**. In most of North America, yellowthroats show a dull whitish or pale brownish belly region that contrasts with the yellow throat and upper breast; Mournings are more solidly yellow below. Yellowthroats are smaller and have a proportionately longer tail and shorter undertail coverts. Compare also with other dull olive and yellow warblers, such as **ORANGE-CROWNED** (especially gray-headed *orestera* and *celata*).

 VOICE

SONG is typically two-parted, with the second part slightly lower in pitch and containing fewer syllables: *churry-churry-churry-chory-chory*. Many variations exist, although song variation is less than in MacGillivray's. In some songs the second part with the lower notes is longer than the first. Other songs have notes all on one pitch (these may suggest Kentucky Warbler). Uniform songs have been found to dominate in the western part of the range and two-parted songs to dominate farther east. Spring migrant males may sing frequently. Flight songs, somewhat more complex than typical songs delivered from perches, have been described.

The **CALL NOTE** is quite distinctive and is probably the best single way to tell this species from MacGillivray's. Mournings call frequently, especially in response to pishing. The call is a sharp, rather scratchy *chit* or *vit* (also *chet, jip*) similar to one of the common notes given by the Bewick's Wren (*Thryomanes bewickii*). This call can be given in a loosely organized series when the bird is agitated. Another call, a higher and less harsh *tsip,* is given when the nest or young are approached. The **FLIGHT NOTE** is a thin, sharp *seep,* less buzzy than the flight call of Connecticut.

 ## BEHAVIOR

This is a secretive species that spends most of its time (when not singing) on or near the ground. It moves on the ground or low in the vegetation by hopping. Forages mainly by gleaning foliage for insects and spiders. Singing males, even spring migrants, will often start singing from low in the vegetation and work their way higher to more exposed perches in shrubs or trees before diving back into the undergrowth. On the breeding grounds they often sing from exposed perches 80 ft. or more above the ground. In threat display around nest, they flick their wings rapidly outwards and may fan or flip their tails. Mournings are generally solitary and territorial on the winter grounds.

The **NEST** is difficult to find; it is placed on or near the ground (very exceptionally higher, to 30 ft.), within dense tangles of briars or herbaceous vegetation. The nest is built of fibers and leaves, lined with grass, rootlets, and hair.

 ## HABITAT

For **BREEDING**, this boreal species reaches greatest abundance in the dense second-growth vegetation that thrives after fires, windfalls, or forest clearing (as for power line right-of-ways). It also occurs in wet bottomland woods with a dense growth of ferns, skunk-cabbage, marsh marigold, etc; they usually avoid areas with standing water. Second-growth habitats contain dense tangles and brambles, including blackberry, raspberry, and young saplings. These areas may be occupied with 2–4 years of deforestation and are suitable until a closed canopy develops. Dominant trees may be deciduous or coniferous. Other habitats occupied include dense thickets of aspen, birch, and cherry, and montane cranberry bogs.

WINTER birds occur in dense thickets, forest edges, coffee plantations, and overgrown weedy pastures, often near water. **MIGRANTS** are typically fond of dense, brushy thickets and woodland edges, and dense ragweed thickets.

BREEDS from ne. B.C. (where local), extreme se. Yukon, n. Alta., cen. Sask., cen. Man., n. Ont., cen. Que., Nfld. (including extreme s. Lab.), south to cen. Alta., se. Sask., s. Man., extreme n. N.D., e. Minn., s. Wisc. (also rare and local in n. Ill.), s. Mich., ne. Ohio, n. Pa., s. N.Y., nw. Mass., cen. N.H., and cen. Me. Also breeds at higher elevations in the Appalachians in W. Va., extreme w. Md., and nw. Va. A pair was noted for several summers in the 1980s in w. N.C. (near Jenkins), and there are summer records for the Indiana Dunes region of n. Ind.

WINTERS from s. Nicaragua south and east through Costa Rica and Panama to w. Colombia (but not in e. lowlands away from the Andes), w. Venezuela (and once in Sierra Parima in se.), and e. Ecuador. Generally winters below 6,000 ft., although often somewhat higher in the northern Andes. One January record for Oaxaca, Mexico. Within the U.S. there are two exceptional winter records, both in Calif.: an immature male in Los Angeles Co. 26 December 1981 to 28 January 1982, and an adult male in Orange Co. 31 December 1994 to 25 February 1995.

This is a circum-Gulf **MIGRANT** (like, for example, Nashville Warbler), which is unusual among warblers that winter primarily in s. Central America and South America. This avoidance of a Gulf crossing adds a good deal of distance to the migration. The spring migration route is through e. Mexico and s., cen., and e. Texas, but it is decidedly rare on the upper Texas coast and in sw. La. Migration then proceeds north through the prairie states east to the Ohio Valley. It is very scarce east of the Appalachians and south of New England in spring. The fall route is roughly a reverse of the spring route, but the Mourning is much more numerous on the upper Texas coast and sw. La. and decidedly more regular on the East Coast south of New England. Of the "eastern" warblers, this is by far the scarcest in the southeastern states, being very rare or casual from the Carolinas south to Fla. and west along the Gulf Coast to se. La. S.C., for example, has only four records. In the Southeast the majority of the records are from fall. Throughout its range, true migration patterns are somewhat obscured by the species' secretive nature.

SPRING MIGRATION is, along with Connecticut, the latest of all our warblers. The earliest arrival in Texas and other southern states is usually in very late April; late April records exist north to Mo., Ill., and Ont. Published reports from mid-April (and even to late March) seem unlikely and require documentation. More typical spring arrivals in the South are in the first or second weeks of May. The earliest arrivals in the upper Midwest and s. New England are usually in the first week of May, and in most of New England and in Man. in the second week of May. More typical arrivals average a week or so later. The peak of spring movement is from mid-May (Texas) to the last third of May and into the first week of June farther north (30 birds once recorded at Pt. Pelee, Ont., on 2 June). Most birds probably do not arrive at the northernmost nesting areas until nearly mid-June. Late stragglers are noted into the first week of June in Texas and to nearly mid-June in most other regions.

In FALL MIGRATION, the first individuals are noted south of the breeding grounds in early August (exceptionally to 30 July in Missouri), but more typical arrivals (as in upper Midwest and Northeast) are in the third week of August. Migration builds to a rapid peak at the very end of August and the first week of September in most areas; most birds have passed through by mid-September, with small numbers continuing through the end of the month and stragglers into the first few days of October. Strictly casual after this, with late dates for most eastern states ranging from about the end of the first week of October to the end of the month. One was recorded as late as 2 November in Ohio, and one found dead

MOURNING WARBLER
Oporornis philadelphia

in Mass. on 20 December was considered "probably" this species. A record for James Bay, Ont., on 22 September is late for that latitude. Stragglers occur into late October in the southern states.

VAGRANT to western North America, with most records being from Calif. Of 99 Calif. records, about half are from the Farallon Is., where (as with Connecticut Warbler) this species is far more easily detected than in its normal migration haunts. All but 18 Calif. records are for fall (late August to early November, but especially September); the spring records are mostly from mid-May to mid-June. Strictly casual elsewhere in the West, recorded in Colo., Mont., Wyo., N.M., Ariz., and Nev. There are sight records for Ore. and Wash. There are two September specimens from Alaska (Fairbanks, Middleton Is.). There is an early June specimen from off s. Baja Calif., and an October sighting for Punta Eugenia, Baja Calif. Sur.

There are three specimens from Greenland.

STATUS AND CONSERVATION

Given the transitional nature of many of its preferred breeding habitats, populations of this species may cycle locally, but overall numbers appear stable; forest clearing has probably resulted in higher populations at present than prior to the 1700s. Rarely parasitized by Brown-headed Cowbirds.

SUBSPECIES

No subspecies described. A mosaic pattern of variation in adult males has been noted in presence or absence of eye-arcs and in lore color (Newfoundland birds having largest percentage of dark lores). Wing-minus-tail measurements average slightly lower in the western part of the breeding range (all birds with wing-minus-tail of under 10 mm were from Ontario west in this study).

TAXONOMIC RELATIONSHIPS

Closely related to the MacGillivray's Warbler, and some authors have considered the two conspecific. Most purported hybrids may be variant Mournings. Near overlap in breeding ranges occurs in ne. British Columbia and w.-cen. Alberta.

A specimen thought to represent a hybrid with Connecticut Warbler is most likely an aberrant Mourning. Has hybridized with warblers of two other genera: Canada Warbler and Common Yellowthroat. A purported hybrid with Blue-winged Warbler instead appears to involve Kentucky × Blue-winged parentage.

SPRING ADULT MALE: Crown and sides of head gray; slightly paler gray on the sides of the throat. Darker gray in the loral region, and blackish there in a minority of birds throughout the range. A small proportion of birds through most of the species' range show thin but evident white eye-arcs. Gray of the crown and nape contrasts fairly sharply with the olive green of the remainder of the upperparts (slightly brighter and yellower on the rump and uppertail coverts). Feathers of the chin and throat darker gray than those of the face and crown, with some pale gray tips. There is a variable patch of black feathering across the chest at the lower border of the gray throat, which is sharply cut off from the yellow of the lower breast. Pale gray feather tips impart a scalloped effect within this black patch in all but the most heavily worn birds. In the darkest birds the chin and throat are almost the same color as the black chest. The remainder of the underparts are rather bright yellow, with a wash of olive on the flanks. The undertail coverts are yellow. The wings appear unmarked olive; the inner webs of the flight feathers are dusky brown. The tail is olive with yellow-olive edges to the rectrices. **FIRST SPRING MALE:** Very similar to spring adult male and generally not distinguishable in the field. Averages slightly duller on the upperparts, with a more blended border between the gray hindneck and olive back. The throat and lores average paler gray, and the black chest patch averages smaller. The more worn and tapered rectrices are evident in the hand. **SPRING ADULT FEMALE:** Head, including crown and hindneck, light gray; pale gray to grayish white on the throat. Eye-arcs lacking in most birds, but many show thin whitish arcs. There is an inconspicuous thin whitish or pale gray-buff supraloral stripe. The throat may include a few pale yellow feathers. Upperparts, wings, and tail as in spring adult male. The gray or gray-brown chest contrasts fairly sharply with the yellow

Mourning Warbler. Adult male in Santander, Colombia, in May. (Photo: J. Dunning/VIREO)

Mourning Warbler. First fall in New York in September. (Photo: Arthur Morris/Birds as Art)

of the underparts. The remainder of the underparts as in spring adult males, but yellow is slightly paler and duller. **FIRST SPRING FEMALE:** Generally quite similar to spring adult females, but many individuals are noticeably duller, with a strong olive-brown wash to the crown, more pale yellow in the throat, and more brown in the chest. There is more of a tendency to show thin whitish eye-arcs. Rectrices relatively worn and tapered. **FALL ADULT MALE:** Very similar to spring adult male, but the dark gray and black feathering on the throat and chest is more strongly veiled with pale gray feather tips, and the crown and hindneck are slightly washed with olive-brown. **FIRST FALL MALE:** Upperparts, including crown and hindneck, uniform olive, somewhat duller and browner than fall adult male. Lores grayish, with a thin pale yellow-buff supraloral streak and thin whitish eye-arcs. Throat color varies from whitish with a hint of pale yellow to rich yellow. The yellow of the throat continues through the center of the breast and blends with the yellow of the remaining underparts; the sides of the breast are brownish olive, forming an indistinct partial hood. Some first fall males show a few black feathers on the lower throat and the chest, but these can be almost completely obscured by yellowish or gray-buff feather tips. When visible, such spots confirm the bird as a first fall male, but roughly half the individuals show no such spotting. In a few young males the underlying black spotting on the chest is strong enough to form a complete hood separating the pale throat from the yellow underparts. **FALL ADULT FEMALE:** Similar to spring adult female, but the crown and hindneck are more strongly washed with olive-brown, and the gray of the face is tinged with pale brown. There is often some pale yellow in the throat, with the throat ground color varying from white to pale gray or buff. Also, there is a greater tendency to show whitish eye-arcs, often almost forming a complete ring. Quite similar to first fall male, but throat averages whiter, head with more gray, and rectrices truncate. **FIRST FALL**

FEMALE: Very similar to first fall male and generally not distinguishable in the field. Black always lacking in lower throat and chest region, but as noted above, such black may be absent or obscured in many first fall males. Throat color ranges from yellow-buff (nearly as bright as the yellow of the lower underparts) to very pale gray-buff with only a hint of a yellow wash. As in first fall male, this color washes through the breast so that there is no fully hooded effect. General color of upperparts and underparts averages slightly duller than in first fall male. **JUVENILE:** Olive-brown above; deep grayish tawny olive on the underparts, paler and more yellowish on the belly and undertail coverts. Inconspicuous buffy eye-ring. **BARE PARTS:** Upper mandible of bill dusky to blackish; lower mandible and tomium contrastingly paler, usually pinkish to yellowish pink. Legs and feet pinkish. Eyes dark brown.

The prebasic molt occurs primarily on the breeding grounds in July and August; it is complete in adults and partial in hatching-year birds (not involving the flight feathers). The prealternate molt is limited, taking place from February to April.

 REFERENCES

GENERAL: Cox 1960, Pitocchelli 1993, Veit and Petersen 1993.
DISTRIBUTION: Sutton 1967 (supposed Connecticut × Mourning Warbler hybrid).
ECOLOGY, BEHAVIOR, VOCALIZATIONS, AND CONSERVATION: Pitocchelli 1990.
IDENTIFICATION: Curson 1992, Kowalski 1983, Lanyon and Bull 1967, Phillips and Holmgren 1979, Pyle and Henderson 1990.
PLUMAGES: Hailman 1968, Pitocchelli 1990 and 1992.
SYSTEMATICS: Bledsoe 1988, Cox 1973, Graves 1988, Hall 1979, Patti and Myers 1976.

MacGILLIVRAY'S WARBLER   PL. 23

Oporornis tolmiei

5.25 in. (13 cm). MacGillivray's is the close western counterpart of the Mourning Warbler. Males are generally distinguished from the latter species by their bold white eye crescents and black lores; female and immature plumages of the two species are very similar. In distinguishing the two species, particular attention should be paid to the extent and shape of the eye-arcs, throat and breast color and pattern, tail length and undertail covert extent, and vocalizations. The breeding ranges of MacGillivray's and Mourning closely approach each other in e.-cen. British Columbia and w. cen. Alberta, but hybridization is limited or absent. This widespread but skulking western species shows slight geographical variation in color and measurements. It has been recorded as a vagrant to the Midwest and East.

This species was originally decribed by Townsend, and named *Sylvia tolmiei* after fellow naturalist and medical doctor William Tolmie, who collected the first specimen. Audubon independently named it for Scottish ornithologist William MacGillivray, but Townsend's name had nomenclatural priority. Audubon's tribute to MacGillivray has been preserved in the species' English name.

DESCRIPTION

Generally olive above, including the unmarked wings and tail, and bright yellow on the underparts. The head is gray, with a hooded appearance. Prominent white arcs are shown above and below the eye in all plumages; these are thickest and most prominent in adult males because they are set off from the black lores; adult males show variable slaty mottling on the lower throat. Females and immatures are pale gray to whitish (rarely dingy yellowish) on the throat, but retain a hooded appearance with a complete band of gray or olive-gray across the chest. The yellow underparts are somewhat more tinged with olive on the sides and flanks than in corresponding plumages of Mourning. There is little seasonal plumage change in adults; adults can readily be sexed, but immature males and females are very similar.

This is the most slender and long-tailed *Oporornis*, with considerable extension of the tail beyond the longest undertail coverts (averaging about 22 mm, as opposed to 10.5–15.0 mm in other *Oporornis*). It shares the weakly bicolored bill (dark upper mandible and pale yellowish pink lower mandible), and pinkish legs with its congeners.

SIMILAR SPECIES

Distinctions from the closely related and very similar **MOURNING WARBLER** are discussed under that species. Problematic birds (many females and immatures, as well as variant adult male Mournings) should be carefully examined for eye-arc shape, throat color, chest pattern, and undertail covert length; vocalizations (song, call notes) provide the surest means of field identification.

Gray-headed **ORANGE-CROWNED WARBLERS** with yellowish underparts, particularly birds of the race *orestera*, can be confused with MacGillivray's. Note the finer, sharper bill (lacking the pale pinkish lower mandible) and thinner and duller grayish legs of

Orange-crowned. Orange-crowned shows indistinct streaks on breast, a hint of a dark eye line, an indistinct split eye-ring rather than conspicuous eye-arcs, and a small patch of pale yellow at the bend of the wing. Also, Orange-crowned differs in more acrobatic and arboreal behavior and in sharp *tik* call note. Compare also with superficially similar **NASHVILLE WARBLER** (which has yellow throat, complete white eye-ring, fine sharp bill, and tail-wagging habit).

♪ VOICE

SONG is more variable than that of Mourning; some versions are similar in the two species, but MacGillivray's song is generally recognizable by the more varied ending. As in Mourning, the song usually consists of two parts: first, a series of 3–5 similar short, rough, or slightly trilled notes, followed by 2–3 notes on a different pitch. A typical rendition might be *trree trree trree trree swit swit* or *churry churry churry tree tree*. Unlike Mourning, in which the concluding series of notes is consistently lower pitched than the first series, MacGillivray's has a variable ending: higher pitched or lower pitched than the first series, with notes in the ending series often distinctly slurred or even double-noted: *sweet sweet sweet peachy peachy* or *chur chur chur swee swee ti-di.* Occasional males, at least on Vancouver Is., British Columbia, consistently give a loose trill suggesting (and perhaps learned from?) the song of "Audubon's" Yellow-rumped Warbler. MacGillivray's is known to give a flight song. Unlike Mourning, MacGillivray's rarely sings in spring migration.

CALL NOTE is a sharp, loud *tik* or *tsik,* sharper than the calls of other western warblers. The call resembles some calls of the Common Yellowthroat but lacks the burry *j* quality usually found in the latter species' calls. Especially sharp versions may suggest calls of a waterthrush, *Seiurus.* The call is distinctly different from the hollower, flatter *jip* or *vit* note of the Mourning and is a key feature separating the two species. Call note is frequently given in migration.

FLIGHT NOTE is a penetrating *tseep* without any buzzy tones; it resembles the flight note of Mourning.

🦅 BEHAVIOR

Like others of its genus, a skulking bird that spends much time well within dense brush and thickets. However, it is generally easier to observe than Mourning or Connecticut warblers, because it is readily "pished" into view and because habitats occupied in

migration are often rather open (including desert scrub). Movements are rather quick and furtive; the tail is often switched sideways. On the breeding grounds, males usually sing from well within dense vegetation; often, however, they will work up to more visible perches near the top of a shrub or well up into a tree (exceptionally to 45–60 ft.), dropping back into the understory at any disturbance. Singing birds frequently shift perches. Foraging is primarily by gleaning of bark and foliage in dense, often moist vegetation, usually within 3–6 ft. of the ground; some foraging occurs on the ground. Food consists of a variety of insects. Wintering birds are territorial, not usually joining in mixed-species flocks.

The **NEST** is a cup placed just off the ground in a shrub or clump of annual growth. It consists of grasses, fibers, rootlets, and hair, woven around vertical stalks which anchor it.

 ## Habitat

BREEDING habitat varies considerably through the species' range, but always includes dense shaded deciduous thickets. Birds along the Pacific Coast breed on moist, fog-shrouded, brushy, north-facing slopes and in canyon bottoms; they favor dense thickets of poison oak or blackberry or other shrubs and tangles within or adjacent to oak woodlands or willow riparian associations. In the wetter northwestern coastal areas, they are more broadly distributed in dense, low tangles in forest openings, burned-over areas, power line right-of-ways, and clear-cuts. In montane areas in California they breed within coniferous forests in riparian thickets (especially willow) along streams, around seeps and springs, and around the margins of meadows where there is dense undergrowth beneath the conifers. Other montane breeding habitats in the interior West, including Rocky Mountains, include the shrubby understory of aspen woodlands, and dense ravine and streamside associations of willow, chokecherry, wild rose, etc. They are more broadly distributed in thickets near water in the northern part of the interior breeding range, usually within or adjacent to forests of Douglas-fir, lodgepole pine, etc. Cutover areas and burns are often occupied once thick brush is established. The isolated populations in ne. Mexico breed in mixed pine-oak-chaparral associations in ravines on the northern slopes of mountains around 8,000–10,500 ft. elevation.

WINTERS in a wide variety of habitats that provide dense cover, including dense thickets, scrub, arid and humid forest undergrowth, forest edge, second growth, grown-over fields and clearings. Winters from lowlands to as high as 9,400 ft. **MIGRANTS** occur widely but seek dense cover where available.

BREEDS from se. Alaska, sw. and s.-cen. Yukon, nw. and e.-cen. B.C., sw. Alta., and the Cypress Hills of se. Alta. and sw. Sask. southward as follows: to s. Calif. (on the coast very locally to Santa Barbara Co. and in the mountains to the San Gabriel, San Bernardino, and San Jacinto mtns.), in the Great Basin and Rocky Mtns. south to n. and e.-cen. Ariz. (and Pinaleño Mtns. in se.), and s. N.M., and, as an isolated population, in se. Coahuila and s. Nuevo Leon in e.-cen. Mexico. Breeds east to the Cypress Hills, the eastern flank of the Rocky Mtns., and the Black Hills (S.D.).

WINTERS in the Cape District of Baja Calif. Sur and widely through mainland Mexico from Sonora and Nuevo Leon south (both on the coastal slopes and in the interior); absent from the Yucatan Peninsula. Winters south through Central America to w. Panama (casually to cen. Panama); winters mainly at higher elevations in the southern winter range. A very small number winter very rarely in s. Calif. and casually north to coastal n. Calif. Also winters casually in s. Ariz. and in coastal Texas and the hill country of s.-cen. Texas.

SPRING MIGRATION mainly begins in early April, with the earliest passage being primarily through s.-cen. and sw. Ariz. and s. Calif. (this movement involves the nominate subspecies); the earliest migrants are noted during the last week of March, exceptionally back to about 18 March. The first breeding birds on the cen. Calif. coast have usually arrived by 10 April; arrivals are progressively later to the north, with birds usually not on territory in coastal B.C. until late April or early May. Spring arrivals in the interior portions of the breeding range are usually from about the second week of May in the south to late May at the northern end of the range in Alta. The spring migration is quite prolonged, with no sharp peak. In the deserts of s. Calif. and s. Ariz., where the largest numbers of migrants are noted, the bulk of the migration is in May, with a few noted into early June. Relatively few birds are found on the immediate coast of s. Calif. in spring. Spring migrants are fairly common east through N.M. and w. Texas. In the w. Great Plains (w. Okla., w. Kans., e. Colo., w. Neb.) this species is a rare or very uncommon transient, mainly during the last three weeks of May; it is casual farther east in the plains states and in e.-cen. Texas.

FALL MIGRATION begins through much of the West in early August (rarely in very late July); this southbound movement is earlier than the more easterly movement of the related Mourning Warbler. There is no strong peak to fall migration, but most pass through from late August to mid-September. Small numbers pass through the southwestern states until early October, with a few until mid-October (and casually later). Departure from the northern breeding grounds is complete in September (rarely to late September, and with 11 October and 24 November records for interior B.C.). Although fall migrants are numerous in montane areas, large numbers also pass through the lowland deserts.

VAGRANT east of the normal range, but status in the East confused by the close similarity to Mourning Warbler. Casual in La., with eight records in fall, winter, and spring, and on the upper Texas coast. There are single spring records from Minn., Mo., and Ont. There are four late fall records (but no specimen) from Mass., and one was banded and photographed in coastal Ga. One winter sighting from Fla. may have pertained to MacGillivray's. Late fall and winter *Oporornis* in the East should be scrutinized and documented very carefully, as MacGillivray's is more likely than Mourning at this season. There are additional reports, including both sight records and netted birds, from other eastern states, but many of these may apply to variant Mournings.

MacGILLIVRAY'S WARBLER
Oporornis tolmiei

Also recorded casually in the Northwest Territories, s. Alaska (August records for Anchorage and Copper River Valley) and n. Alaska (1 July and 12 September records for Barrow). Casual in ne. B.C. and in Sask. (away from Cypress Hills breeding area).

STATUS AND CONSERVATION

Populations appear to be stable, and the species' acceptance of brushy habitats, which are successional to logging, suggests that widespread declines are unlikely. Populations at the southern limit of the range in coastal central California, the mountains of southern California (where perhaps a recent colonist), and in Mexico are all small and fragmented, and could be vulnerable.

SUBSPECIES

Minor variations in plumage and measurements (particularly tail length) have resulted in the recognition of as many as four subspecies of MacGillivray's Warblers. Most current workers recognize only two. Nominate *tolmiei* is the brighter yellow and green bird of the Pacific coastal states, and *monticola* encompasses the interior breeding populations that are duller above and paler yellow below but variable in measurements (especially tail length). Nominate *tolmiei* is the brightest subspecies, more yellow-olive on the upperparts and deeper yellow on the underparts (tending toward orange-yellow in adult males). It breeds along the Pacific Coast from British Columbia to cen. California, and in the mountains of the Pacific states south through the Cascades and Sierra Nevada to the higher mountains of s. California. The bulk of the early (April) spring movement of this species through sw. Arizona and s. California involves this subspecies. The name *intermedia* has been applied to the more inland, montane populations of nominate *tolmiei*, based on their slightly duller plumage than coastal birds (thus, intermediate toward *monticola*).

The subspecies *monticola* occupies the remaining, interior portion of the species' breeding range, from e. British Columbia and sw. Saskatchewan south to Arizona and New Mexico (and in Coahuila and Nuevo Leon, Mexico). *O. t. monticola* averages duller and grayer on the upperparts and paler, more greenish yellow on the underparts than *tolmiei*. Tail length is variable within *monticola*; the longest tailed populations of the species occupy the southern portion of the range of *monticola* (from se. Oregon and sw. Wyoming south); these long-tailed birds are the least similar to Mourning Warbler in overall tail length and in wing-minus-tail measurement. *O. t. monticola* in the northern part of the range are as short-tailed as nominate *tolmiei*. The name *austin-smithi* has been applied to these shorter-tailed birds. *O. t. monticola* is a later and more easterly spring migrant than nominate *tolmiei*. The winter ranges of the two subspecies have not been satisfactorily delineated, but *monticola* appears to winter mainly in the highlands of cen. and s. Mexico, whereas *tolmiei* occurs more widely from sw. Mexico to Panama.

TAXONOMIC RELATIONSHIPS

This species has been considered conspecific with Mourning Warbler by some authors, but there seems little justification for this in light of consistent differences in plumages, measurements, and vocalizations, and the absence or scarcity of intergrades. The breeding ranges of the two species approach each other closely in w. Alberta (as at Athabasca River west of Edmonton) and limited sympatry may exist near Dawson Creek in e.-cen. British Columbia. In these regions, there are usually open lodgepole pine forests between the breeding areas of the two species; these relatively dry forests lack breeding populations of either species. Replacement of spruce forests with commercial pine may further widen the gap between the two species' breeding ranges in many areas.

PLUMAGES AND MOLTS

SPRING ADULT MALE: Forehead, crown, and hindneck deep gray (slightly bluish), contrasting sharply with the olive green of the remaining upperparts. Rump and uppertail coverts slightly brighter yellow-olive than the back. Lores and a very narrow strip across the

MacGillivray's Warbler. Male in California in May. (Photo: Herbert Clarke)

forehead just above the bill flat black; this black is variable in extent, sometimes coming down under the anterior part of the eye and onto the chin. Thick, bold white arcs above and below the eye. Remainder of head deep gray, contrasting with the white eye-arcs and the black lores. Extreme uppermost chin white (not normally visible in the field); remaining chin and throat slate gray, becoming darker, almost blackish slate, on the lower throat and often the center of the throat. These darkest feathers have pale gray fringes, giving a mottled effect; these pale fringes may be vertically aligned to give a suggestion of pale streaking through the slaty throat. Reduced pale fringing is shown as the spring and summer season progresses. The lower breast, belly, and undertail coverts are rich, deep yellow; the sides and flanks are washed with olive. Upper wing coverts olive; flight feathers dusky, with yellow-olive outer webs. Underwing coverts olive-yellow, bend of wing bright yellow. Rectrices dusky olive with yellow-olive edges. **FIRST SPRING MALE:** Similar to spring adult male but averaging slightly duller, with gray of crown slightly tinged with brownish olive. Many first spring males retain much light gray-buff on the chin and throat, particularly in early spring. Rectrices of immatures noticeably more pointed than those of adults and are also noticeably more worn in spring birds. **SPRING ADULT FEMALE:** Crown and hindneck deep gray, tinged lightly with olive-brown and showing slight contrast with the olive of the remaining upperparts. Lores and sides of head gray, with a very indistinct pale gray supraloral streak. Evident, thick white arcs above and below the eye. Chin whitish; throat and upper breast pale gray, sometimes tinged slightly buffy on the center of the throat. Lower breast, belly, and undertail coverts bright yellow, slightly paler than yellow of male; sides and flanks washed with olive. Wings and tail as in spring males. **FIRST SPRING FEMALE:** Very similar to spring adult female but with rectrices more pointed and worn. On average, slightly more brownish olive on the crown and

MacGillivray's Warbler. Female in California in April. (Photo: Larry Sansone)

MacGillivray's Warbler. First fall female in California in August. (Photo: Larry Sansone)

neck, with these areas contrasting even less strongly with the olive back. The lower margin of the hood on the breast averages less well-defined. **FALL ADULT MALE:** Very similar to spring adult male, but feathers of crown tipped with brownish olive, and with broader pale gray fringes to the slaty feathers of the throat. **FIRST FALL MALE:** Gray of forehead, crown, and hindneck slightly tinged with olive-brown; some contrast with olive green back. Rump and uppertail coverts somewhat brighter yellow-olive. Sides of head gray; indistinct loral streak pale grayish white. Distinct whitish eye-arcs, which may rarely be extensive enough to form a nearly complete eye-ring. Chin and throat very pale gray, becoming darker gray, slightly mottled with whitish on the lower throat, forming a hood border. A few individuals that show slaty feathers in the lower breast are reliably sexed as males, but such coloring is usually concealed if present. Sides and flanks olive; lower breast, belly, and undertail coverts moderately bright yellow. In the hand, first fall birds show considerably narrower and more tapered rectrices than adults. **FALL ADULT FEMALE:** Resembles spring adult female, but the crown and hindneck are more strongly washed with olive-brown, and the chin and throat show a stronger buffy tinge. Differs from first fall female in its stronger gray wash on the head and chest and, in the hand, by rectrix shape. **FIRST FALL FEMALE:** Resembles first fall male, but forehead, crown, and hindneck more strongly tinged with olive-brown, with little or no contrast to the olive green back. Sides of the head gray, slightly tinged with brownish olive; distinct creamy white eye-arcs. Indistinct supraloral streak pale grayish buff. Thick, dull whitish eye-arcs, which may very rarely form a nearly complete eye-ring. Chin and throat very pale gray, slightly tinged with buffy. In a few individuals there is a slight but evident dingy yellow wash on the chin and throat. Upper breast pale gray, with indistinct whitish spotting, forming an indistinct but complete lower hood. Sides and flanks washed olive. Lower breast, belly, and undertail coverts bright yellow. **JUVENILE:** Brownish olive above; head brownish. Brownish olive below, washed yellowish on the belly. **BARE PARTS:** Bill brownish black on upper mandible and tip of lower mandible; base of lower mandible and cutting edge of both mandibles pale yellowish pink to grayish pink. Eyes very dark brown. Legs and feet vary from grayish pink or brownish pink to rather bright pink; soles paler.

The prebasic molt occurs on the breeding grounds in July and August; it is complete in adults but does not involve the flight feathers in hatching-year birds. A limited prealternate molt takes place from February to April.

 REFERENCES

GENERAL: Pitocchelli 1995.
DISTRIBUTION: Ely 1962.
ECOLOGY, BEHAVIOR, VOCALIZATIONS, AND CONSERVATION: Hutto 1981, McNicholl 1980, Morrison 1981, Shuford 1993, Pitocchelli 1990.
IDENTIFICATION: Curson 1992, Kowalski 1983, Lanyon and Bull 1967, Phillips and Holmgren 1979, Pyle and Henderson 1990.
PLUMAGES, MOLTS, AND MORPHOLOGY: Hailman 1968, Pitocchelli 1990.
SYSTEMATICS: Behle 1985, Phillips 1947, Cox 1973, Hall 1979, Patti and Myers 1976.

COMMON YELLOWTHROAT   PL. 24

Geothlypis trichas

5 in. (12.7 cm). The Common Yellowthroat is perhaps our most widespread warbler, being common in wet brushy habitats, weedy fields, and marshes through most of North America; it breeds in all 49 mainland states and in all of Canada's provinces and territories. The adult male has a distinctive black-masked appearance, but females and immature males are more subtly marked in brownish olive and pale yellow. This warbler is wrenlike in behavior, skulking low in the underbrush or within reeds; singing males, however, can be quite conspicuous and often even perform an energetic flight song. Geographical variation is considerable throughout North America; this variation is evident in both males and females and involves the extent of yellow on the underparts, the color of the upperparts, the color of the pale "frontal band" across the forecrown, and other characters.

The upperparts, including the wings and tail, are entirely olive, olive-gray, or olive-brown, depending on subspecies and degree of plumage wear. The chin, throat, and breast are bright yellow in males, but paler yellow, buffy yellow, or even creamy whitish in females. The extent of yellow on the underparts varies geographically, but there is some whitish in the belly of most races. The flanks are tinged brownish, strongly so in fresh fall plumage. Most males are readily distinguished from females by a distinctive black mask from the forehead back through the eyes and auriculars, although this mask is poorly defined or nearly absent in immature males and may very rarely be present in females. Males have a pale "frontal band," variably gray or whitish (or whitish tinged with pale yellow in some populations), separating the black forehead and mask from the olive rear crown and neck.

This is a fairly slender warbler with relatively short wings and a moderately long, somewhat rounded tail. Tail extension beyond the longest undertail coverts averages about 21–22 mm, about the same as in MacGillivray's Warbler but longer than in other *Oporornis*. Rictal bristles are poorly developed in males and lacking or virtually lacking in females.

SIMILAR SPECIES

The black mask easily separates the adult male from other warblers except for the geographically restricted **BAHAMA** and **BELDING'S YELLOWTHROATS** (for distinctions, see those species); also see **GRAY-CROWNED YELLOWTHROAT**, which has black mainly restricted to the lores. Compare male also with **KENTUCKY WARBLER** (see below).

Female and immature birds are trickier and may easily be confused with several other plain warblers. The most likely confusion species are in the genus *Oporornis*. Common Yellowthroats are slimmer, smaller bodied, and relatively longer tailed and shorter winged than any *Oporornis*, although **MACGILLIVRAY'S WARBLER** overlaps it in tail length and tail extension beyond the undertail coverts. All *Oporornis* are rather uniformly yellow on the underparts (bright in most species but duller and paler in Connecticut); virtually all Common Yellowthroats show some white in the belly region, and some races are extensively white there. Beware, however, southwestern *chryseola* yellowthroats, which may be almost completely yellow through the belly. **CONNECTICUT WARBLER** shares the brownish-tinged upperparts and complete eye-ring with female yellowthroats, but is much larger, chunkier, and longer-winged, shows a bolder eye-ring, and walks on the ground and on tree limbs. Female **MOURNING** has a yellow throat and often shows a thin, complete eye-ring but is more uniformly yellow below, lacking white in the belly region, is brighter olive above, is relatively shorter-tailed, and has a different call note. Fall immature male Common Yellowthroats with black-flecked faces can be confused with the larger, chunkier **KENTUCKY WARBLER**; the latter is more uniformly bright yellow on the underparts and brighter olive green above. On Kentucky note the distinct yellow supraloral line that wraps around and under the eye; very rare variant adult male Common Yellowthroats show a thin yellow supraloral line, and this trait could possibly occur in first fall males as well.

VOICE

The loud and familiar **SONG** consists of a rhythmic series of rich notes of two to six phrases, uttered about twice per second, such as *witchity-witchity-witchity-witch; which is it, which is it, which is it; wee-witchity, wee-witchity, wee-witchity,* etc. Variation is extensive, especially in the number and type of notes per phrase, both among and within local populations. Some geographic trends in song pattern are also evident, with eastern birds giving four- to six-noted phrases more frequently than midwestern and western birds, which give mostly two- or three-noted syllables. Some variations in the song may resemble songs of Kentucky Warbler and even various sparrows, wrens, and buntings.

This species frequently gives a flight song in which the male flies 15 ft. or more straight into the air giving a series of sputtering *pit!* notes and, as he nears the apex of the flight, a rapid, bubbly series of phrases often followed by the more typical song phrases; the flight during song delivery is quite jerky.

CALL NOTE is a husky *djip, tschep,* or *tidge,* with seemingly innumerable minor variations; it is usually distinctive in its raspy quality, but sharper versions may closely resemble the typical *tsik* call of MacGillivray's. Other call notes given include a sharp *pit* (like the introductory notes to the flight song) and a rapid, sputtering series of *chip* notes, heard on the breeding grounds; the latter is often mistaken for the song of the Sedge Wren (*Cistothorus platensis*). The **FLIGHT NOTE** is a low, unmusical, buzzy *dzip* or *zzeet.*

BEHAVIOR

Common Yellowthroats are usually seen on or near the ground and are especially fond of working through dense tangles of damp weedy growth or stands of reeds or rushes; they often perch and climb on vertical stalks. The behavior is wrenlike, with nervous actions and frequent cocking and twitching of the tail. When on the ground, the yellowthroat hops rather than walks. The flight is jerky, and when flushed the bird usually flies low and quickly to a nearby patch of dense cover. They are inquisitive warblers that readily respond to pishing. They forage by gleaning insects low in the vegetation or off the surface of mud or damp ground. After the nesting season, they may forage somewhat higher in shrubs and low trees. Singing males may be conspicuous, often singing from exposed perches atop reeds or shrubs and occasionally giving flight songs.

The **NEST** is a loose, bulky cup of grasses, sedges, rootlets, and other fine material, usually well concealed on or near the ground or just above water. When floodwaters are high, nests are sometimes built higher (exceptionally to 20 ft.). Males are occasionally polygynous.

HABITAT

In the wetter climates that prevail over most of the eastern and northern parts of its **BREEDING** range, the yellowthroat is widespread in a variety of damp weedy, brushy, or marshy habitats. The greatest numbers are reached in cattails and other dense marsh vegetation, but the species is also common in weedy fields, brushy second growth and forest edge, swamps, brambles, bogs, dense herbaceous growth in the understory of open forests, and a variety of other habitats. In the drier regions of the West, where wet habitats are more restricted, yellowthroats occur mainly in marshy stream and pond margins and flooded lowland riparian thickets. The subspecies *sinuosa* of the San Francisco Bay area is largely restricted to salt marsh habitats, and the extralimital *modesta* of western Mexico occurs mainly in salt marsh and mangroves.

WINTER habitats generally resemble those used during the breeding season; the northernmost wintering birds usually occupy extensive marshes. **MIGRANTS** are found in an even broader range of habitats, but still prefer dense cover. Migrants in the West may occur in arid situations.

DISTRIBUTION

BREEDS commonly through most of North America, north to Glacier Bay in se. Alaska, c. Yukon, sw. Dist. of Mack., n. Sask., cen. Man., n. Ont., cen. Que., the Canadian Maritime Provinces, and Nfld. (small numbers). The breeding range extends south through the U.S., although it is local in much of the arid Southwest, greatly reduced in the Rio Grande Valley of s. Texas, and absent from the Florida Keys. Breeds south in Mexico to n. Baja Calif., along the coast from s. Sonora to Colima, and through the central plateau regions at least rarely to Oaxaca.

WINTERS mainly from the southern U.S. south through Central America and most of the West Indies. Within the eastern U.S. it winters most commonly from the Carolinas south through Fla. and west across the Gulf states through s.-cen. and coastal Texas; it is much scarcer away from the coastal plain in these states. Small numbers winter locally farther inland in the Southeast, as in s. Ark. A few yellowthroats linger at least through the early winter much farther north along the Atlantic Coast (to N.S., casually in Nfld.), as well as around the southern Great Lakes (especially Lake Erie). These northern, lingering birds are rarely noted after early January, which may reflect mortality through the winter but also diminished observer effort after the Christmas Bird Counts. Casual in early winter elsewhere in the interior of e. North America, with some records involving individuals at feeding stations. This species certainly attempts to winter farther north in larger numbers than any warbler other than Yellow-rumped. In w. North America winters mainly in s. Ariz., along the Colorado River and other marshy areas of se. Calif., and along the coastal slope of s. and cen. Calif. north regularly to Sonoma Co. Occurs very rarely as far north as B.C. and in the interior north to Nev., N.M., and Colo.; a few winter along the Rio Grande in w. Texas. Yellowthroats winter south through Mexico and Central America to cen. Panama, and casually to e. Panama, Colombia, and the Netherlands Antilles. They also winter throughout the Greater Antilles, on islands in the western Caribbean, and on Bermuda; they are rare winter visitors to the Virgin Is. and casual in the Lesser Antilles (Antigua, Guadaloupe, and Dominica). Single records from Venezuela and Tobago are not fully satisfactory.

In SPRING MIGRATION the various subspecies move, collectively, on a broad front. Migrants can be abundant in the East through s. Texas, the Gulf Coast, and Fla. They are abundant along the Atlantic Coast, with spring concentrations usually exceeding those in fall; this is one of the few warbler species that is a truly common migrant along the Atlantic Coast in spring. In e. North America, migration begins in Fla. and along the Gulf Coast in the latter half of March (early March in southernmost Fla.). Over the rest of the South, arrival is from late March to early April. In the southern Midwest (Okla., s. Mo., Tenn., Ky.) most birds arrive in early to mid-April, with arrivals through the rest of the Midwest typically in the third week of April. From Wisc. through the Great Lakes and New England, spring arrivals are usually during the first week of May, with many April records. Arrivals at the northern end of the breeding range are usually from about 10 to 25 May. In the West, spring migration is under way by early March, but the earliest migrants may arrive in Calif. and s. Ariz. in late

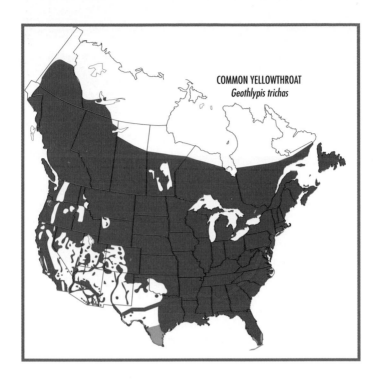

COMMON YELLOWTHROAT
Geothlypis trichas

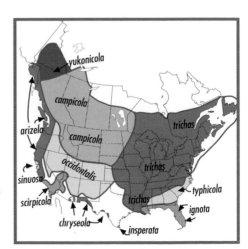

yukonicola

campicola

campicola

arizela

occidentalis

sinuosa

scirpicola

chryseola

insperata

trichas

trichas

trichas

typhicola

ignota

Generalized breeding distribution of Common Yellowthroat subspecies.

February; arrival over most of the interior West takes place in early May (with a few birds in late April). At the latitude of Mont., Alta., and interior B.C., spring arrivals are usually during the latter half of May. By contrast, populations breeding along the coast of the Pacific Northwest arrive as early as early to mid April, even as far north as se. Alaska. Spring migration is protracted in both the East and the West, extending into late May and even early June, even in the southern states. Migration peaks in the southern states are from mid-April to early May; over much of the interior of the continent, migration peaks during the first two weeks of May, while peaks in the northern Midwest and New England are from mid- to late May.

FALL MIGRATION occurs mainly from mid-August to late October. Peak movements in the upper Midwest and New England are in September, with many birds still moving through in early October. Virtually all birds have departed from the northernmost portions of the breeding range by the end of September. Peak fall passage in Fla. is from late September to mid-October. Yellowthroats can be numerous in fall in Bermuda, peaking in late October. Little is known of peak movements in the West, but these likely occur in late September and early October. Small numbers of migrants are noted north of the wintering range through the end of October, with a few into early November.

VAGRANT to the south of the normal wintering range, as noted above. Casual north of the breeding range in cen. Alaska (Harding Lake in June), south coastal Alaska (fall), n. Man. (Churchill), Kugong Is. in Hudson Bay, n. Lab. Five records for the w. Palearctic, all in the U.K. (three in fall, one wintering, one in spring). Also recorded three times in fall in Greenland. Undoubtedly the various subspecies wander outside of their normal range, but there are few specific records of such vagrancy. Surprisingly, there are no published records of the widespread eastern subspecies *trichas* in the West, despite its abundance and long migrations; such birds are undoubtedly overlooked. Birds identified as belonging to the interior western subspecies *occidentalis* and *campicola* have been collected in Fla.

STATUS AND CONSERVATION

Abundant through most of its range, especially in the East. The highest breeding densities are in New England and adjacent portions of eastern Canada, but densities in portions of the Midwest are nearly as high. Populations are stable in most regions, and slight increases have been noted in many areas. However, regional declines and even local extirpation have occurred in parts of the South and West. The most severe decline has been in Texas, where the subspecies *insperata* has been virtually extirpated and other races have been greatly reduced. Over much of the West, where wetlands are scarce and localized, this species has declined with the draining of wetlands and channelization of rivers. However, the species is considerably adaptable, and "new" habitat along irrigation channels and around reservoirs is quickly colonized. The subspecies *sinuosa*, resident in salt marshes in the San Francisco Bay area, is a candidate for federal Endangered status, as is *insperata*.

This is one of the most frequent cowbird hosts among our warblers, with first broods especially frequently parasitized. Some local declines are undoubtedly due in part to cowbirds. Yellowthroats, like Yellow Warblers, may recognize cowbird eggs and build new nests over the parasitized clutch. This egg recognition may be a consequence of the fact that both species occurred with cowbirds in the plains regions before cowbirds underwent their major range expansion.

SUBSPECIES

Geographic variation is more extensive in the Common Yellowthroat than in any North American warbler apart from the Yellow Warbler. Some 15 subspecies are widely recognized, though many of these are poorly defined, and many workers believe that this species has been "oversplit." As many as 14 additional subspecies have been proposed, but the validity of most has not been widely accepted. Geographical variation involves north-south and east-west clines in upperpart color, the shade and extent of yellow on the underparts, flank color, frontal band color and breadth, size, and wing and tail proportions. Most of these differences are subtle, and differences within populations due to season are often greater than differences between populations.

Three subspecies are generally recognized in eastern North America: nominate *trichas* breeds from the northern part of the species' range south to e. Texas and sw. La., the northern portions of the Gulf states, and se. Virginia; *typhicola* breeds on much of the southeast coastal plain from cen. Alabama northeast to e. North Carolina; and *ignota* breeds along the Gulf and southern Atlantic coasts from se. Louisiana and coastal Ga. south through Florida. Additional subspecies have been named from within the range of nominate *trichas*, but they are not generally recognized today; the subspecies name *brachidactylus* is often applied to the breeding yellowthroats from the eastern Great Plains, the Midwest, e. Canada, New England, and the Appalachian region, but it is perhaps best merged with *trichas*. An additional subspecies, *insperata*, is limited to the Rio Grande Valley of s. Texas and adjacent n. Tamaulipas. The majority of the wintering birds in e. Mexico, Central America, and the West Indies are *trichas* (inclusive of *brachidactylus*). *G. t. typhicola* winters mainly along the Gulf Coast and in ne. Mexico, and *ignota* is largely resident.

Through the interior of w. North America are the widespread subspecies *campicola*, which breeds from nw. and cen. Canada south to the northern Rocky Mtn. and Great Plains states, and *occidentalis*, which breeds south of *campicola* to e.-cen. California, s.-cen. Arizona, s. New Mexico, and nw. Texas. The paler and grayer more northerly populations of *campicola* are sometimes referred to as *yukonicola*. The race *chryseola* breeds from se. Arizona, sw. New Mexico, and w. Texas south into n. Mexico. These subspecies appear to winter mainly in n. and w. Mexico and adjacent portions of the southwestern U.S.

Along the Pacific Coast, *arizela* breeds from the northern extreme of the species' range in se. Alaska south through cen. California; it winters mainly from n. California to nw. Mexico. More southerly *scirpicola* breeds from s.-cen. California south to n. Baja California, and east mainly through the Colorado River Valley to s. Nevada, sw. Utah, w. Arizona, and the Colorado River delta; it almost completely withdraws from the northern, interior portions of its range in winter. The very local *sinuosa* breeds in salt marshes in the San Francisco Bay region; it is partially migratory, recorded in winter south to s. California.

In general terms, eastern and midwestern birds are brighter olive on the upperparts, birds of the western interior are paler and grayer or browner above, and West Coast birds are brownish olive. Within the East, the more northerly birds tend to be darker and greener above, with a trend toward paler and browner dorsal plumage to the south. Within the western interior, the more northerly birds are paler and grayer, whereas those to the south, culminating in *chryseola*, are brighter yellow-olive. Along the Pacific Coast there is a cline from darker birds in the north to paler and brighter birds in the south; *sinuosa* of the San Francisco Bay area is darkest above and brownest on the flanks. The frontal band of all eastern birds is pale gray, while that of western birds is whitish; in the southwestern race *chryseola,* the whitish frontal band is slightly tinged with pale yellow on the sides. Frontal band width is variable, but averages broader in western birds.

The extent and shade of yellow on the underparts is variable, with eastern birds generally being moderately to extensively yellow, western interior birds having richer but relatively restricted yellow (even orange-tinged in *campicola* and *occidentalis*, with

*Common Yellow-
throat. Adult male
trichas in Ohio in
September. (Photo:
Steve and Dave
Maslowski)*

the color often not extending below the upper breast), and Pacific Coast birds being richly yellow of intermediate extent. *G. t. chryseola* is the most extensively yellow of all U.S. subspecies. These differences are most obvious in males but are somewhat paralleled in females. Females of *campicola* and *occidentalis* have very restricted yellow below, and some may completely lack yellow, instead being creamy whitish. Northern *campicola* ("*yukonicola*") are the palest of all Common Yellowthroats.

Along the Atlantic Coast, there are slight trends in the extent of yellow on the underparts, more with northerly birds showing intermediate amounts, central Atlantic Coast birds showing less yellow, and Florida birds showing the most extensive yellow. The northeasternmost birds are the palest yellow on the underparts.

Geographical trends in size are slight and complex; northerly, more migratory populations tend to be slightly longer winged. *G. t. sinuosa* is the smallest subspecies.

TAXONOMIC RELATIONSHIPS

One case of hybridization with Mourning Warbler has been described. The Common Yellowthroat is closely related to the Bahama and Belding's yellowthroats. These and some additional Mexican taxa have all been considered conspecific by some earlier workers; conversely, some workers consider the subspecies *chapalensis* of Common Yellowthroat from Lake Chapala, Jalisco, to be a separate species. The genus *Geothlypis* is sometimes enlarged to include *Oporornis*.

The nominate race from eastern North America is described below; see Subspecies for the appearance of other subspecies. **SPRING ADULT MALE:** Upperparts olive with a slight brownish tinge from the center of the crown through the back, dullest and brownest on the crown and nape. Olive of the back grades to slightly brighter olive green on the rump and uppertail coverts. Forehead black, back to the anterior edge of the eye; this black is separated from the olive-brown center of the crown by a "frontal" band of pale gray about 3–5 mm in width. The black forehead continues down through the lores and malar region and back through the auriculars, forming a distinct mask. The area around the eye is black, with no pale eye-ring. In very rare variants there may be a yellow supraloral streak back to the eye, dividing the black of the forehead from the black of the lores. The pale frontal band extends back and downward, framing the top and rear of the black auricular region. The chin, throat, and breast are bright yellow, extending as a wash of paler yellow down through the center of the belly. The undertail coverts are bright yellow. The flanks are strongly tinged with gray-brown, this color washing into the vent area, where it is mixed with creamy or white. The wings are brownish olive, with the flight feathers edged brighter olive. The tail is olive, narrowly edged yellowish olive on the outer webs of the rectrices. **FIRST SPRING MALE:** Very similar to spring adult male and generally not distinguishable in the field. Many individuals show some brown mixed in the black forehead and mask and at least traces of a buffy eye-ring. In the hand, most individuals show somewhat more worn and tapered rectrices than adults. **SPRING ADULT FEMALE:** Upperparts entirely dull olive, tinged with brown or reddish brown on the forecrown; slightly brighter olive on the rump and uppertail coverts. Forehead, lores, and auricular area dusky

Common Yellow-throat. Male occidentalis/campicola in California in April. (Photo: Herbert Clarke)

Common Yellow-throat. Male chryseola *in Arizona in May. (Photo: Rick and Nora Bowers)*

to gray-brown, with a hint of a pale gray-buff supercilium and eye-ring. The auricular area contrasts rather sharply with the pale yellow chin, throat, and upper breast, and usually imparts a slight masked effect. The remainder of the underparts are dull whitish, strongly tinged with dull gray-brown or brownish olive on the sides and flanks and becoming dull yellow on the undertail coverts. The wings and tail are unmarked dull olive, with thin olive-yellow fringes. Very rare variants may show a male-like black mask, and many birds show a ghost of a mask pattern and frontal band. **FIRST SPRING FEMALE:** Very similar to spring adult female, and most individuals are probably not distinguishable. On average, first spring females are less yellow on the throat and breast and have a more uniform crown and face, lacking the ghost of a male-like pattern present in many spring adult females. In the hand, the rectrices may appear more worn and tapered. **FALL ADULT MALE:** Closely resembles spring adult male, but upperparts are somewhat darker and browner, and the flanks are strongly washed with brown. The yellow of the underparts is slightly washed with buffy, and in very fresh birds there are some thin gray tips to the black feathers of the mask. **FIRST FALL MALE:** Upperparts olive with a brownish tint; crown strongly brownish. Chin, throat, and breast bright yellow, paling to creamy whitish on the belly. Flanks strongly washed with brownish; undertail coverts yellow. The lores, cheeks, and sometimes the forehead are variably blackish, but this black is partially veiled by buffy or pale gray feather tips in fresh plumage. There is no pale frontal band, but the face shows a pale gray or buffy eye-ring and a postocular stripe, that angles downward, forming a rear border to the blackish cheeks. With feather wear the mask appears more solidly black by midwinter, and a prealternate molt results in a fully masked plumage by late winter. Some first fall males are more extensively black on the forehead and mask than described above and may not be separable from fall adult males, though

Common Yellow-throat. Female trichas in New Jersey in September. (Photo: Kevin T. Karlson)

the black is more heavily veiled with brown or gray feather tips. In the hand, rectrices of first fall birds may appear more tapered than those of adults. **FALL ADULT FEMALE:** Very similar to spring adult female, but the flanks are more strongly washed with brown, and the upperparts have more of a brownish tinge. Usually brighter yellow on the throat and breast than first fall females. **FIRST FALL FEMALE:** The dullest and least yellow plumage. The upperparts are entirely olive-brown, and the chin, throat, and breast are buff or yellowish buff. The sides and flanks are extensively washed with buffy brown. There is an indistinct buffy eye-ring. **JUVENILE:** Upperparts, throat, and breast brownish olive; underparts dull buffy brown, paler on the belly. Two irregular cinnamon-buff wing bars. Yellow begins to appear on the chin, throat, and breast shortly after fledging. **BARE PARTS:** Bill of adult male blackish (spring and summer) to slaty brown, with some flesh or pale brown at the base of the lower mandible. Bills of females and first fall males browner, with more extensive yellowish on the lower mandible. Eyes brown to blackish brown. Legs and feet vary from dark brown to pale brown.

The prebasic molt occurs on the breeding grounds; it is complete in adults but in hatching-year birds does not involve the flight feathers in most populations (some flight feathers may be molted in the first prebasic molt in some southern populations, but evidence is conflicting). A partial prealternate molt occurs, at least in immature males.

 REFERENCES

GENERAL: Stewart 1953.
DISTRIBUTION: Atwood 1992, Shuford 1993 (*G. t. sinuosa*).
ECOLOGY, BEHAVIOR, VOCALIZATIONS, AND CONSERVATION: Atwood 1994, Borror 1967, Marshall and Dedrick 1994 (*G. t. sinuosa*), Shuford 1993 (*G. t. sinuosa*).
PLUMAGES, MOLTS, AND MORPHOLOGY: Blake 1969, Ewert and Lanyon 1970, Taylor 1976.

SYSTEMATICS: Behle 1950, Behle and Aldrich 1947, Bledsoe 1988, Chapman 1890, Marshall and Dedrick 1994 (*G. t. sinuosa*), Parkes 1954, Van Rossem 1941.

BELDING'S YELLOWTHROAT PL. 25

Geothlypis beldingi

5.5 in. (14 cm). This large yellowthroat is endemic to the central and southern parts of the Baja California peninsula and is unrecorded within the U.S. or the mainland of Mexico. It is found mainly in freshwater marshes and wet riparian tangles, habitats that are generally quite restricted within its range. Overall it resembles a large, long-billed Common Yellowthroat but is more extensively yellow below, and males generally show a yellow border behind the black mask. There are two distinct subspecies, *goldmani* from the central part of the peninsula and nominate *beldingi* from the Cape district, with an apparent gap between the two. Sometimes called the Peninsular Yellowthroat.

 DESCRIPTION

Generally olive green above (brighter in males than females) and extensively bright yellow below. Males show a typical yellowthroat's black forehead and mask, bordered by lemon yellow (Cape district) or pale creamy yellow (central peninsula). Females show some whitish in the belly, especially birds of the central peninsula. This is a large, heavy and rather long-tailed yellowthroat with a long and fairly thick bill. Immature males closely resemble adults, and seasonal variation in appearance is only slight.

 SIMILAR SPECIES

Migrant and winter COMMON YELLOWTHROATS occur through the range of Belding's. Belding's is larger and substantially longer billed than even the largest Common Yellowthroats. In plumage, male nominate Belding's from the Cape district are easily told by the clear yellow frontal band and border to the black mask and by the extensive yellow throughout the underparts. *G. b. goldmani* from the central peninsula should be told with care from Common Yellowthroats. Especially similar is the Common Yellowthroat subspecies *chryseola* from border regions of the sw. U.S. and n. mainland Mexico; *chryseola* is unknown in the Baja California range of

Belding's, but could occur in winter. *G. t. chryseola* is extensively yellow below, and males usually show some yellow in the frontal band, but Belding's is still noticeably larger, with a heavier and longer bill. *G. t. scirpicola* of cen. and s. California does overlap Belding's in winter and may occasionally show a hint of yellow in the frontal band; again note much larger size and heavier bill of Belding's.

Female Belding's are best told from Common by size and structural differences. On Belding's, the face, superciliary region, supraloral area, and forehead are usually paler than the corresponding areas on Common and are often tinged with pale yellow. Belding's is geographically widely separated from the similar but much smaller ALTAMIRA YELLOWTHROAT (*G. flavovelata*) of ne. Mexico, which is sometimes considered a race of Common; it is even farther removed from the large, heavy-billed BAHAMA YELLOWTHROAT.

 ## VOICE

The SONG is much richer and more powerful than the song of the Common Yellowthroat, with a somewhat different phrasing: *wi te-wich-uh, wi te-wich-uh...,* or *ch-ch-wee? ch-ch-wee? ch-wee-chew.* The phrasing is different from that of typical Common Yellowthroat songs but can sometimes be matched by Commons. The rich quality suggests a Northern Cardinal (*Cardinalis cardinalis*). A flight song is occasionally given. CALL NOTE is a harsh *djip* or *chek,* very similar to the call of a Common Yellowthroat but perhaps slightly deeper and fuller. Also gives a Common-like dry rattle.

 ## BEHAVIOR

A skulking bird of marshes and wet tangles, generally similar in behavior to Common Yellowthroat. Presumably forages by gleaning in marsh vegetation and on damp ground, as in Common.

The cup NEST is made of grasses and reed strips and lined with fine fibers and hairs; it is placed low in cattails or other reedy growth. Clutch size (usually 2–3 eggs, but up to 4) averages smaller than that of Common.

HABITAT

RESIDENT mainly in freshwater marshes of bulrushes and cattails and also in dense low growth along streams. Such habitat is very limited within the range of *goldmani* of the cen. part of the peninsula, and only slightly more widespread in the Cape district range of nominate *beldingi.* Although not normally found in extensive coastal salt marshes and mangrove associations, it does routinely occur in scrubby mangrove growth at the inland edge of coastal estuaries.

 DISTRIBUTION

Endemic to the Baja California peninsula, with the more northerly subspecies *goldmani* being generally resident from the vicinity of San Ignacio (in the center of the peninsula at 27° 17' N) south to Comondu (about 26° N), and nominate *belding* resident in the Cape region from La Paz south. No records elsewhere. One winter record of *goldmani* from the Cape district (AOU 1957) suggests at least limited movement in that form. The type locality of *goldmani* was incorrectly given as San Ignacio Lagoon; the species is in fact unrecorded from the west coast of the peninsula.

 STATUS AND CONSERVATION

No information, but overall population size is probably no more than a few thousand birds. The limited habitat in the central peninsula range of *goldmani* makes that subspecies potentially vulnerable to the degradation of wetlands. Nominate *beldingi* is probably more numerous (it is not restricted to one "very small marsh" at San Jose as has been suggested) but suitable habitat is still limited and scattered. Parasitism by cowbirds is not recorded; the Brown-headed Cowbird is rare in the breeding season in the cen. and s. Baja California peninsula, but is perhaps expanding its range southward.

 SUBSPECIES

The brighter nominate race *beldingi* of the Cape district is described below. Male *goldmani* differ in being somewhat duller olive above and paler yellow below, with a tendency toward white in the center of the belly. The frontal band varies from creamy white to pale yellow but lacks the bright lemon yellow of nominate birds. Female *goldmani* are duller and grayer on the upperparts and paler yellow below; the facial area is pale gray, usually lacking yellow or buff tinges.

TAXONOMIC RELATIONSHIPS

Relationships within the genus *Geothlypis* are not well understood. Belding's has in the past been considered conspecific with the smaller Altamira or Yellow-crowned Yellowthroat (*G. flavove-*

lata) of northeastern Mexico; Altamira, in turn, is often considered a race of the Common Yellowthroat. Some authorities have suggested conspecificity of Belding's with the Common Yellowthroat, in which case *goldmani* would represent intergradation between the two groups. But despite its plumage tendencies toward Common, *goldmani* certainly appears distinct in its overall size, bill size, and song, and other workers have suggested that relationships of Belding's may actually lie with certain Mexican forms and even the Bahama Yellowthroat.

PLUMAGES AND MOLTS

Nominate birds are described below; see Subspecies for characters of *goldmani*. **SPRING ADULT MALE:** Forehead, lores, and auricular and malar regions black, forming a distinctive mask. Broad but indistinct lemon yellow frontal band forms a border to the black forehead, and the black auricular area is entirely surrounded by bright yellow. The width of the black forehead varies with the individual. Underparts bright yellow tinged with olive-brown on the flanks; no white in the belly area. The yellow of the frontal band merges gradually into the olive-brown crown; the yellow of the sides of the neck, behind the black mask, continues upward as a partial collar behind the crown. Remaining upperparts rather bright olive green, slightly paler on the uppertail coverts. Wings and tail olive green, edged with light yellow-olive. **FIRST SPRING MALE:** Probably indistinguishable from spring adult male, though in the hand, flight feathers appear more worn. Some may show a trace of a whitish eye-ring. **SPRING ADULT FEMALE:** Upperparts dull olive green, tinged slightly with brown, especially on the crown. Chin, throat, breast, and upper belly rich yellow, lightening to pale buffy yellow or dull whitish in the center of the belly. Flanks washed with gray-buff. Supraloral region and broad (but indistinct) supercilium pale buffy yellow; auricular region grayish. Some females, perhaps older birds, show a hint of a pale buffy yellow frontal band and dark gray feather bases on the forehead. Wings and tail unmarked olive, edged with light yellow-olive. **FIRST SPRING FEMALE:** Like spring adult female; in the hand may show duller, more worn flight feathers. **FALL ADULT MALE:** In fresh plumage shows a more extensive brown wash on the flanks than spring birds, and may be tinged brownish on the upperparts. The yellow frontal band is slightly veiled with grayish white feather tips. **FIRST FALL MALE:** Resembles fall adult male, but black forehead and mask are more limited, and veiled with grayish or yellowish; most show a pale eye-ring. **FALL ADULT FEMALE:** Like spring adult female, but flanks extensively tinged with brown, and a stronger brownish tinge to the upperparts. **FIRST FALL FEMALE:** Resembles fall adult female, but averages duller and more brownish above, and the yellow of the underparts is more strongly tinged with buff. **JUVENILE:** Brownish olive above; dull buffy brown below, paler on the belly. Rusty

buff tips to median and greater coverts form two wing bars. **BARE PARTS:**
Bill of male is black in spring and summer; in females and fall and winter
males, bill is dark brown, paler at the base of the mandible. Legs and feet
pinkish. Eyes dark brown.

A complete prebasic molt takes place in late summer after the breeding
season in adults; the prebasic molt of hatching-year birds presumably
does not include the flight feathers. There is no evidence of any prealternate molt in adults, but immature males probably replace some head
feathers in the late winter or early spring.

 REFERENCES

DISTRIBUTION: Howell and Webb 1992.
IDENTIFICATION: Kaufman 1979.
SYSTEMATICS: Behle 1950, Brewster 1902, Oberholser 1917, Todd 1911.

BAHAMA YELLOWTHROAT   PL. 25

Geothlypis rostrata

5.5 in. (14 cm). This large yellowthroat is an endemic resident of
the Bahamas, with four subspecies recognized from the various
islands. There are several reports of this species from Florida, but
none has been fully substantiated. The population of the subspecies *tanneri* on Grand Bahama is geographically the most likely source of potential vagrants to Florida. The Bahama Yellowthroat differs from the Common Yellowthroat in its larger size,
large and heavy bill, coloration, behavior, and habitat. Unlike the
mainland species, it is a bird of pine woodland understory and
hardwood thickets rather than marshes and wet scrub.

 DESCRIPTION

Males are generally olive above and bright yellow below, with a
typical black yellowthroat "mask" and forehead. Males of the different subspecies vary in details of the head pattern, such as the
amount of yellow in the supercilium and the degree of development of the frontal band. Immature males show an adultlike
plumage by their first fall, unlike most Common Yellowthroats.
Females are generally olive above and mostly yellow below, with
extensive olive or brownish on the flanks. Structural differences
from the Common Yellowthroat include larger overall size, a heavier and longer bill that shows a stronger curvature to the culmen

and a stronger upward gonydeal angle, and, sometimes, a hint of a "bump" on the forehead that differs from the Common's flatter head shape.

The subspecies *tanneri* of Grand Bahama and the Abacos is described below.

SIMILAR SPECIES

Very similar to the **COMMON YELLOWTHROAT**, and any suspected Bahama Yellowthroats on the mainland would have to be carefully distinguished from this common and widespread species. Bahama Yellowthroat is a larger and more heavily built bird, with a robust, long, thick bill that shows definite curvature on the culmen and a slight upward angle at the gonys. Common Yellowthroats of the race *ignota* from Florida are slightly longer billed than other eastern subspecies, but the bill does not approach the length and thickness of the Bahama's. The richer and much more extensive yellow on the underparts of the male Bahama, including the entire belly, is a good distinction from all eastern populations of Common Yellowthroat. In most subspecies of Bahama Yellowthroat, including those of Grand Bahama, the pale frontal band between the black forehead and grayish or olive-gray crown is indistinct or absent, although there is a rather well-defined yellowish border to the black auriculars beginning at the eye. Female Bahamas are closely similar to female Common Yellowthroats and are best identified by overall size and the bill shape characters noted above. They are more extensively yellow on the underparts, but the yellow of the belly is partially obscured by the extensive olive-gray of the flanks. At least some females show a yellow suffusion on the forehead and some gray around the rear of the auricular.

The Bahama's richer song and different call note (see below) are also useful distinctions from Common Yellowthroat, and its more sluggish behavior may aid in identification. Note habitat differences (below) in Bahamas.

VOICE

SONG is similar to the Common Yellowthroat in pattern (*wi-chi-tu, wi-chi-tu, wi-chi-tu*), but somewhat richer in quality and usually delivered more slowly. A quieter whisper song, including short trills and sputtering notes, has been described, but flight songs are apparently unknown in this species. The **CALL NOTE** is quite distinct from the Common Yellowthroat, a rather sharp and full *tuck* or *chyimp*, lacking the *sh* or *j* qualities of the Common. A rapid chatter or rattle call, similar to the rattle of a Common, is also given.

Behavior

The movements of this species are markedly sluggish and slow compared to its mainland counterpart. It is often tame and easily approached. The diet consists of both insects and berries; they occasionally catch and eat anole lizards.

The **NEST** is a cup variably placed near the ground or in one case in a tree stump, and in another case 3 ft. from the top of a 20 ft. pine in a mature pine stand in which the understory had been recently burned. Little additional information exists on the species' behavior.

Habitat

The typical habitat of this species on Grand Bahama and Great Abaco is the scrubby undergrowth of open Caribbean pine forests; dominant undergrowth plants in this habitat include the thatch palm (*Thrinax morrisii*) and bracken fern. It also occupies low coppice, a fairly dense association of hardwoods, especially where surrounded by pine woods and where the understory is dense; yellowthroat densities are low in extensive stands of high, uninterrupted coppice. Yellowthroats in marshes on the Bahamas are likely to be migrant or wintering Common Yellowthroats; likewise, yellowthroats in ornamental plantings around settlements are most often Commons.

Distribution

RESIDENT on the major northern Bahama Islands. Fairly common on Grand Bahama and Great and Little Abacos and offshore cays (*tanneri*), apparently the only islands where healthy populations still exist. Also found on New Providence (*rostrata*, now nearly extirpated), Andros (*exigua*, scarce), Eleuthera (*coryi*, uncommon), and Cat Is. (*coryi*, fairly common). There is no proven evidence of any migratory movements, even from island to island.

VAGRANTS reported three times in Fla. and adjacent waters. The first report was of a bird handled and released at Loxahatchee National Wildlife Refuge on 19 October 1968; no photographs, detailed descriptions, or measurements were obtained. A second report involved a sight record from the Panhandle of w. Fla. on 8 October 1974; no details were published. Finally, remains identified as those of a Bahama Yellowthroat were found in the stomach of a tiger shark (*Galeocerdo cuvier*) captured on the night of 11 May 1976 just off Melbourne Beach on the central east coast of Fla.; the shark's stomach also contained remains of a Yellow-billed Cuckoo (*Coccyzus americanus*) and a Mourning Dove

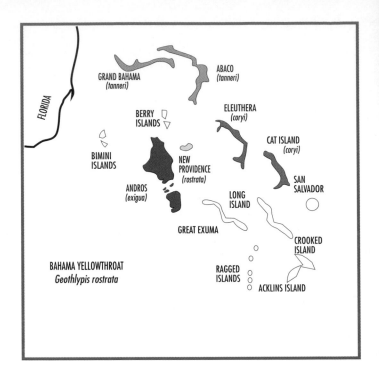

GRAND BAHAMA
(tanneri)

ABACO
(tanneri)

FLORIDA

BERRY
ISLANDS

ELEUTHERA
(coryi)

CAT ISLAND
(coryi)

BIMINI
ISLANDS

NEW
PROVIDENCE
(rostrata)

SAN
SALVADOR

ANDROS
(exigua)

LONG
ISLAND

GREAT EXUMA

CROOKED
ISLAND

BAHAMA YELLOWTHROAT
Geothlypis rostrata

RAGGED
ISLANDS

ACKLINS ISLAND

(*Zenaida macroura*). Even if correctly identified, the yellowthroat could conceivably have been consumed near the Bahama Islands, as tiger sharks can travel long distances in short periods.

ᴵᴵᴵᴵ STATUS AND CONSERVATION

This species remains rather common and presumably stable on Grand Bahama and Great Abaco and some of their offshore cays, but populations on other islands have been reduced. The subspecies *exigua* on Andros is now scarce; *coryi* has been greatly reduced on Eleuthera (and needs study here), but is still readily found on Cat Is. Nominate *rostrata* on New Providence is rare and seriously threatened. Habitat destruction of pinelands and coppice scrub has probably been the main factor in the species' decline. Shiny Cowbirds arrived in the Bahamas in 1994, so parasitism may perhaps become a population threat.

This species shows rather marked interisland variation. The ranges of the four currently recognized subspecies are outlined under Distribution above. In comparison to *tanneri*, male nominate *rostrata* from New Providence have a pale gray tinge to the crown, only faintly yellow-tinged superciliaries that extend across the forecrown as a very pale gray frontal band in most birds, a yellow-olive back, and yellow flanks. Males on Andros, *(exigua,* formerly treated as part of nominate *rostrata),* are the smallest Bahama Yellowthroats and are darker than New Providence birds, with a darker gray crown and gray superciliaries that do not continue to form a frontal band. In *coryi* from Eleuthera and Cat Is., males are much brighter than the other races, with brighter olive-yellow upperparts, yellow superciliary stripes, brighter yellow underparts, yellow-green flanks, and little if any gray in the olive crown. Cat Is. *coryi* are shorter-tailed and slightly brighter than Eleuthera birds. Plumage variation among females is more subtle, but *coryi* is paler yellow-olive above and brighter yellow below than other subspecies, and *tanneri* and *exigua* are the darkest on the upperparts. Specimen samples have been insufficient to convincingly show measurement differences. A second form ("*maynardi*") suggested to be sympatric with nominate *rostrata* on New Providence in fact represents adult individuals of *rostrata*.

🧬 TAXONOMIC RELATIONSHIPS

Although early workers who failed to appreciate the effects of plumage wear recognized several species of yellowthroats on the Bahamas, all were later lumped as one species, the Bahama Yel-

Bahama Yellowthroat. Male tanneri *on Grand Bahama, Bahamas, in April. (Photo: Bruce Hallett)*

lowthroat. Some subsequent authors have considered the Bahama Yellowthroat to be conspecific with the Common Yellowthroat of North America, but differences in plumage, size, behavior, habitat, and call notes suggest that it is distinct. One worker suggested that the yellowthroats of the Bahamas were more closely related to the various Mexican species of yellowthroats than to the Common.

✒ PLUMAGES AND MOLTS

SPRING ADULT MALE: Crown, hindneck, and upperparts olive green. There is an indistinct pale gray frontal band, tinged with yellow, just behind the black forehead. This frontal band continues as a more distinct pale yellowish border from the eye back along the posterior border of the mask. The forehead, lores, and auricular and malar regions are black, forming a typical yellowthroat "mask." The underparts are rather bright yellow, becoming slightly paler in the center of the lower belly and washed with grayish olive on the rear sides and flanks. The undertail coverts are yellow. The wings and tail are plain olive. **FIRST SPRING MALE:** Generally indistinguishable from spring adult male, but spring birds showing duller and more worn flight feathers and less yellow in the supercilium are probably first spring birds. **SPRING ADULT FEMALE:** Upperparts grayish olive, grading to brownish olive on the crown; forehead and forecrown strongly washed with brown. Lores and auricular area grayish brown, with a hint of a pale grayish supercilium, often extending down around the rear of the auricular, and broken whitish eye-ring. Throat and breast rather bright, rich yellow, becoming pale yellow on the lower belly; undertail coverts yellow. Flanks washed with olive-brown. Wings and tail unmarked olive. **FIRST SPRING FEMALE:** Indistinguishable in the field from spring adult female, but

Bahama Yellowthroat. Female tanneri *on Grand Bahama, Bahamas, in March. (Photo: Jon Dunn)*

in the hand, flight feathers may appear more worn. **FALL ADULT MALE:** Much like spring adult male, but the flanks are more strongly washed with brown. **FIRST FALL MALE:** Differs from fall adult males in having somewhat duller upperparts and, presumably, a less distinct pale border to the mask. **FALL ADULT FEMALE:** Like spring adult female, but flanks are more strongly washed with brown. **FIRST FALL FEMALE:** Presumably similar to fall adult female, but upperparts browner and yellow of the underparts duller, buffier. **JUVENILE:** Undescribed. **BARE PARTS:** Males have completely black bills at least from late winter through early summer; females and fall and winter males have brownish black upper mandibles and show some gray or flesh at the tomium and base of the lower mandible. The legs and feet are deep grayish pink. Eyes are dark brown.

The timing of the prebasic molt is imperfectly known, but it is usually complete by September; this molt is presumably incomplete in hatching-year birds and complete in adults. There is apparently no prealternate molt.

 REFERENCES

DISTRIBUTION: Dodrill and Gilmore 1978, King et al. 1979, Sykes 1974.
ECOLOGY, BEHAVIOR, VOCALIZATIONS, AND CONSERVATION: Baltz 1994.
IDENTIFICATION: Kaufman 1984.
SYSTEMATICS: Bangs 1900, Bonhote 1903, Schwartz 1970, Todd 1911.

GRAY-CROWNED YELLOWTHROAT   PL. 25

Geothlypis poliocephala

5.5 in. (13.3 cm). This widespread warbler of Mexico and Central America was formerly resident in the Brownsville area of southernmost Texas but disappeared from there around the end of the 19th century; well-documented records from that area may involve the same individual. Superficially yellowthroat-like, this warbler is distinguished from other *Geothlypis* yellowthroats by its thick, bicolored bill with a strongly curved culmen, its long, graduated and expressive tail, and its voice and behavior; it probably deserves placement in its own genus, *Chamaethlypis*. It is a bird of open grassy and weedy fields with scattered bushes; it does not occupy marshes. The Gray-crowned Yellowthroat has gone by a host of other common names, including Ground Chat, Thick-billed Yellowthroat, and Meadow Warbler.

DESCRIPTION

Generally grayish olive to brownish olive above and yellow below, lightening to whitish on the belly and washed with brown on the sides and flanks. Crown gray but partly to completely veiled with brown in some plumages. In males the lores are black, with the black extending back just under the eye; these areas are slaty gray in females. In northern birds there is a fairly conspicuous split white eye-ring. Fall birds are strongly washed with brown on the upperparts, sides, and flanks. The more worn body plumage of spring and early summer is decidedly grayer.

This is a moderately large, slender warbler with a long, graduated tail. The wings are relatively short, and the wing tip is the most rounded of any of our warblers. The bicolored bill is thick, with a strong decurvature to the culmen.

SIMILAR SPECIES

Superficially similar to the COMMON YELLOWTHROAT, especially to immature males of the latter species which may have the black mask largely restricted to the lores and the area below the eye. Easily told from all Common Yellowthroats by the thick bill distinctly decurved along the culmen. Note that the bill of Gray-crowned is distinctly bicolored — blackish or dark brown on the upper mandible and pale fleshy-yellow on the lower mandible. The northern races of Gray-crowned Yellowthroat show a distinct eye-ring, broken broadly in front by the dark lores; the indistinct eye-rings of female and immature male Common Yellowthroats are usually complete or nearly so. See below under Voice, which is completely diagnostic. Gray-crowned Yellowthroats are skulkers like Commons, but when sitting up often adopt a more vertical posture; they may expressively cock and wave the long tail but are generally less wrenlike in shape and action than Commons.

The YELLOW-BREASTED CHAT is considerably larger and longer tailed than the Gray-crowned Yellowthroat and has an even thicker bill. The chat is also brighter and more extensively yellow on the breast, and always shows a white supraloral line, which joins the white eye-ring to form a spectacled appearance.

VOICE

The SONG is a long, rich, and musical warble suggestive of *Passerina* buntings, Blue Grosbeak (*Guiraca caerulea*) or Orchard Oriole (*Icterus spurius*). The up-and-down phrases are somewhat variable in pattern, and the length of the song is similarly variable; the phrasing of some songs suggests that of the Common Yellowthroat's song, but the quality differs in its richness and both scratchy and fluty overtones. The song is usually given from atop a weedstem, shrub, or low tree, but may sometimes be given in flight. A variety of **CALL NOTES** are given, all of which are quite different from calls of other yellowthroats. Commonly heard is a distinctive high, grating *chee-dee, dee-deet,* or *cheed-l-eet,* with the last note slightly higher than the first. Also given is a descending series of three-syllabled notes, such as *jee-jee-jeu, jee-jee-jeu . . .* or *peet-a-loo, peet-a-loo . . . .* A single *chee* is also given.

 BEHAVIOR

Generally a rather secretive bird, skulking in the grasses and other low vegetation. Feeds mainly by gleaning for insects in the vegetation, but occasionally sallies after flying insects. Males are most easily located while singing or calling, when they usually perch openly on a grass stem, low shrub, small tree, or even utility wire. Often flicks, pumps, or switches the tail; the tail is occasionally cocked and moved from side to side. Perching birds sometimes adopt a rather vertical posture with tail held pointing downward. When agitated, it perches prominently and erects the crown feathers, giving the head a peaked look.

The **NEST** is a well-concealed cup in a tussock of grass, less than a meter off the ground; it is constructed of grasses and dead leaves and lined with fine fibers.

 HABITAT

This is primarily a bird of tall, dense grasses with some scattered shrubs or low trees; the taller woody vegetation is used mainly for singing perches. Occupied habitats are often human-created successional grasslands. Its former habitat in s. Texas consisted of dense grassy openings within the subtropical thorn scrub of the Rio Grande delta area. In the bulk of its Neotropical range it may also inhabit weedy fields and pastures, bracken fern, low growth on arid slopes, cane fields, and weedy hedgerows. Gray-crowned Yellowthroats do not occur in salt grass, nor do they normally occur in marshes of cattails and bulrushes, where Common Yellowthroats thrive.

 DISTRIBUTION

RESIDENT from cen. Sinaloa in w. Mexico and s. Tamaulipas in e. Mexico southward mainly in the lowlands through Mexico (including Yucatán peninsula) to w. Panama. Locally extends to higher elevations, even to 7,400 ft. in Panama. It was formerly resident in the lower Rio Grande Valley in extreme s. Texas and was probably fairly common there, with some 30 specimens and several egg sets taken in the late 1800s. After a long hiatus, two records were documented by photos in s. Texas in 1988 and 1989: a singing bird photographed at Sabal Palms Sanctuary east of Brownsville February–April 1988, and another (or possibly the same individual) there May–July 1989; this is near where numerous specimens were obtained nearly a century earlier. Additionally there were single-observer sight records in Cameron Co. in April 1988 and Hidalgo Co. in March 1989; these were accepted by the Texas Bird Records Committee. A bird present near San Ygnacio (above Falcon Dam) from mid-November 1995 through spring 1996 was originally identified as this species, but may have been a hybrid with Common Yellowthroat (see Taxonomic Relationships below).

STATUS AND CONSERVATION

The elimination of the resident population in southernmost Texas was probably related to habitat modification as a result of changing agricultural practices and overgrazing. Similar habitat modification in adjacent northern Tamaulipas suggests that the northernmost subspecies *ralphi* may be in some jeopardy. Such declines seem surprising in light of the species' tendency to inhabit early-successional grassy habitats. In the remainder of its range, populations of the Gray-crowned Yellowthroat are relatively stable, and the species has undoubtedly increased in some areas with the clearing of tropical forests. This species has been a host of Brown-headed and Bronzed cowbirds, but the extent of cowbird parasitism is unclear.

SUBSPECIES

The northernmost subspecies, *ralphi*, is the one recorded in Texas and is described below; *ralphi* is the palest and grayest of all of the forms; the gray of the crown is relatively light, and the black lores do not extend across the forehead, or do so only as a thin strip immediately above the bill. G. p. *ralphi* is resident mainly in Tamaulipas and e. San Luis Potosi, formerly extending north into southernmost Texas; recent records in Texas almost certainly pertain to this subspecies. The nominate race *poliocephala* is resident in the coastal lowlands of w. Mexico from Sinaloa south to w. Oaxaca and inland in the Rio Balsas drainage to the states of Mexico and Morelos. It is similar to *ralphi* but slightly more olive (less gray) above, slightly brighter yellow below, and very slightly smaller. G. p. *palpebralis* occurs from cen. Veracruz south through the Atlantic lowlands of Mexico, including the Yucatán peninsula, to n. Costa Rica; *caninucha* occurs on the Pacific slope east of the Isthmus of Tehuantepec and south to Honduras. Both of these subspecies are considerably more olive above than *ralphi* and *poliocephala*, and are brighter and more extensively yellow on the underparts; males have more extensive black across the forehead that merges into a dark gray crown. The split white eye-ring is reduced in some *caninucha* and absent in many. The subspecies *icterotis* of w. Nicaragua and w. Costa Rica and *ridgwayi* of e. Costa Rica and w. Panama, poorly differentiated from each other, are generally similar to *caninucha* but are somewhat brighter yellow below, deeper blue-gray on the crown, and lack any white around the eye.

TAXONOMIC RELATIONSHIPS

For stability we follow the AOU in including this species within *Geothlypis*. The monotypic genus *Chamaethlypis* has been merged with *Geothlypis* by various workers for over 100 years. It differs from all *Geothlypis* yellowthroats in its bill (thick, bicolored, and with a decurved culmen), graduated tail, distinct call notes, and grassy upland habitats. *Chamaethlypis* was erected to emphasize certain structural similarities of the Gray-crowned Yellowthroat to the Yellow-breasted Chat. Although claims of a close relationship between *Chamaethlypis* and *Icteria* have been refuted satisfactorily, we still feel that the distinctions above perhaps argue for the retention of the monotypic genus *Chamaethlypis*.

The individual present in San Ygnacio, Texas, in 1995–1996 was much like a Gray-crowned Yellowthroat in plumage, but showed some structural (especially bill) characters of Common Yellowthroat; its call note was much like that of the latter species. It was identified initially as a Gray-crowned, but was certainly not a "pure" bird of that species; it may have been a hybrid with Common Yellowthroat, and was paired with a female Common in the spring.

PLUMAGES AND MOLTS

SPRING ADULT MALE: Crown gray, slightly tinged with olive-brown on top but purer gray on the sides; auriculars, hindneck, and back plain olive-brown with a slight grayish cast; rump and upper tail coverts slightly brighter olive. With continued wear, the upperparts become grayer as the spring and summer progress. Lores, extending partway back under the eye, jet black; the black of the lores does not, or just barely, meets across the top of the bill. Chin and throat clear yellow, becoming paler yellow on the breast; the sides of the breast and flanks are washed with buffy brown.

Gray-crowned Yellowthroat. Male ralphi *on 19 February 1988 at Sabal Palms Sanctuary, Cameron Co., Texas. (Photo: Greg W. Lasley)*

The belly is creamy whitish, washed slightly with pale yellow. The undertail coverts are pale yellow like the breast. The bend of the wing is pale yellow. The plain dusky wings have the flight feathers edged with yellowish olive when fresh. The tail is fairly bright olive. **FIRST SPRING MALE:** Probably indistinguishable from spring adult male, but flight feathers and especially rectrices appear more worn. **SPRING ADULT FEMALE:** Similar to spring adult male, but the black of the lores is replaced by slaty gray and is slightly less extensive, never extending across the forehead. The crown is even more strongly washed with brown, with little clear gray showing on the sides of the crown. **FIRST SPRING FEMALE:** Probably indistinguishable from spring adult female, but flight feathers more worn. **FALL ADULT MALE:** Similar to spring adult male, but the crown and upperparts are strongly washed with rich brown, with only limited clear gray on the forecrown and sides of the crown. The yellow of the breast is washed with buffy brown, and the sides and flanks are more strongly and extensively washed with buffy brown than in spring birds. **FIRST FALL MALE:** Similar to fall adult male, but black of the lores is usually less extensive, the breast is more strongly washed with buffy brown, and the upperparts are even browner. **FALL ADULT FEMALE:** Similar to spring adult female, but extensively washed with brown on the upperparts, sides, and flanks. The slaty lores have some pale gray-buff feather tips and are thus even less evident than in spring birds. **FIRST FALL FEMALE:** The dullest and brownest plumage, with the slaty of the lores very reduced or even absent. The upperparts are entirely brown, with no gray showing on the crown. The yellow of the underparts is pale and strongly washed with buff. The dullest birds have the clear yellow of the underparts restricted to the chin and malar area, with the breast, belly, and undertail coverts being buffy with only a hint of pale yellow. The split eye-ring is creamy in color. **JUVENILE:** Brown above and buffy below, with two thin buffy wing bars. **BARE PARTS:** Upper mandible dark brownish slate in adult males, somewhat duller and browner in females and immatures, but always contrasting with the pale pinkish tan lower mandible and tomium. Legs and feet pinkish brown. Eyes dark brown.

In northern populations there is a complete prebasic molt which takes place after breeding in adults; the prebasic molt of hatching-year birds does not involve the flight feathers. There is a partial prealternate molt.

 REFERENCES

DISTRIBUTION: Oberholser 1974.
SYSTEMATICS: Eisenmann 1962, Ridgway 1894.

HOODED WARBLER PL. 26

Wilsonia citrina

5.25 in. (13.3 cm). This striking warbler is a familiar breeding bird in the understory of southeastern forests, but it also ranges north through much of the eastern U.S. A bold black and yellow hood is present in males and to some degree in many females; all individuals show a dark loral spot. The large dark eye, standing out boldly on the yellow face, is distinctive; in fact, one study showed the Hooded's eye size to be the largest among 32 species of warblers analyzed, a character possibly related to its preference for deeply shaded habitats. Extensive white in the tail is readily visible as the bird frequently flicks the tail feathers open and shut. The bill is larger than that of other *Wilsonia* warblers. On the wintering grounds, primarily on the Yucatán peninsula and adjacent regions of Mexico and Central America, most birds maintain well-defined feeding territories.

 DESCRIPTION

A black hood, extending from the crown through the hindneck and throat, setting off the yellow face and forehead, is present in males; adult females also show a variable amount of black in the hood. The underparts are bright yellow and the upperparts yellow-olive in all plumages. All birds show much white in the outer three pairs of rectrices, this varying slightly by age and sex. All plumages also show a spot of blackish or dusky olive in the lores. Aging is usually difficult; there is only very subtle seasonal change in appearance.

This is a medium-sized warbler with a fairly long, square-tipped tail, stout legs, and a relatively large bill for a *Wilsonia*. The dark eye is large and conspicuous.

Females without black on the head can resemble some female **WIL-SON'S WARBLERS**. Briefly, Wilson's is smaller, smaller-billed, lacks white in the tail, and lacks the dark loral spot; for a more detailed discussion see under that species. In Hooded, the distinctive hood markings easily identify males and many females but note the slight similarity to **"LAWRENCE'S"** (Blue-winged × Golden-winged) **WARBLER**; from this hybrid Hooded is told by its yellow face, plain wings, lack of dark auricular patch. Males of the probably extinct **BACHMAN'S WARBLER** have a yellow chin and black chest patch that does not join black of forecrown; Bachman's is smaller, with a finer and slightly decurved bill, an eye-ring, whitish under-tail coverts, and less white in the shorter tail. The **YELLOW WARBLER** shares the characteristic of a prominent dark eye on a blank yellow face but differs in having distinct pale yellow edges to the flight feathers, yellow tail spots, and (often) fine streaking on the breast.

♪ VOICE

The **SONG** is a short, loud series of whistled notes with an emphatic ending. It typically starts with two (or more) sets of paired notes and ends with a two- or three-note phrase with the first or second note accented and the last note dropping in pitch. Representations include: *tawee tawee tawee TEE-to*; *wee-tee, wee-tee, WEE-tee-you*; or *wee-see, wee-see, wee-SEE-you*. Another version, *wee-tee, wee-tee, WEE-to-WEE*, rises in pitch throughout, with the last note strongly emphasized. An individual male may sing several different song types, but most frequently repeats one particular song; female song has been recorded. The **CALL NOTE** is a sharp, loud *chink* or *chip*, suggestive of the common contact note of the California Towhee (*Pipilo crissalis*); the call is also reminiscent of that of Louisiana Waterthrush and Prothonotary Warbler, and to some suggests an exceptionally sharp, loud version of the call of Orange-crowned Warbler. During aggressive interactions a more complex *chippity-chup* note is given. Note that calls attributed to this species in Borror and Gunn's published recordings appear to be of Kentucky Warbler. **FLIGHT NOTE** apparently not described.

🐦 BEHAVIOR

An excellent field character is this species' habit of rapidly opening and shutting its tail with a lateral movement, revealing the extensive white in the outer three pairs of rectrices; this tail-flashing occurs at a rate of more than once per second. This species has a relatively low foraging beat, usually staying within 5–10 ft. of the ground and often foraging on the ground itself. Birds habitually remain well within the forest understory; the flashing of the white in the tail often reveals a bird's presence in such deeply shaded habitats. Foraging behaviors include sallying, hover-gleaning, and gleaning; prey consists almost entirely of arthropods. Males on the breeding grounds characteristically choose a song perch that is quite high in the canopy and usually somewhat concealed; some song perches are more in the open. Hoodeds are persistent singers, singing well into midday, and are often the last warblers to cease singing in the evening. Males may sing on the breeding grounds well into September, and are occasionally noted to sing in fall migration.

Wintering birds are known to be strongly territorial, but individuals also accompany mixed species flocks. "Wing droop" and "head switch" displays are given by territorial wintering birds.

The **NEST** is usually in a patch of shrubs (rhododendron, laurel, cane, palmetto) within 3–6 ft. of the ground. The neat, compact nest cup is covered on the outside with numerous dead leaves, resulting in a rather bulky but well camouflaged structure. Both nest predation and cowbird parasitism rates are high at Hooded Warbler nests, and renestings are frequent, often extending through the end of the summer.

HABITAT

BREEDS in both upland and bottomland woodlands, the key habitat features being the presence of a well-developed shrubby understory beneath extensive mature, shaded forests. Such habitats especially occur along streambottoms and ravines and in floodplains. In the Deep South this species is common in swamp woods of tupelo and cypress, with an understory including palmetto and cane; it also occurs in ash and maple woods and in pine woods with an adequate understory. Through the remainder of the breeding range it uses mixed forests of red maple, beech, oaks, and white pine, again with appropriate understory and abundant saplings; pine plantations are occupied in some regions. Drier upland woods of oak and hickory are used only locally. In the Appalachian and Allegheny mountains it nests in laurel and rhododendron thickets, and in portions of the Great Lakes region it is found mainly in shaded ravines and gorges. In the pine barrens of New Jersey it nests in cedar swamps. **WINTERS** in a variety of lowland tropical evergreen forests with well-developed undergrowth, including forest edge and second-growth habitats.

To a great extent, winter males and females segregate by habitat, with males favoring taller, more humid forests and females occurring in drier, more open woodlands and even shrubby fields. MIGRANTS are not encountered in numbers away from the Gulf Coast, but where found tend to be low in dense thickets and the undergrowth of woodlands.

DISTRIBUTION

BREEDS in e. North America mainly south of the Great Lakes; especially common in the South. Breeds from e. Kans. (very local), ne. Okla. (Tulsa area), Mo. (locally), Iowa (mainly se.), cen. Wisc., Mich. (mainly s.), s. Ont., N.Y., Conn. (mainly in south; formerly north to Mass.), and R.I. south to cen. (very local) and e. Texas and nearly to the coast in the Gulf states and n. Fla. Breeds casually west and north to s. Minn. and Mass.; formerly bred in se. Neb. Has summered in Colo. and the southwestern states, well west of the normal breeding range; breeding was documented in 1992 in s. Calif.

WINTERS in the lowlands mainly from e. Mexico (s. Veracruz, with a few north to s. Tamaulipas) south to the Caribbean region of Honduras and Nicaragua, with the largest numbers occurring on the Yucatán peninsula and adjacent regions. Also winters (uncommonly) in sw. Mexico, east of the isthmus; a few winter in w. Mexico north to Nayarit. Small numbers winter south to Costa Rica (locally to 4,000 ft.) and Panama (rare; mainly w. and cen.). Casual south to n. Colombia, n. Venezuela, Netherlands Antilles, and Trinidad. Winters regularly in small numbers on Bermuda and in the Bahamas and Greater Antilles; casual in winter in the Lesser Antilles. Casual in winter as far north as the s. U.S., with records for Fla., Texas, La., and S.C.; an early December record for the New York City region may represent a late fall migrant. There are about six winter records for s. Calif., as well as two for Wash. and a December record for B.C.

SPRING MIGRATION is almost exclusively trans-Gulf, with the major spring passage being through the upper Texas coast and coastal La.; smaller numbers are found on the s. Texas coast and east to Fla. (Panhandle and Keys). Spring migrants appear as early as mid-March on the Gulf Coast and in Fla., and exceptionally in early March. Males may appear on the southernmost breeding grounds (including e. Texas) by the last week of March. Arrivals in Ark., Tenn., s. Mo., and Ky. are usually during the first half of April (exceptionally to the third week of March in Ark.), with most breeders on territory by late April. In the Midwest (s. portions of Ohio, Ind., and Ill.), the n. Appalachian region, and the

Mid-Atlantic states, birds typically arrive during the latter half of April. Breeding birds arrive at the northern end of the breeding range around 5–15 May. Spring overshoots may appear in the northern part of the range much earlier than outlined above (exceptionally even as early as late March), with such events usually correlated with the passage of strong southerly storms. Regular spring overshoot to Mass. (mainly late April to late May) and N.S. (about 20 spring records, mostly in April and exceptionally as early as 6 April); casual spring overshoot to s. Que. In spring, this species is noted in significant numbers only along the Gulf Coast, with the peak spring passage from early to (especially) mid-April; elsewhere it is uncommon to rare as a migrant. Peak numbers of migrants in more northerly areas are during the first half of May. Late migrants have been noted as late as mid-May from the Gulf Coast and casually as late as early June farther north (to 14 June at Pt. Pelee, Ont.).

FALL MIGRATION is slightly more eastward than that in spring and is more spread out over time. Migrants can be noted quite early,

HOODED WARBLER
Wilsonia citrina

with individuals having been noted in Fla. in the first half of July and small numbers being regular there by the end of July. The last birds have usually departed their breeding territories by early September (a few to mid-month). In general it is casual, rare, or very uncommon as a fall migrant away from the Gulf Coast; the main movement through the Gulf Coast is more easterly than in spring. In the Midwest and Great Lakes regions it is much less numerous in fall than in spring. Only in New England and the Canadian Maritimes is it somewhat more frequent in fall. Peak fall movements take place during September, with small numbers into early October. The latest fall dates from most regions are from the latter half of October, with casual late November records even as far north as s. Ont. There is one early December record for the New York City area.

VAGRANT well west of its normal range. Casual in spring and fall on the Great Plains, with a few records (mainly spring) north to Man. and Sask. Recorded from all western states except Mont.; most records are for spring. In Calif. there are some 338 records, ⅔ from spring; most are from the south. Some 80 birds were recorded in Calif. during spring and summer 1992 alone. Spring records from the West are mainly in May (a few in April, and many records well into the summer); fall records are mainly in September and October, with a few late August and November records. Several winter records for the West are noted above. Records exceptionally far north include two from James Bay (Moose River mouth, Ont., and North Twin Is., Northwest Territories), one from Churchill, Man., and three from Nfld.

EXCEPTIONAL VAGRANT to the British Isles, with records for the Isles of Scilly (20–23 September 1970) and St. Kilda (10 September 1992).

STATUS AND CONSERVATION

Populations seem to be stable overall. Some local increases are perhaps related to the enrichment of the forest understory following selective cutting, treefalls after strong winds, and gypsy moth damage. Conversely, declines in parts of the range (e.g., Mississippi River bottomlands in the southern Midwest) have resulted from extensive forest clearing. In some southern pine forests, management practices involve the burning of undergrowth, which adversely affects this species. Hooded Warblers require extensive forest tracts (about 30–50 acres, but regionally variable); therefore they are especially susceptible to forest fragmentation and its attendant increases in nest predation and cowbird parasitism. As such it is an important indicator species of forest quality. Parasitism rates by Brown-headed Cowbirds are high in many regions, but this species' tendency to rear second broods late in the season may partially offset the effects of parasitism. The preference (at least by males) for mature forests in winter suggests that tropical deforestation adversely affects this species.

 ## SUBSPECIES

No subspecies recognized; no geographical variation reported.

 ## TAXONOMIC RELATIONSHIPS

Relationships within the genus *Wilsonia* are unclear; the Hooded Warbler seems not to be particularly closely related to the other two species placed in that genus.

PLUMAGES AND MOLTS

SPRING ADULT MALE: Forehead, forecrown, and face bright yellow. Black extending from the top of the crown back through the hindneck and around the sides of the neck to the chin and throat, forming a striking hood. Small loral spot dusky black. The black hindneck contrasts sharply with the back and remaining upperparts, which are bright yellow-olive. The rounded lower border of the black hood is sharply set off from the bright yellow underparts. Wings dusky olive, with the coverts and flight feathers edged glossy yellow-green. Tail dusky olive with the three outer rectrices extensively white on the inner webs and a spot of white on r3; tail thus appears white from below. **FIRST SPRING MALE:** Indistinguishable in the field from spring adult male. In the hand, many birds can be told by

Hooded Warbler. Adult female (L), male (R) in Ohio in June. (Photo: Steve and Dave Maswlowski)

Hooded Warbler. First spring female in Ontario in May. (Photo: Jim Flynn)

the duller, more olive-brown color of the flight feathers and more tapered rectrices; the extent of these differences depends on the number of juvenal flight feathers and rectrices that are retained (variable). **SPRING ADULT FEMALE:** Variable in the extent of black in the hood, but always with less black than males. The most extensively hooded females closely resemble males but have olive green on the hindneck and some yellowish on the chin. In typical adult females, the black is confined to the front of the crown, down the sides of the neck (outlining the rear part of the yellow face), and variably onto the throat. In minimally black adult females there is a faint outline to the hood and some black extending onto the sides of the lower throat (but with a clear yellow chin and upper throat). Variation in the amount of black in the hood of females in definitive basic plumage is apparently not related to age. Loral spot dusky olive. Remaining upperparts bright yellow-olive, underparts yellow. White in the tail less extensive than in adult male, with only limited white on r4 and usually none on r3. **FIRST SPRING FEMALE:** Similar to spring adult female and indistinguishable in the field from some, but plumage nearly always lacks black; the "hood" is outlined on the forecrown and sides of the neck with dark olive; this dark outline comes to a point on the sides of the throat. Dusky olive loral spot; auriculars may be faintly tinged with olive. Upperparts yellow-olive; entire underparts yellow. Extent of white in the tail as in first fall female. **FALL ADULT MALE:** Very similar to spring adult male, but black hood and throat feathers sometimes show faint, thin yellow tips. **FIRST FALL MALE:** Very similar to fall adult male, but thin greenish yellow tips to black crown and throat feathers usually more evident. **FALL ADULT FEMALE:** Very similar to spring adult female, but plumage fresher. **FIRST FALL FEMALE:** As first spring female, but plumage fresher. **JUVENILE:** This plumage held only briefly on the breeding grounds. Extensively brownish olive above; dull buff below, with breast mottled with light yellow. Wings olive, with coverts edged brownish. White in tail as in first fall birds. **BARE PARTS:** Bill black in adults, tinged brown on the mandible and tomium in fall birds and immatures. Legs light tan-pink. Eyes blackish brown.

The prebasic molt takes place on the breeding grounds; it is complete in adults but usually partial in hatching-year birds, involving the body plumage, some remiges, and usually the rectrices. A prealternate molt is lacking; the very slight plumage change from fall into spring is due to the wear of greenish feather tips on head.

 REFERENCES

GENERAL: Evans and Stutchbury 1994.

DISTRIBUTION: Austen et al. 1994, Gartshore 1988, Gunn and Crocker 1951.

ECOLOGY, BEHAVIOR, VOCALIZATIONS, AND CONSERVATION: Evans et al. 1996, Lynch et al. 1985, Powell and Rappole 1986, Rappole and Warner 1980.

PLUMAGES, MOLTS, AND MORPHOLOGY: Eaton et al. 1963, Morton 1989.

WILSON'S WARBLER PL. 26

Wilsonia pusilla

4.75 in. (12 cm). The Wilson's Warbler is a small bright green and yellow warbler that is remarkably active in behavior. It frequently hover-gleans and flycatches, flipping its long tail expressively in an up-and-down or circular gnatcatcher-like movement. The beady blackish eye stands out conspicuously on the blank face. In males a round black cap or "yarmulke" is obvious, and a suggestion of this cap is present in many females. This is one of the most numerous warblers in western North America, but it is generally uncommon in the East. Three subspecies are recognized, differing slightly in size, plumage, vocalizations, and ecology.

 DESCRIPTION

Bright olive green to yellow-green above, yellow (to brilliant golden yellow) below. No strong plumage markings except a black cap on males (variably reduced in most adult females and many first fall males, more obscure or lacking in immature females). Sexing of birds in the field may be difficult because of variability in the extent of the black cap in females, both geographically and within populations; there is little seasonal variation in plumage. Males average about 5 percent larger than females. This species shows slight geographical variation in the color of the upperparts and underparts, the extent of black in the cap of females, and size.

This is a small warbler with a rather long, slightly rounded tail, a small but relatively wide bill, and well-developed rictal bristles. The legs are thin and delicate looking.

 SIMILAR SPECIES

The most likely candidate for confusion is the immature female **HOODED WARBLER**, which is larger, has a considerably larger blackish bill and dusky lores, and shows extensive white in the tail (accentuated by frequent flicking of outer tail feathers) in all plumages. The auriculars of Hoodeds look yellower, showing more contrast with the olive of the crown and nape; this and its relatively larger eye impart a different face pattern than Wilson's. Male and older female Hooded Warblers are easily told by black on the hood; beware of the effect of missing facial and chest feathers on Wilson's, which can give the appearance of dark coloration.

The **ORANGE-CROWNED WARBLER** has a thinner, more sharply pointed bill and a dark eye line (unlike the blank-looking face of Wilson's); Orange-crowned is much duller in plumage and often softly streaked below, though bright western *lutescens* Orange-crowneds are nearly as bright as the dullest immature female Wilson's (which tend to be eastern *pusilla,* not likely to be found with *lutescens* Orange-crowned). Also note the pale broken eyering of Orange-crowned, with the eye standing out less on the face. Overall shape also differs, with Orange-crowned being shorter tailed; Orange-crowned does not wave tail. Calls differ, Orange-crowned giving a sharp *tik*.

The **YELLOW WARBLER** is similar in having a bold dark eye standing out on the face. Yellows with uniformly yellow underparts (lacking red streaks) can suggest immature female Wilson's. Note the very different wing pattern of Yellow, with prominent pale edges to wing coverts and tertials, as well as the yellow tail spots. The tail of Yellow is much shorter than that of Wilson's, with undertail coverts extending much closer to the tail tip. Yellow has a subdued tail wag but lacks expressive tail waving of Wilson's. Calls differ, Yellow giving a slurred *chip* call and a buzzy *zeet* flight note.

 VOICE

The **SONG** consists of one or more rapid series of abruptly slurred *chip* notes, but there is considerable regional variation in pattern. Eastern *pusilla* gives a rather weak series that changes pitch (usually dropping) slightly toward the end, such as *chi chi chi chi chi chi chi chi chet chet.* Compare with the more even and vigorous trill of the Palm Warbler (which often shares breeding habitat in e. Canada, Maine). In contrast, the song of West Coast *chryseola* is a more vigorous and staccato series that builds in volume and often in speed toward the end, but that usually shows little obvious change in pitch: *chi chi chi chi chit chit CHIT CHIT CHIT*. The song of *pileolata* does not appear to be well described but is generally intermediate in quality between those of *pusilla* and *chryseola*. Variant songs throughout the species' range may be more distinctly two- or three-parted: *chi chi chi chi chi chet chet sip sip sip*; some of these variants may suggest songs of nominate *ruficapilla* Nashville Warbler.

CALL is a highly distinctive, somewhat nasal *timp* or *chimp*, suggesting note of western North American Winter Wren (*Troglodytes troglodytes pacificus*), but not doubled as is usually the case in the wren. Also, a sharper, slurred *chip* or *tsip* when flushed and as **FLIGHT NOTE** (and occasionally when perched); this note recalls a soft Lark Sparrow (*Chondestes grammacus*) note and is sometimes given in a rapid series.

 BEHAVIOR

Extremely active, with frequent sallying and hover-gleaning and nearly constant flitting from twig to twig. The tail is constantly quickly flipped forward over the back or laterally in a circular motion, much like a gnatcatcher. The wings are also frequently flicked. Foraging by gleaning, hover-gleaning, and sallying usually takes place at medium levels but foraging near (occasionally on) the ground and high in treetops is also frequent. Foraging height appears to average lower in the East. Food consists mainly of insects (especially leafhoppers) and spiders, but some berries are eaten in summer and fall. Very tame, inquisitive, and confiding, especially around the nest; responsive to "pishing." Migrants of the nominate race in the East are often encountered in association with Canada Warblers. Winter birds are usually solitary and territorial but will also join mixed species flocks.

NESTS are geographically somewhat variable in structure and placement. In eastern *pusilla* and presumably most populations of *pileolata*, the nest is placed on or near the ground, often in a clump of moss or tussock of sedges at the base of a small tree or shrub. The nest cup is made almost entirely of fine grasses, often with some leaves or hair. Montane populations of the Pacific Coast race *chryseola* are similar in their nesting behavior, but in at least some coastal populations birds tend to place their nests about 1–3 ft. off the ground; these coastal nests are bulkier cups incorporating twigs, fine stems, and leaves. Pacific Coast populations have a relatively long breeding season and are often double-brooded; single broods are the norm elsewhere in the species' range. Polygyny is not rare in Sierra Nevada, California, populations.

 HABITAT

BREEDING habitat is geographically variable, but in all cases involves dense ground cover and low shrubs in relatively wet situations. Nominate *pusilla*, in the eastern boreal portion of the species' range, inhabits relatively open wet areas such as bogs, pond margins, and beaver ponds, with an extensive shrubby growth of alder, willow, dwarf birch, and stunted conifers (black spruce, tamarack); low ground cover, including mosses (such as sphagnum) and Labrador-tea is abundant within such habitats. In the western boreal regions, *pileolata* is widespread in low, thick deciduous vegetation (especially willow and alder) within rather open areas around streams and ponds. Western montane populations of *pileolata* and *chryseola* are found in thickets of willows, alders, and other shrubs at or near treeline as well as in montane meadows, along steep ravines and avalanche slopes, and along stream bottoms and lake shores. Pacific Coast *chryseola* have variable habitat preferences. They breed in dense coniferous forests where canopy gaps and clear-cuts permit a dense shrub layer to develop, as well as in thickets of rhododendron, Sitka alder, and dense young conifers, maples, and alders. They also breed in moist, well-developed broadleaf woodlands (alders, willows, cottonwoods) with a well-developed understory (poison oak, brambles, nettles), especially along lowland and foothill watercourses. In some areas they occupy dense, moist, north-slope coastal scrub with no overstory.

In **MIGRATION,** found in a variety of thickets and scrubby woodlands, with deciduous growth preferred.

WINTER birds within the U.S. (where rare) are found mainly in willow thickets and other moist, scrubby growth (including bamboo thickets). South of our region they winter in moist lowland and highland habitats. The wide variety of occupied habitats includes gardens, plantations, scrubby fields, woodland borders and gaps, second growth, humid forests, treeline scrub, and even stunted vegetation above treeline. They are especially common in winter in highlands of Central America.

 DISTRIBUTION

BREEDS from w. and n. Alaska east through the forest and scrub regions of Canada to Nfld., and south through the Pacific states to s. Calif., in the montane West to w. Colo. and n. N.M., and in the East south to ne. Minn., n. New England. Nominate *pusilla* breeds from Dist. of Mack. and possibly n. Yukon, and n. and e. Alta. (east of the Rocky Mtns.) eastward across the boreal forests to n. Que., cen. Lab., and N.S.; breeds south to cen. Sask., s. Man. (scarce), ne. Minn. (rare), extreme nw. Wisc. (Apostle Is.), n. Mich. (local, upper peninsula only), s.-cen. Ont., ne. N.Y. (rare, Adirondacks), ne. Vt. (rare), n. N.H., and cen. Me. The race *pileolata* breeds over much of Alaska (north to the south slope of the Brooks Range and west on the Seward Peninsula to about 166° W and to the base of the Alaska Peninsula), s. Yukon, B.C. (including Queen Charlotte Is., but excluding sw. coastal region), and w. Alta., and then south through the Rocky Mtns. and mountains of the Great Basin to e. Wash., e. Ore., ne. Calif., cen. Nev., s.-cen. Ut., Colo., and n.-cen. N.M. (San Juan and Sangre de Cristo mtns.). Pacific Coast *chryseola* breeds from sw. B.C. south (mainly west of the Cascade crest) along the coastal slope to Santa Barbara Co., Calif. (and formerly to San Diego Co., with some recent records), and through the Sierra Nevada (including extreme w. Nev.) to the San Gabriel and San Bernardino mtns. of s. Calif. (where now scarce). Breeding *chryseola* in the southern part of its range on the Pacific Coast may arrive as early as mid-March, but northern nesting *pusilla* and *pileolata* arrive on breeding grounds after mid-May (many *pusilla* even in early June).

WINTERS mainly from n. Mexico (a few to the s. U.S.) south to w. Panama. Nominate *pusilla* winters primarily on the Caribbean slope from ne. Mexico south at least to Costa Rica. Birds of this subspecies also winter regularly from the Rio Grande Valley of s. Texas north and east along the Gulf Coast to se. La. (and very rarely east to Fla., where somewhat more regular in the south than the north). There are a handful of mid- and late winter records as far north as Ky., Ont., Conn., and N.S. *W. p. pileolata* winters mainly from nw. Mexico (Sinaloa and Durango) south (mainly in the highlands) to w. Panama. *Pileolata* and *pusilla* have been found wintering together commonly in the lowlands of s. Veracruz, Mexico. Most *chryseola* winter from nw. Mexico (s. Baja Calif., Sonora) south along the Pacific slope and highlands to w. Panama. Small numbers of Wilson's Warblers (subspecies mostly undetermined, but winter specimens from Calif. and Ariz. include both *chryseola* and *pileolata*) winter along the Pacific Coast of North America, especially in willow thickets on the cen. Calif. coast; they are annual in nw. Calif. and casual north to sw. B.C. One spent an entire winter at Kodiak, Alaska. Also casual in winter in the interior Southwest, with additional December records north and east to Colo. and N.M. Recorded once in late fall in Colombia.

In **MIGRATION,** generally abundant in the West but uncommon in the East; spring daily counts in the Southwest may reach several hundred birds, whereas high counts in the East seldom exceed a few dozen individuals even at prime migrant traps.

The **SPRING MIGRATION** of eastern *pusilla* is circum-Gulf. Birds move north through s. Texas, the Texas hill country, and n.-cen. Texas but are rare on the upper Texas coast and casual east through the Gulf region to Fla. and elsewhere in the Southeast. This is one of our later spring warblers. A very few birds arrive in Texas in mid-April (most earlier records may pertain to overwintering birds); birds arrive on the Texas coast after the third week of April and don't reach the Great Lakes in any numbers until early May, peaking in mid-May. There are scattered mid-April records well to the north, such as an 1 8 April record for N.S. and a 6 April record for n. Indiana. For much of the Midwest and East (north to s. New England) spring arrivals are in the first few days of May. Arrivals in the n. Great Lakes region, n. New England, and the Canadian Maritimes are usually during the third week of May, while birds arrive on the northernmost breeding grounds in late May and very early June. Spring migration peaks are late, being in mid-May in n.-cen. Texas and the s. Midwest and the last third of May in the n. Midwest and New England. The bulk of the spring movement is west of the Appalachian Mtns. The species is decidedly rare in spring along the Atlantic Coast south of N.J., Del., and Md. Small numbers of spring migrants are still passing through the n. U.S. through the first third of June.

The race *pileolata* parallels nominate *pusilla* in **SPRING** timing, although numbers begin moving north a little earlier. They move on a rather broad front from the w. Great Plains through much of the West (except the immediate Pacific Coast). The earliest migrants in w. Texas (almost certainly *pileolata*) have been noted by the last few days of March, but typically first arrive in the Southwest during the second week of April. Typical arrivals over much of the montane West are in the first half of May (a few records to mid-April), but usually in late May at the highest elevations. Alaska breeders arrive around 1 0–2 0 May. Peak spring migration over much of the Southwest (including e. Calif.) is from early to mid-May, with considerable passage still taking place in late May (and a few birds into early June).

Spring migration of chryseola is decidedly earlier than that of the other two races. Virtually all of the spring movement is through s. Arizona and the Pacific Coast states. The earliest migrants have arrived in s. Ariz. as early as the end of February, but more typical arrivals there and in s. Calif. are during the first third of March. Coastal Calif. breeders arrive on territory from

WILSON'S WARBLER
Wilsonia pusilla

WILSON'S WARBLER
Wilsonia pusilla

mid- to late March (or early April in nw. Calif.). At the northern end of the breeding range (sw. B.C.) birds arrive in late April and early May. Peak movements of migrant *chryseola* in the Southwest are from late March to mid-April, with some movement through the end of April and the very beginning of May.

FALL MIGRATION of eastern *pusilla* largely retraces the spring routes, with a slight eastward shift that yields more birds along the Atlantic Coast and eastern Gulf Coast. This race is regular in fall in Bermuda and casual in the Bahamas and Greater Antilles. The earliest southbound migrants are normally noted in mid-August (casually in late July in s. Canada and the n. U.S.). Peak fall movement is from the end of August to mid-September, with small numbers passing through into early October. A few are noted to late October and casually to late November, particularly in coastal New England and the Canadian Maritimes. Specimens attributed to *pusilla* have been collected west to Idaho, Ore., and Ariz. (primarily in late May, but with some fall records as well); many of these, particularly from the Northwest, may in fact be dull *pileolata*.

Fall migrant *pileolata* move broadly through the West; they are more numerous in fall on the w. Great Plains than in spring. They appear from mid-August (a few to early August) to mid-October, generally peaking during the first half of September (earlier in Alaska). Noted rarely to late October and casually into November (even as far north as se. Alaska). *W. p. pileolata* is reported from specimens as far east as Mo., Minn., and Miss.; also recorded from Bering Sea islands (mainly fall).

W. p. chryseola is a somewhat earlier fall migrant than the other races, with some birds appearing away from breeding areas as early as about 10 July; more typically, fall arrivals appear in early August. Fall migration extends through September, peaking from late August through mid-September. As in spring, the bulk of the fall migration is through the Pacific states and Arizona.

VAGRANT north to Arctic Alaska, n. Baffin Is. (73° N), Greenland (September 1975), and sw. England (13 October 1985); these records likely pertain to nominate *pusilla*.

Status and Conservation

Local declines and increases have been noted from Breeding Bird Survey data, but no broad trends are evident for *pusilla* and *pileolata*. West Coast *chryseola* has disappeared from most of the coastal lowlands south of Santa Barbara Co., California, because of destruction of lowland riparian thickets and the effects of cowbird parasitism; this species is an especially frequent cowbird host in that region. The emergence of dense second-growth scrub following clear-cutting has probably led to local increases in the Pacific Northwest. The species' use of a variety of second-growth, scrubby, and high-elevation habitats in winter makes it relatively immune to declines resulting from winter habitat modification.

SUBSPECIES

There is moderate geographical variation in size, upperpart color, brightness of the yellow underparts, extent of olive on the face, extent of black in the cap of females, and vocalizations. Three subspecies are recognized: nominate *pusilla* breeding from District of Mackenzie and n. and e. Alberta eastward; *pileolata* from Alaska, n. and interior British Columbia, and nw. Alberta south through Rocky Mtns. and Great Basin to ne. California; and *chryseola* on Pacific Coast from sw. British Columbia south to s. California (see Distribution). Possible intergradation between *pusilla* and *pileolata* in n. Yukon should be investigated. Also, the boundaries of *pileolata* and *chryseola* in e. California need clarification. Wilson's mirrors the Orange-crowned Warbler in its geographical variation, with the brightest birds on the West Coast, the dullest in the boreal regions, and largest birds of intermediate brightness in the montane West.

Eastern nominate *pusilla* is described below. It is intermediate in size but dullest in plumage. It averages darker and duller green on the upperparts; the underparts are a duller, less intense yellow than in the two western races, and the forehead and lores are duller yellow. Female *pusilla* average less black on the crown than in western races, and many adult and all first fall birds lack contrast between the crown and forehead. The thin yellow eye-ring is most evident in this race because of a more extensive wash of

Wilson's Warbler. Male pusilla *in New York in September. (Photo: Douglas Whitman)*

olive through the face and a touch of olive in the lores (especially in females and immatures).

W. p. pileolata, from Alaska south through the montane regions of the West, is the largest race, though size differences are too small to be useful in the field. Wing chords average about 2 mm longer than in *pusilla.* It is much like *pusilla* on the upperparts, though averaging slightly brighter green. It is much brighter yellow on the forehead and underparts than *pusilla,* with a hint of rich cadmium color, thus approaching *chryseola*; there is only a very slight olive wash on the underparts. The forehead and lores are clear yellow, and there is only a slight olive wash to the sides of the head. Some dull *pileolata* are probably indistinguishable in plumage from *pusilla.* Female *pileolata* appear to be intermediate between *pusilla* and *chryseola* in the extent of black shown by females, but like all races are quite variable in this feature. Adult females may show black caps up to 14 mm in length. About ⅔ of first fall females lack any black in the cap, as do a few first spring females.

Pacific Coast birds, *chryseola,* are bright yellow-green on the upperparts and uniformly deep cadmium yellow on the underparts. The forehead is contrastingly bright yellow even in most first fall female *chryseola*; it may be almost bright yellow-orange in adult males. Females average more black on the cap than in other races; about ⅓ of first basic females lack any black in the cap, but nearly all first spring females show some black. In adult females the black of the cap may measure up to 14 mm. Wing chords are similar to or slightly smaller than those of *pusilla.*

TAXONOMIC RELATIONSHIPS

Relationships within genus not well understood, although this species appears to be more closely related to Canada than to the more similarly plumaged Hooded Warbler.

PLUMAGES AND MOLTS

The following descriptions are of the eastern nominate race. **SPRING ADULT MALE:** Yellow forehead contrasting sharply with a neat, shiny black cap patch. Hindneck and upperparts bright olive green. A bright yellow supercilium extends broadly above and behind the eye. The lores, auricular region, and sides of face are yellowish olive. Thin, inconspicuous yellow eye-ring. Underparts bright lemon yellow, washed variably with olive on the sides and flanks. Wing coverts olive green; flight feathers dusky olive. Tail dusky olive, with rectrices edged brighter olive green; the unmarked tail appears all dark from below. **FIRST SPRING MALE:** Essentially identical to spring adult male; a few birds may show limited green feather tips at the rear of the black cap. Rectrices more pointed and worn; flight feathers and primary coverts somewhat browner and more worn than in adult. **SPRING ADULT FEMALE:** Similar to spring adult male, but the black is usually limited to the front half of the cap, or may be nearly or completely absent. Forehead tinged with olive, not sharply contrasting with any black that may be present in the cap. Lores tinged olive. The black of the cap does not exceed 8 mm from front to back (in contrast to males, in which the black extends at least 11 mm); the black present in the cap is generally flatter, less shiny than that of males. (Black in cap averages more extensive in the two western subspecies; see under Subspecies). **FIRST SPRING FEMALE:** Like spring adult female, but black of the cap even more reduced, and absent in about 50 percent of individuals. Forehead and face even more strongly tinged olive. Rectrices, flight feathers, and primary coverts browner and more worn than in adult. **FALL ADULT MALE:** Nearly identical to alternate adult male; a few narrow green feather tips found within the black cap, usually in the rear portion, in a minority of individuals. **FIRST FALL MALE:** Resembles fall adult male, but green tips on black cap are more extensive, usually extending throughout the cap and obscuring the rear border of the cap; black of cap flatter, less shiny. **FALL ADULT FEMALE:** Like alternate adult female, but with green tipping to any black present in cap feathers. **FIRST FALL FEMALE:** Forehead dull olive or yellowish olive, with little or no contrast with the olive cap. (Forehead averages brighter, showing more contrast with cap in the two western subspecies; see Subspecies.) Black is nearly always absent on the cap. Sides of face strongly washed with olive and lores tinged olive, making the thin yellow eye-ring more conspicuous. Underparts duller and paler yellow than in fall adults. **JUVENILE:** Dull olive-buff nearly throughout, paling to yellowish buff on the belly and undertail coverts. Two buffy wing bars. This plumage has largely been replaced by the olive and yellow first basic plumage by the time the young have fledged. **BARE PARTS:** Bill blackish on maxilla, yellowish with

Wilson's Warbler. Male chryseola *in California in March. (Photo: P. La Tourrette/VIREO)*

Wilson's Warbler. Female pileolata in California in May. (Photo: Larry Sansone)

duller brown tip on mandible; legs and feet tan-pink; eye blackish brown, standing out prominently on face.

The prebasic molt takes place on the summer grounds; it is complete in adults but partial in hatching-year birds (not involving flight feathers and rectrices). A limited prealternate molt (mainly involving head feathers) takes place in late winter and early spring.

 REFERENCES

DISTRIBUTION: Ramos and Warner 1980.
ECOLOGY, BEHAVIOR, VOCALIZATIONS, AND CONSERVATION: Stewart 1973, Stewart and Darling 1972, Stewart et al. 1977.
IDENTIFICATION: Kaufman 1991.
PLUMAGES, MOLTS, AND MORPHOLOGY: McNicholl 1977, Stewart 1972.

CANADA WARBLER
PL. 27

Wilsonia canadensis

5.25 in. (13.3 cm). This active warbler, breeding in cool, moist thickets within the boreal and Appalachian regions, is blue-gray (to olive-gray) above and mostly yellow below, with a pale spectacle and a variable necklace of streaks across the breast. It often holds its long tail slightly cocked, with the wings slightly drooped. As in all *Wilsonia*, it has evident bristles around the bill and frequently forages with short "flycatching" sallies. It tends to forage low, and during migration is often found in association with Wilson's Warblers. This is an inquisitive bird, quick to investigate intruders in the nest area. The Canada Warbler is a late migrant in spring and a rather early one in fall.

DESCRIPTION

All plumages show evenly grayish upperparts, yellow underparts with white undertail coverts, a conspicuous eye-ring and yellow supraloral stripe, and a necklace (bold to almost lacking) of short streaks. Tail spots are lacking in all plumages. Considerable variation has been reported within all age and sex classes; this condition is probably the norm for warblers, but most species await intensive study. Because of this variation, sexing of some individuals is unreliable in the field. These is little seasonal variation in appearance.

This is a moderately long-tailed warbler. The wide-based bill is slightly decurved along the culmen. Males average slightly larger than females, a difference not discernible in the field.

SIMILAR SPECIES

Some dull females may recall Nashville or dull female Magnolia warblers. **NASHVILLES** always lack breast streaks, but streaks may be absent in extremely dull Canadas, and Nashvilles may get dirt smudges on the breast that resemble streaks; Nashvilles are easily told by their bright yellow undertail coverts and strong olive green or yellow-green wash on the wing coverts, rump, and uppertail coverts. Nashvilles (western *ridgwayi*) frequently wag their tails (which are short compared to the tails of Canadas). Even the dullest **MAGNOLIA WARBLERS** show thin whitish wing bars, bold white on the basal half of the outer tail feathers, and a yellowish rump patch.

KENTUCKY WARBLER recalls Canada in face pattern, but lacks breast streaking, is yellow through the entire underparts, and has olive green (not grayish) upperparts.

GOLDEN-CROWNED WARBLER (vagrant to s. Texas) is similar in general coloration but differs in head pattern, showing a yellowish supercilium and thin black lateral crown stripes. Juvenile Canadas may closely resemble juvenile **WILSON'S WARBLERS** and are best identified by association with adults.

VOICE

The **SONG** is a variable, sputtery, staccato series of notes which invariably starts with a *tchup* or *chip* note and often ends with a similar note; there are 5–15 notes, and consecutive notes are rarely on the same pitch. One example is *chup-chuppity-swee-*

ditchee. Songs are quite variable among individuals; a given individual's repertoire size is large (up to 11 song types), and several different songs may be sung in succession. A flight song is occasionally given. Generally sings until mid-July, with some renewal of singing later in summer. The song recalls that of Magnolia Warbler, but is longer, less sweet in tone and with different introduction. Some song elements (*chuppity, swee-ditchee, witchity*) are suggestive of Common Yellowthroat, but the yellowthroat's song is much more regular and repetitive in pattern.

CALL NOTE is a sharp *tchup* or *tik*, recalling the common note of a Lincoln's Sparrow (*Melospiza lincolnii*) or the boreal and northwestern groups of the Fox Sparrow (*Passerella iliaca*). **FLIGHT NOTE** said to be a high *zzee*.

 BEHAVIOR

This is an active, inquisitive warbler, which generally forages low in the understory. The long tail is sometimes held slightly cocked (and is sometimes flipped about), with the wings slightly drooped. While foraging they make frequent short sallies within the shrub canopy for flying insect prey; they also glean leaves and twigs for arthropods. Most activity is within 15 ft. of the ground. Singing birds will sometimes ascend higher, but songs are usually given from the shrubby understory. Canada Warblers are highly responsive to pishing. Birds become extremely agitated when an observer enters their territory, chipping vigorously and constantly and often giving distraction displays with tail fanned and wings fluttering. Winter birds accompany mixed-species foraging flocks and sometimes attend army ant swarms.

The well-concealed **NEST** is a bulky cup of grasses, leaves, fibers and twigs, lined with hair, rootlets, leaves, and fine grasses. The nest is placed on or very near the ground, in a clump of mosses or grasses, and often at the base of a log, stump, or rock. This species is normally single-brooded.

 HABITAT

BREEDS in cool, shaded, moist woodlands, thickets, and swamps, generally where there is a dense brushy understory and moist ground cover with a hardwood or conifer overstory; often found along streamsides or in cool, moist ravines. Over much of the boreal region it breeds in deciduous thickets in the understory of forests of maples, eastern white pines, balsam fir, and northern white cedar. They are most likely to be found at forest edges or openings, ponds, bogs, and streams. In the Appalachians they occupy rhododendron thickets within forests of hemlock, etc. At

lower elevations they are found in hemlock ravines with an understory of mountain laurel and rhododendron; also locally in deciduous swamps and areas of dense young deciduous growth. In the
highest Appalachians (the species breeds to 6,300 ft. in North
Carolina) they use tangled, stunted growth and wet mossy areas.
Typically breeds in denser woodland with taller timber than does
the Wilson's Warbler.

WINTERS in dense growth along the edges and within openings of
humid and semi-humid forests in montane regions, including
cloud forests, rain forests, and second growth. **MIGRANTS** show a
preference for dense thickets, briars, and wet areas, usually in
woodland edges and openings. Fall migrants may also use tall
weedy growth.

▼ Distribution

BREEDS from ne. B.C., extreme se. Yukon, and n. Alta. east across
boreal Canada to Que. and N.S. Breeds south to cen. Alta., s.
Man., n. Minn., cen. (locally s.) Wisc., n. Ill. (local), n. Ind., and
Ohio (mainly ne.). Probably also breeds irregularly in ne. N.D.
(Pembina Hills) and ne. Iowa. Breeds south in the Appalachian
Mtns. to w. N.C., extreme nw. S.C. (possibly), e. Tenn., extreme
se. Ky., and ne. Ga. In the Atlantic coastal states it breeds south to
n. N.J. and (locally) Long Island, N.Y.

WINTERS almost exclusively in n. South America east of the crest
of the Andes, in Colombia, e. Ecuador, e. Peru, Venezuela
(including Tepui region of s. Venezuela), and extreme n. Brazil
(Roraima). Winters rarely north to Panama and casually north to
Costa Rica. A mid-December record for Honduras may pertain to
a late fall straggler; winter records for Mexico (Oaxaca) are questionable. There are no credible winter records for the U.S.,
although stragglers have been noted into December.

SPRING MIGRATION is among the latest for our warblers and is primarily through Central America, e. Mexico (but generally absent
from the Yucatán peninsula), and south coastal Texas. Some birds
appear to fly across the westernmost Gulf of Mexico, as small
numbers appear regularly on the upper Texas coast and in sw. La.
It is rare farther east on the Gulf Coast and is seen only very
rarely or casually in Fla., the Bahamas, and Greater Antilles. In
spring, the first birds arrive in south Texas in mid-April, but the
main passage is from late April to mid-May. There are a handful
of late March and early April reports for the U.S., some of which
may be correct. There is a 10 April specimen from Mass. There
are late April records over much of e. North America (as far north
as n. Wisc., s. Ont., and Me.), but normal arrivals are during the
second week of May. Across the boreal regions the first arrivals

are usually during the last third of May. Peak movements are in early May in e. Texas, mid-May from n. Texas to Ky., and about 20–25 May over most of the other areas outside the breeding range. Significant numbers still pass through the s. Great Lakes region and New England into early June, with stragglers to mid-June (a few records even later).

The **FALL MIGRATION** route largely retraces that of spring, but the species is more regular on the e. and cen. Gulf Coast at this season. An early fall migrant, this species is noted casually away from breeding areas in late July, more regularly in early August, and in numbers around 10–15 August. Peak fall movement over most of eastern North America is during the last week of August and the first week of September. Most have departed the boreal regions by the end of August, and only a few birds are still passing through interior e. North America after mid-September; a count of 75 at High Island on 26 September shows that the species can still be numerous on the upper Texas coast late in the month. It is casual after early October, with a few records into November (exceptionally to late November in n. Texas and Sault Ste. Marie, Ont.).

CANADA WARBLER
Wilsonia canadensis

CASUAL in migration west of the cen. Great Plains (probably annual in extreme ne. Mont.). Very rare but regular vagrant to Calif., mainly in fall (235 records, mostly from early September through October, with a few into November and one in early December); about 25 spring records, from the end of May through June. Recorded from all western states (except Idaho and Wash.) and sw. B.C. About 20 records for Colo. (divided equally between spring and fall), five for N.M., eight records (all fall) for Ariz., and five for Ore.; fewer records for the other western states. There is a November record for Clipperton Is., two records for the n. slope of Alaska (July, September), and a record for s. Dist. of Mack.

A rare fall migrant on Bermuda, and very rare in the Bahamas; otherwise strictly casual in the West Indies (and perhaps no valid records from the Lesser Antilles). Rare fall vagrant to Nfld. (may breed rarely in sw.). Recorded in Greenland (three times) and sw. Iceland (29 September 1973).

 ## STATUS AND CONSERVATION

Sharp population declines have been noted within portions of the range, such as in Pennsylvania. These declines are probably due primarily to fragmentation of breeding habitat; because this is not a breeding bird of deep continuous forests, however, it may actually have benefited in some areas from limited forest clearing. This species appears to be stable over much of its range and seems relatively immune to problems generated by modification of winter habitat. Parasitism by Brown-headed Cowbirds is rather frequent.

 ## SUBSPECIES

No geographical variation described; no subspecies recognized.

TAXONOMIC RELATIONSHIPS

Probably most closely related to Wilson's Warbler, but the relationships within *Wilsonia* (and of *Wilsonia* to other genera) are not well understood. Has hybridized with Mourning Warbler.

 ## PLUMAGES AND MOLTS

SPRING ADULT MALE: Forehead and forecrown black, with thin gray feather tips; center of crown variably spotted with black. The lores and anterior portion of the auriculars are black, forming a continuous black border between the gray hindneck and rear auricular and the yellow throat. A broad yellow supraloral line connects with a complete eye-ring that is variably white or yellow but usually mixed (yellow above, white below). Some individuals show a short pale yellow median stripe on the forehead. The throat, breast, and belly are bright yellow; the undertail coverts are pure white. There is a series of thick black streaks forming a necklace across the breast. The remainder of the upperparts are pure blue-gray with no hint of olive or brown. The wing coverts are blue-gray; the flight feathers are dusky gray, edged with blue-gray. Many adult males are less strongly marked with black on the face and breast, and occasional birds are paler yellow on the underparts. **FIRST SPRING MALE:** Much like spring adult male, but with a slight hint of an olive wash on the back, and with the black streaking across the chest averaging thinner and less extensive. The flight feathers are more worn and brownish in appearance. **SPRING ADULT FEMALE:** Forehead gray, with a slight yellow tinge; black on the grayish crown and cheeks is absent or limited to a few small spots on the forecrown and a dull blackish area under the eye. Supraloral stripe somewhat thinner and duller yellow than in spring male, eye-ring slightly less bold. The necklace of breast streaks is diffuse, but some black is present in the necklace of the majority of spring adult females. Upperparts even gray, sometimes very slightly tinged olive. The yellow underparts average paler than in adult males. **FIRST SPRING FEMALE:** Like spring adult female, but forehead more strongly tinged yellow-green; upperparts more often tinged with olive or brownish. Necklace markings grayish, ill-defined. Flight feathers and primary coverts duller and more worn. **FALL ADULT MALE:** Closely resem-

bles spring adult male, but more extensive bluish gray feather edgings obscure much of the black on the crown, yielding the appearance of sparse black flecks. Slight veiling of the black breast streaks by yellow feather tips. Thin olive-yellow feather tips on the dorsal feathering, if present, are usually not visible in the field. **FIRST FALL**

Canada Warbler. Adult male in Texas in May. (Photo: Rick and Nora Bowers)

Canada Warbler. First fall female in Ohio in September. (Photo: Steve and Dave Maslowski)

MALE: Forehead tinged yellowish green; the grayish crown lacks any black spotting; there may be some black present on the anterior and lower portions of the auriculars. Back tinged with olive. The streaking across the breast is usually gray or mixed gray and black, thinner and less sharp than in adult males. Flight feathers brownish. The dullest birds may not be distinguishable from first fall females, but usually show darker and more distinct spots in the necklace. **FALL ADULT FEMALE:** Virtually identical to spring adult female, but the gray of the upperparts is somewhat more veiled with yellow or olive (especially on forehead, center of back), and the necklace streaks are slightly veiled with yellow. **FIRST FALL FEMALE:** Nearly all first fall females lack black in the plumage. The forehead, crown, and cheek are gray, strongly tinged with yellowish olive; there is a thin yellowish supraloral stripe, and the whitish eye-ring is tinged with pale yellow. There is no sharp border between the gray nape and the yellowish throat. The upperparts are strongly tinged with olive-brown. The breast is very faintly and diffusely marked with short grayish streaks; extremely dull individuals are virtually unmarked on the breast, showing only some inconspicuous stippling. Flight feathers brownish. **JUVENILE:** Generally brownish on the head and upperparts, paler buffy brown on the underparts, paling to whitish on the undertail coverts. Obscure buffy wing bars. **BARE PARTS:** The bill is dark gray-brown to slaty above, paler tan (often with a gray-brown tip) below. Legs pale, varying from bright pinkish tan to pale yellowish or tan color. Eyes dark brown.

The prebasic molt takes place on the breeding grounds, prior to the southbound migration. It is complete in adults and partial in hatching-year birds (not involving the flight feathers and primary coverts). The prealternate molt is quite limited in adults, with breeding-season plumage attained largely through wear; it is probably more extensive in first-year birds.

 REFERENCES

DISTRIBUTION: Brauning 1992.
ECOLOGY, BEHAVIOR, VOCALIZATIONS, AND CONSERVATION: Brauning 1992.
PLUMAGES, MOLTS, AND MORPHOLOGY: Rappole 1983.

RED-FACED WARBLER

Cardellina rubrifrons

5 in. (12.7 cm). Primarily a northwestern Mexican species, the Red-faced Warbler ranges northward in summer to moderate and high elevations of the mountains along our southwestern border in Arizona and New Mexico. Our only warbler with bright red on the face, its identification is straightforward. Its shape and mannerisms suggest a Wilson's or Canada warbler, and some workers consider the monotypic genus *Cardellina* to be closely related to *Wilsonia*. The mostly gray and white coloration, acrobatic feeding behavior, and short thick bill give this warbler a chickadee-like appearance.

 DESCRIPTION

Generally gray above and white below, with a striking red and black face pattern and a white patch on the rump. The sexes are similar, though males average brighter and deeper red than females; immature birds are only slightly duller than adults. There is little seasonal change in appearance. Structurally, the Red-faced Warbler has a relatively long, square-tipped tail and long, pointed wingtips. The bill is rather short and thick, with a noticeably decurved culmen; rictal bristles are prominent.

 SIMILAR SPECIES

The red and black face pattern easily distinguishes it from all other warblers. The only other warbler with red in the plumage normally encountered within its U.S. range is the PAINTED REDSTART, which is completely different in plumage pattern and is also different in posture and behavior. Brief views, with the bird's face hidden, might cause one to mistake it for a CHICKADEE or TITMOUSE (*Parus*).

♩ VOICE

The variable **SONG** is a clear and energetic series with an emphatic ending, often suggesting a Yellow or Chestnut-sided's song in pattern (and the emphatic ending can recall the song of a Hooded Warbler). The song begins with a variable series of assorted thinner notes and ends with from one to several sharply slurred notes: *wi tsi-wi tsi-wi si-wi-si-whichu.* The number and arrangement of notes in the song are highly variable. Singing Yellow Warblers, whose songs can be similar, rarely occur in the same montane habitats. Flight song has been noted.

CALL NOTE is a sharp *chup* or *tchip,* suggestive of the call of a Black-throated Gray Warbler.

FLIGHT NOTE is unknown.

BEHAVIOR

An active warbler, often waving around its long tail. It typically forages by gleaning for insects at the tips of twigs, often in acrobatic, chickadee-like fashion; it also frequently sallies after flying insects. Foraging occurs widely from low shrubs to high in trees, but usually is at middle levels. Like *Wilsonia,* rather tame and responsive to pishing. In late summer, fall, and winter Red-faced Warblers will join mixed-species flocks, often with only one Red-faced per flock.

The **NEST** is placed on the ground, usually well concealed in a depression at the base of a tree, roots, log, or rock on a canyon slope. It is a loose cup of rootlets, grasses, dead leaves, hair, and bark.

HABITAT

BREEDS on heavily wooded montane slopes and canyons where there is a mixture of conifers (spruces, firs, Douglas-firs, and pines) and oaks (both live oaks and deciduous Gambel oaks); at its highest breeding elevations may also occur in aspen groves where intermixed with conifers. Generally found above 6,600 ft., but down to about 5,900 ft. in shaded canyons with mixed live oaks and Douglas-firs. Most foraging takes place in oaks, but Red-faceds also utilize conifers.

WINTERS in similar oak-conifer habitats, and in cloud forest, humid pine-evergreen forests, and to a lesser extent in semi-deciduous woodlands of foothills.

BREEDS from nw. Ariz. (Hualapai Mtns.) and n.-cen. Ariz. (San Francisco Peaks, Bill Williams Mtn., and possibly the north rim of the Grand Canyon, where recorded in summer), and sw. N.M. (and Sacramento Mtns.; has nested in Sandia Mtns.) south through the mountains of se. Ariz. and thence through the Sierra Madre Occidental, Sinaloa, and Durango in Mexico. Arrives in the mountains of s. Ariz. as early as about 1o April, but arrivals farther north are usually in late April.

WINTERS in the highlands of w. and cen. Mexico from Sinaloa to Oaxaca and from Chiapas through Guatemala, w. Honduras, and El Salvador. There is a late February record from the Santa Catalina Mtns. in se. Ariz. that may pertain to a wintering bird.

SPRING MIGRANTS are rarely noted, although in cold springs a few individuals are sometimes seen in foothill woodlands below breeding habitat. Spring lowland records in Ariz. and N.M. are

RED-FACED WARBLER
Cardellina rubrifrons

mostly from late April to mid-May (exceptionally to early June). **FALL** departure from breeding grounds is poorly known, but probably mainly from August through the third week of September. The few fall lowland records in Ariz. and N.M. are from early August to 11 October.

CASUAL in Texas (15 records) and Calif. (11 records). Texas records are mostly from Chisos Mtns. (Big Bend region), but also recorded in El Paso, in Bastrop Co., and on the lower Texas coast (Laguna Atascosa NWR); they are mostly for spring (early May to early June), with three additional August records. In Calif. about half the records are for mid-May to early July in the mountains (San Gabriel Mtns., Clark Mtn., New York Mtns.); the remainder are for the lowlands (two from the interior and two from the coast in late spring, two from the coast in fall); northernmost is a late August record for the Farallon Is. There are September sight records for the Spring Mtns. in s. Nev. **VAGRANT** also to sw. Colo. (3 June 1994, Durango Co.), cen. Colo. (3 May 1993, Jefferson Co.); sw. Wyo. (29 April–3 May 1989, Green River), and La. (27–30 April 1990, Cameron Parish).

 STATUS AND CONSERVATION

No information; populations appear to be stable, although they may be vulnerable to logging. There has been some northward expansion of the breeding range in Arizona and New Mexico in the 20th century. No parasitism by cowbirds recorded.

SUBSPECIES

This species is monotypic; a southern race, *bella*, described from the species' winter range in Guatemala, is clearly based on seasonal variation and is not considered valid.

 TAXONOMIC RELATIONSHIPS

The genus *Cardellina* is monotypic. The long tail and acrobatic behavior suggest a close relationship between *Cardellina* and *Wilsonia*, and some workers have suggested that these two genera are perhaps best merged. The similarities, including the well-developed rictal bristles, may be due to convergence, however, reflecting similar foraging behavior. The thick bill and decurved culmen of Red-faced are dissimilar to *Wilsonia*. A close relationship between *Cardellina* and the Neotropical highland genus *Ergaticus* (Red and Pink-headed warblers) has been suggested.

SPRING ADULT MALE: Forehead, forecrown, eye-ring, loral region, chin, throat, uppermost breast, and sides of neck bright red. Center and rear crown, extending down through the sides of the head and auricular region are jet black. Small patch of white on the hindneck. Upperparts medium gray except for a patch of white on the rump. Remaining underparts white, tinged gray on the sides of the breast and flanks. Many individuals, especially earlier in spring, are tinged with pale pinkish across the lower breast. Wing coverts and flight feathers generally gray; median coverts tipped with white, forming a single wing bar. Rectrices grayish, unmarked. With plumage wear through the late spring and summer, any traces of pinkish on the lower breast disappear, and the single wing bar often becomes obsolete. **FIRST SPRING MALE:** Indistinguishable in the field from spring adult males; some individuals are slightly paler, more orangish red than typical adults, but many are as bright as adults. In the hand, the rectrices may appear slightly more worn than in adults, but this is not always reliable. **SPRING ADULT FEMALE:** Very similar to spring adult male. On average slightly paler, oranger red on the face, a difference that is sometimes evident between members of a pair. **FIRST SPRING FEMALE:** Probably indistinguishable from first spring male and spring adult female, but averages duller; in the hand, rectrices may appear slightly more worn than in spring adults. **FALL ADULT MALE:** Resembles spring adult male, but plumage is fresher, so there is a more evident wash of pink through the breast, often extending into the belly region. **FIRST FALL MALE:** Red of forehead, chin, throat, and sides of neck averages duller than in fall adult male, but varies from orange-red to a bright red that matches brightest adults. Black of cap not as shiny as in fall adult male. Slight wash of brownish on the upperparts. **FALL ADULT FEMALE:** Resembles spring adult female, but plumage fresher, with an evident wash of pink through the breast on some individ-

Red-faced Warbler. In New Mexico in June. (Photo: Larry Sansone)

uals. **FIRST FALL FEMALE:** Dullest plumage, with red of forehead, chin, throat, and sides of neck paler, more orange than spring adults (dull salmon color in dullest birds). Black of cap and auriculars dull, not shiny. Gray wash across breast. Slight tinge of brown on the upperparts. **JUVENILE:** Gray-brown above; rump whitish. Head and breast brown, belly pale gray. Two buffy wing bars. In first prebasic molt, black of cap appears before red of face. **BARE PARTS:** Bill dull blackish, slightly paler at base of mandible; bill of first fall immatures paler. Legs and feet pinkish gray. Eyes dark brown.

The prebasic molt occurs from late June to August on the breeding grounds; it is complete in adult but does not involve flight feathers in hatching-year birds. There is no prealternate molt.

 REFERENCES

GENERAL: Martin and Barber 1995.
DISTRIBUTION: Lasley et al. 1982.
ECOLOGY, BEHAVIOR, VOCALIZATIONS, AND CONSERVATION: Franzreb and Franzreb 1983.

PAINTED REDSTART PL. 28

Myioborus pictus

5¼ in. (13.3 cm). This unique, flashy warbler, colored black, white, and red, is a summer resident in shaded pine-oak canyons in our southwestern mountains. It is one of the most beautiful members of a showy Neotropical highland and foothill genus whose members are sometimes known as "whitestarts." Tame and accommodating, it is intensely active, often creeping along trunks, branches, and rocks with wings partly spread and tail fanned widely. This eye-catching behavior may aid the redstart in flushing up insect prey. The juvenal plumage is retained longer than in most of our other warblers, and young birds lacking red on the breast may be seen independently of adults well into early fall (but not as late as fall migration). Painted Redstarts regularly stray into California, and there are also records in several northern and eastern states and provinces.

 DESCRIPTION

Head, upperparts, upper breast, sides, and flanks black; bright red patch on lower breast and upper belly; conspicuous white patch on median and greater secondary coverts; much white in outer three pairs of rectrices. All post-juvenal plumages are similar. Males average slightly brighter red on the underparts than females, but this difference is seldom evident in the field. There is no prealternate molt, and essentially no seasonal change in appearance apart from the normal effects of feather wear. Juveniles lack red.

The bill is rather broad at the base, and the rictal bristles are well developed.

SIMILAR SPECIES

A striking species to which the term "unmistakable" is perhaps better applied than to any other North American Warbler. The only truly similar species is the SLATE-THROATED REDSTART, a vagrant from Mexico to our southwestern border. For distinctions, see under that species. Beginners and overzealous birders might mistake poorly seen SPOTTED TOWHEES (*Pipilo maculatus*) for adults, and perhaps BLACK PHOEBES (*Sayornis nigricans*), DARK-EYED JUNCOS (*Junco hyemalis*), or alternate male LARK BUNTINGS (*Calamospiza melanocorys*), for the juveniles.

VOICE

SONG is a somewhat variable series of rich, usually two-parted syllables, concluding with one or more single-syllable inflected notes. The overall effect is of a rather low-pitched, rich warble. Renditions include *weeta weeta weeta wee* or *chee che-wee che-weeta weeta chew*. Several variations may be sung by a single bird. Notes are delivered rather slowly (3–6 per second). Songs are given mostly by males, but females will sing in response to male song or in duets with their mate. Overwintering birds in the U.S. have been known to sing frequently. The CALL NOTE is distinctive, a scratchy, whistled *sheu, sreeu, wheeu,* or a richer *cheree* or *chew-elee*; these are reminiscent of calls of Pine Siskin (*Carduelis pinus*) and are unique among our warblers. A high, slightly downslurred *seet* is given at least by juveniles.

BEHAVIOR

A very active warbler, moving along trunks and major branches, among twigs, or on the ground with wings partly spread and tail flashed open or held widely spread. This flashing of white plumage marks is presumed to aid in foraging by flushing up insect prey, but may also help members of a pair or family group locate each other in the shadowy understory. A foraging bird often turns from side to side with each hop. Flight is generally rather weak and fluttery. Much time is spent foraging on trunks, fallen logs, and boulders, but foraging at middle heights within the tree canopy is common as well. Hover-gleaning and acrobatic gleaning are common. Short sallies after flying insects are frequent; longer sallies (up to 50 ft.) have been observed. Singing birds may choose high perches in pines, etc.

The members of a pair usually forage in close proximity; in the nonbreeding season Painted Redstarts may join mixed-species flocks in the pine-oak forests; apart from family groups, they are rarely seen in intraspecific flocks. Polygyny has occasionally been observed.

The **NEST** is a bulky cup, well hidden on the ground; it is usually placed on an embankment, often near water. It may be hidden under rocks, grass tufts, ferns, or large roots. The female builds the nest of bark, fibers, grasses, and hairs. Rarely, nests may be in vines well off the ground. Second broods may be frequent.

 ## Habitat

BREEDS in pine-oak forests in mountains and foothills. Dominant trees may include emory, silverleaf, Gambel and Arizona white oaks, ponderosa pines, Douglas-firs, Arizona sycamores, cottonwoods, and alders. Favored sites have a high diversity of plants in the understory. Throughout, this species has a strong preference for shaded habitats with a well-developed overstory and steep canyon slopes. It is especially numerous in the lusher growth near water in canyon bottoms. South of our region, the species breeds in somewhat more arid pine and oak woodlands. There is some tendency for upslope movement into pine-spruce-fir habitats late in summer (mainly late July to September). **MIGRANTS** are only rarely observed outside of breeding habitat. Vagrants have been noted in a variety of open wooded habitats and plantings.

 ## Distribution

BREEDS in montane habitats, generally from about 5,000 ft. to 7,000 ft., in n., cen., and se. Ariz. (north to Hualapai Mtns., Mogollon Rim, and White Mtns.), sw. N.M. (Mogollon highlands, Magdalena, San Mateo, Peloncillo, and Animas mtns.), and sw. Texas (irregularly in Chisos Mtns., once in Davis Mtns.). It occurs more rarely in summer in n.-cen. N.M. and s. Nev. (especially the Spring Mtns.), and in the mountains of s. Calif. (especially the San Bernardino Mtns., breeding documented there and in the Laguna Mtns. of San Diego Co.).

South of our area, breeds locally throughout the highlands of Mexico to Guatemala, Honduras, and n.-cen. Nicaragua.

WINTERS from s. Sonora and s. Nuevo Leon south through the remainder of the breeding range; also winters rarely but regularly in the mountains of se. Ariz. There are about 20 winter records for Calif.

Only rarely noted in **MIGRATION**, even in lowland areas adjacent to breeding mountains. The majority of lowland migrants are recorded in spring, mostly from mid-March through April. The earliest arrivals on the breeding grounds in se. Ariz. are in mid-March, with most birds having arrived by late April. In the northernmost breeding areas the first arrivals are in late March or early April. Very few fall migrants are noted in the lowlands; most such records are for September.

VAGRANT well to the west, north, and east of the breeding range. There are about 107 records for Calif., all but two in s. Calif., about half for the coastal slope; coastal slope records are almost all for fall and winter while the majority of the mountain and interior lowland records for Calif. are for spring. Casual in sw. Ariz.,

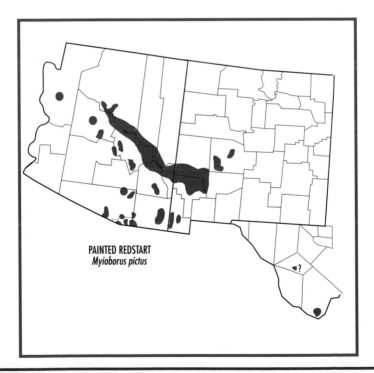

PAINTED REDSTART
Myioborus pictus

sw. Ut., Colo., and s.-cen., se., and s. Texas (including twice in spring on the upper Texas coast). Recorded once in Baja Calif. (October). There are several **EXCEPTIONAL** records well north of the normal range. Recorded in B.C. (November), Mont. (Nov.), Wisc. (April), Mich. (Nov.), s. Ont. (Nov.), Ohio (Nov.), N.Y. (late fall), Mass. (mid-October), La. (three records, November–March), Miss. (fall), Ala. (late September), and Ga. (mid-April).

STATUS AND CONSERVATION

No information. Abundant within appropriate shaded pine-oak habitat, and no evidence of any significant population declines. Deforestation and excessive grazing undoubtedly cause local declines. There is only one published instance each of brood parasitism of this species by Brown-headed and Bronzed cowbirds.

SUBSPECIES

There is minor geographical variation in plumage. Birds north of the Isthmus of Tehuantepec, including all those in our region, belong to the nominate subspecies, described below. South of the Isthmus, from Chiapas to Nicaragua, is the subspecies *guatemalae*, which is distinguished by having slightly less white in the rectrices and lacking white margins on the tertials.

TAXONOMIC RELATIONSHIPS

The Painted Redstart does not seem to be particularly closely related to any of the other members of the genus *Myioborus*, being rather distinct in vocalizations and many aspects of its plumage. This species was long placed incorrectly in the genus *Setophaga*, along with the American Redstart. But the Painted has been convincingly shown to belong with the Neotropical redstarts of the genus *Myioborus*; similarities to *Setophaga* in wing-spreading and tail-flashing behavior represent a convergence of feeding styles. Among the many characters distinguishing these genera is the different pattern of retention of juvenal plumage: it is ephemeral in *Setophaga*, being largely replaced by fledging age, whereas it is retained longer in *Myioborus* (particularly *M. pictus*) than nearly all other wood-warblers.

PLUMAGES AND MOLTS

SPRING ADULT MALE: Entire head, throat, upper breast, and upperparts jet black with a very slight gloss. There is a thick white arc just below the eye. The center and lower breast and uppermost belly are bright red, contrast-

Painted Redstart. Adult in Arizona in September. (Photo: Rick and Nora Bowers)

ing sharply with the black chest, sides, and flanks. The lower flanks are slate gray. The longer, underlying undertail coverts are mostly black; the shorter coverts overlying these are mostly white with blackish centers; the general effect in the field in this region is of a variable mixture of slate and white. The lesser wing coverts are slaty; the median coverts are broadly tipped with white, and the greater coverts are completely white on the outer webs, forming a conspicuous white forewing patch. The tertials and inner secondaries are bordered with white on the outer webs. The remainder of the remiges are blackish. The axillars and underwing coverts are white. Visible portions of the outer two pairs of rectrices are pure white; the third pair (r4) is white on the outer web and tipped with white on the inner web. **FIRST SPRING MALE:** Distinguished from spring adult male in the hand by somewhat browner flight feathers and more tapered rectrices. **SPRING ADULT FEMALE:** Essentially identical to spring adult male, but on average the red of the breast is a very slightly paler, more orange tone. This difference might occasionally be noticeable in the field between members of a pair when direct comparison is possible, but there is considerable overlap in the brightness of the sexes. **FIRST SPRING FEMALE:** Like spring adult female but show somewhat browner flight feathers and more tapered rectrices in the hand. **FALL ADULT MALE:** Very similar to spring adult male, but plumage fresher, with white edges of the tertials and inner secondaries cleaner and more prominent. **FIRST FALL MALE:** Like fall adult male; distinguishable in the hand by flight feather and rectrix criteria noted above. **FALL ADULT FEMALE:** Very similar to spring adult female, but plumage fresher, with white edges of the tertials and inner secondaries cleaner and more prominent. **FIRST FALL FEMALE:** Like fall adult female; distinguishable in the hand by flight feather and rectrix criteria noted above. **JUVENILE:** Head and upperparts dull black; white arc under the eye. Breast dull slaty, feathers tipped with dull gray-brown; lower breast and belly slaty, irregularly spotted with dull grayish buff. Vent area and undertail coverts mottled grayish. **BARE PARTS:** Bill black; iris very dark brown; legs and feet slaty black.

The prebasic molt occurs on the breeding grounds from July to October. It is complete in adults, but in hatching-year birds does not appear to involve the flight feathers. The first prebasic molt does not occur until several weeks after fledging, so that juveniles lacking red on the underparts are routinely seen in late summer (birds from late broods), often independent of adults. Prealternate molt absent.

 REFERENCES

ECOLOGY, BEHAVIOR, VOCALIZATIONS, AND CONSERVATION: Marshall and Balda 1974, Marshall 1957.
SYSTEMATICS: Parkes 1961.

SLATE-THROATED REDSTART

Myioborus miniatus

5.25 in. (13.3 cm). This widespread and variable Neotropical species ranges from northern Mexico southward well into South America. In our area it has been documented from se. Arizona and se. New Mexico, with an additional sight record for the Chisos Mtns. in w. Texas. Like the related Painted Redstart, the Slate-throated is a very active bird that fans its tail, flashes bold white markings, and droops and spreads its wings. The lack of a white patch on the wing, the slate gray upperparts, and the more restricted white in the tail easily distinguish it from the Painted Redstart. Mexican birds, including individuals recorded within the U.S., have red on the breast and belly; from Guatemala through Panama there is a transition from birds with orange-red underparts to those with yellow underparts.

 DESCRIPTION

Generally slate gray on the upperparts, head, throat, and flanks, with a chestnut crown patch and red lower breast and belly. Much white in the outer three rectrices. There is slight sexual dimorphism in plumage, but no seasonal change in appearance apart from slight effects of wear. First-basic birds closely resemble adults. The juvenal plumage is distinct from all subsequent plumages.

Like the Painted Redstart, this species is a rather long-tailed warbler, and the bill is broad-based and flattened; the rictal bristles are long and prominent. The tail is distinctly graduated in shape, with the outer rectrices about 1 cm shorter than the central pair.

SIMILAR SPECIES

Somewhat similar to the **PAINTED REDSTART** but readily told by the following characters: The wings are completely slate gray, with no white patch on the coverts and no white edges to the tertials. The upperparts and face are slaty rather than jet black. There is a chestnut patch on the crown in all post-juvenal plumages; this is lacking in the Painted Redstart but may be difficult to see in the Slate-throated. Slate-throated lacks the white arc under the eye that is so conspicuous in Painted. The red of the underparts of Painted is deeper but slightly more restricted. Finally, the tail of Slate-throated shows less white, and the tail is slightly more graduated in shape. Juvenal Slate-throated (only seen on breeding grounds) is told from juvenal Painted by lack of white wing patch, less extensive white in tail. Vocalizations of the two species differ; see below.

VOICE

SONG is a variable series of sweet *s-wee* notes that often accelerates toward the end and usually ends with one or more notes on a different pitch. Examples include *s-wee s-wee s-wee s-wee s-wee s-chi s-chi s-chi*; *s-weet s-weet s-weet swee-wee-we-wee sweet*; or *sweet sweet sweet sweet ch-wee ch-wee*. Although the song pattern can suggest Painted Redstart, the quality is altogether different — thinner and higher — and mostly consists of single slurred notes rather than 2–3-syllable notes. Various versions of the song can suggest Yellow-rumped ("Audubon's") or Magnolia warblers. **CALL NOTE** is a single high *chip* or *tsip,* suggestive of the *chip* note of a Chipping Sparrow (*Spizella passerina*). Other renditions of the call include *tsit, pik,* and *chet.* **FLIGHT NOTE** unknown.

BEHAVIOR

A confiding and very active warbler, generally similar to the Painted Redstart in habits. The white-edged tail is fanned as conspicuously as by the Painted Redstart and is often held fanned for several seconds during a foraging bout; it may also be flashed open and shut. This redstart hops, flits, and switches its body from side to side as it forages, and frequently pursues insects with short aerial sallies. On average, foraging appears to take place lower in the vegetation than by the Painted; the Slate-throated is much less of a trunk and branch specialist, spending relatively more time in foliage, on finer twigs, on the ground, and in the air. Often probes dead leaf clusters. At least in southern populations, may remain paired through the year; often joins mixed-species flocks and sometimes associates with the Painted Redstart.

The **NEST** is well concealed on the ground or streambank; it is a roofed cup made of grasses, needles, and mosses.

HABITAT

RESIDENT in humid montane coniferous forest, humid evergreen forest, cloud forest, and mixed forest, including pine-oak woodlands. Where it overlaps with Painted Redstart, Slate-throated tends to occur in lusher, more humid habitats. In South America it occurs in a variety of humid forests, particularly lower montane cloud forest, but is successful in edge situations and second growth and is relatively tolerant of disturbance. Through the northern portion of its range it generally occurs from elevations of 3,300 ft. to 10,000 ft. There is a tendency for some downslope movement in the **WINTER**, with birds descending into the pine-oak belt from higher elevation coniferous forest, or even into humid foothill (and rarely coastal) habitats below the pine-oak belt. The Arizona and Texas records come from mixed pine-oak-riparian habitats in shaded canyons, areas also favored by the Painted Redstart. The New Mexico specimen was taken at a willow-lined stock tank in a desert valley.

DISTRIBUTION

Primarily **RESIDENT** north in Mexico to sw. Chihuahua (and adjacent se. Sonora) in the Sierra Madre Occidental, and to sw. Tamaulipas (and less commonly to s. Nuevo Leon and se. Coahuila) in the Sierra Madre Oriental. The range then extends south through the highlands of Mexico, including the Pacific highlands of Guerrero, Oaxaca, and Chiapas, and thence south through the highlands of Guatemala, El Salvador, Honduras, n.-cen. Nicaragua, Costa Rica, and Panama. In South America found from Colombia east to the mountains of n. Venezuela, and in the Tepui regions of s. Venezuela, Guyana, and extreme ne. Brazil; also found south in the Andes to s.-cen. Bolivia.

Some seasonal movement is suggested by **WINTER** records outside of the known breeding range in Sonora, coastal sightings in San Blas, Nayarit, and by the U.S. records outlined below.

In the U.S. it has been documented on only a very few occasions, all in spring. An adult female was collected at Stevens Tank, Lea Co., extreme se. N.M., on 16 April 1962. One was photographed in Miller Canyon, Huachuca Mtns., Ariz., 10–15 April 1976 and another was photographed in Madera Canyon, Santa Rita Mtns., on 26 May 1996. There are sight records for Cave Creek Canyon, Chiricahua Mtns., Ariz., on 2 May 1978 and 29 March 1993. One was well seen at Boot Spring in the Chisos Mtns., Texas, 26 and 30 April 1990 (and possibly again on 15 May) and accepted for the Texas "provisional list" (since no photographs were obtained). Additional sight records from se. Ariz., s. N.M., and w. Texas have lacked sufficient documentation for acceptance.

STATUS AND CONSERVATION

There is no information on population trends, but this common and widespread species is probably not threatened anywhere in its range; it is successful in disturbed habitats in lower montane regions in South America. There are no published instances of cowbird parasitism.

SUBSPECIES

Some 12 subspecies have been described, of which only the most northerly are red below; the name "Red-bellied Redstart" has been used for these red northern birds. Nominate *miniatus* (described below) occurs through most of the species' Mexico range, south to the Isthmus of Tehuantepec. A distinct subspecies, *molochinus*, is resident in the Sierra de Tuxtla of s. Veracruz. It is diagnosed by its deeper slate upperparts, brighter red underparts, whiter undertail coverts, less extensive white in the outer rectrices, and relatively shorter tail. The subspecies *intermedius* is resident east of the Isthmus in Chiapas and cen. Guatemala. It is slightly darker slate on the upperparts than nominate *miniatus*, and the red of the underparts is paler, being more of a deep salmon color. The white in the tail is less extensive, being very limited on r4 and never extending to the tip of r3. In this race and all that follow, the undertail coverts are mainly white or pure white, rather than mottled with slaty. The subspecies *hellmayri* (Pacific montane Guatemala to sw. El Salvador) is even more orange than *intermedius*; it resembles the following subspecies but averages slightly larger. *M. m. connectens* (resident in the remainder of El Salvador and in Honduras) is orange underneath. Birds from Costa Rica and w. Panama (races *comptus* and *aurantiacus*) are deep yellow-orange below, tinged tawny across the breast. They are deep slaty above and have as much white in the tail as nominate *miniatus*; they are essentially monomorphic, with both sexes showing slaty black on the forehead and sides of the crown patch. South American subspecies, such as the widespread *ballux* (which extends west to extreme se. Panama) and *verticalis*, are yellow below and have more extensive white in the tail than the more northerly subspecies. They are also essentially monomorphic; these races vary subtly in the shade of yellow on the underparts, the amount of white in the tail, and the amount of black in the forehead and sides of the crown.

 ## TAXONOMIC RELATIONSHIPS

There is a taxonomically confusing array of *Myioborus* redstarts in South America that are probably closely related to the Slate-throated Redstart (and to each other) but generally occur at higher elevations. The Painted Redstart seems to be the taxonomic outlier, and it may possibly deserve generic rank, but a close relationship between Slate-throated and Painted may yet be demonstrated.

 ## PLUMAGES AND MOLTS

SPRING ADULT MALE: Forehead and forecrown dull black. Patch on center and rear of crown chestnut. Nape, back, rump, and uppertail coverts slate

Slate-throated Redstart. Subspecies miniatus *in Oaxaca, Mexico, in December. (Photo: R. K. Bowers/VIREO)*

gray; longest uppertail coverts dull black. Sides of face and neck slate gray. Loral region, chin, and throat dull black, with some black extending laterally to the upper sides. Breast and belly bright vermilion red. Sides and flanks slate gray. Lower belly and undertail coverts mottled slaty and white. Wing coverts slate gray; flight feathers dusky slate, edged with gray. Tail blackish; outer rectrix mostly white on the outer web, and white on the distal half of the inner web. The fifth rectrix is white on the distal third, and there is a spot of white at the tip of the fourth rectrix. The third rectrix may also show a tiny amount of white at the tip. **FIRST SPRING MALE:** Not safely distinguishable from spring adult male; rectrices may average slightly more worn, and flight feathers may average more brownish. **SPRING ADULT FEMALE:** Similar to spring adult male and perhaps not always distinguishable in the field. However, spring females generally have the black of the forehead, loral region, and throat replaced by dark slaty, and the chestnut crown patch averages paler and less extensive. The red of the underparts averages paler in females. **FIRST SPRING FEMALE:** Not distinguishable from spring adult female, apart from slight average differences in rectrix and flight feather wear (see under first spring male). **FALL ADULT MALE:** As spring adult male, but plumage fresher. **FIRST FALL MALE:** Not distinguishable from fall adult male. **FALL ADULT FEMALE:** As spring adult female, but plumage fresher. **FIRST FALL FEMALE:** Not distinguishable from fall adult female. **JUVENILE:** Dull slaty above and below, paler on the breast, belly, and undertail coverts, where mottled with cinnamon brown. Wing and tail pattern as in first fall birds. **BARE PARTS:** Bill black; eyes dark brown; legs and feet blackish.

A complete prebasic molt occurs in late summer; the prebasic molt of hatching-year birds appears to be partial, not involving the flight feathers. There is apparently no prealternate molt.

 REFERENCES

GENERAL: Curson et al. 1994, Ridgely and Tudor 1989.
DISTRIBUTION: Harris 1964.
SYSTEMATICS: Wetmore 1942.

FAN-TAILED WARBLER

PL. 29

Euthlypis lachrymosa

5.75 in. (14.6 cm). This large warbler is endemic to Mexico and northern Central America. It has been recorded casually in late spring, summer, and early fall in se. Arizona; there is also an early winter record for n. Baja California. The long graduated tail, tipped with white, is frequently fanned open and moved about. The head is distinctly marked with a yellow crown and white eye-arcs and a white supraloral spot against a blackish face. Fan-tailed Warblers stay on or near the ground, where they are among the few wood-warblers to walk. The genus *Euthlypis* is closely related to *Basileuterus* and is merged into that genus by some authors.

 ## DESCRIPTION

Generally gray above and yellow, tinged tawny, below; white markings around eyes and on tail tip. There is very little age and sex variation in plumage, and geographic variation is slight. This long-legged warbler has a long, slightly graduated tail.

 ## SIMILAR SPECIES

The long, graduated tail clearly shows a white tip as it is fanned and flicked open; this pattern is unique among our warblers. The distinctive coloration should also prevent confusion with other warblers: the upperparts are unmarked dark gray, and the yellow underparts are washed with tawny across the breast. No other warbler in our area shows the distinctive head pattern of white eye-arcs combined with a prominent white loral spot.

The somewhat larger **YELLOW-BREASTED CHAT** might cause confusion with poor views; chats have more restricted yellow on the under-parts, lack the yellow crown patch, have a much thicker bill, lack white on the tail tip, have a different distribution of white on the face, and do not walk on the ground. **SLATE-THROATED REDSTART** has more extensive white in the tail, slate gray throat, and lacks the white head markings; Mexican populations (and birds recorded in the U.S.) are red to orange-red below, not yellow like Fan-tailed.

 ## VOICE

SONG is a series of sweet notes that usually ends with a sharp up-slur or down-slur. The general effect is a song that begins with rather weak notes and builds to a louder, slurred ending. Renditions include: *che che che a-wee wee che-cheer* and *su-wee su-wee su-wee chu*. Some songs are reminiscent of those of Swainson's Warbler. **CALL NOTE** is a distinctive, high, thin *tsew, seep, sieff* or *schree*; the call is not especially loud but is given frequently and often the best way to locate the bird. A shorter *si* note is also given. **FLIGHT NOTE** undescribed.

Behavior

An active warbler with the distinctive habit of holding its boldly marked tail partially fanned, swinging it in a downward side-to-side arc or an up-and-down motion. Habitually forages on or near the ground, often around rocky streambottoms or fallen logs. On the ground it walks, shuffles, or takes short hops, and frequently makes quick, short upward sallies. Generally found alone or in pairs, sometimes joining mixed-species flocks; within much of its range it is most readily found in association with army ant swarms, a circumstance that does not occur in our area; a dozen or more birds may gather at these swarms.

The few described **NESTS** were open cups, unlike the domed nests of *Basileuterus*. They were constructed of dried leaves, fine grasses, pine needles, and fibers, and placed on the ground on shaded slopes well hidden under forest floor debris. Little is known of the nesting biology of this species.

 Habitat

RESIDENT in moist, shady steep-walled ravines, canyons, and barrancas, as low as 150–300 ft. elevation but locally up to about 6,000 ft. Forest cover may vary from evergreen to semi-deciduous, but the important habitat component is a shaded understory with a rocky substrate.

The Arizona records have come from steep-walled canyons with fairly lush vegetation in foothill and lower montane areas. The one record of a vagrant in Baja California was from planted trees on a ranch in a region of arid scrub.

Distribution

Mainly **RESIDENT** locally on the Pacific slope of Mexico from e.-cen. Sonora and sw. Chihuahua south to Oaxaca, and on the Atlantic slope of Mexico from s. Tamaulipas to s. Veracruz and extreme n. Oaxaca. Also resident from w. Chiapas east and south through the Pacific slope of Guatemala and Honduras, interior El Salvador, and w.-cen. Nicaragua. Populations in Sonora and Chihuahua are apparently present only in summer (May to July), withdrawing southward in fall and winter.

CASUAL late spring, summer, and early fall vagrant to se. Ariz. and adjacent n. Sonora; records in this region fall between 19 May and 8 June, with an additional record for 5–8 September. The six Arizona records are from canyons near the Mexican border: two from Guadalupe Canyon (including a specimen), two from the

Huachuca Mtns., one from Sycamore Canyon in the Pajaritos Mtns., and one from the Whetstone Mtns.; the ne. Sonora record was only five miles south of the Arizona border. One exceptional record of a specimen taken 31 December 1925 near the coast of nw. Baja Calif. at Santo Domingo, northeast of San Quintin.

📊 STATUS AND CONSERVATION

Nowhere common, but probably not especially threatened because of the ruggedness of its habitat. No records of cowbird parasitism.

🦋 SUBSPECIES

There is slight clinal variation mainly involving the color of the upperparts. These differences are subtle and without clear geographical breaks; many authors consider it to be monotypic. Birds from west Mexico, from Sonora and Chihuahua south to Jalisco (and including U.S. and Baja California individuals) are sometimes separated as *E. l. tephra*; these are described above. Nominate birds from e. Mexico south to Guerrero, Oaxaca, and Veracruz are somewhat darker slaty on the upperparts, lacking olive tones; they show deeper and more extensive black in the facial markings than *tephra*, and the white supraloral spot averages smaller. Southern birds (to which the name *schistacea* has been applied, occurring from w. Chiapas to Honduras and Nicaragua), are even darker above than nominate birds.

🧬 TAXONOMIC RELATIONSHIPS

The monotypic genus *Euthlypis* seems closely related to the widespread genus *Basileuterus*; some workers merge *Euthlypis* into that genus. In some aspects of plumage and behavior, *Euthlypis* appears to "bridge" *Basileuterus* with the tropical redstarts of the genus *Myioborus*.

🪶 PLUMAGES AND MOLTS

SPRING ADULT MALE: Forehead, sides of crown, loral region, and upper malar region (to below front of eye) black, except for a white supraloral spot. Short white arcs above and below the eye. Bright yellow patch in the center of the crown, slightly obscured (especially toward the rear) by dark gray feather tips. Sides of head and neck, nape, and remaining upperparts dark gray with a very slight tint of olive on the back. Chin and throat deep

Fan-tailed Warbler. In Oaxaca, Mexico, in March. (Photo: J. Dunning/VIREO)

yellow (becoming whitish on extreme upper chin). Breast and sides deep tawny, grading into bright yellow belly and vent region. Undertail coverts whitish, tinged pale yellow. Sides of breast deep olive-gray; flanks olive-gray mixed with tawny. Thigh feathering grayish. Wing coverts dark gray; flight feathers dark dusky slate. Rectrices slaty, tipped with white, narrowly on outer web, more broadly on inner web; white of central pair of rectrices lacking or very limited. **SPRING ADULT FEMALE:** Nearly identical to spring adult male, but black of forehead, loral region, and sides of crown averages somewhat duller slaty; blackish of lores does not extend as far into the malar region. **FIRST SPRING:** Not safely distinguishable from adults; in the hand, the flight feathers may appear somewhat browner and more worn than adults. **FALL ADULT:** Resembles spring individuals of respective sex, but in fresher plumage may show more dark gray tips to the yellow crown feathers and thin pale gray tips to the median and greater wing coverts. **FIRST FALL:** Resembles fall adults, and probably not distinguishable in field. Black markings on head probably average duller and more limited than fall adults of respective sex. **JUVENILE:** Overall sooty gray, shading to pale yellow-buff on the belly and undertail coverts; two pale wing bars. White tips on long tail are distinctive. **BARE PARTS:** Bill is black in adults; bills of juveniles and first fall birds are brownish. Eyes dark brown. Legs and feet pinkish tan.

A prebasic molt (complete in adults, partial in hatching-year birds) probably takes place after the breeding season. No prealternate molt known.

 REFERENCES

DISTRIBUTION: Binford 1989, Grinnell and Lamb 1927, Levy 1962.
SYSTEMATICS: Dickey and Van Rossem 1926, Monroe 1968, Van Rossem 1934.

Basileuterus culicivorus

5 in. (12.7 cm). This is the most widespread member of the species-rich Neotropical warbler genus *Basileuterus*; it has been recorded casually in fall, winter, and spring in the Rio Grande Valley of extreme southern Texas. The overall coloration, olive-gray above and yellow below, suggests an Orange-crowned Warbler or a *Wilsonia*, but note the distinctive head pattern. This species usually stays low within dense undergrowth and is often best located by its distinctive call notes. Also known as "Stripe-crowned Warbler."

DESCRIPTION

All age and sex classes are very similar, and seasonal variation is almost nonexistent. The northernmost subspecies *brasherii* is the one recorded in Texas and is described below. Generally olive-gray above and yellow below, with plain grayish wings and tail. The distinctive head pattern shows two blackish lateral crown stripes enclosing a yellow (sometimes orangish) median crown stripe. There is a yellowish olive supercilium between the lateral crown stripes and the grayish auriculars. The amount of orangish color in the median crown stripe is individually variable within *brasherii*, but this is not distinctly related to age or sex.

This is a fairly heavy-bodied and long-tailed warbler with relatively short, rounded wings. The bill is of moderate thickness and is fairly broad, with a slightly curved culmen.

SIMILAR SPECIES

ORANGE-CROWNED (especially) and WILSON'S WARBLERS are superficially similar in their generally olive or olive-gray upperparts, yellowish underparts, and lack of wing bars or tail spots. Golden-crowned is easily told by the distinctive head pattern of blackish lateral crown stripes outlining a broad yellow (sometimes orangish) median crown stripe and bordered below by a yellowish supercilium. Compare also with WORM-EATING WARBLER, which is buffy (not yellow) below and on the pale median crown stripe and supercilium; Worm-eating is shorter tailed and heavier billed. The call notes of Golden-crowned are unique among our warblers (see below).

VOICE

The **SONG** (which has only rarely been heard within the U.S.) consists of 5–7 rather clear, whistled notes, ending with a distinct upslur: *see-whew-whew-wee-see?* or *wee-wee-wee-wee-see-weee?* The quality and pattern of the song can be suggestive of Hooded Warbler's.

CALL NOTES are dry and wrenlike in quality, with the slightly buzzy *chut, tuck,* or *tack* note, often doubled or run into a scolding series. Also gives a more liquid churring rattle. A very vocal species, with calls often given continuously for long periods.

BEHAVIOR

Usually encountered alone or in pairs; Texas records have often involved birds with mixed-species foraging parties of titmice and other passerines. Within their main Neotropical range they are often an important "leader" species in mixed-species flocks of antwrens, antvireos, redstarts, etc. They forage actively in low (especially) and medium levels of forest understory, usually by gleaning foliage but also by probing into leaf tangles and occasionally sallying for insects. Known to sometimes take berries. Golden-crowned Warblers are restless birds, often jerking and flicking open their tails and flicking their wings. Generally somewhat retiring, they can be inquisitive and usually respond well to pishing.

The **NEST** (not known north of Mexico) is a domed structure with a side entrance; it is built of rootlets, fibers, strips of palm leaves, mosses, etc., and is well hidden on the forest floor.

HABITAT

Found in the understory of humid evergreen and semi-deciduous forests of lower mountain slopes and foothills (locally to about 8,000 ft. in Mexico) and (in the extreme northern part of its range) along gallery forests of coastal plains. Also occurs in coffee plantations and in second-growth habitats. The Texas records are from wooded resacas and river-bottom growth.

DISTRIBUTION

RESIDENT in Mexico on the Atlantic slope foothills from Nuevo Leon (north to the vicinity of Sabinas Hidalgo, about 60 miles west of Falcon Dam, Texas) and cen. Tamaulipas south through the Isthmus region and most of the Yucatán peninsula; also in w. Mexico from se. Nayarit to Colima, Guerrero, Oaxaca, and s. Chiapas. In Central America occurs from Guatemala and Belize east and south through Honduras (mainly Caribbean slope), Costa Rica, and Panama (Pacific slope). Also widespread in South America, mainly in highlands, from Venezuela and Colombia south to e. Bolivia, Paraguay, Uruguay, and ne. Argentina.

CASUAL, mainly in winter, in the lower Rio Grande Valley in s. Texas, with eight accepted records. Accepted Texas records span the period 23 October to 19 March; these include two January 1892 specimens, plus seven sight and photo records since 1979. Several additional reports have not been submitted to the Texas Bird Records Committee; these include two September records and a 15 April record that are likely correct.

 ## STATUS AND CONSERVATION

No information. No record of cowbird parasitism.

SUBSPECIES

Three rather well-marked subspecies groups exist; these are perhaps distinct at the species level. The name "Stripe-crowned Warbler" has been suggested for the northern *culicivorus* group, which ranges from ne. Mexico south to Panama. Birds of this group are characterized by yellowish supercilia, olive-gray upperparts, and variably yellowish to dull orangish median crown stripes; geographical variation within the *culicivorus* group is minor. The northernmost subspecies *brasherii* (described below) occurs in ne. Mexico south to Hidalgo and n. Veracruz; Texas records pertain to this race. Birds from cen. Veracruz, Puebla, and Oaxaca, east and south to nw. Costa Rica, belong to nominate *culicivorus*, which is very similar to *brasherii* but with upperparts averaging slightly darker olive-gray and the lateral crown stripes averaging slightly broader. Birds from Nayarit to Colima in w. Mexico have been separated as *flavescens*; these average slightly brighter yellow on the head stripes and underparts than nominate *culicivorus*, but this subspecies has been merged into *culicivorus*. Birds from the Pacific slope of Oaxaca and Chiapas have been described as *ridgwayi*; they are intermediate in appearance between *flavescens* and nominate *culicivorus*. Birds from Costa Rica (except nw.) to w. Panama, *goldmani*, are slightly more olive (less gray) above than nominate *culicivorus*. There is a general trend within the *culicivorus* group of increasing frequency of orangish in the median crown stripe as one goes south.

The two South American groups are sometimes considered to

be specifically distinct from the northern *culicivorus* group. The *cabanisi* group ("Cabanis' Warbler") is found in n. South America from Colombia to nw. Venezuela. These birds (up to four subspecies recognized) have gray upperparts, grayish white supercilia, and (usually) yellowish median crown stripes. The *aurocapillus* group ("Golden-crowned Warbler") resembles *cabanisi* but is olive above and usually shows an orangish median crown stripe; up to five subspecies are recognized within this group, which ranges from Trinidad, Venezuela, and e. Colombia south to e. Bolivia, Uruguay, and ne. Argentina.

TAXONOMIC RELATIONSHIPS

This species has close allies in South America, of which the closest appears to be the White-bellied Warbler, *B. hypoleucus;* the Three-banded Warbler *(B. trifasciatus)* is also closely related and is sometimes treated as conspecific with Golden-crowned.

PLUMAGES AND MOLTS

SPRING ADULT: Broad stripe down center of crown yellow, usually slightly obscured by olive-gray feather tips. In some individuals this area is strongly suffused with orangish, especially anteriorly. The immediate forehead is grayish olive. There is a black stripe on each side of the crown, extending from the side of the forehead (where narrow) all the way back to the side of the nape. Below this, a broad supercilium, forward through the supraloral area, is rather dull yellowish olive. There is a split yellow eyering and a gray loral spot; the auricular area is grayish olive, indistinctly mottled with pale yellowish. The upperparts are uniformly olive-gray. The underparts, from the chin through the undertail coverts, are fairly bright

Golden-crowned Warbler of culicivorus *group. In Azu, Panama, in February. (Photo: D. Wechsler/VIREO)*

yellow, tinged with olive on the sides of the breast and flanks. The wing coverts are olive-gray like the back; bend of wing bright yellow. The flight feathers of the wing and tail are unmarked dusky gray. **FIRST SPRING:** Probably indistinguishable from spring adult, although flight feathers may appear somewhat browner and more worn. **FALL ADULT:** Essentially identical to spring adult, but the yellow or orangish color of the median crown stripe is usually somewhat more veiled by olive-gray feather tips, and overall plumage is fresher. **FIRST FALL:** Probably indistinguishable from fall adult, but at least some first fall birds show somewhat more obscure lateral crown stripes. **JUVENILE:** Head and upperparts generally brownish olive; lores somewhat darker than the sides of the head. Throat and breast paler olive-buff, with the underparts becoming more yellowish on the lower breast and belly. Two tawny wing bars. **BARE PARTS:** Bill dark brown, paler flesh on the lower mandible. Legs and feet fleshy pink. Eyes dark brown.

A complete molt takes place after breeding; extent of the first prebasic molt in hatching-year birds not known. There is evidence of a limited prealternate molt.

 REFERENCES

DISTRIBUTION: Arvin 1980, Langham 1980.
ECOLOGY, BEHAVIOR, VOCALIZATIONS, AND CONSERVATION: Buskirk 1972.
SYSTEMATICS: Phillips 1966, Todd 1929.

RUFOUS-CAPPED WARBLER PL. 29

Basileuterus rufifrons

5 in. (12.7 cm). The northernmost member of a diverse Neotropical genus of warblers, the Rufous-capped is a very rare vagrant to the border region of w. and s. Texas and in southeastern Arizona (with one record of attempted nesting). The face pattern is distinctive, with a rufous cap and cheek patch, white supercilium, and bright yellow throat. Perhaps even more distinctive is the species' habit of cocking and waving its long and remarkably thin tail in a manner suggestive of a wren or gnatcatcher. It prefers brushy habitats, especially in mountain and foothill canyons.

 DESCRIPTION

Generally olive-gray to olive above, yellow on the throat and breast, and whitish on the remaining underparts. The head is distinctly patterned, with rufous on the crown and auriculars, a white supercilium and moustachial region, and blackish lores. All post-juvenal plumages are essentially similar, with males showing only very slight average differences from females. There is some geographical variation in the intensity and extent of rufous on the head, extent of yellow on the underparts, upperpart color, and tail length; northern *caudatus* is described under Plumages. Central and South American populations show much more extensive yellow on the underparts and are now usually regarded as a separate species, the Chestnut-capped Warbler *(B. delattrii)*.

Structure is distinctive, with a rather short and thick bill with a noticeable decurvature to the culmen; the wings are relatively short and rounded, and the tail is long and composed of uniquely thin, spindly rectrices. The legs are quite long.

 ## SIMILAR SPECIES

Not likely to be confused with any other North American warbler. The combination of the rufous cap, white supercilium, rufous cheeks, and yellow throat and chest sharply contrasting with the whitish belly make identification easy within our area, although there are somewhat similar *Basileuterus* within its Neotropical range. The long, spindly tail that is cocked nearly vertically is also unlike most other warblers. In silhouette it may suggest a WREN, GNATCATCHER, or WRENTIT *(Chamaea fasciata)*.

 ## VOICE

SONG is a rapid, variable series of chips, usually changing in pitch and pace once or twice, especially toward the end; the effect is often one of alternating series of chips and trills. The song is not especially musical in quality. Some versions of song are reminiscent of certain goldfinches *(Carduelis)*. The song is quite different from those of other *Basileuterus* warblers, including the closely related Chestnut-capped Warbler (see Subspecies).

CALL NOTE is a *chick* or *tik*, sometimes doubled or run into a rapid series, *chit-chit-chit-chit*. The hard call suggests call of a Lincoln's Sparrow *(Melospiza lincolnii)*. Also gives a higher *tsi* call. FLIGHT NOTE unknown.

 ## BEHAVIOR

The posture is distinctive, with the tail cocked at an angle from 45° to nearly vertical, as noted above. Usually found singly or in pairs, apparently remaining paired throughout the year. Forages in dense brush, often close to the ground; gleans foliage for insects and spiders, often with deliberate movements and much scanning. Like most other *Basileuterus,* the Rufous-capped Warbler is inquisitive and responds well to pishing.

The **NEST** is a domed structure with a side entrance; it is made of fibers and other plant material and placed on a steep bank among litter, rocks, or logs.

Habitat

Restricted to brushy habitats, usually in foothill regions and lower mountain slopes and canyons, including second growth and coffee plantations. It occurs in brushy clearings within foothill and lower mountain woodlands (locally to 8,200 ft.), but avoids deep forests; it is absent from lowland thorn scrub habitats. U.S. sightings have primarily come from canyon bottoms bordered by brushy thorn scrub or oak slopes.

Distribution

RESIDENT in w. Mexico from n. Sonora and w. Chihuahua, and in e. Mexico from e. Nuevo Leon, south through most of the foothill, mountain, and central highland regions of Mexico to e. Chiapas, w. Guatemala, and in s. Belize. The related Chestnut-capped Warbler (considered conspecific with the Rufous-capped by many authors) occurs from se. Chiapas and s. Guatemala through El Salvador, Honduras (mainly Pacific slope) and w. Nicaragua, Costa Rica and Panama, extending south to n. and w. Colombia and w. Venezuela.

CASUAL north into the U.S., where recorded in se. Ariz. and w., cen., and s. Texas. The seven Ariz. records come mainly from canyons in the lower portions of the Chiricahua, Huachuca, and Whetstone mtns., and in the Pajaritos Mtns. west of Nogales. The records extend from March to mid-August, and one involves a single bird that built a nest and laid two eggs in Cave Creek Canyon (Chiricahua Mtns.) in 1977. Two singing males were in French Joe Canyon, Whetstone Mtns., during spring and summer 1995 and a pair was there in 1996. In Texas the 11 records are concentrated in the Big Bend region, with an individual returning for several years in Santa Elena Canyon 1976–1979, one in Campground Canyon 1973–1975, another in Big Bend 26 Oct 1980, and one there 8 May 1993. Also recorded from Webb Co. (two males with enlarged gonads taken May 1980), Falcon Dam, Val Verde Co., Kendall Co. (se. Edwards Plateau), Uvalde Co., and on the coast at Corpus Christi. This species is a common resident in the Sierra Picachos near Cerralvo, Nuevo Leon, about 50 miles southwest of Falcon Dam, but is evidently absent from the mountains of Coahuila south of the Big Bend region.

🏛 STATUS AND CONSERVATION

No specific information; generally common. The species' preference for brushy habitats and edges, rather than deep forest interior, makes it relatively safe from habitat loss. There is a recorded case of parasitism by Bronzed Cowbird *(Molothrus aeneus)* on Rufous-capped Warbler of the w.-cen. Mexican race *dugesi*.

🦅 SUBSPECIES

A widespread species, with a trend toward increasing yellow on the underparts and face toward the south. Extensively yellow southern birds (s. Guatemala south) are often considered a separate species, the Chestnut-capped or Delattre's Warbler *(Basileuterus delattrii)*.

Arizona records presumably belong to the northernmost race *caudatus*, described below. This subspecies occurs in nw. Mexico, from Sonora and Chihuahua south to Sinaloa (where it intergrades with the following race). The very similar *dugesi* is slightly more olive above and marginally shorter tailed; it ranges in w. and cen. Mexico from Sinaloa south and east to Morelos, Guerrero, and Oaxaca. Also very similar is the ne. Mexican race *jouyi*, which is probably the subspecies represented by the s. Texas records and perhaps also those from the Big Bend region. *B. r. jouyi* occurs from Nuevo Leon and w. Tamaulipas south to Hidalgo and Puebla; it differs, on average, from *caudatus* in its slightly darker and more olive upperparts, slightly deeper green wing panel formed by the edges of the primaries and secondaries, slightly deeper wash of gray-brown on the sides and flanks, and slightly deeper and more extensive rufous crown. Nominate *rufifrons* is the form occurring from cen. Veracruz and the southern Mexican plateau south to cen. Oaxaca, Chiapas, and cen. Guatemala. It is decidedly more olive green (less gray) on the upperparts than the above three races, showing some contrast between the gray hindneck and the greenish back; the wing coverts and flight feathers are edged with bright olive green; the chestnut cap and auriculars are deeper in color, with this color more extensive through the center of the crown; the flanks are a deeper, richer brown; the yellow of the underparts is deeper and brighter; and the tail is relatively shorter. The race *salvini*, which occurs from se. Veracruz southeast to n.-cen. Guatemala and disjunctly in s. Belize, resembles nominate *rufifrons* but is much more extensively yellow below, with yellow washing through the entire belly region; its flanks are more deeply washed with buff.

The related Chestnut-capped Warbler, *B. delattrii*, has often been considered conspecific with the Rufous-capped Warbler. It differs from Rufous-capped in its entirely bright yellow underparts, bright yellow-olive upperparts, more extensive rufous in the auriculars and yellow in the submoustachial region, shorter tail (shorter than wing), and vocalizations. There are three subspecies of Chestnut-capped found from the Pacific region of Guatemala south to northernmost South America.

TAXONOMIC RELATIONSHIPS

The long tail and thin rectrices set it somewhat apart from other *Basileuterus* (even leading to the recognition of a separate genus at one point), but generic separation certainly does not seem warranted. The Chestnut-capped Warbler *(B. delattrii)*, noted above under Subspecies, is closely related and considered by many authorities to be conspecific. The Golden-browed Warbler *(B. belli*, endemic to Central America from n. Mexico to Honduras), is superficially similar in plumage, but its relationships with *rufifrons* and *delattrii* are uncertain.

PLUMAGES AND MOLTS

SPRING ADULT MALE: Forecrown and sides of crown rich rufous. Thin, short whitish median forehead streak. Center of crown grayish olive tinged with pale rufous; rear crown grayish olive. Conspicuous white supercilium extending from the bill to well behind the eye. Lores and feathering

Rufous-capped Warbler. Nominate rufifrons *in Oaxaca, Mexico, in December. (Photo: R. K. Bowers/VIREO)*

immediately around and behind the eye slaty black. Cheeks rich rufous. Moustachial and submoustachial region mottled grayish and white, separating the rufous cheeks and blackish lores from the yellow throat and breast. The uppermost chin is white. Remaining upperparts grayish olive, becoming grayer with feather wear. Lower border of the yellow breast sharply set off from the whitish belly. Sides and flanks grayish buff, this color deepest on the flanks. Undertail coverts light grayish buff. Wing coverts olive-yellow; bend of wing yellow. Primaries and secondaries dusky, narrowly edged with pale yellow-olive. Rectrices dusky olive, edged with olive-yellow. **FIRST SPRING MALE:** Probably only distinguishable in the hand from adult by relatively more worn flight feathers. **SPRING ADULT FEMALE:** Essentially identical to adult male, but on average the rufous of the center of the crown is less extensive, with the olive-gray of the rear of crown extending farther forward. **FIRST SPRING FEMALE:** Probably only distinguishable in the hand from adult by relatively more worn flight feathers. **FALL ADULT MALE:** Like spring adult, but fresher plumage is tinged more strongly with olive-brown on the upperparts (less gray) and shows a stronger brownish wash on the flanks. **FIRST FALL MALE:** Probably not distinguishable from fall adult male. **FALL ADULT FEMALE:** Like spring adult, but fresher plumage is tinged more strongly with olive-brown on the upperparts (less gray) and shows a stronger brownish wash on the flanks. **FIRST FALL FEMALE:** Probably not distinguishable from fall adult female. **JUVENILE:** Brownish olive above, including crown; buffy on the breast, becoming paler buff-white on the belly. White supercilium, olive auricular region, slate gray lores. Two cinnamon-buff wing bars. **BARE PARTS:** Bill black, tinged slightly brown at the base of the lower mandible. Eyes dark brown. Legs and feet grayish pink to fleshy pink.

A prebasic molt takes place after breeding. It is complete in adults; extent of the first prebasic molt in hatching-year birds unknown. No prealternate molt known.

 REFERENCES

DISTRIBUTION: Arnold 1980.
SYSTEMATICS: Dickey and Van Rossem 1938, Todd 1929.

YELLOW-BREASTED CHAT
PL. 30

Icteria virens

7 in. (17.8 cm). The chat is by far the largest wood-warbler, and is set apart from our other warblers by many aspects of behavior, song, and plumage. Its taxonomic relationship to the rest of the

wood-warblers has long been controversial. Although many workers have questioned its place in the Parulidae, recent genetic work appears to confirm that it is a warbler, albeit an aberrant one. Skulking and secretive thicket-dwellers, chats are most easily seen when males are singing, which they often do on a high, bare branch or even in flight. The bill is very heavy, with a strongly curved culmen. The song, a medley of whistles, harsh scolds, and chatters, is completely unlike that of any other warbler. Chats are widespread over much of North America south of Canada but are declining in much of their range.

 ## DESCRIPTION

All plumages show plain olive green to olive-gray upperparts, a deep yellow throat and breast, and a whitish spectacle contrasting with the dark lores and auricular area. The exceptional size and thick bill with a strongly curved culmen set the chat apart structurally from all other North American warblers. The tail is somewhat graduated (about 10 mm from tip of outer rectrices to tip of longest, central rectrices). Sex and age variation is minor, and there is little seasonal change in appearance apart from plumage freshness and bill color. There is moderate geographical variation, mainly involving the color of the upperparts and the length of the tail. The description below applies to the nominate eastern race.

 ## SIMILAR SPECIES

The chat is not likely to be confused with any other warbler, although it can suggest an outsized yellowthroat. From the **COMMON YELLOWTHROAT**, note the much larger size, heavier bill, facial markings, and (from males) the lack of black in the auriculars. See also **GRAY-CROWNED YELLOWTHROAT**. Because beginning birders often do not recognize the Yellow-breasted Chat as a warbler, confusion with female **TANAGERS, ORIOLES,** or **YELLOW-THROATED VIREO** is possible. The skulking behavior differs from the actions of the more arboreal tanagers and orioles. The curved culmen and white facial markings differ from our orioles; and the long tail and the cheek and throat contrast should prevent confusion with our tanagers.

 ## VOICE

The **SONG** of the Yellow-breasted Chat is a bizarre and highly distinctive collection of harsh notes, whistles, cackles, mews, catcalls, and *caw* notes. Harsh *cheh-cheh-cheh-cheh* and higher *tu-*

tu-tu-tu series are frequently incorporated into the song. The notes are often widely spaced, even hesitant sounding. The song cannot be confused with that of any other warbler, though it may resemble the ramblings of a mockingbird or thrasher (family Mimidae). The pacing is much slower than that of any mimid. Songs may be given through much of the day, but also frequently at night. Apart from the male's singing, chats are rather quiet warblers. **CALL NOTES** are not frequently heard; they sometimes give a harsh *chough* , *cheow,* or *chak* note and a more nasal *air* note, and a sharp *cuk* or *cuk-cuk-cuk.* **FLIGHT NOTE** apparently not given (but males frequently give flight songs).

🦅 BEHAVIOR

Chats are generally extremely shy and retiring, skulking birds, and are usually found alone. Even singing males on the breeding grounds can be real skulkers, although they may be more conspicuous by virtue of their frequent choice of conspicuous song perches and, especially, their habit of giving flight songs. Flight songs may last for several seconds. The male, in song throughout, usually launches vertically into the air with deep, slow wingbeats, dangling legs, strongly pumping tail, and head held high; alternatively he may employ this exaggerated flapping flight while traveling horizontally between exposed song perches. The yellow underwing coverts show conspicuously during these song flights. The male's black mouth lining is sometimes displayed to the female, with the male perched below the female, opening his gape fully and moving the body slowly from side to side. Chats on breeding territories also sing frequently at night, unlike most warblers. The Yellow-breasted Chat possesses several behavioral traits unique or rare among warblers; it is among the few warblers to scratch under the wing and is the only warbler known to hold food in its feet.

Foraging takes place low within dense thickets, mainly by gleaning insects from foliage; occasionally forages on the ground. In late summer and fall it feeds to a large extent on small fruits, such as the fruits of honeysuckle, wild strawberry, blackberry, mulberry, chokecherry, sumac, and nightshade.

The **NEST** is a bulky though well-hidden structure of dead leaves, grasses, and shreds of bark placed 3–6 ft. off the ground in a bush or low sapling; thorny shrubs (such as multiflora rose) or briar patches are often chosen for nest placement; in the West nests are often placed in dense tangles of wild grape.

HABITAT

Throughout its **BREEDING** range the chat requires dense tangles and thickets, usually at the edge of deciduous woodlands. Eastern birds favor thickets, briar patches, willow clumps, multiflora rose brambles, and other thorny clumps for breeding. Such thickets may either be in lowland floodplains or in upland regions far from water, and are often in second growth following forest clearing, burns, windfalls, or mining. Some taller trees or snags are required for song perches. Western populations are more closely tied to streamside thickets of willows, mesquite, mulefat, and other riparian species, with tangles of grapevines, etc. In some areas of the Southwest they use exotic salt cedar stands, especially where mixed with honey mesquite and an understory of arrowweed. In the prairie regions they prefer impenetrable thickets of buffalo berry, hawthorn, and rose under stands of cottonwoods.

Chats **WINTER** in thickets, second growth, and forest edge. **MIGRANTS** also tend to occupy heavy, tangled cover; they are not often detected.

 DISTRIBUTION

BREEDS from sw. and s.-cen. B.C., se. Alta., s. Sask., w. N.D., S.D., Iowa, s. Minn. (a few records), s. Wisc., s. Mich., extreme s. Ont. (regular at only a few localities), and w. and s. N.Y. (and until recently Conn. and R.I.) south through much of the U.S. to n. Baja Calif., n. Sinaloa, the central Mexican plateau (to Zacatecas), w. and e. Texas (but absent from much of the remainder of the state), the Gulf Coast states (but scarce on the immediate Gulf Coast), and n. Fla.

WINTERS in the lowlands of the Pacific and Atlantic slopes of Mexico and Central America, from Sinaloa and s. Tamaulipas south to w. Panama. Generally occurs below 5,000 ft. elevation. Casual in winter north to s. Ariz., s. Texas and the southern portions of the Gulf states. Curiously, it is recorded regularly (especially in late fall and early winter) along the Atlantic Coast north to Mass., and regularly at least into December in the Canadian Maritime Provinces and Nfld. It also occurs casually in winter in the interior of e. North America, north to Ill., Ind., Ohio, and once each in Iowa, Mich., and s. Ont. Exceptional in late fall and winter on the West Coast, where there are but a few records (north to Ore.).

SPRING MIGRATION is surprisingly late, given the relatively southerly breeding distribution of this species. In the East it is primarily a trans-Gulf migrant and is noted only rarely in peninsular Fla. It arrives on the Gulf Coast mainly in mid-April, with a few appearing in early April. Average arrivals in s. Mo., Tenn., and Ky. are around 20 April, and typical arrivals in Ill., Ind., and Ohio are closer to 1 May. At the northern end of the breeding range in the Midwest, arrivals vary from early to mid-May; there are a few exceptional records of early April overshoots in the Midwest region. Arrivals in the northeastern part of the breeding range are in early May. Western birds arrive in Calif. and s. Ariz. in mid-April (rarely early April). At the latitude of Ore., n. Ut., and Colo., arrivals are mostly in early May. Arrivals in the northernmost breeding range in the West are in the latter half of May. Spring migrants are uncommonly encountered away from migrant traps on the Gulf Coast and western desert oases, so most of the timing scheme above applies to the return of birds to breeding territories.

FALL MIGRATION is poorly documented because of the species' secretive nature; it goes largely undetected once singing ceases (usually in mid-July, but into August in portions of the Southwest). The main period of fall movement over much of North America is from late August (a few to mid-August) to late September, with stragglers recorded to late October or later. Eastern birds possibly use a trans-Gulf route again in fall, as evidenced by up to two dozen birds noted in single day along the upper Texas coast in September. Western birds appear to move south on a broad front, although migrants are generally scarcer near the coast.

CASUAL to w. Wash., e. N.D., s. Man., n. Minn., n. Wisc., n. Mich. (including Upper Peninsula), n. Ont. (north to s. James Bay), Que., Vt. (one nesting record), and N.H. Annual in small numbers in Mass., especially along the outer coast and offshore islands from mid-August to October, occasionally to November. This pattern of apparent northward fall movement is well defined in coastal Maine and especially the Canadian Maritime Provinces, with hundreds of records concentrated along south-facing beaches. This northward movement extends north to Nfld. (where a few have even attempted to winter). Sightings into early winter in coastal New England and the Maritimes are routine, particularly at feeders. A few have successfully overwintered in Mass. Away from this northeastern region, northern extralimital vagrants are about evenly divided between late spring and fall. Rare but regular fall vagrant to Bermuda (occasionally wintering) and is casual in fall and winter in the Bahamas; at least one winter record for Cuba and a probable winter record for Grand Cayman. Three fall specimens from Greenland.

YELLOW-BREASTED CHAT
Icteria virens

⅃ STATUS AND CONSERVATION

Yellow-breasted Chats have declined precipitously over much of their range, although they still occupy at least sparsely most of their historical range. Negative trends have been noted for most eastern states and much of the Midwest, and there has been near total withdrawal from s. New England. Reasons for the decline are not clear but probably reflect a reduction of dense shrubby second growth through urbanization and the maturation of regenerating forests. Populations are generally stable in much of the West, although urbanization, flood control, and perhaps cowbirds have greatly reduced populations in California and some adjacent regions.

A rather frequent host of Brown-headed Cowbirds, although chats at least sometimes appear to distinguish cowbird eggs and destroy them or abandon parasitized nests.

Moderate geographical variation mainly involves tail length and the color of the upperparts, and to a lesser extent the richness of the yellow underparts. Most authorities recognize only two subspecies within our area. Nominate *virens* occurs through the eastern portion of the range and is described below. It breeds from cen. Texas, the eastern portions of the plains states, and the Great Lakes region eastward, and winters from Tamaulipas and Guerrero south to w. Panama.

The western subspecies *auricollis* (including "*longicauda*"), sometimes colloquially known as the "Long-tailed Chat," occupies the w. North American range from w. Texas, the w. Great Plains, and s. Saskatchewan westward; it breeds south to cen. Sonora. It winters primarily in w. Mexico and is recorded south only to Guatemala. Specimens assigned to western *auricollis* have been taken in winter in Georgia and Massachusetts. *I. v. auricollis* is characterized by a longer tail and grayer, less green, upperparts. The tail of *auricollis* averages 6 mm longer than that of the corresponding sex of *virens*; the tail is longer than the wing in *auricollis* (the reverse is true of *virens*). *I. v. auricollis* males may average deeper yellow below, more frequently tending toward orange, than nominate birds. Additionally, the white submoustachial stripe averages broader in western birds. Within the west there is a subtle cline from more olive-backed birds in the north to grayer-backed birds in the southwest; the name *longicauda* has been applied to these northern birds, but few authorities now recognize its distinctness. The subspecies name *danotia* has been applied to birds in cen. and s. Texas and adjacent Coahuila, which may be smaller and greener-backed than "*longicauda*" to the northwest; today this race is generally merged with nominate *virens*. Mexican birds from southern Sonora (and presumably adjacent Sinaloa) have been given the name *tropicalis;* this race, also not generally recognized today, averages even grayer than *auricollis* and tail length is equal to wing length, rather than longer.

 TAXONOMIC RELATIONSHIPS

The affinities of the Yellow-breasted Chat have long been debated, although it is now generally recognized that the chat is a parulid, albeit an aberrant one. Its unusual parulid characters include its large size, distinctive bill shape, behavior, and molts; it also has some distinctive skeletal characters. Postulated relationships with the manakins, vireos, tangers, "honeycreepers," and other groups occur in the literature. Within the warblers, chat affinities are unclear. They share some characteristics of shape with the Neotropical *Granatellus* chats, and the Gray-crowned Yellowthroat *(Geothlypis [Chamaethlypis] poliocephala)* seems, superficially at least, to link the more typical yellowthroats with *Icteria.*

PLUMAGES AND MOLTS

SPRING ADULT MALE: Forehead and forecrown olive green, the former washed with gray and sometimes with some blackish flecking (in rare variants, the forehead and crown are almost solid black). Remainder of crown, nape, back, and rump deep olive green (to olive-gray in western birds; see under Subspecies above). Lores black, bordered below by a short white submoustachial streak and above by a white supraloral line that extends back around the eye, forming a white "spectacle." Auricular area and sides of neck slaty gray. Chin and throat, down through lower breast, deep bright yellow (in some variants tinted or blotched with orange-yellow, possibly diet related). Remainder of underparts whitish, with grayish olive flanks. Wings and tail dusky, edged olive green; underwing coverts bright yellow. **FIRST SPRING MALE:** Essentially identical to spring adult male, but averages slightly duller on the upperparts. In the hand, the inner 3–6 primaries appear more worn than the remaining outer primaries; there is a gap of 3mm or more between the tips of the innermost fresh primary and the outermost worn (juvenal) primary. **SPRING ADULT FEMALE:** Resembles spring adult male, but the upperparts are paler and duller olive and the underparts are less intensely yellow. The face pattern is more subdued, with the lores dark gray rather than black. Bill color differs (see Bare Parts below). **FIRST SPRING FEMALE:** Essentially indistinguishable from spring adult female but averaging duller. In the hand may be

Yellow-breasted Chat. Male virens *in Ontario in May. (Photo: Arthur Morris/Birds as Art)*

*Yellow-breasted Chat.
Male* auricollis *in
California in May.
(*Photo: Brian E.
Small)

aged by wing measurement as in first spring male. **FALL ADULT MALE:** In fresh
fall plumage the yellow of the underparts, especially on the breast, is very
slightly veiled with olive; the sides of the head and neck are washed with
olive or brownish, and the flanks show a strong buffy brown tinge. Bill
color also changes seasonally (see Bare Parts). **FIRST FALL MALE:** Resembles
fall adult male, but yellow of underparts more strongly veiled with olive,
lores gray rather than black, sides and flanks even more strongly washed
with brown, and upperparts darker and duller (browner). **FALL ADULT FEMALE:**
Resembles spring adult female, but in fresher plumage the yellow of the
underparts is veiled with olive, and the flanks are strongly tinged with
buff-brown. **FIRST FALL FEMALE:** The dullest post-juvenal plumage encountered, being similar to but somewhat duller than the fall adult female. The
upperparts are dull brownish olive. Yellow of underparts veiled with olive;
sides and flanks extensively washed with pale brown. **JUVENILE:** Upperparts
deep, dull olive-gray; spectacles lacking; underparts mottled with white
and grayish olive, lacking yellow; flanks buffy brown. At most, only traces
of this plumage may be encountered away from the breeding grounds. If
attending adults are not present, this plumage can be confusing because
of the lack of yellow and the fact that the chat's size and shape can lead to
confusion with nonwarblers such as orioles, tanagers, or vireos. **BARE
PARTS:** Bill black in breeding adult male, with some gray at the base of the
mandible; dark brown in winter adult males. Adult female's bill is even
browner, with some yellowish pink on the basal half of the mandible. Bills
of immature birds are brown above, pale yellow below. The mouth lining
is black in spring males but pinkish in spring females and (presumably) all
fall birds. Legs and feet slate black (adults) to slate-brown (immatures).
Eyes dark brown.

The prebasic molt of adults is complete and occurs mainly on the
breeding grounds (July to October). In hatching-year birds the first preba-

sic molt includes some or most of the outer primaries, the tertials, and (variably) some or all secondaries and rectrices. Unlike most other North American warblers, spring plumage is acquired by wear; there is no prealternate molt. Orange-breasted variants found locally appear to result from a diet rich in honeysuckle *(Lonicera)* before the late summer prebasic molt.

 ## REFERENCES

GENERAL: Petrides 1938, Phillips 1974.

DISTRIBUTION: Austen et al. 1994, Dennis 1967.

ECOLOGY, BEHAVIOR, VOCALIZATIONS, AND CONSERVATION: Burtt and Hailman 1978, Dennis 1958.

PLUMAGES, MOLTS, AND MORPHOLOGY: Blake 1962, Dwight 1899, Mulvihill et al. 1992, Phillips 1974.

SYSTEMATICS: Burtt and Hailman 1978, Ficken and Ficken 1962, Sibley and Ahlquist 1982, Van Rossem 1939.

ACKNOWLEDGMENTS
GLOSSARY
BIBLIOGRAPHY
REFERENCES
INDEX

ACKNOWLEDGMENTS

Over a decade has passed since the idea of this book was first enthusiastically discussed among three friends, Eirik A. T. Blom, Jon L. Dunn, and Cindy House. Kimball L. Garrett was soon asked to join our venture. We shortly found out, however, that it was one thing to talk about writing and illustrating a book and another to sit down and actually do it. Fortunately for us, Rick Blom's energy and passion kept the book from floundering. In 1990 artist Thomas R. Schultz joined the group. A major reorganization of the book and its research methods took place around that time. Unfortunately, duties and commitments elsewhere led Rick in another direction, eventually leading to his withdrawal as an author. We are indebted to Rick and his boundless enthusiasm in those early years of the warbler field guide. He is a keen observer of birds, regularly contributing his knowledge through his written contributions.

Researching and producing this guide would not have been possible without the incredible cooperation of the staff of the Division of Birds at the National Museum of Natural History (Smithsonian Institution) in Washington, D.C. We thank all those associated with this premier collection for accommodating our numerous visits and providing specimens for the artists. In particular we are grateful to J. Philip Angle, Richard C. Banks, M. Ralph Browning, Roger Clapp, James Dean, Carla Dove, Bonnie Farmer, Gary R. Graves, Storrs L. Olson, and Richard Zusi. Bonnie, especially, did a phenomenal amount of leg work for our visits, loans, and data requests; Jim and Phil were also of constant assistance.

A number of other ornithological research collections proved invaluable in the preparation of this guide. The library and specimen collections of the Natural History Museum of Los Angeles County were constant reference sources in the writing of the species accounts and introductory text. Other collections (and their staff) which we used extensively for this guide, or which were consulted by reviewers, are as follows: Field Museum of Natural History, Chicago (David Willard); Carnegie Museum of Natural History in Pittsburgh, Penn. (Kenneth C. Parkes); University of Wisconsin Zoological Museum at Madison (Frank Iwen); Moore Laboratory of Ornithology at Occidental College, Los Angeles (John Hafner and Jim Northern); the Burke Memorial Museum at the University of Washington, Seattle (Chris Wood, Sievert Rohwer); Western Foundation of Vertebrate Zoology, Camarillo, Calif. (Jon Fisher, Walter Wehtje, Lloyd Kiff); Museum of Natural Science, Louisiana State University, Baton Rouge, La. (J. V. Remsen, Steve Cardiff, and Donna Dittmann); and the Cincinnati Museum of Natural History (Bob Kennedy).

Countless friends and colleagues supplied key information, ideas, or advice for the guide; many reviewed portions of the manuscript. We first single out those who provided frequent advice, voluminous information, and guidance: Bruce H. Anderson provided much information on Florida from the manuscript of the now-published *Birdlife of Florida*; John C. Arvin reviewed draft accounts from several primarily Neotropical warbler species. Giff Beaton provided numerous photographs and helpful migration data from n. Georgia. Louis R. Bevier provided assistance and advice on many matters, and allowed us an early look at the now-published Connecticut breeding bird atlas. M. Ralph Browning was of great help with the difficult Yellow Warbler complex. Charles R. Duncan provided JLD with the opportunity to co-teach a warbler course with him under the Institute of Field Ornithology at the University of Maine at Machias, and gave much advice during the book project, including a detailed review of draft accounts for the *Dendroica virens* group. Gary R. Graves reviewed draft accounts for Swainson's and Black-throated Blue warblers and provided much information on wood-warbler hybrids. George A. Hall reviewed a number of early draft species accounts. Bruce Hallett provided hundreds of reference photographs; in particular his material on Bahama Yellowthroat and *flavescens* Yellow-throated Warbler was invaluable for reference. Paul Hamel reviewed draft accounts for Bachman's and Cerulean warblers. Steve N. G. Howell and Sophie Webb provided us with an advance draft of the warbler accounts from the excellent Mexico field guide and reviewed draft species accounts and sketches of the primarily Mexican species. Kenn Kaufman reviewed much of the text, giving many helpful suggestions. Greg Lasley provided much information about Texas warbler distribution and provided many reference photos. Paul Lehman reviewed all of the maps and was of tremendous general help with distribution. Bruce Mactavish gave us much appreciated insight and data from the Newfoundland region. Bruce Peterjohn reviewed almost the entire manuscript in fine detail and gave exhaustive, helpful comments; he provided Breeding Bird Survey information and reviewed maps for eastern North America, as well as giving a great deal of much-appreciated advice. Kenneth C. Parkes reviewed several early draft species accounts and provided helpful critiques of some plates and much specific information on Blue-winged and Golden-winged warbler hybrids. Peter Pyle reviewed portions of the manuscript and provided us with a careful review of our plumage and molt treatments; he also provided drafts of warbler accounts from the much-anticipated second edition of his aging and sexing guide. J. V. Remsen, Jr., answered innumerable queries quickly and insightfully; he reviewed much of the manuscript, gave detailed information on Louisiana, advice on our treatment of behavior and provided us with information from the 7th edition of the AOU Check-list. In many ways Van provided a directional beacon we strived to follow. Chuck Sexton provided much information on Golden-cheeked Warbler. Fred A. Sharpe's manuscript on birds of the Olympic Peninsula, Washington, was an invaluable source, and we are grateful to him and George A. Gerdts for providing this. Dominic Sherony provided much helpful advice on the introductory text and helped obtain numerous reference photos. David Sibley and Michael O'Brien helped with much general information and provided useful comments on flight calls. James L. Stasz provided unpublished information on Magnolia Warbler plumages. Paul W. Sykes reviewed our account of Kirtland's Warbler. Guy Tudor lit a fire under the authors at just the right time to get the researching and writing on track. Richard West provided information from a forthcoming book on the birds of Delaware. Anthony White provided much useful reference material, particularly about the Bahamas, and provided JLD with the opportunity to study Bahama Yellowthroats and *flavescens* Yellow-throated Warblers; Tony's bird-finding guide to the Bahamas is nearing completion. Alan Wormington's unparalleled knowledge of Ontario and adjacent regions was an invaluable source of information and ideas.

Among those who also provided information, including copies or drafts of their publications, answered queries, or gave advice we also thank Jonathan Alderfer, Parker Backstrom, Ilze Balodis, Margaret Bain, Robert A. Behrstock, Gordon Berkey, Chuck Bernstein, H. David Bohlen, Richard Cannings, Roger B. Clapp, Robert J. Conn, Dave Cook, Mel and Arlie Cooksey, Stuart Cuberhatch, Bob Curry, Michael E. DeCapita, Paula Dimond,

Paul Donahue, Robert A. Duncan, Stephen W. Dunn, Shawneen Finnegan, Tom Frillman, Jean Gauthier, Nicolas Gagnon, Daniel D. Gibson, Mary Gustafson, Robert A. Hamilton, J. C. Hanagan, Robert Harlan, Phill Holder, Jeff Kingery, Hugh E. Kingery, Mary Alice Koeneke, Peter Landry, Laurie B. Larson, Charles T. LaRue, Stephen A. Laymon, Ian A. MacLaren, Joe T. Marshall, Glen Mahler, Guy McCaskie, Jim Morgan, C. P. Nicholson, Brainard L. Palmer-Ball, Jr., Ron Pittaway, Kenneth M. Prytherech, Don Roberson, Jim Stasz, Will Russell, Susan Rust, Shirley L. Scott, Andrew Sigler, Dan Singer, Muriel Smith, Robert Spahn, David A. Spector, Stuart Tingley, Thede Tobish, Philip Unitt, John W. Vanderpoel, Richard E. Webster, Jerry Weinrich, Claudia P. Wilds, Chris Woodson, and Kevin Zimmer. Over the long course of preparation of this guide, we have been aided by numerous others whom we have not mentioned, and to them we are also grateful.

Sue Tackett researched the range maps; rough drafts were reviewed by a number of regional and state authorities, to whom we are extremely grateful; many of these reviewers also provided important information for our Distribution sections. The reviewers and their regions or species of expertise area as follows: **Alberta:** Peter Sherrington, Cliff A. Wallis, C. R. Wershler; **British Columbia:** R. Wayne Campbell; **Manitoba:** Rudolf F. Koes, Herbert Copland, Peter Taylor, Manitoba Museum of Man and Nature's Prairie Nest Record Card Scheme; **Newfoundland:** Bruce Mactavish, **Northwest Territories:** Jacques Sirois; **Ontario:** Alan Wormington; **Quebec:** Yves Aubry; **Saskatchewan:** Robert Kreba; **Yukon:** Cameron D. Eckert, Wendy Nixon, Pamela Sinclair; **Alabama:** Greg Jackson; **Alaska:** Daniel D. Gibson, Brina Kessel, Thede Tobish; **Arizona:** Troy E. Corman, Alan M. Craig, David Jasper, Chuck LaRue, Narca A. Moore-Craig, Robert Morris, Gary H. Rosenberg; **Arkansas:** Norman Lavers, Michael Mlodinow, Helen Parker, Max Parker, William M. Shepherd; **California:** Richard A. Erickson, Robert A. Hamilton, Jo Heindel, Matt T. Heindel, Tom Heindel, Michael A. Patten, David Yee, Sue Yee; **Colorado:** Robert Righter; **Connecticut:** Louis R. Bevier; **Florida:** P. William Smith, Noel Wamer; **Delaware:** Richard L. West; **Georgia:** Giff Beaton, Malcolm F. Hodges, Jr.; **Idaho:** Brad Hammond, Terry McEneaney, Susan Potla, Charles Trost; **Illinois:** Vernon Kleen; **Indiana:** Kenneth J. Brock, James A. Haw, Charles E. Keller; **Iowa:** Brian Blevius, Jim Dinsmore, Steve Dinsmore, Kelly McKay, Peter C. Petersen, James D. Wilson; **Kansas:** Bill Busby, Charles Ely, Earl S. McHugh, Sebastian Patti, Max C. Thompson; **Kentucky:** Brainard L. Palmer-Ball, Jr.; **Louisiana:** David P. Muth, J. V. Remsen, Jr., David A. Wiedenfield; **Maine:** Charles D. Duncan, Peter D. Vickery; **Maryland:** Kathleen Klimkiewicz, Michael O'Brien; **Massachusetts:** the late Richard A. Forster; **Minnesota:** Kim R. Eckert; **Mississippi:** Malcolm F. Hodges, Jr., Terry Schiefer, Judith A. Toups; **Missouri:** Mark B. Robbins; **Montana:** Charles M. Carlson, Daniel Casey, Terry McEneaney; **Nebraska:** Barbara Padelford, Loren Padelford, Richard C. Rosche, B. J. Rose; **Nevada:** Art Biale, J. L. Cressman, Marian D. Cressman, Leonard Hoskins, Larry A. Neel; **New Hampshire:** Paula Dimond, Walter G. Ellison; **New Jersey:** Bill Boyle, Jr., **New Mexico:** Jim Black, John Parmeter, Hart Schwartz, Barry Zimmer; **New York:** Paul DeBenedictis, Walter G. Ellison; **North Carolina:** Harry E. LeGrand; **North Dakota:** Gordon Berkey, Ron Martin; **Ohio:** Mary Gustafson, Larry O. Rosche; **Oklahoma:** William A. Carter, Joseph A. Grzybowski, James C. Hoffman, Jim Norman, Darrell Pouge; **Oregon:** Jeff Gilligan, Steve Summers; **Rhode Island:** Scott C. Tsagarakis; **South Carolina:** Jon Cely, Dennis M. Forsythe; **South Dakota:** Richard Peterson, Paul F. Springer, Nathaniel R. Whitney; **Tennessee:** C. P. Nicholson; **Texas:** Keith A. Arnold, John Arvin, Karen Benson, Kelly B. Bryan, Mark A. Elwonger, William J. Graber III, Carl B. Haynie, Richard Kinney, Greg W. Lasley, Mark Lockwood, Guy Luneau, Brad McKinney, Brent Ortego, Paul Palmer, Willie Sekula, Chuck Sexton, Kenneth D. Seyffert, Roland Wauer, Matt White, David E. Wolf, Barry Zimmer; **Utah:** Al Schnurrer, Ella Sorenson, Steve Summers; **Vermont:** Walter G. Ellison; **Virginia:** Roger B. Clapp; **Washington:** Eugene Hunn, Dennis Paulson, Bill Tweit; **West Virginia:** George A. Hall; **Wisconsin:** Jim Baughman, John Bielefeldt, Randy Hoffman, Robbye Johnson, Fred Lesher, Mike Mossman, Sam Robbins; **Wyoming:** Helen Downing, Forest Luke, Terry McEneaney, Oliver K. Scott, Rick Steenberg. Kirtland's Warbler: Paul W. Sykes, Jr.; Golden-cheeked Warbler: Chuck Sexton.

Larry Rosche worked hard and skillfully to produce the final maps; his work was aided by Sherry Rosche. We are grateful to Dan Cole of the National Museum of Natural History for his initial advice on the production of the maps.

The color photographs that appear in this guide, and those additional photographs used for reference, are the work of many of North America's finest photographers. For supplying reference photos we thank, in addition to those mentioned above, Jonathan Alderfer, Sid Bardht, Jack Bartholmai, Richard Bowen, Robert A. Behrstock, Giff Beaton, Joe Bens, David Blue, H. David Bohlen, O. G. Chapin, Richard L. Ditch, Victor Fazio, Jim Greaves, Kevin Griffith, Bruce Hallett, Matt T. Heindel, Kevin T. Karlson, Greg W. Lasley, Curtis Marantz, David Nurney, Michael A. Patten, Thomas Perry, Brian G. Prescott, Gary H. Rosenberg, Larry Sansone, Alan Sawinska, Ray Schwartz, Dominic Sherony, Sharon M. Skelly, Monte M. Taylor, Richard E. Webster, Douglas

Whitman, John Wilson, and Kevin J. Zimmer. Many important reference photos were obtained at Elizabeth Brooks's banding station.

The staff at Houghton Mifflin Company has shown remarkable patience and given wonderful guidance throughout this project. Harry Foster shepherded this guide along skillfully and tactfully; Susan Kunhardt and Lisa White provided superb editing. In particular, Lisa White's cheerfulness and efficiency through the arduous editing and production phases were nothing short of heroic. In addition to designing the book, Anne Chalmers worked closely with Larry Rosche on the maps. The late Roger Peterson reviewed the plates and early drafts of the species accounts, and his warm support for the project was an inspiration.

We are grateful to Kathy C. Molina for preparing the index.

The numerous cross-country trips necessary to research this guide would have been intolerable, if not impossible, without the logistical support provided by Silvia and Edwin Bierly (who were our frequent and gracious hosts during our work at the Smithsonian), Marshall Howe and Janet McMillen, Bruce Peterjohn and Mary Gustafson, Rich Pacer and T. J. Myers, Lee and Patricia Blom, Hal Wierenga, Charles and Mary Lofgren, Greg Septon, and Tony and Trina White also kindly provided hospitality.

JLD is thankful for the inspiration, advice, and encouragement received before and during this project and his years in the field studying warblers from Priscilla Dunn, the late Lloyd Dunn, Giff Beaton, Bruce Hallett, Matt T. Heindel, Charlotte Mathena, Shirley L. Scott, and Guy Tudor.

KLG thanks his wife Kathy Molina for her constant support and encouragement, and Lewis and Jean Garrett for understanding and nurturing a child's infatuation with birds. Logistical support from the Research and Collections Division of the Natural History Museum of Los Angeles County was much appreciated. Co-workers John Heyning, Dave Janiger, and Mark Wimer provided just the right amount of levity to help the writing along; Nan Lillith helped with many paperwork tasks.

CJH thanks her husband, Eric Derleth, her parents, the late Howard and Millie House, her sister, Lynn Thompson, and her family, Janet McMillen and Marshall Howe for the years of moral support and encouragement in her artistic endeavors; Dr. Kenneth C. Parkes for his critique of her plates, and the following who assisted in various ways: Betsy Potter, Willie D'Anna, Barbara Dowell, Deanna Dawson, Jonathan Alderfer, John and Karen Confer, Alison England, staff of Southwestern Research Station, and Michael Bierly.

TRS would like to express his thanks to the many friends who have provided stimulating companionship in the field over the past 25 years, for all have contributed in various ways to his development as a birder and bird artist. He would also like to thank the members of his family, especially his parents, who did so much to make it possible for him to pursue his life's passion. Last, he extends his deepest gratitude and appreciation to his wife Wendy and his two sons for their constant support and patience through seemingly endless years of work on this project.

GLOSSARY

GEOGRAPHICAL TERMS

Allegheny region. Mountain and plateau subset of the Appalachian region in Pennsylvania, West Virginia, western Maryland, and western Virginia.

Appalachian region. Highland region of eastern North America from southern Quebec south to northern Georgia, northeastern Alabama.

boreal regions. Wooded northern part of North American continent from interior Alaska east through the northern portions of the Canadian Prairie Provinces and much of Manitoba, Ontario, and Quebec (and adjacent border states in the United States from Minnesota to northern New England).

Canadian Shield. Large region of eastern Canada centered on Hudson Bay, northward from northern Saskatchewan east through much of Quebec; also adjacent northeastern Minnesota and the Adirondack Mountains in New York. The southern limit of many boreal species.

circum-Gulf. Refers to migration primarily overland on the west side of the Gulf of Mexico (*see* **trans-Gulf**).

Deep South. Gulf states plus all of Florida, southern Georgia, and much of lowland South Carolina.

Delmarva Peninsula. Landmass between Chesapeake Bay and Delaware Bay, including Delaware, eastern Maryland, and an isolated portion of northeastern Virginia.

East. North America roughly east of the 100th meridian.

eastern Great Plains. Region from northern Texas north through much of Oklahoma, Kansas, Nebraska, and the Dakotas.

Florida Panhandle. Westward extension of Florida along the Gulf of Mexico coast.

Great Basin. Western landlocked basin including much of Nevada and adjacent eastern California and northwestern Utah.

Great Lakes states. Northern states of the U.S. bordering the Great Lakes.

Great Plains states. Central North American region extending from northern Texas to North Dakota, including North Dakota, South Dakota, the eastern sections of Montana, Wyoming, and Colorado, and most of Nebraska, Kansas, and Oklahoma.

Gulf states. States bordering the Gulf of Mexico (Louisiana, Mississippi, Alabama; and Gulf coasts of Texas and Florida).

Maritime Provinces. Provinces of New Brunswick, Prince Edward Island, and Nova Scotia in eastern Canada.

Mid-Atlantic region. Atlantic coastal region from Virginia north to Long Island, New York.

Midwest. Region from Missouri and Iowa east through Illinois and Indiana to Ohio and western Kentucky, and north to the southern portions of Minnesota, Wisconsin, and Michigan.

Neotropics. In the broad sense, all of the Americas south of the United States–Mexico border.

New England. Northeasternmost United States, including Maine, Vermont, New Hampshire, Massachusetts, Rhode Island, and Connecticut.

Northeast. New England and adjacent New York, northeastern Pennsylvania, and northern New Jersey.

Piedmont. Plateau from southeastern Pennsylvania and Maryland south to Georgia and northern Alabama, lying between the Atlantic coastal plain and the Appalachian Mountains.

Prairie Provinces. South-central Canada including Alberta, Saskatchewan, and Manitoba; the true prairie regions are restricted to southern Alberta, southern Saskatchewan, and southwestern Manitoba.

Rocky Mountain states. New Mexico, Colorado, Wyoming, and Montana, and portions of adjacent Arizona, Utah, and Idaho.

South. General region from the southern Midwest and Carolinas south through the Gulf states and Florida.

Southern (Lower) Midwest. Central and western Kentucky and much of Missouri north to the southern portions of Ohio, Indiana, and Illinois.

Southwest. Region from southeastern California east through Arizona and New Mexico to the Big Bend region of western Texas; also adjacent southern Nevada and southwestern Utah.

trans-Gulf. Migration across the Gulf of Mexico (*see* **circum-Gulf**).

Upper Midwest. Iowa and northern portions of Illinois, Indiana, and Ohio north to southern Minnesota, central Wisconsin, and central Michigan.

West. North America roughly west of the 100th meridian.

western Great Plains. Region from northeastern New Mexico and eastern Colorado north through eastern Wyoming and eastern Montana; also adjacent western portions of Oklahoma, Kansas, Nebraska, and South Dakota.

PARTS OF A WARBLER

alula. Feathers at the "wrist" of the wing attached to the first digit ("thumb"); these inconspicuous feathers lie just anterior to the greater primary coverts on the folded wing.

auricular. Feathering on side of head covering ear openings; "cheek."

bend of wing. Marginal coverts along the "wrist" of the wing.

cheek. Auricular region on side of head.

culmen. Upper ridge of upper mandible (maxilla).

eyelid. Narrow feathered arc(s) above and/or below eye.

lateral crown stripes. Contrasting dark feathering along the sides of the crown; the upper border of the supercilium.

loral area, lores. Region between the bill and the eyes.

malar stripe, malar region. The area forming the lateral border of the chin and upper throat, sometimes marked dark feathering.

mantle. Upper back.

maxilla. Upper mandible.

moustachial stripe. A contrasting dark lower border of the auricular.

panel (on wing). Contrastingly pale region on folded wing formed by pale outer webs of remiges.

postocular stripe. A contrastingly dark stripe extending back from the eye (*see* **transocular stripe**).

primary coverts. Feathers overlying the base of the primaries; their color and relative state of wear can be important aging characters.

primary projection. Extension of primary tips beyond the tertials and secondaries on the folded wing.

rectrix (pl. rectrices). Tail feathers; in warblers there are six pairs of rectrices.

remex (pl. remiges). Long "flight feathers" of the wing, consisting of the primaries, secondaries, and tertials.

rictal bristles. Stiff hairlike feathers around the gape of the mouth, frequent in birds that capture flying insects.

secondary coverts. Lesser, median, and greater rows of coverts overlying the base of the secondary feathers.

shaft streaks. Contrasting (usually dark) area along the central shaft (rachis) of a feather.

split eye-ring. Pale feathered ring around eye that is interrupted at the front and rear.

submoustachial stripe. A contrastingly pale stripe between the moustachial and malar stripes.

subocular crescent. Arc of contrastingly light or dark feathers curving under the eye, below the eye-ring or eye-arcs.

supercilium (superciliary). Contrasting pale stripe over the eye, from the supraloral region back to behind the eye.

supraloral area. Area immediately above the lores; anterior-most part of the supercilium.

tail projection. Extension of the rectrices (tail feathers) beyond the tail coverts.

tail spots. Contrasting (usually white) areas on the outer one or more pairs of rectrices, visible on the spread tail and from below on the folded tail.

tertials. Innermost secondaries.

transocular stripe. Eye line; a contrastingly dark stripe extending from the lores through and behind the eye.

OTHER TERMS

albinistic. Completely lacking pigment, thus appearing white (feathers) or pinkish (bare parts).

allopatric. Species (or subspecies) having non-overlapping breeding ranges.

alternate plumage. Breeding plumage acquired through a prealternate molt.

basic plumage. Fall and winter (most species) or year-round plumage acquired through the prebasic molt.

bobbing. Down and up tail movement; we try to avoid the frequently used term *wagging* for this behavior because of the implication of a side-to-side movement.

Breeding Bird Survey. Roadside survey sponsored by United States Fish and Wildlife Service (U.S. Geological Survey Biological Resources Division) to monitor North American bird populations.

brood parasite. A species in which the female lays her eggs in the nests of other, "foster," host species; most notably, in North America, the cowbirds *(Molothrus)*.

call note. Simple vocalization, especially the "chip" and "flight" notes of warblers.

chenier. Habitat along western Gulf Coast; well-known fallout sites for trans-Gulf migrants.

dimorphic. Having two distinct plumage types (e.g., distinct male, female plumages).

flight note. Simple call, usually a high *see* or *zzeet* note, generally given in flight.

hawk (verb). *see* **sally**.

hover-glean. Term often used for sally-hover, in which prey is gleaned from a surface while the foraging bird is airborne.

intergradation. Genetic mixing, as in a region where two subspecies (more rarely, species) interbreed.

leucistic. Having reduced pigment in plumage, therefore appearing paler than normal, often nearly whitish.

melanistic. Abnormally dark plumage.

monotypic. A species having no named subspecies.

nominate. In a polytypic species, the subspecies which bears the same name as the specific epithet.

paramo. Open habitats above treeline in the higher mountains of South America.

pishing. Sounds made by birders to bring small birds such as warblers into view, e.g., *psshhh, psshhh, psshhh*. . . Such sounds may mimic a mild "heads up" alarm call given by some songbirds.

polygyny. Mating system in which a male has two or more mates, either simultaneously or sequentially within a breeding season.

polytypic. A species having named subspecies.

prealternate molt. Limited to extensive molt, usually from late winter to early spring, in which an alternate, or breeding plumage is acquired.

prebasic molt. Extensive molt (usually complete in adult birds, but involving mainly the body feathers and some coverts in hatching-year birds) occurring in late summer or early fall, usually on the breeding grounds, in which the basic plumage is acquired.

refugia (Pleistocene). Postulated remnant woodland habitat areas during peak glacial periods.

resaca. Small isolated wooded wetlands in southern Texas.

sally (verb). Aerial maneuver for prey capture; the misleading term *flycatch* is commonly employed in this context, but few warblers actually catch true flies.

song. Complex vocalizations, usually only given by male wood-warblers, which function largely in territorial establishment and maintenance, and in mate attraction.

sympatric. Species (or subspecies) having overlapping breeding ranges.

taiga. Far northern coniferous forest.

tepui. Isolated sandstone table-top mountains in southern Venezuela and adjacent Brazil and Guyana.

BIBLIOGRAPHY

The following references apply to the introductory chapters.

American Ornithologists' Union. 1957. *A.O.U. Check-list of North American Birds,* 5th ed. Baltimore, Md.: Lord Baltimore Press.

———. 1983. *A.O.U. Check-list of North American Birds,* 6th ed. Lawrence, Kans.: Allen Press, Inc.

Behle, W. H. 1985. Utah birds: geographic distribution and systematics. Occasional Paper No. 5, Utah Museum of Natural History

Bent, A. C. 1953. Life histories of North American wood warblers. Bulletin of the United States National Museum 203:1 734.

Borror, D. J. and W. W. H. Gunn. 1985. *Songs of the Warblers of North America.* Ithaca, N.Y.: Cornell Laboratory of Ornithology, Library of Natural Sounds.

Bledsoe, A. H. 1988. Nuclear DNA evolution and phylogeny of the New World nine-primaried oscines. *Auk* 105:504–515.

Burtt, E. H., Jr. 1986. An analysis of physical, physiological, and optical aspects of avian coloration with emphasis on wood warblers. *Ornithological Monographs* 38:1–126.

Chapman, F. M. 1917. *The Warblers of North America,* 3rd ed. New York: D. Appleton.

Cook, R. E. 1969. Variation in species density of North American birds. *Systematic Zoology* 18:63–84.

Curson, J., D. Quinn, and D. Beadle. 1994. *Warblers of the Americas: an Identification Guide.* Boston: Houghton Mifflin.

DeSante, D. F., and P. Pyle. 1986. *Distributional Checklist of the Birds of North America.* Lee Vining, Calif.: Artemisia Press.

Escalante, P., A. M. Sada, and J. R. Gil. 1996. *Listado de nombres comunes de las aves de Mexico.* Mexico: Comision Nacional para el Conocimiento y Uso de la Biodiversidad.

Ficken, M. S., and R. W. Ficken. 1962. The comparative ethology of wood warblers: a review. *Living Bird* 1:103–121.

Friedmann, H., L. Griscom, and R. T. Moore. 1957. Distributional check-list of the birds of Mexico, Part II. *Pacific Coast Avifauna,* No. 33.

Friedmann, H., and L. F. Kiff 1985. The parasitic cowbirds and their hosts. *Proceedings of the Western Foundation of Vertebrate Zoology,* Vol. 2, No. 4.

Getty, S. 1993. Call notes of North American wood warblers. *Birding* 25:159–168.

Griscom, L., and A. Sprunt, Jr., eds. 1957. *The Warblers of America.* New York: Devin-Adair.

Harrison, H. H. 1984. *Wood Warbler's World.* New York: Simon and Schuster.

Howell, S. N. G., and S. Webb. 1995. *A Guide to the Birds of Mexico and Northern Central America.* Oxford: Oxford University Press.

Keast, A., and E. S. Morton, eds. 1980. *Migrant Birds in the Neotropics.* Washington, D. C.: Smithsonian Institution Press.

Lowery, G. H., Jr., and B. L. Monroe Jr. 1968. Family Parulidae, in *Check-list of Birds of the World,* Vol. 14. R. A. Paynter Jr., ed. Cambridge, Mass.: Museum of Comparative Zoology.

MacArthur, R. H. 1958. Population ecology of some warblers of northeastern coniferous forests. *Ecology* 39:599–619.

Male, M., and J. Fieth. 1996. *Watching Warblers* (video). Blue Earth Films.

Mayr, E., and L. L. Short. 1970. Species taxa of North American birds. *Publications of the Nuttall Ornithological Club,* No. 9.

Mengel, R. M. 1964. The probable history of species formation in some northern wood warblers (Parulidae). *Living Bird* 3:9–43.

Mengel, R. M. 1965. The birds of Kentucky. Ornithological Monographs, No. 3. American Ornithologists' Union.

Morse, D. H. 1985. Habitat selection in North American parulid warblers. In *Habitat Selection in Birds,* M. L. Cody, ed. New York: Academic Press.

————. 1989. *American Warblers.* Cambridge, Mass.: Harvard University Press.

Nolan, V., Jr. 1978. The ecology and behavior of the Prairie Warbler *Dendroica discolor. Ornithological Monographs* 26:1–595.

Oberholser, H. C. 1974. *The Bird Life of Texas.* Austin: University of Texas Press.

Parkes, K. C. 1978. Still another parulid intergeneric hybrid (*Mniotilta × Dendroica*) and its taxonomic and evolutionary implications. *Auk* 95:682–690.

Parkes, K. C. 1989. Sex ratios based on museum collections — a caution. *Colonial Waterbirds* 12:130–131.

Price, J., S. Droege, and A. Price. 1995. *The Summer Atlas of North American Birds*. London: Academic Press.

Pyle, P., S. N. G. Howell, R. P. Yunick, and D. F. DeSante. 1987. *Identification Guide to North American Passerines*. Bolinas, Calif.: Slate Creek Press.

Pyle, P., N. Nur, and D. F. DeSante. 1994. Trends in nocturnal migrant landbird populations at Southeast Farallon Island, California 1968–1992. *Studies in Avian Biology* 15:58–74.

Rea, A. 1983. *Once a River*. Tucson: University of Arizona Press.

Remsen, J. V., Jr., and S. K. Robinson. 1990. A classification scheme for foraging behavior of birds in terrestrial habitats. *Studies in Avian Biology* No. 13:144–160.

Robbins, C. S. 1964. A guide to the aging and sexing of wood warblers (Parulidae) in fall. *Eastern Bird Banding Association News* 27:199–215.

Sibley, C. S., and B. L. Monroe Jr. 1990. *Distribution and Taxonomy of the Birds of the World*. New Haven, Conn.: Yale University Press.

Spector, D. A. 1992. Wood-warbler song systems: a review of paruline singing behaviors. *Current Ornithology* 9:199–238.

Stein, R. C. 1962. A comparative study of songs recorded from five closely related warblers. *Living Bird* 1:61–71.

Sutton, G. M. 1967. *Oklahoma Birds*. Norman: University of Oklahoma Press.

Unitt, P. 1984. *The Birds of San Diego County*. Memoir 13. San Diego Society of Natural History.

Wood, D. S. 1992. Color and size variation in eastern White-breasted Nuthatches. *Wilson Bulletin* 104:599–611.

Wormington, Alan. 1994. *Notes on the Status and Distribution of Ontario Warblers*. Unpublished manuscript.

REFERENCES

The following references are cited in the species accounts.

Airola, D. A., and R. H. Barrett. 1985. Foraging and habitat relationships of insect-gleaning birds in a Sierra Nevada mixed-conifer forest. *Condor* 87:205-216.

Aldrich, J. W. 1942. Specific relationships of the Golden and Yellow Warblers. *Auk* 59:447-449.

Ambuel, B., and S. A. Temple. 1982. Songbird populations in southern Wisconsin forests: 1954 and 1979. *Journal of Field Ornithology* 53:149-158.

American Ornithologists' Union. 1957. *A.O.U. Check-list of North American Birds,* 5th ed. Baltimore: Lord Baltimore Press.

―――. 1983. *A.O.U. Check-list of North American Birds,* 6th ed. Lawrence, Kans.: Allen Press, Inc.

Amos, E. J. R. 1991. *A Guide to the Birds of Bermuda.* Warwick, Bermuda: Corncrake.

Arnold, K. A. 1980. Rufous-capped Warbler and White-collared Seedeater from Webb County, Texas. *Bulletin of the Texas Ornithological Society* 13:27.

Arvin, J. C. 1980. The Golden-crowned Warbler: An 88-year-old 'new' species for the avifauna of the United States. *Birding* 12:10-11.

Atwood, J. L. 1992. Inferred destinations of spring migrant Common Yellowthroats based on plumage and morphology. In *Ecology and Conservation of Neotropical Migrant Landbirds,* edited by J. M. Hagan and D. W. Johnston. Washington, D.C.: Smithsonian Institution Press.

―――. 1994. Endangered small landbirds of the western United States. In *A century of avifaunal change in western North America,* edited by J. R. Jehl Jr., and N. K. Johnson. Studies in Avian Biology no. 15.

Austen, M. J. W., M. D. Cadman, and R. D. James. 1994. *Ontario*

Birds at Risk: Status and Conservation Needs. Don Mills: Federation of Ontario Naturalists and Port Rowan: Long Point Bird Observatory.

Bain, M. 1996. A mystery warbler in southern Ontario. *Birders Journal* 5:134–135.

Baird, J. 1958. Yellow-throated Warblers collected in sycamores along the Delaware River in New Jersey. Urner Ornithology Club Field Observer 7:1-3.

_____. 1967. Arrested molt in Tennessee Warblers. *Bird-Banding* 36(3):169-179.

Baltz, M. E. 1994. Shiny Cowbirds (*Molothrus bonairensis*) on North Andros Island, Bahamas. *El Pitirre* 7:4.

Bangs, O. 1900. Notes on a collection of Bahama birds. *Auk* 17: 283-293.

_____. 1918. A new race of the Black-throated Green Warbler. *Proceedings of the New England Zoological Club* 6:93-94.

_____. 1925. The history and characters of *Vermivora crissalis* (Salvin and Godman). *Auk* 42:251-253.

Banks, R. C., and J. Baird. 1978. A new hybrid warbler combination, Yellow-rumped (*D. coronata*) × Bay-breasted (*D. castanea*). *Wilson Bulletin* 90:143-144.

Bankwitz, K. G., and W. L. Thompson. 1979. Song characteristics of the Yellow Warbler. *Wilson Bulletin* 91:533-550.

Barber, R. D. 1985. A recent record of Bachman's Warbler in Florida. *Florida Field Naturalist* 13:64-66.

Barlow, C. 1899. Nesting of the Hermit Warbler in the Sierra Nevada Mountains, California. *Auk* 16:156-159.

Barrowclough, G. F. 1980. Genetic and phenotypic differentiation in a wood warbler (Genus *Dendroica*) hybrid zone. *Auk* 7:655-668.

Beatty, H. A. 1943. Records and notes from St. Croix, Virgin Islands. *Auk* 60:110-111.

Behle, William H. 1950. Clines in the yellow-throats of western North America. *Condor* 52:193-219.

_____. 1985. *Utah birds: geographical distribution and systematics*. Occasional Publication No. 5, Utah Museum of Natural History.

Behle, W. H., and J. W. Aldrich. 1947. Description of a new yellowthroat (*Geothlypis trichas*) from the northern Rocky Mountain-Great Plains region. Proceedings of the Biological Society of Washington 60:69-72.

Bennett, S. E. 1980. Interspecific competition and the niche of the American Redstart (*Setophaga ruticilla*) in wintering and breeding communities. In *Migrant Birds in the Neotropics: Ecology, Behavior, Distribution and Conservation*, edited by A.

Keast and E. S. Morton. Washington, D.C.: Smithsonian Institution Press.

Benzinger, J. 1994a. Hemlock decline and breeding birds I. Hemlock Ecology. *Records of New Jersey Birds* 20:2–12.

_____. 1994b. Hemlock decline and breeding birds II. Effects of Habitat Change. *Records of New Jersey Birds* 34–51.

Bermingham, E., E. S. Rohwer, S. Freeman, and C. Wood. 1992. Vicariance biogeography in the Pleistocene and speciation in North American wood warblers: a test of Mengel's model. Proceedings of the National Academy of Sciences USA 89:6624-6628.

Binford, L. C. 1971. Identification of Northern and Louisiana waterthrushes. *California Birds* 2:1-10.

Black, C. P. 1975. The ecology and energetics of the northern Black-throated Blue Warbler *(Dendroica caerulescens caerulescens)*. Ph.D. dissertation, Dartmouth College.

Blake, C. H. 1954. Leg color of Blackpoll and Bay-breasted Warblers. *Bird-Banding* 25:16.

_____. 1962. Wing length of Yellow-breasted Chat. *Bird-Banding* 33:43.

_____. 1969. Notes on the Common Yellowthroat. *EBBA News* 32:45.

Blake, C. H., and J. M. Cadbury. 1969. An old warbler. *Bird-Banding* 40:255.

Blake, E. R. 1949. The nest of the Colima Warbler in Texas. *Wilson Bulletin* 61:65–67.

Bledsoe, A. H. 1988. A hybrid *Oporornis philadelphia* × *Geothlypis trichas*, with comments on the taxonomic interpretation and evolutionary significance of intergeneric hybridization. *Wilson Bulletin* 100:1-8.

Boertmann, D. 1994. An annotated checklist to the birds of Greenland. *Bioscience* 38:51-54.

Bohlen, H. D. 1989. *The Birds of Illinois*. Bloomington and Indianapolis: University of Indiana Press.

Bonhote, J. L. 1903. On a collection of birds from the northern islands of the Bahama group. *Ibis* (8th Series) 3: 273-315.

Borror, D. J. 1967. Song of the yellowthroat. *Living Bird* 6:141-161.

Bradley, R. A. 1980. Avifauna of the Palos Verdes Peninsula, California. *Western Birds* 11:1-24.

Bradshaw, C. 1992. Mystery photographs. *British Birds* 85:647-649.

Braun, M. J., D. D. Braun, and S. B. Terrill. 1986. Winter records of the Golden-cheeked Warbler *(Dendroica chrysoparia)* from Mexico. *American Birds* 40:564-566.

Brauning, D. W. 1992. *Atlas of Breeding Birds in Pennsylvania.* Pittsburgh: University of Pittsburgh.

Brewer, R., G. A. McPeek, and R. J. Adams. 1991. The Atlas of Breeding Birds of Michigan. Michigan state University Press.

Brewster, W. 1889. Descriptions of supposed new birds from western North America and Mexico. *Auk* 6:85–98.

———. 1891. Notes on Bachman's Warbler *(Helminthophila bachmani). Auk* 8:149-157.

———. 1902. Birds of the Cape region of Lower California. *Bulletin of the Museum of Comparative Zoology* 41, no. 1

Briskie, J. V. 1995. Nesting biology of the Yellow Warbler at the northern limit of its range. *Journal of Field Ornithology.* 66:531-543.

Brodkorb, P. 1934. A hybrid in the genus *Dendroica. Auk* 51:243.

Brown, R. E., and J. G. Dickson. 1994. Swainson's Warbler *(Limnothylpis swainsonii).* No. 126 in *The Birds of North America,* edited by A. Poole and F. Gill. Philadelphia: Academy of Natural Sciences; Washington, D.C.: American Ornithologists' Union.

Browning, M. R. 1978. An evaluation of the new species and subspecies proposed in Oberholser's *Bird Life of Texas. Proceedings of the Biological Society of Washington* 91:85-122.

———. 1994. A taxonomic review of *Dendroica petechia* (Yellow Warbler). *Proceedings of the Biological Society of Washington* 107(1):27-51.

Brush, A. K., and N. K. Johnson. 1976. The evolution of color differences between Nashville and Virginia's Warblers. *Condor* 78:412-414.

Burleigh, T. D. 1944a. The bird life of the Gulf Coast region of Mississippi. Lousiana State University Museum of Zoology, Occasional Papers 20:329–490.

———. 1944b. Description of a new hybrid warbler. *Auk* 61:291-293.

Burleigh, T. D., and H. S. Peters. 1948. Geographical variation in Newfoundland birds. *Proceedings of the Biological Society of Washington* 61:119.

Burtt, E. H., and J. P. Hailman 1978. Head-scratching among North American wood-warblers (Parulidae). *Ibis* 120:153-170.

Busby, D. G., and S. G. Sealy. 1979. Feeding ecology of a population of nesting Yellow Warblers. *Canadian Field-Naturalist* 57:1760-1681.

Buskirk, W. H. 1972. Ecology of bird flocks in a tropical forest. Ph.D. dissertation, University of California, Davis.

Carlson, C. W. 1981. The Sutton's Warbler — a critical review and summation of current data. *Atlantic Naturalist* 34:1-11.

Chamberlain, E. B. 1958. Bachman's Warbler in South Carolina. *Chat* 22:73–74, 77.

Chapman, F. M. 1890. On the eastern forms of *Geothlypis trichas. Auk* 7:9-14.

_____. 1925. The relationships and distribution of the warblers of the genus *Compsothlypis*: a contribution to the study of the origin of Andean bird life. *Auk* 42:193-208.

Chappell, C. B., and B. J. Ringer. 1983. Status of the Hermit Warbler in Washington. *Western Birds* 14:185-196.

Chipley, R. M. 1980. Nonbreeding ecology of the Blackburnian Warbler. In *Migrant birds in the Neotropics,* edited by A. Keast and E. S. Morton. Washington, D.C.: Smithsonian Institution Press.

Clark, K. L., and R. J. Robertson. 1981. Cowbird parasitism and evolution of anti-parasite and anti-predator strategies in the Yellow Warbler. *Wilson Bulletin* 93: 249-258.

Clench, M. H. 1973. The fall migration route of Kirtland's Warbler. *Wilson Bulletin* 85:417-428.

Collins, S. L. 1983. Geographic variation in the habitat structure of the Black-throated Green Warbler *(Dendroica virens). Auk* 100:382-389.

Confer, J. L. 1992. Golden-winged Warbler. No. 20 in *The Birds of North America,* edited by A. Poole and F. Gill. Philadelphia: Academy of Natural Sciences; Washington, D.C.: American Ornithologists' Union.

Confer, J. L., and K. Knapp. 1979. The changing populations of Blue-winged and Golden-winged warblers in Tompkins County and their habitat selection. *Kingbird* 29:8–14.

_____. 1981. Golden-winged Warblers and Blue-winged Warblers: the relative success of a habitat specialist and a generalist. *Auk* 98:108-114.

Contreras-Balderas, A. J., J. A. Garcia-Salas, and J. I. Gonzalez-Rojas. 1995. Additional records of owls and wood warblers from Mexico. *Wilson Bulletin* 107:765.

Cox, G. W. 1960. A life history of the Mourning Warbler. *Wilson Bulletin* 72:5-28.

Cox, G. W. 1973. Hybridization between Mourning and Mac-Gillivray's Warblers. *Auk* 90:190-191.

Craig, J. 1984. Comparative foraging ecology of Louisiana and Northern waterthrushes. *Wilson Bulletin* 96:173-183.

_____. 1985. Comparative habitat uses by Louisiana and Northern waterthrushes. *Wilson Bulletin* 97:347-355.

_____. 1987. Divergent prey selection in the two species of waterthrushes, *Seiurus. Auk* 104:180-187.

Crook, J. R. 1984. Song variation and species discrimination in Blue-winged Warblers. *Wilson Bulletin* 96: 91-99.

Curson, J. 1992. Identification of Connecticut, Mourning and MacGillivray's Warblers in female and immature plumages. *Birders Journal* 1:275-278.

———. 1993. Identification of Northern and Louisiana waterthrushes. *Birders Journal* 2:126-130.

Curson, J., D. Quinn, and D. Beadle. 1994. *Warblers of the Americas.* Boston: Houghton Mifflin.

DellaSala, D. A. 1986. Polygyny in the Yellow Warbler. *Wilson Bulletin* 98: 152-154.

Dennis, J. V. 1958. Some aspects of the breeding ecology of the Yellow-breasted Chat. *Bird-Banding* 39:169-183.

———. 1967. Fall departure of the Yellow-breasted Chat (*Icteria virens*) in eastern North America. *Bird-Banding* 38:130-135.

DeSante, D. F., and D. G. Ainley. 1980. *The Avifauna of the South Farallon Islands, California.* The Cooper Ornithological Society. Lawrence, Kans.: Allen Press, Inc.

Dick, J. A., and R. D. James. 1996. Rufous crown feathers on adult male Tennessee Warblers. *Wilson Bulletin* 108: 181-182.

Dickey, D. R., and A. J. van Rossem. 1926. A southern race of the Fan-tailed Warbler. *Condor* 28:270-271.

———. 1938. The birds of El Salvador. *Field Museum of Natural History Publication,* Zoology Series 23:1-609.

Dobkin, D. S. 1994. Conservation and management of Neotropical migrants in the Northern Great Plains. Moscow: University of Idaho Press.

Dodrill, J. W., and R. G. Gilmore. 1978. Land birds in the stomachs of Tiger Sharks. *Auk* 95:585-586.

Doepker, R. V., R. D. Earle, and J. J. Ozoga. 1992. Characteristics of Blackburnian Warbler, *Dendroica fusca,* breeding habitat in upper Michigan. *Canadian Field Naturalist* 106:366–371.

Doherty, P. 1992. Golden-winged Warbler: new to the western Palearctic. *British Birds* 85:595-600.

Ducharme, C., and J. Lamontagne. 1992. Un cas d'hybridation chez les parulines? *Dendroica caerulescens* × *Dendroica petechia. Québec Oiseaux* 4:1-6.

Duncan, R. A., and W. E. Weber. 1985. The Yellow Warbler: a diurnal circum-Gulf fall migrant. *Florida Field Naturalist* 13:20-22.

Dwight, J. 1899. Sequence of plumages; illustrated by the Myrtle Warbler (*Dendroica coronata*) and the Yellow-breasted Chat (*Icteria virens*). *Auk* 16:217–220.

Eaton, S. W. 1953. Wood warblers wintering in Cuba. *Wilson Bulletin* 63:169-174.

———. 1957a. A life history study of *Seiurus noveboracensis* (with notes on *Seiurus aurocapillus* and the species of *Seiurus* compared). Science Studies St. Bonaventure University 19:7-36.

_____. 1957b. Variation in *Seiurus noveboracensis*. *Auk* 74:229-239.

_____. 1958. A life history study of the Louisiana Waterthrush. *Wilson Bulletin* 70:211-236.

_____. 1995. Northern Waterthrush (*Seiurus noveboracensis*). No. 182 in *The Birds of North America*, in *The Birds of North America*, edited by A. Poole and F. Gill. Philadelphia: Academy of Natural Sciences; Washington, D.C.: American Ornithologists' Union.

Eaton, S. W., P. D. O'Connor, M. B. Osterhaus, and B. Z. Anicete. 1963. Some osteological adaptations in Parulidae. Pages 71–83 in *Proceedings of the XIII International Ornithological Congress*, edited by C. G. Sibley. American Ornithologists' Union.

Eisenmann, E. 1962. On the genus *"Chamaethlypis"* and its supposed relationship to *Icteria*. *Auk* 79:265-267.

Elder, D. H. 1991. Breeding habitat of the Connecticut Warbler in the Rainy River District. *Ontario Birds* 9:84-86.

Ely, C. A. 1962. The birds of southeastern Coahuila, Mexico. *Condor* 64:34-39.

Embody, G. S. 1907. Bachman's Warbler breeding in Logan County, Kentucky. *Auk* 24:41-42.

Engels, T. M., and C. W. Sexton. 1994. Negative correlation of Blue Jays and Golden-cheeked Warblers near urbanizing area. *Conservation Biology* 8:286-290.

Enright, S. D. 1995. Magnolia Warbler in Scilly: new to Britain and Ireland. *British Birds* 88:107-108.

Evans Ogden, L. J., and B. J. Stutchbury. 1994. Hooded Warbler (*Wilsonia citrina*). No. 110 in *The Birds of North America*, edited by A. Poole and F. Gill. Philadelphia: Academy of Natural Sciences; Washington, D.C.: American Ornithologists' Union.

_____. 1996. Constraints on double brooding in a neotropical migrant, the Hooded Warbler. *Condor* 98:736–744.

Ewert, D. N., and W. E. Lanyon. 1970. The first prebasic molt of the Common Yellowthroat (Parulidae). *Auk* 87:362-363.

Ficken, M. S. 1962. Agonistic behavior and territory in the American Redstart. *Auk* 62:189-206.

_____. 1963. Courtship of the American Redstart. *Auk* 80:307-317.

Ficken, M. S., and R. W. Ficken. 1962. Some aberrant characters of the Yellow-breasted Chat. *Auk* 79:718-719.

_____. 1965. Comparative ethology of the Chestnut-sided Warbler, Yellow Warbler, and American Redstart. *Wilson Bulletin* 77:363-375.

_____. 1966. Notes on mate and habitat selection in the Yellow Warbler. *Wilson Bulletin* 78:232-233.

_____. 1967. Age-specific differences in the breeding behavior and ecology of the American Redstart. *Wilson Bulletin* 79:188-199.

_____. 1968a. Ecology of Blue-winged Warblers and Golden-winged Warblers, and some other *Vermivora*. *American Midland Naturalist* 79:311-319.

_____. 1968b. Courtship of Blue-winged Warblers, Golden-winged Warblers and their hybrids. *Wilson Bulletin* 80:161-172.

_____. 1968c. Reproductive isolating mechanisms in the Blue-winged Warbler–Golden-winged Warbler complex. *Evolution* 22:166-179.

_____. 1968d. Singing behavior of Blue-winged and Golden-winged warblers and their hybrids. *Behavior* 28:149-181.

_____. 1968e. Territorial relationships of Blue-winged Warblers, Golden-winged Warblers, and their hybrids. *Wilson Bulletin* 80:442-451.

Ficken, R. W., M. S. Ficken, and D. H. Morse. 1968. Competition and character displacement in two sympatric pine-dwelling warblers (*Dendroica*, Parulidae). *Evolution* 22:307-314.

Foster, M. S. 1967a. Pterylography and age determination in Orange-crowned Warbler. *Condor* 69:1-12.

_____. 1967b. Molt cycles of the Orange-crowned Warbler. *Condor* 69:169-200.

Foy, R. W. 1974a. Aging and sexing American Redstarts in fall. *EBBA News* 37:43-44.

_____. 1974b. Aging and sexing American Redstarts in fall: a note of caution. *EBBA News* 37:128.

Franzreb, K. E., and B. J. Franzreb. 1983. Foraging ecology of the Red-faced Warbler during the breeding season. *Western Birds* 14:31-38.

Friedmann, H., and L. F. Kiff. 1985. The parasitic cowbirds and their hosts. *Proceedings of the Western Foundation of Vertebrate Zoology* vol. 2, no. 4.

Gartshore, M. E. 1988. A summary of the breeding status of Hooded Warbler in Ontario. *Ontario Birds* 6:85-89.

George, W. G. 1962. The classification of the Olive Warbler, *Peucedramus taeniatus*. *American Museum Novitates*, 2103:1-41.

Gill, F. B. 1980. Historical aspects of hybridization between Blue-winged and Golden-winged warblers. *Auk* 97:1-18.

_____. 1987. Allozymes and genetic similarity of Blue-winged and Golden-winged warblers. *Auk* 104:444-449.

Gill, F. B., and B. G. Murray Jr. 1972a. Discrimination behavior and hybridization of the Blue-winged and Golden-winged warblers. *Evolution* 26:282-293.

_____. 1972b. Song variation in sympatric Blue-winged and Golden-winged warblers. *Auk* 89:625-643.

Gochfield, M. 1974. Status of the genus *Vermivora* (Aves Parulidae) in the Greater Antilles with new records from Jamaica and Puerto Rico. *Caribbean Journal of Science* 14:177–181.

Godfrey, W. E. 1951. Comments on the races of the Myrtle Warbler. *Canadian Field Naturalist* 65:166-167.

Goodman, S. M. 1982. Age and sexual morphological variation in the Kirtland's Warbler (*Dendroica kirtlandii*). *Jack-Pine Warbler* 60:144-147.

Graber, J. W., R. R. Graber, and E. L. Kirk. 1983. *Illinois Birds: Wood Warblers*. Biological Notes No. 118. State of Illinois, Department of Energy and Natural Resources.

Graves, G. R. 1988. Evaluation of *Vermivora* × *Oporornis* hybrid wood-warblers. *Wilson Bulletin* 100: 285–289.

_____. 1992. A case of aggregated nest placement and probably polygyny in the Swainson's Warbler. *Wilson Bulletin* 104:370-373.

_____. 1993. A new intergeneric wood warbler hybrid (*Parula americana* × *Dendroica coronata*; Aves: Fringillidae). *Proceedings of the Biological Society of Washington* 106:402-409.

_____. 1996a. Censusing wintering populations of Swainson's Warblers: surveys in the Blue Mountains of Jamaica. *Wilson Bulletin* 108:94-103.

_____. 1996b. Hybrid wood warblers, *Dendroica striata* × *Dendroica castanea* (Aves: Fringillidae: Tribe Parulini) and the diagnostic predictability of avian hybrid phenotypes. *Proceedings of the Biological Society of Washington* 109(2):373-390.

Graves, G. R., M. A. Patten, and J. L. Dunnl. 1996. Comments on a probable gynandromorphic Black-throated Blue Warbler. *Wilson Bulletin* 108:178-180.

Greenberg, R. 1984. The winter exploitation systems of Bay-breasted and Chestnut-sided warblers in Panama. *University of California Publications in Zoology* 116:1-107.

_____. 1987a. Development of dead-leaf foraging in a tropical migrant warbler. *Ecology* 68:130-141.

_____. 1987b. Seasonal foraging specialization in the Worm-eating Warbler. *Condor* 89:158-168.

Grinnell, J. 1905. Status of the Townsend's Warbler in California. *Condor* 7:52-53.

Grinnell, J., and C. C. Lamb. 1927. New bird records from lower California. *Condor* 29:124-126.

Gunn, W. W. H., and A. M. Crocker. 1951. Analysis of unusual bird migration in North America during the storm of April 4-7, 1947. *Auk* 68:139-163.

Hailman, J. 1968. A male MacGillivray's-like *Oporornis* warbler banded at Brigantine, New Jersey, in June. *Bird-Banding* 39:316-317.

Hall, G. A. 1979. Hybridization between Mourning and Mac-Gillivray's Warblers. *Bird-Banding* 50:101-107.

_____. 1994. Magnolia Warbler *(Dendroica magnolia)*. No. 136 in *The Birds of North America,* edited by A. Poole and F. Gill. Philadelphia: Academy of Natural Sciences; Washington, D.C.: American Ornithologists' Union.

_____. 1996. Yellow-throated Warbler *(Dendroica dominica)*. No. 223 in *The Birds of North America,* edited by A. Poole and F. Gill. Philadelphia: Academy of Natural Sciences; Washington, D.C.: American Ornithologists' Union.

Hamel, P. B. 1986. *Bachman's Warbler: A Species in Peril.* Washington, D.C.: Smithsonian Institution Press.

_____. 1995. Bachman's Warbler *(Vermivora bachmanii)*. No. 150 in *The Birds of North America,* edited by A. Poole and F. Gill. Philadelphia: Academy of Natural Sciences; Washington, D.C.: American Ornithologists' Union.

Hamel, P. B., and R. G. Hooper. 1979. Bachman's Warbler—the most critically endangered. *Proceedings of First South Carolina Endangered Species Symposium, 1976.*

Hamel, P. B., and S. A. Gauthreaux Jr. 1982. The field identification of Bachman's Warbler *(Vermivora bachmanii Audubon)*. *American Birds* 36:235-240.

Hann, H. W. 1937. Life history of the Ovenbird in southern Michigan. *Wilson Bulletin* 48:145-237.

Hardy, J. W., and T. Webber. 1975. A critical list of type specimens of birds in the Moore Laboratory of Zoology at Occidental College. Contributions in Science no. 273. Natural History Museum of Los Angeles County.

Harris, A. 1990. Palm Warblers use upland cutovers as nesting habitat in northwestern Ontario. *Ontario Birds* 8:84-87.

Harris, B. K. 1964. First United States record for the Slate-throated Redstart, and first specimens of various species for New Mexico. *Auk* 81:227-229.

Harshman, J. 1994. Reweaving the tapestry: what can we learn from Sibley and Ahlquist (1990)? *Auk* 111:377–388.

Heathcote, D. R., and K. Kaufman. 1985. Crescent-chested Warbler in Arizona, a first for the United States. *American Birds* 39:9-11.

Hellmayr, C. E. 1935. Catalogue of birds of the Americas. Field Museum of Natural History, Zoological Series 13, part 8:1-541.

Highsmith, R. T. 1989. The singing behavior of Golden-winged Warblers. *Wilson Bulletin* 101: 36-50.

Hix, G. E. 1916. Louisiana Waterthrush eating fish. *Copeia* 30:31.

Hobson, K. A., and S. G. Sealy. 1972. Female song in the Yellow Warbler. *Condor* 92:259-261.

Holmes, R. T. 1986. Foraging patterns of forest birds: male-female differences. *Wilson Bulletin* 98:196–213.

_____. 1994. Black-throated Blue Warbler *(Dendroica caerulescens)*. No. 87 in *The Birds of North America,* edited by A. Poole and F. Gill. Philadelphia: Academy of Natural Sciences; Washington, D.C.: American Ornithologists' Union.

Holmes, R. T, T. W. Sherry, and S. E. Bennett. 1978. Diurnal and individual variability in the foraging behavior of American Redstarts *(Setophaga ruticilla)*. *Oecologia* 36:171-179.

Holmes, R. T., T. W. Sherry, and L. Reitsma. 1989. Population structure, territoriality and the overwinter survival of two migrant warblers in Jamaica. *Condor* 91:545–561.

Holmes, R. T., T. W Sherry, P. P. Marra, and K. E. Petit. 1992. Multiple brooding and productivity of a Neotropical migrant, the Black-throated Blue Warbler *(Dendroica caerulescens)* in an unfragmented temperate forest. *Auk* 109:321–333.

Hooper, R. G., and P. B. Hamel. 1977. Nesting habitat of Bachman's Warbler — a review. *Wilson Bulletin* 89:373-379.

Howard, D. V. 1968. Criteria for ageing and sexing Bay-breasted Warbler in fall. *Bird-Banding* 39:132.

Howell, A. H. 1930. Description of a new subspecies of the Prairie Warbler with remarks on two other unrecognized Florida races. *Auk* 47:41-43.

Howell, S. W., and S. Webb. 1992. Noteworthy bird observations from Baja California, Mexico. Western Birds 23:153–163.

_____. 1995. *A Guide to The Birds of Mexico and Northern Central America.* Oxford: Oxford University Press.

Hubbard, J. P. 1965. Migration of the Black-throated Blue Warbler in southern Michigan. *Jack-Pine Warbler* 43: 162-163.

_____. 1969. The relationships and evolution of the *Dendroica coronata* complex. *Auk* 86:393-432.

_____. 1970. Geographical variation in the *Dendroica coronata* complex. *Wilson Bulletin* 82:355-369.

Hunt, P. D. 1996. Habitat selection by American Redstarts along a succession gradient in northern hardwoods forest: evaluation of habitat quality. *Auk* 113:875-888.

Hurley, G. F., and J. W. Jones II. 1983. A presumed mixed Baybreast × Blackburnian meeting in West Virginia. *Redstart* 50:108-111.

Hutto, R. L. 1981. Seasonal variation in the foraging behavior of some migratory wood warblers. *Auk* 98:765-777.

Jackson, W. M., C. S. Wood, and S. Rohwer. 1992. Age-specific plumage characters and annual molt schedules of Hermit Warblers and Townsend's Warblers. *Condor* 94:490-501.

Jaramillo, A. 1995. Townsend's and Hermit warblers in eastern Canada. *Birders Journal* 4:232–236.

Jewett, S. G. 1944. Hybridization of Hermit and Townsend's warblers. *Condor* 46:23-24.

Johnson, K. W., J. E. Johnson, R. O. Albert, and T. R. Albert. 1988. Sightings of Golden-cheeked Warblers *(Dendroica chrysoparia)* in northeastern Mexico. *Wilson Bulletin* 100:130-131.

Johnson, N. K. 1976. Breeding distribution of Nashville and Virginia's Warblers. *Auk* 93:219-230.

Johnston, D. W. 1976. Races of Palm Warbler killed at a Florida TV tower. *Florida Field Naturalist* 4:22-24.

Kahl, R. B., T. S. Baskett, J. A. Ellis, and J. N. Burroughs. 1985. Characteristics of summer habitats of selected non-game birds in Missouri. University of Missouri, Columbia Agric. Exp. Sta. Res. Bull. 1056.

Kaufman, K. 1979a. Comments on the Peninsular Yellowthroat. *Continental Birdlife* 1:38-42.

_____. 1979b. Identifying "Myrtle" and "Audubon's" warblers out of breeding plumage. *Continental Birdlife* 1:89-92.

_____. 1984. Notes from the Bahamas: identification of two potential Florida vagrants. *Birding* 16:112-114.

_____. 1990a. *Advanced Birding*. Boston: Houghton Mifflin.

_____. 1990b. Answers to June photo quiz. *Birding* 22:194-197.

_____. 1991. Yellow Warbler and its ID contenders. *American Birds* 45:167-170.

King, W. B., N. F. R. Snyder, M. Segnestan, and J. Grantham. 1979. Noteworthy ornithological records from Abaco, Bahamas. *American Birds* 33:746-748.

Kirkconnell, A., G. E. Wallace, and O. H. Garrido. 1996. Notes on the status and behavior of the Swainson's Warbler in Cuba. *Wilson Bulletin* 108:175-178.

Kirkconnell, A., and O. H. Garrido. 1996. La Candelita *Setophaga ruticilla* (Aves: Parulidae) nidificando en Cuba. *El Pitirre* 9:5.

Klein, N. K., and W. M. Brown. 1994. Intraspecific molecular phylogeny in the Yellow Warbler *(Dendroica petechia)* and implications for avian biogeography in the West Indies. *Evolution* 48:1914-1932.

Kowalski, M. P. 1983. Identifying Mourning and MacGillivray's warblers: geographical variation in the MacGillivray's Warbler as a source of error. *North American Bird Bander* 8:56-57.

_____. 1986. Weights and measurements of Prothonotary Warblers from southern Indiana, with a method of ageing males. *North American Bird Bander* 11:129-131.

Kricher, J. C. 1995. Black-and-white Warbler *(Mniotilta varia)* No. 158 in *The Birds of North America,* edited by A. Poole and F. Gill. Philadelphia: Academy of Natural Sciences; Washington, D.C.: American Ornithologists' Union.

Kroll, J. C. 1980. Habitat requirements of the Golden-cheeked Warbler: management implications. *Journal of Range Management* 33:60-65.

Kroodsma, D. E., R. C. Bereson, B. E. Byers, and E. Minear. 1989. Use of song types by the Chestnut-sided Warbler: evidence for both intra- and inter-sexual functions. *Canadian Journal of Zoology* 67: 447–456.

Lack, D. 1976. *Island Biology, Illustrated by the Landbirds of Jamaica.* Oxford: Blackwell Scientific Publications.

Lamb, C. C. 1925. The Socorro Warbler added to the A.O.U. checklist. *Condor* 27:36-37.

Lambert, A. B., and R. B. H. Smith. 1984. The status and distribution of the Prairie Warbler in Ontario. *Ontario Birds* 2:99-115.

Langham, J. M. 1980. Golden-crowned Warbler in Texas: A documented record for the ABA Checklist area. *Birding* 12:8-9.

Lanning, D. V., J. T. Marshall Jr., and J. T. Shiflett. 1990. Range and habitat of the Colima Warbler. *Wilson Bulletin* 102:1-13.

Lanyon, W. E. 1966. Melanism in the Ovenbird. *Wilson Bulletin* 78:474-475.

Lanyon, W. E., and J. Bull. 1967. Identification of Connecticut, Mourning and MacGillivray's Warblers. *Bird-Banding* 38:187-194.

LaRue, C. T. 1994. *Birds of Northern Black Mesa, Navajo County, Arizona.* Provo, Utah: Brigham Young University.

Lasley, G. W., D. A. Easterla, C. W. Sexton, and D. A. Bartol. 1982. Documentation of the Red-faced Warbler *(Cardellina rubrifrons)* in Texas and review of its status in Texas and adjacent areas. *Bulletin of the Texas Ornithological Society* 15:8-14.

Lawrence, L. de K. 1948. Comparative study of nesting behavior of Chestnut-sided and Nashville Warblers. *Auk* 65:204-219.

_____. 1953. Notes on the nesting behavior of the Blackburnian Warbler. *Wilson Bulletin* 65:135–144.

Leck, C. 1983. Black-throated Gray Warbler in the northeast. *Records of New Jersey Birds* 9(2):22-23.

Lefebvre, G., B. Poulin, and R. McNeil. 1992. Abundance, feeding behavior, and body condition of Neoarctic warblers wintering in Venezuela mangroves. *Wilson Bulletin* 104:400-412.

Lehman, P. 1987. Immature Blackburnian and Cerulean Warblers: a cautionary note. *Birding* 19:22-23.

Lein, M. R. 1978. Song variation in a population of Chestnut-sided Warblers *(Dendroica pensylvanica)*: its nature and suggested significance. *Canadian Journal of Zoology* 56:1266-1283.

_____. 1980. Display behavior of Ovenbirds *(Seiurus aurocapillus)* I. Non-song vocalizations. *Wilson Bulletin* 92:312–329.

Lemon, R. E., R. Cotter, R. C. MacNally, and S. Monette. 1985. Song repertoires and song sharing by American Redstarts. *Condor* 87:457-470.

Lentz, J. E. 1993. Breeding birds of four isolated mountains in southern California. *Western Birds* 24:201–234.

Levy, S. H. 1962. The first record of the Fan-tailed Warbler in the United States. *Auk* 79:119-120.

Lewis, T. J., D. G. Ainley, D. Greenberg, and R. Greenberg. 1974. A Golden-cheeked Warbler on the Farallon Islands. *Auk* 91:411-412.

Lowery, G. H., Jr., and B. L. Monroe Jr. 1968. Family Parulidae in *Check-list of Birds of the World,* vol. 14, R. A. Paynter Jr. Cambridge, Mass.: Museum of Comparative Zoology.

Lucas, F. A. 1894. The tongue of the Cape May Warbler. *Auk* 11:141-144.

Lynch, J. F., E. S. Morton, and M. E. van de Voort. 1985. Habitat segregation between the sexes of wintering Hooded Warblers *(Wilsonia citrina). Auk* 102:714-721.

Lynch, J. M. 1981. Status of the Cerulean Warbler in the Roanoke river basin of North Carolina. *Chat* 45:29-35.

MacArthur, R. H. 1958. Population ecology of some warblers of northeastern coniferous forests. *Ecology* 39:599-619.

Mactavish, B. 1996. Hybrid Hermit × Townsend's Warbler in Newfoundland. *Birders Journal* 5:33–34.

Marshall, J., and R. P. Balda. 1974. The breeding ecology of the Painted Redstart. *Condor* 76:89-101.

Marshall, J. T., Jr. 1957. Birds of pine-oak woodland in southern Arizona and adjacent Mexico. *Pacific Coast Avifauna* no. 32.

Martin, T. E., and P. M. Barber. 1995. Red-faced Warbler *(Cardellina rubrifrons).* No. 152 in *The Birds of North America,* edited by A. Poole and F. Gill. Philadelphia: Academy of Natural Sciences; Washington, D.C.: American Ornithologists' Union.

Mason, C. R. 1976. Cape May Warblers in Middle America. *Auk* 93:167-169.

Mayfield, H. F. 1960. *The Kirtland's Warbler.* Bloomfield Hills, Mich.: Cranbrook Institute of Science.

_____. 1972. Winter habitat of Kirtland's Warbler. *Wilson Bulletin* 84:347-349.

_____. 1992. Kirtland's Warbler. No. 19 in *The Birds of North America,* edited by A. Poole and F. Gill. Philadelphia: Academy of Natural Sciences; Washington, D.C.: American Ornithologists' Union.

Mayr, E., and L. L. Short Jr. 1970 Species taxa of North American birds. *Publications of the Nuttall Ornithology Club* no. 9.

McCabe, T. T., and A. H. Miller 1933. Geographic variation in the Northern Water-thrushes. *Condor* 35:192-197.

McCracken, J. D. 1991. Status report on the Louisiana Waterthrush in Canada. Ottawa: Committee on the Status of Endangered Wildlife in Canada.

McLaren, I. A. 1981. *The Birds of Sable Island, Nova Scotia.* Nova Scotian Institute of Science.

McNair, D. B., and W. Post. 1993. Autumn migration route of Blackpoll Warblers: evidence from southeastern North America. *Journal of Field Ornithology* 64:417-425.

McNicholl, M. K. 1977. Measurements of Wilson's Warblers in Alberta. *North American Bird Bander* 2(3):108-109.

_____. 1980. Songs of MacGillivray's and Townsend's warblers in coastal British Columbia. *Western Birds* 11:157-159.

McWilliams, J. M. 1996. Bay-breasted Warbler *(Dendroica castanea).* No. 206 in *The Birds of North America,* edited by A. Poole and F. Gill. Philadelphia: Academy of Natural Sciences; Washington, D.C.: American Ornithologists' Union.

Meanley, B. 1966. Some observations on habitats of the Swainson's Warbler. *Living Bird* 3:151-165.

_____. 1971. Natural history of the Swainson's Warbler. *North American Fauna* 69:vi,1-90. United States Department of the Interior.

Meanley, B., and G. M. Bond. 1950. A new race of Swainson's Warbler from the Appalachian Mountains. *Proceedings of the Biological Society of Washington.* 63:191-193.

Mengel, R. M. 1964. The probable history of species formation in some northern wood warblers (Parulidae). *Living Bird* 3:9-43.

Michigan Department of Natural Resources. 1992. Michigan's bird of the Jack Pine: Kirtland's Warbler. 12 pp. [includes color plate of plumages].

Miller, A. H. 1942. Differentiation of the Oven-birds of the Rocky Mountain region. *Condor* 44:185-186.

Miller, W. D., and L. Griscom. 1925. Notes on Central American birds with descriptions of new forms. American Museum Novitates 183:1-14.

Moldenhauer, R. R. 1992. Two song populations of the Northern Parula. *Auk* 109:215-222.

Moldenhauer, R. R., and D. J. Regelski. 1996. Northern Parula *(Parula americana)*. No. 215 in *The Birds of North America*, edited by A. Poole and F. Gill. Philadelphia: Academy of Natural Sciences; Washington, D.C.: American Ornithologists' Union.

Monroe, B. L. Jr. 1968. A distributional survey of the birds of Honduras. Ornithological Monographs no. 7. American Ornithologists' Union.

Moore, F. R. 1990. Prothonotary Warblers cross the Gulf of Mexico together. *Journal of Field Ornithology* 61:285-287.

Moore, R. T. 1941. New races of flycatcher, warbler and wrens from Mexico. *Proceedings of the Biological Society of Washington*. 54:35-42.

_____. 1946. The status of *Dendroica auduboni nigrifrons* in the United States. *Auk* 63:241-242.

Morrison, M. L. 1981. The structure of western warbler assemblages: analysis of foraging and habitat selection in Oregon. *Auk* 98:578-588.

_____. 1982. The structure of western warbler assemblages: ecomorphological analiyisis of Black-throated Gray and Hermit warblers. *Auk* 99:503-513.

_____. 1983. Analysis of geographic variation in the Townsend's Warbler. *Condor* 85:385-391.

_____. 1990. Morphological and vocal variation in the Black-throated Gray Warbler in the Pacific Northwest. *Northwestern Naturalist* 71:53-58.

Morrison, M. L., and J. W. Hardy. 1983a. Hybridization between Hermit and Townsend's Warblers. *Murrelet* 64:65-72.

_____. 1983b. Vocalizations of the Black-throated Gray Warbler. *Wilson Bulletin* 95:640-643.

Morse, D. H. 1966. The context of songs in the Yellow Warbler. *Wilson Bulletin* 78:444-455.

_____. 1967a. Competitive relationships between Parula Warblers and other species during the breeding season. *Auk* 84:490-502.

_____. 1967b. The contexts of songs in the Black-throated Green and Blackburnian warblers. *Wilson Bulletin* 79:62–72.

_____. 1967c. Foraging relationships of Brown-headed Nuthatches and Pine Warblers. *Ecology* 48:94-103.

_____. 1968. A quantitative study of foraging of male and female spruce-woods warblers. *Ecology* 49:779-784.

_____. 1971. The foraging of warblers on isolated small islands. *Ecology* 52:216-228.

_____. 1974. Foraging of Pine Warblers allopatric and sympatric to Yellow-throated Warblers. *Wilson Bulletin* 86:474-477.

_____. 1977. The occupation of small islands by passerine birds. *Condor* 79:399-412.

_____. 1978. Populations of Bay-breasted and Cape May warblers during an outbreak of the spruce budworm. *Wilson Bulletin* 90:404-413.

_____. 1993. Black-throated Green Warbler *(Dendroica virens)*. No. 55 in *The Birds of North America,* edited by A. Poole and F. Gill. Philadelphia: Academy of Natural Sciences; Washington, D.C.: American Ornithologists' Union.

_____. 1994. Blackburnian Warbler *(Dendroica fusca).* No. 102 in *The Birds of North America,* edited by A. Poole and F. Gill. Philadelphia: Academy of Natural Sciences; Washington, D.C.: American Ornithologists' Union.

Morton, E. S. 1980. Adaptations to seasonal changes by migrant land birds in the Panama Canal Zone. In *Migrant Birds in the Neotropics,* edited by A. Keast and E. S. Morton. Washington, D.C.: Smithsonian Institution Press.

_____. 1989. Female Hooded Warbler plumage does not become more male like with age. *Wilson Bulletin* 101:460-462.

Mulvihill, R. S., K. C. Parkes, R. C. Leberman, and D. S. Wood. 1992. Evidence supporting a dietary basis for orange-tipped rectrices in the Cedar Waxwing. *Journal of Field Ornithology* 3:212-216.

Munson, C. R., and L. W. Adams. 1984. A record of ground nesting by the Hermit Warbler. *Wilson Bulletin* 49:27.

Murray, B. G. 1965. On the autumn migration of the Blackpoll Warbler. *Wilson Bulletin* 93:85-92.

Murray, B. G., Jr., and F. B. Gill. 1976. Behavioral interactions of Blue-winged and Golden-winged warblers. *Wilson Bulletin* 88:231-254.

Nice, M. M. 1932. Habits of the Blackburnian Warbler in Pelham, Massachusetts. *Auk* 40:92–93.

Nisbet, I. C. T. 1970. Autumn migration of the Blackpoll Warbler: evidence for long flight provided by regional survey. *Bird-Banding* 41:207-240.

Nolan, V., Jr. 1978. Ecology and behavior of the Prairie Warbler *(Dendroica discolor).* Ornithological Monographs no. 26.

Nolan, V., Jr., and R. E. Mumford. 1965. Analysis of Prairie Warblers killed in Florida during nocturnal migration. *Condor* 67:322-338.

Norris, R. A. 1952. Postjuvenal molt of tail feathers in the Pine Warbler. *Oriole* 17:29-31.

Oberholser, H. C. 1917. A new subspecies of *Geothlypis beldingi. Condor* 19:182-184.

———. 1921. A revision of the races of *Dendroica auduboni*. *Ohio Journal of Science* 21(7):240-248.

———. 1930. Notes on a collection of birds from Arizona and New Mexico. *Scientific Publications of the Cleveland Museum of Natural Science* 1:83-124.

Oliarnyk, and Robertson. 1996. Breeding behavior and reproductive success of Cerulean Warblers in southeastern Ontario. *Wilson Bulletin* 108:673–684.

Olson, S. L. 1980. Geographic variation in the Yellow Warblers (*Dendroica petechia*: Parulidae) of the Pacific Coast of Middle and South America. *Proceedings of the Biological Society of Washington* 93:473-480.

Osterhaus, M. B. 1962. Adaptive modifications in the leg structure of some North American warblers. *American Midland Naturalist* 68:474-486.

Ouellet, H. 1967. The distribution of the Cerulean Warbler in the province of Quebec. *Auk* 84:272-274.

Parker, T. A. III. 1994. Habitat, behavior and spring migration of Cerulean Warbler in Belize. *American Birds* 48:70-75.

Parkes, K. C. 1951. The genetics of the Golden-winged × Blue-winged warbler complex. *Wilson Bulletin* 63:5-15.

———. 1953. The Yellow-throated Warbler in New York. *Kingbird* 3:4-6.

———. 1954. Notes on some birds of the Adirondack and Catskill Mountains, New York. *Annals of the Carnegie Museum* 33:149-178.

———. 1961. Taxonomic relationships among the American redstarts. *Wilson Bulletin* 73:374-379.

———. 1968. Some bird records from western Pennsylvania. *Wilson Bulletin* 80:100-102.

———. 1978. Still another parulid intergeneric hybrid (*Mniotilta* × *Dendroica*) and its taxonomic and evolutionary implications. *Auk* 95:682-690.

———. 1979. Plumage variation in female Black-throated Blue Warblers. *Continental Birdlife* 1:133-135.

———. 1983. Three additional hybrid combinations in North American Birds. Abstract of paper presented at the 101st stated meeting of the American Ornithologists' Union, New York, N.Y.

———. 1985. Audubon's mystery birds. *Natural History* 94(4):88-92.

———. 1991. Family tree: tracing the genealogy of Brewster's and Lawrence's warblers. *Birder's World* 5:34-37.

Parkes, K. C., and R. W. Dickerman. 1967. A new subspecies of Mangrove Warbler (*Dendroica petechia*) from Mexico. *Annals of the Carnegie Museum* 39:85-89.

Pashley, D. N. 1988. Warblers of the West Indies. I. The Virgin Islands. *Caribbean Journal of Science* 24:11–22.

———. 1990. Warblers of the West Indies. II. The Western Caribbean. *Caribbean Journal of Science* 24:112–126.

Pashley, D. N., and R. B. Hamilton. 1990. Warblers of the West Indies. III. The Lesser Antilles. *Caribbean Journal of Science* 26:75-97.

Patten, M. A. 1993. A probable bilateral gynandromorphic Black-throated Blue Warbler. *Wilson Bulletin* 105:695-698.

Patti, S. T., and M. L. Myers. 1976. A probable Mourning × MacGillivray's Warbler hybrid. *Wilson Bulletin* 88:490-491.

Paynter, R. A., Jr. 1957. Birds of Laguna Ocotal. *Bulletin of the Museum of Comparative Zoology* 116:249-285.

Petit, K. E., M. D. Dixon, and R. T. Holmes. 1988. A case of polygyny in the Black-throated Blue Warbler. *Wilson Bulletin* 100:132-134.

Peterson, J. J., G. W. Lasley, K. B. Bryan, and M. Lockwood. 1991. Additions to the breeding avifauna of the Davis Mountains. *Bulletin of the Texas Ornithological Society* 24(2): 1991.

Petit, K. E., and K. A. Tarvin. 1990. First record of Prothonotary Warbler from Galápagos Islands, Ecuador. *American Birds* 44:1094.

Petit, L. J. 1989. Breeding biology of Prothonotary Warblers in riverine habitat in Tennessee. *Wilson Bulletin* 101:51-61.

Petit, L. J., D. R. Petit, K. E. Petit, and W. J. Fleming. 1990. Intersexual and temporal variation in foraging ecology of Prothonotary Warblers during the breeding season. *Auk* 107:133-145.

Petrides, G. A. 1938. A life history study of the Yellow-breasted Chat. *Wilson Bulletin* 50:184–189.

Phillips, A., J. Marshall, and G. Monson. 1964. *The Birds of Arizona*. Tucson: University of Arizona Press.

Phillips, A. R. 1947. The races of MacGillivray's Warbler. *Auk* 64:296-300.

———. 1962. Notas sistemáticas sobre aves Mexicanas, I. Anales del Instituto Biologica de la Universidad de Mexico. 32:333–381.

———. 1966. Further systematic notes on Mexican birds. *Bulletin of the British Ornithologists' Club* 86:125-131.

———. 1974. The first prebasic molt of the Yellow-breasted Chat. *Wilson Bulletin* 86:12-15.

Phillips, A. R., and M. Holmgren. 1979. The second DMNH/CFO taxonomy clinic. *Colorado Field Ornithologists Journal* 13:92-100.

Pitocchelli, J. 1990. Plumage, morphometric, and song variation in Mourning *(Oporornis philadelphia)* and MacGillivray's *(O. tolmiei)* warblers. *Auk* 107:161-171.

_____. 1992. Plumage and size variation in the Mourning Warbler *(Oporornis philadelphia)*. *Condor* 94:198-209.

_____. 1993. Mourning Warbler *(Oporornis philadelphia)*. No. 72 in *The Birds of North America,* edited by A. Poole and F. Gill. Philadelphia: Academy of Natural Sciences; Washington, D.C.: American Ornithologists' Union.

_____. 1995. MacGillivray's Warbler *(Oporornis tolmiei)*. No. 159 in *The Birds of North America,* edited by A. Poole and F. Gill. Philadelphia: Academy of Natural Sciences; Washington, D.C.: American Ornithologists' Union.

Pittaway, R. 1995. Recognizable forms: subspecies of the Palm Warbler. *Ontario Birds* 13:23-27.

Place, A. R., and E. W. Stiles. 1992. Living off the wax of the land: bayberries and Yellow-rumped Warblers. *Auk* 109:334-345.

Porneluzi, P., J. C. Bednarz, L. Goodrich, N. Zawada, and J. Hoover. 1993. Reproductive performance of territorial Ovenbirds occupying forest fragments and a contiguous forest in Pennsylvania. *Conservation Biology* 7:618-622.

Powell, G. V. N., and J. H. Rappole. 1986. The Hooded Warbler. In *Audubon Wildlife Report,* edited by R. L. DiSilvestro. New York: National Audubon Society.

Prather, J. W., and A. Cruz. 1995. Breeding biology of Florida Prairie Warblers and Cuban Yellow Warblers. *Wilson Bulletin* 107:475-484.

Proctor-Gray, E., and R. T. Holmes. 1981. Adaptive significance of delayed attainment of plumage in male American Redstarts: tests of two hypotheses. *Evolution* 35:742-751.

Pulich, W. M. 1976. *The Golden-cheeked Warbler: A bioecological study.* Austin: Texas Parks and Wildlife Department.

Pulich, W. M., D. H. Riskind, R. Wahl, and B. Thompson. 1989. The Golden-cheeked Warbler in Texas. Brochure 4000-377. Texas Parks and Wildlife Department.

Pyle, P., and P. Henderson. 1990. On separating female and immature *Oporornis* in fall. *Birding* 22:222-229.

Pyle, P., and R. P. Henderson. 1991. The Birds of Southeast Farallon Island: Occurrence and Seasonal Distribution of Migratory Species. *Western Birds* 22:41–84.

Rabenold, K. N. 1980. The Black-throated Green Warbler in Panama: a geographic and seasonal comparison of foraging. In *Migrant Birds in the Neotropics,* edited by A. Keast and E. S. Morton. Washington, D.C.: Smithsonian Institution Press.

Radabugh, B. E. 1974. Kirtland's Warbler and its Bahama wintering grounds. *Wilson Bulletin* 86:374-383.

Ramos, M. A., and D. W. Warner. 1980. Analysis of North American subspecies of migrant birds wintering in Los Tuxtlas, southern Veracruz, Mexico. In *Migrant Birds in the Neotropics,* edited by A. Keast and E. S. Morton. Washington, D.C.: Smithsonian Institution Press.

Rappole, John H. 1983. Analysis of plumage variation in the Canada Warbler. *Journal of Field Ornithology* 54:152-159.

Rappole, J. H., and D. W. Warner. 1980. Ecological aspects of migrant bird behavior in Veracruz, Mexico. In *Migrant Birds in the Neotropics,* edited by A. Keast and E. S. Morton. Washington, D.C.: Smithsonian Institution Press.

Raveling, D. G. 1965. Geographic variation and measurements of Tennessee Warblers killed at a TV tower. *Bird-Banding* 36:89-101.

Raveling, D. G., and D. W. Warner 1965. Plumages, molt and morphometry of Tennessee Warblers. *Bird-Banding* 36:169-179.

———. 1978. Geographic variation of Yellow Warblers killed at a TV tower. *Auk* 95:73-79.

Regelski, D. J., and R. R. Moldenhauer. 1996. Discrimination between regional song forms in the Northern Parula. *Wilson Bulletin* 108:335–341.

Remsen, J. V., Jr. 1986. Was Bachman's Warbler a bamboo specialist? *Auk* 103:216-219.

Remsen, J. V., Jr., M. Ellerman, and J. Cole. 1989. Dead-leaf-searching by the Orange-crowned Warbler in Louisiana in winter. *Wilson Bulletin* 101:645-648.

Richardson, M., and D. W. Brauning. 1995. Chestnut-sided Warbler *(Dendroica pensylvanica).* No. 190 in *The Birds of North America,* edited by A. Poole and F. Gill. Philadelphia: Academy of Natural Sciences; Washington, D.C.: American Ornithologists' Union.

Ridgely, R. S., and G. Tudor. 1989. *The Birds of South America.* Vol. I: the Oscine Passerines. Austin: University of Texas Press.

Ridgway, R. 1894. Description of a new *Geothlypis* from Brownsville, Texas. *Proceedings of United States National Museum* 16:691-692.

Rimmer, C. C. 1988. Timing of the prebasic molt of Yellow Warblers at James Bay, Ontario. *Condor* 90:141-156.

Ripley, S. D., and A. Moreno. 1980. A recent sighting of Bachman's Warbler in Cuba. *Birding* 12:211-212.

Robbins, C. S., K. Dawson, and B. A. Dowell. 1989. Habitat area requirements of breeding forest birds of the middle Atlantic states. *Wildlife Monographs* no. 103. The Wildlife Society.

Robbins, C. S., J. R. Sauer, R. S. Greenberg, and S. Droege. 1989. Population declines in North American birds that migrate to the Neotropics. *Proceedings of the National Academy of Sciences* 86:7658-7662.

Robbins, C. S., J. W. Fitzpatrick, and P. B. Hamel. 1992. A warbler in trouble: *Dendroica cerulea*. In *Ecology and Conservation of Neotropical Migrant Landbirds,* edited by J. M. Hagan III and D. W. Johnston. Washington, D.C.: Smithsonian Institution Press.

Robbins, S. D. 1974. New light on the Connecticut Warbler. *Passenger Pigeon* 36:110-115.

Robbins, S. D., D. W. Sample, P. W. Rasmussen, and M. J. Mossman. 1996. The Breeding Bird Survey in Wisconsin: 1996–1991. *Passenger Pigeon* 58:81–179.

Robbins, S. D., Jr. 1991. *Wisconsin Birdlife: Population & Distribution, Past & Present*. Madison: University of Wisconsin Press.

Roberson, D. 1980. *Rare Birds of the West Coast*. Pacific Grove, Calif.: Woodcock Publications.

Robinson, S. K. 1995. Rare Summer Birds of the Lowden-Miller State Forest: Is this really Illinois? *Meadowlark* 4:16-18.

Robinson, W. D. 1995. Louisiana Waterthrush (*Seiurus motacilla*). No. 151 in *The Birds of North America,* edited by A. Poole and F. Gill. Philadelphia: Academy of Natural Sciences; Washington, D.C.: American Ornithologists' Union.

Rohwer, S. 1994. Two new hybrid *Dendroica* warblers and new methodology for inferring parental species. *Auk* 111:441-449.

Rohwer, S., W. P. Klein Jr., and S. Heard. 1983. Delayed plumage maturation and the presumed prealternate molt in American Redstarts. *Wilson Bulletin* 95:199-208.

Russell, K. B. 1976. Migrant Golden-winged Warbler with a bivalent repertoire. *Auk* 93:178-179.

Schaeffer, F. 1974. Chin spots in Louisiana Waterthrush. *EBBA News* 37(3-4):128.

Schnell, G. D., and L. D. Caldwell. 1966. Xanthochroism in a Cape May Warbler. *Auk* 83:667-668.

Schwartz, A. 1970. Subspecific variation in two species of Antillean birds. *Quarterly Journal of the Florida Academy of Science* 33:221-236.

Schwartz, P. 1964. The Northern Waterthrush in Venezuela. *The Living Bird* 3:169-184.

Sciple, G. W. 1950. Recent record of Bachman's Warbler, *Vermivora bachmanii* from Gulf Coast of Mississippi. *Auk* 67:520.

Scott, W. E. D. 1888. Bachman's Warbler (*Helminthophila bachmanii*) at Key West, Florida in July and August. *Auk* 5:428-430.

Sealy, S. G. 1979. Extralimital nesting of Bay-breasted Warblers: response to forest tent caterpillars? *Auk* 96:600-603.

_____. 1985. Analysis of a sample of Tennessee Warblers window-killed during spring migration in Manitoba. *North American Bird Bander* 10:121-124.

Seidel, G. E., and R. C. Whitmore. 1982. Effect of forest structure on American Redstart foraging behavior. *Wilson Bulletin* 94:289-296.

Sexton, C. 1992. Rare, local, little-known, and declining North American breeders: the Golden-cheeked Warbler. *Birding* 24:373-376.

Shanahan, D. 1992. Notes on calls of breeding Connecticut Warblers. *Ontario Birds* 10:115–116.

Sharpe, F. A. 1993. *Olympic Peninsula Birds, the Songbirds.* Behavioral Ecology Research Group, Simon Fraser University, Burnaby.

Sherry, T. W. 1979. Competitive interactions and adaptive strategies of American Redstarts and Least Flycatcher in northern hardwood forests. *Auk* 96:265-275.

Sherry, T. W., and R. T. Holmes. 1985. Dispersion patterns and habitat responses of birds in northern hardwood forests. In *Habitat Selection in Birds,* edited by M. L. Cody. New York: Academic Press.

Short, L. L., Jr. 1963. Hybridization in the wood warblers *Vermivora pinus* and *V. chrysoptera. Proceedings of the XIII International Ornithological Congress,* pp. 147–160.

Short, L. L., Jr., and C. S. Robbins. 1967. An intergeneric hybrid wood warbler (*Seiurus* × *Dendroica*). *Auk* 84:534-543.

Shuford, W. D. 1993. *The Marin County Breeding Bird Atlas, a Distributional and Natural History of Coastal California Birds.* Point Reyes Bird Observatory, Bolinas: Bushtit Books.

Shuler, J. 1977a. Three recent records of Bachman's Warbler. *Chat* 41:11-12.

_____. 1977b. Bachman's Warbler habitat. *Chat* 41:19-23.

_____. 1977c. Bachman's phantom warbler. *Birding* 9:245-250.

Shuler, J., P. Nugent, J. Trochet, and J. van Os. 1978. Bachman's Warbler observations continue in I'On Swamp. *Chat* 42:23-24.

Sibley, C. G., and J. E. Ahlquist. 1982. The relationships of the Yellow-breasted Chat (*Icteria virens*) and the alleged slowdown in the rate of macromolecular evolution in birds. *Postilla* no. 187.

_____. 1990. *Phylogeny and Classification of Birds.* New Haven and London: Yale University Press.

Sibley, D. 1994. A guide to finding and identifying hybrid birds. *Birding* 26:162-177.

Smith, P. W., S. A. Smith, P. G. Ryan, and R. Cassidy. 1994. First report of Virginia's Warbler from the Bahama Islands, with comments on other records from the West Indies and eastern North America. *El Pitirre* 7:2–3.

Smith, T. M., and H. H. Shugert. 1987. Territory size variation in the Ovenbird: the role of habitat structure. *Ecology* 68:695-704.

Sogge, M. K., W. M. Gilbert, and C. Van Riper III. 1994. Orange-crowned Warbler *(Vermivora celata)*. No. 101 in *The Birds of North America,* edited by A. Poole and F. Gill. Philadelphia: The Academy of Natural Sciences; Washington, D.C.: The American Ornithologists' Union.

Spector, D. A. 1991. The singing behavior of Yellow Warblers. *Behavior* 117:29-52.

Spellman, C. B., R. E. Lemon, and M. M. J. Morris. 1987. Color dichromatism in female American Redstarts. *Wilson Bulletin* 99:257-261.

Staicer, C. A. 1989. Characteristics, use, and significance of two singing behaviors in Grace's Warbler *(Dendroica graciae)*. *Auk* 106:49-63.

Stein, R. C. 1962. A comparative study of songs recorded from five closely related warblers. *Living Bird* 1:61-74.

Stenger, J. 1958. Food habits and available food of Ovenbirds in relation to territory size. *Auk* 75:335-346.

Stevenson, H. M. 1938. Bachman's Warbler in Alabama. *Wilson Bulletin* 50:36-41.

_____. 1972. The recent history of Bachman's Warbler. *Wilson Bulletin* 84:347.

_____. 1978. Bachman's Warbler, *Vermivora bachmanii* (Audubon). In *Rare and Endangered Birds of Florida,* v. 2 (Birds), edited by H. W. Kale. Gainesville: University of Florida.

_____. 1982. Bachman's Warbler . . . rarest North American bird? *Florida Wildlife* 35:36-39.

Stewart, R. E. 1953. A life history study of the yellowthroat. *Wilson Bulletin* 65:141-161.

Stewart, R. M. 1972. Determining sex in western races of adult Wilson's Warbler: a reexamination. *Western Bird Bander* 47:45-48.

_____. 1973. Breeding behavior and life history of the Wilson's Warbler. *Wilson Bulletin* 85:21-30.

Stewart, R. M., and K. Darling. 1972. Breeding biology of the Wilson's Warbler in the high Sierra and on the coast. *Pt. Reyes Bird Observatory Newsletter* 24:3-5.

Stewart, R. M., M. R. P. Henderson, and K. Darling. 1977. Breeding ecology of the Wilson's Warbler in the High Sierra Nevada, California. *Living Bird,* 16th Annual.

Stiles, F. G., and R. G. Campos. 1983. Identification and occurrence of Blackpoll Warblers in southern Middle America. *Condor* 85:254-255.

Stiles, F. G., and S. M. Smith. 1980. Notes on bird distribution in Costa Rica. *Brenesia* 17:137-156.

Sturm, L. 1945. A study of the nesting activities of the American Redstart. *Auk* 62:189-206.

Sutton, G. M. 1967. *Oklahoma Birds: Their Ecology and Distribution, with Comments on the Avifauna of the Southern Great Plains.* Norman: University of Oklahoma Press.

Sykes, P. W., Jr. 1974. First record of Bahama Yellowthroat in the United States. *American Birds* 28:14-15.

_____. 1997. A closer look: Kirtland's Warbler. *Birding* 29:48–62.

Sykes, P. W., Jr., C. B. Kepler, D. A. Jett, and M. E. DeCapita. 1989. Kirtland's Warblers on the nesting grounds during the post-breeding period. *Wilson Bulletin* 101:545-558.

Taylor, W. K. 1970. Analysis of Ovenbirds killed in central Florida. *Bird-Banding* 43:15-19.

_____. 1973. Aging of Ovenbirds by rusty-tipped tertials and skull ossification. *EBBA News* 36:71-72.

_____. 1976. Variations in the black mask of the Common Yellowthroat. *Bird-Banding* 47:72-73.

Terrill, S. B. 1985. A sight record of the Crescent-chested Warbler from lowland Sonora. *American Birds* 39:11.

Terrill, S., K. P. Able, and M. A. Patten. 1992. Changing seasons. *American Birds* 46:1109-1111, 1182.

Terrill, S. B., and R. D. Ohmart. 1984. Facultative extension of fall migration by Yellow-rumped Warblers (*Dendroica coronata*). *Auk* 101:427-438.

Terrill, S. B., and R. L. Crawford. 1988. Additional evidence of nocturnal migration by Yellow-rumped Warblers in winter. *Condor* 90:261-263.

Thomas, B. G., E. P. Wiggers, and R. L. Clawson. 1996. Habitat selection and breeding status of Swainson's Warblers in southern Missouri. *Journal of Wildlife Management* 60: 611-616.

Todd, W. E. C. 1911. The Bahaman species of *Geothlypis. Auk* 28: 237-253.

_____. 1929. A revision of the wood-warbler genus *Basileuterus* and its allies. *Proceedings of the U. S. National Museum.* 74:1-95.

_____. 1963. *Birds of the Labrador Peninsula and Adjacent Areas.* Toronto: University of Toronto Press.

Tramer, E. J., and T. R. Kemp. 1980. Foraging ecology of migrant and resident warblers and vireos in highlands of Costa Rica. In *Migrant Birds in the Neotropics,* edited by A. Keast and E. S. Morton. Washington, D.C.: Smithsonian Institution Press.

Ulrich, D., and S. Ulrich. 1981. Observations on the 1980 Indiana Sutton's Warbler. *Atlantic Naturalist* 34:12–13.

United States Fish and Wildlife Service. 1990. Endangered Species Technical Bulletin 15(6).

Van Horn, M. A., and T. M. Donavan. 1994. Ovenbird (*Seiurus aurocapillus*). No. 88 in *The Birds of North America,* edited by A. Poole and F. Gill. Philadelphia: Academy of Natural Sciences; Washington, D.C.: American Ornithologists' Union.

Van Rossem, A. J. 1934. Critical notes on middle American birds. *Bulletin of the Museum of Comparative Zoology* 77:387-490.

_____. 1935. The Mangrove Warbler of northwestern Mexico. *Transactions of the San Diego Society of Natural History* 8:67-68.

_____. 1939. A race of the Yellow-breasted Chat from the tropical zone of southern Sonora. *Wilson Bulletin* 51:156.

_____. 1941. Critical notes on some yellowthroats of the Pacific southwest. *Condor* 32:297-300.

Veit, R. R., and W. R. Petersen. 1993. *Birds of Massachusetts.* Massachusetts Audubon Society.

Vidal, R. M., C. Macias Caballero, and C. D. Duncan. 1994. The occurrence and ecology of the Golden-cheeked Warbler in the highlands of northern Chiapas, Mexico. *Condor* 96:684-691.

Wahl, R. R., D. D. Diamond, and D. Shaw. 1990. The Golden-cheeked Warbler: a status review. Albuquerque, N.M.: United States Fish and Wildlife Service.

Walkinshaw, L. H. 1938. Nesting studies of the Prothonotary Warbler. *Bird-Banding* 9:32-46.

_____. 1941. The Prothonotary Warbler: a comparison of nesting conditions in Tennessee and Michigan. *Wilson Bulletin* 53:3-21.

_____. 1953. Life history of the Prothonotary Warbler. *Wilson Bulletin* 65:152-168.

_____. 1957. Distribution of the Palm Warbler and its status in Michigan. *Wilson Bulletin* 69:338-351.

_____. 1959. The Prairie Warbler in Michigan. *Jack Pine Warbler* 37:54-63.

_____. 1983. *Kirtland's Warbler: The Natural History of an Endangered Species.* Bloomfield Hills, Mich.: Cranbrook Institute of Science.

Wallace, D. I. M. 1980. A review of waterthrush identification with particular reference to the 1968 British record. In *The Frontiers of Bird Identification,* edited by J. T. R. Sharrock. Macmillan.

Wauer, R. 1985. *A Field Guide to Birds of the Big Bend.* Austin: Texas Monthly Press.

Wayne, A. T. 1907. The nest and eggs of Bachman's Warbler

Helminthophila bachmani (Aud.) taken near Charleston, South Carolina. *Auk* 24:43-48.

Webster, J. D. 1958. Systematic notes on the Olive Warbler. *Auk* 75:469-473.

_____. 1961. A revision of Grace's Warbler. *Auk* 78:554-566.

_____. 1962. Systematic and ecological notes on the Olive Warbler. *Wilson Bulletin* 74:417-425.

Welsh, D. A. 1971. Breeding and territoriality of the Palm Warbler in a Nova Scotia bog. *Canadian Field Naturalist* 85:31-37.

Wetmore, A. 1942. Descriptions of three additional birds from southern Veracruz. *Proceedings of the Biological Society of Washington.* 55:105-108.

_____. 1949. Geographical variation in the American Redstart (*Setophaga ruticilla*). *Journal of the Washington Academy of Science.* 39:137-139.

Wetmore, A., and B. H. Swales. 1931. Birds of Haiti and the Dominican Republic. Bulletin 155, U. S. National Museum.

Whitcomb, R. F., C. S. Robbins, J. F. Lynch, B. L. Whitcomb, M. K. Klimkiewicz, and D. Bystrak. 1981. Effects of forest fragmentation on avifauna of eastern deciduous forests. In *Forest Island Dynamics in Man Dominated Landscapes,* edited by R. L. Burgess and D. M. Sharpe. Ecological Studies 41, New York: Springer-Verlag.

Whitney, B. 1983. Bay-breasted, Blackpoll and Pine Warblers in fall plumage. *Birding* 15(6):219-222.

Whitney, B. M. 1994. The Blackburnian Warbler *Dendroica fusca* in South America, with a record from Santa Cruz Dept., Bolivia. *Cotinga* 2:36-37.

Widmann, O. 1897. The summer home of Bachman's Warbler no longer unknown. *Auk* 15:305-309.

Wiedenfeld, D. A. 1991. Geographical morphology of male Yellow Warblers. *Condor* 93:712-723.

_____. 1992. Foraging in temperate and tropical breeding and wintering male Yellow Warblers. In *Ecology and Conservation of Neotropical Migrant Landbirds,* edited by J. M. Hagan III and D. W. Johnston. Washington, D.C.: Smithsonian Institution Press.

Williams, J. M. 1996. Nashville Warbler (*Vermivora ruficapilla*). No. 205 in *The Birds of North America,* edited by A. Poole and F. Gill. Philadelphia: The Academy of Natural Sciences; Washington, D.C.: The American Ornithologists' Union.

Williams, T. C. 1985. Autumnal bird migration over the windward Caribbean Islands. *Auk* 102:163-167.

Wilson, W. H., Jr. 1996. Palm Warbler (*Dendroica palmarum*). No. 238 in *The Birds of North America,* edited by A. Poole and

F. Gill. Philadelphia: Academy of Natural Sciences; Washington, D.C.: American Ornithologists' Union.

Winker, K., D. W. Warner, and A. R. Weisbrod. 1992. The Northern Waterthrush and Swainson's Thrush as transients at a temperate inland stopover site. In *Ecology and Conservation of Neotropical Migrant Landbirds,* edited by J. M. Hagan III and D. W. Johnston. Washington, D.C.: Smithsonian Institution Press.

Woolfenden, G. E. 1967. A specimen of Golden-cheeked Warbler from Florida. *Auk* 84:115.

Wormington, A. 1994. *Notes on the Status and Distribution of Ontario Warblers.* Unpublished manuscript.

Wunderle, J. M. R. 1978. Territorial defense of a nectar source by a Palm Warbler. *Wilson Bulletin* 90:297–299.

Wunderle, J. M., Jr. 1992. Sexual habitat segregation in wintering Black-throated Blue Warblers in Puerto Rico. In *Ecology and Conservation of Neotropical Migrant Landbirds,* edited by J. M. Hagan III and D. W. Johnston. Washington, D.C.: Smithsonian Institution Press.

Yocum, C. F. 1968. Status of the Hermit Warbler in northwestern California. *Murrelet* 49:27.

Yunick, R. P. 1989. Some comments on Yellow-rumped Warbler molt. *The Kingbird* 39:100–101.

Zach, R., and J. B. Falls. 1977. Influence of capturing a prey on subsequent search in the Ovenbird (Aves: Parulidae). *Canadian Journal of Zoology* 55:1958-1969.

———. 1978. Prey selection by captive Ovenbirds (Aves: Parulidae). *Journal of Animal Ecology* 47:929-943.

———. 1979. Foraging and territoriality of male Ovenbirds (Aves: Parulidae) in a heterogeneous habitat. *Journal of Animal Ecology* 48:33-52.

Zimmer, J. T. 1948. The specific name of the Olive Warbler. *Auk* 65:126-127.

Zimmer, K. 1985. *The Western Birdwatcher.* Englewood Cliffs, N.J.: Phalarope Books (Prentice Hall).

INDEX

We provide the page number on which each species account begins and (in bold face) the number of the plate(s) that portray the species. Maps and photographs are placed within the species accounts.

Basileuterus culicivorus, 589, **Pl. 29**
  rufifrons, 593, **Pl. 29**
Cardellina rubrifrons, 568, **Pl. 28**
Chamaethlypis poliocephala (see *Geothylpis poliocephala*)
Chat, Yellow-breasted, 598, **Pl. 30**
Dendroica caerulescens, 257, **Pl. 10**
  castanea, 375, **Pl. 18**
  cerulea, 401, **Pl. 16**
  chrysoparia, 291, **Pl. 13**
  coronata, 267, **Pl. 12**
  discolor, 356, **Pl. 19**
  dominica, 325, **Pl. 17**
  fusca, 392, **Pl. 16**
  graciae, 334, **Pl. 17**
  kirtlandii, 349, **Pl. 20**
  magnolia, 240, **Pl. 11**
  nigrescens, 282, **Pl. 15**
  occidentalis, 316, **Pl. 14**
  palmarum, 366, **Pl. 20**
  pensylvanica, 232, **Pl. 10**

  petechia, 210, **Pls. 8, 9**
  pinus, 340, **Pl. 19**
  striata, 383, **Pl. 18**
  tigrina, 248, **Pl. 11**
  townsendi, 307, **Pl. 14**
  virens, 298, **Pl. 13**
Euthlypis lachrymosa, 584, **Pl. 29**
Geothlypis beldingi, 525, **Pl. 25**
  poliocephala, 535, **Pl. 25**
  rostrata, 529, **Pl. 25**
  trichas, 512, **Pl. 24**
Ground-Chat (see Gray-crowned Yellowthroat)
Helmitheros vermivorus, 435, **Pl. 21**
Icteria virens, 598, **Pl. 30**
Limnothlypis swainsonii, 442, **Pl. 21**
Mniotilta varia, 411, **Pl. 15**
Myioborus miniatus, 579, **Pl. 28**
  pictus, 573, **Pl. 28**
Oporornis agilis, 484, **Pl. 22**
  formosus, 475, **Pl. 22**
  philadelphia, 493, **Pl. 23**
  tolmiei, 502, **Pl. 23**

Ovenbird, 448, **Pl. 21**
Parula americana, 195, **Pl. 7**
   pitiayumi, 204, **Pl. 7**
   superciliosa, 190, **Pl. 29**
Parula, Northern, 195, **Pl. 7**
   Tropical, 204, **Pl. 7**
Peucedramus taeniatus, 109, **Pl. 30**
Protonotaria citrea, 427, **Pl. 1**
Redstart, American, 418, **Pl. 27**
   Painted, 573, **Pl. 28**
   Slate-throated, 579, **Pl. 28**
Seiurus aurocapillus, 448, **Pl. 21**
   motacilla, 468, **Pl. 21**
   noveboracensis, 457, **Pl. 21**
Setophaga ruticilla, 418, **Pl. 27**
Undertail patterns, **Pls. 31, 32**
Vermivora bachmani, 117, **Pl. 1**
   celata, 154, **Pl. 4**
   chrysoptera, 133, **Pl. 2**
   crissalis, 180, **Pl. 6**
   lawrencii, 140
   leucobronchialis 140, **Pl. 3**
   luciae, 185, **Pl. 6**
   peregrina, 145, **Pl. 4**
   pinus, 125, **Pl. 2**
   ruficapilla, 166, **Pl. 5**
   virginiae, 174, **Pl. 5**
Warbler, Audubon's, 267, **Pl. 12**
   Bachman's, 117, **Pl. 1**
   Bay-breasted, 375, **Pl. 18**
   Black-and-white, 411, **Pl. 15**
   Blackburnian, 392, **Pl. 16**
   Blackpoll, 383, **Pl. 18**
   Black-throated Blue, 257, **Pl. 10**
   Black-throated Gray, 282, **Pl. 15**
   Black-throated Green, 298, **Pl. 13**
   Blue-winged, 125, **Pl. 2**
   Blue-winged × Golden-winged hybrids, 140, **Pl. 3**
   Brewster's, 140, **Pl. 3**
   Canada, 560, **Pl. 27**

Cape May, 248, **Pl. 11**
   Cerulean, 401, **Pl. 16**
   Chestnut-sided, 232, **Pl. 10**
   Colima, 180, **Pl. 6**
   Connecticut, 484, **Pl. 22**
   Crescent-chested, 190, **Pl. 29**
   Fan-tailed, 584, **Pl. 29**
   Golden, 210, **Pl. 9**
   Golden-cheeked, 291, **Pl. 13**
   Golden-crowned, 589, **Pl. 29**
   Golden-winged, 133, **Pl. 2**
   Grace's, 334, **Pl. 17**
   Hermit, 316, **Pl. 14**
   Hooded, 541, **Pl. 26**
   Kentucky, 475, **Pl. 22**
   Kirtland's, 349, **Pl. 20**
   Lawrence's, 140, **Pl. 3**
   Lucy's, 185, **Pl. 6**
   MacGillivray's, 502, **Pl. 23**
   Magnolia, 240, **Pl. 11**
   Mangrove, 210, **Pl. 9**
   Mourning, 493, **Pl. 23**
   Myrtle, 267, **Pl. 12**
   Nashville, 166, **Pl. 5**
   Olive, 109, **Pl. 30**
   Olive-backed (*see* Tropical Parula)
   Orange-crowned, 154, **Pl. 4**
   Palm, 366, **Pl. 20**
   Parula (*see* Northern Parula)
   Pine, 340, **Pl. 19**
   Prairie, 356, **Pl. 19**
   Prothonotary, 427, **Pl. 1**
   Red-faced, 568, **Pl. 28**
   Rufous-capped, 593, **Pl. 29**
   Swainson's, 442, **Pl. 21**
   Tennessee, 145, **Pl. 4**
   Townsend's, 307, **Pl. 14**
   Townsend's × Hermit hybrids, 321, **Pl. 14**
   Virginia's, 174, **Pl. 5**
   Wilson's, 549, **Pl. 26**
   Worm-eating, 435, **Pl. 21**
   Yellow, 210, **Pls. 8, 9**
   Yellow-rumped, 267, **Pl. 12**

Yellow-throated, 325, **Pl. 17**
Waterthrush, Louisiana, 468,
    Pl. 21
  Northern, 457, **Pl. 21**
Wilsonia canadensis, 560, **Pl. 27**
  citrina, 541, **Pl. 26**
  pusilla, 549, **Pl. 26**

Yellowthroat, Bahama, 529, **Pl.**
    25
  Belding's, 525, **Pl. 25**
  Common, 512, **Pl. 24**
  Gray-crowned, 535, **Pl. 25**
  Peninsular (*see* Belding's)

THE PETERSON SERIES®

PETERSON FIELD GUIDES®

BIRDS

ADVANCED BIRDING (39) North America 53376-7
BIRDS OF BRITAIN AND EUROPE (8) 66922-7
BIRDS OF TEXAS (13) Texas and adjacent states 26252-6
BIRDS OF THE WEST INDIES (18) 67669-X
EASTERN BIRDS (1) Eastern and central North America
36164-8
EASTERN BIRDS' NESTS (21) U.S. east of Mississippi River 48366-2
HAWKS (35) North America 44112-9
WESTERN BIRDS (2) North America west of 100th meridian
and north of Mexico 51424-X
WESTERN BIRDS' NESTS (25) U.S. west of Mississippi River 47863-4
MEXICAN BIRDS (20) Mexico, Guatemala, Belize, El
Salvador 48354-9
WARBLERS (49) North America 78321-6

FISH

PACIFIC COAST FISHES (28) Gulf of Alaska to Baja California 33188-9
ATLANTIC COAST FISHES (32) North American Atlantic coast 39198-9
FRESHWATER FISHES (42) North America north of Mexico 53933-1

INSECTS

INSECTS (19) North America north of Mexico
18523-8
BEETLES (29) North America 33953-7
EASTERN BUTTERFLIES (4) Eastern and central North America
63279-X
WESTERN BUTTERFLIES (33) U.S. and Canada west of 100th meridian, part of
northern Mexico 41654-X
EASTERN MOTHS North America east of 100th meridian 36100-1

MAMMALS

MAMMALS (5) North America north of Mexico 24084-0
ANIMAL TRACKS (9) North America 18323-5

ECOLOGY

THE ECOLOGY OF EASTERN FORESTS (37) Eastern North America 47953-3
THE ECOLOGY OF WESTERN FORESTS (45) Western U.S. and Canada 46724-1
VENOMOUS ANIMALS AND POISONOUS PLANTS (46) North America north of
Mexico 35292-4

PLANTS

EDIBLE WILD PLANTS (23) Eastern and central North America 31870-X
EASTERN TREES (11) North America east of 100th meridian 46732-2
FERNS (10) Northeastern and central North America, British Isles and
    Western Europe 19431-8
MEDICINAL PLANTS (40) Eastern and central North America 46722-5
MUSHROOMS (34) North America 42102-0
PACIFIC STATES WILDFLOWERS (22) Washington, Oregon, California, and
    adjacent areas 31662-6
ROCKY MOUNTAIN WILDFLOWERS (14) Northern Arizona and New Mexico to
    British Columbia 18324-3
TREES AND SHRUBS (11A) Northeastern and north-central U.S. and south-
    eastern and south-central Canada 17579-8
WESTERN TREES (44) Western U.S. and Canada 46729-2
WILDFLOWERS OF NORTHEASTERN AND NORTH-
    CENTRAL NORTH AMERICA (17) 18325-1
SOUTHWEST AND TEXAS WILDFLOWERS (31) 36640-2

EARTH AND SKY

GEOLOGY (48) Eastern North America 66326-1
ROCKS AND MINERALS (7) North America 72777-4
STARS AND PLANETS (15) 53759-2
ATMOSPHERE (26) 33033-5

REPTILES AND AMPHIBIANS

EASTERN REPTILES AND AMPHIBIANS (12) Eastern and central North America
    58389-6
WESTERN REPTILES AND AMPHIBIANS (16) Western North America, including
    Baja California 38253-X

SEASHORE

SHELLS OF THE ATLANTIC (3) Atlantic and Gulf coasts
    and the West Indies 69779-4
PACIFIC COAST SHELLS (6) North American Pacific coast, including Hawaii
    and the Gulf of California 18322-7
ATLANTIC SEASHORE (24) Bay of Fundy to Cape Hatteras 31828-9
CORAL REEFS (27) Caribbean and Florida 46939-2
SOUTHEAST AND CARIBBEAN SEASHORES (36) Cape Hatteras to the Gulf Coast,
    Florida, and the Caribbean 46811-6

PETERSON FIRST GUIDES®

ASTRONOMY 46790-X
BIRDS 40684-6
BUTTERFLIES AND MOTHS 67072-1
CATERPILLARS 56499-9
CLOUDS AND WEATHER 56268-6
DINOSAURS 52440-7
FISHES 50219-5
INSECTS 35640-7
MAMMALS 42767-3
REPTILES AND AMPHIBIANS 62232-8
ROCKS AND MINERALS 56275-9
SEASHORES 61901-7
SHELLS 48297-6
SOLAR SYSTEM 52451-2
TREES 65972-8
URBAN WILDLIFE 67069-1
WILDFLOWERS 40777-X
FORESTS 71760-4

PETERSON FIELD GUIDE COLORING BOOKS

BIRDS 32521-8
BUTTERFLIES 34675-4
DESERTS 67086-1
DINOSAURS 49323-4
ENDANGERED WILDLIFE 57324-6
FISHES 44095-5
FORESTS 34676-2
INSECTS 67088-8
MAMMALS 44091-2
REPTILES 37704-8
SEASHORES 49324-2
SHELLS 37703-X
TROPICAL FORESTS 57321-1
WILDFLOWERS 32522-6

PETERSON NATURAL HISTORY COMPANIONS

LIVES OF NORTH AMERICAN BIRDS 77017-3

AUDIO AND VIDEO

EASTERN BIRDING BY EAR
cassettes 50087-7
CD 71258-0

WESTERN BIRDING BY EAR
cassettes 52811-9
CD 71257-2

EASTERN BIRD SONGS, Revised
cassettes 53150-0
CD 50257-8

WESTERN BIRD SONGS, Revised
cassettes 51746-X
CD 51745-1

BACKYARD BIRDSONG
cassettes 58416-7
CD 71256-4

MORE BIRDING BY EAR
cassettes 71260-2
CD 71259-9

WATCHING BIRDS
Beta 34418-2
VHS 34417-4

PETERSON'S MULTIMEDIA GUIDES: NORTH AMERICAN BIRDS
(CD-ROM for Windows) 73056-2

PETERSON FLASHGUIDES™

ATLANTIC COASTAL BIRDS 79286-X
PACIFIC COASTAL BIRDS 79287-8
EASTERN TRAILSIDE BIRDS 79288-6
WESTERN TRAILSIDE BIRDS 79289-4
HAWKS 79291-6
BACKYARD BIRDS 79290-8
TREES 82998-4
MUSHROOMS 82999-2
ANIMAL TRACKS 82997-6
BUTTERFLIES 82996-8
ROADSIDE WILDFLOWERS 82995-X
BIRDS OF THE MIDWEST 86733-9
WATERFOWL 86734-7
FRESHWATER FISHES 86713-4

WORLD WIDE WEB: http://www.petersononline.com

PETERSON FIELD GUIDES can be purchased at your local
bookstore or by calling our toll-free number, (800) 225-3362.

Then referring to title by corresponding ISBN number,
...ace with 0-395.